The Urbana Free Library

To renew: call 217-367-4057
or go to "*urbanafreelibrary.org*"
and select "Renew/Request Items"

TERRORIST ATTACKS ON AMERICAN SOIL

TERRORIST ATTACKS ON AMERICAN SOIL

From the Civil War Era to the Present

J. Michael Martinez

ROWMAN & LITTLEFIELD PUBLISHERS, INC.

Lanham • Boulder • New York • Toronto • Plymouth, UK

Published by Rowman & Littlefield Publishers, Inc.
A wholly owned subsidary of The Rowman & Littlefield Publishing Group, Inc.
4501 Forbes Boulevard, Suite 200, Lanham, Maryland 20706
www.rowman.com

10 Thornbury Road, Plymouth PL6 7PP, United Kingdom

British Library Cataloguing in Publication Information Available

Library of Congress Cataloging-in-Publication Data

Martinez, J. Michael (James Michael)
  Terrorist attacks on American soil : from the Civil War era to the present / J. Michael
Martinez.
    p. cm.
  Includes bibliographical references.
  ISBN 978-1-4422-0323-5 (cloth : alk. paper)— ISBN 978-1-4422-0324-2 (electronic)
  1. Terrorism—United States—History. I. Title.
  HV6432.M379 2012
  363.3250973—dc23

                                                                      2012020138

∞™ The paper used in this publication meets the minimum requirements of
American National Standard for Information Sciences—Permanence of Paper
for Printed Library Materials, ANSI/NISO Z39.48-1992.

Printed in the United States of America

This book is for my granddaughter,
Brianna Marie Carter, a terror in her own
right—but a good, beautiful, loving, joyful "terror."

That high All-Seer that I dallied with
Hath turn'd my feigned prayer on my head
And given in earnest what I begg'd in jest.
Thus doth he force the swords of wicked men
To turn their own points on their masters' bosoms.

—William Shakespeare, King Richard III, Act V, Scene i

CONTENTS

List of Illustrations   ix

Acknowledgments   xi

Introduction: Understanding Terrorism   1

PART I   THE NINETEENTH CENTURY

1 "A Sight Which Can Never Be Forgotten": The Mountain
Meadows Massacre (1857)   13

2 "The Gentle, Kindhearted Bioterrorist": Luke Pryor Blackburn
and the Yellow Fever Plot (1864–1865)   45

3 "We May Suspect That Race Was the Cause of the Hostility":
The Colfax Massacre (1873)   71

PART II   THE MODERN ERA

4 "The McNamaras Have Betrayed Labor": The *Los Angeles Times*
Bombing (1910)   97

5 "An Explosion Just Like the Sound of a Gatling Gun": The Wall
Street Bombing (1920)   123

6 "A President Has to Expect These Things": The Truman
Assassination Attempt (1950)   149

7 "The Klan Is Back on the Market": The Sixteenth Street
Bombing and the Civil Rights Movement (1963)   175

8 "You Don't Need a Weatherman to Know Which Way
the Wind Blows": Weatherman and the Counterculture
Movement (1960s)   205

PART III   POSTMODERN TERROR

9 "A Revolution against the Industrial System": The Unabomber
(1970s–1990s)   239

10 "How Charged with Punishments the Scroll": The Oklahoma
City Bombing (1995)   275

11 "There Is a Bomb in Centennial Park; You Have Thirty
Minutes": Eric Robert Rudolph (Late 1990s)   319

12 "The System Was Blinking Red": The Radical Islamic Movement
and the September 11 Attacks   361

PART IV   CONCLUSION

The Lessons of Terrorism   417

References   431

Index   453

About the Author   475

LIST OF ILLUSTRATIONS

1   Joseph Smith, founding prophet of the Church of Jesus Christ of Latter-Day Saints   18

2   Mormon leader Brigham Young   26

3   John D. Lee, a central figure in the Mountain Meadows Massacre   34

4   Luke Pryor Blackburn, "Dr. Black Vomit"   47

5   Jacob Thompson, head of the Confederate clandestine operations in Canada   56

6   White supremacist groups active in Louisiana in the 1870s   83

7   Drawing of the aftermath of the Colfax riot in *Harper's Weekly*, May 10, 1873   89

8   Famed U.S. labor leader Samuel Gompers   104

9   John J. and James B. McNamara in San Quentin Prison   114

10   Prominent defense attorney Clarence Darrow   118

11   The chaotic scene following the 1920 Wall Street explosion   126

12   Metal slugs and bomb fragments from the scene of the 1920 Wall Street explosion   127

13   Puerto Rican Nationalist Party member Oscar Collazo loaded into an ambulance   162

14   Griselio Torresola's body in the Washington, D.C., morgue   164

15   President Harry Truman shown with his wife and daughter   166

16   The Sixteenth Street Baptist Church following the bombing
     on September 15, 1963   191
17   A victim's funeral following the Sixteenth Street Baptist
     Church bombing   197
18   Members of the Congress of Racial Equality (CORE) march
     in Washington, D.C.   199
19   The University of Texas chapter of the Students for a Demo-
     cratic Society (SDS) demonstrates against the Vietnam War   211
20   Prominent Weather Underground Organization activists
     march on October 11, 1969, to protest the trial of the Chicago
     Seven   213
21   Composite sketch of the Unabomber   251
22   U.S. Marshals escort the Unabomber, Ted Kaczynski, to the
     federal courthouse in Helena, Montana   263
23   FBI agents escort Timothy McVeigh from the courthouse in
     Perry, Oklahoma   297
24   A Herblock cartoon depicts the horrors of the Oklahoma City
     bombing   299
25   The Oklahoma City Memorial honoring victims, survivors,
     and rescuers from the April 19, 1995, terrorist attack   309
26   A Mike Luckovich cartoon depicts the defiant attitude of
     Olympic organizers and athletes following the Centennial
     Olympic Park bombing   333
27   Bombing suspect Eric Rudolph takes a "perp walk" from the
     Cherokee County jail in Murphy, North Carolina   350
28   United Airlines Flight 175 moments before it crashed into
     the South Tower of the World Trade Center on September
     11, 2001   383
29   The scene at the Pentagon following the September 11, 2001,
     terrorist attacks   393
30   Osama bin Laden appears on the Al Jazeera television net-
     work on October 7, 2001   397

ACKNOWLEDGMENTS

As I have learned repeatedly throughout my career, no one writes a book without considerable assistance. First and foremost, I extend heartfelt and undying appreciation to the wonderful staff at Rowman & Littlefield, especially Carrie Broadwell-Tkach, associate editor for American history; Laura Grzybowski, associate editor, and Megan Barnett, assistant editor, production; Niels Aaboe, formerly executive editor; Grace Baumgartner, editorial assistant; and copyeditor Matt Evans.

I also appreciate the marketing assistance I received from Liz Kula of webdesignsbyliz.com. She created my website and has kept it up to date as I have struggled to build my career. Liz has been an invaluable asset.

I would be remiss if I did not acknowledge the advice and assistance I received from numerous librarians, researchers, and archivists. In alphabetical order, I extend thanks to the following professionals: Sarah Alex, director of programs, the Herb Block Foundation; Jim Baggett, head, Department of Archives and Manuscripts, Birmingham Public Library; Janice Davis, archives technician, Harry S. Truman Library; Kevin Grace, head archivist, Archives and Rare Book Library, the University of Cincinnati; Paula Mitchell, archivist at the Gerald R. Sherratt Library, Southern Utah University; Silka Quintero, Accounts and Permissions, the Granger Collection; Bobbie Reynolds, paralegal, Intellectual Property Office, Church of Jesus Christ of Latter-Day Saints; Marianne Sugawara, Permissions Department, Creators Syndicate; Pauline Testerman, audiovisual archivist,

Harry S. Truman Library; Brooke M. Thomas, sales and service representative, Getty Images; and Erin Tikovitsch, Rights and Reproductions, the Chicago History Museum.

As always, my family and friends have provided tremendous support. I especially thank Loren and Polly Mead; Martha and Dick Pickett; Bob and Peggy Youngblood; the late Charles DuBose and his wife, Glenda; Wallace and Leila Jordan; Dr. William D. Richardson of the University of South Dakota; Keith W. Smith; Chuck and Lisa Redmon; Cheryl Schmidt; Sheila Traub; Shirley Hardrick; Anthony Gallagher; and Greg Perkowski.

I have been blessed to enjoy such wonderful support. Of course, any errors or omissions in fact or interpretation are my responsibility alone.

INTRODUCTION

Understanding Terrorism

Since then, at an uncertain hour,
That agony returns;
And till my ghastly tale is told,
This heart within me burns

—Samuel Taylor Coleridge, *The Rime of the Ancient Mariner*, Part VII

One afternoon during the late 1990s, I was driving my car while my eight-year-old stepdaughter sat in the backseat. I was navigating through heavy traffic on Interstate 85 near Atlanta, Georgia, during rush hour, a harrowing experience for even the most steely, experienced driver. For some reason I can no longer recall, I was in an especially foul mood that day. I normally played the radio or chatted with my stepdaughter, but on that late autumn afternoon, we were silent, each of us lost in thought.

Suddenly, seemingly out of the blue, a pickup truck raced past my car and swerved into my lane. Fearing an imminent collision, I slammed on the brakes, eliciting a cacophony of horn blowing from the cars following behind me. I am not what my mother used to call a "potty mouth," but now and again I can spew forth expletives in the same league with a sailor on shore leave.

This was one of those occasions. Before I realized I had uttered anything aloud, a creative menagerie of colorful words and phrases, some of which were repeated over and over for effect, filled the car. One word in particular performed triple duty as noun, verb, and adjective.

When I recovered my composure and realized what I had said, I glanced in the rearview mirror. My stepdaughter's eyes were large ovals, and her mouth was frozen in an O of surprise. Realizing that I had violated one of my own cardinal rules about watching one's language, I felt the need to explain the outburst.

"I should not have said what I just said," I told her. "Sometimes, however, when we get upset, we say things we would not normally say."

"Why are you upset?" she asked.

It was a valid question. "I don't know if you saw the truck that cut in front of us," I replied, pointing to the monstrosity zigzagging in and out of the lanes ahead. "But he came very close to hitting us. I was so scared and upset that I spoke without realizing it."

She nodded, although she did not look entirely convinced by the logic of the explanation.

"Whoever is driving the truck is a bad guy," I said, feeling a bit lame and embarrassed by my excuse. "Sometimes really bad guys bring out the worst in us."

"Why is he a bad guy?"

"He's bad because he could have hurt us. He's dangerous."

She nodded, now apparently getting the point. "Oh, he's like Eric Rudolph," she said matter-of-factly.

I could not help but chuckle. Eric Rudolph, the Olympic Park bomber, had been in the news recently, especially because we lived near Atlanta, where his initial bombings occurred. Despite the ubiquitous press coverage, I was surprised that an eight-year-old knew anything about him.

She squinted at me, deeply suspicious that I was making fun of her. "What's so funny?" she asked.

"How do you know about Eric Rudolph?"

As I watched her in the rearview mirror, my stepdaughter sighed and rolled her eyes, exasperated with me and my stodgy ways. "Oh, Daddy," she said, "everybody knows about Eric Rudolph."

"Oh, I see. Well, I don't think the guy driving the pickup truck is quite as bad as Eric Rudolph."

I mention this anecdote because it illustrated to me how much terrorism has affected our culture. I doubt my eight-year-old stepdaughter—or most Americans, for that matter—could have identified winners of the Nobel Peace Prize or leading cancer researchers or anyone holding a high-ranking federal position aside from the president or vice president of the United

States. Yet she was acquainted with a disaffected serial terrorist who desired nothing so much as to maim and kill innocent people. Like so many alienated souls, Eric Rudolph nursed a deep, unrelenting, all-encompassing anger, an anger that pushed him to lash out and inflict his pain on others. This little nobody who could have been expected to grow up, live his life, pursue his career, raise his family, retire, and die unheralded had become a well-known symbol of at least one aspect of popular culture.

Everybody knows about Eric Rudolph. If that is true, perhaps terrorism pays off in some ways even as it is self-defeating in other ways. Perhaps infamy is a coin of the realm.

Beginning with that long-ago incident, I have often reflected on how much terrorism has penetrated the American consciousness. Moreover, throughout the years, I have wanted to explore the question of whether terrorism pays off. The short answer, as I discuss within these pages, is maybe. Maybe it pays off; it depends on the terrorists' goals. This book examines twelve separate, presumably emblematic, and often disparate cases of terrorism to address this and other questions.

Terrorism has become a high-profile subject—much more so than it was in the 1990s when my stepdaughter and I discussed Eric Rudolph. The horrendous events of September 11, 2001, heightened an awareness of terrorism unlike any other catastrophe in American history. It is a date forever enshrined in our national memory. Just as the Japanese attack on Pearl Harbor and President Kennedy's assassination are emblazoned on the American psyche, so too were the terrorist attacks on symbolic targets in New York City and Washington, D.C., and the plane crash in Shanksville, Pennsylvania. Some episodes can never be forgotten, nor should they be.

Yet terrorism is not a new phenomenon, despite increased attention paid to the issue. It has long plagued organized societies. In the aftermath of the September 11, 2001, terrorist attacks, Americans as well as many citizens around the world have desperately sought assurances that never again will noncombatants be harmed by zealots intent on advancing a radical or nonmainstream political agenda. Some political leaders have promised that government policies will be created to "keep Americans safe again." Indeed, the administration of President George W. Bush justified enactment of the controversial USA Patriot Act and the indefinite detention of suspected terrorists at the Guantanamo Bay naval base as necessary components of an American "war on terror." Historians realize, however, that the use of terror tactics is older than the republic. The leaders of a nation can never guarantee citizens' safety and security. The best they can do is to develop policies and safeguards that will minimize the likelihood of a terrorist attack and mitigate the effects after an attack occurs.

As they seek assurances that future attacks can be dispelled, citizens must first grapple with one major difficulty: no consensus exists about the definition of terrorism. It is difficult to utter promises of "never again" if the concept remains muddled. What exactly will never again occur? How do we know terrorism when we see it? Some commentators choose to include wartime atrocities in the definition. Debates can rage about whether the Japanese attack on Pearl Harbor in 1941 constituted terrorism or whether the forcible removal of the Cherokee Indians along the Trail of Tears in the 1830s was a terrorist act perpetrated by the Jackson and Van Buren administrations against a group of people based solely on race. To open this door is to raise a host of questions ranging from the use of relocation centers to detain Japanese-Americans during World War II, the FBI's COINTELPRO activities against members of the civil rights movement as well as other groups, and the Bush administration's reliance on the USA Patriot Act to detain enemy combatants without the benefit of a civilian trial. Although these are important issues worthy of consideration, *Terrorist Attacks on American Soil* focuses on acts outside of a military situation and exercised by substate agents against civilians. The only exception to this nonmilitary context is the yellow fever plot, but if one considers the Confederate States of America an illegitimate government (as Lincoln did during the Civil War), and if the use of a biological agent is viewed as an indiscriminate weapon that potentially harms noncombatants of all stripes, the episode falls within the definition of terrorism stated here.

Terrorism is defined broadly in this book as an act of violence or a threat of violence undertaken by substate, nongovernmental agents against citizens and other noncombatants to achieve a moral, social, political, religious, or ethnic objective, but even this articulation is not precise. An act of violence employed by one citizen or a group of citizens against another citizen or group of citizens would appear to be a matter best addressed through ordinary criminal law administered by the American judicial system. Yet if the definition is expanded to include other features, such as determining the psychology, motivations, demography, ideology, organization, leadership, and operations of "terrorists," the definition becomes unwieldy and unworkable, a bulky behemoth that, in attempting to encompass a wide array of factors constituting "terrorism," becomes overly inclusive and virtually meaningless. Ideally, a definition should be broad, but not too broad, and should allow for moral condemnation of terrorism without stifling legitimate political dissent, even offensive or "disloyal" discourse.

In his book *Inside Terrorism*, a well-known researcher on terrorism, Bruce Hoffman, discusses the changing definition of the term. During the French Revolution, "terror" was a positive term denoting the revolutionary spirit of the age as monarchs fell and democratic governments, often employing violent techniques, rose up in their stead. The concept became associated with revolution, and organized groups formed to fight for liberation from colonialism or to shake off the yoke of repressive political regimes. Toward the end of the twentieth century, economics was added to the definition; terrorists fought to disrupt markets and commerce. As the definition evolved, a multitude of sources developed different definitions. Hoffman's book includes a chart containing 109 definitional elements of terrorism compiled from his extensive research into the subject. The only universally agreed-upon proposition by the dawn of the twenty-first century was that "terrorism" was a pejorative description of violent political acts undertaken by weak perpetrators.[1]

The United Nations (UN) has struggled to define terrorism so that nation-states can agree on a common understanding for law enforcement purposes, but the task has been contentious. In 2002, the UN Comprehensive Convention on International Terrorism developed a draft definition that attracted its share of defenders as well as detractors:

Any person commits an offence within the meaning of this Convention if that person . . . unlawfully and intentionally . . . causes: (a) Death or serious bodily injury to any person; or (b) Serious damage to public or private property, including a place of public use, a State or government facility, a public transportation system, an infrastructure facility or the environment; or (c) Damage to property, places, facilities, or systems referred to in paragraph 1 (b) of this article, resulting in major economic loss, when the purpose of the conduct, by its nature or context, is to intimidate a population, or to compel a Government or an international organization to do or abstain from doing any act.[2]

Two years later, the UN Security Council adopted Resolution 1566, which characterized "terrorist acts" as

criminal acts, including against civilians, committed with the intent to cause death or serious bodily injury, or taking of hostages, with the purpose to provoke a state of terror in the general public or in a group of persons or particular persons, intimidate a population or compel a government or an international organization to do or to abstain from doing any act, which constitute offences within the scope of and as defined in the international conventions and protocols relating to terrorism, are under no circumstances justifiable by considerations of a political, philosophical, ideological, racial, ethnic, religious or other similar nature.

The resolution called on nation-states to punish such offenses through appropriate mechanisms in their respective criminal justice systems.[3]

The U.S. Federal Bureau of Investigation (FBI) defines domestic terrorism as "the unlawful use of force or violence against persons or property to intimidate or coerce a government, the civilian population or any segment thereof, in furtherance of political or social objectives."[4] As with the UN efforts, the FBI definition focuses on the unlawful nature of the overt acts, the reliance on violence or the threat thereof, the focus against civilians, and the desire to effect social and/or political change beyond the context of the act itself.[5]

As imprecise as these definitions are, the common elements suggest a conceptual framework. Each episode that qualifies as "terrorism" must involve violence or the threat thereof. The violence or threat must violate the positivist law of the area where the act occurs. One or more civilians must be the intended target or the recipient of collateral damage. Even if the actor does not intend to harm civilians, if the act is so reckless and indiscriminate that it is likely that civilians will be injured or killed, the incident can still be deemed a terrorist attack. Finally, the violence or threat must be employed in service of another, presumably broader goal (whether it is moral, social, political, religious, or ethnic) aside from the act itself. A person who kills his or her lover in a moment of anger does not look beyond the incident when the violence occurs; hence it is a "heat of passion" crime that does not qualify as terroristic. A terrorist incident must be designed to effect moral, social, political, religious, or ethnic change. The attack is carried out by weak individuals or groups that believe they have no recourse but to lash out violently.[6]

According to a 1985 Rand Corporation report, five pieces of information are available about attacks properly labeled "terrorism": the place where the action occurred, the tactics employed, the type of target involved, the nationality of the target population, and the number of fatalities directly or indirectly attributable to the action. Eyewitness accounts, forensic evidence, newspaper reports and other contemporaneous accounts, and police reports can provide some or all of this information. Owing to the presence of these five pieces of information, valuable data exist on a variety of high-profile episodes.[7]

Data compiled about terrorist attacks can be examined using analytical tools employed by scholars to explore public policy. Analysts trace policies through three distinct phases: formulation, implementation, and evaluation. In step one, policy analysts examine the origins of a policy—how the need arose, how the question was framed, how it became part of the policy agenda, and why persons initiated the policy in the first place. In the implementation phase, analysts observe the evolution from creating a policy (thought) to carrying it out (deed). They desire to understand the variables involved in this evolution, including the challenges in assembling the requisite personnel and materiel, the means by which the operation is financed, the resistance encountered, and the unintended consequences that invariably occur. In the evaluation phase, policy analysts provide a postevent or after-action assessment of the nature of the policy to determine why some steps failed and others succeeded.[8] Applying this same tripartite analytical construct to terrorism, data on past attacks can be used to trace how the decision to act was formulated, how the action was undertaken, and how well it achieved the desired objectives.

The initial question is to ask why some people feel compelled to develop a plan for initiating an attack when most people refrain from doing so. The terrorist mind-set is poorly understood, and numerous motives seem to exist. Occasionally, people are compelled to engage in violence because ignorance and poverty provide them with few peaceful options. Some religious terrorists embrace violence because they believe the deity will be pleased. Still other explanations suggest that people who are disenfranchised and feel little or no stake in the political, economic, and social system are filled with hate; therefore, they lash out at the groups or symbols they believe have oppressed or aggrieved them. Some attackers may wrestle with mental illness. Still other terrorists act as though they were operating any business or corporate enterprise. They have a well-defined mission statement, an overall strategy, and a series of tactics designed to achieve their goals. They engage in fund-raising activities and employ workers with the appropriate skills necessary to fulfill the group's mandate. Some terrorists are well-educated, competent, rational human beings. In short, terrorists act for many reasons, some of which are difficult to fathom in general and can only be understood in context.

Although the mind-set is almost impossible to fathom, analysts can assess indicators that suggest a mind-set. From such assessments it appears that some offenders labeled "terrorists" are separatists, some are ideologically driven, and some evince characteristics of both types. A "separatist" is a person residing in a particular area who shares a common culture with surrounding inhabitants but who believes that an outside force—the government, a religious group, a faction such as homosexuals, abortion rights advocates, or elites—has rendered life under the *status quo ante* intolerable. A transnational separatist aims his wrath at a foreign nation-state because he believes agents of the state are his oppressors. An ideologically driven terrorist believes that a wealthy, bourgeois, or ruthlessly elite enemy posess an ongoing threat to social, political, and/or religious reform; the traditional methods of expressing discontent are hopelessly corrupted or were never effective in the first place. Of the twelve cases in this book, many loners can be characterized as separatists, while groups often are motivated by ideology. As the chapters indicate, some overlap occurs.

The plan eventually moves from initial conceptualization to implementation. This evolution represents a quantum leap. Anyone, including ordinary citizens who do not intend to act, can place pen to paper and sketch out an idea for striking at one's enemies. Carrying out a plan requires a level of organization and strategy that transcends the willingness or ability of most disaffected parties. In reconstructing the event, it is necessary to examine how the actors recruited personnel, financed equipment, transported men and materiel from one point to another, and controlled external parties and events until the plan could be put into place. In some instances, a "lone wolf" separatist will implement the scheme with little or no assistance from third parties. An ideological terrorist sometimes, although not always, relies on an extensive network of operatives and financiers to advance a complex, multifaceted attack that depends on coordinated timing and execution.

Examining overt acts and the immediate aftermath can reveal much about the nature of an attack. When a perpetrator undertakes an act, he or she decides whether to claim responsibility for the act or attempt to disavow all knowledge and escape detection. For some terrorists, the purpose is to strike fear into the hearts of the target population. Claiming responsibility becomes a significant part of the campaign of terror. When Puerto Rican nationalists attempted to assassinate President Truman, they did not hate the man; they sought to attack a symbol of American executive power and authority. Their purpose was to publicize the plight of their island and the tyrannical impulses of the U.S. government. Claiming credit was integral to the plan. In fact, publicity, not a high body count, was the point. The Wall Street bombing in 1920, in contrast, was an apparent attempt to create fear among Wall Street financiers and inflict as many casualties as possible. The perpetrators never claimed responsibility and were never discovered. One reason the event continues to interest researchers is that it seemed to herald a new age where terrorists sought to increase the body count without explanation.

Insofar as the body count is concerned, terrorist acts can be evaluated in terms of lethality. Was the incident designed as a symbolic act, or was the purpose to inflict the maximum number of casualties? Assessing the lethality of the act can reveal much about the organization, leadership, demography, ideology, psychology, funding, communications, and environment of the perpetrators even in situations where responsibility is not claimed. The crucial analysis requires an understanding of the context in which terrorist attacks occur. With this information in hand, the researcher generally can construct a timeline to examine the episode from inception to the act itself to the aftermath.

This book examines selected attacks on American soil since the years just before the U.S. Civil War by placing terrorism into historical context and tracing each episode from its initial formulation through its implementation to its evaluation to determine whether any common elements of terrorism exist. Because the topic is large and complex, no book can purport to be an exhaustive history of terrorism or a definitive account of how and why terrorists do what they do. Accordingly, *Terrorist Attacks on American Soil* presents a representative sampling of attacks and seeks to understand the lessons that can be learned from those events.

Some events, such as the 1995 Oklahoma City bombing, the Unabomber's decades-long campaign of violence, the September 11, 2001, terrorist attacks—and yes, Eric Rudolph—are well known to a large percentage of the American public. Others, such as the Mountain Meadows Massacre, Luke Pryor Blackburn's yellow fever plot, and the *Los Angeles Times* bombing, date from an earlier epoch; consequently, all but the most knowledgeable students of history probably know little or nothing about these attacks. Despite the varying levels of visibility, I have strived to select emblematic events.

As an example, consider that many race riots occurred during the Gilded Age, that period between the end of the U.S. Civil War and the early years of the twentieth century. This book focuses on a race riot known as the Colfax Massacre. The selection of the Colfax incident is not designed to minimize other riots that occurred or to suggest that all nineteenth-century race riots were alike in terms of the causes, the events themselves, the casualties, or the consequences. Instead, the Colfax Massacre is a representative case, just as the other episodes described in these pages stand as representatives of larger trends in terrorist activities.

A researcher investigating terrorism soon discovers that he will never get to the root causes of, or fashion suitable solutions to, all instances of violent mischief. The best he can do is sift through representative cases and muse over the causes and consequences. By exploring the myriad contexts of attacks on American soil and reflecting on the indicia of terrorism, I hope to suggest the means by which we can understand terrorist attacks of the past as well as the range of possibilities for future terrorist attacks.

Everybody knows about Eric Rudolph, indeed. Maybe that is true; maybe it is not. But how many people know about other salient terrorist attacks in American history? Join me as we look back to a veritable rogues' gallery of characters and situations that ultimately led to the present state of affairs.

NOTES

1. Hoffman, *Inside Terrorism*, 20–41.

2. See, for example, Hmoud, "Negotiating the Draft Comprehensive Convention on International Terrorism," 1031–43, and Rostow, "Before and After," 475–90.

3. United Nations Security Council Resolution 1566 (2004). See also Wilkinson, *Terrorism versus Democracy*, 2–3.

4. See, for example, Flaherty, "Youth, Ideology, and Terrorism," 209–30; Hewitt, *Understanding Terrorism in America*, 14; Hoffman, *Inside Terrorism*, 38; McCann, *Terrorism on American Soil*, 7–8.

5. Hewitt, *Understanding Terrorism in America*, 14; Hoffman, *Inside Terrorism*, 38–40.

6. Lutz and Lutz, *Terrorism in America*, 1–2.

7. Cordes et al., *A Conceptual Framework for Analyzing Terrorist Groups*, 16–17.

8. See, for example, Sapru, *Public Policy: Formulation, Implementation, and Evaluation*.

I

THE NINETEENTH CENTURY

1

"A SIGHT WHICH
CAN NEVER BE FORGOTTEN"

The Mountain Meadows Massacre (1857)

Hence then, and evil go with thee along,
Thy offspring, to the place of evil, hell;
Thou and thy wicked crew: there mingle broils,
Ere this avenging Sword begin thy doom,
Or some more sudden vengeance wing'd from God
Precipitate thee with augmented pain.

—John Milton, *Paradise Lost*, Book VI

September 11 would become an infamous date in American history during the twenty-first century, but in 1857, with the storm clouds of an eastern civil war gathering and public attention focused on a schism between North and South, it earned its initial place in history. Few Americans recognized that mass murder was on the western horizon. The "darkest deed of the nineteenth century" occurred in one of the most beautiful, idyllic spots on the continent. Mountain Meadows, a regular stop on the Old Spanish Trail from Santa Fe to points farther west, existed as a lush, picturesque grassland oasis isolated from civilization. Pioneers who braved that desolate land were always cognizant of possible Indian attack, especially in remote areas, but the episode that unfolded on a long-ago September 11 commenced not as a struggle between whites and Native Americans, although some of the latter participated in the slaughter. The incident involved the Church of Jesus Christ of Latter-Day Saints (or the "Mormon Church," to use the vernacular term) and civilians traveling westward during the antebellum era. Utah was still a territory in the 1850s, an area plagued by an escalating conflict between the U.S. government and a militia group, the Nauvoo Legion, operated by the Mormon Church.[1]

THE MORMON PLIGHT

Much has been written about the Mormons; they remain a frequently misunderstood, often persecuted religious sect. To their defenders, they are pious and devout Christians who seek to do the Lord's will, just as devoted to God as other Christians and people of faith across all denominations and religions, but they have been bitterly attacked by ignorant, vicious opponents intent on destroying the church and its adherents. To detractors, Mormons are a dangerous cult filled with blasphemers who originally practiced polygamy and continue to threaten mainstream Christianity with their strange ideas and customs. Middle ground has seldom been found between Mormons and their critics. Before they settled in the Utah Territory, church members were denigrated as pariahs, constantly forced from their homes and communities when they gained too much power and influence to suit their neighbors' sensibilities.[2]

Even the terminology is contested. "Mormon" is an imprecise term that refers to the Church of Jesus Christ of Latter-Day Saints. Founding father Joseph Smith Jr. established a precursor, the Church of Christ, on April 6, 1830, in upstate New York. He was, and remains, one of the most controversial religious leaders in American history. A young man of no distinct lineage and lacking a formal education, Smith was raised by unconventional parents. His father professed his faith in deism while his mother embraced Christian Primitivism. Originally from Vermont, the Smith clan migrated to western New York in hopes of eking out something more than a meager existence. The family was never quite able to make a go of farming, a sorry state of affairs which meant that young Joseph occasionally was hungry during his formative years. His literal hunger for sustenance would be superseded in time by his figurative hunger for religious comfort, which led to the creation of a new order.[3]

It was a fortuitous time to relocate to upstate New York. During the first half of the nineteenth century, the area experienced a religious revival known as the Second Great Awakening. The First Great Awakening in the mid-eighteenth century had done much to ignite religious fervor among the British colonists. Revivalist preachers had excited audiences with dazzling oratory and rich, evocative narratives about heaven and hell. The second period, to some extent, was a continuation of the first; the latter was especially important because it spread the idea of democratization among individuals and religious congregations. For much of the history of organized Christianity in North America, a believer would look to a wise, learned minister to explain the cryptic, confusing nature of scripture. In some religious denominations, the clergy trained for years to master Latin, Greek, and Hebrew as well as the arcane, esoteric points of theology. This emphasis on the difficulties in understanding God and his commandments interposed doctrinaire requirements between worshippers and their God. The Second Great Awakening sparked an interest in evangelical religion that allowed even the least educated believer to understand the scriptures No longer was guidance from a learned man of the cloth necessary for the pious to understand the word of God. A lay minister could lead the way.[4]

Charles Grandison Finney was arguably the most popular evangelical minister of the Second Great Awakening, and his experience served as a useful model for anyone intent on pioneering a new religion. Finney began his career as a lawyer in upstate New York when, at the age of twenty-nine, he experienced a road-to-Damascus revelation after a bright light filled his law office one fine day. As Finney saw things, the brilliant beam heralded the eternal spirit of Jesus Christ. He emerged from the experience ready to set aside the trappings of his former life in exchange for a higher calling. Rejecting the Calvinism and Unitarianism of his neighbors, Finney used his considerable charisma and oratorical skills to pioneer a new style of Presbyterianism. Based on an evangelistic form of revivalism, the "New Measures" eventually attracted a large group of disciples known as the "Holy Band." During the remaining five decades of his life, Finney held innumerable tent revivals for the Holy Band. In the process, he became the forerunner of the modern televangelist appealing to a popular lay audience. Finney eventually served as the head of Oberlin College in Ohio and authored an influential manual on conducting revivals.[5]

Finney was not the only well-known evangelical minister of the Second Great Awakening, but his ascension during Joseph Smith's adolescence undoubtedly made Finney a role model. As a young man growing up in the "burned-over district" of western New York—so named because numerous revivals had taken place there—young Joseph possessed so much charisma and religious faith that he seemed to be cut from the Finney mold. Smith came of age at a time when some Americans were obsessed with the possibility that gifted denizens possessed magical powers that could assist in the quest for buried treasure. He appeared to possess the gift. While still in his teens, he developed a reputation as a "glass looker," a fellow who could practice folk medicine and interpret signs leading to long-lost riches.[6]

Smith chose a mystical path when an itinerant magician and diviner visited the community to search for buried treasure and recover lost household items in exchange for a fee. The diviner possessed magic stones that, he claimed, told him where to search. Smith was enthralled, for here was a man after his own heart. The dour subsistence farmers of western New York focused their eyes downward, struggling to scratch out a living from the soil. Young Joseph preferred to focus his eyes on the heavens, dreaming of a more glorious future than the prosaic prospects that awaited most farmers. Smitten with this charismatic figure, the young man spent time with the diviner trying to understand how the magical stones worked. Amazingly, he soon acquired magic stones of his own. Although he was never able to retrieve gold, much to the consternation of neighbors who paid him to provide assistance, Joseph Smith launched a career that would make him one of the most important religious leaders of the nineteenth century.[7]

He did not set out to found a religion, but the idea arose, he later claimed, in 1820 when the fourteen-year-old boy was visited by two "personages," God the Father and Jesus Christ. This initial visit convinced the boy that the traditional view of Christianity as the trinity of Father, Son, and Holy Spirit could not be true. He had seen two separate personages at the same time, which demonstrated to his satisfaction that traditional Christian doctrine was lacking in key respects. Revisionist historians have claimed that it was natural for an imaginative, possibly mentally disturbed adolescent troubled by denominational arguments within his own family to seek solace in visions and dreams. Less skeptical observers contend that such dismissive interpretations discount the mystical, religious value of Smith's encounters. They suggest that all religious pioneers are denounced as insane or frauds at the outset; only later, after the religion becomes institutionalized, do the founder and his disciples appear in a more favorable light. Because the founders of ancient religions long ago passed from flesh and blood into mythology, they possess a legitimacy that time has yet to bestow on Smith. His supporters argue that in centuries to come Smith will be as revered among non-Mormons as he is among true believers.[8]

Whatever his motivations, Smith's divine experiences increased as he matured. Three years after his initial vision, an angel, Moroni, appeared, explaining that the North American continent was the site of God's interaction with an ancient race. Moroni told Smith that a series of thin gold plates were buried in Cumorah, a hill near the Smith home. During the next four years, young Joseph attempted to retrieve the plates, which reputedly revealed the word of God, but apparently he was not ready to complete his religious awakening. When he finally discovered the plates in 1827, they contained inscriptions about God's revelations to indigenous North Americans in a language that only Smith could translate. He set to work. The translation, known as the Book of Mormon, appeared in March 1830, a month before Smith established his first church.⁹

The Book of Mormon could be read as a sequel to the original Holy Bible. It revealed that Native Americans were the Lost Tribe of Israel. Written in the style of the King James Version of the Bible, the work nonetheless reflected the tenor of the times, encapsulating the rising nationalism and patriotism of the early nineteenth century with a decidedly American optimism. Rationalists, then and now, balked at what they viewed as thinly veiled chicanery, but over the years true believers flocked to Smith's side. Whether the prophet genuinely believed in such mythology or was simply a well practiced charlatan remains a point of contention to this day. Even Smith's own father-in-law, Isaac Hale, feared that the latest episode was yet another scam in a long line of scams perpetrated by a bizarre young fanatic.¹⁰

Within a few years, Smith and his wife moved on from his father-in-law's property. He had been tried in court for "disorderly conduct," and several newspapers had denounced the Book of Mormon as blasphemous. Realizing he had worn out his welcome and would risk reprisals if he stayed in New York, in 1831 the prophet moved on to Kirtland, Ohio. From there, the Latter-Day Saints, as they came to be called, became a force to be reckoned with on the frontier, eventually gathering between 1,500 and 2,000 followers. Kirtland proved to be an inviting destination after Sidney Rigdon, a preacher there, converted his entire congregation to Mormonism. With a ready-made church awaiting his arrival, Smith found sanctuary at a low point in his career. Rigdon became his close confidant and adviser after the move.¹¹

Never satisfied to remain stationary, the peripatetic Smith searched for the true Zion throughout the American Midwest. After he was tarred and feathered for supposedly making improper advances to a seventeen-year-old girl in 1832, Smith's desire to find a permanent home acquired an increased sense of urgency. He dispatched an expedition to Missouri, but when he separated from his flock, rival leaders arose to challenge Smith's authority. Eventually, a rift developed between Mormons living in Ohio and their Missouri brethren as adherents fought to control their own branch of the church.¹²

Even as he struggled to retain control over his church, Smith exacerbated internal tensions over two issues that plagued the church for much of its

Joseph Smith, founding
prophet of the Church of
Jesus Christ of Latter-Day
Saints. Courtesy of Spe-
cial Collections, Gerald R.
Sherratt Library, South-
ern Utah University.

history: the use of violence and the practice of plural marriage. Insofar as
violence was concerned, Smith professed his desire to live in peace, but he
recognized that he and his followers could not turn the other cheek indefinitely. He demonstrated his departure from the pacifist school of thought
among Christians when he assembled a paramilitary force trained in military tactics and maneuvers.[13]

Polygamy became one of the most repellent and frightening aspects of
Mormonism for nonbelievers. Smith kept the practice secret in public but
privately defended it using a concept known as the "New and Everlasting
Covenant," which extended beyond notions of earthly law. Earthly mar-
riages were contracts and nothing more unless they were grounded in the
new covenant. The covenant had to be sealed through a series of anoint-
ments. Conveniently, only Smith could seal the covenant. After a man
and woman entered the covenant, they would be promised exaltation, or
godhood after death. The ultimate manifestation of the new covenant was
through polygamy, which allowed a human being to transcend earth and
even an angelic state to become a god.[14]

As the church's profile and power grew, neighbors became alarmed at the strange sect. It was difficult to separate truth from fiction when rumors of the group's bizarre religious practices circulated, but it was clear that Mormons were unwelcome in most tight-knit, mainstream Christian communities spread across the frontier. Smith established a pattern that would govern the group during his tenure: he would set up shop, build his power base, proclaim himself a community leader, and excite hysteria among neighboring towns. Eventually, angry and frightened neighbors banded together to drive the strange interlopers away from the vicinity. The pattern first emerged when Smith fled from Ohio to avoid financial problems and soon found himself and his followers barred from Missouri.

Any discussion of the violence practiced by Mormons against outsiders must acknowledge the violence perpetrated against the group during these early years. In virtually every community where the church took refuge, fearful residents lashed out, frequently employing violence. The Mormons could not look to law enforcement and community leaders for protection because often these forces were the perpetrators. Critics subsequently denounced church leaders for employing terror tactics, but a convincing rejoinder is that the group armed its members in self-defense against state-tolerated terrorism on the American frontier.

By the late 1830s, Smith and the Mormons had set up residency in a swampy area at Nauvoo, Illinois. Once again demonstrating a penchant for self-aggrandizement, he announced that he was both mayor of the town and commander of his own militia, the Nauvoo Legion. In 1843, he announced his candidacy for the American presidency. Smith was at the height of his influence, but a precipitous fall was not far in the future.[15]

In 1844, a local newspaper, the *Nauvoo Expositor*, in its one and only issue, raised a hue and cry about Smith's power as well as his commitment to polygamy. Incensed by the revelations, Smith ordered the Nauvoo Legion to destroy the press. This reckless act—reminiscent of the tactics employed by a mob that had murdered an Illinois abolitionist, Elijah Lovejoy, in Alton, Illinois, in 1837—only increased public outrage over the growth of the Mormon Church. Smith reacted by declaring martial law and mobilizing the Nauvoo Legion, although eventually he realized he could not raise more forces than the state militia. Outnumbered, Smith had little choice but to surrender to the governor.[16]

While incarcerated in the town of Carthage and awaiting trial for inciting to riot, Smith plotted to have the Nauvoo Legion break him out of jail. He did not realize how unpopular he had become with the frontier denizens outside the Mormon Church. His increasingly erratic, unpopular behavior, coupled with his public pronouncements that he was running for president, had finally irrevocably incensed the masses. Rumors spread that his followers would spring him from jail. The wild stories only heightened local concerns. Driven by fears that Mormonism was a dangerous sect and acting against the backdrop of the intolerant nineteenth-century frontier, an enraged mob rushed into the jail and brutally murdered Smith and his older brother, Hyrum. Joseph Smith, glass looker, religious zealot, prophet, and founding father of Mormonism, was martyred at the age of thirty-eight.[17]

Many fledgling religions have withered and died when their founder passed from the scene, but the Mormons survived largely because one man, Brigham Young, emerged as a strong successor to the martyred Smith. Young and Smith shared many traits. Both had been born early in the nineteenth century—Young in 1801, Smith in 1805—to farming families in Vermont. Both came of age in the religiously fertile burned-over district of New York. Both men sought solace in the church. Both men were charismatic, larger-than-life figures capable of inspiring fierce devotion among their followers and intense hatred among their critics.[18]

The ninth of eleven children, Young endured a hardscrabble existence, especially after his mother died of tuberculosis when Brigham was fourteen years old. The family moved frequently, eventually settling in central New York. As with so many citizens of that era, he spent his early years as a farmer. Young read the Book of Mormon not long after Smith published it, and he was entranced. At last he had found a faith he could embrace and a church that would welcome him into the fold. He abandoned the Methodist faith to join the Mormon Church. Within a few years, Young's first wife had died and he had traveled to Canada as well as to Kirtland. Even among the zealous Mormons of those early years, Brigham Young excelled. In 1835, he was ordained a member of the Quorum of the Twelve Apostles, a high council that traveled around preaching the gospel "to all nations, kindred, tongues, and people."[19]

He was a frequent traveler, spending each summer proselytizing on behalf of the cause and returning in the winter months to fortify the Mormon Church in Kirtland. During the 1830s, Young proved to be an industrious, indefatigable church member, assisting in the construction of the Kirtland Temple, attending the School of the Prophets, and serving as an able aide to Joseph Smith. Perhaps Young's greatest service to Smith occurred when the community challenged Smith's leadership. Brigham Young vehemently defended his friend and mentor—so much so that Young was forced to flee to Missouri with his family in December 1837 to avoid angry reprisals. Fleeing from encroaching enemies was another common bond between Joseph Smith and his eager disciple.[20]

The Missouri relocation provided a temporary respite; by the summer of 1838 it was clear that many of the Saints' new neighbors were growing increasingly hostile toward the church. Young demonstrated his leadership skills under these trying circumstances. The major church leaders, including Joseph Smith, his brother Hyrum, and Sidney Rigdon, were imprisoned at a crucial moment for the Latter Day Saints, for the flock was on the move. As the senior member of the Quorum of Twelve, Young took control of the group's evacuation to several Illinois communities. Between 8,000 and 12,000 church members joined the exodus. Young also worked with members of the Committee on Removal to develop the Missouri Covenant, which required signatories to make their resources available so the church could remove every person to safety who wished to leave Missouri. This early test of his leadership was an important proving ground for Brigham Young. Although he did not know it at the time, it was a dress rehearsal for a longer journey that awaited the group in the 1840s.[21]

Young and his family followed Joseph Smith and the bulk of the faithful to Commerce (rechristened Nauvoo), Illinois, in the spring of 1839. Shortly thereafter, the Quorum of Twelve departed to England to proselytize the British. Once again, the faithful lieutenant's abilities were on full display. During his year abroad, Young baptized between 7,000 and 8,000 converts, distributed 5,000 copies of the Book of Mormon as well as 3,000 hymnals, and assisted almost 1,000 converts in immigrating to Nauvoo. He emerged as a natural leader and potential successor to Joseph Smith.[22]

Young's stature was enhanced by his successes. When he returned to Nauvoo, he was directed to oversee land purchases, construction projects, and the settlement of immigrants. After initial reluctance, he accepted the concept of plural marriage. Indeed, he became one of the most well-known polygamists of the church; by the end of his long life, he had acquired fifty-five wives, all but one of whom he married after joining the church. He fathered fifty-six children from sixteen of his wives. He once stated that when he originally learned of the concept of polygamy, "it was the first time in my life that I desired the grave." In time, his outlook changed.[23]

By the mid-1840s, Young had become one of the most important church leaders. Joseph Smith trusted his friend and adviser implicitly, even confiding in him the inevitability of moving out west to the Rocky Mountains. In 1844, perhaps realizing that his life was imperiled, Smith told other members of the Twelve Apostles they must "bear off this kingdom" if something happened to him. In May of that year, Young departed on his usual summer mission. In his absence, Joseph Smith met his death exactly as he had feared.[24]

By the time Joseph Smith died in 1844, Young was a strong candidate to become Smith's successor, but he was not the heir apparent. To the faithful, Young's personality was remarkably similar to Smith's. Charismatic, supremely confident, and ruthless when the situation so required, he used his powerful presence to good effect. In 1847, Young faced down a challenge to his authority from a competitor, eventually leading his followers out of Illinois toward points farther west. He understood, as Smith had, that it was time to move on before neighboring communities began to organize and threaten Mormon safety. Gathering the flock and herding believers across the continent created an added benefit: They looked to Young as their Moses, delivering them from a land of oppression. Their shared sense of persecution united the band in the wake of the prophet's death, thereby ensuring the religion would survive.[25]

The Mormons had intended to depart on their journey in April 1846, but they accelerated the schedule by two months to avoid additional conflicts with a restless state militia. February was bitterly cold and hardly the ideal time to undertake a dangerous western trek, but the Mormon pioneers believed they had little choice. Following a meandering route through Iowa, Nebraska, and Wyoming, they arrived in the Salt Lake Valley on July 24, 1847. After struggling through innumerable hardships, the small, solidified band, now fully united in their suffering, settled permanently in Utah. Thereafter, their northerly route became known as the Mormon Trail.[26]

The Mormons deemed Utah a suitable destination because it was outside the territorial boundaries of the country, at least when the pioneers set forth on their journey. Following the war with Mexico, the calculus changed as the 1848 Treaty of Guadalupe Hidalgo ceded a large swath of land to the United States, including the area containing Utah. Recognizing that he could not ignore the change, Brigham Young dispatched emissaries to Washington, D.C., to propose that the state of "Deseret" be created. The plan was for Young to serve as the new governor. After the federal government rejected his plan to create a new state, Young was mollified when he discovered that Utah would form a territorial government in 1850. As the most prominent white settler in the territory, he was a natural, if not quite perfect, fit for territorial governor. Few alternatives existed. It took a special kind of person to head into the far-flung corners of the continent, which meant that a territorial governor must be found or imported from more suitable environs. Life was hard; the weather was unpredictable; fate was fickle. So few other white settlers populated the territory in large numbers that the Mormons would be useful representatives of the federal government—or so it seemed at the outset. In 1851, Young won his appointment as the territorial governor.[27]

He and his band forged an uneasy relationship with federal officials. As the 1850s progressed, it became clear that the territorial governor did things his own way, often disregarding Washington's instructions. Young shared much in common with his predecessor, including authoritarian tendencies, a desire not to separate church and state, and a belief in the virtues of polygamy. During a period known as the Mormon Reformation, prominent Mormons began to speak of "blood atonement" as a means of reforming their lives and their commitment to God. Although this concept was not universally accepted, the fierce, frightening rhetoric worried some outsiders who viewed the Latter-Day Saints with suspicion and mistrust. Outsiders were not certain they understood what the Mormons meant by the phrase "blood atonement," but it sounded ominous and dangerous.[28]

These features of 1850s Mormonism inevitably heightened tensions between the territorial governor and the government of the United States. Although Governor Young and the presidential administrations in Washington repeatedly quarreled over the Mormon leader's unwillingness or inability to compromise on separating church and state, the uneasy truce might have continued into the foreseeable future had politics not reared its ugly head as a result of the 1856 presidential election. Trouble began when Democrat James Buchanan defeated John C. Fremont of the newly formed Republican Party in November of that year. During the campaign, the Republicans attacked Buchanan on numerous issues, including the Democratic candidate's inability or unwillingness to attack the "twin relics of barbarism," slavery and polygamy. A "Doughface"—that is, a Northern man who supported slavery—Buchanan would not interfere with the peculiar institution, but he could secure a political advantage by demonstrating his aversion to polygamy. As a symbolic act, the president dismissed Brigham Young as the territorial governor and appointed a successor, Alfred Cumming, to serve in Young's stead. Buchanan instructed federal troops to escort the new administrator to his post.[29]

This absurd crisis was not the politically tone deaf president's first miscalculation, nor, regrettably, would it be his last. Lacking an understanding of conditions in Utah or the Mormons' long-held sense of persecution, to say nothing of the group's growing sense of outrage, Buchanan failed to appreciate the consequences of his seemingly inconsequential act. Not only were the Latter-Day Saints outraged that their leader had been snubbed by officials in Washington, but they resented unilateral action without even a pretense of consulting with them. Moreover, some Mormons mistook the name "Cumming" for R. W. Cummins, an anti-Mormon activist from Missouri. The idea that a bitter enemy would govern the Mormons' home territory was horrifying. Although he had no way of foreseeing future events, James Buchanan inadvertently created the conditions that would culminate in a massacre during the late summer of 1857.[30]

In the same way that Birmingham police chief Bull Connor would later serve as a unifying symbol of evil for civil rights marchers in the 1960s, James Buchanan was cast as the villain in Brigham Young's morality play. The administration's blustery, inept posturing was a godsend for the embattled Mormon leader. Young was battling numerous intractable problems that confronted western settlers of the nineteenth century. After suffering through a drought and an infestation of grasshoppers that severely curtailed the group's farming ventures, the Mormon leader told his people that God was punishing them for losing their righteousness. When he learned of the president's hasty action of sending a replacement governor under armed escort, Young ordered his flock to store grain and hoard ammunition in preparation for the dark days ahead. In his apocalyptic view of the pending confrontation, federal troops would enter the territory to exterminate the group. This standoff was not simply a dispute between government officials over western policy; it was a battle for the survival of Mormonism. Young was defiant. He would not be removed from office absent force. When the Mormon-dominated Utah legislature realized that the U.S. Army might soon appear to enforce the president's order, they reactivated the Nauvoo Legion.[31]

Paranoia became the order of the day. As the church mobilized for war, Young and his followers destroyed records and harassed federal officials traveling through the territory. Fierce, vituperative rhetoric filled the churches and town squares of the hamlets littered throughout the region. In southern Utah, church elder George A. Smith discovered a natural talent for demagoguery as he preached a message of vengeance against the invaders who dared to encroach on Mormon lands. He also sought assistance from Indians in preparing for war. Mormon communities went on high alert as they awaited the coming clash between their forces of good arrayed against the forces of evil represented by the U.S. Army and its agents.[32]

Forced to confront a developing crisis largely of his own making, Buchanan instructed additional troops to move into the Utah Territory to install the president's new man in office and quell the rising rebellion. At a time when the Mormon leader was trying to motivate his flock and instill a sense of camaraderie in the Latter-Day Saints, the administration's decision to engage in military action created a "rally 'round the flag" sentiment that Young used to good advantage.

Recalling the enemy's violence directed at Mormons in the years preceding their trek to Utah—especially the slaughter of the Smith brothers in 1844—Young portrayed a possible confrontation as nothing less than a battle of good against evil. Playing on his constituents' fears, he repeatedly predicted that the Latter-Day Saints would be extirpated if they did not fiercely resist the federal encroachment. The seeds of a violent conflict had been planted and nurtured.[33]

THE BAKER-FANCHER PARTY AND THE MOUNTAIN MEADOWS MASSACRE

As rumors of the U.S. Army's impending arrival spread through small, close-knit frontier communities, Mormon leaders suspected new emigrants and strangers of spying on behalf of the U.S. government. One group attracted special attention from a band of Mormons living 280 miles south of Salt Lake City. An extended wagon train from Arkansas, thereafter known as the Baker-Fancher party, moved into southern Utah. This group of 140 pioneers heading to California had the misfortune to be accompanied by poor timing and scurrilous rumor. A revered Mormon apostle, Partley Pratt, had recently been murdered in Arkansas. When the anxious Latter-Day Saints learned that the new interlopers were Arkansans, word circulated that some of the party had participated in Pratt's murder. In the aftermath of the horrors to come, would-be Mormon apologists recounted at least one heated episode with the Baker-Fancher party during which one or more travelers boasted of complicity in Pratt's murder. It is difficult to assess these claims. No evidence exists that anyone associated with the Baker-Fancher party was directly involved in the Pratt killing, although it cannot be ruled out altogether. Perhaps angry emigrants spewed forth a torrent of vitriolic words designed to aggravate their Mormon detractors or the Mormons who reported the incidents sought to justify subsequent atrocities. Other widely circulated rumors accused the party of poisoning Mormon cattle, insulting the church and its leaders, tormenting women, and threatening to inflict violence against Mormon settlements in southern Utah. Whatever the origins of the tales, the arrival of this particular wagon train in this particular place at this particular time inarguably ratcheted up tensions.[34]

Brigham Young's role in the ensuing violence has long been debated. Historians recognize that Young was not a direct participant. He was hundreds of miles away when the confrontation occurred and, frontier communications being relatively primitive in 1857, he was not in a position to

Mormon leader Brigham Young. Courtesy of Special Collections, Gerald R. Sherratt Library, Southern Utah Uiversity.

direct the action. Nonetheless, he set the stage for the massacre with his incautious public statements and his long-standing antipathy for Gentiles who would interfere with Mormon affairs.[35]

On September 1, in advance of the Baker-Fancher arrival, Young convened a meeting of southern Indian chiefs. Recognizing that the appearance of white settlers could only portend negative repercussions for local tribes, the Indians listened patiently as the Mormon president instructed them to seize travelers' cattle as their wagons rolled along the "south route," which everyone knew was the trail through southern Utah toward California. Whether Young knew his instructions would trigger violence, as his critics have charged, or whether he was merely figuratively firing a shot across the government's bow is open to interpretation.[36]

Three days later, the Fanchers and their traveling companions arrived in Cedar City, Utah, a southern village along the trail. Their arrival did not go unheralded. Isaac Haight, second in command of the Iron Brigade, the Nauvoo Legion's force in southern Utah, and president of the Cedar City Stake of Zion (making him the highest Mormon ecclesiastical official in southern Utah), gathered his flock to discuss an appropriate response to this intrusion. Hardly a timid fellow, the fiery Haight, once described as "a terror to evildoers," informed his followers that it was "the will of all in authority" to arm the Paiute Indian tribe and urge them to "kill all or part" of the Baker-Fancher party. It was important that the slaughter appear to be the work of Indians alone. Despite the work of subsequent apologists who argued that the affair got out of hand in the heat of the moment, it was clear that the more radical Mormon faction was thinking ahead to craft a suitable explanation for posterity.[37]

With the wheels set in motion, Haight directed his Indian interpreter, Nelphi Johnson, to "stir up" the Indians and thereby "give the emigrants a good hush." Haight defended the seemingly indefensible. "There will not be one drop of innocent blood shed, if every one of the damned peck are killed," he argued, "for they are the worse lot of outlaws and ruffians that I ever saw in my life."[38]

Events escalated in coming days. On September 6, as Brigham Young preached from Salt Lake City that the Mormons were not subject to the laws of the United States, Isaac Haight mounted the pulpit to extol the virtues of shedding "my last drop of blood in defense of Zion." Casting the Fanchers as villains, the zealous man of God explained that the Mormons must defend themselves from their would-be enemies. On the same day he spoke these words, the would-be enemies encamped in an idyllic spot known as the Mountain Meadows.[39]

The meadows were a neck-like valley approximately one mile wide and six miles long nestled between small southern Utah hills. A fresh spring of clear, cool water bubbled through the lush vegetation and wild grasses, reinforcing many a visitor's description of the area as an oasis along the often harsh, brutal landscape of the old Santa Fe Trail. It was little wonder that a wagon train would choose the Mountain Meadows as the site for a temporary respite from the travails of a long journey to California.[40]

Events spiraled out of control on September 7 as the Baker-Fancher party was sitting down to breakfast. Someone fired a shot toward the travelers, striking a child. Behind a nearby ridge, between forty and fifty marauders, some of whom were Paiutes and others were Mormons disguised as Native Americans, fired on the wagon train. The pioneers were heavily armed; they returned fire. Had they gathered their possessions and fled the area immediately, the massacre might never have occurred. Because they failed to recognize the impending Mormon threat, the Baker-Fancher party circled the wagons and planned a defense. This strategy was effective in situations where an Indian attack lasted a few hours or days, but it was unsustainable in the long term. In the ensuing days, the precariousness of the Baker-Fancher predicament became clear as the scene degenerated into a siege.[41]

Despite the antipathy the Latter-Day Saints displayed toward this unwelcomed band of transients, not every Mormon agreed that violence was justified. With dissension spreading in the ranks, the southern Utah leaders decided to clothe themselves with the imprimatur of the Mormon leadership. Haight dispatched a courier on the six-hundred-mile round trip to Salt Lake City to confer with President Young and ask for guidance. Owing to poor roads and an almost nonexistent transportation infrastructure, the trek was undertaken entirely on horseback, requiring six days to complete. By the time an order arrived from Brigham Young directing his flock not to attack the wagon train, the deed was done. Critics have argued that the timing was too convenient; it allowed Young to enjoy plausible deniability in avoiding responsibility for the massacre. Haight could have waited to receive the president's reply if he had genuinely needed instructions before carrying out his plan.[42]

The decision makers did not act in the heat of passion; they knew their actions would be scrutinized. Over three days, from September 8 through 10, Haight repeatedly discussed the matter with William H. Dame, his superior in the Nauvoo Legion. Dame was a co-founder of the Mormon town of Parowan and an influential member of the high council, a group comprised of twelve men who helped coordinate policy in the Mormon territory. Although a naturally timid fellow who preferred to avoid difficult policy questions, Dame nonetheless held a variety of important posts within the governing structure of the church. He could be counted on to support any policy he believed to advance the Mormon cause. If Dame had insisted that the Baker-Fancher party must be allowed to depart in peace, the massacre probably would not have occurred. Whatever his personal predilections, Dame reputedly remarked that "my orders are that all the emigrants [with the exception of young children] must be done away with."[43]

By September 11, all parties were weary from the exchange of gunfire. The emigrants trapped inside the circle of wagons were low on supplies as well as desperate to nurse their sick and wounded. In the meantime, the Paiute Indians gradually wandered off. They initially had been emboldened by the prospect of divvying up the pioneers' goods if the group left them behind in a mad dash for safety, but as the siege dragged on, the Native Americans grew disenchanted. The attack had not gone as well as the Mormons had promised. For their part, Mormon leaders were dismayed as the Paiutes departed. The plan was to blame the attack on the Indians. Although the Paiutes might yet serve as convenient scapegoats for posterity, their absence certainly would complicate matters.[44]

If necessity is the mother of invention, Mormon leaders on the scene devised a new scheme that took into account the need for ending the stalemate. Major John Higbee, the leader in charge of the Mormon forces at Mountain Meadows, instructed two Nauvoo Legion soldiers, John D. Lee and William Bateman, to approach the wagon train under a flag of truce. They were inspired choices. At forty-five years of age, Lee, like many Mormons, had suffered through terrible hardships in his youth and desperately sought spiritual solace through numerous organized religious groups until he embraced, and in turn was embraced by, the Latter-Day Saints. He had been with the church through its wilderness years. After journeying across the mountains to Utah, he was a devoted Mormon, one of the most zealous in the territory. For his part, Bateman was a leader in southern Utah owing to his position as the Cedar City constable. He represented law and order on the frontier.[45]

Reasoning with the band was the surest way to gain their trust. The envoys were to promise the pilgrims a deal too attractive to refuse under the circumstances. If Fancher and his followers would lay down their arms and surrender their possessions, including the wagons and cattle, to the Paiutes, the Mormons would escort them, unharmed, to Cedar City, thirty-five miles away. It was a humiliating, potentially devastating setback for pioneers who, in some cases, had brought all their worldly goods on the perilous journey, but it was the only realistic option for the hapless travelers. They could not hold out against the siege much longer.[46]

When the two men approached the wagon train, an intrepid pioneer met them halfway as he hoisted a white rag on a stick. The emigrant leader, Alexander Fancher, was already dead, so the identity of the correspondent has been the subject of conjecture since that time. In any case, he spoke with the two Mormons for about fifteen minutes before leading Lee and another group of men inside the wagons. The sight of well-fortified pioneer stock was unnerving, but Lee continued with the plan. Outlining the surrender terms, he used all his argumentative skill to sell the band on the scheme.[47]

Although some of the party remained suspicious of the "deal," it did not take much persuasion to arrange the surrender despite the travelers' fears for their safety. "If the emigrants had had a good supply of ammunition they would never have surrendered," Lee later speculated. "I do not think we could have captured them without great loss, for they were brave men and very resolute and determined." Because they were almost out of ammunition and supplies, the question was whether they would lay down their arms now, when generous terms might be had, or continue to fight and risk being overwhelmed by an enraged, superior force that would give no quarter in its hour of triumph.[48]

And so began one of the most devious, shameful acts in nineteenth-century American history. The beleaguered travelers surrendered their firearms because they trusted the Mormon promises of safe passage. Samuel McMurty, a Nauvoo Legion soldier, grabbed the reins of one emigrant wagon as the youngest children crawled inside. The most seriously wounded men and a woman occupied another wagon. The women and older children followed behind the second wagon as the men, marching in single file and accompanied by a Mormon guard, brought up the rear. Lee walked between the two wagons so he could direct events from the front of the wagon train. Major Higbee directed events from the back. The specific ordering should have alerted the emigrants that something was amiss. Separating the injured from the healthy made sense, but moving children away from their parents would have seemed inexplicable if the ultimate purpose was to escort the group to a safe haven.[49]

Although a few men muttered cautious words of protest, most emigrants appeared relieved that the standoff had ended without further bloodshed. They were weary from the fighting and had to be hurried along, but eventually the band got moving. Unbeknownst to them, a group of Paiutes hid from sight less than a mile away. For the scheme to work, the assailants needed the element of surprise to subdue their captives.[50]

Even the most hardened, zealous Mormon hesitated in the face of a monumental act of treachery. Major Higbee was slated to call a halt at a strategic point on the trail—a signal for the carnage to commence—but he did not call out the command immediately. Later, he explained that he hoped for a last-minute reprieve from high-ranking church leaders. No reprieve came. As the emigrants shuffled past the original site for the command, it was clear the plan would fail if the killing did not commence; the element of surprise would be lost. Lee later chastised Higbee for the unconscionable delay that imperiled the scheme.[51]

After marching for a quarter mile past the ideal spot, the Baker-Fancher party began to relax, believing their Mormon protectors would be true to their word. It was a sad mistake. As the group shuffled along a small hill, Higbee somehow found the gumption to act. "Halt," he called. No sooner had he spoken than a volley of gun fire echoed across the meadows as each Mormon guard shot the emigrant man marching at his side. The gunfire lasted no more than a few minutes, but in that short time the men were cut down with astonishing rapidity.[52]

A second wave of killing came at close quarters. If anything, it was worse than the initial bloodshed, for it involved unarmed, helpless women and children. Nelphi Johnson gave the order for his men to rush at the defenseless captives who had just witnessed their fathers, brothers, husbands, uncles, and comrades cut down before them. As the ambushers raced forward, emitting "hideous, demon-like yells," they fell on their victims with relish. Nancy Huff, who was spared because she was four years old, recalled years later the horror that unfolded before her. "I saw my mother shot in the forehead and fall dead. The women and children screamed and clung together. Some of the young women begged the assassins after they had run out on us not to kill them, but they had no mercy on them, clubbing their guns and beating out their brains." Another eyewitness remembered that the "women and children were knocked down with stones, clubs, and gun barrels, struck in the neck and butchered like hogs." One hundred and twenty men, women, and children died that day.[53]

The aftermath of the massacre would reverberate for decades. Immediately following the event, some participants, notably John D. Lee, bragged of their ferocity in doing what needed to be done, distasteful though it might have been. They would have occasion to recant. When word arrived that Brigham Young had ordered the emigrants to pass through the area unmolested and it became clear the world looked upon the deed as an abomination, previously boastful Mormons and Paiutes developed spotty memories or confessed to taking part solely on the periphery. Some Mormon leaders contended that the Indians had been the only actual participants, thereby exonerating the Mormon leadership of southern Utah. Few observers believed such a transparent falsehood.[54]

Seventeen children—none over seven years of age—survived the butchery. The Mormons gathered up the shell-shocked youngsters and transported them to Mormon homes to spend time until they could be doled out to families willing to raise them to adulthood. It was a cruel irony that some of the men who slaughtered their parents subsequently welcomed the children into their homes.[55]

As for the site itself, the Indians had been promised a share in the bounty. They scoured the scene immediately following the murders to procure whatever goods they could carry. As Lee described it, "The bodies of men, women and children had been stripped entirely naked, making the scene one of the most loathsome and ghastly that can be imagined."[56]

Brigham Young had not wanted the Baker-Fancher party harmed, at least not by Mormons, but it was too late to change what had happened. Still oblivious to the slaughter, on September 15 he defiantly ordered the Nauvoo Legion to resist federal troops if they entered Utah Territory. When he learned of the episode, Young was no fool; he immediately recognized that the repercussions could be dire. If the U.S. Army had been restrained in its past dealings with the Latter-Day Saints, it might be more aggressive in the wake of stories about the slaughter of innocents. In time, the Mormon leader tried to reconcile his conscience with the massacre, for surely he knew that no small measure of the responsibility was his. Even if Brigham Young had not ordered the killings, he had set the tone of hostility that drove his fellow citizens to wield the bloody sword. "I asked the Lord if it was all right for the deed to be done, to take the vision of the deed from my mind, and the Lord did so, and I feel first rate. It is all right. The only fear I have is from traitors." It was a convenient reworking of historical memory and a masterful act of self-deception.[57]

Exactly as Young had feared, press reports dwelled on the brutality of the crime. Then, as now, newspapers reveled in gruesome details of catastrophic events as a means of capturing reader interest. John Aiken, a mail carrier who passed through the Mountain Meadows not long after the event, was among the first to provide grist for the mill. He described a grisly scene where wolves feasted on carcasses left to rot in the sun. Newspaper editors anxious to prolong stories of the carnage used their opinion pages to call for a government investigation of the crime. The *San Francisco Bulletin* urged the federal government to pursue "a crusade against Utah which will crush out this beast of heresy forever." Congress, never known to shy away from headlines, launched an investigation.[58]

The following month, the Nauvoo Legion harassed soldiers moving into the territory, burning more than fifty army wagons on October 5. The Mormons were playing a dangerous game, and they knew it. Trained soldiers, emboldened by growing public disgust over what was being called the Mountain Meadows Massacre, might exact vengeance for atrocities, real and imagined, perpetrated by an unpopular religious sect. Anticipating a bloody campaign in the spring, army forces established winter quarters at Fort Bridger with the expectation of moving on to Salt Lake City when the weather improved. When spring rolled around, reinforcements arrived and the soldiers set out to engage the Mormons. Only Brigham Young could forestall further violence and bloodshed. He knew when to back away from his overheated rhetoric. Before the army arrived in the territory, he announced that he would step aside as the territorial governor. The foolish "Utah War" had ended.[59]

For all of his righteous fury, Brigham Young realized that he and the Mormons would be judged harshly by posterity if the complete story of the massacre became public knowledge. After interviewing John Lee about the massacre, Young submitted a report to the commissioner of Indian affairs implicating the Paiutes and exonerating the Mormons of southern Utah. In a deposition during Lee's subsequent trial, the crafty Mormon leader even used his removal as territorial governor to good advantage. In explaining why he had not prosecuted Lee or any Mormon leader who planned or participated in the massacre, he said, "because another governor had been appointed by the president of the United States, and was then on the way here to take my place, and I did not know how soon he might arrive; and because the United States judges were not in the territory." Casting himself in the role as a dutiful public servant who sought only to cooperate to the best of his ability, Young went on to say, "Soon after Governor Cumming arrived I asked him to take Judge Cradlebaugh, who belonged to the southern district, with him, and I would accompany them with sufficient aid to investigate the matter and bring the offenders to justice."[60]

Although no one outside the Mormon community believed the self-serving narrative, the continued promise of an armed conflict between the U.S. Army and the Mormons prevented a federal investigation until 1859. The investigation fell under the command of Brevet Major James Henry Carleton, a career army officer who had fought in the war with Mexico and served on the plains. While serving as commander of the First Dragoons stationed at Fort Tejon, California, he was ordered to march to southern Utah and head the investigative team. At the massacre site, he discovered partial skeletons and women's hair strewn across the brush. According to Carleton's subsequent report, he found children's bones still nestled in their mothers' arms, "a sight which can never be forgotten."[61]

Determined to be thorough, Carleton met with local settlers as well as Paiutes. During these interviews, he heard a variety of views and conflicting stories. He came away convinced that the Indians had not acted alone, despite Brigham Young's assertions to the contrary. Carleton's May 1859 report placed blame squarely on the Mormons. Jacob Forney, superintendent of Indian affairs for Utah, filed a subsequent report agreeing with Carleton's findings. Forney took an additional step to resolve the issue by transporting the surviving children from their temporary lodgings with the Mormons back to Arkansas to live with relatives.[62]

For his part, Major Carleton directed his men to bury the bones in a cairn so that animals and the elements would no longer desecrate the remains. Two years later, Brigham Young ordered the cairn torn down so the monument would not serve as a fresh reminder of the controversy. Young reputedly said, "Vengeance is mine and I have taken a little." Whether he actually uttered such a statement is disputed.[63]

In the aftermath of these investigations, a federal judge, John Cradlebaugh, arrived in Provo, Utah, in 1859, toured the Mountain Meadows site,

John D. Lee, a central figure in the Mountain Meadows Massacre. Courtesy of Special Collections, Gerald R. Sherratt Library, Southern Utah University.

and ordered that Isaac Haight, John Higbee, and John D. Lee, architects of the massacre, be arrested and put on trial. The suspects fled before they could be apprehended. A frustrated Judge Cradlebaugh charged Brigham Young as an "accessory before the fact" owing to his efforts to instigate trouble between the Indians and emigrants passing through the Utah territory. Mormon territorial probate court judge Elias Smith, thought to be sympathetic to the Latter-Day Saints, ordered Young to be arrested, probably to ensure his trial before a favorable Mormon court. When formal charges were not filed, Young went free and never faced prosecution.[64]

Interest in the massacre gradually decreased, especially when a civil war erupted in the eastern United States. By the late 1860s, as attention returned to the episode, the Mormon Church excommunicated Isaac Haight and John D. Lee. In 1874, a territorial grand jury indicted nine suspects, although Lee was the only defendant to be tried, convicted, and executed for his part in the massacre.[65]

CAUSES AND CONSEQUENCES

The massacre continues to fascinate modern audiences owing to the fear and hysteria that have accompanied Mormonism in the decades since Smith first produced the Book of Mormon. Many nineteenth-century contemporaries believed the Latter-Day Saints were a band of dangerous religious fanatics who deceived an emigrant party with promises of safety, only to kill everyone except seventeen small children with no compunction. In light of the circumstances leading up to the grisly episode, it is difficult to justify the Mormons' actions. The Baker-Fancher party and other emigrants did not directly threaten settlers in Utah. Although rumors circulated that the travelers may have poisoned cattle and some members reputedly boasted of committing atrocities against Mormons in the past, no evidence exists that these acts ever occurred. Even if they did occur, the slaughter of 120 unarmed people who were induced to surrender under false pretenses, including many women and children, was hardly a proportional response. In the words of three historians who have written of this episode, "The Mountain Meadows Massacre stands as one of the darkest events in Mormon history."[66]

The question here is whether the actions of the Mormon instigators constituted terrorism. As discussed in the introduction, defining an act as "terrorism" is not merely a semantics game; it is essential to understanding the central case of a terrorist act. Understanding the central case may assist in explaining the root causes, and potential solutions, to the problem of terrorism.

An act of terrorism, as the name implies, is intended to strike terror into the hearts of the civilian population. Since the rise of the modern nation-state, a large number of terrorist acts have been perpetrated by state actors such as Germany under Adolf Hitler, the Soviet Union under Joseph Stalin, Communist China under Mao Tse-tung, and Cambodia under Pol Pot, to name a few notorious examples. The advantage of state-sponsored terrorism—if such heinous acts can be said to contain advantages—is that the identity of the actors involved, if not the facts surrounding the acts themselves, is relatively clear. Substate terrorism presents problems because the identity and motivations of the actors are not always clear. Even if substate actors do not believe they are acting as terrorists, an act can still be characterized as terroristic if the goal is to achieve a social, political, or religious end through the threat or use of violence aimed at civilians. The matter is further complicated by the realization that some enterprises such as the Cosa Nostra or various criminal rings may eschew social, political, or religious purposes in favor of strictly monetary designs and yet engage in acts of terror. Al Capone's organization in 1920s Chicago did not seek to influence the political process through terror except as a means to the end of amassing a large fortune.[67]

The Mormons would recoil—in fact, did recoil—at the characterization of their actions on September 11, 1857, as "barbaric," "savage," "beastly," or, in modern parlance, "terroristic." On numerous occasions before the slaughter, prominent Mormons railed against their enemies and promised retribution. During a Pioneer Day celebration in Cedar City two months before the murders, participants hoisted banners sporting phrases such as "A terror to evil-doers" and "Zion's Avengers." With the benefit of hindsight, it is tempting to read these public displays as evidence of the group's terroristic intent. The twenty-first-century notion of terrorism, however, is different from what nineteenth-century denizens meant by such provocative language. Typical writings from the antebellum era are rife with florid prose, partially influenced by the Romantic literature of the day. A lack of restraint in written communications does not a terrorist make. Were that the case, many a practitioner of purple prose who went on to engage in violence would be labeled a "terrorist."

To give the Mormons their due, they had been victims of numerous acts of violence since their earliest days as an organized group. Their initial efforts to arm themselves occurred as self-defense measures employed against hostile neighbors. Even the dispute with the U.S. Army in 1857 and 1858 eventually ended with a peaceful resolution. They did not set out for the Utah Territory to slaughter infidels or conquer native peoples. In fact, most accounts describe their relations with Native Americans as mutually beneficial and convivial. Despite the criticism heaped on the church by its detractors, they were reluctant warriors.[68]

Unlike the central case of terrorism, where perpetrators often proudly accept credit for their work, the Mormons tried to hide their involvement after the fact. Perhaps John D. Lee and others who had a hand in the planning and commission of the crime boasted of their prowess, but the braggarts knew their claims were suitable only for a select audience of like-minded individuals; they were careful to limit the number of parties involved. Realizing that even some of their fellow Mormons rejected the actions of September 11, they obfuscated their intentions before and after the episode occurred. This kind of aversion to public scrutiny is not what one thinks of as classic terrorist behavior, at least not as the concept came to be understood in later times. Whatever can be said about the events of that day, the episode was not a quintessential case of terrorism.[69]

Several common characteristics of group violence existed in the Mountain Meadows Massacre. The first characteristic was an intense desire to retaliate against one's tormentors—not simply to defend oneself against outsiders, but to take the fight to the enemy. To understand, although not necessarily excuse, what happened, it is crucial to consider the tenor of the times. The Mormons had long suffered from persecution, which is not factually disputed even by critics who contend that the group was the cause of much of its troubles. The Latter-Day Saints had been herded out of one home after another and chased across the midwestern states by armed militia in some instances. Group members had been subjected to violence on innumerable occasions. The founder, Joseph Smith, had been brutally murdered at the hands of a mob. Critics argue that much of the fear and mistrust directed at the religious group resulted, at least in part, from the Mormon penchant for antagonizing neighboring communities. After the practice of polygamy became widely known, the Mormons' strange practices, once dismissed by charitable observers as eccentric and off-putting, were interpreted as blasphemous and threatening. It was a religious age. Many frontier families clung to their long-held religious beliefs, for those beliefs were almost all they had. For the fundamentalist who believed that the Christian Bible was the revealed word of God, unassailable and literally true (despite the thorny problem of multiple translations), the Mormons were a dangerous, radical cult that needed to be eradicated. Their blasphemous talk of Native Americans as the Children of Israel was too much for some communities to tolerate.[70]

Even if the Mormons brought some of their misfortune on themselves, an unfortunate inability to play well with others does not justify violence. For their part, the Mormons frequently gave as well as they got. No one seemed willing or able to step back and break the cycle of violence. When neighbors attacked the Mormons, they returned the attack, thereby inviting another wave of violence. The aphorism attributed to Gandhi—an eye for an eye makes the whole world blind—was anathema to the nineteenth-century frontier where violence was an acceptable form of dispute resolution.[71]

Assuming that the Mormons were victims of ruthless violence, does persecution justify retaliation? In Anglo-American criminal law, a widely held doctrine of self-defense allows a party under attack to use reasonable forced to repel the attack. Even if the attack would not have been fatal, the party under attack is deemed to have used reasonable force if he or she believed, under the circumstances, that such force was necessary to preserve his or her life. Only when the party under attack becomes the aggressor does the analysis change. A party under attack that fends off the assault and thereafter chases the attacker in an effort to extract vengeance has now moved from being the aggrieved party to being the aggrieving party.[72]

Although the Latter-Day Saints were bombarded by their enemies and sought shelter from the storm in the Utah Territory, the group's plight was not altogether unwelcome to its members. For a religious group whose members view themselves as the chosen people, suffering has an ennobling effect. Brigham Young used the Mormon experience of persecution to advance his goals. In the long tradition of demagogues throughout the ages who have used their enemies' transgressions as justification for all manner of repugnant acts, the Mormon president claimed that he and his followers acted in self-defense. The preemptive strike as a means of ensuring no further attacks owing to the *in terrorem* effect is a convenient rationale for a group that views itself as beleaguered.[73]

Fundamentalist groups of all sorts, especially those that believe they have been persecuted, objectify and even vilify nonmembers. This worldview casts "us" against "them," with "them" being outsiders who do not understand the perspective of "us" and therefore do not share the group's values. In fact, outsiders are downright antagonistic to the group's values. The more threatened the group is by real or imagined outsider actions, the more likely it is that a dispute will turn violent. If violence becomes commonplace, individuals inside the group become desensitized. It is considerably less repugnant for "us," the group, to slaughter an objectified "them" when violence is deemed an appropriate course of action than it is for individuals to kill other individuals absent this framework. The demonization of outsiders, coupled with a culture of violence, is a recipe for what can be defined loosely as "terrorism."[74]

The Utah Mormons were fed a steady diet of righteous anger and indignation at what had been done to them by nonbelievers in their creed. God was punishing them for their lapses in faith and judgment; how else could one explain the pests that threatened their crops? If the group would only reaffirm its righteousness and get right with the church and with God, the members might yet experience better days ahead.

The Baker-Fancher party represented the worst form of outsiders. These emigrants were from Arkansas—the land where Parley Pratt had been cut down—and rumor had it that some of that holy man's killers were among the party. Another rumor suggested that the Fanchers had poisoned Mormon cattle. It was possible the travelers were not innocent emigrants in the first place. They might have been spies sent by the soon-to-arrive U.S. Army to reconnoiter the area and channel sensitive military intelligence to the invaders. If this string of unsubstantiated conspiracy theories sounds absurd from the remove of many decades, at the time it engendered a level of hysteria that infused almost every action the Mormons undertook in the summer and fall of 1857.[75]

Another characteristic of group violence is the presence of authoritarian leadership. By all accounts, Brigham Young was an authoritarian leader who seldom brooked dissent. His personality required that he assume the mantle of unquestioned leadership, but it was more than that. The internecine struggle for a successor to Joseph Smith resulted in some Mormon offshoots setting up denominations elsewhere. If Young hoped to solidify the church and secure his position as the undisputed leader, he had to act decisively, authoritatively. When the band set out for the western territory in the bitter cold of February, a strong leader was required to guide the way. After the Mormons were ensconced in the Utah Territory, they faced multiple threats to their existence. The harsh climate and infestations meant that their existence was constantly imperiled. Repeated demands from several presidential administrations in Washington, D.C., intruded into Mormon business throughout the 1850s, ensuring that the group would have to satisfy the very government that had sheltered their tormentors and the murderers of their prophet a decade earlier. Finally, the inexorable movement of federal troops across the landscape cast a shadow over everything the Mormons did in the weeks and months leading up to the Mountain Meadows Massacre.[76]

As the years passed and Brigham Young managed to hold the church together, he tightened his grip on power. The numerous external crises he faced only convinced his followers of the need to retain a single leader with the authority to provide for their security against dangerous outside forces. If these external crises had not occurred, it is possible that Young would have needed to manufacture a bogeyman so he could hold his flock together.[77]

Yet another characteristic of group violence naturally stems from the constant presence of an authoritarian leader. Citizens learn their behavior through a complex socialization process; the desire to follow the group, which is often present under an authoritarian regime, results from living, day in and day out, under a system where individuality is viewed, at best, as off-putting and, at worst, dangerous. Brigham Young developed a rigid hierarchy of control in his Utah theocracy; the Mormon people learned to obey their leaders with few or no questions. When prominent men such as William H. Dame, Isaac Haight, and John D. Lee implemented a plan to trick and kill the Baker-Fancher party, it was unlikely that anyone lower in the hierarchy would disobey their orders. Even those who might have been inclined to speak up by temperament had learned that obedience was a prized attribute. In any event, the most iconoclastic individuals deliberately were left out of the decision-making process lest they raise an alarm.[78]

A discussion of these characteristics does much to explain what happened that September day in southern Utah, although the full permutations and combinations that led to slaughter may never be known with certainty. It still does not answer the central question of whether the Mormons were terrorists. As with the other cases recounted in this book, some aspects of the Mormon example suggest that the group engaged in terrorism, at least in that time and place. The masterminds behind the slayings attempted to justify their actions as self-defense in the larger sense that the Baker-Fancher party and their ilk represented a threat to the Mormon way of life even if the unarmed men, women, and children butchered that day were not a specific, immediate threat. If a legitimate, specific claim of self-defense is set aside, the incident appears to have been driven by a misguided amalgamation of motives: a desire to exact vengeance against the few braggarts who boasted of killing Parley Pratt, a desire to send a message to the U.S. Army and others who would encroach on Mormon rights and lands, and a general expression of the Mormon ferocity that had been nurtured by decades of abuse and persecution.[79]

Even this explanation is not correct. Assuming the Mormons sought to send a message to would-be interlopers, their subsequent efforts to cover up what happened muted what otherwise would have been a clear warning to all who followed the Baker-Fancher expedition into southern Utah. Sending a message to the U.S. Army that violence is an appropriate standard of action would seem to be the height of folly, bordering on suicide. Avenging Pratt's death by slaughtering women and children who could not have taken part in that episode simply does not make sense. Perhaps, as has been said in other times and in a variety of contexts, when the times are frightening and people are hysterical, matters can get out of hand. Acts that otherwise would be condemned as horrendous and beyond the pale briefly enter the province of acceptable behavior. Such acts may not be part of a larger design of terrorism, but they nonetheless can constitute terroristic acts.

NOTES

1. Bancroft, *History of Utah, 1540–1886*, 543–44; Walker et al., *Massacre at Mountain Meadows*, 3–4.

2. Arrington and Bitton, *The Mormon Experience*, xiii–xvi; Krakauer, *Under the Banner of Heaven*, 3–8; Walker et al., *Massacre at Mountain Meadows*, 6–7.

3. Arrington and Bitton, *The Mormon Experience*, 9–14; Krakauer, *Under the Banner of Heaven*, 61–62; Walker et al., *Massacre at Mountain Meadows*, 6–7.

4. Howe, *What Hath God Wrought*, 312–13.

5. Hambrick-Stowe, *Charles G. Finney and the Spirit of American Evangelicalism*, 1 21.

6. Arrington and Bitton, *The Mormon Experience*, 5–7; Howe, *What Hath God Wrought*, 313; Krakauer, *Under the Banner of Heaven*, 55–56.

7. Arrington and Bitton, *The Mormon Experience*, 5–7; Krakauer, *Under the Banner of Heaven*, 56.

8. Bushman, *Joseph Smith*, 41; Krakauer, *Under the Banner of Heaven*, 55–57.

9. Arrington and Bitton, *The Mormon Experience*, 8–12; Bushman, *Joseph Smith*, 44–45; Howe, *What Hath God Wrought*, 313–14; Krakauer, *Under the Banner of Heaven*, 57–58

10. Arrington and Bitton, *The Mormon Experience*, 19–21; Bushman, *Joseph Smith*, xx, 35–36; Howe, *What Hath God Wrought*, 313–15.

11. Arrington and Bitton, *The Mormon Experience*, 21; Bushman, *Joseph Smith*, 89–90.

12. Bushman, *Joseph Smith*, 178–79; Walker et al., *Massacre at Mountain Meadows*, 8.

13. Krakauer, *Under the Banner of Heaven*, 5–6; Walker et al., *Massacre at Mountain Meadows*, 6–8.

14. Bushman, *Joseph Smith*, 442–43; Krakauer, *Under the Banner of Heaven*, 5–6.

15. Arrington and Bitton, *The Mormon Experience*, 22; Bushman, *Joseph Smith*, 221; Howe, *What Hath God Wrought*, 318.

16. Bushman, *Joseph Smith*, 539–42; Howe, *What Hath God Wrought*, 725–26.

17. Arrington and Bitton, *The Mormon Experience*, 22; Bushman, *Joseph Smith*, 551–52; Howe, *What Hath God Wrought*, 725–26; Krakauer, *Under the Banner of Heaven*, 131–33, 191–92.

18. Howe, *What Hath God Wrought*, 726–27; Krakauer, *Under the Banner of Heaven*, 192–96.

19. Arrington, *Brigham Young: American Moses*, 48–52; Arrington and Bitton, *The Mormon Experience*, 22; Howe, *What Hath God Wrought*, 726–27; Krakauer, *Under the Banner of Heaven*, 193–96.

20. Arrington, *Brigham Young: American Moses*, 62; Walker et al., *Massacre at Mountain Meadows*, 17–18.

21. Arrington, *Brigham Young: American Moses*, 70; Krakauer, *Under the Banner of Heaven*, 105–7.

22. Arrington and Bitton, *The Mormon Experience*, 22; Howe, *What Hath God Wrought*, 319; Krakauer, *Under the Banner of Heaven*, 105–7; Walker et al., *Massacre at Mountain Meadows*, 13.

23. Arrington, *Brigham Young: American Moses*, 121; Howe, *What Hath God Wrought*, 730–31.

24. Arrington and Bitton, *The Mormon Experience*, 22; Bushman, *Joseph Smith*, 551–52; Howe, *What Hath God Wrought*, 725–26; Krakauer, *Under the Banner of Heaven*, 131–33, 191–92.

25. Arrington, *Brigham Young: American Moses*, 113–17; Bushman, *Joseph Smith*, 89–90; Howe, *What Hath God Wrought*, 726–27; Krakauer, *Under the Banner of Heaven*, 198–201.

26. Arrington, *Brigham Young: American Moses*, 145–46; Howe, *What Hath God Wrought*, 727–29; Walker et al., *Massacre at Mountain Meadows*, 18–20.

27. Arrington, *Brigham Young: American Moses*, 226–30; Howe, *What Hath God Wrought*, 801–11.

28. Arrington, *Brigham Young: American Moses*, 361–62; Krakauer, *Under the Banner of Heaven*, 196–97; Walker et al., *Massacre at Mountain Meadows*, 23–24.

29. Bagley, *Blood of the Prophets*, 79–80; Furniss, *The Mormon Conflict*, 95–96; Poll and Hansen, "'Buchanan's Blunder,'" 121–31; Walker et al., *Massacre at Mountain Meadows*, 27–30, 38.

30. Furniss, *The Mormon Conflict*, 62–68; Krakauer, *Under the Banner of Heaven*, 206–8; Szasz and Szasz, "Religion and Spirituality," 364; Walker et al., *Massacre at Mountain Meadows*, 38.

31. Arrington, *Brigham Young: American Moses*, 175, 189; Howe, *What Hath God Wrought*, 730.

32. Arrington, *Brigham Young: American Moses*, 307; Bagley, *Blood of the Prophets*, 83–87; Krakauer, *Under the Banner of Heaven*, 217–18; Walker et al., *Massacre at Mountain Meadows*, 49–53.

33. Arrington, *Brigham Young: American Moses*, 261–62; Szasz and Szasz, "Religion and Spirituality," 364.

34. Arrington, *Brigham Young: American Moses*, 493; Arrington and Bitton, *The Mormon Experience*, 166; Bagley, *Blood of the Prophets*, 70–71; Bancroft, *History of Utah, 1540–1886*, 544–48.

35. Bagley, *Blood of the Prophets*, 87–88; Bancroft, *History of Utah, 1540–1886*, 543–44; Walker et al., *Massacre at Mountain Meadows*, 70–71.

36. Bagley, *Blood of the Prophets*, 83–88; Krakauer, *Under the Banner of Heaven*, 218–19.

37. Bagley, *Blood of the Prophets*, 155–56; Krakauer, *Under the Banner of Heaven*, 219; Walker et al., *Massacre at Mountain Meadows*, 57–59, 136–40.

38. Quoted in Walker et al., *Massacre at Mountain Meadows*, 164–65, 180–81.

39. Krakauer, *Under the Banner of Heaven*, 219–20; Walker et al., *Massacre at Mountain Meadows*, 149–51.

40. Bancroft, *History of Utah, 1540–1886*, 549–50; Walker et al., *Massacre at Mountain Meadows*, 3–4.

41. Bancroft, *History of Utah, 1540–1886*, 550; Krakauer, *Under the Banner of Heaven*, 219–20.

42. Krakauer, *Under the Banner of Heaven*, 211–17; Walker et al., *Massacre at Mountain Meadows*, 156.

43. Bagley, *Blood of the Prophets*, 155–56; Walker et al., *Massacre at Mountain Meadows*, 178–79.

44. Bancroft, *History of Utah, 1540–1886*, 551–52; Krakauer, *Under the Banner of Heaven*, 222–23; Walker et al., *Massacre at Mountain Meadows*, 192 93.

45. Bancroft, *History of Utah, 1540–1886*, 548 49, 564–68, Walker et al., *Massacre at Mountain Meadows*, 194–95.

46. Arrington, *Brigham Young. American Moses*, 278–79; Bancroft, *History of Utah, 1540–1886*, 552.

47. Bancroft, *History of Utah, 1540–1886*, 555–56; Walker et al., *Massacre at Mountain Meadows*, 195.

48. Bancroft, *History of Utah, 1540–1886*, 555; Krakauer, *Under the Banner of Heaven*, 222; Walker et al., *Massacre at Mountain Meadows*, 196.

49. Bancroft, *History of Utah, 1540–1886*, 555; Walker et al., *Massacre at Mountain Meadows*, 196–97.

50. Krakauer, *Under the Banner of Heaven*, 222; Walker et al., *Massacre at Mountain Meadows*, 195–98.

51. Arrington, *Brigham Young: American Moses*, 278–79; Bagley, *Blood of the Prophets*, 150; Bancroft, *History of Utah, 1540–1886*, 555–56; Walker et al., *Massacre at Mountain Meadows*, 199.

52. Bagley, *Blood of the Prophets*, 150–53; Krakauer, *Under the Banner of Heaven*, 222–23; Walker et al., *Massacre at Mountain Meadows*, 199 203.

53. Bagley, *Blood of the Prophets*, 153–55; Bancroft, *History of Utah, 1540–1886*, 556–57; Krakauer, *Under the Banner of Heaven*, 223.

54. Krakauer, *Under the Banner of Heaven*, 224–25; Walker et al., *Massacre at Mountain Meadows*, 212–16.

55. Bagley, *Blood of the Prophets*, 154–55; Bancroft, *History of Utah, 1540–1886*, 557–58; Walker et al., *Massacre at Mountain Meadows*, 212, 216–17.

56. Krakauer, *Under the Banner of Heaven*, 242–43; Walker et al., *Massacre at Mountain Meadows*, 213–17, 221.

57. Arrington, *Brigham Young: American Moses*, 415; Krakauer, *Under the Banner of Heaven*, 211–16, 220–21, 230; Poll and Hansen, "'Buchanan's Blunder,'" 121–31; Walker et al., *Massacre at Mountain Meadows*, 183–86.

58. Bagley, *Blood of the Prophets*, 157, 191, 243; Bancroft, *History of Utah, 1540–1886*, 559.

59. Bagley, *Blood of the Prophets*, 181; Furniss, *The Mormon Conflict*, 143–44.

60. Quoted in Bancroft, *History of Utah, 1540–1886*, 558.

61. Krakauer, *Under the Banner of Heaven*, 229–30; Walker et al., *Massacre at Mountain Meadows*, 3–5, 193.

62. Bancroft, *History of Utah, 1540–1886*, 557–58; Walker et al., *Massacre at Mountain Meadows*, 4.

63. Bancroft, *History of Utah, 1540–1886*, 558–59; Walker et al., *Massacre at Mountain Meadows*, 4.

64. Arrington, *Brigham Young: American Moses*, 276–78; Bancroft, *History of Utah, 1540–1886*, 558–62.

65. Arrington, *Brigham Young: American Moses*, 280–81; Bancroft, *History of Utah, 1540–1886*, 568–69; Krakauer, *Under the Banner of Heaven*, 245–48; Walker et al., *Massacre at Mountain Meadows*, 227–31.

66. Walker et al., *Massacre at Mountain Meadows*, ix–xvi.

67. Symeonidou-Kastanidou, "Defining Terrorism," 15–18.

68. Walker et al., *Massacre at Mountain Meadows*, 131.

69. Krakauer, *Under the Banner of Heaven*, 224–25; Walker et al., *Massacre at Mountain Meadows*, 227–29.

70. Arrington, *Brigham Young: American Moses*, 111; Bancroft, *History of Utah, 1540–1886*, 228–35; Krakauer, *Under the Banner of Heaven*, 127–33.

71. Walker et al., *Massacre at Mountain Meadows*, 6–16.

72. Samaha, *Criminal Law*, 137–48.

73. Arrington, *Brigham Young: American Moses*, 113–17; Bushman, *Joseph Smith*, 89–90; Howe, *What Hath God Wrought*, 726–27; Krakauer, *Under the Banner of Heaven*, 194–96; Walker et al., *Massacre at Mountain Meadows*, 28–32, 99–100.

74. Symeonidou-Kastanidou, "Defining Terrorism," 18–23; Walker et al., *Massacre at Mountain Meadows*, xiv–xv.

75. Arrington, *Brigham Young: American Moses*, 493; Bagley, *Blood of the Prophets*, 70–71; Bancroft, *History of Utah, 1540–1886*, 546–47; Walker et al., *Massacre at Mountain Meadows*, 30–32, 124–25.

76. Arrington, *Brigham Young: American Moses*, 121, 145–46, 175, 189; Howe, *What Hath God Wrought*, 727–29; Walker et al., *Massacre at Mountain Meadows*, 18–20.

77. Arrington, *Brigham Young: American Moses*, 145–46; Walker et al., *Massacre at Mountain Meadows*, 16–32.

78. Krakauer, *Under the Banner of Heaven*, 219–25; Walker et al., *Massacre at Mountain Meadows*, xiii–xv, 143–48.

79. Arrington, *Brigham Young: American Moses*, 493; Arrington and Bitton, *The Mormon Experience*, 166–67; Bagley, *Blood of the Prophets*, 70–71; Bancroft, *History of Utah, 1540–1886*, 546–47; Krakauer, *Under the Banner of Heaven*, 215–17; Walker et al., *Massacre at Mountain Meadows*, 30–32, 124–25.

2

"THE GENTLE, KINDHEARTED BIOTERRORIST"

Luke Pryor Blackburn and the Yellow Fever Plot (1864–1865)

Presumptuous man! The reason wouldst thou find,
Why formed so weak, so little, and so blind?

—Alexander Pope, *An Essay on Man*

Luke Pryor Blackburn comes down through history as a schizophrenic figure: humanitarian and monster, hero and villain, angel and devil existing side by side. As with most human beings, his character was a mixture of noble and base motives. He was a man of science and reason who succumbed to emotion and passion in the service of a goal for which he willingly turned his back on his Hippocratic oath. During most of his professional life, he was a well-regarded medical doctor who dedicated his considerable talents to caring for his patients and bettering his community, frequently at great physical and pecuniary risk. A bas-relief on his gravestone depicts him as a Good Samaritan in recognition of his Herculean efforts to combat yellow fever and improve hospital conditions throughout the antebellum South. He championed quarantines as a means of arresting the spread of the dread disease, and he worked tirelessly to alleviate suffering. He lived in a time when the medical establishment knew little of infectious diseases, how they were spread, or how they could be treated successfully, yet he constantly sought to understand the debilitating sicknesses that ravaged his fellow man.[1]

Blackburn was an ambitious fellow, and he was not satisfied to confine his efforts to medicine. In his twilight years, he turned to politics as an outlet for his energies. As governor of the commonwealth of Kentucky from 1879 until 1883, he also became known as a progressive proponent of prison reform. Nineteenth-century penitentiaries were almost unspeakably horrible places. The eighty-year-old Frankfort penitentiary was nicknamed "Kentucky's Black Hole of Calcutta" owing to appalling conditions inside the prison walls. Inmates were stuffed into small, unsanitary pits that offered little in the way of nutritious food, health care facilities, or opportunities for reintegration into society upon the completion of a prison sentence, assuming the prisoner survived the squalid conditions. Governor Blackburn championed prison reform despite the politically controversial nature of such work. Then as now, hard-nosed citizens were disinclined to invest much time or money into improving the lot of convicted offenders. In modern parlance, being "soft" on crime was a political liability, yet "Lenient Luke" persevered in arguing for prison reform. He also issued more than 1,000 pardons, a small percentage of the petitions he received, but still a number to evoke venomous reactions from his political opponents and opportunists of every stripe. Despite the unpopularity of the cause and the likelihood that it limited his prospects for a political career in the future, Blackburn would not yield.[2]

These are the actions of a man unafraid to make unpopular decisions in the service of what he believes to be a higher purpose. Perhaps it was this same sense of duty and honor that contributed to the darker side of Luke Pryor Blackburn's character. For all his good works, during the American Civil War the Confederate partisan earned the title "Dr. Black Vomit" for his scheme to send yellow fever–infected clothing to Northern cities to sicken Union troops and civilians. Abraham Lincoln reputedly was a target of one shipment of garments. The good doctor's insidious plan is regarded as one of the earliest attempts at waging biological warfare in American history.[3]

It is difficult to reconcile Blackburn's actions during wartime with the other episodes of his life. In the final analysis, perhaps the best that can be said is that he was blinded by his commitment to the Confederate cause. As the other chapters of this book discuss, the committed partisan who eventually is branded a "terrorist" shares with other such committed souls a belief in the righteousness of his cause and the dastardly character of the "other." Dr. Blackburn knew human suffering up close and personal. He had witnessed firsthand the ravages of infection and the awful toll that yellow fever, cholera, smallpox, and other infectious diseases took on the

Luke Pryor Blackburn, "Dr. Black Vomit." Courtesy of the Kentucky Historical Society.

human body. Yet, in hatching a plot to infect his enemies, he set aside what he knew of good deeds and elevated his desire for Confederate victory over the humanity of his enemies. In so doing, he earned a place in a book about the causes and consequences of terrorism.[4]

THE SCOURGE OF YELLOW FEVER

The old proverb suggests that "all is fair in love and war." The statement is not altogether true, at least not insofar as war has been practiced by civilizations labeled "decent" throughout history. In many epochs, warfare occurred according to defined rules that participants were expected to follow. Sometimes large armies would clash on a field of battle and the last group standing would be the victor. Maneuvering soldiers as though they were chess pieces was a highly prized attribute of warfare during the Napoleonic age. For Native Americans in some eras, humiliating the enemy was the objective, not slaying opposing combatants. Involving noncombatants or triggering what today is called "collateral damage" were signs of a sloppy, imprecise army. The rules were not hard and fast; some unintended consequences were inevitable. Still, warfare required skill and dexterity. It was a focused, limited affair.[5]

Despite the record of combatants who pledged to adhere to prescribed rules of engagement, innumerable others have acted without a sense of restraint or concern for the judgment of history. Biological warfare is especially worrisome because all thought of precision or skill is abandoned. The disease cuts through the population without discriminating between the identities of the respective combatants. A plot to infect one's enemies with yellow fever was especially insidious in the nineteenth century because the disease was so prevalent and deadly. As far back as Christopher Columbus's second expedition to the New World, the disease was known as a scourge. Observers recounted the horrors of yellow fever as it swept through Mexico in 1648, probably having been imported on slave ships from West Africa. It ravaged the Caribbean in the centuries that followed. An epidemic that swept through the southern United States in 1801 may have contributed to Napoleon's decision to sell the Louisiana territory to the Jefferson administration. By 1900, perhaps as many as ninety epidemics had spread throughout the country. Even rumors of the poorly understood affliction caused citizens to quake in fear.[6]

It was little wonder they feared the disease; the mortality rate was between 30 and 50 percent. Infectious diseases were poorly understood; doctors were unaware that hemorrhagic disease is transmitted by infected mosquitoes. The practice of rubbing clothing on infected persons and passing along the soiled garments to infect others was widespread. It was not until 1900 that Dr. Walter Reed identified the culprit as a mosquito, *Aedes aegypti*. Dr. Reed also found that the illness was transmitted when a human host suffered a bite.[7]

Yellow fever is frightening because it seemingly appears overnight and ravages its victims quickly. Once contracted, the virus incubates for between three and six days. The resultant infection occurs in an acute phase that causes fever, muscle pain, backache, headache, shivers, loss of appetite, nausea, and vomiting. Most patients suffer through these symptoms and recover after three or four days. Yet approximately 15 percent of infected patients enter a second phase after remission. High fever returns to these hapless souls; they develop jaundice and vomit violently. In some cases, blood oozes from the patient's mouth, nose, and eyes. Blood is clearly visible in the vomit and feces, although it can appear as a dark color owing to hemorrhaging mucous membranes, hence the description of "black vomit." The victim's kidney function deteriorates, and about half the patients die a horrible death within ten to fourteen days.

Yellow fever resembles malaria, typhus, dengue, and hepatitis, which complicates diagnosis. In the modern era, blood tests can detect yellow fever antibodies produced in response to the infection, but nineteenth century physicians did not know these things. By the time they realized the patient was infected with yellow fever, the disease was left to run its course, and a victim lived or died on his own. Quarantines could halt its spread, but the lengthy incubation phase meant that the infection probably had already occurred by the time symptoms appeared, especially among itinerant populations.[8]

From an early age, Luke Pryor Blackburn was familiar with yellow fever and attendant infectious diseases. He spent his early medical career fighting to protect the lives of his patients on the frontier. By all accounts, he was a dedicated and caring professional, a man who never hesitated to set aside his own personal interests in the interests of his patients. Yet he was willing to infect his enemies with a terrible disease if it served a higher cause.[9]

BLACKBURN'S LIFE AND TIMES

Luke Pryor Blackburn was born on June 16, 1816, to a prominent family on the Kentucky frontier. The son of a self-made lawyer and cousin to the legendary congressional lion Henry Clay, young Luke came of age with all the privileges available to children of the era. He did not enjoy a formal education, but he had access to classic books as well as prominent men in his family and community, and they taught him well. At the age of sixteen, he began a two-year apprenticeship with his uncle, Churchill Blackburn, a well-regarded physician in Paris, Kentucky. It was a propitious time to embark on a career in medicine; few physicians lived west of the Alleghenies. A man trained in diseases of the body would be valuable, an esteemed member of his community.[10]

As a physician's apprentice, young Luke Blackburn first encountered infectious diseases when Asiatic cholera erupted in Kentucky in 1832. Cholera had swept through Europe in the late 1820s and early 1830s before appearing in the United States. The death toll among a vulnerable population was high—1,400 in Norfolk, 3,500 in New York City, and 5,000 in New Orleans—but it might have been worse had an early frost not arrested its spread. As was often the case in the early nineteenth century, nature's remedies were vastly superior to human medications.[11]

Physicians were at a loss to combat infectious diseases; their understanding of the cause of illness, never mind the treatment, was poor. Worse than the gaps in their knowledge was the fallacious reasoning that led the most sophisticated minds of the day to surmise that gases produced by rotting vegetation and standing water caused sickness and death. These erroneous conclusions induced the populace to flee inland to escape swampy, low-lying areas. In their haste to be secure, frightened citizens carried the infection to other parts of the state, territory, and country.

A new wave of cholera erupted in central Kentucky during the summer of 1833. Of the 6,000 residents of Lexington, two-thirds fled for more hospitable environs. Despite all efforts to avoid the disease, more than five hundred citizens died. Paris, Kentucky, was hit especially hard by what a contemporary observer described as a disease "with almost unparalleled malignity." Although he was not yet a full-fledged physician, Blackburn, by all accounts, performed heroically. Yet it was a hopeless enterprise. Medicine was so primitive and the causes of cholera so poorly understood that more than 10 percent of the town's population succumbed.[12]

At the end of his apprenticeship, the young physician-to-be matriculated at Transylvania University. To earn his medical degree, Blackburn attended classes and submitted a thesis, "Cholera Maligna," partially based on his firsthand experiences and observations. Reflecting the conventional wisdom of the antebellum medical community, the thesis suggested that cholera struck people who were vulnerable owing to impoverished diets and "intemperance." Consuming rotten vegetables, "bad water," and acidic beverages led to the appearance of symptoms and the illness and death that followed. These medical bromides earned Luke Pryor Blackburn a medical degree in March 1835, three months shy of his nineteenth birthday.[13]

The adolescent doctor established a medical practice in downtown Lexington immediately after graduation. No sooner had he opened his doors than infectious disease once again swept through the countryside with a vengeance. Doctor Blackburn demonstrated his courage and professional dedication by remaining in the city to care for infected patients even as more prominent physicians fled to the relative safety of the countryside. One contemporary observer characterized the young doctor as the "kindest and most gentle yet bravest man" the fellow had ever met. At great personal risk, and apparently with no thought of remuneration, Blackburn "entered homes of the sick and dying, and many did he bring back from the jaws of death by his skill and intrepid nerve." Here was a professional who was well on his way toward earning the title of "Good Samaritan" that would one day adorn his gravestone.[14]

Except for these sporadic accounts of his early career, many details of the man's prewar life have been lost to history. In November 1835, Doctor Blackburn married his distant cousin, Ella Gist Boswell, and the couple produced their only child, a son, two years later. A physician's position on the frontier was neither luxurious nor lucrative. Consequently, the good doctor searched for a means of augmenting his meager income. He invested his savings in an enterprise to manufacture hemp products, but the business failed, leaving the young family in dire financial straits. After serving a single, undistinguished term in the Kentucky House of Representatives in the 1840s, Blackburn relocated to Natchez, Mississippi. It was early in 1846, and he was not yet thirty years old.[15]

Natchez was a bustling center of commerce for the Cotton South, the best and worst of what the region had to offer. A gracious, quiet elegance could be found in its profusion of colonnaded, antebellum mansions and fine families. For the refined Southerner, the stately buildings and gentle ways of its residents represented the best of a Southland that would be romanticized in later years. Natchez was these things, but it was so much more. It also sported a robust, rowdy waterfront and a thriving racetrack that attracted gamblers from neighboring communities and states. People traveled from miles around to gain or lose their fortunes in the leading city of the Magnolia State. The bustling slave market was among the largest in the region, reinforcing the attitudes and values of the antebellum South.

The Blackburns and the Boswells fit into the town's social stratum as if they had lived there for generations. Luke Blackburn thrived, earning more than $10,000 in a single year, a princely sum for that time and place. He helped to create a temperance society in addition to serving as an agent for Kentucky purchasers and winning election as an honorary captain of a local militia company, the Natchez Fencibles. Aside from his medical practice, he managed the Natchez hospital, demonstrating a tenacity that would serve him well throughout his life. Disgusted at typical medical facilities, which he found to be "disagreeable, dull, dirty places," Blackburn vowed that a hospital under his care would be "conducted very differently." It was.[16]

As a prominent citizen, the doctor hobnobbed with Mississippi's leading citizens, including Jefferson Davis. For all his elite connections, Blackburn was known to treat freed Negroes and waive or reduce his fee for patients who could not pay for his services. He insisted that the Natchez Hospital accept charity cases, even servants from local plantations and notoriously transient river men who seldom possessed funds to settle their bill.

Ella Blackburn hoped to return to the Bluegrass State, but she recognized that her husband's status and income potential were greater in Natchez. She had never seen him "as happy and contented as he is now," in no small measure because "rich, poor, high, low respect him. No one can say a word against him, and it is quite a by-word in town to be as temperate as Dr. B." Two years after his arrival in the Mississippi town, he won election as the Natchez health officer. Blackburn proved to be an indefatigable doctor who time and again lived up to the sobriquet of a "Good Samaritan" during his Natchez years.[17]

As yellow fever spread through Mississippi and the Deep South in the 1850s, Blackburn carefully recorded information on the disease and its aftereffects. He was a proponent of quarantine to prevent the spread of the fever, a measure that in turn received praise from citizens anxious to protect public health and businessmen concerned about the loss of income and depressed commercial opportunities. Always pleased to demonstrate his hard-won knowledge and intellectual abilities, Blackburn shared his recommendations with numerous audiences throughout the years, notably the Southern Commercial Convention, which met in New Orleans in January 1855.[18]

In September 1856, he accompanied his eighteen-year-old son, Cary, to Philadelphia so the young man could commence an apprenticeship with Dr. Samuel David Gross, a well-known medical doctor. During the trip, Blackburn assisted health officials in Long Island with combating a yellow fever epidemic that had recently erupted. When he returned home, he was alarmed to find his wife of almost twenty-one years suffering from an undiagnosed fever. Because Natchez was surrounded by low-lying swampland infested with mosquitoes, the area was a breeding ground for numerous tropical diseases. Ella Blackburn died of an unnamed tropical disease in November 1856. Her passing left Luke Pryor Blackburn in a state of deep depression. The man who had devoted much of his life to combating infectious diseases had lost his beloved wife to the enemy he could not vanquish.[19]

At the urging of friends concerned about his state of mind, the widowed doctor embarked on a European visit, which included trips to Rome and Paris. In letters of introduction, his colleagues characterized Blackburn as a "gentleman of the highest standing socially and professionally" who was "crowned with honors" by "the elite of Natchez." The tenacious man of medicine used his time well. Combining business with pleasure, he inspected European hospitals to learn how doctors there treated infectious diseases.[20]

Aside from his professional pursuits, Blackburn recovered his mental health during his sojourn to the Continent. While still overseas, the forty-one-year-old physician met and courted a twenty-four-year-old Kentucky woman, Julia Churchill, who was traveling through Europe with her sister and her niece. The vivacious young lady ended Blackburn's depressive period and convinced him to try his hand at matrimony again. In November 1857, the couple returned to the United States to discuss marriage plans with Julia's parents. Not long thereafter, they were wed at the bride's home. Despite his affinity for Natchez, the town held bad memories. In January 1858, the doctor and his bride relocated to New Orleans.[21]

Luke Pryor Blackburn's professional career and equanimity were recognized by all who knew him before the outbreak of the Civil War. It was his actions during the war that called his reputation and character into question, and even then the nature of his intentions and involvement are disputed. Little is known of his wartime activities during the first two years of the rebellion, although he seems to have acted as an agent for Kentucky governor Beriah Magoffin in acquiring guns from Louisiana to defend the commonwealth. That he was a partisan Confederate cannot be doubted, but it is curious that he did not offer his services to the Confederate medical department. Clearly, a forty-five-year-old man was too old for a front-line position, at least until the South grew desperate toward the end of the war.

Continuing his civilian activities, Blackburn turned up as an aide-de-camp for Confederate general Sterling Price in Mississippi. As was true with many Confederate military officers, Price was desperately short of supplies. He dispatched Blackburn to travel around the South speaking to groups in hopes of acquiring arms for the troops. The doctor succeeded in procuring 8,000 guns, some of which had to be repaired before they were put into the field. Writing the general to report on the success of his mission, Blackburn also noted that 30,000 additional arms had recently arrived in Southern ports.[22]

In February 1863, Mississippi governor John J. Pettus created a commission "to get all of Mississippi's soldiers together in one ward or hospital so that their wants may be attended to without so much loss or inconvenience in the transportation of articles sent to them." Recognizing Blackburn's experience in working with infectious diseases, the governor asked the physician to serve as one of the two commissioners on the project. Blackburn spent several months traveling from hospital to hospital in Mississippi and Alabama. His plan to create a single ward for infected soldiers never came to fruition, but the task convinced him that he could best serve the Confederate States of America (CSA) by using his medical knowledge to good effect. He traveled to Richmond and approached the secretary of war about serving as general inspector of hospitals and camps. Demonstrating a selfless nature, Blackburn explained, "I am willing to take this position without pay or rank." Blackburn's offer, for whatever reasons, was refused, leaving him to support the war effort in other ways. He provided assistance to soldiers wounded during the siege at Vicksburg before turning up as Mississippi's Confederate agent in Canada to acquire supplies for blockade runners.

In his effort to provide supplies, Blackburn found a ship, filled it with ice, and made his way to Mobile. Governor Pettus directed that the ship be used to exchange cotton in Cuba for arms and other commodities useful to the Southern Confederacy, but Union sailors intercepted the vessel before it could depart from Mobile Bay. Blackburn's status as a civilian saved him from imprisonment.[23]

THE CANADIAN CABAL

Canada, especially the area around Toronto, was the locus of a small cadre of Confederates that sought to wreak havoc on Union cities and towns. Their efforts intensified in 1864 when the CSA's plight worsened. As Southern armies faltered and the conflict ground into its fourth year, the Confederate leadership searched for a means of bringing the war to the enemy. General Robert E. Lee had tried repeatedly to transport the horrors and privations of war to the Northern populace through his 1862 Maryland campaign and his 1863 excursion into Pennsylvania, but the sour misfortunes of war had forced him back into Virginia. With the exception of Jubal Early's last-ditch effort to menace Washington, D.C., the days when the Army of Northern Virginia could push Union troops away from Southern territory had ended. If the Confederates hoped to take the offensive, they would have to devise modest attacks against their foe. To this end, Confederate secretary of state Judah P. Benjamin allocated $1 million to initiate a campaign of attack on federal arsenals, liberate Union military prison camps, and harass Northerners, including civilians, who had few resources with which to defend themselves. President Jefferson Davis approved the expenditure and was well aware of the Canadian effort. The Confederacy eventually created the Special and Secret Service Bureau to legitimize clandestine activities.[24]

At President Davis's behest, a prominent Southerner, Jacob Thompson, agreed to spearhead the Canadian campaign. In an April 1864 letter, the Confederate president instructed his friend and colleague to "proceed at once to Canada, there to carry out the instructions you have received from me verbally." Thompson was a well-known Southern partisan who had been born and raised in North Carolina. He graduated from the University of North Carolina and practiced law before he moved to Mississippi at the suggestion of his brother, Dr. James Thompson, who already lived in the Magnolia State. During the antebellum years, Thompson earned his living practicing law and growing cotton. He also served as a Democratic congressman throughout the 1840s. During that time, he became friends with a fellow member of Congress from Mississippi, Jefferson Davis. Because he supported James Buchanan's nomination for president during the 1856 Democratic convention in Cincinnati, Thompson accepted a position as secretary of the interior as his reward. He was a well-respected, successful member of the prewar planter elite, a man thoroughly inculcated with Southern values.[25]

For all of his ties to the Cotton South, Jacob Thompson was a pragmatic man. He understood that the vicissitudes of war would harm all Americans. He remained in the Buchanan cabinet, possibly so he could leak information to Southern partisans, even as many of his friends and colleagues left to defend the Southland from perceived federal encroachment. Initially opposed to the idea of secession, he resigned from the Buchanan administration after he learned of the president's decision to dispatch a ship, the *Star of the West*, to resupply Union defenders ensconced at Fort Sumter in the mouth of Charleston Harbor. Although resupplying a single federal outpost was hardly tantamount to war, and Fort Sumter was little more than a symbol of federal authority nestled next to a leading southern city, the president's action convinced Thompson and his colleagues that the struggle between North and South had entered a new, more belligerent stage.[26]

Once he had taken the first step away from the Union and embraced the newly created Southern Confederacy, Thompson devoted his considerable energies to undermining his former government. In the early war years, he served valiantly with the Confederate States Army in battles in Tennessee and Mississippi, notably Vicksburg, Corinth, Tupelo, Grenada, and the Tallahatchie River. Anxious to use his talents to good advantage, he won election to the Mississippi legislature late in 1863.[27]

When Davis approached him about the Canadian enterprise in 1864, the newly elected state legislator set aside his other duties to render what service he could to the cause. Thompson's orders were to drum up support for the Confederate states by contacting sympathetic Northern leaders for assistance in launching a series of covert operations against the Union. He corresponded with influential newspaperman Horace Greeley when that

Jacob Thompson, head of the Confederate clandestine operations in Canada. Courtesy of the Library of Congress.

irascible editor visited Niagara Falls to explore terms of peace. Unlike the pro-Confederate privateers, guerrillas, raiders, and marauders who occasionally terrorized Northerners on the frontier and in the border states, Thompson and his colleagues enjoyed the imprimatur of the Confederate government in whatever activities, violent or otherwise, they chose to pursue. They were no mere ruffians shooting up the countryside for the sake of relieving boredom or scoring points against the enemy. They were directed to develop a strategy for assisting the larger war effort. Thompson coordinated planning and logistics for a wide range of Confederate attacks on vulnerable Northern targets and installations, but he was not involved in every scheme. He set the wheels in motion, but he left the practical implementation to others. Thompson's official, albeit secret, sanction meant that the Canadian operation was a legitimate military operation in wartime, at least in the eyes of the participants, but it required him to use stealth and cunning.[28]

Thompson believed the capture of a Union war vessel would do much to erode Northern morale. One plan called for his associates to capture the U.S. gunboat *Michigan* on the Great Lakes and commandeer the vessel so it could attack the Union prisoner-of-war camp on Johnson's Island in Lake Erie. Freeing thousands of Confederates and arming them for a fight would strike terror into the hearts of U.S. citizenry even if the plan failed. Alas, Union spies or reluctant rebels infiltrated the Confederate ranks and exposed the plan before it could be implemented. Union officials in Detroit were surprised to encounter a shadowy figure who claimed to be a "refugee rebel soldier" reporting that "the officers and men of the steamer *Michigan* had been tampered with" by Confederate spies "in expectation of getting possession of your steamer."[29]

The Confederate cabal in Canada was nothing if not tenacious. During the summer of 1864, Thompson worked with a group, the Order of the Sons of Liberty, to trigger uprisings coinciding with Clement L. Vallandigham's return to Ohio from his well-known exile. Ideally, the Sons would unleash a Northwest Conspiracy and encourage western states to break away from the Union. A Democrat and former congressman from Ohio, Vallandigham was a leading critic of the Lincoln administration and a well-known Copperhead. The Copperheads were Northern "peace Democrats" who called for an immediate end to the war even if it meant negotiating a settlement with the Southern Confederacy. For this reason, Confederate secret agents sought to create an alliance with the Copperheads to hasten the day when the war would end and the Confederate States of America would be allowed to exist in peace without interference from its former parent.[30]

Vallandigham was the leading Copperhead, a rabble-rouser who delivered long-winded diatribes against virtually every military policy of his government. President Lincoln, a frequent subject of Vallandigham's tirades, had suspended the writ of habeas corpus, which allowed the U.S. government to arrest critics and hold them without benefit of trial. It was only a matter of time before the contentious Ohio politician crossed swords with the administration. When Vallandigham spoke out against the war once too often in 1863, he found himself under arrest for his "habit of declaring sympathies for the enemy." General Ambrose Burnside ordered the cantankerous Copperhead taken into custody. Although he was not Vallandigham's fan and he did not wish to undermine his general officer, Lincoln was worried that the arrest would become a cause célèbre among the administration's detractors. To placate those who condemned the government as heavy-handed and oblivious to the requirements of constitutional due process, the president changed Vallandigham's sentence from imprisonment to exile, ordering the infuriating Copperhead delivered to the Confederacy. It was an inspired punishment. If the loudmouthed Copperhead was so enamored of the Confederate States of America, he would be escorted at the point of a bayonet to the land of his desires.[31]

Confederate authorities were not sure what they should do with their new resident. They need not have worried. Vallandigham recognized that his gifts were best suited to criticism of the Northern administration, not direct participation in the Southern war effort. He was a man of words, not actions. He would not take up arms when his pen and tongue were the weapons of choice. As soon as he could arrange it, Vallandigham traveled to Bermuda and eventually to Canada, where he declared himself a candidate for governor of Ohio. He would campaign for office in absentia, a touch of political theater that would allow him to call attention to the vagaries of Lincoln's government. As the toast of Copperheads throughout the North and partisans across the South, Vallandigham discovered that Ohio voters were not as disloyal to the Union as he had hoped. In misjudging the mood of the electorate, Vallandigham lost his gubernatorial bid in 1863. He remained a proud, defiant troublemaker. A year later, the man-in-exile returned to Ohio and even ventured to the 1864 Democratic National Convention in Chicago.[32]

Thompson hoped to use Vallandigham's high profile to rally anti-Union sentiment and assist in recruiting operatives for the Southern cause. Unfortunately for him, his confederates in the Order of the Sons of Liberty lacked the organizational skills and leadership to parlay Vallandigham's return to the United States into an effective campaign of terror. In the final analysis, the spirit was willing, but the flesh was weak. Without effective leadership and direction, the group floundered and missed opportunities to inflict damage on Union targets.[33]

Vallandigham was not the only Copperhead who presented an opportunity for Confederate agents. Like many Southern partisans, Jacob Thompson realized that Democratic victories in key elections could tip the balance of public opinion against the Lincoln administration and thereby undermine support for vigorously prosecuting the war. He contributed $40,000 to the gubernatorial campaign of Democrat James C. Robinson, a Peace Democrat who shared Vallandigham's disdain for the Lincoln administration. Thompson also sent money to the "Copperhead Convention" of August 1864 in Peoria, Illinois. As a pièce de résistance, he advanced a plot to destabilize U.S. currency by converting greenbacks into gold and shipping the gold to England so he could transfer it into currency to be used for buying additional U.S. gold. The plan failed to work.[34]

The United States was scheduled to hold national elections in November 1864, including a presidential contest that pitted Abraham Lincoln against his former military commander, Democrat George B. McClellan. Thompson recognized that Election Day, November 8, was an opportune time to strike terror into the hearts of voters. The terrorist seeks to disrupt the normal course of business by convincing citizens that they may be wounded or killed as they go about their daily lives. To accomplish the goal, Thompson planned to promote armed insurrections in New York City and Chicago. He might have succeeded but for Union spies who alerted military officials. The federal government dispatched 10,000 soldiers to guard polling places and patrol the cities. His scheme foiled, Thompson pushed his operatives to burn New York City following the election. Confederate agents managed to start several fires and temporarily caused panic, but the plot never achieved the scale of destruction he had intended. Despite Thompson's best efforts, his campaign was little more than a nuisance for Union military officials.[05]

As the war wound to a close in 1865, the collapsing Confederate government sent an emissary, Edwin Gray Lee, to relieve Thompson of his duties. Recognizing that his service was at an end, Thompson refunded some of his funds to Lee and deposited the remaining $400,000 in a British financial institution for use by the Confederate States government. It was too little money too late in the game to be of much value. On May 2, Thompson learned that the new U.S. president, Andrew Johnson, had issued a proclamation listing possible conspirators in the Lincoln assassination. Thompson's name was included on the list.

Fearing capture and possible execution, Thompson fled to Europe. He remained outside of the country until 1869. When he returned to his Mississippi plantation, Thompson found the property in ruins. He eventually moved to Memphis, Tennessee, where he lived until his death in 1885.[36]

DR. BLACK VOMIT AND THE YELLOW FEVER PLOT

Luke Pryor Blackburn was one of many partisans who contacted Jacob Thompson in Canada. Blackburn enjoyed a distinct advantage over his brethren, however; he was a trained physician who had witnessed the devastation that disease could inflict on the human body. As he whiled away his time in service to the Southern cause, inspiration struck, and Dr. Blackburn hatched the scheme that would earn him epithets in years to come. No doubt drawing on his experience combating infectious diseases and illustrating his antipathy toward the U.S. government and its citizens,

he mulled over the idea of infecting clothing with yellow fever and sending the items to prominent civilian and military leaders in the North. Although Blackburn's exact motivations remain obscure, he probably shared
his brother James's feeling, expressed in an 1861 letter, that "I hold every
Union traitor as my enemy" and therefore "I intend to begin the work of
murder in earnest, and if I ever spare one of them may hell be my portion.
I want to see Union blood flow deep enough for my house to swim in it."[37]

The idea of infecting the enemy with yellow fever, or any number of
dread diseases, did not originate with Blackburn, although he seems to
have masterminded the 1864 plot. Vulnerable citizens had debated ways of
driving off their tormentors with the threat of infection. Children in New
Orleans, a city especially prone to outbreaks of disease owing to its position
as a port city and gateway to Confederate destinations, were known to taunt
Union soldiers with calls, "Yellow Jacks will grab them up and take them all
away." Rebels forced to submit to General Benjamin "Beast" Butler's iron
rule of the Crescent City could smirk at their captors with promises of a
hasty, ignominious burial when the Yankee devils fell victim to the scourge
of the Black Vomit.[38]

An outbreak of yellow fever in Bermuda, site of a Confederate wharf and
office, in April 1864 presented Blackburn with the opportunity he needed
to test his theories of germ warfare. Once again offering his medical skills
to the Confederate cause, the determined doctor found a more recep-
tive audience than he had in previous years. Departing in mid-April from
Halifax, Nova Scotia, he arrived in Bermuda as the epidemic reached its
peak. He spent three months carefully and methodically collecting soiled
garments worn by yellow fever victims. Blackburn was especially interested
in acquiring clothing stained with "black vomit," the distinctive stomach
contents coughed up by hemorrhaging patients in the most severe stages
of the disease. Interspersing the patients' clothing with clean garments in
eight large trunks, he proposed to mail the contaminated packages to un-
suspecting Northern victims.[39]

That a man of medicine and seemingly high moral character could have
been driven to hatch such an insidious plot and take proactive steps to bring
it to fruition says much about the grim nature of warfare and the desperate
straits already apparent in the Confederate war effort by the summer of
1864. It also speaks volumes about Dr. Luke Pryor Blackburn's willingness
to betray his Hippocratic oath in service of a political cause. He was so
blinded by the virtues of the Southern position that he could not or would
not consider a higher duty to the family of man.

The exact nature of the plot remains a subject of no small dispute, but
the matter first came to light owing to the testimony of one Godfrey Joseph

Hyams on two separate occasions, first during Dr. Blackburn's trial for attempted murder in Canada and later during the investigation of the Lincoln assassination. Although Hyams's testimony differed in a few minor details between the two inquests, a general outline of the plot emerged. Described as an "Israelitish" man—that is, a fellow "of the Jewish persuasion"—the slight gentleman of dark complexion and crossed eyes explained that Dr. Blackburn asked him to participate in a plot to send trunks filled with yellow fever–infected clothes to key Northern leaders during the summer of 1864.

Hyams was something of a shadowy figure, and his veracity was always questionable. The fellow used the alias "J. H. Harris" when he offered to sell the names of traitorous Copperheads to Union informers. He first came to prominence on April 5, 1865, nine days before Lincoln was shot, when he entered the office of the U.S. Consul in Toronto offering to trade information on a terrorist plot in exchange for a pardon for his activities serving the clandestine Canadian-based operations of the Southern Confederacy. He requested financial compensation as well. The consul, David Thurston, was not sure what to do with this character or his story, for it might be a hoax to swindle money from government agents. Erring on the side of caution, Thurston passed along the information to Secretary of State William H. Seward. Eventually, the U.S. government agreed to Hyams's demands in exchange for his testimony at a military tribunal.

Credible information about his background gradually emerged. Hyams had moved from London to New York City in 1852, but he was not the sort of man who could sit still for long. He eventually settled in Arkansas and tried his hand as a shoemaker and leather cutter. In the 1860s, he professed allegiance to the Northern cause until a Union officer occupying Helena, Arkansas, during the war insulted Hyams's wife. Preferring neutrality to open conflict with the Union, Hyams relocated to Canada with his family in June 1863. As the months dragged on, Hyams found that he missed the South and sought a return to aid the Confederate war effort. To that end, he contacted a recruiting agent, a Mr. Slaughter, who put Hyams in touch with Reverend Stuart Robinson. Robinson introduced Hyams to Dr. Blackburn.[40]

At this point, Hyams's account became difficult to verify. His association with the Kentucky-bred physician was a sensational story of biological warfare aimed against Northern military and civilian targets. According to Hyams,

About the middle of December, 1863, I made the acquaintance of Dr. Blackburn; I was introduced to him by the Rev. Stewart [sic] Robinson, at the

Queen's Hotel, in Toronto. I knew him by sight previously, but before that had had no conversation with him. I knew that he was a Confederate, and was working for the rebellion. . . . He took me upstairs to a private room. . . . He then told me he wanted me to take a certain quantity of clothing consisting of shirts, coats, and underclothing into the States, and dispose of them by auction. I was to take them to Washington City, to Norfolk, and as far South as I could possibly go, where the Federal Government held possession and had the most troops.[41]

Assuming the story was true, Hyams was not Blackburn's only confidant. The doctor previously had discussed the plan with a Confederate runner in Bermuda who, stunned by the vicious scheme, "shouted, not in the choicest of language, to leave the office." In the meantime, Edward Swan, a resident of Saint George, Bermuda, learned of the plot and agreed to store the trunks while Blackburn sailed for Canada to complete his arrangements. Apparently, it was during this foray to Canada that Blackburn secured Hyams's assistance.[42]

As Hyams described his participation, he received a letter from Blackburn in May 1864 asking Hyams to borrow money to travel to Montreal and meet the doctor. The meeting occurred in July, when Blackburn instructed his confederate to remove eight trunks and a valise from the steamer *Alphia*. Blackburn took possession of three trunks, and Hyams transferred the remaining five to his hotel room. Hyams refused to accept the valise of elegant shirts that Blackburn had designated for delivery to President Lincoln. At Blackburn's suggestion, Hyams chewed camphor and smoked cigars in his hotel room so he could avoid the deleterious effects of the contaminated clothing while he repacked the trunks.[43]

After he repacked the clothing, Hyams and an officer from the *Alphia* bribed another officer to assist them in smuggling the baggage on board the steamer *Halifax*. Hyams and the trunks arrived in Boston a week later. After checking into the Astor House Hotel, Hyams arranged for the trunks to be sent to Philadelphia, New York, Washington, and Norfolk. Trunk number 2 was designated for delivery to Washington, D.C. Blackburn's assessment was that trunk number 2 was so infected that it could "kill at sixty yards." It wound up at Wall and Company Auction House on Ninth Street and Pennsylvania Avenue. One of the two trunks delivered to Norfolk was slated for transport to New Bern, North Carolina. Because New Bern had fallen under federal control, Hyams persuaded a sutler named Myers to carry the trunk for him.[44]

After Hyams distributed the trunks, he returned to Toronto. On August 13, he met with Clement C. Clay and James P. Holcombe, Thompson's representatives. Holcombe told Hyams that Blackburn was in Montreal, so Hyams sent a telegram asking for a meeting. They met in Toronto on the 16th along with Lieutenant Bennett H. Young, a Southern escapee from Chicago's Camp Douglas Union prison. On October 19, 1864, Young led twenty-five Confederates in an attack on St. Albans, Vermont, as part of a plan to terrorize Northern cities near the Canadian border. Blackburn's apologists have argued that Hyams was an unreliable witness and surely exaggerated the nefarious activities that occurred during these meetings, but the presence of Jacob Thompson's agents suggests that the doctor's intentions were hardly benign.[45]

Hyams met with Blackburn before the doctor left for another trip to Bermuda. Concerned that Hyams might be duplicitous, Blackburn required his agent to produce bills of sale from the auction houses demonstrating that Hyams had sent the trunks. Satisfied that the task had been completed, Blackburn promised his confederate that $60,000 would be forthcoming from Jacob Thompson's operation. In the meantime, Blackburn wrote Hyams a check to meet his immediate expenses. The two men engaged in all sorts of fanciful speculation, if Hyams is to be believed. Blackburn apparently offered to introduce his co-conspirator to Napoleon III, the emperor of France, as part of a scheme to interfere in affairs in Mexico.[46]

It is difficult to know the extent to which Blackburn was in cahoots with Jacob Thompson and the Canadian cabal, but clearly the plot to infect Northern denizens with infectious diseases had not ended. On his next trip to Bermuda, Blackburn apparently sought to reprise his role as a biological terrorist, even investigating the possibility of sending smallpox in the next shipment. On this trip, he acquired three trunks filled with soiled clothing. He directed a laborer named William Blackman to transport the new trunks to Saint George and store them until the summer weather would, in his erroneous view, increase the virulence of the disease. The plan was to ship the infected material to New York.[47]

Blackburn's movements in the last half of 1864 are difficult to trace, although he turned up in Boston in November as part of a plot to set fire to the city. The doctor remained anonymous, working in the shadows, until a disgruntled Hyams, upset at not being paid the compensation he had been promised, walked into the U.S. Consulate in Toronto and exposed the plot. The "great rascal," as Blackburn once labeled Hyams, was not necessarily a credible source, but even if only half of what he said were true, it was a cold-blooded scheme. The generally sympathetic, pro-Confederate press begrudgingly admitted that the plan was "an outrage against humanity."[48]

Aside from the case brought against him in Toronto, Blackburn was swept up in the investigation into the Lincoln assassination. By that time, his beloved Southern Confederacy was defunct, and his personal fortunes were at a low ebb. He suddenly found himself labeled with the epithet "Dr. Black Vomit." The humanitarian who had done so much to comfort his patients and explore effective treatments for infectious diseases was denounced as a man willing to perpetrate crimes against humanity in the service of a political cause.[49]

To buttress his dubious credibility, Hyams told his interrogators of a plot by Jacob Thompson and his agents to buy a steamer, the *Georgian*, and direct the ship to sail "among the fishing vessels of the U.S. to attack and destroy them." The purpose of the plan was to terrorize civilians working on Lake Michigan in a move similar to Thompson's plans for the *Michigan*. As with the other scheme, the *Georgian* plot proved to be a pipe dream. To hide the transaction, William L. "Larry" MacDonald, another Confederate agent working in Canada, arranged for a sympathetic Canadian politician to purchase the steamer and convey it to the Confederacy. The scheme went awry when the *Georgian* experienced a series of mechanical failures that prevented her from being put into service. In addition, rumors circulated that the ship would be used to secure the escape of Confederate captives held in the Johnson's Island Union prison. The Canadian government eventually seized the ship and handed it over to the U.S. government.[50]

Hyams was not finished telling his spy tales. He also exposed a plot to use lumps of coal as explosive devices on the *Georgian*. In his Toronto safe house, Larry MacDonald was experimenting with a new bomb hidden inside pieces of coal. When the hollowed-out coal was mixed with real coal, theoretically the device would remain hidden until it detonated. Hyams's credibility was enhanced when Canadian police raided the safe house and found the coal bombs buried under the floorboards. If Hyams's story about the bombs proved to be true, presumably the rest of his testimony should be believed.[51]

In the postwar hysteria that accompanied the Lincoln assassination investigation, the question naturally arose whether Jefferson Davis and the Confederate administration in Richmond had planned and executed the murder. With plots uncovered in Canada, it was reasonable to assume that Davis was the guiding hand behind all manner of nefarious activities. This supposition gained traction when Union colonel Edward Hastings Ripley, one of the first Union troops to occupy Richmond after the Confederates fled in April 1865, discovered a coal bomb in Davis's office at the White House of the Confederacy. If the Confederate president was aware of the

Canadian plots to inflict terror on Northern civilians, what other matters did he know about? Although no conclusive proof ever established a link between the Davis administration and the Lincoln assassination—John Wilkes Booth apparently directed his own substate conspiracy—the issue was debated endlessly.[52]

By coincidence, Hyams told authorities about Blackburn's yellow fever plot on the same day that Lincoln was assassinated. Charles Allen, the U.S. consul in Bermuda, wired details of the plot to Washington, D.C. Later, as Judge Advocate General Joseph Holt prepared his case against the Lincoln conspirators before a military tribunal, he considered all manner of evidence concerning Confederate conspiracies. Anxious to inquire whether Jacob Thompson and Luke Blackburn had been involved in the Lincoln assassination plot, the Bureau of Military Justice ordered their arrest. Because both men were hiding in Canada at the time, they were beyond the reach of American authorities. Nonetheless, Thompson and Blackburn had no way of knowing whether U.S. officials would strike a deal with their Canadian counterparts to extradite them. So great was the desire to apprehend Dr. Black Vomit that an unfortunate Indian herbal doctor named Francis Tumblety was arrested in St. Louis and held in the Old Capitol Prison for three weeks because his alias, J. H. Blackburn, was suspiciously similar to the name of the notorious Confederate conspirator. Although Tumblety eventually won his release, his travails illustrated the eagerness of U.S. authorities to catch the architect of this "outrage against humanity."[53]

Canadian authorities arrested Dr. Blackburn for violating his host nation's neutrality in the American Civil War. He could not be charged with conspiracy to commit murder under Canadian law because the charge only applied if the intended victim were a head of state, and evidence that Lincoln was the target was simply too tenuous. Although few records exist of the Canadian trial, Blackburn apparently was acquitted because it was unclear whether the infected trunks had ever been stored within the jurisdiction of the court.[54]

Despite his acquittal in a Canadian court, the doctor remained fearful of retribution owing to the public anguish over Lincoln's murder. He remained abroad until 1867, when he attempted to mend fences so he could return to U.S. soil. Learning of a yellow fever epidemic racing through New Orleans and Galveston in the fall of 1867, he penned a letter to President Andrew Johnson. "I have had much experience in the treatment of this disease and feel confident I could render essential service to my suffering and dying countrymen," he explained without commenting on the irony of offering to help the nation eradicate the same disease he once sought to unleash inside its borders. In what appeared to be a statement of contrition, Blackburn wrote, "If it is, Mr. President, consistent with your duty to accept my offer, my conduct shall be such as to meet and merit your approbation."[55]

Secretary of State William H. Seward responded in a letter to the U.S. consul in Toronto, who had assured the Johnson administration that Blackburn had sworn an oath of loyalty to the United States. Seward wrote of his outrage that the "fiend" who had masterminded the yellow fever plot would now seek to make amends for his crimes. Despite Seward's refusal to entertain a presidential pardon for the doctor, Blackburn quietly returned to the United States that fall. He spent time working to combat yellow fever in Louisville before he and his wife settled in Arkansas. They remained there until late 1872 or early 1873, when they returned to their plantation home.[56]

By the time he died in 1887, Dr. Blackburn had repaired his tarnished reputation, at least among Southern partisans eager to forgive his wartime zeal in consideration of his good works as a physician and his reform-minded tenure as governor of Kentucky. Everything about his professional career before and after the war suggested that the yellow fever plot was an aberration. In the long decades since the scheme was exposed, Blackburn's supporters have contended that Godfrey Hyams and men of his ilk were hardly credible witnesses. Perhaps the affair was greatly exaggerated or manufactured from whole cloth. Much of the evidence has disappeared or been lost to history. As a consequence, the yellow fever plot remains a shadowy, indistinct episode, one more example of the intrigue that accompanies war.[57]

ASSESSING THE CHARACTER AND ACTIONS OF LUKE PRYOR BLACKBURN

Blackburn is a difficult figure to assess. One historian has labeled him "the gentle, kindhearted bioterrorist." The description seems apt. His record as a physician before and after the Civil War was exemplary. His courageous efforts to reform prisons while he served as governor of Kentucky in the early 1880s produced encomiums regarding his character and conduct. All who knew the hardworking, compassionate doctor of medicine found him to be a spirited, empathetic, dedicated public servant. Yet, in a supreme irony, he also became the architect of what would have been an abominable, unspeakable crime if it had succeeded. His thought process was odd. By the time Blackburn formulated his plan, the Southern Confederacy was crumbling. Even if the scheme had succeeded, it is questionable whether the act would have rendered practical assistance to the Southern cause.[58]

Blackburn's actions fit our conceptual framework for "terrorism" with one possible exception. He was an ideologically driven actor who did not acknowledge responsibility for his actions. In fact, he struggled assiduously to protect himself against retribution or answering for his actions in a court of law. Blackburn shares in common with other substate actors labeled "terrorist" the passion and commitment of a true believer. Many a true believer does not consider himself a terrorist. He is fighting for an important cause when other avenues of dissent are unavailable. If disaffection cannot be registered through peaceful means, the committed activist may deem violence a legitimate tool of protest. This committed soldier in the Confederate army sought to drive up the number of casualties while also striking at a symbolic target, the president of the United States.

The common feature of terrorism as it is discussed in this book involves targeting civilians. From his perspective, Luke Pryor Blackburn was engaged in a military operation directed by a foreign government against the United States. He intended to undermine the U.S. war effort by striking at the commander in chief as well as military subordinates. Such actions were not "terroristic" as that term is understood today because Blackburn was fighting a wartime enemy. The characterization of his actions goes to the heart of the issue. If the CSA was not a separate entity and if its military personnel were nothing more than rabble-rousers, as Lincoln always contended, the actions resemble terrorism. If the CSA was a separate nation and Blackburn was a military officer in service of the nation-state, the characterization of his actions might change.

Even a nation-state can employ terrorist tactics; the crucial issue is the target population. Blackburn sought to undermine the U.S. military. He did not specifically attack civilians. Yet the use of a biological weapon is indiscriminate. If yellow fever had been transmitted through infected clothing, it was possible, even likely, that civilians would have been infected—perhaps members of the president's family, his domestic advisers, and even the postal employees who delivered the package. Civilians not infected by the parcel might have learned of the incident, and the threat of a violent death would have spread terror throughout the land.

Blackburn is not a quintessential terrorist, but he meets the requirements of the definition. In times of armed conflict and strife, when passions run high and patriotic fervor supplants the normal reasoning process, the true believer, even the kindhearted type, can rationalize behavior that otherwise would be rejected as anathema. The story of Luke Pryor Blackburn is a reminder that even a conscientious, gentle, humanitarian man of science can become a fiend under the right circumstances.

NOTES

1. Steers, "Risking the Wrath of God," 69.

2. Baird, *Luke Pryor Blackburn*, 78–102; Soodalter, "Partisan, Terrorist, Soldier, Spy," 39.

3. Quoted in Crosby, *The American Plague*, 128.

4. Crosby, *The American Plague*, 43; Singer, *The Confederate Dirty War*, 80; Soodalter, "Partisan, Terrorist, Soldier, Spy," 39.

5. Carr, *The Lessons of Terror*, 7–11, 31–33, 151–53.

6. Steers, "Risking the Wrath of God," 66.

7. Crosby, *The American Plague*, 162–65.

8. Crosby, *The American Plague*, 9–11; Steers, "Risking the Wrath of God," 66.

9. Soodalter, "Partisan, Terrorist, Soldier, Spy," 39.

10. Baird, *Luke Pryor Blackburn*, 2.

11. Baird, *Luke Pryor Blackburn*, 3–6; Steers, *Blood on the Moon*, 46–47.

12. Baird, *Luke Pryor Blackburn*, 4–5.

13. Baird, *Luke Pryor Blackburn*, 6; Steers, *Blood on the Moon*, 46–47; Tidwell et al., *Come Retribution*, 185.

14. Baird, *Luke Pryor Blackburn*, 6–7.

15. Baird, *Luke Pryor Blackburn*, 7–8; Steers, *Blood on the Moon*, 46–47; Tidwell et al., *Come Retribution*, 185.

16. Baird, *Luke Pryor Blackburn*, 7–8.

17. Baird, *Luke Pryor Blackburn*, 8–10; Steers, "Risking the Wrath of God," 69.

18. Baird, *Luke Pryor Blackburn*, 15, 17; Crosby, *The American Plague*, 40–41.

19. Baird, *Luke Pryor Blackburn*, 17–18.

20. Baird, *Luke Pryor Blackburn*, 18.

21. Baird, *Luke Pryor Blackburn*, 18–19.

22. Baird, *Luke Pryor Blackburn*, 20–21; Steers, *Blood on the Moon*, 47; Tidwell et al., *Come Retribution*, 185.

23. Baird, *Luke Pryor Blackburn*, 21; Steers, *Blood on the Moon*, 46–47.

24. Bakeless, *Spies of the Confederacy*, 247; Callahan, *A Diplomatic History of the Southern Confederacy*, 225; Nelson, "Thompson, Jacob," 608; Tidwell et al., *Come Retribution*, 20–22.

25. Quoted in Flood, *1864*, 302. See also Bakeless, *Spies of the Confederacy*, 5–6; Callahan, *A Diplomatic History of the Southern Confederacy*, 225–26; Nelson, "Thompson, Jacob," 607–8; Tidwell, *April '65*, 32; Tidwell et al., *Come Retribution*, 20–22.

26. Bakeless, *Spies of the Confederacy*, 5–6; Flood, *1864*, 302–3; Nelson, "Thompson, Jacob," 607.

27. Nelson, "Thompson, Jacob," 607–8.

28. Callahan, *A Diplomatic History of the Southern Confederacy*, 225–26; McPherson, *The Political History of the United States*, 301–2; Nelson, "Thompson, Jacob," 608–9; Singer, *The Confederate Dirty War*, 11–13; Steers, *Blood on the Moon*, 46; Tidwell, *April '65*, 32–33; Tidwell et al., *Come Retribution*, 20–22.

29. Flood, *1864*, 303; Steers, *Blood on the Moon*, 72.

30. Nelson, "Thompson, Jacob," 608–9; Singer, *The Confederate Dirty War*, 21–22; Tidwell et al., *Come Retribution*, 183.

31. Callahan, *A Diplomatic History of the Southern Confederacy*, 221; Flood, *1864*, 127–28, 246; Singer, *The Confederate Dirty War*, 29.

32. Callahan, *A Diplomatic History of the Southern Confederacy*, 221; Flood, *1864*, 246; Nelson, "Thompson, Jacob," 608; Singer, *The Confederate Dirty War*, 29.

33. Nelson, "Thompson, Jacob," 608; Tidwell et al., *Come Retribution*, 198.

34. Flood, *1864*, 303; Nelson, "Thompson, Jacob," 609.

35. Flood, *1864*, 331; Nelson, "Thompson, Jacob," 608–9; Pittman, *The Assassination of President Lincoln and the Trial of the Conspirators*, 53–54; Singer, *The Confederate Dirty War*, 53.

36. Nelson, "Thompson, Jacob," 609; Steers, *Blood on the Moon*, 101; Tidwell et al., *Come Retribution*, 406–7.

37. Quoted in Baird, *Luke Pryor Blackburn*, 22. See also Steers, "Risking the Wrath of God," 62, 64; Tidwell et al., *Come Retribution*, 185–89.

38. Singer, *The Confederate Dirty War*, 80–82; Soodalter, "Partisan, Terrorist, Soldier, Spy," 38–39; Tidwell, *April '65*, 32–33; Tidwell et al., *Come Retribution*, 406–7.

39. Baird, *Luke Pryor Blackburn*, 21–25; Pittman, *The Assassination of President Lincoln and the Trial of the Conspirators*, 54–55; Steers, "Risking the Wrath of God," 60–61; Tidwell et al., *Come Retribution*, 185–87.

40. Pittman, *The Assassination of President Lincoln and the Trial of the Conspirators*, 54–57; Steers, "Risking the Wrath of God," 60–61; Tidwell et al., *Come Retribution*, 185–86.

41. Quoted in Pittman, *The Assassination of President Lincoln and the Trial of the Conspirators*, 54.

42. Baird, *Luke Pryor Blackburn*, 25–26; Pittman, *The Assassination of President Lincoln and the Trial of the Conspirators*, 55–56; Steers, "Risking the Wrath of God," 64–65.

43. Baird, *Luke Pryor Blackburn*, 25–27; Pittman, *The Assassination of President Lincoln and the Trial of the Conspirators*, 55.

44. Baird, *Luke Pryor Blackburn*, 29–30; Pittman, *The Assassination of President Lincoln and the Trial of the Conspirators*, 55–56; Steers, "Risking the Wrath of God," 64–66.

45. Baird, *Luke Pryor Blackburn*, 27–30; Pittman, *The Assassination of President Lincoln and the Trial of the Conspirators*, 55–56; Steers, "Risking the Wrath of God," 64; Tidwell et al., *Come Retribution*, 186.

46. Baird, *Luke Pryor Blackburn*, 30; Pittman, *The Assassination of President Lincoln and the Trial of the Conspirators*, 56; Steers, "Risking the Wrath of God," 64; Tidwell et al., *Come Retribution*, 186–87.

47. Baird, *Luke Pryor Blackburn*, 29–31; Steers, "Risking the Wrath of God," 64–65; Tidwell et al., *Come Retribution*, 187.

48. Baird, *Luke Pryor Blackburn*, 28–29; Singer, *The Confederate Dirty War*, 79–80; Steers, *Blood on the Moon*, 49–50; Steers, "Risking the Wrath of God," 65.

49. Baird, *Luke Pryor Blackburn*, 31–32; Soodalter, "Partisan, Terrorist, Soldier, Spy," 39; Steers, *Blood on the Moon*, 47–50; Steers, "Risking the Wrath of God," 67–69.

50. Pittman, *The Assassination of President Lincoln and the Trial of the Conspirators*, 56; Steers, "Risking the Wrath of God," 65.

51. Steers, "Risking the Wrath of God," 65.

52. Steers, *Blood on the Moon*, 90; Steers, "Risking the Wrath of God," 65.

53. Baird, *Luke Pryor Blackburn*, 26–27; Steers, "Risking the Wrath of God," 65. Francis Tumblety was later a suspect in the Jack the Ripper killings in London in 1888. See, for example, Kauffman, *American Brutus*, 385.

54. Baird, *Luke Pryor Blackburn*, 26–32; Soodalter, "Partisan, Terrorist, Soldier, Spy," 39; Steers, "Risking the Wrath of God," 65–68.

55. Quoted in Baird, *Luke Pryor Blackburn*, 33. See also Steers, "Risking the Wrath of God," 60, 69.

56. Baird, *Luke Pryor Blackburn*, 36–37; Soodalter, "Partisan, Terrorist, Soldier, Spy," 39; Steers, "Risking the Wrath of God," 69.

57. Baird, *Luke Pryor Blackburn*, 115–16; Soodalter, "Partisan, Terrorist, Soldier, Spy," 39; Steers, "Risking the Wrath of God," 69; Tidwell et al., *Come Retribution*, 187.

58. Blackburn is labeled the "gentle, kindhearted bioterrorist" in Soodalter, "Partisan, Terrorist, Soldier, Spy," 39.

3

"WE MAY SUSPECT THAT RACE WAS THE CAUSE OF THE HOSTILITY"

The Colfax Massacre (1873)

With sword so shining and so sharp, it caused
Terror to me on this side of the river.

—Dante Alighieri, *The Divine Comedy: Purgatorio*, Canto XXIX

The episode that became known in American history as the "Colfax Massacre" was one of many violent confrontations between blacks and whites during the Reconstruction era. Owing to the large number of freedmen killed and wounded as well as its culmination in a historic U.S. Supreme Court case that reaffirmed white supremacy throughout the nation, the Colfax incident became a landmark event, another sad chapter in the life of the republic. It also presents a thorny problem in the study of terrorism. Substate terrorism is generally thought of in terms of an insurgency fighting against established society, a small group of disaffected activists that uses violence as a means of calling attention to the group's message and subverting the mainstream power structure. Colfax presents the opposite scenario. Mainstream society, at least in the Southern region of the United States during the waning days of the nineteenth century, employed violence against a black insurgency, although the insurgency often fought back vehemently. In this reversal of the usual situation, the identities of the "terrorist" and the "terrorized" become muddled.[1]

Political officials in the nineteenth century would dispute the characterization of violence employed by whites against a black minority as terroristic. "Terrorism" as the term is used today involves violence or a threat of violence that violates the positivist law and harms civilians in service of another, presumably broader, moral, social, political, religious, or ethnic goal. By this definition, whites in positions of power during the post-Reconstruction era would contend that blacks seeking to challenge the status quo were "terrorists" in the sense that blacks violated white supremacy laws to secure greater political rights. The concept of a small band of alienated persons undermining the stability of the regime through violence and threats of violence is frightening to the populace and is usually considered the sine qua non of terrorism. Observers who contemplate the causes and effects of terrorism after the fact typically consider the issue from the perspective of the established ruling party—a perspective that automatically assumes the illegitimacy of the terrorist position. Critics of terrorism as a political tactic bemoan the failure of the disaffected parties to participate in political life through the normal channels of participation. To the so-called terrorists, however, the normal channels of expressing discontent are closed or severely limited, which partially explains the reason the aggrieved parties choose to act outside of mainstream society. In the twenty-first century, champions of equal justice under law argue that a small band of disenfranchised people struggling to secure its fair share of political and economic power against a far larger, pertinacious force is not necessarily terroristic, but from the perspective of a society where inequality had long been a legally protected and recognized social norm, the conclusions are not so clear. The Colfax episode suggests that assessing terrorism and identifying the aggrieved parties and their transgressors can be challenging.[2]

PRESIDENTIAL VERSUS CONGRESSIONAL RECONSTRUCTION

To understand how the Colfax Massacre occurred, it is necessary to understand the broader context of American Reconstruction during the 1860s and 1870s. The roots of the confrontation stretch back to the waning days of the Civil War. In April 1865, the United States had reached a crossroads; the Southern Confederacy had not yet been defeated, but with the surrender of General Robert E. Lee at Appomattox Court House on April 9, the end was near. The American president, Abraham Lincoln, was dead, the victim of an assassin's bullet. His untested successor, Andrew Johnson, entered the presidency facing one of the most difficult periods in national memory. He would have to reconstruct a country ripped apart by civil war.[3]

Against this backdrop, the Radical Republicans, a small but vocal political minority serving in Congress, sought to remake American institutions so that former slaves could take part in political life absent the handicaps imposed on them by their previous condition of servitude. It was wishful thinking to believe that white supremacists throughout the land would willingly abandon social relations that had served them and their forbears for decades, if not centuries. The Radicals had battled with President Lincoln about the terms and conditions of Reconstruction policy. Although sympathetic to their goal of lifting up an impoverished race and providing for their future well-being, Lincoln understood as few of his contemporaries did that radically altering the social strata would disrupt the lives and fortunes of innumerable people who felt they had suffered enough from the sour vicissitudes of war. A political leader must not stray too far in front of the electorate, no matter how worthy the cause or the desired end result.[4]

To the Radicals' way of thinking, the kindhearted Lincoln, though well-meaning, was simply unequal to the task of fiercely punishing the traitorous South for having seceded in the first place. At critical junctures throughout four years of war, they pressed the president to move beyond political moderation. As battlefield victory seemed ever more certain, they turned their attention to reconstructing the nation—not as it had been before the firing on Fort Sumter, but as it might be when the traitorous rebels were brought to heel.[5]

For the Radicals, the administration's efforts to plan for a postwar republic were disappointingly pedestrian. Lincoln's original Reconstruction scheme, announced in December 1863, had been remarkably generous— too generous for some tastes—to the vanquished foe. By affirming an oath to support the U.S. Constitution and agreeing to obey all federal laws, including those abolishing slavery, Southerners could rejoin the United States. Rather than treat the defeated warriors as prisoners or second-class citizens, Lincoln would allow Confederates to enjoy all property rights "except as to slaves." Even worse in the Radicals' view, when the number of citizens affirming the oath in a particular state equaled or exceeded 10 percent of the votes cast in the 1860 election, newly made loyalists could establish a state government.[6]

The Radicals believed that these lenient terms were a recipe for disaster. The moment the Southern elite reestablished control over state governments, they would reinstate slavery in everything but name. If this occurred, the Old South would be alive and well. What had the war been about if the nation returned to its old ways of thinking and acting? The freedmen who had been unshackled from bondage would find themselves becoming second-class citizens under the thumb of brutally oppressive white regimes if the federal government squandered a golden moment to alter government and society in fundamental ways. For the Radicals, the burning question during the latter half of April 1865 was whether the new president, Andrew Johnson, would continue Lincoln's misguided policies.[7]

With Lincoln dead and buried, the new man sitting in the president's chair was a great unknown. He was a Southerner and a Democrat, but he had stayed loyal to the Union, which won him the vice presidency and eventually the presidency. Initially, his muscular rhetoric against the rebels suggested he was a fellow who would fit the Radical mold. Time and again, he promised to bear down on the rebels with all the might of the conquering army, thereby enforcing a reformulation of American society. In early meetings with Radical leaders, he insisted he was committed to punishing traitors. Radical senator Benjamin Wade of Ohio, a frequent Lincoln critic, was grateful to find a sympathetic chief executive. "Mr. Johnson, I thank God that you are here," he said. "Lincoln had too much of the milk of human kindness to deal with these damned rebels. Now they will be dealt with according to their deserts."[8]

The Radicals' amicable relationship with the president was short-lived. They were stunned when Johnson issued a proclamation of amnesty on May 29, 1865. Although they had begun to realize that the new president did not stand for everything they had hoped he would, the measure was an abrupt departure from Johnson's promises to punish the traitors. With the exception of high-ranking civilian and political leaders, he offered to pardon all Southerners for their actions in supporting the Southern Confederacy during the war. As if the pardon were not bad enough, the president appointed pro-Southern provisional state governors. This lenient proclamation was closer in spirit and tone to Lincoln's original 10 percent plan than the harsh executive action the Radicals preferred.[9]

Congress was not in session when Johnson issued his proclamation, but the Radicals wasted no time in preparing a rebuttal. When the legislators convened in December 1865, leading members of Congress, including Senator Wade, Congressman Henry Winter Davis of Maryland, Senator Charles Sumner of Massachusetts, and Congressman Thaddeus Stevens of Pennsylvania, moved to reverse the president's permissive Reconstruction measures. Aside from their concern for the welfare of the freedmen, they were worried that if the Southern states reentered the Union too quickly, the region's congressmen and senators would join forces with Northern Democrats to build a legislative coalition; thus, Republicans would lose control of the legislative process. To prevent the return of Southern legislative power, the Radicals joined forces with moderate Republicans to champion a series of bills strengthening punitive policies toward the South.[10]

Their first two bills were hardly radical, but they served notice to the administration that the federal government must afford protections to emancipated slaves. Senator Lyman Trumbull of Illinois, chairman of the Judiciary Committee, sponsored a bill to extend the life of the Freedmen's Bureau, the federal agency designed to assist freed slaves in negotiating labor contracts and establishing a plan for becoming integrated into American life. When Lincoln signed the bill establishing the Freedmen's Bureau in March 1865, the agency was supposed to only last a year. Nine months into its tenure, it was clear that the plight of the freedmen remained desperate; they required continued assistance in securing clothing, housing, and education. No other agency of the federal government, except possibly the military, was well situated to alleviate the problems of the former slaves.[11]

Republicans introduced a second initiative, the Civil Rights Bill of 1866, to augment the Thirteenth Amendment to the U.S. Constitution, which abolished slavery throughout the country in December 1865. Section two of the amendment declared that "Congress shall have power to enforce this article by appropriate legislation." A civil rights bill, modest by twenty-first-century standards, recognized all persons born in the United States, with the notable exception of Native Americans, as national citizens entitled to the "full and equal benefit of all laws" without regard to race. U.S. district attorneys, U.S. marshals, and other federal officials were authorized to file suit in federal courts to ensure compliance. The Radicals saw the bill as a necessary first step toward reducing or eliminating discrimination and violence against the freedmen.[12]

Much to the Republicans' dismay, President Johnson vetoed both the bill extending the Freedmen's Bureau as well as the Civil Rights Bill of 1866. He explained in his veto message for the civil rights bill that the federal government could not constitutionally consolidate its power to protect any group, regardless of their prior circumstances, from discrimination. To afford blacks special treatment would violate the Constitution. Johnson wrote that "the distinction of race and color is by the bill made to operate in favor of the colored and against the white race." Reflecting the prejudice of the age, he expressed concerns about racial intermarriage and his belief that former slaves lacked a basic understanding of "the nature and character of

our institutions." In his view, the federal government had no role in securing freedoms for blacks beyond abolishing the institution of slavery.[13]

The president's break with the Radicals was complete. The angry Jaco-
bins joined forces with moderates to override both vetoes. They were not
satisfied with a piecemeal victory, though. Eventually, the Republican-
dominated Joint Committee on Reconstruction proposed a constitutional
amendment to define national citizenship as "all persons born or natu-
ralized in the United States." Although the Thirteenth Amendment had
eradicated slavery, this new measure once and for all dispatched with the
concept of counting former slaves as three-fifths of white citizens, as had
been the case under the Constitution under the Great Compromise. The
amendment also forbade any state from abridging the rights of U.S. citizens
or denying them "the equal protection of the laws" absent "due process of
law." Moreover, it declared that any state denying a person's right to vote,
excepting untaxed Native Americans, persons convicted of a crime, or
"participants in the Rebellion," would find its congressional representation
reduced proportionally. Persons who "engaged in insurrection or rebellion"
or who had "given aid or comfort to the enemies" of the Union could not
hold "any office, civil or military, under the United States, or under any
State." The proposed amendment repudiated Confederate debt and af-
firmed "the validity of the public debt of the United States" and directed
that "Congress shall have power to enforce, by appropriate legislation, the
provisions of this article."[14]

The Constitution can be amended after two-thirds of both houses of
Congress submit a proposed change to the states and three-fourths of the
states ratify the amendment either through their state legislatures or in
special conventions called to consider the amendment. In June 1866, both
houses of Congress provided the necessary two-thirds votes. The proposed
Fourteenth Amendment was sent to the states for ratification. There it
encountered problems.[15]

President Johnson, now unmistakably opposed to the Radicals' position,
immediately attacked the proposal. In addition, he lent his presidential
prestige to a new National Union Party comprised of conservative Republicans and Democrats anxious to prevent the Radicals from seizing control of
federal Reconstruction policy from the president. Johnson was never content to stay above the level of bare-knuckle politics, though. To galvanize
support, he also embarked on an eighteen-day train tour to publicize his
opposition. Johnson's disastrous "swing around the circle"—taking his case
to the people to circumvent dissident elements in Congress—forever after
became a case study in how not to whip up support for a presidential posi-

tion. Crowds were hostile, and Johnson returned their hostility. His verbal tirades and self-indulgent harangues compelled the *New York Tribune* to label him an "irritated demagogue" following the president's exchange of epithets with hecklers.[16]

In the meantime, the Fourteenth Amendment failed to secure necessary support in three-fourths of the states owing to the Southern states' refusal to sound the death knell of the white aristocracy. Through political maneuvering that required states to adopt the amendment prior to rejoining the Union, the Republican coalition managed to secure ratification by July 1868. The goal was accomplished by enacting the first Reconstruction Act of 1867. If the South would not ratify the Fourteenth Amendment, Southern state governments would have to be reconstituted. The act divided the eleven former states of the Southern Confederacy, except Tennessee, into five military districts under the command of a military officer under orders to hold elections for constitutional conventions. When the new state constitutions were written, they were submitted to Congress for approval. After Congress approved a state's newly created constitution and the state agreed to adopt the Fourteenth Amendment, the state was restored to the Union.[17]

Southerners decried despotic rule, arguing that military units parading on their streets was tantamount to an imperialistic nation launching a de facto military takeover of a conquered province. They also protested that the Fourteenth Amendment was being forced on them. President Johnson agreed, remarking that Southerners "were to be trodden under foot 'to protect niggers.'" As a logical argument, the protesters had a point. If they were to rejoin the Union as full partners in the American republic, this rough treatment was not calculated to engender warm feelings of nationalism and pride in their common heritage. In light of the outcome of the war, however, vanquished Confederates had little choice but to comply. The subsequent veneration of the Fourteenth Amendment did little to assuage the anger that white Southerners nursed as they watched the Radical faction in Washington ride roughshod over the Union as it was. Many outbreaks of violence, including the Colfax Massacre, occurred as an expression of the anger and resentment that whites felt about having to acknowledge the right of black Americans to equal treatment under the law.[18]

The federal government continued to intervene in state affairs despite the unpopularity of such actions in the South. Congress enacted a second Reconstruction Act on March 23, 1867. The second measure directed district commanders to register eligible voters as a prelude to electing delegates to the state constitutional convention. Success depended on local commanders convincing the local citizenry that federal Reconstruction policy was in everyone's best interests, but it was a hard sell to Southerners still incensed at the Union war victory. White Southerners, many of whom were Confederate veterans, recoiled at military authorities imperiously dictating laws and contravening home rule.[19]

By extending political rights to blacks, Republican leaders threatened the social strata carefully constructed by white Southerners over many generations. Realizing that radical change was afoot, many newly emancipated slaves organized Union Leagues as a mechanism for making their voices heard in political affairs and consolidating their power within the community. The leagues increased white Southerners' anxiety as they watched the groups organize voter registration drives and support Republican policies and officials. Matters grew worse with the appearance of Northerners who arrived to teach school and help administer state governments. Derisively labeled "carpetbaggers," an allusion to the large number of interlopers who carried their belongings in cheap carpetbags, these do-gooder whites who mingled with freedmen undermined traditional Southern mores. Southern Unionists who lent a sympathetic hand to the Republicans were decried as "scalawags," an epithet linked to the little town of Scalloway in the Shetland Islands where a poor-quality, scrubby cattle was reputed to originate.[20]

A third bill, this one enacted in March 1867, extended the Radicals' Reconstruction efforts by attempting to limit President Johnson's ability to remove cabinet members who were holdovers from the Lincoln administration and not necessarily loyal to the new chief executive. Titled the Tenure of Office Act, the measure prohibited the president from removing from office any federal official who had received Senate confirmation. On its face, the act was constitutionally deficient. Article II, Section 2, Clause 2 of the U.S. Constitution directs that the president "shall nominate, and with the Advice and Consent of the Senate, shall appoint Ambassadors, other public Ministers and Consuls, Judges of the supreme Court, and all other officers of the United States, whose Appointments are not herein otherwise provided for, and which shall be established by Law." The Constitution is silent on whether Senate approval is required for removing officials. Presumably, if the Founders had intended to insist on Senate approval before removing a federal official from office, they would have included the requirement in Article II somewhere near the requirement of Senate confirmation for appointments.[21]

Johnson contended that the Tenure of Office Act was unconstitutional because only a constitutional amendment could impose additional constraints on presidential appointments. To drive home the point, the president originally vetoed the act. The Republican-controlled Congress overrode his veto. Never content to avoid a confrontation, Johnson suspended Secretary of War Edwin M. Stanton, a favorite of the Radical Republicans, without securing the necessary Senate approval. This deliberate refusal to obey the new law infuriated his critics, but judging by Democratic gains in state elections during the fall of 1867, the president appeared to enjoy widespread public support. As a Johnson loyalist explained, "Any party with an abolition head and a nigger tail will soon find itself with nothing left but the head and the tail."[22]

Johnson was on politically dangerous ground. When Stanton's suspension came before the Senate for review, as required by the Tenure of Office Act, the Radicals persuaded their colleagues not to grant authorization for the dismissal. The matter might have ended there if the odious Stanton had been left in his office, but Johnson would have none of it. Without missing a beat, he violated the act by dismissing Stanton, regardless of the consequences.[23]

This act of open defiance was exactly the pretext the Radicals needed to challenge the president. They previously had accused him of engaging in all manner of malfeasance, but so far the charges had been little more than allegations of gross incompetence and buffoonery. Now, in their view, articles of impeachment were warranted owing to a blatant violation of statutory law. The man from Tennessee had failed to "play the part of Moses for the colored people," the *Nation* wryly observed, so he played the part "for the impeachers."[24]

Republican leaders in the House of Representatives filed eleven articles of impeachment, nine of which related to the violation of the Tenure of Office Act. Article 10 denounced the president's "inflammatory and scandalous harangues" against Congress, and the eleventh article summarized the accusations. With a vote of 126 to 47 in favor of preparing articles of impeachment for a trial in the U.S. Senate, "on Monday, February 24, 1868, the House of Representatives of the Congress of the United States, resolved to impeach Andrew Johnson, President of the United States of high crimes and misdemeanors, of which, the Senate was apprised and arrangements made for trial."[25]

It was the first time in American history that Congress had impeached a president of the United States. Article II, Section 4, of the Constitution states that a president, vice president, "and all civil Officers of the United States, shall be removed from Office on Impeachment for, and Conviction of, Treason, Bribery, or other high crimes and Misdemeanors." According to the Constitution, the House of Representatives prepares the Articles of Impeachment and the Senate, presided over by the Chief Justice of the

U.S. Supreme Court, "shall have the sole Power to try all Impeachments." Two-thirds of the members present must agree to remove the president from office.[26]

The impeachment was an unabashedly partisan affair. Horace Greeley, influential editor of the *New York Tribune*, called Johnson "an aching tooth in the national jaw, a screeching infant in a crowded lecture room." The Radicals called him "an ungrateful, despicable, besotted traitorous man— an incubus." General William T. Sherman said, "He is like a General fighting without an army."[27]

Johnson was a less-than-stellar president, but it was difficult to justify removing a president for incompetence. The Founders deliberately wrote the provisions on impeachment to make it difficult to remove a high-ranking federal official. They did not seek to turn the affair into a partisan strategy to maneuver around a disagreeable president. Regrettably, a partisan political effort is exactly what the Johnson impeachment proceedings became.[28]

Despite the congressional opposition to the president, public support for impeachment waned. Eventually, seven moderate Republican senators, led by Senator William P. Fessenden of Maine, changed their votes in favor of acquittal. The "Treacherous Seven," as the Radicals labeled the defectors, turned the tide in Johnson's favor. On May 16, 1868, thirty-five senators voted for removal and nineteen against. This tally was one vote short of the necessary margin to convict the president. Despite the Radicals' best efforts, the infuriating Andrew Johnson would serve out his term as president of the United States.[29]

The impeachment battle was the zenith of Radical political power. In the aftermath of the debacle, their power declined. The grand old man of the Radical Republicans, Thaddeus Stevens, died within months of the acquittal, and his colleagues gradually retired or lost power through the electoral process. After the election of Ulysses S. Grant as president in 1868, the nation began a slow, gradual movement away from Reconstruction policies. The Radicals, once so certain and righteous in their cause, were seen by some detractors as power-hungry would-be demagogues. They constantly cajoled the moderates in their party when cooler heads ought to have prevailed, thereby imperiling carefully crafted policies. Personally ambitious to a fault and intoxicated with power, these men of extremes failed to appreciate the virtues of negotiation and compromise. In time, historians reassessed the Radicals, sometimes depicting them as principled men who refused to yield on moral issues because to do so would have been an act of hypocrisy.[30]

As the Radicals' political power and influence declined, moderate Republicans looked to a standard bearer who promised to mend fences within the party: Ulysses S. Grant. He was a nonideological, middle-of-the-road candidate, a political newcomer who theoretically would halt the bickering between Republican factions. Although no one realized it at the start of Grant's tenure, he was committed to two conflicting goals: first, uniting the party, and second, pursuing a vigorous Reconstruction policy. He was pledged to protect the freedmen without alienating the South in the process. As time would demonstrate vividly, they proved to be mutually exclusive objectives.[31]

For all of the well-documented failures of his administration, Grant showed political courage in supporting ratification of the Fifteenth Amendment and in intervening in state affairs to confront the Ku Klux Klan in several Southern states, notably in South Carolina in 1870. Earlier that same year, he appointed a friend of the freedmen when he selected Amos T. Akerman as his second attorney general.[32]

Despite these efforts, Grant was a disappointment to the Radicals. As the war receded into history and a new generation of political leaders emerged to control the Republican Party, interest in aggressively protecting blacks waned. Grant seemed to please no one as his first term drew to a close. Conservatives found him too committed to Reconstruction and the Radical position. The Southern press denounced him as a despot promoting puppet state governments infested with carpetbaggers. The Radicals were displeased as well; in their view, he was a plodding, cautious, naive titular leader who surrounded himself with sycophants. In trying to please everyone, he risked pleasing no one.[33]

The Liberal Republican faction within the party contested Grant's re-election bid in 1872, a fissure that caused, at least in part, the administration's retreat from Reconstruction policies during the second term. The party schism served notice that the end of Reconstruction was at hand. Grant handily won reelection, but his last four years in office were engulfed by political scandals as well as an economic crisis.[34]

While shifting political winds hurt former slaves, the economy exacerbated their troubles. It is no exaggeration to say that the Panic of 1873 occurred at a time when support for Reconstruction was declining, and the financial downturn further undermined support for the freedmen. The crisis began as a result of the railroad construction boom following the war. Railroad companies had laid more than 35,000 miles of track between 1866 and 1873. Anxious to promote new growth, the Johnson and Grant administrations provided generous grants and subsidies to the railroads. Unfortunately for investors and speculators, the good times could not last indefinitely. In September 1873, Jay Cooke, a wealthy investor who had gambled that a second transcontinental railroad would be built, suddenly announced his ruination. When he could not obtain an expected $300 million government loan to finance additional construction, Cooke could no longer operate his cash-starved business, and he declared bankruptcy on September 18. The collapse of Jay Cooke & Company sent the economy into a downward spiral. As federal officials struggled to deal with the crisis, their attention turned away from Reconstruction in the states. The Republican Party, once hailed as the "Party of Lincoln," gradually became the party of business interests. The freedmen were left to fend for themselves against increasingly emboldened white supremacists in the Southern states.[35]

THE STRUGGLE FOR RECONSTRUCTION IN LOUISIANA

As the Radicals fought to wrest control of Reconstruction away from President Johnson, the states underwent their own Reconstruction struggles. Louisiana, one of the first states to surrender to Union forces during the war, had experienced Reconstruction longer than surrounding areas. Lincoln had attempted to implement his so-called 10 percent plan there during the war, although the results were not promising. The president had hoped to demonstrate that reconstructing a state could be accomplished without treating the area as a conquered territory, but recalcitrant residents were complicating the task. Even as the victorious Union army attempted to allow former slaves to partake in the political life of the state, embittered Southerners did their best to disenfranchise blacks.[36]

In 1866, when Radical Republicans attempted to reconvene a state constitutional convention in New Orleans, violence erupted between blacks and whites, foreshadowing the violence and bloodshed that would become common in the ensuing years. In the midst of this chaos, a former slave owner from Louisiana, William Smith Calhoun, cast his lot with the Republicans. When he engaged in a dispute about the placement of a ballot box in a Democratic stronghold, Calhoun managed to have the votes collected at a Republican plantation store. Predictably, white Democrats were furious when Republicans won the vote tally. Recriminations between both sides made it clear that an undercurrent of violence lay beneath the surface. Incensed whites tossed the ballot box into the Red River and had their nemesis arrested for voter fraud. From there, matters escalated. In the wake of the murder of a black Republican election commissioner, Calhoun persuaded the legislature to carve out a new district, Grant Parish, named for Union war hero Ulysses S. Grant, from parts of Winn Parish and Rapides Parish.[37]

It was clear that state Republicans faced a hostile citizenry. Indeed, Calhoun's troubles mirrored the troubles of the state governor, Henry C. Warmouth. Originally hailing from Illinois, the carpetbagger governor found himself under siege by angry whites after he installed a black Union veteran, William Ward, as commander of a regiment of the state militia. Later, Warmouth's political expediency propelled him into the Liberal Republican camp in an effort to retain political power. During the 1872 election season, the Liberal Republicans favored a rapprochement with white Democrats in an effort to close the wounds inflicted by the Civil War and the excesses of Radical Republicans. As a Liberal Republican, Warmouth backed the Democratic gubernatorial candidate, John McEnery, as his successor against the Republican candidate, William Pitt Kellogg. The

White supremacist groups active in Louisiana in the 1870s. Courtesy of the Library of Congress.

disputed election resulted in both sides claiming victory, although eventually a Republican federal judge decided that Kellogg was the victor. Grant dispatched federal troops to protect the new governor's administration.[38]

Kellogg's ascension into the governor's chair despite the previous governor's opposition inaugurated a new period of pitched violence between the forces of radicalism and reactionary whites who sought to return to the Union as it was before the outbreak of hostilities. Armed confrontations between McEnery's people and Kellogg's people became common. As Warmouth had done before him, Kellogg attempted to prop up the Republican Party by appointing prominent party members to positions of power, including registrar posts, to ensure that ballot boxes were not stuffed with Democratic votes. When both Republicans and Democrats claimed to have won local elections in Grant Parish—a black Republican Union veteran named William Ward, a former slave, claimed to be police chief while white Democrat Christopher Columbus Nash, a Confederate veteran, argued that he was the rightful office holder—the dispute dragged on until Republicans seized the parish courthouse in Colfax on the evening of March 25, 1873. Fearing bloodshed, they began fortifying the building against attack and preparing for a siege from local white supremacists.[39]

The battles between Democrats, all of whom were white, and Republicans, many of whom were black, had created a large reservoir of bitterness and resentment among local whites. They were infuriated because the recently freed blacks inside the courthouse dared to rise up against their former masters. The audacity of this assault on the established social order was more than many whites could bear. Nash and his confederates hatched a plan to storm the courthouse and punish the miscreants for their dastardly deeds. On April 1, James Hadnot, a well-known white supremacist in postwar Louisiana, arrived in Colfax to help organize whites against the offending Negroes and ensure the continuation of white supremacy.[40]

Recognizing their precarious position, blacks armed their own forces and launched a preemptive strike against several white supremacist leaders. A running street battle ensued between Negroes who refused to be denied their rights and whites who sought to protect the white regime. The two sides eventually entered into peace negotiations, but the good faith of everyone concerned was questionable. Stories, some real and some imagined, of atrocities perpetrated on both sides only inflamed tensions. The sensational tale of a black man, Jesse McKinney, shot in the head while repairing a fence especially outraged Negroes who realized they might face such a fate if local whites gained the upper hand. McKinney supposedly "cried like a pig" while his murderers danced about in a festive air. This vignette, brought to the negotiating table in the midst of discussions, ended the session with much acrimony among all participants.[41]

Shortly before Easter Sunday, William Ward and his men hopped onto a steamship bound for New Orleans. Depending on who told the story, either they sought to abandon blacks ensconced in the Colfax courthouse owing to cowardice or they were on a mission to gather U.S. troops from Governor Kellogg. In any case, in their absence, blacks in Colfax resolved to hold off their assailants until help arrived. For their part, whites outside the courthouse traveled downriver to the town of Alexandria and acquired a wheeled cannon to use in the assault.[42]

A few days later, on Easter, Christopher Columbus Nash assumed control of the white paramilitary forces. Addressing his troops as a general officer would prepare his subordinates for battle, he outlined the plan for dislodging the blacks from the courthouse. He also warned them that they might be prosecuted for treason if they participated in the Colfax struggle. Twenty-five men departed from the ranks after this speech, but the remaining three hundred followed their commander to the courthouse grounds. It was around noon, and the time had come to end the standoff.[43]

Nash demanded that the men inside surrender. When they refused, he allowed women and children surrounding the courthouse thirty minutes to disperse. When they had departed, Nash's men fired rifles into the building. The defenders returned fire. The resulting stalemate frustrated everyone. To resolve the impasse, the white supremacists rolled the cannon into place, which caused several blacks inside the building to panic. According to later reports, approximately sixty defenders bolted from the courthouse, headed for the nearby woods, and jumped into the river.[44]

Nash and his men were not satisfied to allow the escapees to find solace in the water. White attackers on horseback gave chase, shooting the panicked black men before they crossed to the other side. Emboldened by the chase and enthralled by the killing, the troops returned to the scene of the standoff. Afterward, the militia forced a black prisoner to set fire to the courthouse. The aftermath remains a source of contention.[45]

Inside the burning building, the freedmen had no option but to surrender. They hoisted white flags through the windows indicating that they would come outside. The shooting halted momentarily, but the carnage was far from over. At some point shortly after the white flags appeared, someone shot white supremacist James Hadnot. Whites outside the building insisted it was the blacks inside the courthouse. Blacks insisted that Hadnot's comrades in arms accidentally shot him. Whatever happened, enraged white supremacists fired their rifles at the black defenders as the latter streamed from the courthouse. Blacks who were not killed immediately supposedly were taken prisoner, only to be shot and killed later. Only one man, Levi Nelson, survived the slaughter when he managed to crawl away without attracting attention.[46]

After the state militia arrived, they found the smoldering ruins of the Colfax courthouse as well as the bodies of black defenders strewn throughout the nearby grounds. Despite the poor condition of the remains, it was obvious that the men had been shot in the back. Some corpses had been beaten almost beyond recognition. One man's body had been mauled with a knife. About fifteen or twenty bodies floated in the river. A search for suspects revealed that the whites who participated in the massacre, anticipating repercussions, had fled. With all the conflicting reports, the number of dead and wounded was never established clearly or completely.[47]

The Colfax slaughter became riveting news throughout the nation, and indeed around the world. Reactions varied, depending on the orientation and political predilections of the reader. For Republicans, especially those of a radical bent, it was a frightening warning that efforts to remake the South after the war largely had failed. Despite the Radicals' legislative initiatives to ensure equal treatment for the races, the hearts and minds of whites steeped in a tradition of white supremacy would not easily be altered. With the Grant administration's retreat from enforcing the Reconstruction-era laws, the Colfax episode suggested that the federal government would leave it to the states to police themselves—even if it meant abandoning the freedmen in their hour of need.[48]

For white supremacists, the Colfax Massacre carried an encouraging message. Although the architects of the massacre eventually were apprehended and tried for their actions, they succeeded in keeping blacks in their place. Across the South, the lesson for "uppity Negroes" was to be careful when they dared to oppose the white power structure. Legal slavery may have ended with the end of the war and the ratification of the Thirteenth Amendment, but social relations between the races need not undergo radical change.[49]

REPERCUSSIONS OF THE MASSACRE

Federal prosecutors eventually indicted ninety-seven suspects, charging them with violating Section 6 of the Enforcement Act of 1870, which prohibited conspirators from denying citizens their constitutional rights. U.S. attorney general George Williams had instructed Justice Department attorneys that prosecutions must be limited to the most culpable defendants. To go after every member of the mob would inundate the department with cases and exhaust its resources. The limited resources hampered prosecutors, especially when they found that one man who was reported dead, Levi Nelson, was very much alive. If casualty reports were fraught with error, determining the facts and proving a case against the perpetrators would be difficult. An editor of the unsympathetic *Alexandria Democrat*, Edward Biossat, sardonically observed that "one main negro swearer, Nelson by name, was actually killed in the fight, but some stray Gabriel's last trumpet blew him alive again." Prosecutors had no margin for error in making a case against the offenders.[50]

The men tried for their part in the murders found support from their friends and neighbors in the white community. Although some defendants, including William Cruikshank and J. P. Hadnot, the eighteen-year-old son of the "martyred" James Hadnot, had financial means, others were destitute. They need not have worried. Whites who had dared to combat black rabble-rousers were hailed as heroes; local elected officials and private institutions enthusiastically raised money for their legal expenses. J. P.'s classmates at the Pineville military academy, which later became Louisiana State University, scheduled a theatrical performance to raise money. Local women solicited funds door to door. Defense attorneys offered their services *pro bono publico*. White supremacists closed ranks to protect their own from the legal process.[51]

In the trials that followed, the defense enjoyed substantial advantages. Local whites packed the galleries and cheered the defendants, often hissing when the prosecutors spoke. Defense attorneys found their courtroom tables in inundated with flowers. Prosecutors and jurors were accosted on the streets throughout the proceedings, and the judge was denounced as a party hack and a drunk.[52]

Despite the prosecution's instructions to preserve resources and try cases on the cheap, it was clear their witnesses, most of whom were black, would need protection if they were to appear in court. Calling on U.S. marshals to provide escorts, prosecutors ensured they would be able to mount a case despite the prevailing atmosphere of hostility. Eventually, 140 people paraded through the court to describe what they had seen in the days leading up to the massacre and during the massacre itself. The ordeal was taxing. Some witnesses suffered physical beatings and ostracism from local whites in the aftermath of the trials.[53]

Each side sought to make the most of strategy, but, again, the defense held an advantage. Prosecutors struggled to show a connection between the race of the victims and the actions undertaken by white supremacists. Such a causal nexus was required under interpretations of the applicable federal constitutional and statutory provisions of the time. The problem was that the defense contended that race was not an issue. They argued that the attackers had acted because the threat of armed men seizing control of the Colfax courthouse required the resumption of law and order. Whites who fired on blacks inside the building would have acted exactly the same, defense attorneys argued, regardless of the race of the lawbreakers. Although everyone was aware that race was the underlying cause of the melee, the defense relied on a wink and a nod to suggest that race played no part in the episode.[54]

One defendant won an acquittal; a mistrial occurred for eight other defendants. At a new trial, three men were convicted of conspiracy and sixteen other charges. The consolidated cases came up on appeal to the U.S. Supreme Court, and in a five-to-four decision, the justices held that the indictments were faulty because the Enforcement Act was a federal statute, but the charges in the case did not involve a denial of federal rights. Chief Justice Morrison Waite wrote the majority opinion in *United States v. Cruikshank* finding that the First Amendment right of assembly and the Second Amendment right to bear arms protected citizens from federal abuses, which did not occur in Colfax. In Waite's view, the due process and equal protection rights protected by the Fourteenth Amendment applied only to states, not to individuals. Because individuals carried out the massacre and state officials never participated, the indictments were invalid. As for the claim that white citizens interfered with the black victims' right to vote, the court dismissed the complaint because the evidence did not adequately demonstrate that race played a role in the incident. "We may suspect that race was the cause of the hostility," Waite observed, "but it was not so averred. This is material to a description of the substance of the offence, and cannot be supplied by implication."[55]

Cruikshank became a controversial case in nineteenth-century American jurisprudence. Supporters argued that it was a powerful defense of state rights and wholly in line with a strict constitutional interpretation of federalism during that epoch. Modern historians have concluded that the opinion was part of a line of cases eviscerating the Civil War amendments and enforcement acts as part of the march toward legal segregation of the races. The court's opinion was widely regarded as permission for white supremacists throughout the South to reestablish the rule that had been interrupted by the Civil War and Reconstruction. Louisiana citizens received the message loud and clear. In later years, the state saw the rise

Drawing of the aftermath of the Colfax riot in *Harper's Weekly*, May 10, 1873. Courtesy of the Granger Collection, New York.

of "white line" paramilitary organizations such as the White League, which used violence and terror to ensure that blacks were kept in their place as second-class citizens. Other Southern states witnessed the rise of rifle clubs and similar armed, quasi-legitimate adjuncts to state governments firmly under the control of Democratic Party loyalists who were determined to protect the rights of the white race.[56]

MAKING SENSE OF THE COLFAX MASSACRE

The episode at Colfax, Louisiana, was not the only armed confrontation between blacks and whites during the Reconstruction era, but it stands out in the annals of the time owing to its ferocity as well as the large number of freedmen killed. Even by the standards of the era, when black lives counted for little in the white supremacist South, the carnage was remarkable. From the perspective of the twenty-first century, it is deeply disturbing that one group of Americans could slaughter another group of Americans owing to racial strife.[57]

The Colfax Massacre shares one feature with many of the episodes in this book, namely the use of terror to keep a group of people in line with the desires of those who would employ violence to achieve their ends. What makes this case unusual is the condition of the Southern states after the end of Reconstruction. The concept of terrorism usually evokes images of a small, determined, weak group of malcontents ready to risk their lives to achieve a goal that is unachievable through the normal channels of political participation. This image persists because many modern episodes of terrorism have been initiated by exactly such bands of fanatical comrades in arms united by extremist ideals and with little to lose in their everyday lives.[58]

For about eighty years, beginning in the 1870s, the American Southland was a region caught in the grip of apartheid. The Colfax Massacre was one episode in the struggle of white supremacists to solidify control over second-class citizens of a darker hue. The perpetrators of the Colfax violence were not a small group of disaffected outsiders; they were representatives of the white elite. Although the front-line soldiers in this struggle were rough around the edges and of a lesser social class than the white elite, they played their part in the white power structure. The terrorists were the regime leaders, and the insurgents were the blacks who dared to rise against the status quo.[59]

Whites of the era, of course, saw matters quite differently than later observers less afflicted by racial prejudice and, with the benefit of hindsight, possessing a deeper understanding of equality of opportunity. White Southerners of the nineteenth century viewed blacks as dangerous fanatics. Many former slaves had lost their supposed docile demeanor in the aftermath of Appomattox. The fixed social positions of the races, so strong and secure for generations, had become muddled. People of color no longer knew their place in the God-given scheme of things. For whites who had been reared to see themselves as the rightful rulers of the earth, blacks were "terrorists" because they undermined the status quo.[60]

The Colfax Massacre is different from other examples of terrorism in this book as well. Had white supremacy been a concept limited to a large percentage of the citizenry in the Cotton South, the idea might be dismissed as yet another strange pathology of the American Southland. We might yet look to William Faulkner as the quintessential prophet of a curious region south of the Mason-Dixon Line. Yet it is clear in the wake of the massacre that other white citizens—even those who did not live in the South and ostensibly shared no affinity for Dixie—agreed with the ideal that blacks must be kept in an inferior social and legal position. The *Cruikshank* case stands out as an example of the power of governmental institutions—in this case, the U.S. Supreme Court—to affect the daily lives of a large number of citizens by providing the imprimatur of the federal government on a brutal instrument of social control. The Colfax Massacre served notice to blacks that Southern whites would use whatever means were necessary to keep them in their place, and *Cruikshank* indicated that whites throughout the country would support their Southern brethren in that endeavor.[61]

Finally, this case presents a challenge to the traditional understanding because terrorist tactics tend to be used by the weak. In this case, whites were the elites, the leaders of Southern society. The freedmen were marginalized and weak in 1870s Louisiana. Yet "weak" need not be limited to numerical inferiority. White citizens believed they were oppressed owing to losses on the battlefield in the Civil War, the emancipation of the slaves, and the erosion of the antebellum social structure. White Southern leaders had reemerged from Reconstruction to assume the mantle of political power, but they feared that their way of life was slipping away. Keeping the freedmen under control through violence may not have fallen under the standard definition of "terrorism," but for the reasons discussed here, it should qualify.

NOTES

1. Keith, *The Colfax Massacre*, xi–xviii.
2. Khan and Azam, "Root Causes of Terrorism," 66–71.
3. Kauffman, *American Brutus*, 240–41, 278–80; Leonard, *Lincoln's Avengers*, 33; Peterson, *Lincoln in American Memory*, 14; Winik, *April 1865*, 355–59.
4. Trefousse, *The Radical Republicans*, 280–307.
5. Brands, "Hesitant Emancipator," 58; Donald, *Lincoln*, 362–63; Goodwin, *Team of Rivals*, 463; Green, *Freedom, Union, and Power*, 155–56; McPherson, *Tried by War*, 108; Trefousse, *The Radical Republicans*, 224; White, *A. Lincoln*, 493.
6. Goodwin, *Team of Rivals*, 589–90; Hesseltine, *Lincoln's Plan of Reconstruction*, 35–50; Trefousse, *The Radical Republicans*, 283–86; White, *A. Lincoln*, 613–14; Williams, *Lincoln and the Radicals*, 301–3.
7. Burg, "Amnesty, Civil Rights, and the Meaning of Liberal Republicanism," 34; Currie, "The Reconstruction Congress," 385; Foner, *Reconstruction*, 224–27; Simkins and Roland, *A History of the South*, 255–59.
8. Quoted in Martinez, *Carpetbaggers, Cavalry, and the Ku Klux Klan*, 41. See also Beale, *The Critical Year*, 48–52.
9. Calabresi and Yoo, "The Unitary Executive during the Second Half-Century," 739–41; Foner, *Reconstruction*, 183–84; Henry, *The Story of Reconstruction*,

46–48; Hyman, *The Radical Republicans and Reconstruction*, 246–47; Means, *The Avenger Takes His Place*, 201–16; Simkins and Roland, *A History of the South*, 256–58.

10. Calabresi and Yoo, "The Unitary Executive during the Second Half-Century," 740–41; Foner, *Reconstruction*, 224–27; Simkins and Roland, *A History of the South*, 257–58; Trefousse, *The Radical Republicans*, 325–30.

11. Currie, "The Reconstruction Congress," 390–91; Harrison, "New Representations of a 'Misrepresented Bureau,'" 215–16; Simkins and Roland, *A History of the South*, 261.

12. Kaczorowski, "Congress' Power to Enforce Fourteenth Amendment Rights," 199–205.

13. Currie, "The Reconstruction Congress," 398–99; Simpson, *The Reconstruction Presidents*, 96–99.

14. Belz, *Reconstructing the Union*, 304; Foner, *Reconstruction*, 251–52; Henry, *The Story of Reconstruction*, 208–10; Kendrick, *The Journal of the Joint Committee of Fifteen on Reconstruction*, 115; Stampp, *The Era of Reconstruction*, 136–37.

15. Bartley, "The Fourteenth Amendment," 474; Bryant, "Unorthodox and Paradox," 564–65; Currie, "The Reconstruction Congress," 407; Henry, *The Story of Reconstruction*, 332–33; Klarman, *From Jim Crow to Civil Rights*, 19–20; Trefousse, *The Radical Republicans*, 405–8.

16. Quoted in Simpson, *The Reconstruction Presidents*, 107; Mantell, *Johnson, Grant, and the Politics of Reconstruction*, 94. See also Beale, *The Critical Year*, 13; DeWitt, *The Impeachment and Trial of Andrew Johnson*, 110–26; Henry, *The Story of Reconstruction*, 194–96; Martinez, *Carpetbaggers, Cavalry, and the Ku Klux Klan*, 43; Tulis, *The Rhetorical Presidency*, 87–93.

17. Currie, "The Reconstruction Congress," 408–14; Foner, *Reconstruction*, 275–80; Henry, *The Story of Reconstruction*, 219–21.

18. Quoted in Foner, *Reconstruction*, 276. See also Currie, "The Reconstruction Congress," 411–12; Henry, *The Story of Reconstruction*, 216; Simpson, *The Reconstruction Presidents*, 113–17; Trefousse, *The Radical Republicans*, 355–61.

19. Currie, "The Reconstruction Congress," 416–18; Henry, *The Story of Reconstruction*, 213–14; Simpson, *Let Us Have Peace*, 172–73.

20. Rable, *But There Was No Peace*, 95; Warmouth, *War, Politics and Reconstruction*, 70–71.

21. Calabresi and Yoo, "The Unitary Executive during the Second Half-Century," 758–59; Tulis, "The Two Constitutional Presidencies," 94–101.

22. Quoted in Stewart, *Impeached*, 324. See also Currie, "The Reconstruction Congress," 414–17; Foner, *Reconstruction*, 333; Henry, *The Story of Reconstruction*, 255; Simpson, *The Reconstruction Presidents*, 112–13; Trefousse, *The Radical Republicans*, 356–57.

23. Currie, "The Reconstruction Congress," 443; Simpson, *The Reconstruction Presidents*, 122–23; Stewart, *Impeached*, 134–37; Trefousse, *The Radical Republicans*, 381–83.

24. Foner, *Reconstruction*, 337–38; Martinez, *Carpetbaggers, Cavalry, and the Ku Klux Klan*, 51–52; Simpson, *The Reconstruction Presidents*, 126–28; Trefousse, *The Radical Republicans*, 399–404.

25. Currie, "The Reconstruction Congress," 444–45; DeWitt, *The Impeachment and Trial of Andrew Johnson*, 373–74; Stewart, *Impeached*, 148–49; Trefousse, *The Radical Republicans*, 383–84

26. Calabresi and Yoo, "The Unitary Executive during the Second Half-Century," 755–56; Currie, "The Reconstruction Congress," 451–52; Foner, *Reconstruction*, 334–35; Stewart, *Impeached*, 77–81; Tulis, *The Rhetorical Presidency*, 90–91.

27. Quoted in Foner, *Reconstruction*, 334. See also Currie, "The Reconstruction Congress," 451–52; Stewart, *Impeached*, 315–24.

28. Calabresi and Yoo, "The Unitary Executive during the Second Half-Century," 755–56; DeWitt, *The Impeachment and Trial of Andrew Johnson*, 385; Stewart, *Impeached*, 159–62.

29. Calabresi and Yoo, "The Unitary Executive during the Second Half-Century," 756–57; Currie, "The Reconstruction Congress," 449; Henry, *The Story of Reconstruction*, 308–9.

30. Bartley, "The Fourteenth Amendment,"478–79; DeWitt, *The Impeachment and Trial of Andrew Johnson*, 597–99; Foner, *Reconstruction*, 343–45; Henry, *The Story of Reconstruction*, 333–34; Stewart, *Impeached*, 305–6; Trefousse, *The Radical Republicans*, 436–37.

31. Shaw, "Leadership Lessons from the Life of Ulysses S. Grant," 29, 33–34; Simpson, *Let Us Have Peace*, 1–9; Smith, *Grant*, 24, 26–33, 157.

32. Calabresi and Yoo, "The Unitary Executive during the Second Half-Century," 759–60; Simpson, *The Reconstruction Presidents*, 139–40; Smith, *Grant*, 468–69.

33. Scaturro, *President Grant Reconsidered*, 75–76; Smith, *Grant*, 430–33; Trefousse, *The Radical Republicans*, 424–25.

34. Burg, "Amnesty, Civil Rights, and the Meaning of Liberal Republicanism," 43–47; Foner, *Reconstruction*, 488–94.

35. Foner, *Reconstruction*, 512–13; Henry, *The Story of Reconstruction*, 500; Smith, *Grant*, 583.

36. Goodwin, *Team of Rivals*, 589–90; Hesseltine, *Lincoln's Plan of Reconstruction*, 35–50; Trefousse, *The Radical Republicans*, 283–86; White, *A. Lincoln*, 613–14.

37. Dray, *Capitol Men*, 28–32; Keith, *The Colfax Massacre*, 63; Lemann, *Redemption*, 12.

38. Keith, *The Colfax Massacre*, 80–81; Rable, *But There Was No Peace*, 123; Warmouth, *War, Politics and Reconstruction*, 161.

39. Dray, *Capitol Men*, 142–43; Keith, *The Colfax Massacre*, 37–38, 86–88; Lemann, *Redemption*, 12; Rable, *But There Was No Peace*, 142.

40. Dray, *Capitol Men*, 146; Keith, *The Colfax Massacre*, 37, 87, 92; Lemann, *Redemption*, 12.

41. Dray, *Capitol Men*, 144; Keith, *The Colfax Massacre*, 88–92.

42. Keith, *The Colfax Massacre*, 95.

43. Keith, *The Colfax Massacre*, 97–99; Lemann, *Redemption*, 16.

44. Keith, *The Colfax Massacre*, 99–101.

45. Keith, *The Colfax Massacre*, 101–3; Lemann, *Redemption*, 18–19.

46. Dray, *Capitol Men*, 146; Keith, *The Colfax Massacre*, 103; Lemann, *Redemption*, 18–19.

47. Keith, *The Colfax Massacre*, 111–12; Rable, *But There Was No Peace*, 127–28.

48. Keith, *The Colfax Massacre*, xiii–xvi; Lemann, *Redemption*, 19–24; Rable, *But There Was No Peace*, 129–31.

49. Dray, *Capitol Men*, 147–50; Lemann, *Redemption*, 28–29.

50. Keith, *The Colfax Massacre*, 135.

51. Keith, *The Colfax Massacre*, 136; Lemann, *Redemption*, 23–25.

52. Keith, *The Colfax Massacre*, 136–46.

53. Keith, *The Colfax Massacre*, 138–39; Lemann, *Redemption*, 24–25.

54. Huhn, "The Legacy of *Slaughterhouse, Bradwell*, and *Cruikshank* in Constitutional Interpretation," 1071–72; *United States v. Cruikshank*, 92 U.S. 542, 548 (1876).

55. Quoted at 92 U.S. 542, 556. See also 92 U.S. 542, 546–59.

56. Huhn, "The Legacy of *Slaughterhouse, Bradwell*, and *Cruikshank* in Constitutional Interpretation," 1051–52; Keith, *The Colfax Massacre*, xiii–xvii; Martinez, *Carpetbaggers, Cavalry, and the Ku Klux Klan*, 200–201.

57. Dray, *Capitol Men*, 142–50; Keith, *The Colfax Massacre*, xiii–xvii; Lemann, *Redemption*, 12–20; Rable, *But There Was No Peace*, 127–28.

58. Foner, *Reconstruction*, 550–52; McCann, *Terrorism on American Soil*, 5–8; Rable, *But There Was No Peace*, 126–28.

59. Foner, *Forever Free*, 214–15; Dray, *Capitol Men*, 352–73; Woodward, *The Strange Career of Jim Crow*, 3–10.

60. Henry, *The Story of Reconstruction*, 363–65; Martinez, *Carpetbaggers, Cavalry, and the Ku Klux Klan*, 109–11.

61. Foner, *Reconstruction*, 559–63; Henry, *The Story of Reconstruction*, 544–53; Keith, *The Colfax Massacre*, 153–71.

II

THE MODERN ERA

4

"THE MCNAMARAS HAVE BETRAYED LABOR"

The *Los Angeles Times* Bombing (1910)

And what rough beast, its hour come round at last,
Slouches towards Bethlehem to be born?

—William Butler Yeats, "The Second Coming"

On October 1, 1910, the offices of the *Los Angeles Times* exploded in a fiery conflagration that terrorized a nation—the result of a dynamite charge placed by a member of the International Association of Bridge and Structural Workers. The resultant investigation captured the imagination of a generation of Americans. The act was widely denounced as "the crime of the century," one of at least a half dozen violent acts in the twentieth century that received that description. Even a century after the event, the *Los Angeles Times* bombing ranked as the fourth deadliest attack ever to have occurred on American soil. Despite the hyperbolic characterization, the bombing represented a period of unrest that has seldom been equaled in American labor history. During the early 1900s, sporadic acts of violence resulted from labor disputes between workers and management. The former contended that their working conditions were dangerous and degrading and their wages were barely above the subsistence level. The latter argued that they provided conditions and compensation commensurate with the skill of the labor force, and that increased costs associated with improving employees' labor conditions would severely undermine the competitiveness of American businesses.[1]

Before the case ended, it had captured headlines owing to the appearance of the legendary trial attorney Clarence Darrow and the divisive nature of the trial and its aftermath. In many modern accounts, observers report that terrorists always seek media attention for their deeds. These accounts suggest that perpetrators single out high-profile, symbolic targets to ensure maximum public attention. This conventional wisdom explains why the Unabomber sought an outlet for his manifesto, why Eric Rudolph planted a bomb in Centennial Olympic Park in Atlanta, and why the 9/11 terrorists attacked the World Trade Center and the Pentagon. Yet the *Los Angeles Times* bombing is the exception that proves the rule. The bombers in that case targeted a high-profile newspaper not solely to trigger increased media attention, but because the newspaper had been so critical of the U.S. labor movement.[2]

As the investigation led to a group of suspects in the labor movement, it was clear the case was emblematic of a larger fissure in American society. The battle between labor and management was reflected in the *Los Angeles Times* case, and the outcome undoubtedly would affect the progress, or lack thereof, of labor relations in the United States in the years to come. Initially reluctant to become involved, Darrow agreed to represent the defendants after he received a personal plea from Samuel Gompers, the famous labor activist. After the end of the trial, Darrow found himself charged with jury tampering. He spent much of his personal fortune and several years attempting to clear his name. Although he was eventually acquitted of all charges, the case haunted him for the remainder of his life. Questions remain about whether the great advocate was guilty of the offense.[3]

BACKGROUND

At the beginning of the twentieth century, California workers in industries outside of Hollywood and the entertainment field were struggling to form unions to improve their wages and labor conditions. The iron workers union, first organized in 1886, was among the most tenacious. Iron workers were seasonal and generally unskilled, which meant they suffered through the most difficult working conditions of any group. Beginning in 1902, the union demonstrated its newfound clout by winning a strike against a subsidiary of the powerful U.S. Steel Corporation. The victory helped the union organize iron industry employees across the nation in less than a year.[4]

Steel industry executives were not satisfied to allow workers to unionize without a fight. U.S. Steel and the American Bridge Company created the National Erectors' Association to champion an open shop as a means of breaking the power of the unions. The anti-union movement, which authorized the use of labor spies, strikebreakers, and detective agencies to infiltrate and investigate unions, proved to be enormously successful. By the end of the decade, union membership was declining, and labor organizers were desperate to increase their membership rolls and regain their lost momentum.[5]

Violence was the order of the day. For opponents of the labor movement, union organizers were rabble-rousers, little more than riffraff who sought to interfere with freedom of contract and the ability of businessmen to respond to market conditions in whatever manner they deemed appropriate. These meddlesome organizers, most of whom were probably socialists or communists, were undermining American capitalism and threatening the national economy. In the face of such a threat, management was justified in employing extreme tactics, including the use of force. Labor organizers viewed managers as wealthy opportunists who would stop at nothing, including exploiting their workers, to maximize profits. As long as workers were unable to voice protest or participate in management decisions, they would be paid a paltry wage and left to scratch out a subsistence living as best they could. Leaders of the labor movement believed they must strike for improved working conditions in some instances, and meet violence with violence in all instances. By the dawn of the twentieth century, neither side seemed willing or able to negotiate.[6]

Metal workers in Los Angeles were on strike during the fall of 1910 to protest management's draconian wage and labor provisions. *Los Angeles Times* owner and publisher Harrison Gray Otis, a well-known conservative Republican, became a high-profile opponent of the strike. As was the case with many wealthy supporters of management, Otis was incensed at the audacity of the metal workers. Rank-and-file members had little education and few other employment prospects; they were lucky to be employed in the first place. If they knew what was good for them, they would never go on strike. With the power of the press at his command, Otis frequently published editorials denouncing unions and attempting to galvanize public opinion against organized labor. The problem, as most managers saw it, came not from the common laborer. The essential problem was that labor leaders were agitators; they stormed into a community and upset the normally placid laborer with false promises of huge pay increases and unreasonably luxurious working conditions. What was needed, then, was a voice of reason to expose the ludicrous claims of labor organizers and thereby undermine their legitimacy. Harrison Gray Otis saw himself as that voice.

Owing to Otis's high-profile position and his vehement rhetoric, he became a convenient target of labor supporters who no longer believed they could operate within the overly restrictive confines of the law.[7]

So effective were his voice and pen that Otis became well known throughout the country as an anti-union man. His numerous editorials in the *Los Angeles Times* railed against labor agitators in the most incendiary, florid prose imaginable. Otis was a man who brooked no dissent and never allowed for the possibility that his opinions might be erroneous or that his opponents might have a point of view worth considering. Time and again, he called for business and government to band together and destroy the unions at whatever costs were necessary.[8]

Early on the morning of October 1, 1910, union workers struck back at Otis and his empire. When a bomb exploded in the offices of the *Los Angeles Times* at Broadway and First Street in Los Angeles, it did not take much intuition to realize that labor organizers probably were involved. Presumably the device had been rigged to detonate when no one was in the building—this was not an act of terrorism designed to target innocent victims as the attacks on the World Trade Center were on September 11, 2001—but, nonetheless, employees were still inside in the wee morning hours. They were attempting to produce the next edition of the newspaper.[9]

The bomb collapsed the southern wall of the structure, which triggered a chain reaction. Without the load-bearing southern wall in place, the weight of the printing presses caused the floor to collapse, which in turn tumbled onto the floor below, which also collapsed. With the collapsing floors cascading on top of one another, the heating system and the gas mainline in the building ignited. Newspaper employees were trapped inside with the fire. Some desperate victims leapt from upper stories in the building to escape the searing heat. Eventually, twenty-one souls perished owing to the explosion, and the building sustained $500,000 worth of damage.[10]

Police officers investigating the incident discovered a second bomb at Otis's house. They were able to move the device to another location and detonate it without causing injury to anyone. Later, investigators turned up a third device at the home of Felix J. Zeehandlaar, secretary of the Merchants and Manufacturers Association. Zeehandlaar was another outspoken critic of organized labor. Police were unable to detonate the bomb owing to a weak battery, but at least no one else was injured.[11]

In the immediate aftermath of the episode, Otis was understandably furious and distraught. He used his pulpit to denounce the bombing as the crime of the century and to characterize the perpetrators as anarchists, cowardly murderers, and leeches on society. The striking iron workers were careful to denounce the action in public as well. Sensing his precarious public standing and a possible backlash against the labor movement, Samuel Gompers, president of the American Federation of Labor (AFL), joined in the chorus of public outrage. Everyone, it seemed, sought a quick resolution to the case. The police assured an anxious citizenry that all available resources would be used to hunt down the bombers and bring them to justice.[12]

It was far easier to excoriate the act than to locate the perpetrators. As weeks passed and no arrests were made, rumor and innuendo became the order of the day. Conspiracy theorists alleged that Harrison Otis or members of his staff had plotted and carried out the bombing as a method of undermining the momentum of organized labor. In this version of the facts, anti-unionists could use public outrage as a pretext for aggressively moving against labor organizers. In many of the tales of terrorism throughout this book, observers have argued that the victims of violent terrorist attacks were in fact the perpetrators. Blaming the victim becomes a convenient method of resolving a case that, at least initially, appears insoluble. In the *Los Angeles Times* bombing, a more probable alternative scenario was the suggestion that a severed natural gas line triggered the explosion and fire. Investigators eventually demonstrated that dynamite caused the explosion; however, the natural gas explosion rumor proved to be stubbornly persistent.[13]

THE INVESTIGATION AND COURT PROCEEDINGS

Recognizing that he needed assistance to crack the case, Los Angeles mayor George B. Alexander sent a wire to a private detective, William J. Burns, asking him to investigate. Burns was approaching fifty years of age and had become a well-known criminal investigator. He had honed his skills during a career that included stints on the St. Louis police force and in the U.S. Secret Service. The William Burns International Detective Agency was renowned because of the founder's prowess in solving difficult, infamous cases. Never one to shy away from the limelight, the dapper, red-haired detective immediately agreed to assist Los Angeles authorities in identifying and apprehending the responsible parties. With the famous detective on the case, it was only a matter of time before the villains were caught and dragged into court.[14]

Burns was nothing if not indefatigable. He had investigated the nationwide wave of iron manufacturing plant bombings for at least four years on behalf of the National Erectors' Association, and he was convinced that this latest episode was part of a pattern. Events soon confirmed his insight. During his investigation, Burns found that iron workers union member Ortie McManigal had participated in the bombing campaign on orders from union leaders. Always alert to the weaknesses of others, Burns realized that several union leaders, including President Frank M. Ryan and his associate, James B. McNamara, were heavy drinkers who enjoyed consuming prodigious amounts of alcohol while hunting for game. Along with a fellow spy, Burns joined McNamara and several union members on a hunting expedition. During the trip, Burns surreptitiously snapped J. B.'s picture. He later showed the photograph to a hotel clerk in downtown Los Angeles and found that the man recognized McNamara as a "J. B. Bryce," a hotel guest who had checked in around the time of the bombing.[15]

Prosecutors convened a grand jury to investigate the episode, and more than two hundred witnesses appeared. Three names continually appeared: J. B. Bryce, A. M. Schmidt, and David Caplan. The three men were known to have been in Los Angeles immediately following the bombing, although they disappeared shortly thereafter. In April 1911, six months after the bombing, Burns and his son, along with police officers from Detroit and Chicago, confronted Ortie McManigal and James B. McNamara, the elusive "J. B. Bryce." After the men were arrested, McManigal proved to be the weak link in the conspiracy chain. He simply could not endure Burns's aggressive questioning. McManigal eventually confessed that he and James B. McNamara had planted the dynamite in the building.[16]

With two suspects finally in custody, the case came together. Burns learned that James B. McNamara's brother, John, secretary of the International Association of Bridge and Structural Iron Workers, had ordered the bombing campaign from his headquarters in Indianapolis, Indiana. Armed with this new information, on April 22, 1911, Burns traveled to John McNamara's offices with fifteen investigators and detectives from the Indianapolis Police Department. At around 6 that evening, law enforcement officials executed a search warrant on the offices. During the search, they found approximately one hundred pounds of dynamite in a box in the basement. Harry Graff, the building custodian, later told investigators that he remembered John McNamara asking if he could store boxes in the basement. Burns and his investigators also uncovered letters and papers that clearly suggested John McNamara's involvement in the bombing. Having captured his man, Burns placed the suspect under arrest.[17]

Organized labor was under siege. Among other things, James B. McNamara faced charges that he masterminded the *Los Angeles Times* bombing while John McNamara was bound over for trial for sabotaging the

Llewellyn Iron Works plant in Los Angeles. Representatives of the national labor movement were incensed at the treatment of the McNamaras. In their view, the brothers had not been afforded their constitutional protections. Labor leaders quickly defended the McNamaras and castigated law enforcement personnel for their aggressive methods, arguing that William J. Burns should not have been employed to bring the defendants back to California. From their perspective, Burns had kidnapped James McNamara and transported him across state lines. Both defendants had been arrested based on a questionable confession and tyrannical police tactics.[18]

Despite labor's objections—or perhaps because of them—law enforcement personnel moved aggressively to try the defendants as soon as possible. John D. Fredericks, the Los Angeles district attorney, led an experienced prosecution team. He employed three able deputy prosecutors, chief deputy W. Joseph Ford; Oscar Lawler, a former U.S. attorney; and Earl Rogers, another experienced prosecutor who would later assume a high-profile position as a defense attorney in a collateral matter. The men wasted no time investigating the facts and preparing their case. In light of public outrage about the bombing and the voluminous evidence against them, the defendants seemed to be in dire straits.[19]

This break in the case captured headlines around the nation. Pro-labor forces collected money to ensure a proper criminal defense for the McNamara brothers. Recognizing that this was a crucial legal proceeding that would do much to determine the fate of organized labor, union officers strongly encouraged members to contribute money to the McNamara defense fund. Samuel Gompers publicly vowed that he would do everything within his power to ensure a fair and vigorous defense for the defendants. He immediately began to search for the best criminal defense attorney in the nation.[20]

In 1910, Clarence Darrow was widely regarded as the preeminent attorney in the United States. Born and raised in Ohio, he began his career as a traditional small-town lawyer during the late 1870s and early 1880s. After he moved to Chicago, the young attorney made a name for himself working on behalf of corporations, and later, in a reversal, on behalf of trade unions. He represented Eugene Debs, the famous American socialist, in the wake of the 1894 Pullman Strike, and associated with many prominent socialist and progressive thinkers and activists afterward. He represented woodworkers in Wisconsin in a famous 1898 case as well as the United Mine Workers in Pennsylvania during the anthracite coal strike of 1902. In the early 1900s, Darrow also won fame representing the Western Federation of Miners, including the notorious William "Big Bill" Haywood. Darrow

Famed U.S. labor leader Samuel Gompers. Courtesy of the Chicago History Museum.

subsequently handled landmark criminal cases defending individuals, often poor and disenfranchised, against the power of the state.[21]

Gompers realized that it would be a public relations triumph to recruit Darrow for the McNamara brothers' defense team. Aside from Darrow's well-known courtroom manner, his name and reputation for championing labor causes boded well for the defendants. Nothing in the case would assist the cause of the labor movement as much as having Clarence Darrow, champion of the working man, take on the cause of the McNamaras, innocent victims of management's Machiavellian machinations.

Darrow understood the value of his name and the politics associated with the case. Aside from grave misgivings about inserting himself into such a politically charged matter, his health was poor, and he was reluctant to accept a strenuous assignment. Worried that Darrow could not be brought around, Iron Workers' president Frank Ryan turned to another attorney, Job Harriman, to provide a defense in Darrow's stead. When Gompers learned of this arrangement, he traveled to Chicago and met with Darrow. Using all the force of his charismatic personality and his legendary powers of persuasion, Gompers argued that only Darrow could provide the level and quality of representation needed to ensure a victory for the McNamara brothers. Yielding to Gompers's entreaties, Darrow agreed to serve as the lead defense attorney. Job Harriman, meanwhile, remained on the defense team as Darrow's assistant. LeCompte Davis, a former Los Angeles County district attorney, and Cyrus F. McNutt, a pro-union judge from Indiana, also signed on to the defense team.[22]

When the McNamaras were arraigned on May 5, 1911, they pleaded not guilty. Not surprisingly, after turning state's evidence, McManigal did not appear at the arraignment. Darrow, recognizing that he had a difficult case on his hands, informed his supporters that he would need $350,000 to conduct an adequate defense. The AFL executive council immediately went to work raising the money. They were masters at fund-raising and public relations. Among other things, the group produced pins, buttons, and other commercial items designed to generate revenue. Labor Day 1911 became known as "McNamara Day," an opportunity for pro-union marchers to take to the streets in thirteen major cities. The film *A Martyr to His Cause* arguably became the most successful defense tool. It was the country's first feature-length worker-made film, and it depicted John McNamara as an innocent victim of insidious anti-union forces. Focusing on his idyllic family life and the brutal police procedures that framed an innocent man, the film was propaganda raised to a high art form. The film played to packed audiences after its release in September 1911; however, the producers withdrew the film from circulation after the McNamaras changed their plea in November 1911, thereby altering the course of the trial.[23]

Jury selection commenced on October 25, 1911. As Darrow worked through the process of voir dire and learned more about his client, James B. McNamara, he concluded that the case could not be won. Despite his lifelong efforts to champion labor, Darrow was under no illusions; the movement remained unpopular among many Americans. Labor leaders often appeared in the media as cartoonish villains, little more than anarchists threatening the American way of life. To counteract this popular misconception, Darrow realized he would have to change the story. He worked as much as anyone to portray his clients as innocent victims of a harsh, oppressive judicial system driven by bias and emotion. Realizing that his job was as much in the realm of public relations as in a court of law, the attorney sought out opportunities to present the McNamara brothers to the world as symbols of the common man being railroaded by an overzealous prosecution team.[24]

He spent hours working with his clients in expectation of the trial. During those discussions, Darrow took a measure of his witnesses. It became clear that James would not be able to withstand rigorous cross-examination. Part of a defense attorney's task is to gauge how well his client will perform under the stress of testifying in a court of law. A client who projects sincerity and intelligence will perform nicely before a jury. If a client appears duplicitous or otherwise insincere, he can lose credibility in jurors' eyes regardless of other facts of the case. In Darrow's view, James B. McNamara would be a disaster in the courtroom. He did not appear sincere, and he was unable to keep his stories straight. Darrow knew he would have to prevent his client from testifying.[25]

To make matters worse, the defense learned that prosecutors had collected voluminous evidence that strongly suggested the McNamaras were guilty. The brothers faced twenty-one charges in state court. In addition, U.S. attorney general George W. Wickersham was prepared to file federal charges. Owing to the overwhelming weight of the evidence, defense attorneys began to contemplate a plea bargain. Darrow remained committed to the cause of the labor movement, but the evidence indicated that the McNamara brothers were guilty of the bombing. A defense attorney, no matter how gifted, cannot work miracles in the face of virtually unassailable evidence.[26]

The case had become a cause célèbre, and media attention was ferocious. Darrow knew that even as he tried to control the media, in many ways the media controlled him. When the jury was seated on November 7, events began to spiral out of control. Well-known muckraking journalist Lincoln Steffens arrived at the Los Angeles jail to interview the McNamara brothers. During his discussion with the defendants, Steffens claimed they confessed their guilt to him. Darrow was outraged by this communication, but his health was declining and he had lost faith in the case. If his clients so easily and quickly confessed to Steffens, it was only a matter of time before they confessed to the prosecution or fell victim to their own inconsistent stories. Ultimately, he acquiesced when the brothers cooperated with Steffens. Darrow even agreed to explore the possibility of arranging lenient prison terms for his clients in exchange for an end to the AFL labor strike.[27]

Prosecutors had a strong case, and they knew it. It was the kind of case that could make a career for an ambitious prosecuting attorney, especially if it were brought to trial. Lead prosecutor John Fredericks, when he learned of Darrow's attempts to forge a plea bargain, initially balked at the suggestion. In his opinion, if either McNamara brother escaped a substantial prison term, the state's leniency would send a message to criminals everywhere that Los Angeles County would tolerate violent behavior. In addition, he did not wish to be excoriated as the prosecutor who allowed the crime of the century to go unpunished.

Every prosecutor realizes that the jury is unpredictable; even a seemingly airtight case can fail. Cases involving high media visibility, while they can make a career, can break a career as well. Recognizing the divisive nature of the case, Fredericks reluctantly agreed to accept a compromise. If James B. McNamara received a life sentence, his brother could secure a shorter term in prison. From the prosecution's perspective, it was not an ideal compromise, but it would ensure a victory and forestall the momentum of the labor movement. Los Angeles business interests would be served, and John Fredericks would be a hero to conservative supporters.[28]

When the brothers learned of the plan, James was reluctant to accept any deal that did not allow his brother to go free. As is often the case with defendants, they initially believed they could escape prosecution if they stuck to their stories, no matter how preposterous. It was not to be. After Darrow explained that few other realistic options were available, James McNamara agreed to accept the deal. In reality, he could do little else.[29]

Because it was a high-profile matter, the proposed resolution met with stiff resistance. Darrow and the defense team had hoped that a plea agreement would end the case, yet prosecutors apparently experienced buyers' remorse. Fredericks and his men insisted on an admission of guilt in open court. They might have allowed the defendants to plead guilty absent public allocution, but such a compromise would have left doubt as to the perpetrators and their motive. If prosecutors hoped to arrest the momentum of the labor movement in California, and perhaps beyond, they needed an unequivocal public pronouncement of guilt.

Defense attorneys recognized they were bargaining from a position of weakness. With the facts arrayed against them and unreliable clients as witnesses, not to mention generally unsympathetic public opinion, they had few alternatives but to agree to the prosecution plan. The defense position was further weakened when Clarence Darrow himself was accused of bribing a juror after his chief investigator was arrested for bribery. Darrow had been seen handing money to the investigator shortly before the alleged bribery attempt.[30]

The jury tampering episode remains shrouded in a mystery brought on by conflicting accounts. It seems the defense attorneys' lead investigator, Bert Franklin, visited the home of Robert Bain, a juror in the case. Franklin was a former employee of the U.S. Marshal's office as well as a former detective for the Los Angeles County Sheriff's Department and was known as a seasoned investigator. Darrow originally hired the man to examine the backgrounds of potential jurors owing to Franklin's extensive contacts and experience in city and county administration. In an early meeting, Darrow provided Franklin with a list of 125 men in the initial jury pool. Franklin's initial task was to gather information about the potential jurors' attitudes toward organized labor as well as their social, political, and religious views. This kind of investigation was legal and routinely conducted for civil and criminal cases. Approaching jurors and offering money for a particular verdict, of course, was patently illegal.

Bert Franklin was seventy years old in 1911, and his salad days were long behind him. He was also in desperate financial straits and on the lookout for a means to augment his meager income. His personal difficulties apparently prompted Franklin to approach Robert Bain with a proposition. Although Bain was not home when the investigator arrived, Franklin spoke to Bain's wife. During that conversation, the investigator learned that Mr. and Mrs. Bain had recently purchased a home with a $1,800 mortgage, which they were having difficulty paying. Bert Franklin understood their predicament all too well. Seizing the opportunity, he offered to make an overdue payment on the Bain home in exchange for a vote of acquittal in the McNamara case. It would be strictly a quid pro quo transaction. As long as no one informed the prosecutors, the dirty deed could be accomplished to the satisfaction of all parties to the deal. When Bain returned home and learned of the incident, his reaction was ambiguous. Some sources later indicated that Bain was furious with Franklin for attempting to purchase his vote and thereby assail his personal integrity. Other sources suggested a muted response. In any case, Bain invited Franklin to return to his house, at which point the investigator handed the juror $500. It was an important case, crucial to the success of the labor movement; Franklin agreed to supply another $3,500 after Bain voted to acquit the McNamaras. Bain later told prosecutors that Franklin said Clarence Darrow had provided $20,000 to bribe potential jurors.[31]

Another juror, George Lockwood, also told the prosecution team that Bert Franklin had offered cash in exchange for an acquittal. Unlike Robert Bain, Lockwood was not content to accept money in exchange for his vote. He immediately reported the malfeasance to prosecutor John Fredericks. Recognizing an opportunity to corroborate Lockwood's tale, Fredericks arranged a sting. Lockwood agreed to meet with Franklin on a street corner in downtown Los Angeles to accept the bribe. Fredericks's men would be waiting to apprehend the villain.[32]

Three days before the beginning of the McNamara trial, on November 28, 1911, Franklin and a friend, C. E. White, appeared in downtown Los Angeles to consummate the deal. The plan was similar to the arrangement with Robert Bain, except White would act as an intermediary. With Franklin waiting nearby, White was supposed to hand Lockwood $500 with the promise of an additional $3,500 after the McNamara brothers were acquitted. The agreement seemed simple enough, at least in theory.

As White and Lockwood were completing the transaction, Franklin emerged from a nearby saloon. He recognized the Los Angeles detectives who had been hired to spy on the conspirators. In a frantic effort to flee the scene and avoid capture, Franklin urged Lockwood and White to follow him down the street. Even as the chaotic transaction unfolded, another individual hurried toward the group. The individual turned out to be Clarence Darrow. Before he could speak, Darrow was interrupted by a detective who arrived and immediately arrested Bert Franklin. The detective transported Franklin, Lockwood, and White to the prosecutor's office, but Darrow did not accompany them. At the police station, Lockwood and White readily agreed to testify against Bert Franklin; thus they were released immediately. Darrow appeared and posted $10,000 in bail money to secure Bert Franklin's release. He also hired a well-known defense attorney and former governor of California, Henry Gage, to represent Franklin.[33]

This latest news in an already sensational case spread rapidly around the country, although Darrow's involvement was kept secret. Two months later, Franklin pleaded guilty to jury tampering. He also testified that Clarence Darrow had known about, and approved, the bribery. Because Darrow had been present when Franklin was arrested, it seemed plausible that the great attorney knew of the scheme. Accordingly, Fredericks and his team arrested Darrow and bound him over for trial.[34]

While these collateral matters developed, prosecutors and defense attorneys resolved the original case. Bowing to the inevitable, on December 1, 1911, the McNamara brothers changed their pleas to guilty in open court. James B. McNamara confessed to murder because he set the bomb that destroyed the *Los Angeles Times* building on October 1. John McNamara admitted to having destroyed the Llewellyn Iron Works on December 25. At the time, they agreed with their famous defense attorney that pleading guilty was the best course of action. They would come to regret the decision.[35]

THE AFTERMATH

Union supporters who had contributed funds to the McNamara defense felt betrayed by the guilty pleas. Regardless of the guilt or innocence of the defendants, the contributors had expected Darrow and his team to mount a vigorous defense that would expose corrupt management practices and

Otis's sharp business practices. When the McNamaras openly admitted their culpability, they reversed the expected roles. The confessions undermined labor's claim that management continually victimized the masses. An admission that organized labor employed violence, incredibly and inadvertently, created sympathy for the wealthy class. Trade unions lost momentum and whatever modicum of public support they had enjoyed prior to 1911.

In retrospect, as they became aware of the backlash among their union friends and supporters, the McNamaras came to see the deal as flawed. They were under fire for harming the labor movement by refusing to fight the charges against them at whatever cost. During a subsequent interview, John complained about Darrow's representation as well. He claimed the attorney kept the defendants isolated from the public and oblivious to the impact of a guilty plea. Had the McNamaras known that public opinion was less virulently anti-union than they had been led to believe, they would not have entered a guilty plea for the bombings, or so the brothers claimed in the aftermath of the court proceedings. This change of heart was a convenient reinterpretation with the benefit of hindsight, and it did much to harm Darrow's public reputation.[36]

Samuel Gompers was another disaffected party who denigrated Darrow's representation. As he later recounted the story, the labor leader learned of the news as he was traveling by rail in New Jersey. An Associated Press reporter boarded his train, woke him up, and handed him a dispatch indicating that the McNamara brothers had pleaded guilty. Gompers was livid. Expressing astonishment and outrage, he remarked that "the McNamaras have betrayed labor." He was also upset with Darrow, regarding the decision to plead guilty as a deliberate betrayal of the American labor movement. One of the reasons that Gompers had asked Darrow to lead the defense team was that he believed the Chicago attorney was the most aggressive advocate in the nation and a well-known friend to labor. Regardless of the facts of the case, Gompers believed that Darrow should have zealously represented the McNamara brothers as symbols of the common laborer. This was no ordinary case; therefore, the ordinary considerations of a defense attorney handling a routine criminal matter did not apply.[37]

When the court sentenced the defendants on December 5, James B. McNamara received a life term while his brother received fifteen years. Owing to the verdicts, management redoubled its efforts to destroy the power of the unions in California. Throughout the nation, the labor movement did not recover for decades. In the wake of the McNamara case, scores of labor workers faced charges of conspiracy and interstate transportation of explosives.[38]

Clarence Darrow's troubles were only beginning. He was indicted on two charges of jury tampering on the basis of Bert Franklin's testimony. Never a wealthy man even in the best of times, he soon found himself destitute. Desperate for financial assistance, Darrow asked the AFL to assist in raising funds for his defense. Samuel Gompers was still upset about Darrow's handling of the McNamara case; he refused to help. The great champion of the little man was himself a little man, but he had no Clarence Darrow waiting to represent him *pro bono publico*. He was left to fend for himself.[39]

As Darrow pondered his defense, he received an intriguing proposition from a former client. A year earlier, a poor woman had approached the attorney and asked if he would defend her son, George Bissett, who had been convicted of murder and sentenced to life in prison. Busy with other cases, Darrow had initially refused to assist the woman; however, he eventually accepted the case for free. Bissett had been convicted of murdering a police officer and wounding another officer in a bar shootout in June 1909. During the murder trial, Bissett emphatically insisted he had shot no one. As it turned out, Bissett had fired at the police officers after they had shot at him first. Relying on a self-defense argument, Darrow persuaded the Supreme Court of Illinois to reverse the conviction and remand the case for a new trial. During the new trial, Darrow defended Bissett and won an acquittal.

Now, a year later, George Bissett appeared, unbidden, in Darrow's Los Angeles office. It must have been quite a shock to look up and find the man standing in his doorway. The grateful former client, having heard that his defender was in need of assistance, explained that he had brought dynamite and had hatched a plan to kill Bert Franklin to help Darrow escape his troubles. If George Bissett could not repay his attorney with money, he could offer an in-kind contribution. Touched by the man's pledge of loyalty, Darrow explained that it was not appropriate to kill Franklin, regardless of the reasons. "All along through my life I have had many warm demonstrations of friendship," Darrow later wrote, "but this was the first time any man had offered to kill someone for me. I looked at George, and thought of this rough, unlettered man riding two thousand miles on car tops and bumpers and in seriousness offering to risk his life out of gratitude for what I had done for him. I did my best to show my appreciation of this most astounding proffer." As tempting as the offer was, Darrow talked Bissett out of going through with the scheme. The two men would cross paths again five years later when Bissett was arrested for stealing $500,000 from a government building in Minneapolis. Once again, Darrow represented the man in criminal court. In that case, Darrow was able to finagle a two-and-a-half-year prison term, a relatively light sentence under the circumstances. In 1912, however, the lawyer and his client transacted no further business apart from Bissett's initial proffer of assistance.[40]

Recognizing that he needed expert legal counsel during the bribery trial, Darrow managed to scrape together the funds to retain defense attorneys Horace Appel, Harry Dehm, Jerry Geisler, and Earl Rogers. Rogers was an especially well-known Los Angeles defense attorney. A legendary member of the California bar, he was an innovator in every sense of the word. In an era when ballistics and forensics were in their infancy, Rogers championed the use of scientific methods in courts of law. His secret weapon, if it could be called that, was thorough preparation. He typically immersed himself in all manner of scientific literature; in fact, Rogers knew as much about anatomy as the coroners and medical professionals he cross-examined in court. He was fond of reenactments and demonstrations. No fact or detail was too minuscule to be overlooked when preparing a case. Aside from his well-deserved reputation as an able legal advocate, Rogers was known as a frequent imbiber. A saying arose among members of the California bar: "I would sooner have Earl Rogers drunk defending me than any other lawyer sober." Darrow himself had once labeled Rogers "the greatest lawyer of his time."[41]

In an interesting twist of fate, Rogers's law office was located directly across the street from the *Los Angeles Times* building. He had been working in his office when the bomb went off. Rushing to the scene only moments after the explosion, Rogers had seen the horrific damage done to the building and heard the screams of victims burned by the fire. He never forgot the human tragedy, recounting to his daughter how he bore witness to the "faces appearing in the windows of the editorial and city rooms like distraught fugitives from a graveyard." Owing to his firsthand experiences with the devastation of the bombing, his representation of management in previous cases, and his work with the prosecution team in the early stages of the McNamara case, Earl Rogers could not be expected to represent labor unions or their chief advocate, Clarence Darrow. Yet he signed on to defend Darrow against the bribery charges.[42]

As Darrow and Rogers prepared for trial, they debated the strengths and weaknesses of the prosecution's evidence. Another defense attorney working on the case, Jerry Geisler, suggested that the prosecution's strongest evidence was Darrow's presence at the scene of the bribery attempt. Rogers agreed. It would be difficult to argue that the defendant knew nothing of Bert Franklin's activities since Darrow had been present when the arrest occurred. "We must make it work for us," Rogers said. The defense would have to provide a plausible explanation of why the attorney had suddenly appeared on the scene if he were innocent of bribing anyone. When pressed, Darrow claimed he had received an anonymous call indicating that the prosecution would try to frame Bert Franklin. Therefore, according to Darrow, he rushed to the scene to warn his investigator of a potential trap. It never occurred to him that the prosecution might be after the Mc-Namaras' lead attorney and that the anonymous call was part of the sting. Realizing he could work with this explanation, Rogers suggested that if Darrow had intended to bribe anyone, he would have been smart enough not to show up at exactly the moment when the illegal activity occurred. A prosecution setup was the only explanation that made sense under the circumstances. It was a compelling argument.[43]

With two of the most prominent and influential attorneys of their generation working on the same case, it was inevitable that egos would clash. Darrow was offended when Rogers suggested that the great man's actions were foolish. With the benefit of hindsight, rushing to the scene had been an exceedingly poor idea. At the time, however, Darrow had been anxious to assist his investigator. Determined to transform a vice into a virtue, Rogers recommended that the defense allege that prosecutors had set their sights on bigger game than Darrow alone. The defense's theory of the case was that John Fredericks and his men had staged the elaborate bribery attempt as a means to discredit Clarence Darrow, Samuel Gompers, and the entire American labor movement.[44]

Darrow's fortunes waxed and waned as he prepared for trial. He was dismayed to learn that a detective he had brought with him from Chicago, John Harrington, intended to cooperate with prosecutors. After having worked as the chief investigator for the McNamara defense team from April until December 1911, this former investigator for the Chicago city railway was poised to damage Darrow's credibility immeasurably. Earl Rogers and his lawyers could only speculate on Harrington's motives. Perhaps the man was upset because Darrow had refused to provide a substantial pay increase, or he may have been fearful that he himself would be implicated in the bribery case. In any event, Harrington agreed to spy on his former employer. At one point, he had met Darrow in a hotel room that had been bugged with a microphone supplied by prosecutors. Two stenographers wearing headphones listened in on the conversation from an adjacent room. The prosecution's trick, later dubbed the "Dictograph Trap," lasted four days and produced a total of between ten and twelve hours of recordings.[45]

With all the machinations and manipulations, the bribery trial was long and complicated; it lasted thirteen weeks. Darrow eventually won an acquittal, but the prosecution was tenacious. Fredericks and his team filed additional charges against Darrow. A second trial ended in a hung jury. Although Darrow actively practiced law for many years afterward, his reputation was tarnished by the McNamara affair and the contentious aftermath.[46]

Clarence Darrow was not the only character in the *Los Angeles Times* bombing to suffer through a difficult period. Ortie McManigal found himself ostracized and denounced as a traitor to the labor cause. He claimed he never would have confessed except that William J. Burns had promised to support McManigal's family while poor Ortie was incarcerated. Realizing he was considered a pariah to his former friends and colleagues, McManigal eventually moved to Honduras to seek gainful employment. In 1932, he returned to Los Angeles and worked as a watchman in the County Hall of Records under an alias, W. E. Mack. It was no small irony that a man who once plotted to blow up Los Angeles County buildings should be hired to watch over them. The denouement was even more ironic; when W. E. Mack retired in 1944, the Los Angeles County Board of Supervisors passed a resolution commemorating the loyal employee for his "long, faithful and efficient services rendered to the people of this county."[47]

John J. McNamara and James B. McNamara in San Quentin Prison. Courtesy of the Archives and Rare Books Library, University of Cincinnati Libraries.

As might be expected, the McNamara brothers faced the most ignominious fate of all. Following their sentencing, both men were transferred to San Quentin state prison near San Rafael, California. James B. McNamara became enamored of the Communist Party and, much to his surprise, became a darling of the Left. Despite his newfound identity as a political martyr, James spent the remainder of his life behind bars. He died of cancer in San Quentin prison on March 9, 1941.[48]

John J. McNamara earned parole after serving ten years in prison. He rejoined the union and kept a low profile until 1925, when he was indicted for blackmail and operating an illegal still. He escaped trial and conviction when the charges against him were dismissed owing to an illegal search warrant. Three years later, he was expelled from the union for allegedly stealing two hundred dollars. John died in Butte, Montana, on May 8, 1941, two months after his brother's death.[49]

The prosecution team, and two men in particular, emerged from the case with grand prospects. As the detective who cracked the case, William J. Burns added substantially to the luster of his reputation. He eventually became known as "America's Sherlock Holmes" when he assisted in a number of high-profile criminal cases in the ensuing years. He also served as director of the Bureau of Investigation (BOI), the predecessor agency of the Federal Bureau of Investigation (FBI), from 1921 to 1924. Aside from his natural talents as an investigator, Burns repeatedly demonstrated an uncanny knack for generating favorable publicity. His successor at what became the FBI, J. Edgar Hoover, took note of the benefits attendant to public acclaim and self-aggrandizement. In many ways, Burns was the prototype for the 1930s man of action, the G-man who stopped at nothing to apprehend criminals and protect the public.[50]

The ambitious prosecutor, John D. Fredericks, also fared well after the *Los Angeles Times* bombing case, although not as well as he had planned. Fredericks had hoped to ride the favorable headlines and management goodwill into the governor's mansion in 1914. He ran a credible campaign and certainly seemed popular enough in the aftermath of the McNamara sentencing. But it was not to be. He lost the gubernatorial election, much to his chagrin, although he later served as a U.S. congressman for two terms before resuming his law practice.[51]

CONCLUSION

As with each episode discussed in this book, the issue in the *Los Angeles Times* case is whether the incident qualifies as terrorism. Each of the common elements of terrorism was present, although the last two elements require additional discussion. The act was violent and it violated the law. As for the third element, the bombers sought to destroy the newspaper, but killing innocent civilians apparently was not the objective. The plan was to destroy some or all of the building while it was vacant, but an accident caused a large number of casualties. Whatever the initial motivation, when the perpetrators planted the explosives, they knew or should have known that despite their best efforts, civilian injuries and deaths were distinct possibilities under those circumstances. Anyone who employs violence risks the possibility of what Timothy McVeigh, among others, called "collateral damage." Such damage is reasonably foreseeable.

The question of whether a broader cause was involved remains problematic. On one hand, destroying the hated newspaper could be viewed as a practical goal in the ongoing war between labor and management. Therefore, this incident was a matter of criminal law and not a terrorist attack. On the other hand, striking at a prominent target in the middle of the night makes a bold political statement: Enemies of labor beware. You are not safe. Reasonable minds can differ on the proper interpretation. One might also conclude that the *Los Angeles Times* building was an attractive target because its destruction accomplished both a practical and a political objective: a hated newspaper would be placed out of commission, and the violent act would make a bold political statement about the power of the workingman.

When Americans of the twenty-first century think of terrorism, they conjure up the face of a foreign extremist hell-bent on killing and terrorizing the men, women, and children of the West. The events of September 11, 2001, have penetrated the western consciousness, resulting in fear and bafflement about the strange ways of Muslim fundamentalists. It is little wonder, therefore, that the label "terrorist" suggests to Americans of a certain age a person of Middle Eastern descent wearing unusual clothing and adhering to strange beliefs. Yet the *Los Angeles Times* bombing of 1910 demonstrates that terrorism, albeit of a domestic variety, has always been alive and well on American soil.

As this book illustrates repeatedly, no magic formula exists to identify the face of a terrorist. Typically, terrorists are alienated from the larger social and political system they view as threatening to their core values. Because they see no place for their participation in the corrupted political and economic system, terrorists feel justified in acting beyond the normal confines of societal values and institutions. Their actions undermine the social, political, and legal order. This fact, far from being anathema, is heralded as exactly the right prescription for instituting much-needed social change. The socialization process that keeps most citizens in line is, among other things, a missing ingredient in the terrorists' makeup.

Some American labor leaders in the early years of the twentieth century believed that no matter how hard they struggled, they would never achieve parity with the captains of industry. Those titans of the upper class entrenched in economic and political power refused to allow rank-and-file laborers to lobby for decent wages and acceptable working conditions. With every labor achievement in the political and economic realm, management pushed back, sometimes employing violence to accomplish their desired ends. Increasingly frustrated at the stalemate, radical labor leaders suggested that the only way to fight fire was with fire. If management employed strikebreakers and thugs willing to use violence, laborers could not take the high road. They, too, should strive to accomplish their goals at the point of the sword.

Times were changing, and with them, sensibilities changed. No longer satisfied to labor under appalling working conditions while eking out a subsistence wage, rank-and-file workers took to the streets, marching and protesting to call attention to their plight. For a small group of extremists such as the McNamara brothers, public protests would not trigger the desired changes. The political and economic system could not be altered except through violence. This attitude was not born overnight, nor did the laborers who employed violence do so for light or transient causes. Domestic terrorists in the labor ranks believed they had few options available to them, and so they rationalized their actions as necessary and just.

Unlike the 9/11 terrorists, the *Los Angeles Times* bombers did not seek to harm innocents. They deliberately timed the explosion to occur in the wee morning hours. Had they known that people would still be working inside the newspaper offices when the bomb exploded, they likely would have pursued a different course of action. Despite these mitigating factors, violent acts often result in unintended consequences. It was of little comfort to the victims and their families that their assailants harbored theoretically noble motives. For the detached observer, it is important to note that terrorists of the early twentieth century did not display the same penchant for a high body count that terrorists of the twenty-first century so fervently desire.

And what of this dirty business with Clarence Darrow and jury tampering? Some sources strongly contend that he was framed by an overly zealous prosecution team. John Fredericks's tactics certainly offend modern sensibilities and violate subsequent developments in Fourth Amendment

Prominent defense attorney Clarence Darrow. Courtesy of the Library of Congress.

search and seizure law. It is doubtful that much of the evidence he collected against Darrow would survive an exclusionary rule challenge in a modern court of law. But it was a different time, and the tactics of both the prosecution and the defense represented the bare-knuckled legal system of the era. That is not to defend such extreme tactics; it is to acknowledge evolving notions of criminal procedure in the American legal system.

Darrow's detractors—and they are legion—insist that his actions in the McNamara case were hardly atypical. He was caught in the act for once. To those who would assail Darrow's lofty reputation as an advocate of the first order, the McNamara case reveals him to be another Machiavellian, corrupt lawyer who would do anything to win a case. In this version of the facts, Darrow's tarnished reputation was richly deserved. That he escaped a prison cell smacks of injustice for a Darrow critic. That he emerged from the McNamara case with severe damage to his iconic status was, if not justice itself, something very much like justice.

To the dispassionate historian observing the scene a century later, the facts are inconclusive. On one hand, the prosecution failed to prove beyond a reasonable doubt that Clarence Darrow bribed jurors. No smoking gun could be found. On the other hand, Darrow's well-known propensity to immerse himself in the details of every facet of the case suggests that rogue investigators bribing jurors with large sums of money seems unlikely. Bert Franklin and John Harrington were unquestionably zealous characters who pushed the envelope; in fact, these were the very qualities that attracted Darrow to the men in the first place. The question remains, however, whether they engaged in unscrupulous maneuvering at Darrow's behest or took it upon themselves to act absent official sanction. It strains credulity to presume they acted without at least some direction from Darrow and his team, but beyond such a supposition little can be said.[52]

What can be said is that the *Los Angeles Times* bombing remains one of the most infamous and compelling cases of terrorism on American soil. It was also a case handled through the regular criminal courts, not a military tribunal. This point will be discussed again later in this book. For commentators with little historical memory who decried the 9/11 attacks as unprecedented terrorist activities in the United States, the *Los Angeles Times* case undermines the contention that Americans have always been safe within a cocoon of state protection. Terrorism can strike at any time, at any place. Police and defense personnel are well advised to remain cognizant of this fact.

NOTES

1. Cowan, *The People v. Clarence Darrow*, 69–70; Greenstein et al., *Bread & Hyacinths*, 57–60; Klebanow and Jones, *People's Lawyers*, 122; McCann, *Terrorism on American Soil*, 34–35; Rayback, *A History of American Labor*, 219–20.

2. Blum, *American Lightning*, 12–13; Klebanow and Jones, *People's Lawyers*, 108; McCann, *Terrorism on American Soil*, 33–34; Rayback, *A History of American Labor*, 220.

3. Darrow, *The Story of My Life*, 173–74; Farrell, "Darrow in the Dock," 98–111; Klebanow and Jones, *People's Lawyers*, 124; McDougal, *Privileged Son*, 62–63.

4. Adamic, *Dynamite*, 200–203; Greenstein et al., *Bread & Hyacinths*, 60; Rayback, *A History of American Labor*, 219–20.

5. Greenstein et al., *Bread & Hyacinths*, 59–60; Rayback, *A History of American Labor*, 219–20.

6. Burns, *The Masked War*, 44–45; Darrow, *The Story of My Life*, 173.

7. Adamic, *Dynamite*, 204; Cowan, *The People v. Clarence Darrow*, 73; Darrow, *The Story of My Life*, 172; McCann, *Terrorism on American Soil*, 34; Rayback, *A History of American Labor*, 220; Stone, *Clarence Darrow for the Defense*, 267–68.

8. Adamic, *Dynamite*, 204–6; Blum, *American Lightning*, 341; Cowan, *The People v. Clarence Darrow*, 73–74; Kaplan, *Lincoln Steffens*, 186; McCann, *Terrorism on American Soil*, 34.

9. Cowan, *The People v. Clarence Darrow*, 69–70; Klebanow and Jones, *People's Lawyers*, 122.

10. Darrow, *The Story of My Life*, 172; Kaplan, *Lincoln Steffens*, 186; Mandel, *Samuel Gompers: A Biography*, 313; Rayback, *A History of American Labor*, 220.

11. Burns, *The Masked War*, 45; McCann, *Terrorism on American Soil*, 34.

12. Cowan, *The People v. Clarence Darrow*, 100–101; Kaplan, *Lincoln Steffens*, 186; Stone, *Clarence Darrow for the Defense*, 267–68.

13. Adamic, *Dynamite*, 212; Burns, *The Masked War*, 303; Kaplan, *Lincoln Steffens*, 187.

14. Blum, *American Lightning*, 3–4; Burns, *The Masked War*, 44; *Being the Portraits and Biographies of the Progressive Men of the West*, 448; Cowan, *The People v. Clarence Darrow*, 95; Greenstein et al., *Bread & Hyacinths*, 57; Kaplan, *Lincoln Steffens*, 186; McCann, *Terrorism on American Soil*, 35; Rayback, *A History of American Labor*, 220.

15. Blum, *American Lightning*, 3–4, 238; Burns, *The Masked War*, 60–63; Cowan, *The People v. Clarence Darrow*, 93–94; Darrow, *The Story of My Life*, 173; McDougal, *Privileged Son*, 52–53; Stone, *Clarence Darrow for the Defense*, 283.

16. Adamic, *Dynamite*, 214–16; Burns, *The Masked War*, 62–63, 97; Cowan, *The People v. Clarence Darrow*, 94; Darrow, *The Story of My Life*, 173; Greenstein et al., *Bread & Hyacinths*, 58–59; McCann, *Terrorism on American Soil*, 35–36; McDougal, *Privileged Son*, 54; Stone, *Clarence Darrow for the Defense*, 280.

17. Burns, *The Masked War*, 12; Cowan, *The People v. Clarence Darrow*, 95; Mandel, *Samuel Gompers: A Biography*, 311; Rayback, *A History of American Labor*, 220.

18. *Being the Portraits and Biographies of the Progressive Men of the West*, 448; Greenstein et al., *Bread & Hyacinths*, 61; Kaplan, *Lincoln Steffens*, 186; Mandel, *Samuel Gompers: A Biography*, 311–13.

19. *Being the Portraits and Biographies of the Progressive Men of the West*, 448; McCann, *Terrorism on American Soil*, 37.

20. Burns, *The Masked War*, 303; Greenstein et al., *Bread & Hyacinths*, 61; Kaplan, *Lincoln Steffens*, 187; Mandel, *Samuel Gompers: A Biography*, 311.

21. Klebanow and Jones, *People's Lawyers*, 109–10; McDougal, *Privileged Son*, 55.

22. Blum, *American Lightning*, 200–204; Darrow, *The Story of My Life*, 173–74; Greenstein et al., *Bread & Hyacinths*, 61; Klebanow and Jones, *People's Lawyers*, 122–23; McCann, *Terrorism on American Soil*, 36–37; Rayback, *A History of American Labor*, 220.

23. Booker, *A Martyr to His Cause*, 6–7; Greenstein et al., *Bread & Hyacinths*, 61; Kaplan, *Lincoln Steffens*, 186–87; Klebanow and Jones, *People's Lawyers*, 123; McDougal, *Privileged Son*, 54–55.

24. Burns, *The Masked War*, 323–24; Mandel, *Samuel Gompers: A Biography*, 313.

25. Darrow, *The Story of My Life*, 179–81; McDougal, *Privileged Son*, 59–60.

26. Mandel, *Samuel Gompers: A Biography*, 313; McDougal, *Privileged Son*, 59–60.

27. Kaplan, *Lincoln Steffens*, 190–92; Mandel, *Samuel Gompers: A Biography*, 313.

28. *Being the Portraits and Biographies of the Progressive Men of the West*, 448.

29. Darrow, *The Story of My Life*, 182–83; Mandel, *Samuel Gompers: A Biography*, 313; Rayback, *A History of American Labor*, 221.

30. Burns, *The Masked War*, 321; Farrell, "Darrow in the Dock," 98, 100; McDougal, *Privileged Son*, 61–62.

31. Burns, *The Masked War*, 320–21; Cowan, *The People v. Clarence Darrow*, 181–82; McDougal, *Privileged Son*, 58; Stone, *Clarence Darrow for the Defense*, 285.

32. Blum, *American Lightning*, 270–71; Burns, *The Masked War*, 320; Cowan, *The People v. Clarence Darrow*, 235; McDougal, *Privileged Son*, 58; Stone, *Clarence Darrow for the Defense*, 296–98.

33. Blum, *American Lightning*, 271; Cowan, *The People v. Clarence Darrow*, 236–37; Darrow, *The Story of My Life*, 186; Farrell, "Darrow in the Dock," 102; Klebanow and Jones, *People's Lawyers*, 123–24; McCann, *Terrorism on American Soil*, 39; McDougal, *Privileged Son*, 58–59.

34. Blum, *American Lightning*, 297; Klebanow and Jones, *People's Lawyers*, 124; Weinberg and Weinberg, *Clarence Darrow: A Sentimental Rebel*, 263.

35. Burns, *The Masked War*, 92; Darrow, *The Story of My Life*, 183; Farrell, "Darrow in the Dock," 102; Klebanow and Jones, *People's Lawyers*, 123; McDougal, *Privileged Son*, 60; Rayback, *A History of American Labor*, 221; Weinberg and Weinberg, *Clarence Darrow: A Sentimental Rebel*, 178–79.

36. Darrow, *The Story of My Life*, 185; Kaplan, *Lincoln Steffens*, 190–92; McCann, *Terrorism on American Soil*, 38–39.

37. Weinberg and Weinberg, *Clarence Darrow: A Sentimental Rebel*, 174.

38. Burns, *The Masked War*, 321–22; Darrow, *The Story of My Life*, 183; Kaplan, *Lincoln Steffens*, 191.

39. Darrow, *The Story of My Life*, 187; Klebanow and Jones, *People's Lawyers*, 124.

40. Darrow, *The Story of My Life*, 196–97.

41. Darrow, *The Story of My Life*, 188; Farrell, "Darrow in the Dock," 100, 102; Klebanow and Jones, *People's Lawyers*, 124; Stone, *Clarence Darrow for the Defense*, 313.

42. Blum, *American Lightning*, 289.

43. Klebanow and Jones, *People's Lawyers*, 123.

44. Stone, *Clarence Darrow for the Defense*, 311; McDougal, *Privileged Son*, 61–62.

45. Cowan, *The People v. Clarence Darrow*, 297.

46. Darrow, *The Story of My Life*, 189; Farrell, "Darrow in the Dock," 108, 110; Klebanow and Jones, *People's Lawyers*, 124–25; McCann, *Terrorism on American Soil*, 39; McDougal, *Privileged Son*, 62–63.

47. McDougal, *Privileged Son*, 63.

48. "John J. McNamara, Dynamiter, Is Dead," *New York Times*, May 8, 1941; McDougal, *Privileged Son*, 60–61; "McNamara, Bomber, Dies in San Quentin," *New York Times*, March 9, 1941.

49. McDougal, *Privileged Son*, 60–61.

50. Blum, *American Lightning*, 63; McCann, *Terrorism on American Soil*, 35.

51. *Being the Portraits and Biographies of the Progressive Men of the West*, 448.

52. Farrell, "Darrow in the Dock," 98–111; Klebanow and Jones, *People's Lawyers*, 125.

5

"AN EXPLOSION JUST LIKE THE SOUND OF A GATLING GUN"

The Wall Street Bombing (1920)

Soon wild commotions shook him, and made flush
All the immortal fairness of his limbs;
Most like the struggle at the gate of death;
Or liker still to one who should take leave
Of pale immortal death.

—John Keats, "Hyperion"

The early twentieth century was a time of enormous social unrest in the United States, as illustrated by the *Los Angeles Times* bombing case discussed in chapter 4. Yet the *Times* bombing was not an isolated incident; similar acts of violence occurred throughout the country in those years. Almost exactly a decade later, another high-profile bombing, this time on Wall Street in New York City, demonstrated the effect of domestic terrorism on the national consciousness. The latter case involved an ideology frightening to many Americans, namely anarchism, the doctrine that all governments undermine human freedom and therefore must be resisted. For a generation of shell-shocked citizens still trying to recover from the Great War in Europe, the rise and spread of radical ideologies, most of which appeared inexplicable and dangerous to ordinary Americans, seemed to represent a genuine threat to traditional mores. Because the 1920 bombing was never solved, as the *Los Angeles Times* case had been solved, and because the bomb was placed in a heavily traveled area with no regard for what came to be called "collateral damage," the Wall Street episode was far more frightening than many previous cases of public violence. As some observers feared at the time, the incident ushered in a new, more violent era of terrorism on American soil.

THE FACTS

The episode occurred shortly after noon as summer gave way to autumn. Looking back on it, everyone agreed that it was an otherwise ordinary morning with nothing to distinguish it from the mornings that preceded it. The date was Thursday, September 16, 1920. Through the hustle and bustle of a crowd of people, clerks and messengers and buyers and other workers in the financial world prepared for lunch and laid afternoon plans. As they scurried about their business, a horse-drawn wooden cart approached the northern section of Wall Street in the financial district of New York City. Although automobiles had mostly replaced horses in the Big Apple, horse-drawn carts were by no means uncommon. To casual bystanders, a dilapidated cart pulled by an old horse would not have appeared out of place. Such a scene, while unusual in a later time, did not attract undue suspicion in 1920.[1]

The carriage halted at 23 Wall Street on the corner of Broad and Wall streets, the heart of the financial district, an intersection where the U.S. Assay Office and the subtreasury building stood side by side across the street from the J. P. Morgan building. The venerable Morgan building did not display a sign anywhere for passersby to see. It did not need to do so. Anyone who needed to know already knew that the country's most influential bank operated within the walls of the elegant corner building. The House of Morgan, despite the death of its founder, J. Pierpont, in 1913, remained a powerful presence on Wall Street and across the nation.[2]

The area might have been called the "symbolic center of American capitalism," but it was more than that. Thirteen decades earlier, it had served as the seat of power for a fledgling republic. On the northeast corner in 1789, George Washington had sworn an oath as the first chief executive of his country. The first Congress of the United States had met not far away, and legislators had hammered out the constitutional amendments that became known as the Bill of Rights. If any site was emblematic of the country's financial might and its historical promise, it was this small plot situated at the lower end of Manhattan. It was little wonder that the driver chose this spot to conceal hundreds of pounds of metal weights, explosive material, and the timing device in a horse-drawn carriage. An aggrieved terrorist who wished to send a message to the captains of industry could not have found a better spot to ensure that his point would be made in sensational fashion. As an added benefit, numerous pedestrians and occupants of the buildings worked on Wall Street. Such casualties would generate massive publicity and strike terror into many a faint heart. This incident would not be a repeat of the *Los Angeles Times* bombing where the perpetrators were concerned about the human cost. The Wall Street terrorists sought to maximize the human cost.[3]

By most accounts, the driver leapt from the wagon and disappeared into the crowd, although later speculation reflected on whether he had become a willing or inadvertent casualty of the insidious plot. Following the momentous events of September 16, eyewitnesses struggled to recall the man's appearance. All eyewitnesses agreed he sported a swarthy complexion, but no one could say for sure whether he was Jewish, Italian, or some other nationality or race. His height, weight, and other distinguishing characteristics were endlessly debated without consensus. Onlookers could not even agree whether the man had acted alone or had driven the wagon with one or more accomplices. Without additional evidence of the assailant's features, identifying a suspect was an investigative dead end. Too many details were unknown, and they would forever remain a mystery despite later attempts to identify a suspect.[4]

What is known is that the wagon sat at the intersection for only a few minutes. At 12:01 p.m., a bomb tucked inside the wagon exploded. A flashing, roaring conflagration completely obliterated the wooden cart and hurled heavy metal slugs through the air. Traumatized survivors struggled with words that seemed inadequate to describe their experiences. Soldiers home from the Great War in Europe said the explosion reminded them of artillery fire on the field of battle. The head of the Morgan credit department recalled hearing "an explosion just like the sound of a Gatling gun." A Wall Street clerk said it was "the loudest noise I ever heard in my life. It was enough to knock you out by itself." It was as though the earth moved owing to some sort of giant cataclysm, a natural disaster such as an earthquake or monsoon. "I was lifted completely off the ground, and at the same instance a terrible explosion occurred to my right, the terrific force of concussion blowing the hat off my head," an adolescent messenger boy recalled.[5]

Persons and property unfortunate enough to be in the vicinity of ground zero were decimated, for the bomb was designed for maximum destruction. Automobiles were destroyed in their entirety; glass was blown from windows as far as five blocks away; shrapnel was embedded in doors, signposts,

The chaotic scene following the 1920 Wall Street explosion. Courtesy of the Library of Congress.

statues, and people. The only feature left of the poor horse was his hooves, which landed yards away near Trinity Church. J. M. Murphy, among the first witnesses on the scene, recalled the carnage: "I saw a horse on his back with three legs sticking up in the air, an automobile on fire and dead people spread out on the street." Despite the grotesque nature of the carnage, the horseshoes attached to the hooves contained a series of markings that investigators eventually traced to a manufacturer in Buffalo, New York.[6]

In the meantime, the explosion rocked buildings within a half-mile radius of 23 Wall Street. A ball of fire and a cloud of green gas blew out windows throughout the financial district and ignited cloth awnings covering windows twelve stories above the street. The J. P. Morgan building experienced the worst damage; an onlooker recalled seeing "broken glass, knocked over desks, scattered papers, and the twisted remains of some steel-wire screens that the firm had providentially installed over its windows not long before, and that undoubtedly prevented far worse carnage than actually took place."[7]

In the minutes following the explosion, a crowd appeared at the site. What they saw resembled a war zone. For many, the devastation strained credulity. Body parts and shrapnel seemed to be everywhere. A few victims, still conscious and experiencing excruciating pain, cried out for help. At least one man engulfed in fire screamed, "Save me! Save me! Put me out!" A woman eviscerated by flying shards was still alive, but she died when rescuers tried to move her. Witnesses reported watching a woman with no arms cry for help. Even veterans of the Great War who flocked to Wall Street could not remember seeing such human misery and suffering.[8]

As the living victims were transported to the hospital and the dead were carted off to the morgue, it was difficult to determine a proper response. What had happened? Why had it happened? If it was intentional, would other attacks follow? The New York Stock Exchange suspended active trading on the floor as a frightened throng headed for the exits amidst shattered glass and frazzled nerves. Police and fire officials urged gawkers to move away from the site owing to the possibility that a second bomb might be planted nearby. Chaos and confusion reigned supreme, and no one seemed to be in charge during the first minutes after the explosion.[9]

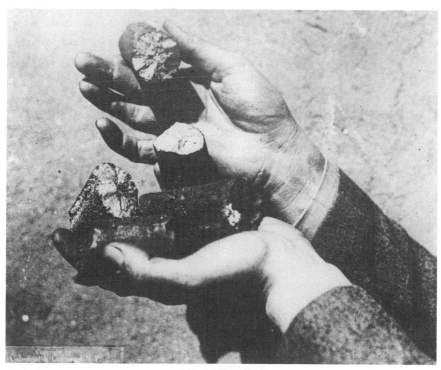

Metal slugs and bomb fragments from the scene of the 1920 Wall Street explosion. Courtesy of the Library of Congress.

As police arrived and sifted through the debris, they discovered the smoldering remains of an automobile that had been thrown onto its side at the corner of Broad and Wall streets. The location and damage suggested that the car had been parked near the epicenter of the blast. Adjacent to the car, investigators found a New Jersey license plate. They also found the remnants of the wagon along with chunks of horseflesh and bits of the harness. Round metal slugs were scattered around the scene as far as five blocks away. Astonished crews discovered that the slugs had been launched as high as the thirty-eighth floor of the Equitable Building. The slugs were hot to the touch.[10]

When investigators later tallied the damage, they discovered that more than thirty people had died owing to the bomb blast. Identifying the deceased was not always a simple affair, but among the known victims, detectives discovered that one J. P. Morgan employee was killed instantly, and another died the next day. The exact number of people who perished as a result of the explosion remains unclear, although some sources place the number as high as forty. As for survivors, more than two hundred people were seriously injured and required hospitalization. Most victims were young employees working in brokerage houses and for the stock exchange as errand boys, stenographers, clerks, secretaries, and junior brokers. Joseph P. Kennedy, father of an American political dynasty, was working in his Wall Street office in the financial district when the bomb exploded, but he escaped injury.[11]

Early in the investigation, authorities were not altogether clear that terrorists were to blame. One theory surfaced that perhaps a delivery wagon had been hauling explosives when an automobile had crashed into the horse cart inadvertently. Several businesses, most notably E. I. du Pont de Nemours and Company, were known to ship dynamite throughout the financial district, so it was possible that the disaster was nothing more than a horrible accident. Because no communications had been received prior to the explosion and because it was difficult to determine the identity of the intended targets, police detectives initially focused on the possibility of negligence. In their view, a terrorist attack would only make sense if it was designed as a means of garnering publicity. The afternoon press coverage seemed to support this view. "The police theory is that the explosion was caused by an automobile colliding with a dynamite wagon," one rag reported. "They do not put any credence in the report that a bomb was thrown at the Morgan office."[12]

Police officers later visited du Pont and the Carl Dittmars Powder Company offices to search for records of explosives shipments with an eye toward pressing criminal charges. It was illegal to deliver explosive devices between sunrise and sunset to avoid exactly this kind of accident. If a company was found to have violated the law, justice would be swift and severe. In addition, agents set out to search for eyewitnesses who either were afraid to come forward or did not realize they had seen something important. "All persons in the vicinity of the scene of the explosion who can give any information, no matter how slight, regarding any of the details, especially regarding vehicles in the street, which might have caused the explosion, or the presence of any suspicious persons at the time of the explosion, should communicate such information to the police at once," a police communiqué announced.[13]

By the end of the first day, after no evidence could be found of missing dynamite shipments and no scenarios involving accidental explosions seemed viable, a new realization emerged. The blast had to be deliberate. This conclusion was first announced by none other than the illustrious William J. Burns, the investigator famous for his role in the 1910 *Los Angeles Times* bombing a decade earlier, described in chapter 4 of this book. His appearance at the crime scene was curious. He was not employed in any official capacity—his claims to represent the Morgan bank were neither confirmed nor denied—but his stature as a public figure ensured that he would be afforded a measure of latitude and respect. Strolling in the debris field, he invited press attention, especially when he offered a new theory on what had happened. "There is not the slightest doubt that it was a bomb which caused the explosion," the great detective told the reporters who hung on his every word. "From my investigation, I am certain that the bomb was in the wagon which was destroyed. There is no other reasonable theory."[14]

Over time, other detectives came to share Burns's view, as did members of the public. While crews picked their way through the debris, they agreed that the timing and location of the explosion strongly indicated that terrorists had struck. The locale seemed too convenient and the damage too deliberate to be an accident. Even as local police came to this realization, the investigation was about to be taken from their hands.[15]

Law enforcement personnel from all levels of government crowded around the scene, but it was unclear which agency should take charge. At the outset, New York City police commissioner Richard E. Enright was the logical choice. As the head of one of the largest police forces in the nation and the highest-ranking local law enforcement officer, Enright should have been first on the scene with his sleeves rolled up, anxious to demonstrate his investigative prowess for all to see. He had been in office for two years

when the Wall Street bomb exploded, ascending to the top spot after enjoying a long career as a constable on patrol. In fact, he was a rarity on the
New York City police force: a rank-and-file policeman who had risen up to
take command of the city's law enforcement apparatus. Unfortunately for
Enright, his public persona was tarnished; he was widely regarded as unfit
for the job, a crony of Mayor John Hylan. His absence from the bombing
site in the immediate aftermath did nothing to endear him to his constituents; they saw him as an unqualified Johnny-come-lately, unaccustomed
to the nitty-gritty work of crime scene investigations. This assessment was
probably unfair—after all, Enright had no way of knowing that his presence would be needed on Wall Street that afternoon—but once the initial
impression was made, it was difficult to rebut.[16]

To make matters worse, Enright suffered by comparison with his immediate predecessor, Arthur Woods, a Harvard-educated professional
educator and lawman extraordinaire who had served as a New York City
police commissioner during the years of the Great War. Woods fortuitously
arrived at the bomb site ahead of his successor and assumed on-site command. He wore the mantle of leadership as though it were his birthright, a
sacred shroud that was his and his alone. Although he was not present in an
official capacity, he retained moral authority from his years in service, and
he did not hesitate to intervene. In the confusing minutes and hours following the blast, Woods was a calming presence, a reminder that someone was
in charge. Marching around the scene, he cajoled police officials to control
the hysterical crowd and preserve the crime scene. When two battalions of
the U.S. Army appeared—called by treasury agents to ensure that no one
looted the gold stored in the subtreasury building—Woods unabashedly assumed command of the confused soldiers, issuing orders to keep onlookers
at bay. Woods's gravitas and willingness to step into a breach of leadership
did not go unrecognized. In a subsequent story, the *Wall Street Journal*
praised the former police commissioner, lamenting his absence from command and lambasting his replacement for, at best, a tardy assumption of
authority and, at worst, an inexcusable dereliction of duty.[17]

This potentially disruptive relationship between the current police
commissioner and his immediate predecessor might have erupted into an
internecine conflict, but, as it turned out, neither Enright nor Woods took
charge of the investigation. Before the day was out, the federal government
had preempted local officials. William J. Flynn, William Burns's predecessor as director of the U.S. Bureau of Investigation, stepped in as the lead
investigator. In one of his first acts, Flynn sifted through data, observed the
scene, and concluded that anarchists were the likely perpetrators.[18]

A heavyset, mustachioed man in his early fifties, and an Irish Catholic in a town largely controlled by Protestants, Flynn had become a well-known government official after U.S. attorney general A. Mitchell Palmer tapped him to investigate a series of bombings in June 1919. Palmer and the press laid it on thick, heralding their man as "the great anarchist expert in the United States," a leader clearly capable of undertaking "the biggest job in the business of crime detection today." The new head of the Bureau of Investigation was surprisingly self-effacing, and the lavish attention embarrassed him.[19]

Flynn was a New York native who had started his career on the city's police force in the early years of the twentieth century. It was a formative period when law enforcement personnel were transitioning from a group of mostly part-time, amateur night watchmen to professional sleuths dedicated to solving crimes using the latest technological advances and crime-solving techniques. As a New York City policeman and later working with the New York branch of the Secret Service, Flynn was at the forefront of the advances in criminal investigation.[20]

He came to the Bureau of Investigation as the agency stood at a crossroads. It was a relatively new organization, created in 1908 as an adjunct to the U.S. Department of Justice, which itself was only established in 1870. The bureau's initial mission was modest. Rather than continually borrowing investigators from the Treasury Department whenever a new case developed, the Justice Department needed its own cadre of agents. During the early years, bureau men devoted their time to low-profile grunt work such as investigating interstate prostitution and anti-trust violations. During the Great War, the bureau had expanded its purview by investigating the activities of suspected radicals, but even this effort had not occurred on a large scale. Flynn wanted to transform his agency into the nation's premier investigatory agency, but in 1920 he was unsure if the Bureau of Investigation possessed the experience or resources to succeed. Moreover, most criminal investigations historically had been handled at the state level. The idea that the federal government would take the lead in a police matter was a novel concept for many Americans, and unsettling to more than a few.[21]

It was an era before media stars, including the celebrated G-men of the 1930s, emerged from the ranks of government agencies to capture the public imagination, and Flynn was no one's idea of a charismatic man of action. Characterized as "phlegmatic," "big-bodied," and "slow-spoken," he was unaccustomed to, and uncomfortable with, heightened media attention. He had come of age in the slower-paced nineteenth century, and he preferred to work absent the glare of the public spotlight. Pressured to join the hyperbole parade, he would only explain, "I'd rather do a thing first and talk about it afterward." It was an admirable sentiment, but it ensured that the bureau's low-key style would not capture headlines unless mistakes were made.[22]

Flynn's initial reaction that anarchists were responsible was logical. The term "anarchism," at least insofar as it describes a political philosophy, does not have a precise meaning, even though the ideology became well known late in the nineteenth century. Since antiquity, the concept of anarchism has meant that all governments, even those founded on the most benign principles of human freedom and political participation, ultimately oppress individuals. The only genuine solution to a totalitarian system of government is to establish a stateless society freed from the shackles of oppression. The difficulty has been that self-styled anarchists have never reached consensus about how a stateless society would operate and whether life in what Thomas Hobbes called a "state of nature" could function other than as a bloody, chaotic free-for-all.[23]

In the United States, the more intellectually adventurous would-be anarchists claimed affinity with Thomas Jefferson, third president and author of that great articulation of human freedom, the Declaration of Independence. Although much of Jefferson's philosophy is difficult to pinpoint—author Joseph J. Ellis dubbed him an "American Sphinx" owing to the multitude of guises and pretensions the Sage of Monticello adopted throughout his long life—it seems safe to conclude that Jefferson argued for decentralized political authority as a means of protecting both individual liberty and property rights, which he understood as rights extending along the same continuum. By exercising local control, yeomen farmers—God's chosen people, as he described them in Query XIX of *Notes on the State of Virginia*—could ensure that maximum human freedom and individual virtue would endure. In a letter he wrote in 1787, shortly before the start of the French Revolution, Jefferson resorted to bombastic language that would warm the cockles of many a terrorist heart. "And what country can preserve its liberties, if its rulers are not warned from time to time, that this people preserve the spirit of resistance? Let them take arms," he argued. "The remedy is to set them right as to the facts, pardon and pacify them. What signify a few lives lost in a century or two? The tree of liberty must be refreshed from time to time, with the blood of patriots and tyrants. It is its natural manure." His incendiary rhetoric inspired intellectually pretentious anarchists to embrace violence as justified in the name of human freedom.[24]

Aside from Jefferson, early-twentieth-century anarchists found inspiration from Josiah Warren, author of "The Peaceful Revolutionist," the first "explicitly anarchist newspaper in the United States," according to some accounts. Henry David Thoreau, a renowned nineteenth-century proponent of civil disobedience, occasionally earns a mention as a social anarchist, although it is not clear he would have accepted the label. Abolitionist Lysander Spooner also earns a nod as an anarchist and philosopher of freedom. Each of these thinkers was essentially a libertarian who wanted nothing so much as to be left alone by government. Pacifism often went hand in hand with anarchism prior to the twentieth century.[25]

The inimitable Emma Goldman was perhaps the best-known anarchist at the turn of the twentieth century, but she was not a committed pacifist. Originally born in the Russian Empire, Goldman moved to New York City in 1885 as a teenager and thereafter became involved in the anarchist movement. She was drawn to the freewheeling ideology in the wake of the Haymarket riot, a sordid episode in which Chicago police clashed with striking workers and some angry soul hurled dynamite at the authorities. During the ensuing melee, eight policemen and numerous civilians died. The incident popularized the stereotype of the "bomb-throwing anarchist" in the public imagination and rallied oppressed workers throughout the world to strike back against the heavy hand of management. Goldman, the freethinking "rebel woman," as some observers described her, came to view all governments as inherently corrupt and destructive of human freedom after she learned of the confrontation. Her admirers saw her as a courageous champion of individualism, even in the face of great personal sacrifice, but to many Americans she was the personification of chaos and disorder, a deeply disruptive force that undermined the social fabric of the nation. Although anarchists were ideologically distinct from communists, philosophical niceties were lost on frightened members of the public who yearned for law and order in the face of sweeping social change. Anarchists, communists, and other radicals, in the minds of many citizens at the turn of the century, threatened to destroy the American way of life and had to be opposed at every turn.[26]

Not all anarchists shared Emma Goldman's dedication to human freedom and dignity as a philosophical commitment. In the first decades of the twentieth century, followers of Luigi Galleani, known as "Galleanists," became prominent practitioners of "propaganda by the deed," the idea that society can only be changed through violent action. Shunted aside were the peaceful protesters who longed for liberty as a means of maximizing human potential, for their tepid efforts to transform society through argumentation and persuasion would not liberate the individual from the omnipotent state. Dedicated Galleanists were known to have masterminded a number of violent acts, especially after the arrest of Nicola Sacco and Bartolomeo Vanzetti, two infamous anarchists charged in a high-profile Massachusetts bank robbery. For anarchists, the Sacco and Vanzetti case was evidence that the powers that be were willing and able to convict innocent men for a crime they did not commit in order to strike at anarchism. Galleani himself briefly came under suspicion for the Wall Street bombing, but he was deported to Italy on another matter before his connection was thoroughly investigated. Months afterward, frustrated detectives would second-guess this decision and seek information on Galleani's whereabouts, but in the early hours after the bombing, the notorious anarchist did not seem to be directly involved in the crime.[27]

When William J. Flynn announced that anarchists were likely behind the Wall Street bombing, he was onto something, and everyone knew it. The question, of course, was which anarchist or group of anarchists should be placed at the top of the list. With Galleani deported and out of commission, police moved to their ranking of likely culprits. The first of the usual suspects was William Dudley Haywood, a founding member of the Industrial Workers of the World (IWW) and a high-profile member of the executive committee of the American Socialist Party. "Big Bill" was a controversial figure who already had known his share of legal troubles. They began in 1905 when someone killed former Idaho governor Frank Steunenberg using a bomb. After a Western Federation of Miners (WFM) member named Albert Edward Horsley, using the alias "Harry Orchard," was implicated in the crime, this shady character agreed to turn state's evidence against other WFM members in exchange for improved treatment in prison. He fingered Haywood, among others, in the murder.

Essentially kidnapped from Denver, Colorado, and placed on trial, Haywood, with fund-raising assistance from the American Federation of Labor, hired Clarence Darrow to represent him. Half a decade before his involvement in the McNamara case, the legendary attorney was at his best. On the stand, he ripped into Harry Orchard's checkered past with a skill and grit that enhanced Darrow's already stellar reputation. Following the masterful cross-examination, Darrow delivered a moving summation that led in no small measure to Haywood's acquittal.[28]

The Steunenberg murder trial was not the end of Haywood's legal woes. During the Great War, as hysteria rose among citizens fearful of domestic subversion, Congress enacted the Espionage Act of 1917, which, among other things, established criminal penalties for persons who "convey information with intent to interfere with the operation or success of the armed forces of the United States or to promote the success of its enemies." The vaguely worded statute, a clear infringement on free speech rights, further criminalized actions designed "to cause or attempt to cause insubordination, disloyalty, mutiny, refusal of duty, in the military or naval forces of the United States, or to willfully obstruct the recruiting or enlistment service of the United States."[29]

Using the espionage statute as a legal pretext, officials from the U.S. Department of Justice raided Industrial Workers of the World meeting halls in September 1917. The raid netted 165 IWW members, and 101 were tried for violating the Espionage Act of 1917. Predictably, Haywood was one of the most prominent defendants. After a five-month trial—the longest criminal proceeding in U.S. history up until that time—Haywood and his co-defendants were found guilty. Haywood and fourteen others received twenty-year prison sentences.[30]

Temporarily free on bail and facing a trial in Illinois on "criminal syndicalism" charges as well as a separate federal charge of "conspiracy to overthrow the government," Prisoner 13106 was dismayed to hear that investigators had placed his name at the top of the list of possible suspects in the Wall Street case. He learned of their suspicions on September 17 as he waited on a train to transport him from Philadelphia to New York. Suffering from poor health and demoralized by the thought of going through additional legal proceedings, the embattled labor leader fled to Chicago where he kept a low profile during the early stages of the investigation. Authorities might have been more zealous in pursuing their number one suspect had William Flynn pressed the matter. As unflappable as ever, the bureau's point man expressed little interest in chasing Haywood to the Windy City. "He is now out on bail, and any time that we want him we can call his bail in," the big man assured an excited press corps. From Flynn's vantage point, aside from Haywood's notoriety, there was little reason to see Big Bill as a viable suspect.[31]

Instead of chasing down the most obvious, if not always promising, leads, Flynn focused his attention on a new development. Not long after the bombing, a letter carrier discovered leaflets inside a mailbox a couple of blocks away from ground zero. The anonymous message indicated that anarchists indeed were responsible for the explosion. Printed in red ink on inexpensive white paper, the leaflets were childish and difficult to take seriously but for the carnage on Wall Street. The message read,

REMEMBER
WE WILL NOT TOLERATE
ANY LONGER

FREE THE POLITICAL PRISONERS
OR IT WILL BE
SURE DEATH FOR ALL OF YOU
—American Anarchist Fighters

No one knew whether the leaflets were a legitimate communication from the perpetrator or an elaborate hoax to throw investigators off the trail of the responsible parties. Whatever the source of the message, the police never satisfactorily discovered who wrote it or why the person left it in the mailbox. They made an elaborate effort to track the source of the communication, visiting numerous printers in a fruitless effort to locate the typeface used in the missive.[32]

The horseshoes seemed to be more promising evidentiary leads than the leaflets. They bore the letters "JHU" and "NOA" about an inch apart on each of the shoes. Police initially thought the letters were initials representing a person's name, but painstaking detective work failed to uncover additional information. Thousands of visits to stables up and down the eastern seaboard revealed that the horseshoes had come from an Italian blacksmith in New York City. Unfortunately, the blacksmith sold innumerable pairs of shoes to innumerable customers. Beyond that fact, investigators uncovered no new information.[33]

Although the police only retrieved a few fragments of the bomb, an explosives expert was able to reconstruct the device. Forensic science was in its infancy, but a Johns Hopkins University experimental physicist, Robert W. Wood, constructed a replica of the bomb. Another expert, Dr. Walter T. Scheele, determined that fifty pounds of blasting gelatin were used in the bombing. Determining how the bomb was constructed, of course, was not the same thing as determining a viable suspect, but it was a starting point in the search for clues. Once again, though, credible leads were few and far between.[34]

Aside from Bill Haywood, the suspect who attracted the most attention in the early days was an odd character named Edwin Fisher, an unlikely anarchist if ever there was one. Fisher was known to admire Emma Goldman, the famous anarchist, and he had voiced suspicion of "all moneyed interests," but these eccentricities hardly suggested that he was a terrorist. Friends were aware of Fisher's "mental derangement" as well as his uncanny ability to forecast future events, but what did it mean? According to some reports, during the week before the explosion, Fisher had warned friends and colleagues to "stay away from Wall Street this Wednesday afternoon." He was always uttering such cryptic pronouncements, and those who knew him thought little of the warning until after the explosion occurred. When law enforcement officials learned of these prophecies, they naturally sought to interview Fisher to determine whether he had been involved in the plot. As investigators spoke with the man, however, it was clear that he had no prior knowledge of the explosion. In fact, police learned of Fisher's numerous prognostications in previous years and his reputation as a bizarre soothsayer. It did not take an extended conversation to recognize that something was not quite right about Edwin Fisher. Investigators found it difficult to believe that this scatterbrained character possessed the necessary skills in organized planning and logistics to be involved in the bombing.[35]

Despite Fisher's unreliability, the strange gadfly's appearance in the case attracted all sorts of crazies from the woodwork. Even seemingly levelheaded citizens were prompted to engage in silly predictions and unsubstantiated suppositions. A scientist at the American Institute for Scientific Research, Dr. Walter F. Prince, suggested that Fisher might have received a "psychic tip" about the events of September 16. For all the color he brought to the case, Edwin Fisher produced no useful leads and played no meaningful part in the official investigation. He was one more dead end in a case filled with dead ends.[36]

After rejecting Haywood and Fisher as credible suspects, police moved down their list of possible desperadoes. One man who briefly excited interest was a bona fide communist born in Russia, Alexander Brailovsky, the anti–Edwin Fisher. This new suspect was conniving and intelligent, and he fit the stereotype of a "typical anarchist" to a T. Brailovsky's militant publication, *Russky Golos*, was enough to inflame even the gentlest skeptic of grand conspiracy theories. In addition, Brailovsky was reputed to have been seen near the bomb site laughing less than an hour after the explosion. Leftists feared that the unsympathetic Russian would become a scapegoat for the powers that be—Attorney General Palmer was known to be monitoring the investigation carefully—but ultimately investigators rejected Brailovsky as the perpetrator. Aside from obvious incongruities—why would the man who set off a major explosion remain near the scene afterward, thereby inviting scrutiny and perhaps capture?—no credible evidence could be found linking this supposedly dangerous radical to the Wall Street bombing.[37]

With renowned detectives such as Flynn and Burns working the case, the public had been confident that a break would occur soon. As the weeks passed and no new leads developed, detectives grew increasingly desperate. Flynn attempted to replicate the tried-and-true method of using undercover operatives to root out new information. In this instance, he relied on spies to infiltrate Italian anarchist circles in New York, but the dangerous operation yielded nothing of value. Occasionally, the undercover men hanging out in bars, coffee houses, barbershops, and meeting halls would gather up membership lists or lists of activists and supporters of various leftist causes, but the follow-up investigations led nowhere. Sometimes a new name would surface and for a while it would raise the investigators' hopes, only to dash them when an alibi proved to be solid or the lead reached a dead end. A dedicated Galleanist named Aldino Felicani, known for his vocal support of Sacco and Vanzetti, surfaced when police learned of his relentless pamphleteering and criticism of the manner in which the judicial system had handled the case involving his colleagues. An interview with Bureau of Investigation agents produced nothing of value, and once again a promising line of inquiry had to be abandoned.[38]

In a desperate attempt to solve the deteriorating case, investigators launched a nationwide search. They were aided—or hindered, depending on one's point of view—by a $100,000 reward for information leading to the arrest of individuals responsible for the bombing. Predictably, they received numerous tips implicating a variety of radical groups, including anarchists, socialists, labor activists, and lone individuals harboring anti-American sentiments. As investigators sifted through the mountain of data and information, they uncovered a twenty-three-year-old Polish immigrant, Florean Zelenska (sometimes Anglicized as "Florian Zelenko"), in Pittsburgh, Pennsylvania. Zelenska first attracted attention when he uttered statements on a train suggesting to passengers that he might be carrying explosives. When police on the train attempted to question him, Zelenska became combative. During the ensuing struggle, they knocked the unruly fellow unconscious. Police later searched his hotel room and found a treasure trove of "radical" Russian propaganda and, far more damning, dynamite, percussion caps, and a fuse. When questioned about these items, Zelenska claimed to be involved in a mining operation. Investigators never found any evidence that the young man had ever worked in mining.[39]

The deeper the police dug into his background, the more likely it seemed that Zelenska was their man. One purported eyewitness claimed to have heard the suspect boast, "See what we did in Wall Street." William Flynn and his men were almost positive they had cracked the case until they discovered that Zelenska, although present in New York City on the day of the bombing, had been nowhere near Wall Street in the moments leading up to the explosion. In addition, they found no evidence linking him to actively violent radical groups. Although investigators eventually charged the young Russian with violating a federal law prohibiting persons from carrying explosives on a train, they were never able to link him to the Wall

Street crime. He was simply one among the hundreds of disaffected, alienated individuals lurking among the citizenry in those discontented days.[40]

As 1920 became 1921 and a new presidential administration led to Attorney General Palmer's departure, police continued searching for the terrorists responsible for the bombing, but their hopes of salvaging the case grew remote. In hopes of reviewing old evidence using a fresh approach, they refocused their efforts on the man who drove the horse cart and parked it at the scene. A flyer based on eyewitness recollections described the man as "28 or 30 years old; 5 feet, 6 inches; medium build; broad shoulders; dark hair; dark complexion; small dark mustache; which at the date of the explosion represented about two week's [sic] growth. He wore a golf cap, pulled down over his forehead, and a khaki shirt turned in at the neck."[41]

The description fit neatly with the conclusion that an Italian anarchist had perpetrated the crime, but its probative value was unclear. In fact, it was difficult to determine whether the description caused investigators to suspect a Galleanist or if suspicions of Galleanist involvement led police to produce the description. In any case, the text became the basis for a widely circulated composite drawing. New evidence, however unreliable, led to new clues, and new clues produced new suspects. One of the names police uncovered as they distributed the drawing was "Vinzenio Leggio," although they were unsure whether the name was actually "Lefi," "Legu," or "Lufi." The trail eventually led detectives to Tito Ligi, who may have used "Vinzenio Leggio" as an alias.[42]

"Federal Agents Think Wall Street Plot Cleared," screamed a headline from the *New York Sun* after the suspect was captured. Ligi loosely matched the general description, and, even more promising, police found two loaded Colt revolvers and a pile of radical literature at Ligi's house. A letter seized on the premises seemed to contain a code with elliptical references to "special work" and a "special job." When subjected to aggressive questioning, the suspect claimed he could not remember where he was between September 8 and 16, 1920, because he moved around frequently. The more the police searched, the more promising the suspect became. They discovered he had been living above an abandoned mine, and they found what appeared to be bomb-making paraphernalia. In the back room of a Scranton, Pennsylvania, restaurant, they recovered a series of sash weights "identical with the fragments of iron scattered through New York's financial center." The evidence against Tito Ligi was piling up rapidly.[43]

Unfortunately for investigators, it was all circumstantial evidence. They could not link Ligi to the scene. Even promising eyewitness testimony began to unravel. Men who had been certain of Ligi's presence on Wall Street during the day of the bombing began to entertain second thoughts. As for the suspect, his radical views were little more than sophomoric platitudes; in fact, Tito Ligi seemed to comprehend few, if any, of the basic tenets of anarchism, or any other radical ideology, for that matter. Reluctant detectives eventually abandoned their case against him, although a Pittsburgh federal court later sentenced Ligi to a year in prison for draft evasion. At least he was behind bars in the event investigators located additional evidence against him and needed to find him quickly.[44]

In December 1921, suspicion fell on a shadowy character named Wolfe Lindenfeld, also known as William Linde, a Polish radical with communist connections in Moscow. Supposedly, agents of the Bureau of Investigation arrested the latest suspect in Warsaw after a physical altercation. As reported on the Associated Press wire on December 16, 1921, Linde confessed to the bombing after enduring hours of interrogation. The idea that Russian spies had carried out a bombing on Wall Street fit with many Americans' paranoia about the growing Red Menace throughout the world. According to the confession, four or five communist agents had been dispatched years earlier to assassinate the legendary financier J. P. Morgan, that great titan of industry. Once again, however, a lead that initially appeared promising led nowhere. Not only did investigators fail to prove Linde's complicity in the bombing, but a deeply chastened William J. Burns, who had replaced William J. Flynn as head of the Bureau of Investigation four months earlier, had to admit that Linde had been employed by Burns's detective agency. If Linde posed a threat to the American way of life, how had he come to be an employee of the "American Sherlock Holmes"? This embarrassing admission damaged Burns's public persona and ensured that Linde would not be prosecuted.[45]

THE CASE GROWS COLD

Several other Italian immigrants and suspected radicals briefly came under suspicion following the Linde debacle, but no leads proved as promising as the initial case against Tito Ligi. Despite all the time and resources devoted to solving the crime, law enforcement personnel eventually conceded that the trail had gone cold. Bitterly disappointed that they had not solved the case, police spent the next two decades periodically investigating clues before they finally closed the case in the 1940s. Until the Oklahoma City bombing in 1995, the Wall Street episode remained the deadliest terrorist attack on American soil. As of this writing, it ranks third behind the 9/11 attacks and the Oklahoma City bombing in terms of casualties.[46]

A young detective working on the Wall Street investigations, J. Edgar Hoover, became fixated on cracking the case. When he ascended into the director's chair at what became the Federal Bureau of Investigation (FBI), Hoover occasionally pursued leads that came to his attention. In 1930, his agents followed up on correspondence with a man named Harry Brant who claimed to have incontrovertible proof of the identity of the responsible parties, although nothing came from this lead. In 1934, a gentleman named Stephen Doyle claimed to know for a fact that the Soviet Union had masterminded the attack as part of an effort to overthrow the U.S. government. FBI agents were always willing to consider new leads, no matter how far-fetched, but as the years passed, none of the subsequent stories proved to be true. Gradually, memories faded and the public became fascinated by other crimes and acts of violence. In 1944, the bureau investigated one final clue when an informant claimed that Edwin Fisher had conspired with the Japanese government to plant the Wall Street bomb. The allegation of Japanese subversion no doubt reflected the hysteria of World War II, but it was clear the claim was not credible. The strange character Edwin Fisher had already claimed enough of the investigators' time and energy.[47]

Although the case remains officially unsolved, amateur sleuths have been unable to resist the urge to speculate on who masterminded the bombing, and why. One of the most promising theories links the episode to the Sacco and Vanzetti indictment nine days before the Wall Street explosion. Paul Avrich, a well-known historian of twentieth-century anarchism, has argued that Mario Buda, sometimes known as "Mike Boda," was an associate of Sacco and Vanzetti and therefore nursed a grievance against the government that had imprisoned the infamous anarchists. Well versed in the use of explosives and other terrorist tactics, Boda possessed the means and motive to perpetrate the crime. Moreover, he matched several eyewitness descriptions of the man seen leaving the scene shortly before the explosion. Documentary evidence is sparse, but Boda was known to have obtained an Italian passport and returned to his homeland shortly after the Wall Street explosion. He never returned to the United States. Avrich presents a forceful argument, and his evidence is powerful, but he cannot conclude definitively that Boda was the perpetrator. In all likelihood, the identity of the bomber(s) will never be known.[48]

CONCLUSION

The Wall Street explosion of 1920 remains an unsolved case despite all the leads that have surfaced throughout the years. Conspiracy theorists and would-be detectives have set forth numerous theories, possible motives, and likely suspects. Some explanations, such as the Mike Boda connection, have been compelling. Yet definitive answers remain elusive to this day. Because no organized group or person stepped forward to claim responsibility and because modern forensic science was still in its infancy at the time of the explosion, the available leads have yielded no incontrovertible evidence. The case is as frustrating in the twenty-first century as it was in the twentieth except that no one is now screaming for a resolution.

Because the culprits were never identified or apprehended, and therefore their motives and objectives are not altogether clear, one might ask whether this case should be included in a book about terrorism in the first place. In light of the symbolic location of the bomb and the antipathy that some Americans, especially anarchists, socialists, and similar organized entities, felt for Wall Street financiers in the post–World War I era, the episode probably was a terrorist attack. The incident involved violence, it violated the law, and it targeted civilians. Whether it was designed to achieve a broader moral, social, political, religious, or ethnic goal remains an open question, but it appears to have been a political statement aimed at the heart of American capitalism.

The case is included here because it was such an important event in American history. Although the episode has faded from the national consciousness, except among crime aficionados and students of domestic terrorism, in its day the case was widely regarded as the "crime of the century." The site of the bomb—at the heart of America's financial district—and the presence of high-profile investigators such as William J. Flynn, William J. Burns, and U.S. attorney general A. Mitchell Palmer ensured that the case would capture headlines during the early 1920s. Subsequent events during that decade, including fallout from the Sacco and Vanzetti case and the rise of criminal syndicates under bosses such as Al Capone, eclipsed press coverage of the Wall Street explosion, but the incident resonated for many years. Citizens believed that their world was changing—and not for the better. The horrors of the Great War, the worldwide influenza epidemic, and the red scares of the postwar period convinced many Americans that the dawning of a new era had revealed the world to be a strange, alien, frightening place. The Wall Street bombing was another part of the new, unsettling landscape. Despite the obscurity of the case during the twenty-first century, the incident contains an object lesson for students of terrorism.[49]

The case represented a turning point in the study of organized violence, although no one recognized that fact at the time. Investigators of that era were astounded that no political or ideological group claimed responsibility for the explosion on Wall Street. Moreover, they were horrified by the deliberate carnage inflicted on innocent bystanders. In a later time, when terrorists actively sought a high body count, the concept of a secret organization deliberately harming innocents without offering prior warning and without immediately claiming responsibility after the fact would not be noteworthy. In 1920, however, law enforcement officials generally assumed that bombers were intent on causing symbolic destruction and capturing media attention for their causes. After all, the model for detonating an explosive device remained the *Los Angeles Times* bombing of 1910. By their own admission, James B. McNamara and his confederates had not intended to harm anyone in that case; their purpose was to lash out at their enemies. The casualties inflicted in 1910 were accidental; a decade later, they were purposive. Although the bombers in the *Los Angeles Times* case had tried to hide their identities, they wanted to send a clear message from labor that management must not be allowed to trample the rights of the American worker.[50]

Unlike the earlier case, the Wall Street bombing represented a new phase in domestic terrorism. Because no person or entity stepped forward to claim responsibility or call attention to a cause and because innocent people were likely to be injured given the location of the bomb, the motives behind the crime differed significantly from previous bombings. In lieu of the destruction serving as a means to an end—namely, a method of calling attention to another issue—destruction was the goal. To those persons directly or indirectly harmed by the explosion, such a distinction may seem meaningless; to students of terrorism, it is an important development.

The terrorist who seeks to send a message without harming innocent bystanders faces formidable obstacles. He must pick a symbolic target and carefully plan its destruction to minimize casualties. As the McNamara case illustrated, this is no mean feat. In many ways, the terrorist who seeks to lash out at enemies, even at the risk of harming bystanders, faces an easier task than the more conscientious activist. The need for advance planning and careful implementation decreases when collateral damage is of no consequence. In fact, the terrorist who seeks to harm his enemies may welcome a large number of casualties. As officials would conclude years later regarding the U.S. war on terror, preventing suicide bombers from achieving their goals is extremely problematic because anti-terrorist officials must be correct in every instance while terrorists only have to achieve their goal once.[51]

The Wall Street bombing contains another useful lesson for modern students of terrorism. Prior to 1920, police officials, when pressed to discuss investigative techniques, emphasized the efficacy of general law enforcement methods. A terrorist was simply another criminal who could be caught using the normal investigative methods employed to fight crime. The fallacy in this assumption is that it presupposes a traditional criminal motive for the terrorist. Although in some cases terrorists are motivated by the usual factors—jealousy, revenge, avarice, or the heat of passion—not every person driven to commit acts of terrorism acts on these motives. Law enforcement personnel have learned through long and bitter experience to investigate the circumstances of a victim's life in searching for an assailant. Thus, an enraged husband will shoot his cheating wife. A disgruntled employee will return to his place of work to exact vengeance against his employer. A desperate, greedy person will walk into a bank with a gun and attempt to abscond with money. Using traditional investigative techniques, police can usually trace cause and effect; the perpetrator leaves a trail that can be traced owing to police perseverance. Even secret conspiracies can be uncovered, in many instances, when police follow up on each and every lead. To use the old adage from World War II, "loose lips sink ships." Police investigators, when they find one conspirator, can often persuade a hapless defendant facing serious prison time to turn state's evidence against his partners in crime.[52]

Modern terrorists, in contrast to the traditional criminal, generally are more disciplined in planning and carrying out their violent activities. This comment is not to suggest that normal investigative techniques fail in every instance. It does suggest, however, that terrorists, because they are not motivated by the same factors as common criminals, may be more difficult to apprehend using traditional investigative techniques employed by the police. As discussed later in this book, the post-9/11 debate over the war on terror focuses precisely on this issue. Because terrorists do not always mirror civilian criminals, they should not be charged, tried, and convicted in civilian courts, or so the argument goes. The lesson here is that terrorists differ from common criminals. They may engage in criminal acts, but they need not be motivated by the *mens rea* found in criminal cases.[53]

Acts of terrorism can be difficult to identify or prevent beforehand because often the grievances of the disaffected are hidden from sight; the first clue that something is amiss is the actual violence itself. Investigators who are unaware of the perpetrators' alienation miss the warning signs because, in their view, no warning signs exist. Criminologists have long recognized triggering factors within society in general and within groups of people in particular that assist in predicting criminal behavior. These assumptions do not hold true for persons suffering from mental illness or for persons who revel in a masochistic desire to destroy themselves, as with suicide bombers. In short, episodes such as the Wall Street bombing demonstrate, if nothing else, the difficulty in using traditional police procedures to solve cases of violence triggered by terrorists.[54]

NOTES

1. McCann, *Terrorism on American Soil*, 62; Watson, *Sacco & Vanzetti*, 77–78.

2. Gage, *The Day Wall Street Exploded*, 30, 31–32; McCann, *Terrorism on American Soil*, 63; McCormick, *Hopeless Cases*, 65; Pernicone, "Luigi Galleani and Italian Anarchist Terrorism in the United States," 189.

3. Gage, *The Day Wall Street Exploded*, 19; McCormick, *Hopeless Cases*, 65.

4. Faber, *Great News Photos and the Stories behind Them*, 32; Gage, *The Day Wall Street Exploded*, 243–44.

5. Avrich, *Sacco and Vanzetti*, 205; Hynd, "The Great Wall Street Explosion," 191; McCormick, *Hopeless Cases*, 66.

6. Faber, *Great News Photos and the Stories behind Them*, 32; Frasier, *Every Man a Speculator*, 330; Gage, *The Day Wall Street Exploded*, 34; Hynd, "The Great Wall Street Explosion," 192; McCormick, *Hopeless Cases*, 66.

7. Avrich, *Sacco and Vanzetti*, 205; Frasier, *Every Man a Speculator*, 330; Gage, *The Day Wall Street Exploded*, 31–33; McCann, *Terrorism on American Soil*, 63.

8. Gage, *The Day Wall Street Exploded*, 33–35; McCann, *Terrorism on American Soil*, 63–64.

9. Faber, *Great News Photos and the Stories behind Them*, 32; Gage, *The Day Wall Street Exploded*, 31–36.

10. Faber, *Great News Photos and the Stories behind Them*, 32; Hynd, "The Great Wall Street Explosion," 191–92.

11. Faber, *Great News Photos and the Stories behind Them*, 32; Hynd, "The Great Wall Street Explosion," 191; McCormick, *Hopeless Cases*, 66.

12. Frasier, *Every Man a Speculator*, 331; Gage, *The Day Wall Street Exploded*, 143–44.

13. Gage, *The Day Wall Street Exploded*, 144–45; Hynd, "The Great Wall Street Explosion," 192.

14. Gage, *The Day Wall Street Exploded*, 148–49; Hunt, *Front-Page Detective*, 153–55; McCormick, *Hopeless Cases*, 8.

15. Frasier, *Every Man a Speculator*, 330–31; Gage, *The Day Wall Street Exploded*, 148–49; Hunt, *Front-Page Detective*, 155.

16. Gage, *The Day Wall Street Exploded*, 133–36; Hickey, *Our Police Guardians*, 89, 101.

17. Gage, *The Day Wall Street Exploded*, 133–34; Hynd, "The Great Wall Street Explosion," 191.

18. McCormick, *Hopeless Cases*, 8; Watson, *Sacco & Vanzetti*, 79.

19. Avrich, *Sacco and Vanzetti*, 166; Gage, *The Day Wall Street Exploded*, 126–27; Hunt, *Front-Page Detective*, 161–62.

20. Gage, *The Day Wall Street Exploded*, 126–27; Melanson, *The Secret Service*, 36–37.

21. *Department of Justice of the United States*, 9–14; Gage, *The Day Wall Street Exploded*, 127–28.

22. Gage, *The Day Wall Street Exploded*, 127; Melanson, *The Secret Service*, 36–37.

23. Aydinli, "Before *Jihadists*, There Were Anarchists," 904–5; McCann, *Terrorism on American Soil*, 64.

24. Quoted in Padover, ed., *Thomas Jefferson on Democracy*, 168. See also Ellis, *American Sphinx*; Jefferson, *Notes on the State of Virginia*, 164–65.

25. Aydinli, "Before *Jihadists*, There Were Anarchists," 920–21; Chalberg, *Emma Goldman*, 25.

26. Chalberg, *Emma Goldman*, 11–26; Dolbeare, *American Political Thought*, 392.

27. Avrich, *Sacco and Vanzetti*, 205–6; McCann, *Terrorism on American Soil*, 64; McGirr, "The Passion of Sacco and Vanzetti," 1085–86, 1089; Pernicone, "Luigi Galleani and Italian Anarchist Terrorism in the United States," 189–90; Watson, *Sacco & Vanzetti*, 199.

28. Conlin, "William D. 'Big Bill' Haywood: The Westerner as Labor Radical," 120–21; Dubofsky, *"Big Bill" Haywood*, 39–40; Gage, *The Day Wall Street Exploded*, 77; Watson, *Sacco & Vanzetti*, 79–80.

29. Conlin, "William D. 'Big Bill' Haywood: The Westerner as Labor Radical," 128–29; Dubofsky, *"Big Bill" Haywood*, 109–13; Gage, *The Day Wall Street Exploded*, 112–13.

30. Conlin, "William D. 'Big Bill' Haywood: The Westerner as Labor Radical," 19–31; Dubofsky, *"Big Bill" Haywood*, 115–21.

31. Dubofsky, *"Big Bill" Haywood*, 132; Watson, *Sacco & Vanzetti*, 78.

32. McCann, *Terrorism on American Soil*, 64; Watson, *Sacco & Vanzetti*, 78–79.

33. Hynd, "The Great Wall Street Explosion," 192; McCann, *Terrorism on American Soil*, 65.

34. Gage, *The Day Wall Street Exploded*, 280; McCann, *Terrorism on American Soil*, 65.

35. Gage, *The Day Wall Street Exploded*, 175–77; McCann, *Terrorism on American Soil*, 65–66.

36. Avrich, *Sacco and Vanzetti*, 205; McCann, *Terrorism on American Soil*, 66.

37. Gage, *The Day Wall Street Exploded*, 185–86; McCann, *Terrorism on American Soil*, 66–67.

38. Avrich, *Sacco and Vanzetti*, 64–66; Gage, *The Day Wall Street Exploded*, 223–24.

39. Gage, *The Day Wall Street Exploded*, 204, 279; McCann, *Terrorism on American Soil*, 66–67.

40. Gage, *The Day Wall Street Exploded*, 204.

41. Gage, *The Day Wall Street Exploded*, 242–44; McCann, *Terrorism on American Soil*, 66–67.

42. Hynd, "The Great Wall Street Explosion," 193; McCormick, *Hopeless Cases*, 112.

43. Gage, *The Day Wall Street Exploded*, 244–45; McCormick, *Hopeless Cases*, 112–13.

44. Gage, *The Day Wall Street Exploded*, 244–45; McCann, *Terrorism on American Soil*, 66–68; McCormick, *Hopeless Cases*, 114–15.

45. Gage, *The Day Wall Street Exploded*, 280–85; McCormick, *Hopeless Cases*, 132–35.

46. Gage, *The Day Wall Street Exploded*, 3–5; McCann, *Terrorism on American Soil*, 67–68.

47. Gage, *The Day Wall Street Exploded*, 324.

48. Avrich, *Sacco and Vanzetti*, 205–7; Faber, *Great News Photos and the Stories behind Them*, 32; McCann, *Terrorism on American Soil*, 67–68; McCormick, *Hopeless Cases*, 98–101; Pernicone, "Luigi Galleani and Italian Anarchist Terrorism in the United States," 189–90.

49. Faber, *Great News Photos and the Stories behind Them*, 32; McCormick, *Hopeless Cases*, 8–9.

50. Burns, *The Masked War*, 321–22; Gage, *The Day Wall Street Exploded*, 312; Klebanow and Jones, *People's Lawyers*, 123.

51. Khan and Azam, "Root Causes of Terrorism," 83–85.

52. McCann, *Terrorism on American Soil*, 1–8.

53. Samaha, *Criminal Procedure*, 528–30.

54. Gage, *The Day Wall Street Exploded*, 6–8; McCann, *Terrorism on American Soil*, 1–8; Samaha, *Criminal Procedure*, 530.

6

"A PRESIDENT HAS TO EXPECT THESE THINGS"

The Truman Assassination Attempt (1950)

America, curious toward foreign characters, stands by its own at all hazards.

—Walt Whitman, "As I Sat Alone by Blue Ontario's Shores"

Harry S. Truman had been president of the United States for five and a half years when two disgruntled would-be assassins tried to kill him on November 1, 1950. Catapulted into the presidency on the death of his popular predecessor, Franklin D. Roosevelt, the man from Independence, Missouri, was widely regarded on his ascension as a little man wearing shoes that were too big for him to fill. After grappling with some of the most daunting crises in American history and winning reelection, Truman had carved out a niche and made the office his own. He had weathered innumerable ups and downs—and he was currently managing a conflict that had erupted on the Korean peninsula—to emerge as a competent, determined, levelheaded, well-respected leader. It would take historians and the public decades to appreciate the many virtues of the plainspoken chief executive, but by 1950 he had settled into a routine that suited him well. He may have been an accidental president, but he had done his best, and his best was good enough for many Americans.[1]

Truman entered his second term in 1949 facing a host of international crises and challenges that would consume the remainder of his presidency. He and his advisers were devastated to learn that the United States no longer enjoyed a nuclear monopoly after the Soviet Union exploded a nuclear device in August 1949. During that same year, Chinese nationalist Chiang Kai-shek and his forces fled China for the safer confines of Formosa, an island off the coast. In Chiang's absence, Mao Tse-tung's communists seized control of the mainland, leading to charges that the United States had "lost China" during Truman's tenure in office. With Americans' concerns over the spreading "Red Menace" increasing, President Truman was under enormous pressure to confront communists in Europe and Asia even if it meant engaging in armed confrontation. He dispatched troops to meet a threat in Korea during 1950, but the president resisted calls for the use of nuclear weapons. In his view, employing such weapons, even in a theoretically limited capacity on the battlefield, would enlarge the conflict and lead to another world war, this time with the potential to annihilate the world. He preferred to support European allies in the North Atlantic Treaty Organization and contain the spread of communism elsewhere. The administration's containment policy was a controversial stance in 1950—Truman and his key advisers were denounced as "soft" on communism and weak appeasers, afraid to stand up to Sino-Soviet aggression—but the wisdom of avoiding a nuclear exchange and containing communism would be borne out across the larger canvas of history later in the twentieth century.[2]

Of all the issues that President Truman faced on that November day in 1950 when two gunmen stormed the building where he napped, the question of nationhood for the island of Puerto Rico was not a top priority. Nonetheless, despite his preoccupation with other pressing issues, he had adopted a more favorable attitude toward Puerto Rico than any other president in U.S. history. Truman had named the first native Puerto Rican as governor of the island, and he had argued in favor of extending Social Security benefits to citizens there. Facing a multitude of domestic and international issues, the president was oblivious to the tumultuous Puerto Rican nationalist forces gathering against him, but he was not an unsympathetic autocrat. As it turned out, the attack was not aimed at Truman the man, but Truman the symbol of American military and political might. It was simply a question of motive meets opportunity that November day. As the White House was being renovated, the president and Mrs. Truman were staying temporarily at nearby Blair House, a residence much less fortified than the traditional presidential compound. Recognizing a prime opportunity to remake American history, two determined Puerto Rican zealots resolved to storm Blair House and cut down a symbol of American imperialism.[3]

Harry Truman was not the first or last American president to be targeted by assassins. The most infamous attack on a president occurred when John

Wilkes Booth shot and killed Abraham Lincoln on April 14, 1865, at Ford's Theatre in Washington, D.C. This notorious deed, coming at the end of the American Civil War, did much to ensure Lincoln's hallowed place in the pantheon of great Americans. Charles J. Guiteau, usually described as a "disgruntled office seeker," assassinated President James A. Garfield in 1881, during Garfield's fifth month in office. Twenty years later, on September 6, 1901, anarchist Leon Czolgosz shot President William McKinley during McKinley's visit to the Pan-American Exposition in Buffalo, New York. The president managed to hang on for eight days before he succumbed to his injuries. On November 22, 1963, President John F. Kennedy was slain by an assassin's bullet as he rode in a motorcade in Dallas, Texas.[4]

The list of unsuccessful presidential attacks, although not as well known as the litany of assassinations, remains alarmingly long. In 1835, Andrew Jackson famously came face to face with an assailant who misfired two pistols aimed at the president at point-blank range. In 1912, a deranged saloon keeper shot former president Theodore Roosevelt in the chest as the Bull Moose candidate campaigned for another term in office. TR survived without major injury because the bullet struck a spectacles case as well as a thick speech folded inside his jacket pocket. Twenty-one years later, President-elect Franklin D. Roosevelt barely escaped an assassin's bullet that killed Chicago Mayor Anton Cermak. More recently, President Gerald Ford faced female would-be assassins on two separate occasions in September 1975. On March 30, 1981, a mentally deranged young man, John Hinckley, shot President Ronald Reagan in the chest in a desperate bid to attract the attention of a comely young actress. Reagan survived the encounter, but he nearly died and was never the same afterward.[5]

The attack on President Truman can be understood as part of a long line of symbolic actions by individuals seeking to attract attention to a political cause. In some cases, the perpetrator nurses a deep-seated grievance against a particular chief executive, as was the case with John Wilkes Booth and his hatred for President Lincoln. In most instances, the assassin appears more interested in drawing attention to a pet cause than in eliminating a particular individual. The surviving assailant in the Truman case later admitted he was not particularly upset with Harry S. Truman the man; he wished to call attention to the plight of beleaguered Puerto Ricans who had been oppressed by the imperialistic United States for far too many years.[6]

The Puerto Rican nationalists' desire to call attention to their cause, if not their methods, was understandable and rational. With the rare exception of scholars or journalists immersed in Latin American affairs, few Americans knew of the history of the island or its tangled relationship with the United

States. Yet for anyone who paid attention to affairs south of the American border, unrest in Puerto Rico was not new. Beginning decades earlier, Puerto Rican nationalists began expressing anger and frustration toward the U.S. government for perceived outrages perpetrated against their island homeland. For members of the Puerto Rican Nationalist Party, attempts to change Puerto Rico from a nonautonomous territory to a partially self-governing commonwealth were infuriating; to their way of thinking, the island was a victim of colonial oppression. In an age when many colonies threw off the yoke of oppression and foreign tyranny, the nationalists sought to sever ties with the patronizing U.S. government and establish a free and independent nation.[7]

THE RISE OF THE PUERTO RICAN NATIONALIST PARTY

Puerto Rico had been a Spanish outpost for centuries, although beginning in the latter half of the nineteenth century, nationalist forces began to build. The first major uprising occurred in 1868. Spanish authorities struggled to put down the revolt, but the seeds of discontent had been sown. In 1897, Spain approved a charter of autonomy allowing Puerto Ricans to establish an independent government. Although this arrangement provided for an unprecedented level of island autonomy, Spain retained authority to appoint a territorial governor and veto legislative decisions that Madrid deemed objectionable. Despite these limitations, the charter was a step forward for independence because it provided for parliamentary elections and a modicum of democratic reforms. Within a year, a new government held elections and began to debate a variety of issues, including budgetary matters and treaty ratifications.[8]

This promising start was not to last. Puerto Rico's large northern neighbor, the United States, greatly expanded its naval forces during the latter half of the nineteenth century based on the premise that a strong navy, modeled on the British Navy, would do much to ensure American power and hegemony in the Western Hemisphere. As part of this expansion, many opportunistic American leaders debated the possibility of annexing land at strategic points within the Caribbean. Beginning in 1894, the U.S. Naval War College developed plans to operate ships in Puerto Rican waters. Because Spain maintained vested interests in Puerto Rico, such activities would risk triggering reprisals from Spanish authorities. Indeed, according to some American officials, war with Spain was a desired result, a pretext for expanding American power into Latin America.[9]

A few Caribbean leaders desired an expanded American presence in the Caribbean. In 1898, two leaders of the Puerto Rican section of the Cuban Revolutionary Party lobbied U.S. president William McKinley to intervene in Puerto Rican affairs. To influence his decision, Revolutionary Party activists provided detailed information on the Spanish military presence in Puerto Rico. Subsequently, U.S. military reconnaissance forces developed maps and other information that would be helpful if the United States chose to invade the island.[10]

The precipitating event that led to warfare between the United States and Spain in the Caribbean occurred on February 15, 1898, when an American battleship, the USS *Maine*, exploded in Havana Harbor, Cuba. Owing in part to sensationalistic press accounts of the episode, punctuated by the war cry "Remember the Maine," the U.S. government sent an ultimatum to Spain insisting on immediate and unconditional withdrawal of forces from Cuba. Rather than submit to such humiliating demands, Spain broke off diplomatic relations with the United States and declared war. On April 25, the U.S. Congress responded with its own declaration of war. Thus began the "Splendid Little War" of 1898.[11]

It was a mismatched affair from beginning to end. Not only were American forces larger and better equipped than their Spanish counterparts, but the proximity of the United States to the field of battle ensured enormous advantages in supplying and transporting troops and matériel. Between May and August 1898, U.S. military forces confronted the Spanish on several islands, including Puerto Rico. By the end of August, the United States had seized effective control of Puerto Rico. In the Treaty of Paris, signed in December 1898 and ratified by the U.S. Senate in February 1899, Spain renounced all claims to Cuba and ceded Guam and Puerto Rico to the United States. As a bonus, the United States gained control over the Philippines in exchange for $20 million.[12]

U.S. intervention in Puerto Rico brought immediate, measurable reforms to the island. The U.S. dollar became the currency. The U.S. Post Office initiated mail service. In many areas, engineers rebuilt and expanded the crumbling infrastructure. With these reforms came greater participation in the political process, including the establishment of political parties. In 1900, the U.S. Congress passed the Foraker Act, named for Senator Joseph B. Foraker of Ohio, which established procedures for governing Puerto Rico. Under the new law, the president of the United States would appoint the island governor. An executive council comprised of thirty-five members would serve as the primary legislative body, and Puerto Rico was authorized to send a resident commissioner as a nonvoting representative to the U.S. Congress. The statute also created a judicial system similar to the Anglo-American model. Charles Herbert Allen, inaugurated on May 1, 1900, served as the first governor. In the meantime, President McKinley appointed the first executive council in June of that year.[13]

Despite these political reforms, the Foraker Act became unpopular with some Puerto Ricans owing to its heavy-handedness. Both Spanish and English were designated as the official languages of the island, with teaching in the schools conducted predominantly in English. Spanish was treated as a secondary course of study. The act placed strict limits on the amount of land that a native Puerto Rican was permitted to own. Moreover, American sugar companies, interested in harvesting sugarcane in Puerto Rico, enjoyed a decided advantage over local farmers. A Puerto Rican plantation owner was required to rely on local banks to finance his operations while American conglomerates could secure financing elsewhere. In effect, this arrangement allowed American companies to procure capital at lower interest rates than were commonly available to Puerto Ricans. In addition, U.S. tariffs imposed on sugar imported from Puerto Rico put local farmers in an untenable position. In many cases, they were forced to sell their holdings to American sugar companies to avoid exorbitant tariffs that all but ate up their profits. For a later generation of Puerto Rican nationalists, this cozy relationship between the U.S. government and American sugar companies was one of many examples of exploitation attributable to arrogant, greedy, and paternalistic policies.[14]

The new climate of reform ensured that political parties would multiply. Among the first parties to emerge, the Partido Independentista, or Independence Party, founded in 1909, lobbied for autonomy from U.S. interference in island political affairs. By subsequent, far-more-radical standards of the Puerto Rican Nationalist Party, it was a muted effort; however, the first nationalist stirrings were signs of things to come.[15]

The same year the Partido Independentista emerged, Congress enacted the Olmsted Amendment when the Puerto Rican legislature failed to pass a budget. The amendment was designed to rectify weaknesses in the original Foraker Act, but it also highlighted Puerto Rico's dependence on the United States, much to the consternation of nationalist forces. Six years later, a group of Puerto Ricans traveled to the United States to argue in favor of greater island autonomy. Their efforts in part led to the enactment of the Jones Act of 1917, which allowed Puerto Ricans to gain restricted U.S. citizenship and made the island an "organized but unincorporated" territory of the United States.[16]

Following enactment of the Jones Act, Puerto Rican citizens critical of the U.S. role in island politics formed the Partido Nacionalista de Puerto Rico, or the Puerto Rican Nationalist Party. This group, led by José Coll y Cuchi, combined a variety of pro-independent organizations, namely the Nationalist Youth and the Independence Association, under a single umbrella. September 17, 1922, was the generally recognized date for the creation of the party. A united organization effectively consolidated nationalist elements into a potent force, with participants unafraid of armed confrontation if necessary. Two years later, Pedro Albizu Campos, a charismatic Harvard-educated lawyer fluent in English, Spanish, French, German, Portuguese, Italian, Latin, and Greek, joined the party and quickly rose through the ranks to become its vice president. Supremely confident and impatient to bring about change, Campos immediately expressed his displeasure with the slow pace of party activities. During the next six years, Campos and Coll y Cuchi quarreled over party leadership. By May 11, 1930, Campos had deposed his rival, who left the party with a number of dissidents. Campos emerged as president.[17]

The newly ordained leader built his party into the largest independent nationalist organization in Puerto Rico. Throughout the 1930s, he repeatedly sounded the clarion call for independence and arranged activities to trigger violent reprisals from authorities. After clashing with civil officials and suffering from what he viewed as government repression, Campos became more militant and outspoken. A veteran of the U.S. Army during World War I, and a bitter ideologue, he believed that the United States was an inescapably racist nation that could never be reformed. As long as the imperialistic Americans interfered in Puerto Rican affairs, island natives would be degraded and humiliated as second-class citizens in their own land. Campos's resentment deepened after he was imprisoned for taking part in violent uprisings during the 1930s, including the assassination of a Puerto Rican police chief. Although the erudite activist was not a mainstream political figure, he galvanized poor and disenfranchised Puerto Ricans who sympathized with his cause.[18]

A series of events in the 1930s engendered sympathy for the party's ideals, if not always for its methods, and demonstrated the party's penchant for violence. On April 6, 1932, a group of nationalists marched to the capital building in San Juan to protest against the Puerto Rican flag, which many Puerto Ricans believed had been forced on them by the Americans. Critics preferred an earlier flag design that predated American intervention. During the April 6 demonstration, a nationalist caught in the pushing and shoving fell from a second-floor balcony and died. The chaotic gathering alarmed many Puerto Rican leaders, who condemned the spirit of lawlessness that seemed to accompany protests by the Puerto Rican Nationalist Party. Although the incident could not be characterized as a riot, the actions of an unruly mob were barely contained.[19]

Worse was yet to come. On October 24, 1935, the day after a student assembly at the University of Puerto Rico declared Albizu Campos a persona non grata, a fight broke out between Campos supporters and local police. Four party members and one policeman were killed. This melee triggered a series of increasingly violent events in the following months and years. On February 23, 1936, two nationalists assassinated Colonel Elisha Francis Riggs, the U.S.-appointed police chief. In retaliation, police officers captured the two assailants, transported them back to police headquarters, and summarily executed them without the benefit of arraignment or trial. Five months later, Campos and several followers received lengthy prison sentences for their part in conspiring to overthrow the U.S. government in Puerto Rico.[20]

The series of escalating confrontations culminated in a bloody affair known thereafter as the Ponce Massacre. On March 21, 1937, a peaceful gathering of Puerto Rican Nationalist Party members in the southern city of Ponce degenerated into a hostile struggle with police. Originally, a parade march had been designed to commemorate the cessation of slavery in Puerto Rico under the authority of the Spanish National Assembly in 1873. Disgruntled party leaders also used the occasion to protest Campos's incarceration. Police officials, concerned that the unruly crowd would riot, waded into the throng with guns drawn. Eventually they opened fire on unarmed citizens, killing twenty and severely injuring more than two hundred others. In some cases, the wounded and dead were shot in the back as they ran from the scene. Investigations into the incident suggested that repressive government actions, a poorly trained police force, and a hostile citizenry created explosive conditions that led to the massacre. General Blanton Winship, the American-appointed governor of Puerto Rico, may have issued the order to fire on the protesters, although this point was widely disputed. Whatever the facts, Campos and his followers lost no time in publicizing the atrocity, characterizing it as but one more example of American arrogance and hostility toward Puerto Rico. The Ponce Massacre would resonate with Puerto Rican nationalists for decades.[21]

Governor Winship became an increasingly unpopular figure. A little more than a year after the Ponce Massacre, on July 25, 1938, the governor ordered a military parade in Ponce to celebrate the American invasion of Puerto Rico. The parade usually occurred in San Juan, but Winship unwisely sought to send a message to nationalists that his administration would not be cowed by continued violence. During the parade, members of the Nationalist Party attempted to assassinate the hated symbol of American hegemony. As Winship rose to give a speech, shots rang out, killing police colonel Luis Irizarry, who sat next to the governor. Predictably, pandemonium reigned. The governor managed to escape unharmed, but more than thirty people suffered injuries.[22]

With Albizu Campos safely tucked away in prison for a decade, the island of Puerto Rico witnessed fewer acts of violence as the 1930s gave way to the 1940s. The Puerto Rican Nationalist Party continued to exist, but without its charismatic leader at the helm, the organization proved to be much less effective than it had been in years past. By the time Campos returned from his prison term in 1947, plans were afoot to make Puerto Rico a commonwealth of the United States.[23]

The year before Campos's return, President Truman had named a new island governor, Jesus T. Piñero. Some nationalists were angry about the regime change. Piñero seemed far too accommodating to the Americans. The point was driven home on June 11, 1948, when Piñero signed the "Ley de la Mordaza" (Gag Law), or Law 53. The new law criminalized the display of the Puerto Rican flag, the singing of patriotic songs, and loose talk of independence. To its numerous detractors, Ley de la Mordaza smacked of the anti-communist laws and loyalty oaths that had become popular in the United States. Although the U.S. Congress enacted legislation to allow Puerto Ricans to vote for their own governor and hold free elections, the Ley de la Mordaza remained a source of indignation for many Puerto Ricans of a nationalist bent.[24]

On July 4, 1950, President Truman signed Public Act 600 allowing Puerto Ricans to draft a constitution as a first step in becoming a U.S. commonwealth. From the standpoint of many Americans, the movement from a protectorate to a commonwealth should have been a welcome development; however, the government's paternalistic action seriously underestimated the fervor among a small group of dedicated nationalists. Back at his party's helm, Campos drafted plans to oppose the increased U.S. presence on the island. As part of this effort, he led a series of protests that became known as the Puerto Rican Nationalist Party Revolts of the 1950s. During the Jayuya Uprising on October 30, nationalist rebels held a town captive for three days. Although the Jayuya Uprising was the best-known nationalist military maneuver of October 1950, it was by no means an isolated incident. Similar armed confrontations occurred in towns throughout Puerto Rico.

U.S. military planes and artillery were employed to put down the rebellion. In the town of Utuado, a determined group of thirty-two nationalists battled local police. When most of the nationalists fell, a group of a dozen retreated to the house of a local man, Damián Torres. Four American P-47 Thunderbolt planes strafed the Torres residence, eventually forcing the nine surviving nationalists to surrender. After the men were taken into custody, they were marched into the town plaza. Stripped of their belts, shoes, and personal belongings, the prisoners were herded behind the police station and gunned down. Four men died. This episode became known as La Masacre de Utuado, or the Utuado Massacre.[25]

In the aftermath of the bloodshed, many nationalist leaders were arrested. Albizu Campos was among them. The Puerto Rican Nationalist Party had enjoyed a renaissance of sorts after their leader had returned from prison in 1947. Just three short years later, their jubilation was cut short. The nationalists were despondent, fearing that the island would forever remain under the yoke of its imperialistic neighbor to the north. For others, however, Campos's latest arrest suggested that other means must be employed to highlight the plight of Puerto Rican nationalists.[26]

THE ASSAULT ON PRESIDENT TRUMAN

Griselio Torresola and Oscar Collazo were two committed ideologues incensed at Campos's persecution and the indignities visited on Puerto Rico during the twentieth century. Torresola hailed from a family committed to the Puerto Rican independence cause, while Collazo had embraced the movement on his own. Meeting up in New York City not long before their attack on Truman, the two men recognized in each other a kindred spirit. They shared an impoverished background and little formal schooling, although Torresola, the younger of the two, was more of a loner and had not enjoyed a stable work history. Each man reveled in his disaffection, and each longed to participate in a dramatic, self-aggrandizing action that would call attention to the cause.[27]

Despite their superficial similarities, they were very different men in temperament and demeanor. Collazo was the more polished of the two, and he had known Campos personally. He had been born in Puerto Rico in 1914, and after his father died he had lived with his brother, a member of the Liberal Party, in Jayuya, the site of the later nationalist uprising. Young Oscar participated in nationalist demonstrations and shared his brother's anger about U.S. domination over Puerto Rico. After he moved to New

York City in 1941, he married a divorcee with two young daughters and began working in a metal polishing factory. Collazo came face to face with his idol, Albizu Campos, when Campos was being treated at a New York City hospital. Collazo was so impressed with this man, and with the nationalist movement, he began working with the New York branch of the Nationalist Party. He eventually became the group's secretary.[28]

Unlike Torresola, Collazo was a calm, orderly gentleman, subsequently described as a devoted husband and father. Whether he was as placid as later accounts suggested, Collazo was at least able to hold a job and participate in society. By contrast, Torresola was unstable, a bit of a thug by most accounts. Whereas Collazo would attract little undue attention because he fit in so well with his surroundings, Torresola was known to excite attention wherever he went. He left trouble in his wake.[29]

In October 1950, when they learned that a popular uprising had failed, Torresola and Collazo were united in their grief and outrage. To these dedicated partisans, the failure of the nationalist movement to secure Puerto Rican independence was yet another humiliation in a long line of humiliations. If their beloved island was to ever enjoy autonomy, an audacious event must publicize their cause. They decided to act. The goal was simple even if implementation proved to be difficult; they must call attention to the plight of the oppressed Puerto Rican by whatever means would capture the most attention. The two men recognized that gunmen assaulting the president of the United States would generate publicity unlike anything else they could do. Because so few Americans understood conditions in Puerto Rico and because official U.S. policy was unlikely to change in the near future, they were desperate to highlight the righteousness of their goal. As Collazo later explained, "by coming to Washington and making some kind of demonstration in the capital of this nation, we would be in a better situation to make the American people understand the real situation in Puerto Rico; that Puerto Rico has no government; there is no Government of Puerto Rico."[30]

The men were not especially upset with President Truman; shooting him seemed to be the most effective means of publicizing their discontent with American policy. "Truman was . . . just a symbol of the system," Collazo later noted. "You don't attack the man, you attack the system." Had another man served as the chief magistrate of the United States, the two nationalists would have been no more or less determined to cut him down with a bullet. Nor were the would-be assassins naive about the repercussions of their act. They recognized that escape would be difficult and that immediate change in American policy was unlikely; nonetheless, they believed that action, any action, was preferable to the status quo. If Puerto Rico was to escape the yoke of American oppression, violence was necessary.[31]

For all of his activist zeal and willingness to engage in violence, Oscar Collazo was not trained in field operations. If he were to take part in the assassination attempt, he would need to prepare assiduously. The first task was to learn to shoot. An accomplished gunman, Torresola instructed his partner on the proper procedure for loading and handling guns, and the two men continually rehearsed. Even as the firearms training progressed, the confederates also studied the layout in and around Blair House. They must know every nook and cranny, every doorway and hallway within the building, if they were to successfully navigate their way through the president's protective force and shoot him dead.[32]

Killing an American president is no easy task, but charging Blair House was considerably less complicated and risky than attacking the White House. Situated across the street from 1600 Pennsylvania Avenue, Blair House was typically used to accommodate official guests of the American government. Because structural defects were being repaired in the White House, Truman and his family had temporarily moved into the guest quarters. The edifice sported a small five-foot yard with a low hedge and a shoulder-high iron fence next to the road. Unbeknownst to the assassins, President Truman's bedroom window was located directly above the main entrance to Blair House and was unprotected.[33]

During the year 1950, Torresola methodically gathered weapons in advance of the assault on the American president. He and Collazo patiently gamed out the scenario, waiting for the right moment to make their move. They recognized a prime opportunity in the fall of that year. On October 31, 1950, they donned new suits, bid farewell to their families, boarded a train southbound, and headed to Washington, D.C.[34]

The following morning, Wednesday, November 1, the two men visited Blair House to assess the strength of the president's security detail and consider their options. Despite the advance planning, Collazo and Torresola hesitated to carry out the plan. They briefly discussed engaging in a demonstration on the steps of Blair House in lieu of firing at the president, but this muted action would not be especially newsworthy. They reiterated their devotion to the cause and their willingness to die on behalf of the Puerto Rican nationalist movement, but beyond these vague assurances, the men seemed lost and uncertain of the best method for achieving their objective. They had reached an impasse. After milling about in front of the house in the morning, they went for lunch and returned to their hotel to mull over their options.[35]

After again resolving to go through with their plan, the two men rode in a taxicab back to Blair House, arriving a few minutes after 2:00 p.m. It was an unusually warm day for early November. Three White House policemen were visibly on duty outside of Blair House, but they appeared inattentive. Aside from the heat, it seemed to be just another average day in a series of average days. Citizens strolled along the sidewalks and cars passed as they always did. As was usually the case, the White House personnel struggled to combat the monotony of guard duty.[36]

And so it began. Against the prosaic backdrop, the confederates had agreed on a two-pronged assault. Dressed in unobtrusive dark business suits, Collazo and Torresola appeared to be young divinity students out for a stroll. Nothing in their appearance or demeanor invited special attention or undue scrutiny. In accordance with their plan, each man approached Blair House from opposite directions. Collazo was supposed to approach the front door while Torresola assaulted the rear entrance. If their scheme had any chance at succeeding, the attack must be well coordinated, and initially they must seem nonthreatening to the White House police force.[37]

At the outset, the plan went like clockwork. Each man arrived at his designated location at precisely the correct time. It was 2:19 p.m. Oscar Collazo brazenly walked up behind capital police officer Donald Birdzell, who was standing on the front steps of Blair House, pointed his Walther P38 semiautomatic nine-millimeter pistol at the officer's back, and pulled the trigger at point-blank range. His lack of training and field experience led to the first significant glitch for the assassins. The novice gunman had failed to cock his pistol; consequently, nothing happened. Panicked, Collazo fumbled with the weapon, pounding on it in a frantic effort to take down the officer. Alerted to the commotion, Birdzell turned to face his assailant at exactly the moment the gun discharged, striking him in the knee. Birdzell went down hard.[38]

Collazo had hoped to dispatch the first officer and immediately proceed toward the front door without delay. Fumbling with the weapon had cost precious seconds and significantly reduced the element of surprise. U.S. Secret Service agent Floyd Boring and White House police officer Joseph Davidson stood in the security booth at the east end of Blair House, not far from Birdzell's position. "I'd come out more or less to chat," Boring later explained. When they heard the gunfire, the two men sprang into action. "It all happened so rapidly," Boring remembered. "I didn't really know what the hell was going on."[39]

As the other officers ran toward the direction of the commotion, Birdzell got to his feet and limped into the street, away from the entrance to Blair

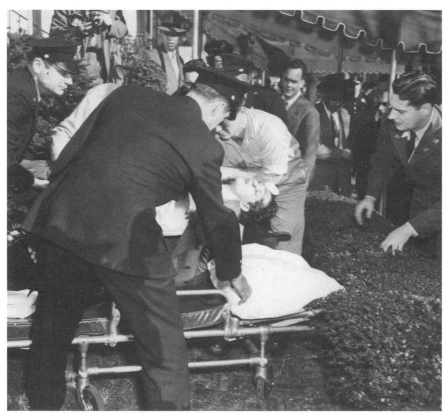

Puerto Rican Nationalist Party member Oscar Collazo loaded into an ambulance. Courtesy of the Granger Collection, New York.

House in a conscious effort to draw the gunman's attention away from the house where President Truman was napping upstairs. This inspired act of grace under pressure caused Collazo to hesitate, thereby providing additional time for Boring and Davidson to arrive on the scene. Instead of charging for the front door, Collazo collapsed onto the steps of Blair House under withering gunfire from Birdzell, Boring, and Davidson. He still intended to gain entry into the building and track down the president, but he was pinned down outside the residence. Even as bullets whizzed around him, occasionally ricocheting off the iron fence, Oscar Collazo fired his gun. He only relented after he was struck by two .38 bullets in the chest and arm. Within minutes, he was surrounded by additional police officers. The grievously wounded would-be killer had missed his opportunity to enter Blair House through the front door.[40]

While Collazo carried out the attack in front of the building, Torresola marched up the west side of Pennsylvania Avenue, approaching a guard booth at the west corner. The strange man apparently began speaking in a loud voice, possibly to divert attention away from Collazo's assault on the front door. Inside the booth, Private Leslie Coffelt turned his head just as his assailant swung inside the small enclosure and fired four shots from a nine-millimeter German Luger semiautomatic pistol. Caught completely by surprise, Coffelt did not have time to reach for his gun. Three shots struck him in the chest and abdomen, and a fourth penetrated his policeman's tunic. Mortally wounded, he slumped in his chair.[41]

White House policeman Joseph Downs, a plainclothes officer who had just paused to talk with Coffelt when the shooting commenced, reached for his weapon as Torresola swung the Luger toward him. Struck in the hip, back, and neck, Downs staggered down the walkway to the basement, opened the door, and crawled inside before Torresola could follow him. This quick-thinking action denied the gunman immediate entry into Blair House. Safely ensconced inside the residence, Downs screamed for help.[42]

In the meantime, Torresola had heard the intense gunfire in front of the building and knew his partner was in trouble. As he rounded the corner of Blair House, he saw Donald Birdzell aiming his service revolver at Oscar Collazo from the south side of Pennsylvania Avenue. Torresola fired his Luger and struck Birdzell in the left knee. Now wounded in both knees, the officer collapsed in pain. He squeezed off several more rounds but finally succumbed to the pain and took no further part in the gun battle.[43]

It was clear that Collazo would not complete the mission, but Torresola might yet gain entry to the house and assassinate the president. If he had immediately charged into the rear entrance, the gunman probably would have found an unobstructed path to the president. Unaware of how close he was to success, he did not take advantage of this golden opportunity. Torresola paused to reload his gun. While he did so, a groggy President Truman, awakened from his nap in the second-floor bedroom, walked over to the window to see what was happening. At the time the president opened his window, Torresola stood approximately thirty feet away. If either man saw the other, he did not acknowledge it.[44]

Truman later understood that a violent confrontation had occurred right outside his bedroom window, but he was unaware of the attack at the time. The president had much on his mind during that November Wednesday. He had recently returned from a meeting with his top general officer, the irascible Douglas MacArthur, on Wake Island in the Pacific Ocean. The two men had plotted strategy for prosecuting the Korean War, a muddled conflict that was not going well. Just that morning, the president had learned from his new CIA director, General Walter Bedell Smith, that the Chinese communists had supplied troops to oppose United Nations troops in North Korea. This unwelcome development was worrisome because it suggested that the war might yet spread to other nations and become World War III. Exhausted from his recent meetings and briefings, Truman had enjoyed a quiet lunch with his wife and mother-in-law before retiring upstairs in Blair House to nap. He was slated to depart at 2:50 p.m. for a ceremony unveiling a statue of British field marshal Sir John Gill at Arlington National Cemetery. His wife and mother-in-law were elsewhere inside Blair House at the time. The president had removed his clothes and was lying on the bed in the front bedroom with the window open during the assault.[45]

Torresola's brief delay to reload his gun allowed Officer Coffelt time to stagger out of the guard booth, aim his pistol at the gunman, and squeeze off one final round. The bullet tore into Torresola's head two inches above

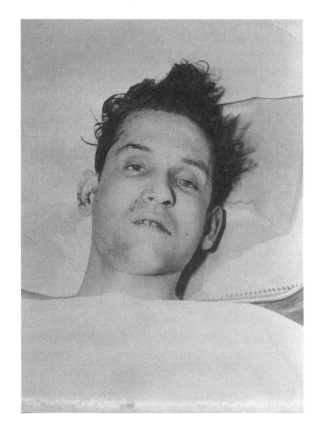

Griselio Torresola's body in the Washington, D.C., morgue. Courtesy of Corbis.

his ear on a slight upward angle, killing him instantly. Leslie Coffelt died four hours later in the hospital. In his last act of heroism, the dying policeman had altered the outcome of the affair. The entire gun battle had lasted less than one minute.[46]

Immediately after the shooting ended, a crowd of people appeared on the scene. Concerned that other assassins might be in the area, a throng of police officers and Secret Service agents converged on Blair House. Alerted to the melee, the White House press corps was not far behind. J. B. West, a White House usher, informed the first lady of the shooting and directed her upstairs. A rumor circulated that Truman had been assassinated, and the story seemed plausible when ambulances appeared in front of Blair House.[47]

With reports of his death greatly exaggerated, the president immediately dressed and bounded down the stairs. He found a chaotic scene, arriving in time to see a group of policemen bending over the prostrate Collazo on the front steps of Blair House. If the president was rattled by the incident, he kept it to himself. According to all accounts, he was composed and unruffled. When someone asked if he still intended to keep his commitment to speak at Arlington National Cemetery, Truman acted as though it had never crossed his mind to cancel the appearance. He responded, "Why, of course."[48]

Within fifteen minutes, he and a group of seven or eight Secret Service agents exited through the back door. The unflappable chief executive delivered his planned speech during the ceremony, never mentioning the incident even as the crowd learned of the assassination attempt through word of mouth. In fact, Truman seemed to have no reaction until he discovered that Officer Coffelt had died. During a subsequent ceremony honoring Coffelt with a plaque placed on the new iron fence in front of Blair House, the genuinely moved, saddened president commented that the fallen officer had been one of the best-liked men on the White House security detail.[49]

When pressed by reporters to comment on the shooting a day later, Truman was philosophical. "A president has to expect these things," he said. He was determined not to let the assassination attempt interfere with his usual routine, which included a morning walk around the city. Despite his best efforts, though, the assassination attempt had changed things. In addition to his usual, heavily armed contingent, Truman now found himself surrounded by at least a dozen additional Secret Service agents. For a man who treasured his privacy and ability to navigate among the citizenry, the president felt more imprisoned than ever before. In public, he remained contemptuous of the failed assassins, remarking that they were as "stupid is they could be." His schedule had been printed in the morning newspaper. Anyone who wished to shoot the man could have waited at the curb until Truman emerged on his way to the ceremony at Arlington National Cemetery. "I know I could organize a better program than they put on," he observed.[50]

On November 5, the president confided to his diary that he retained faith in the goodness of human beings. "Most of the people in the USA are kindly happy people and they show it by smiling, waving and shouting," he wrote. Only days after the attempt on his life, he traveled to St. Louis and observed large groups of people lining the parade route. He might have mingled with the well-wishers, but Truman remained safely locked away inside a well-protected automobile. His security detail would take no additional chances with his safety. Despite his brave public face, Truman was no fool; he knew he had escaped with his life through a combination of luck, the bravery of his security detail, and poor timing on the part of the gunmen. He also knew that he could not be cavalier about following the necessary security arrangements in the future. "Because two crackpots

President Harry Truman shown with his wife and daughter three days after the assassination attempt. Courtesy of Abbie Rowe, National Park Service, the Harry S. Truman Library & Museum, National Archives and Records Administration.

or crazy men tried to shoot me a few days ago my good inefficient guards are nervous," he wrote in his diary. "So I'm trying to be as helpful as I can. Would like very much to take a walk this morning but the S[ecret] S[ervice] . . . and the 'Boss' [his wife, Bess] and Margie [his mother-in-law] are worried about me—so I won't take my usual walk." He ended with a refrain shared by many men who have served as the chief executive of the nation: "It's hell to be president."[51]

THE AFTERMATH

Oscar Collazo survived the November 1 gunfight although his partner did not. He was hit by gunfire multiple times, but he eventually recovered from his injuries. During the subsequent trial, Collazo's attorney advised his client to plead insanity; however, the defendant ignored this advice. As with many politically motivated terrorists, Collazo sought to use his day in court as a forum for espousing his views. In fact, press coverage of the proceedings ensured that his original goal of publicizing the plight of Puerto Rican nationalism would be realized. Charged with homicide in the death of Officer Coffelt as well as several counts of assault with intent to kill, the defendant faced long, difficult odds of acquittal. As everyone expected, he was convicted of all charges and sentenced to death. Ironically, the intended target of Collazo's assassination attempt, President Truman, commuted the sentence to life imprisonment. Truman's motivation remains open to interpretation. Perhaps he intended to extend compassion to his would-be assassin by sparing the man from execution, or perhaps the savvy president sought to deny Collazo a martyr's death. In any case, Collazo avoided the executioner. He remained in prison until 1979, when President Jimmy Carter commuted his sentence.[52]

The world had changed markedly during Collazo's years in prison. Nonetheless, he found isolated enclaves of support. In Chicago, Illinois, in the Puerto Rican Cultural Center, a pro-independence mural proudly included a depiction of Collazo and Torresola, heroes of the Puerto Rican nationalist movement. He also found a sympathetic audience in the person of Cuban president Fidel Castro. Collazo returned to Puerto Rico to live out his years as a symbol of the nationalist ethos. Until his death at the age of eighty on February 21, 1994, he remained committed to the cause of Puerto Rican independence.[53]

The attempted assassination of President Truman was not the last, nor the most dramatic, act of violence that Puerto Rican nationalists leveled against the United States. On March 1, 1954, four partisans—Lolita Lebron, Irving Flores Rodriguez, Rafael Cancel Miranda, and Andres Figueroa Cordero—entered the U.S. Capitol building in Washington, D.C., carrying automatic pistols. Pushing into the visitors' gallery overlooking the floor of the U.S. House of Representatives, the gun-toting zealots happened upon 240 representatives of the 83rd Congress debating an immigration bill. Although Capitol Hill security officers asked if any of the four were carrying cameras, the guards never searched the partisans for weapons. In an era before metal detectors were posted in the lobby of federal buildings, smuggling weapons into the U.S. Capitol was surprisingly easy.[54]

As the oblivious congressmen exchanged barbs, gunfire suddenly erupted throughout the chamber. Bullets ricocheted off marble columns and penetrated wooden tables. Lebron yelled "Viva Puerto Rico Libre," or "Long live free Puerto Rico." Her fellow attackers draped a Puerto Rican flag over a nearby balcony as they continued firing in the House chamber.[55]

While the startled representatives and their staff members threw themselves to the floor or ran for the exits, five men were wounded, one severely. Congressman Alvin Bentley, a Republican from Michigan, suffered a bullet wound to the chest. Emergency room doctors initially believed his injuries to be fatal; however, he survived the attack following surgery. Tennessee congressman Clifford Davis took a bullet in the leg while Iowa congressman Ben Jensen was struck in the back. Both men eventually recovered. George Hyde Fallon of Maryland and Kenneth A. Roberts of Alabama were also injured, but they recovered as well.[56]

Congressman James Van Zandt, a Navy combat veteran, carefully crawled up the stairs and grabbed Rafael Miranda before the assailant could escape. In the meantime, other bystanders sprang into action, subduing the attackers until police arrived. As with the attack on Truman, the Capitol Hill assailants had achieved their goals of publicizing the Puerto Rican independence movement and were unrepentant. Inside her purse, Lebron had written a defiant note explaining her actions: "Before God and the world, my blood claims for the independence of Puerto Rico. My life I give for the freedom of my country. This is a cry for victory in our struggle for independence. . . . The United States of America is betraying the sacred principles of mankind in their continuous subjugation of my country. . . . I take responsible [sic] for all."[57]

With the exception of Andres Figueroa Cordero, who died of cancer in 1975, Lebron and her co-defendants, along with Oscar Collazo, won release from prison when President Carter pardoned the nationalists in 1979. Lebron remained committed to the cause of Puerto Rican nationalism, returning to her island home where she lived until her death in 2010. Throughout the years, she bristled at the term "terrorist," claiming that she and her colleagues did not deserve scorn and derision. "Who calls me a terrorist?" she angrily asked an interviewer toward the end of her life. "The most terrorist country in the world," she said, referring to the United States. "What other country dropped the atomic bomb? And they call me a terrorist. I went to the U.S. in a fight against terrorism."[58]

LESSONS LEARNED

For scholars who study the causes and effects of terrorism, political activism remains one of the most frustrating sources of extremist violence. If the facile thesis that terrorism is directly attributable to poverty and a sense of hopelessness were inarguably true, crafting solutions would be relatively straightforward. If corrupt, authoritarian governments were the sole source of substate terrorism, replacing those governments with more democratically minded regimes would be a sensible solution. If illiteracy, inequality, or religious extremism were the sole culprits, resolving the issue would be possible. Political terrorism complicates matters considerably because it suggests that neither the causes nor the effects of terrorism are linear or easily understood outside their context. Terrorists driven by political motives may be poor religious extremists, or believe themselves to be part of an oppressed minority, but ultimately they see themselves as champions of "the cause" first and foremost. To understand their actions, one must first understand the cause.

In the case of the Puerto Rican nationalists who attacked President Truman, their grievances were rooted in events stretching back decades. One of the assailants, Oscar Collazo, admitted that Truman the man was not the target of the attack. Because the president was a symbol of the U.S. government, he was a convenient target. Truman had already done a great deal for Puerto Ricans, but he was not focused on Caribbean affairs at the time of the attack. Therefore, it is difficult to determine what the president could have done to forestall an assassination attempt. Anything short of immediate autonomy for the island probably would not have placated Collazo and Torresola. Puerto Rican nationalists did not consider themselves terrorists; they were freedom fighters employing violence to call attention to their dire circumstances and the lack of power they had. They did not believe they could use the normal channels of political communication and dissent. For these reasons, identifying and preventing terrorist attacks owing to political causes is always challenging.[59]

Political terrorists, especially would-be assassins, are difficult to thwart because, quite frankly, their cause usually is advanced by the violent act. Collazo and Torresola desperately sought a means for focusing attention on the plight of Puerto Rico. Nothing else they could have done would have been as newsworthy as attacking President Truman. Even if a sympathetic but nonviolent nationalist had intervened to dissuade them from attempting to shoot the president, what words could a conciliator have used to buttress his case? No books, pamphlets, newspaper articles, or public demonstrations would have seared the image of an oppressed Puerto Rico into the American psyche as quickly or unforgettably as a physical assault on the president of the United States. For a rational actor who could never envision undertaking such an extremist, heinous act of violence, the audacity of shooting a president is beyond the pale. Yet as far as the assailants were concerned, the ends justified the means. Political terrorism is commonplace because it works; it captures public attention in a way that no other act can or ever will.

This dismal assessment is not to suggest that terrorism, like the weather, must be stoically endured. As will be discussed in the conclusion of this book, measures can be employed to minimize the possibility of terrorist attacks. When disaffected parties are provided at outlet for expression, some would-be terrorists on the fringes can be convinced to express their grievances through other means. For hard-core extremists, however, nothing short of 100 percent success in advancing the cause will suffice. In those cases, when the causes cannot be controlled, the effects must be mitigated.

NOTES

1. Kane, *Facts about the Presidents*, 366–79; McCullough, *Truman*, 808; Mead, *Special Providence*, 257.

2. Gaddis, *Strategies of Containment*, 24–52; McCullough, *Truman*, 607–8.

3. Kennedy, "Truman Death Aim Denied by Collazo," A32; Kihss, "'Sublime Heroism' Cited in Shooting," A14.

4. June, *Introduction to Executive Protection*, 16–17, 23–26; Kane, *Facts about the Presidents*, 184–86, 230, 270, 415–16; McCann, *Terrorism on American Soil*, 86–87; Millard, *Destiny of the Republic*, 131–32.

5. June, *Introduction to Executive Protection*, 19–21; Kane, *Facts about the Presidents*, 99, 280–81, 358; Wilber, *Rawhide Down*, 79–87.

6. Kennedy, "Truman Death Aim Denied by Collazo," A32; McCann, *Terrorism on American Soil*, 86–87.

7. Dietz, *Economic History of Puerto Rico*, 160–61; Kihss, "'Sublime Heroism' Cited in Shooting," A14; Smith, "Shoot-out on Pennsylvania Avenue," 16–17.

8. Dietz, *Economic History of Puerto Rico*, 75–77; Jimenez de Wagenheim, *Puerto Rico's Revolt for Independence*, xii–xiv.

9. Dietz, *Economic History of Puerto Rico*, 79–80; Foner, *The Spanish-Cuban-American War*, ix.

10. Dietz, *Economic History of Puerto Rico*, 81–82, Graves, *The Spanish-American War*, 8–9.

11. Dietz, *Economic History of Puerto Rico*, 80–82; Graves, *The Spanish-American War*, 10–11.

12. Graves, *The Spanish-American War*, 41.

13. Ayala and Bergad, "Rural Puerto Rico in the Twentieth Century Reconsidered," 67; Dietz, *Economic History of Puerto Rico*, 88–92.

14. Ayala and Bergad, "Rural Puerto Rico in the Twentieth Century Reconsidered," 71–72; Dietz, *Economic History of Puerto Rico*, 88–92; Foner, *The Spanish Cuban-American War*, 267; Pico, *History of Puerto Rico*, 242.

15. Ayala and Bernabe, *Puerto Rico in the American Century*, 56–57.

16. Ayala and Bernabe, *Puerto Rico in the American Century*, 57–58; Brereton and Martinez-Vergne, *General History of the Caribbean*, xxi, 335.

17. Ayala and Bernabe, *Puerto Rico in the American Century*, 105–9; Flores, *The History of Puerto Rico*, xxiii; Pico, *History of Puerto Rico*, 256.

18. Ayala and Bernabe, *Puerto Rico in the American Century*, 105–7.

19. Brereton and Martinez-Vergne, *General History of the Caribbean*, 619.

20. Ayala and Bernabe, *Puerto Rico in the American Century*, 110–11; Flores, *The History of Puerto Rico*, 91; Pico, *History of Puerto Rico*, 256–57.

21. Flores, *The History of Puerto Rico*, 91, 133; Pico, *History of Puerto Rico*, 257.

22. Ayala and Bernabe, *Puerto Rico in the American Century*, 116.

23. Pico, *History of Puerto Rico*, 257–58.

24. Dietz, *Economic History of Puerto Rico*, 233; Flores, *The History of Puerto Rico*, xxiii.

25. Ayala and Bernabe, *Puerto Rico in the American Century*, 165–67; Flores, *The History of Puerto Rico*, 99.

26. Smith, "Shoot-out on Pennsylvania Avenue," 16–17.

27. McCann, *Terrorism on American Soil*, 87–88; Smith, "Shoot-out on Pennsylvania Avenue," 16–17.

28. Clarke, *American Assassins*, 65–66; Hunter and Bainbridge, *American Gunfight*, 112–13; McCann, *Terrorism on American Soil*, 87–88.

29. McCann, *Terrorism on American Soil*, 88; Smith, "Shoot-out on Pennsylvania Avenue," 16–17.

30. Clarke, *American Assassins*, 69; Kennedy, "Truman Death Aim Denied by Collazo," A32; McCann, *Terrorism on American Soil*, 88–89; McCullough, *Truman*, 809–10.

31. McCullough, *Truman*, 812.

32. McCann, *Terrorism on American Soil*, 88–89; McCullough, *Truman*, 810; Smith, "Shoot-out on Pennsylvania Avenue," 17–19.

33. Clarke, *American Assassins*, 71; McCullough, *Truman*, 808–9; Smith, "Shoot-out on Pennsylvania Avenue," 17–19.

34. "Oscar Collazo, 80, Truman Attacker in '50," A16; Smith, "Shoot-out on Pennsylvania Avenue," 17–19.

35. Kennedy, "Truman Death Aim Denied by Collazo," A32; Kihss, "'Sublime Heroism' Cited in Shooting," A14; Smith, "Shoot-out on Pennsylvania Avenue," 18–20.

36. McCann, *Terrorism on American Soil*, 89–90; Smith, "Shoot-out on Pennsylvania Avenue," 18–20.

37. McCann, *Terrorism on American Soil*, 89–90; McCullough, *Truman*, 809–10; Smith, "Shoot-out on Pennsylvania Avenue," 16.

38. McCann, *Terrorism on American Soil*, 90; Smith, "Shoot-out on Pennsylvania Avenue," 18–20.

39. McCullough, *Truman*, 810; Smith, "Shoot-out on Pennsylvania Avenue," 18–20.

40. Hunter and Bainbridge, *American Gunfight*, 106–8; McCullough, *Truman*, 809–10; Smith, "Shoot-out on Pennsylvania Avenue," 18–20.

41. McCullough, *Truman*, 810; Smith, "Shoot-out on Pennsylvania Avenue," 19–21.

42. McCann, *Terrorism on American Soil*, 90–91; McCullough, *Truman*, 810–11.

43. McCann, *Terrorism on American Soil*, 90–91; Smith, "Shoot-out on Pennsylvania Avenue," 19.

44. Hunter and Bainbridge, *American Gunfight*, 160; McCullough, *Truman*, 811; Smith, "Shoot-out on Pennsylvania Avenue," 19–21.

45. Hunter and Bainbridge, *American Gunfight*, 159–60; McCullough, *Truman*, 808–13.

46. McCann, *Terrorism on American Soil*, 91; McCullough, *Truman*, 810; "Oscar Collazo, 80, Truman Attacker in '50," A16; Smith, "Shoot-out on Pennsylvania Avenue," 19–21.

47. McCann, *Terrorism on American Soil*, 91; McCullough, *Truman*, 811; Smith, "Shoot-out on Pennsylvania Avenue," 20–21.

48. McCann, *Terrorism on American Soil*, 91; McCullough, *Truman*, 811.

49. McCullough, *Truman*, 811–12.

50. McCann, *Terrorism on American Soil*, 91; McCullough, *Truman*, 811–13.

51. McCullough, *Truman*, 812–13; Smith, "Shoot-out on Pennsylvania Avenue," 21.

52. McCann, *Terrorism on American Soil*, 91; "Oscar Collazo, 80, Truman Attacker in '50," A16.

53. "Oscar Collazo, 80, Truman Attacker in '50," A16.

54. Kihss, "'Sublime Heroism' Cited in Shooting," A14; McCann, *Terrorism on American Soil*, 93–97.

55. McCann, *Terrorism on American Soil*, 94.

56. Kihss, "'Sublime Heroism' Cited in Shooting," A14; McCann, *Terrorism on American Soil*, 94–95.

57. McCann, *Terrorism on American Soil*, 95.

58. Kihss, "'Sublime Heroism' Cited in Shooting," A14; McCann, *Terrorism on American Soil*, 94–95.

59. Khan and Azam, "Root Causes of Terrorism," 83–85; McCann, *Terrorism on American Soil*, 1–8.

7

"THE KLAN IS BACK ON THE MARKET"

The Sixteenth Street Bombing and the Civil Rights Movement (1963)

Woe! Woe!
Thou hast destroy'd
The beautiful world
With violent blow;
'Tis shiver'd! 'tis shatter'd!

—Johann Wolfgang von Goethe, *Faust*, Part I

Persons unfamiliar with the history of terrorism on American soil may be tempted to assume that foreign subversives are the primary cause of violence directed against Americans. After September 11, 2001, some alarmed citizens succumbed to hysteria. In the search for answers to the root causes of terrorism, it is tempting to attribute mass killings and shadowy conspiracies to foreigners who seek to undermine the American republic. Those presuppositions are sometimes factually accurate. Yet many terrorist attacks in U.S. history have been perpetrated by domestic sources. In the desperate scramble to fortify the nation's borders, figuratively walling out outsiders, we inadvertently leave ourselves vulnerable to the enemy within.

The enemy occasionally consists of citizens struggling to preserve the status quo. Frightened traditionalists, fearful of losing the "American way of life," lash out at what they perceive to be the source of their troubles. This lashing out can be appallingly virulent when convenient targets, often objectified as "the other," are present in the community. As a case in point, consider the grassroots civil rights movement that rose to prominence during the 1950s and 1960s. The movement involved numerous acts of civil disobedience. Although many civil rights protesters professed adherence to a doctrine of nonviolence, the highly visible nature of their activities and the resultant media exposure ensured that reactionary elements, incensed at the assault on traditional values, would resort to physical attacks. Triggering violence was not an ancillary movement goal; it was a primary objective. Nonviolent protesters depended on violent reactions to highlight the justice of their cause. On the few occasions when traditionalist civic leaders refused to sanction violence, such as in the Albany movement of 1961–1962, civil rights leaders floundered in the aftermath of peaceful demonstrations. If fundamental change was to result in a desegregated America, nonviolent demonstrators depended on violent reactionaries to generate worldwide sympathy to the cause.[1]

The annals of the 1960s included many episodes of brutality, some of which met the definition of terrorism, and some of which did not. In fact, the ubiquity of such episodes and the diverse nature of the attacks presented difficulties for students of domestic terrorism. Questions abounded: When was a physical assault a matter for the criminal justice system, and when did the assault rise to the level of a terrorist attack? What happened if the criminal justice system had been perverted by law enforcement personnel who were sympathetic to the attackers? Were the numbers of participants involved—whether as assailants or potential victims—crucial, or were the motivations of the participants the paramount consideration in characterizing an incident as terroristic? Even if an agreed-upon definition of terrorism could be reached, what did it matter in the final analysis?

Assuming that a definition does matter, many episodes that occurred during the civil rights movement probably would qualify as terrorist acts, notably the attack on the Freedom Riders in Alabama in 1961; the murder of the National Association for the Advancement of Colored People (NAACP) activist Medgar Evers in Mississippi in 1963; the murder of three civil rights workers, James Chaney, Andrew Goodman, and Michael Schwerner, in Mississippi in 1964; the shooting death of Viola Liuzzo in Alabama in 1965; and the assassination of Dr. Martin Luther King Jr. in Tennessee in 1968, among others. These stories continue to be told and retold as historians grapple with the meaning of equal justice under law. Many books have been, and will be, written about the civil rights struggle and the terrorist attacks perpetrated against the activists.[2]

A single chapter cannot recount the complex fits and starts of this turbulent period in American history. For the purposes of this book, however, a single incident stands out as emblematic, one of the best known, and most horrific, acts of terrorism that occurred during the twentieth-century civil rights movement. In September 1963, four little girls died as a result of a dynamite blast that rocked the foundations of the Sixteenth Street Baptist Church in Birmingham, Alabama. The bombing, which occurred after four white supremacists under the auspices of the Ku Klux Klan (KKK) deliberately placed explosives near the church basement, highlighted the atrocities sometimes perpetrated against blacks in the United States. The random nature of the victims—four little girls died because they happened to be in the wrong place at the wrong time, but any number of people could have been killed, stoking fears of violence and terror lurking around every corner—was especially dismaying. Although terrorists have a purpose in formulating and implementing their plans, their actions frequently strike fear in the hearts of the populace because they appear to be random. KKK members picked a symbolic target that was important in the black community, but the identity of the specific victims was left to chance. The message to blacks was clear—if you deign to stray beyond the accepted boundaries of segregated communities, you or your loved ones could be struck down when you least expect it. Accordingly, if any act of violence during the civil rights movement would qualify as a "terrorist" attack, surely it was the unprovoked assault on innocent churchgoers worshipping inside the Sixteenth Street Baptist Church.[3]

Opponents of the civil rights movement contended that Dr. King and other civil rights leaders were rabble-rousers and communist sympathizers determined to undermine the American republic. Although this histrionic interpretation largely has been discredited by all but the most partisan, proto-Southern historians of the twenty-first century, the explanation appealed to many mainstream white Americans living in the 1960s. To this way of thinking, the struggles of that decade did not involve a fundamental disparity in the treatment of white and black citizens. Instead, demonstrators who assailed the status quo fundamentally threatened the health and integrity of the nation. The English philosopher Thomas Hobbes once argued that maintaining a strong sovereign, no matter how brutal or undemocratic, was preferable to undermining the legitimacy of that sovereign and potentially reverting to a pregovernment state of nature. For a committed Hobbesian, any attempt at reforming the regime was risky because it potentially eroded the sovereign's legitimacy.[4]

Subsequent philosophers, historians, and activists have rejected Hobbes's defense of the status quo. In fact, the health of the regime is enhanced when incremental reform is allowed, because piecemeal modifications generally forestall violent revolutions. Even incremental reforms, however, may trigger violent reprisals when protectors of the status quo feel threatened by the onslaught of new ideas. Frightened of change, no matter how slow and deliberative, traditionalists justify their actions as necessary to preserving law and order in the community. Thus, if Dr. King and leaders of the civil rights movement insisted on attacking established societal values, participants in the movement must be prepared for violent confrontation.[5]

The Sixteenth Street Baptist Church bombing is a crucial incident in the civil rights movement because even apologists for violence perpetrated against demonstrators would be hard-pressed to justify the brutal murder of four innocent girls. Before Birmingham, mainstream whites living in the 1960s who generally disdained the Ku Klux Klan and the cowardly methods of animalistic, lower-class white supremacists could still tell themselves that Dr. King and the civil rights marchers "had it coming" because they "stirred up trouble." In essence, the average white American could unconsciously embrace the Hobbesian support for a flawed sovereign without necessarily joining the ranks of the white supremacist movement. The Sixteenth Street Baptist Church bombing exposed the unjustifiable brutality of white supremacy. The four girls murdered that day were not rabble-rousers; they had joined no marches; they espoused no ideological or political doctrines; they were not on the front lines of social change. They were four children attending church on a Sunday morning. They were innocent. They had their whole lives ahead of them. They loved, and were loved by, their communities. Their deaths revealed the inequities in the treatment of black citizens in a way that no organized march or rowdy protest or fiery speech ever could. It is no exaggeration to say that the civil rights movement could be divided into two stages: before the Sixteenth Street Baptist Church bombing, and after the bombing.[6]

THE CIVIL RIGHTS MOVEMENT

Black Americans have been a target of systematic violence throughout much of American history. Before the ratification of the Thirteenth Amendment in December 1865, many Negroes had been enslaved and treated as sub-human chattel. Stripped of all legal rights and protections, a slave came to know the harsh language of the lash. The story of slavery across more than two centuries of life on the North American continent was a story of humiliation, degradation, and violence. Defenders of the "peculiar institution" argued that slaves were inherently inferior to whites and therefore were naturally enslaved as part of God's plan for superior creatures to exercise dominion over lesser beings. For the most radical slavery apologists, white slave owners were to be commended for providing food, clothing, shelter, and a way of life for the members of a wretched race. If this explanation strikes modern ears as quaint at best, and offensive at worst, it fared no better among many listeners north of the Mason-Dixon Line during the nineteenth century.[7]

Even if he earned his freedom, a black man in pre–Civil War America faced a world of unremitting racism. Notions of the inferiority of the Negro race were so firmly embedded in the American consciousness that all but the most enlightened of thinkers championed the inequality of the races. Moreover, an egalitarian and philosophical predisposition did not necessarily translate into humane action; staunch advocates of immediate abolitionism often failed to live up to their high handed rhetoric when faced with the realities of living next to, or interacting with, a free person of color. Americans could, and often did, express support for blacks in general and reject the idea of integrating with particular black people. Consequently, freedom in antebellum America was a tenuous concept for persons of a darker hue.[8]

This brief description of the antebellum era does not suggest that all blacks were necessarily victims or that slavery was a monolithic institution. Slaves rebelled against forced labor in numerous ways, large and small. Sometimes they feigned ignorance, mistreated pack animals, destroyed tools and machinery, or ran away from their masters. Outside of the institution, freed people vehemently spoke out against slavery. In 1829, David Walker's pamphlet *Walker's Appeal in Four Articles* provided firsthand details of the inhumanity of human bondage. Former slaves Frederick Douglass, Sojourner Truth, and William Wells Brown, among others, eloquently explained the anti-slavery position through a series of public appearances recounting their lives and experiences as slaves.[9]

The peculiar institution changed as a result of warfare at midcentury. The story of the American Civil War has been told repeatedly and need not be recounted here. Suffice it to say that slavery was a necessary, but insufficient, condition of that conflict. Partisans who argue that the war was caused by constitutional considerations divorced from slavery are disingenuous, while parties who contend that slavery was the sole source of disagreement also distort the historical record. Slavery and race were inextricably tied to the war of 1861–1865. In light of the long-standing tradition of slavery and racism in American history, it is little wonder that numerous issues remained unresolved long after the guns fell silent on the battlefield.[10]

After slavery was outlawed at the end of 1865, race remained a crucial issue in American life. Legal segregation—dubbed "Jim Crow" laws—prevented most blacks from achieving racial equality or economic parity with white citizens. The doctrine of "separate but equal" lived up to the reality of the former but never achieved the promise of the latter. Chapter 3 of this book, which discusses the Colfax Massacre, details to some extent the political struggles during Reconstruction, the time frame in which the black community battled with white supremacists in Louisiana.[11]

"Jim Crow," an epithet applied to the era that commenced a decade after the end of Reconstruction, was a system of laws that kept blacks ensconced in a socially inferior position for generations. The origins of the name remain obscure. Historians believe it can be traced to a popular minstrel song dating from the late 1820s or early 1830s. A white entertainer of the period, Thomas Dartmouth Rice—occasionally known as "T. D." or "Daddy" Rice—performed a song called "Jump Jim Crow" while he wore blackface on stage in 1828. The song "Jump Jim Crow" originally may have referred to a crippled African named Jim Cuff or Jim Crow, who lived at one time in Cincinnati.[12]

As a singer and comedian who delighted in practicing low-brow, broad humor, Rice's performances reflected the crude stereotype of the ignorant, pitiable black man stupidly bumbling through life, much to the merriment of the wise, benevolent whites who looked on the pathetic creature through tears of laughter. Rice frequently was billed as "Daddy Jim Crow." Throughout the 1830s, his act proved to be so popular that many white performers mimicked his style. Minstrel routines sprang up across the country, firmly embedding the image of the amiable black simpleton in the minds of Americans for decades to follow.[13]

Jim Crow laws became prevalent during the 1880s as national political leaders lost interest in protecting blacks from Southern whites who seized control of state governments at the end of federally enforced Reconstruction. In the meantime, when businessmen anxious to promote laissez-faire economic policies revitalized the Republican Party, the party of Lincoln became the party of commerce. Many whites were weary of the war and the struggles that followed; they argued that Reconstruction had solved racial issues as well as they could be solved. It was time to move on to other, more pressing national issues. Blacks clamoring for protection of their rights were left to their own devices.[14]

The period beginning in the 1880s sometimes has been characterized as the "dark night of the Negro." Booker T. Washington, a man born into slavery and reared during the brutal Reconstruction era, was the one shining light to cut through the darkness. Washington made a name for himself by calling for blacks to adhere to a position known as "gradualism." This conservative position suggests that blacks must not pursue radical social change. To do so is to frighten whites and possibly trigger a race war. "I fear the Negro race lays too much stress on its grievances and not enough on its opportunities," Washington told an audience at Fisk University in 1895. In a well-known speech he delivered at the Cotton States and International Exposition in Atlanta, Georgia, on September 18 of that same year, Washington set forth his famous "Atlanta Compromise," urging Negroes to recognize "the importance of cultivating friendly relations with the Southern white man, who is their next-door neighbor." Washington advised, "I would say: 'Cast down your bucket where you are'—cast it down in making friends in every manly way of the people of all races by whom we are surrounded." The only realistic course of action was to seek advancement in "agriculture, mechanics, in commerce, in domestic service, and in the professions."[15]

Washington's supporters praised his approach as pragmatic in light of strained social relations under the Jim Crow regime. This conservative approach, which preempted violent, revolutionary social upheaval, made him the toast of the white world. Under Washington's compromise, blacks would eagerly accept the dirty and demeaning jobs that whites did not desire. Blacks gained something, too; they could scratch out a living without crossing the color line and being harassed—or worse.[16]

Not everyone in the black community shared Booker T. Washington's willingness to compromise. As the twentieth century dawned, W. E. B. DuBois, a classically educated black intellectual from the northern United States, contended that Washington's accommodationist approach was popular with whites because Negroes were transformed into second-class citizens. Negroes would never rise in accordance with their talents as long as legal segregation existed. A man of letters, social activist, and co founder of the NAACP, DuBois penned many influential works, including his seminal *The Souls of Black Folk*, a 1903 polemic attacking the existing social order. "Mr. Washington came with a simple definite programme at the psychological moment when the nation was a little ashamed of having bestowed so much sentiment on Negroes and was concentrating its energies on Dollars," he wrote. "His programme of industrial education, conciliation of the South, and submission and silence as to civil and political rights was not wholly original. . . . But Mr. Washington first indissolubly linked these things; he put enthusiasm, unlimited energy, and perfect faith into this programme, and changed it from a by-path into a veritable Way of Life."[17]

The debate between proponents of gradualism and activists who sought fundamental and immediate change continued well into the new century.

During those years, DuBois's NAACP, established in 1909, used a variety of methods to combat racial discrimination, including litigation, lobbying elected officials, and urging improved education for all Americans to appreciate the value of citizenship and the promise of equality under the law. Despite these efforts, for many black Americans, beginning around 1910 and continuing for six decades thereafter, life in the Southern United States was untenable; a change in geography was needed. Thus began the Great Migration, a time in which nearly seven million blacks relocated from the Old South to the northeastern and midwestern United States.[18]

The Jim Crow regime was so strongly entrenched in American life that few visible signs of change could be identified until shortly after World War II. Even in places where blacks were not restricted by legal segregation, racism was widespread. Vibrant black communities arose in small enclaves inside large cities, but opportunities for advancement were severely restricted outside the confines of these artificial bubbles of prosperity. By the middle of the twentieth century, two Americas existed. In one America, white children were taught they could grow up to be anything their talents and industry would allow. They were encouraged to pull themselves up by their bootstraps and enjoy the blessings of liberty bestowed upon them by the judicious Founding Fathers of the republic. For a white child growing up in the United States during the twentieth century, the future was filled with promise and opportunity; the nation's bounty appeared limitless.[19]

Life in the other America was bleak. Although an exceptional black child could carve out a comfortable niche in highly segregated, colored enclaves, especially inside large cities, the opportunities were limited when compared with his white counterparts. A black man was something less than a man in the eyes of many whites. Black citizens were expected to perform menial labor and remove the burden of drudgery from whites, but they were not expected to succeed in professions that required intellectualism such as law, medicine, business, and artistic pursuits. The record of black achievement undermined the insulting stereotype of an intellectually inferior being who was indolent, shiftless, crooked, and stupid, but few whites chose to look beyond societal prejudices to discover the truth hidden behind the facade.[20]

Beginning in the 1950s, racial relations began to change, albeit gradually. After the United States emerged victorious from World War II and a long period of isolationism in global affairs slowly receded, Americans sensed that the world had changed. No one appreciated this change more than black Americans, many of whom had served in uniform on behalf of their nation during the war. In the words of the old song "How Ya Gonna

Keep 'Em Down on the Farm (After They've Seen Paree)," popular after the First World War, "How ya gonna keep 'em away from harm, that's a mystery / They'll never want to see a rake or plow / And who the deuce can parleyvous a cow? / How ya gonna keep 'em down on the farm / After they've seen Paree?" Having served their country and seen something of the world, Negroes would no longer sit by placidly and allow whites to control crucial aspects of their lives.[21]

Among the first areas of American society to experience unrest was the nation's educational system, which was certainly "separate" but hardly "equal" by any stretch of the imagination. By the early 1950s, black students, parents, and teachers began calling for school integration. On May 17, 1954, the U.S. Supreme Court announced the landmark case of *Brown v. Board of Education*. A unanimous court concluded that "segregation of white and colored children in public schools has a detrimental effect upon colored children. The impact is greater when it has the sanction of the law; for the policy of separating the races is usually interpreted as denoting the inferiority of the Negro group." The court's opinion outraged many whites, who proclaimed May 17 as "Black Monday," but blacks viewed it as the first step in a series of steps designed to dismantle the Jim Crow regime.[22]

Although some groups continued to pursue a strategy of litigation as well as lobbying elected officials, a small but determined subset of black leaders in the 1950s conceived of a more immediate form of protest. In lieu of patiently pursuing incremental social improvements by working within the political and legal system, some activists argued that civil disobedience would lead to systemic change far more quickly and effectively. The concept of mass protest was born.

The purpose of a mass protest was to generate media attention highlighting inequities in the treatment afforded white and black citizens. Presumably, if a large percentage of the citizenry understood the plight of blacks in the American regime, momentum would build to dismantle the segregationist structure in state governments, especially those in the Southern United States. This strategy was risky, however; unlike pursuing a strategy of litigation and lobbying—which depended on political elites to lead the way—mass protests required average black citizens who were often poor, uneducated, and young to put themselves in harm's way. They risked their jobs, their homes, and on occasion their lives.[23]

Although preceded by several notable events, the incident involving Rosa Parks, a secretary of the Montgomery, Alabama, NAACP, is generally regarded as a watershed moment in the modern civil rights movement. On December 1, 1955, Parks was riding on a public bus in Montgomery when the bus driver ordered her to stand up and surrender her seat to a white passenger. Despite her diminutive stature and reserved demeanor, Rosa Parks was not the obsequious black woman she appeared to be. Aside from her work with the NAACP, she had visited the Highlander Center in Tennessee, a school for social activism where civil disobedience and nonviolent protest had been debated with meeting participants. Although she had no way of knowing that December 1 would become a transformative date in the civil rights movement, Parks was a resolute, determined woman who was up to the challenge of defying racially discriminatory laws. She refused to obey the bus driver's order, knowing full well that she would be arrested for her small act of defiance. As expected, the bus driver alerted the police. When the authorities arrived, they placed Parks under arrest. She was tried and convicted of disorderly conduct and violating a Montgomery ordinance.[24]

As news of the incident spread throughout the city, some fifty black leaders decided that this was the opportunity they needed to assault Montgomery's segregationist regime. From these initial stirrings, a new organization, the Montgomery Improvement Association, arose. The association called on the city's black population, estimated at 50,000 people, to boycott Montgomery buses. The group's leaders recognized that blacks generated a significant proportion of the bus company's revenues. Their logic was simple and compelling: If blacks comprised a large percentage of the bus company's customers, they had the right to expect fair treatment. If that treatment was not forthcoming, they would not ride the buses. White leaders, initially recalcitrant, underestimated the resolve of the city's black population. After 381 days, the boycott succeeded. A federal court ordered the buses to be desegregated, and the city fathers repealed the local ordinance segregating blacks and whites.[25]

The Montgomery Improvement Association's victory galvanized the civil rights movement and demonstrated the effectiveness of mass protests. It also transformed a young Baptist minister, the Reverend Dr. Martin Luther King Jr., into a national figure. As the president of the Montgomery Improvement Association, the charismatic, eloquent, well-educated minister sporting a PhD represented a new type of dynamic black leader. A student of Mahatma Gandhi's nonviolent techniques and an idealistic Christian minister, Dr. King preached that oppressed people could take to the streets and effect positive social change without resorting to violence or threatening individual white citizens.[26]

Dr. King's role received sustained media attention, but he was not the sole hero of the civil rights movement during those years. Another milestone in the movement occurred in 1960 when four students from the all-black North Carolina Agricultural & Technical College marched into the Woolworth's department store in Greensboro, North Carolina, sat at a segregated lunch counter, and asked to be served food. The young men—Ezell A. Blair Jr., David Richmond, Joseph McNeil, and Franklin McCain—knew exactly what they were doing. Well dressed, mannerly, and employing nonviolent techniques, their goal was to demonstrate the inequities inherent in segregation laws. Their message would be repeated in numerous sit-ins throughout the South. Such tactics were not new, but the discipline demonstrated by the protesters and the frequency of the sit-ins attracted widespread media coverage. Eventually, demonstrators took the fight to libraries, theaters, museums, parks, and public buildings. Jim Crow's long, uninterrupted reign was under siege.[27]

For some demonstrators, the sit-ins were too passive and required participants to endure all manner of public humiliation without reacting to provocation. Incensed white onlookers sometimes poured food and beverages on the protesters' heads, spat in their food, physically assaulted them, or taunted them with racial epithets. It required a special person to suffer through the assaults without striking back. Some activists preferred to take their message to the streets and test new laws restricting segregation. In 1961, a group of young blacks and whites, under the auspices of the Congress of Racial Equality (CORE), chose to test new laws providing for integrated interstate travel. The participants called their activity "Freedom Rides." The first Freedom Ride was a bus trip from Washington, D.C., to New Orleans, Louisiana, in May 1961. Instead of sitting on a stool at a segregated lunch counter waiting for the fight to come to them, these intrepid souls would go toward the fight of their own accord.[28]

The Freedom Riders anticipated an angry backlash from white supremacists, but even they underestimated the depth of hatred and fear in the white community. What had begun in a tranquil atmosphere deteriorated in Anniston, Alabama, when the bus was firebombed and the passengers barely escaped with their lives. Police officers in Birmingham, Alabama, allowed members of the Ku Klux Klan fifteen minutes without interference to beat the Freedom Riders before the authorities officially intervened. Although the violence suspended the rides temporarily, activists from the Student Nonviolent Coordinating Committee (SNCC) sent representatives to continue the journey.[29]

The violence continued as the Riders made their way through Alabama. Once again, angry white mobs attacked and severely beat the protesters. One of the worst episodes occurred in Montgomery, where white supremacists assaulted SNCC activist John Lewis with a crate. James Zwerg, a white Freedom Rider, received special attention from a mob upset because he was a traitor to his race. They bludgeoned him with a suitcase and knocked out his teeth. Even onlookers who were not part of the Freedom Riders suffered at the hands of the mob. *Life* magazine photographer Don Urbrock was unlucky enough to have his cameras snatched from his hands and used as a weapon against him. Despite the assaults, law enforcement personnel deemed the Riders to be troublemakers; in Jackson, Mississippi, group members were arrested for "breaching the peace" when they used the "whites only" restrooms.[30]

Despite these episodes of brutal violence, young nonviolent activists poured into Mississippi. By the end of the summer of 1961, more than three hundred young people had been jailed in filthy, cramped cells. In some cases, the activists were tortured and forced to engage in hard labor under backbreaking conditions. A new era in the civil rights movement grew out of the Freedom Rides, and a generation of black leaders came to prominence. In addition to John Lewis, many young heroes emerged: Bob Moses, an activist dedicated to increasing voter registration among blacks in Mississippi; Diane Nash, a dynamic, articulate female activist; James Bevel, a charismatic preacher and gifted organizer; and Stokely Carmichael, a daring, intense demonstrator who would later argue for more extreme methods of promoting racial equality. These and many other new faces made up the core of civil rights activists during the 1960s.[31]

During the early 1960s, the civil rights movement achieved many notable successes, but it also lost momentum owing to dissension in the ranks, blunders in strategies and tactics, and the indifference of many mainstream leaders in the white community. Ironically, the movement garnered attention and accomplished its goals whenever merciless segregationists overreacted to civil rights demonstrations. When Laurie Pritchett, the police chief of Albany, Georgia, ensured that white racists and Ku Klux Klansmen did not physically assault protesters and arranged for jailed demonstrators to be transported to faraway holding cells, the resultant peaceful demonstrations failed to capture national headlines. Dr. King was forced to retreat without declaring victory. By contrast, when President Kennedy called out the National Guard so James Meredith could enroll as a student at the University of Mississippi in the fall of 1962, the melee successfully focused attention on the injustices of segregation. When a sniper shot and killed NAACP activist Medgar Evers in the driveway of Evers's home in June 1963, the brutal, cowardly act effectively eroded the public support for Jim Crow. The famous March on Washington in August 1963, coming less than a month before the Sixteenth Street Baptist Church bombing, focused attention on the nation's blacks as never before. Many Americans, having heard only stories of Dr. King's supposed communist affiliation and his penchant for rabble-rousing, caught their first glimpse of the eloquent minister addressing a large and orderly audience with the Lincoln Memorial as a dramatic backdrop.[32]

THE BOMBING AND ITS AFTERMATH

Birmingham, Alabama, was ground zero for the civil rights movement during 1963. The city's police chief, Eugene "Bull" Connor, and the state's governor, George Wallace, were characters straight from central casting. Their fiercely segregationist, racist, and militaristic language and their avowed willingness to protect the white supremacist power structure attracted unprecedented media coverage as they stood up to all manner of enemies—communist agitators, a left-leaning media conglomerate, black rabble-rousers, white scalawags, and representatives of an oppressive federal government. At a time when mature, thoughtful, inclusive, democratic leadership might have reached a political accommodation free from violence and social disruption, these men ratcheted up the stakes in a dangerous game of political one-upmanship. Playing to the fears of the white community, Connor and Wallace, as well as many other local, state, and federal elected demagogues in the Deep South and throughout the rest of the country, refused to consider the possibility of political compromise. As Wallace famously remarked in his inaugural address when he was sworn in as governor in January 1963 on the portico of the Alabama state capitol, where Jefferson Davis had stood when he became president of the Confederate States of America 102 years earlier, "In the name of the greatest people that have ever trod this earth, I draw the line in the dust and toss the gauntlet before the feet of tyranny, and I say segregation now, segregation tomorrow, segregation forever."[33]

In the face of government-sanctioned inequality, civil rights activists tested the Alabama segregation laws throughout 1963. Birmingham had been a city under siege since May, when Dr. King and his colleagues in the civil rights movement had negotiated an end to segregated public lunch counters and restrooms in the city. A well-known black hotel situated not far from the Sixteenth Street Baptist Church had been bombed, as had the home of A. D. King, Dr. King's brother. At the time, 2,500 angry black protesters had taken to the streets to rail against the violence. Three months later, a black lawyer's home had been bombed. It had been a tumultuous time, but as autumn approached, the city seemed to have entered the eye of the hurricane.[34]

In fact, Sunday morning, September 15, 1963, appeared to be just another ordinary day on the west side of Birmingham. Although tensions between whites and blacks remained troubling, few people realized it would become a memorable, historic date. Most citizens, black and white, struggled to feed their families, find meaningful employment, and make ends meet. Their day-to-day lives went on as they had for generations even though segregation was eroding away. Average people for the most part were grateful for a respite from turmoil.[35]

The civil rights movement had achieved successes during the year, but at great cost. The heavy-handedness of Birmingham police chief Bull Connor had worked to the protesters' advantage. For millions of white Americans who had not been attuned to the issues of black America, television images of Connor's men shooting young black girls and boys with fire hoses and unleashing vicious German shepherd dogs demonstrated the brutality of white supremacy. The August 28, 1963, March on Washington, which attracted more than 200,000 people and culminated in Dr. King's celebrated "I have a dream" speech, had done much to publicize and advance the cause of civil rights in the United States. Many trials and tribulations no doubt lay ahead, but blacks in the South could look toward the future with hope in September 1963—hope that would not have been possible a few years earlier.[36]

In many respects, the Sixteenth Street Baptist Church was an obvious target for a terrorist attack. Terrorists throughout time have sought to strike at symbols of their discontent. Even when the loss of life is minimal in terms of numbers, an attack on a symbolic target often demoralizes the terrorists' intended victims. In this case, the Sixteenth Street Baptist Church was a symbol of black affluence in Birmingham. Established in 1873 on the west side of town, the church was a mammoth brick structure situated on the corner of Sixth Avenue North and Sixteenth Street. With a congregation numbering more than four hundred people, the Sixteenth Street Baptist Church was a symbol of the burgeoning black middle class in the South. Numerous affluent black professionals, including attorneys, doctors, dentists, and teachers, worshipped in the historic church. Most famously, Dr. Martin Luther King Jr. had addressed black citizens from the steps of the church during a civil rights demonstration over segregated lunch counters and restrooms in Birmingham during the spring of 1963. As the civil rights protests of the 1960s moved into Birmingham, so many homes and businesses were bombed that the Southern industrial city earned the disparaging nickname "Bombingham." Given its prominence as a symbol of black pride and dignity, it was little wonder that the Sixteenth Street Baptist Church became a target of white supremacists. As the site of mass rallies in the black community, it was hallowed ground.[37]

Unbeknownst to the congregants of the Sixteenth Street Baptist Church that Sunday morning, four members of the United Klans of America, an offshoot of the white supremacist group the Ku Klux Klan, had planted a box of dynamite with a time delay beneath the steps of the church near the basement. The assailants, Bobby Frank Cherry, Thomas Blanton Jr., Herman Frank Cash, and Robert Chambliss, were products of the Old South and were raised on the antiquated notion that the Negro would never be the equal of the white man. Cherry, thirty-three years old at the time, had served in the U.S. Marine Corps, where he had worked with explosives and learned the intricacies of demolitions. Blanton, twenty-five years old, looked up to Bobby Cherry as an older and wiser miscreant. Essentially a follower who did as he was told, Blanton was along for the ride, a terrorist wannabe who was determined to prove himself to his confederates. Forty-five-year-old Herman Cash, a truck driver by profession when he was not terrorizing Southern blacks, was another member of the rank and file, a follower and not a leader. If anyone could have been called the mastermind of the operation, it was Robert Chambliss. At fifty-nine years of age, Chambliss was the old man of the group, and certainly the most experienced terrorist of the lot. Although he would later vehemently proclaim his innocence, "Dynamite Bob" enjoyed a reputation among blacks and whites for ferocity; he was said to have fire-bombed numerous black houses and places of business before the September 1963 incident. An eyewitness later identified Chambliss as the white man he had seen stepping out of a white and turquoise Chevrolet and placing a box under the steps of the church shortly before the bombing.[38]

This act of terrorism was especially horrifying owing to the random nature of the victims. The bombers were not aiming for a particular victim or victims; rather, they sought only to maim or kill targets of opportunity. As will be discussed later in this book, random acts of terrorism wreak havoc far beyond specific, isolated incidents because they seem to lack a reasonable basis. It is difficult to prepare for an attack that appears to be aimed at no one in particular. The attempted assassination of the president or a political figure, while outrageous, nonetheless limits the collateral damage and fear experienced by persons far away from the target. Terrorists who place a bomb beneath the steps of a building traversed by many people intentionally strike fear into the hearts of a multitude. That innocent children might be harmed or killed in such a random attack especially offends the sensibilities.[39]

Minutes after the Klansmen placed the bomb beneath the stairs, the package exploded. At the time, twenty-six children had entered the basement assembly room to prepare for a sermon titled, ironically enough, "The Love That Forgives." Sunday school had ended minutes earlier, and the children were excited about the church service that was scheduled to begin at 10:30. While the adults from the congregation assembled upstairs, the children hurriedly prepared for their roles in the morning service.[40]

Years later, Sarah Collins Cox recalled the scene in the basement restroom when the blast occurred. Twelve years old at the time, Cox was standing with her sister, Addie Mae, who was fourteen, and a friend, Denise McNair, who was eleven years old. They were dressing for the youth pageant. "I remember Denise asking Addie to tie her belt," Cox said. "Addie was tying her sash. Then it happened."[41]

At 10:22 a.m., the bomb exploded in the church basement. Authorities pinpointed the precise time of the blast because a clock inside the church stopped running at that minute. Terroristic threats and promises of violence were nothing new to the movement's adherents or to the Sixteenth Street Baptist Church, for that matter. Parishioners had always taken care to be vigilant and to protect people and property, but it is impossible to protect everyone against all threats all of the time.[42]

The blast from the explosion was so momentous that it rocked the church on its foundation, blowing a hole in the rear wall and destroying the back steps. All but one stained-glass window, which showed Jesus leading a group of small children, were destroyed. In the aftermath of the attack, it was clear that twenty-two people suffered injuries from the blast. Sarah Collins Cox was grievously wounded. "I couldn't see anymore because my eyes were full of glass—23 pieces of glass. I didn't know what happened. I just remember calling, 'Addie, Addie.' But there was no answer. I don't remember any pain. I just remember wanting Addie."[43]

Four young girls perished in the explosion, including Cox's sister, Addie, and her friend Denise McNair. Two other girls, Carole Robertson and Cynthia Wesley, both fourteen years old, also died. Cox was the only girl from the basement restroom to survive the blast. She spent two months in the hospital recuperating from her injuries. When she was finally released, she was only able to see out of her left eye. Doctors inserted a glass eye on the right side of her face.[44]

Immediately following the explosion, a mob of blacks, enraged by the senseless violence, gathered outside the ruins of the church. Anxious white leaders of Birmingham dispatched policemen in riot gear and armed with shotguns to ensure that law and order prevailed. Dr. King had preached on the virtues on nonviolence from the steps of the church, and many believ-

The Sixteenth Street Baptist Church following the bombing on September 15, 1963. Courtesy of the Birmingham, Alabama, Public Library Archives, Catalog # 85.1.22.

ers had heeded his call, but this latest act of terrorism was all too much. The black community in Birmingham had suffered mightily at the hands of white supremacists. How much injury and degradation can one people endure before they take up arms against their oppressors? As the riot grew in intensity, unidentified individuals hurled rocks and bricks at police and overturned cars owned by white citizens. In response, a crowd of 2,000 whites gathered to demonstrate against the desegregation plan for a public high school in a Birmingham suburb.[45]

THE KU KLUX KLAN IN TWENTIETH-CENTURY AMERICA

Onlookers had little doubt that the Ku Klux Klan had been involved in the bombing. Although many whites were upset by the civil rights movement and supported aggressive measures to dissuade Negroes from exercising their constitutional rights, their support tended to be passive. Few citizens of any race or color were willing to cross the line into violent crime. If anyone harbored enough malice to plan and execute such a heinous crime, it would be a Klansman.

The KKK is among the best-known extremist groups in U.S. history. The organization has existed in many forms since the 1860s, although it died out as an active group for approximately four decades following the 1870s. It is difficult to discuss the one true "Klan" because many factions have used the label despite doctrinal differences and brutal internecine struggles among the groups.[46]

The original Ku Klux Klan emerged in the aftermath of the U.S. Civil War. The traditional story is that six ex-Confederate soldiers living in Pulaski, Tennessee, unemployed and bored during the early Reconstruction period, met in late 1865 or early 1866 and formed a social club. The origins of the name are a matter of ongoing dispute, but the most widely accepted account suggests that the founders derived the name from the Greek word *kuklos*, which means "circle." To emphasize their Scotch-Irish ancestry, the circle of brotherhood appropriated the term "clan" but changed the *c* to a *k* to complete the alliteration. Other explanations for the origins of the name are equally jejune; suffice it to say that the founders were pleased with the mysterious, puzzling meaning of the term.[47]

According to most histories of the KKK, the Pulaski den was a social organization similar to a fraternity housed on college campuses. The original members supposedly cavorted around the town engaging in spirited horseplay while dressed in fanciful costumes and conical hats. Klan apologists suggest that the original group harbored no malice toward any individual or race, and their motivations were free from the taint of terrorism. Skeptical historians have questioned this benign view of the group. The KKK, they contend, was founded on the proposition that persons of color must be kept in their place—through violence, if necessary. The argument that the group's founders acted without nefarious purposes seems disingenuous.[48]

Whatever its original purposes, the Klan became a well-known paramilitary organization devoted to ensuring that newly emancipated slaves, the so-called freedmen, did not secure political or legal rights in the Southern states. The transition occurred beginning in 1867, when a former Confederate general officer named George Gordon developed a military-style hierarchical structure for the group. Gordon's plan was for the KKK to exist as an extralegal vigilante organization. Wearing sheets and masks to disguise their identities, participants would visit the homes of freedmen at night to ensure that the "darkies" did not exercise their political rights to lobby for the franchise or arm themselves for a confrontation. What its members could not accomplish under the color of law they would enforce under the cover of darkness.[49]

Also in 1867, the KKK gained legitimacy in the eyes of many discontented whites when former Confederate cavalryman Nathan Bedford Forrest agreed to head the organization as grand wizard. Forrest was a former slave trader who had risen through the ranks during the Civil War to become a Confederate general. By war's end, he had become a legend on both sides of the Mason-Dixon Line. Ulysses S. Grant once remarked that Forrest was the only Confederate cavalry officer who had frightened him during the war. Although Forrest repudiated the group's activities after less than two years, he transformed the budding terrorist organization into an effective mechanism for promoting white supremacy in the Old South.[50]

The Reconstruction-era Ku Klux Klan died out during the 1870s owing to federal prosecutions of KKK leaders, especially in the Piedmont region of South Carolina, as well as new federal legislation designed to protect the freedmen. In addition, as white Southerners "redeemed" state governments throughout the South prior to 1877, the Klan had outlived its usefulness. Because state governments could institute laws enforcing racial segregation, white supremacists could achieve their goals of keeping blacks in line without resorting to extralegal tactics. For many Klan proponents, however, the idea of a "white knight" organization promoting law and order through extremist means was enormously appealing. The KKK died as an active organization during the 1870s, but the group's ideals persisted.[51]

During the early 1900s, a romanticized view of the Ku Klux Klan emerged. Many white Americans conveniently forgot about brutal Klansmen terrorizing, torturing, and killing freedmen during Reconstruction. Instead, they envisioned noble white knights riding to the rescue of good, Christian white families besieged by bestial black men, drunken carpetbaggers, lurid scalawags, and all manner of miscreants hell-bent on destroying the Southern way of life. Thomas Dixon Jr., a lapsed preacher, popularized this notion of the virtuous Kluxer in his popular novel *The Clansman*, first published in 1905. A decade later, D. W. Griffith's epic film *The Birth of a Nation*, based on Dixon's polemic, cleverly portrayed the Ku Klux Klan as defenders of white Christian culture. Griffith rewrote Southern history to show the Klan overcoming innumerable obstacles to vanquish its foes and restore the proper balance to American civilization. At the end of the film, as the victorious Klansmen ride into the sunset, the smiling figure of Jesus

Christ gazes down from the sky on the noble, deserving, white children of God.[52]

In light of this nostalgic view of the secretive terrorist group, it was no wonder that the Ku Klux Klan once again became an active organization. In 1915, a thirty-five-year-old ex-Methodist minister named William Joseph "Doc" Simmons led a group of fifteen men to the top of Stone Mountain, Georgia, a granite outcropping near Atlanta. There, on Thanksgiving night, the group read from the bible and swore allegiance to their new group, the Invisible Empire, reborn as the Knights of the Ku Klux Klan. The Klansmen also burned a sixteen-foot wooden cross as a symbol of celebrating their Christian heritage. Unlike the Reconstruction-era group, which never participated in such a ritual, the new incarnation of the Klan popularized cross burning based on a scene from Dixon's novel *The Clansman*.[53]

The twentieth-century Ku Klux Klan's emphasis on Christian values was specifically designed to appeal to white Southerners raised on fundamentalist and evangelical Christian values in the Bible Belt. Doc Simmons, once described as a man who "was richly endowed with neither character nor ability," also understood that if he wanted to increase group membership, he must cater to the alienation that many white Southerners felt about "big government" as well as their prejudices concerning blacks and other minority groups who seemed to threaten majoritarian white values. During the early years of the revitalized group's existence, Simmons practiced his own peculiar form of demagoguery through long-winded harangues and the distribution of patently racist literature in and around Atlanta.[54]

He was eventually supplanted by Edward Young Clarke, president of the Southern Publicity Association and brother of the managing editor of the *Atlanta Constitution*, the city's major newspaper. Where Simmons's recruiting efforts had been crude and clumsy, appealing only to the least common denominator of poor, uneducated whites, Clarke broadened the group's appeal. With assistance from Elizabeth Tyler, a former Red Cross recruiter, Clarke joined forces with the Salvation Army and the Anti-Saloon League to stage elaborate, sophisticated membership drives. The group eventually moved its headquarters into a spacious building on Atlanta's Peachtree Street.[55]

Unlike the earlier version of the KKK, the new group did not focus merely on keeping black Americans in their place. Capitalizing on fears of immigration following World War I, Clarke argued in favor of nativism. Blacks, Catholics, Jews, and foreigners of all stripes threatened white heritage and undermined the "Christian principles" of "true Americans." Clarke's scare tactics were so successful that he increased Klan membership from fewer than 2,000 people to more than 48,000 members in a year.

By the 1920s, the Ku Klux Klan was one of the most powerful factions in American society. Supposedly even President Warren G. Harding was sworn into the fraternal order in the Green Room of the White House, although many historians have disputed this incredible claim.[56]

The KKK reached its apogee of power and influence during the 1920s; thereafter, membership slowly declined, especially after some rural dens publicly embraced Adolf Hitler's racist ideology during the 1930s. Periodically during the next three decades, group membership spiked upward in response to a perceived threat to white Christian values. After black Americans returned from World War II and began to assume a more prominent role in American life, the Ku Klux Klan enjoyed another brief revival. One Kluxer spoke for many uneducated whites during the late 1940s when he explained that he had joined the group "just to let the niggers know the war is over and that the Klan is back on the market."[57]

Following the U.S. Supreme Court decision in the famous school desegregation case *Brown v. Board of Education* in May 1954 and President Eisenhower's decision to send federal troops into Little Rock, Arkansas, in 1957 to quell racial unrest, the KKK again saw its ranks swell with disaffected white Americans. Even some citizens who were not Klan members shared the group's anger at the federal government's intervention into issues that traditionally had been handled by the states, such as schools and social interaction.[58]

During the 1960s, even as the Klan flourished throughout the country, the group's role in the American landscape remained troubled and contentious. Different factions within the KKK began to fight with each other; splinter groups developed. The United Klans of America (UKA), under the leadership of a charismatic racist from Alabama named Robert Shelton, claimed to have 44,000 members by the mid-1960s. In the meantime, the National Knights of the Ku Klux Klan, led by an Atlanta attorney named James Venable, listed 6,800 members. Another 4,000 or so self-proclaimed Klansmen joined numerous small enclaves scattered throughout the United States. Two of the more colorful groups included the Original Ku Klux Klan of the Confederacy, an Alabama-based racist organization that marched around adorned in Confederate gray robes and claimed an affinity for Nazi storm troopers. The North Carolina Knights of the Ku Klux Klan, headed by a former carnival huckster and wannabe Baptist preacher named James "Catfish" Cole, engaged in a long-running battle with the Lumbee Indians of Robeson County, beginning in the late 1950s.[59]

By the time the Sixteenth Street Baptist Church bombing occurred in September 1963, the Ku Klux Klan was not a unified, hegemonic organization;

it was a series of competing groups united only by their racism and their fear of "foreign elements," strange ideas, and threats to the status quo. The four men who planted the dynamite that day could not claim to champion a fixed ideology or coherent set of values. They were not representatives of an oppressed constituency. They did not act on behalf of a majority of white Americans, even those unsympathetic to the civil rights movement. They were four deeply disturbed individuals, driven by hatred, frightened of change, unwilling or unable to adapt to the modern world, and anxious to hurt anyone who disagreed with them or challenged their perverted worldview. If four innocent children had to die so these men could express their discontent and spread their feelings of hate against blacks, they were not bothered by this result.[60]

THE AFTERMATH OF THE BOMBING

The explosion that September morning sent shock waves through the land. The death of innocent children, whatever their race, disturbed many Americans deeply. Destroying the famous church, a symbol of the desegregation effort, sent an undeniable message to would-be black activists: If you continue the fight against Southern segregation, you had better be prepared to pay with your life.

As community leaders and investigators sifted through the rubble in the aftermath of the blast, they discovered four bodies: eleven-year-old Denise McNair and fourteen-year-old Addie Mae Collins, Carole Robertson, and Cynthia Wesley. The girls had been preparing to sing in the church choir for Sunday services. By indiscriminately attacking the church and striking down innocents who could not have been involved in political activity or "rabble-rousing," the terrorists inadvertently engendered sympathy not only in the black community but among many millions of people of all races and colors. The mainstream news media supported the grieving black community in numerous newspaper editorials and television programs.[61]

The FBI was on the scene immediately. Despite director J. Edgar Hoover's well-known antipathy for civil rights "agitators," he could not afford to neglect such a high-profile case. After all, the victims could hardly be characterized as "agitators" even by the most anti–civil rights bigots. The bureau eventually concluded that four suspects were responsible—white supremacists Robert E. Chambliss, Bobby Frank Cherry, Herman Frank Cash, and Thomas E. Blanton Jr. The Birmingham office recommended that they be prosecuted, but Hoover, never comfortable prosecuting civil

A victim's funeral following the Sixteenth Street Baptist Church bombing. Courtesy of the Library of Congress.

rights matters, decided not to pursue the case. It languished until the bureau closed the file in 1968.[62]

With changing times and sensibilities, Alabama attorney general Bill Baxley reopened the case three years after the FBI had backed away from the investigation. The proceedings dragged on for years. On November

18, 1977, Alabama prosecutors finally won their case, convicting Robert Chambliss of murder. He was sentenced to life in prison. Police reopened the case against the other defendants in 1988, although many more months would elapse before formal charges were filed. Herman Frank Cash remained a prime suspect, but he died in 1994 before he could be prosecuted. On May 17, 2000, Thomas Blanton Jr. and Bobby Frank Cherry were charged with the murder. Blanton was tried, convicted, and sentenced to life in prison on May 1, 2001. A judge originally ruled that Bobby Frank Cherry was mentally incompetent, but eventually prosecutors got that ruling overturned. On May 22, 2002, Cherry was found guilty of four counts of murder and sentenced to life in prison.[63]

In the late twentieth and early twenty-first centuries, murder cases from the civil rights era were reopened as new young prosecutors sought to close an ugly chapter in the story of the American South. The lesson is a valuable one. Anyone who engages in terrorism had better be prepared to pay a price for his or her actions. Even if it appears that the terrorist escaped justice, he or she may be held accountable decades later.[64]

CONCLUSION

Because the victims were innocent black children, the Sixteenth Street Baptist Church tragedy became another disturbing episode in the civil rights battles of the 1960s. The white supremacists who planted the dynamite under the church steps did not intend to further the cause of civil rights, although that is exactly what happened. Those angry, disturbed men sought to lash out at a symbol of black pride and leadership in Birmingham. They were frustrated and frightened by an ascendant black community; they wished to share their pain with representatives of the group they believed had caused the pain. As often happens in cases of terrorism, however, rather than undermining the resolve of the victim, the terrorist act galvanized the community at which it was aimed. The four Kluxers who murdered innocent children that day did more to advance the cause of civil rights than innumerable black protesters marching through the streets of Birmingham could.

This conclusion raises a central question in any analysis of terrorism, namely whether high-profile violent acts accomplish the perpetrators' objectives. If it is true that terrorist acts frequently empower rather than victimize the targets of those acts, why would terrorists continue to employ a disproven method? Presumably, any disaffected person using violent means

Members of the Congress of Racial Equality (CORE) march in Washington, D.C. Courtesy of the Library of Congress.

to accomplish a goal, save a deranged attacker, eventually would recognize the futility of such an act—unless, in some instances, the objective itself is not rational.

Two points merit a discussion here. First, some terrorists, including the Ku Klux Klansmen who planted the dynamite under the church steps in 1963, are unable or unwilling to analyze the likely consequences of their actions. Therefore, although the terrorists can be said to be "rational" in the strict sense, they fail to appreciate the changing tide of history. They have analyzed the situation, but their analysis is faulty because they do not fully understand the historical moment in which they find themselves.

Second, in some situations the violence itself, not the consequences, is the point of the action. For these terrorists, violence is not the means to an end; violence is an end in itself. Some terrorists are so angry, hurt, and dispirited with the political and/or social landscape that lashing out at "others," whatever the consequences, is preferable to the status quo. As we shall see in subsequent chapters, the second type of terrorist proves to be especially insidious because the normal cost-benefit/risk-reward analysis normally associated with criminal confederates does not apply. A person who plants dynamite in one location and flees to a safe haven in another location has weighed the costs and benefits of this action. He or she desires to hurt someone else while preserving his or her own life. By contrast, a suicide bomber seeks to maximize the harm inflicted on others, with little or no regard for his or her physical well-being.

A terrorist act must be judged according to its own rules. In the case of the Sixteenth Street Baptist Church, the terrorists failed to achieve their goals. By any account, the Klansmen hoped to destroy or severely hamper the civil rights movement. Yet the murder of four innocent children had the opposite effect: it demonstrated the righteousness of the black citizenry and the terrible hypocrisy of the brutal white supremacists who sought to deprive blacks of their rightful place in American life.[65]

NOTES

1. Borgeson and Valeri, *Terrorism in America*, 1–16; Branch, *Pillar of Fire*, xiii–xiv; Halberstam, *The Children*, 3–7.

2. Branch, *Parting the Waters*, 412–50; Branch, *Pillar of Fire*, 108, 183, 508–9; Remnick, *The Bridge*, 6–7, 55, 462, 480; Sides, *Hellhound on His Trail*, 164–73; Watson, *Freedom Summer*, 206–11.

3. Bagby, "Two Arrested for 1963 Church Bombing," 6–7; "Four Little Girls, Nobody Knew Their Names," 34; Klubuchar, *1963 Birmingham Church Bombing*, 12–14; Sokol, *There Goes My Everything*, 166.

4. Branch, *Parting the Waters*, 68–69; Hobbes, *Leviathan*, 131, 143–44; McCann, *Terrorism on American Soil*, 103–4; Ridgeway, *Blood in the Face*, 89–93.

5. McCann, *Terrorism on American Soil*, 103–6; McWhorter, "No Trial Closes Injustice's Wounds," 12A.

6. "Four Little Girls, Nobody Knew Their Names," 34; Jones, "Justice for Four Little Girls," 4–6; McWhorter, "No Trial Closes Injustice's Wounds," 12A; Wade, *The Fiery Cross*, 324–25.

7. Ford, "Reconfiguring the Old South," 118–21; Howe, *What Hath God Wrought*, 482; Knowles, "The Constitution and Slavery," 311–13; Luse, "Slavery's Champions Stood at Odds," 385–87; McPherson, *The Struggle for Equality*, 136.

8. Foner, *Forever Free*, 25–26; Ford, "Reconfiguring the Old South," 118–21; Hahn, *A Nation under Our Feet*, 55; Kraditor, *Means and Ends in American Abolitionism*, 3–10.

9. Foner, *Forever Free*, 25–26; Ford, "Reconfiguring the Old South," 118–21; Hahn, *A Nation under Our Feet*, 55; Horton and Horton, *Slavery and the Making of America*, 103–4; Wade, *The Fiery Cross*, 9–11.

10. Cox, *Lincoln and Black Freedom*, 183; Foner, *The Fiery Trial*, 228; McPherson, *Battle Cry of Freedom*, 853–62.

11. Foner, *Forever Free*, 7–8; Wade, *The Fiery Cross*, 112–13; Woodward, *Origins of the New South*, 211–12, 353–54; Woodward, *The Strange Career of Jim Crow*, 7–8.

12. Foner, *Forever Free*, 37–38, 208; Woodward, *The Strange Career of Jim Crow*, 7–8.

13. Foner, *Forever Free*, 27–38; Packard, *American Nightmare*, 14–15.

14. Foner, *Forever Free*, 207–11; Logan, *The Betrayal of the Negro*, 12–13, 83; Packard, *American Nightmare*, 66–68; Simkins and Roland, *A History of the South*, 352.

15. Quoted in Woodward, *Origins of the New South*, 359. See also McPherson, *The Abolitionist Legacy*, 354–57.

16. Foner, *Forever Free*, 211–12; Simkins and Roland, *A History of the South*, 505–6; Woodward, *Origins of the New South*, 357–61.

17. DuBois, *The Souls of Black Folk*, 41–42.

18. Branch, *Parting the Waters*, 32, 563; Lemann, *The Promised Land*, 6–7.

19. Blackmon, *Slavery by Another Name*, 386–94; McCann, *Terrorism on American Soil*, 103.

20. Foner, *Forever Free*, 209; Logan, *The Betrayal of the Negro*, 38–39; Woodward, *Origins of the New South*, 208–13.

21. Logan, *The Betrayal of the Negro*, 314–16.

22. *Brown v. Board of Education of Topeka*, 347 U.S. 483, 494 (1954); See also Branch, *Parting the Waters*, 112–13; Kinshasa, "An Appraisal of *Brown v. Board of Education, Topeka KS* (1954) and the Montgomery Bus Boycott," 18–19.

23. Branch, *Parting the Waters*, 49–53, 284–86; Kinshasa, "An Appraisal of *Brown v. Board of Education, Topeka KS* (1954) and the Montgomery Bus Boycott," 18–20; Metress, "Making Civil Rights Harder," 138–41.

24. Branch, *Parting the Waters*, 128–34; Brinkley, *Rosa Parks*, 106–7; Kinshasa, "An Appraisal of *Brown v. Board of Education, Topeka KS* (1954) and the Montgomery Bus Boycott," 19; Metress, "Making Civil Rights Harder," 149; Parks and Reed, *Quiet Strength*, 23–24; "Rosa Louise McCauley Parks 1913–2005," 64–65; Wade-Lewis, "I Remember Rosa Parks," 2–3; Wilson, "Interpreting the Discursive Field of the Montgomery Bus Boycott," 299–302.

25. Branch, *Parting the Waters*, 143–68; Carson, "To Walk with Dignity," 13–15; Kinshasa, "An Appraisal of *Brown v. Board of Education, Topeka KS* (1954) and the Montgomery Bus Boycott," 19–23; "Rosa Louise McCauley Parks 1913–2005," 64–65.

26. Branch, *Parting the Waters*, 137–41, 203–4; Carson, "Between Contending Forces," 17; Carson, "To Walk with Dignity," 13–15; Wilson, "Interpreting the Discursive Field of the Montgomery Bus Boycott," 321–22.

27. Carson, "Between Contending Forces," 17–18; Flowers, "The Launching of the Sit-In Movement," 53–55; Halberstam, *The Children*, 92–94; Lewis with D'Orso, *Walking with the Wind*, 91–93; Ling, "Racism for Lunch," 36–38.

28. Branch, *Parting the Waters*, 390–93, 412–13; Carson, "Between Contending Forces," 18–19; Catsam, "'Mister, This Is Not Your Fight!'" 93–94; Halberstam, *The Children*, 248–51.

29. Branch, *Parting the Waters*, 417–24; Carson, "Between Contending Forces," 18–19; Catsam, "'Mister, This Is Not Your Fight!'" 93–94; Lewis with D'Orso, *Walking with the Wind*, 140–72; Ling, "Racism for Lunch," 37–38.

30. Catsam, "'Mister, This Is Not Your Fight!'" 93–101; Halberstam, *The Children*, 289–98; Lewis with D'Orso, *Walking with the Wind*, 155–58.

31. Branch, *Pillar of Fire*, 53–57; Carson, "Between Contending Forces," 17–21; Flowers, "The Launching of the Sit-In Movement," 53–56; Halberstam, *The Children*, 3–17; Ling, "Racism for Lunch," 36–38.

32. Branch, *Parting the Waters*, 536–56, 647–72, 827–30; Carson, "Between Contending Forces," 19; Halberstam, *The Children*, 483; Lewis with D'Orso, *Walking with the Wind*, 199–201.

33. Quoted in Sokol, *There Goes My Everything*, 249. See also Anderson, "The Past on Trial," 478–79; Branch, *Parting the Waters*, 737–38; Chalmers, *Hooded Americanism*, 400–401; McCann, *Terrorism on American Soil*, 103–5.

34. Anderson, "The Past on Trial," 478–79; Bagby, "Two Arrested for 1963 Church Bombing," 6–7; McCann, *Terrorism on American Soil*, 104; Stewart, "Historic Church in Store for Revival," 42.

35. Anderson, "The Past on Trial," 478; Bagby, "Two Arrested for 1963 Church Bombing," 6–7; "Four Little Girls, Nobody Knew Their Names," 34; Klubuchar, *1963 Birmingham Church Bombing*, 12–14; McCann, *Terrorism on American Soil*, 105.

36. Branch, *Parting the Waters*, 872–83; McCann, *Terrorism on American Soil*, 103–5; Metress, "Making Civil Rights Harder," 143–44.

37. McCann, *Terrorism on American Soil*, 104; Stewart, "Historic Church in Store for Revival," 42.

38. Bagby, "Two Arrested for 1963 Church Bombing," 6–7; "Four Little Girls, Nobody Knew Their Names," 34; Klubuchar, *1963 Birmingham Church Bombing*, 12–14.

39. Bagby, "Two Arrested for 1963 Church Bombing," 6–7; McCann, *Terrorism on American Soil*, 103.

40. "Four Little Girls, Nobody Knew Their Names," 34; Klubuchar, *1963 Birmingham Church Bombing*, 12–14; Smith, "The Day the Children Died," 87–88; Stewart, "Historic Church in Store for Revival," 42.

41. Quoted in Smith, "The Day the Children Died," 87. See also Jones, "Justice for Four Little Girls," 4–6; McWhorter, "No Trial Closes Injustice's Wounds," 12A.

42. Anderson, "The Past on Trial," 478–79; McKinstry and George, *While the World Watched*, 23; Smith, "The Day the Children Died," 87–88; Stewart, "Historic Church in Store for Revival," 42.

43. Quoted in Smith, "The Day the Children Died," 87. See also "Four Little Girls, Nobody Knew Their Names," 34; Jones, "Justice for Four Little Girls," 4–6; Klubuchar, *1963 Birmingham Church Bombing*, 12–14; McKinstry and George, *While the World Watched*, 16–23; McWhorter, "No Trial Closes Injustice's Wounds," 12A.

44. Eskew, *But for Bombingham*, 319–20; "Four Little Girls, Nobody Knew Their Names," 34; Jones, "Justice for Four Little Girls," 4–6; Klubuchar, *1963 Birmingham Church Bombing*, 12–14; McKinstry and George, *While the World Watched*, 61, 76.

45. Anderson, "The Past on Trial," 479–82; Eskew, *But for Bombingham*, 320; McCann, *Terrorism on American Soil*, 106; McWhorter, "Fearing the Worst," 16–18.

46. Klubuchar, *1963 Birmingham Church Bombing*, 19–20; Martinez, *Carpetbaggers, Cavalry, and the Ku Klux Klan*, ix–x; Ridgeway, *Blood in the Face*, 37–38; Wade, *The Fiery Cross*, vii–ix.

47. Chalmers, *Hooded Americanism*, 8–9; Martinez, *Carpetbaggers, Cavalry, and the Ku Klux Klan*, 7–12; Trelease, *White Terror*, 8–11, 430–31; Wade, *The Fiery Cross*, 32–33.

48. Chalmers, *Hooded Americanism*, 8–10, Klubuchar, *1963 Birmingham Church Bombing*, 19–20; Ridgeway, *Blood in the Face*, 51–52.

49. Horn, *Invisible Empire*, 113; Jones, "The Rise and Fall of the Ku Klux Klan," 17; Martinez, *Carpetbaggers, Cavalry, and the Ku Klux Klan*, 15–16; Trelease, *White Terror*, 13–14; Wade, *The Fiery Cross*, 38–39.

50. Martinez, *Carpetbaggers, Cavalry, and the Ku Klux Klan*, 18–23; Ridgeway, *Blood in the Face*, 51–52; Trelease, *White Terror*, 19–20; Wade, *The Fiery Cross*, 40–41.

51. Chalmers, *Hooded Americanism*, 1–2; Martinez, *Carpetbaggers, Cavalry, and the Ku Klux Klan*, ix–x, 241; Wade, *The Fiery Cross*, 112–16.

52. Martinez, *Carpetbaggers, Cavalry, and the Ku Klux Klan*, 241–46; Ridgeway, *Blood in the Face*, 52; Wade, *The Fiery Cross*, 110–39.

53. Chalmers, *Hooded Americanism*, 28–38; MacLean, *Behind the Mask of Chivalry*, 4–5; Martinez, *Carpetbaggers, Cavalry, and the Ku Klux Klan*, 250–51; Wade, *The Fiery Cross*, 140–47.

54. Chalmers, *Hooded Americanism*, 28–38; MacLean, *Behind the Mask of Chivalry*, 4–5; Ridgeway, *Blood in the Face*, 52; Wade, *The Fiery Cross*, 119–39.

55. Chalmers, *Hooded Americanism*, 31–36; MacLean, *Behind the Mask of Chivalry*, 5–6; Wade, *The Fiery Cross*, 153–57.

56. Chalmers, *Hooded Americanism*, 3–4; MacLean, *Behind the Mask of Chivalry*, xii–xvi; Ridgeway, *Blood in the Face*, 54–55; Wade, *The Fiery Cross*, 165, 186–204.

57. Chalmers, *Hooded Americanism*, 325–34; Wade, *The Fiery Cross*, 276–80.

58. Branch, *Parting the Waters*, 112–13, 222–25; Wade, *The Fiery Cross*, 297–99.

59. Chalmers, *Hooded Americanism*, 366; McCann, *Terrorism on American Soil*, 103–4; Ridgeway, *Blood in the Face*, 75–93; Wade, *The Fiery Cross*, 303–4, 316, 359–60.

60. Klubuchar, *1963 Birmingham Church Bombing*, 12–14; Martinez, *Carpetbaggers, Cavalry, and the Ku Klux Klan*, ix–xi; Ridgeway, *Blood in the Face*, 32–39.

61. Carson, "Between Contending Forces," 20; Eskew, *But for Bombingham*, 319–20; "Four Little Girls, Nobody Knew Their Names," 34; Klubuchar, *1963 Birmingham Church Bombing*, 14; McKinstry and George, *While the World Watched*, 61; McWhorter, "No Trial Closes Injustice's Wounds," 12A; Smith, "The Day the Children Died," 87–88.

62. Drabble, "The FBI, COINTELPRO-WHITE HATE, and the Decline of the Ku Klux Klan Organizations in Alabama," 6–7; "Four Little Girls, Nobody Knew Their Names," 34; Klubuchar, *1963 Birmingham Church Bombing*, 79–80; McWhorter, "No Trial Closes Injustice's Wounds," 12A.

63. McCann, *Terrorism on American Soil*, 106–10; McWhorter, "No Trial Closes Injustice's Wounds," 12A; Stewart, "Historic Church in Store for Revival," 42.

64. "Four Little Girls, Nobody Knew Their Names," 34; McCann, *Terrorism on American Soil*, 108–10.

65. Anderson, "The Past on Trial," 471–504; "Four Little Girls, Nobody Knew Their Names," 34; McCann, *Terrorism on American Soil*, 106–10; McWhorter, "No Trial Closes Injustice's Wounds," 12A; Metress, "Making Civil Rights Harder," 143–45.

8

"YOU DON'T NEED A WEATHERMAN TO KNOW WHICH WAY THE WIND BLOWS"

Weatherman and the
Counterculture Movement (1960s)

The point
Was anger, brother? Love? Dear premises
Vainly exploded, vainly dwelt upon.

—James Merrill, "18 West 11th Street"

During the turbulent decade of the 1960s, left-leaning groups emerged to challenge the status quo, especially in response to U.S. military involvement in Southeast Asia. Many of these so-called counterculture organizations used nonviolent techniques and bitterly criticized America's commitment to engaging in overseas military operations. As the decade progressed, the counterculture grew increasingly frustrated and militant. By the mid-1960s, as the U.S. commitment to military action in Vietnam intensified and the peaceful civil rights movement gave way to the more militant Black Power movement, a small band of young activists willingly embraced the violence they had disavowed years earlier. Organizations that previously would not have been characterized as "terrorist" challenged long-held preconceptions of what it means to be engaged in terrorism.[1]

As a case in point, consider Weatherman, later known as the Weather Underground Organization (WUO), a group of radical leftist anti-war protesters that broke away from the Students for a Democratic Society (SDS) in 1969 to declare war against the U.S. government for engaging in military action in Vietnam. The group's name derives from a lyric in Bob Dylan's

1965 song "Subterranean Homesick Blues": "You don't need a weatherman to know which way the wind blows." WUO activists contended that the only way to reform a deeply corrupted political system, and the only effective means of capturing media attention, was to "fight fire with fire." If the U.S. government insisted on exporting violence overseas, a domestic resistance movement would be forced to employ violence on American soil as a countermeasure. Unlike earlier protest movements, which largely were dedicated to using nonviolent techniques, the WUO and its affiliates eschewed Gandhi's principled, peaceful stance in favor of a more radical approach. A debate arose, and continues to this day, as to whether WUO members were domestic terrorists or legitimate protesters dedicated to reforming a hopelessly flawed political system.[2]

ORIGINS AND PURPOSES

A straightforward description of WUO members and their activities is complicated, as history often is, by competing interpretations of the group, its origins, and members' divergent motives. The traditional interpretation—sometimes labeled the "declension school"—suggests that idealistic college students, increasingly alarmed at the treatment afforded persons of color and the escalating U.S. involvement in the Vietnam War, became radicalized when peaceful protests failed to change societal values. These well-intentioned youngsters, rebelling against the old-fashioned, staid morality of the 1950s, embraced violent revolution as the only effective means of refashioning a hopelessly sullied society. This sympathetic retelling places responsibility on the corrupt powers that be for propelling protesters toward extremism. If the U.S. government had been more amenable to majoritarian criticism, student demonstrators could have worked through the existing political structure to effect incremental change. Because officials occupying high office refused to recognize the legitimate grievances of the masses—indeed, the corrupt leadership intentionally stifled dissent and undermined free speech at every opportunity—anti-war demonstrators, anxious to reform social and political policy and make government decisions more transparent, resorted to the only effective method of capturing attention for their cause. In this manner, according to the declension school, the "good 1960s" of JFK and Camelot, the Peace Corps, peaceful civil rights protests, and the sweet silliness of Flower Power degenerated into the "bad 1960s" of campus takeovers, ghetto uprisings, and bombings aimed at symbols of oppressive governmental power.[3]

Would that history were as simple as a sympathetic retelling would have it. Whether this pro-WUO interpretation remains valid will be the focus of this chapter, but the basic facts must first be recounted. Even at the beginning, the organization was not a warm, fuzzy group dedicated to peaceful ideals achieved through passive, largely white middle-class activism. The SDS was part of the self-proclaimed "Revolutionary Youth Movement" that sought to weaken capitalism through a working-class revolution. SDS members agreed on the ends (forcing the U.S. government to end the war in Vietnam), but the means were a source of contention.[4]

The group's origins could be traced indirectly to the Debsian Socialist Party of the early 1900s. Eugene V. Debs, a controversial American labor leader and perennial presidential candidate, argued against American involvement in World War I and frequently voiced opposition against the darker side of capitalism, which he claimed led to the oppression of the working man. In his view, capitalists, in their never-ending quest to increase profits, always seized control of government mechanisms to promote policies favoring the wealthy class over the working poor. In time, all governments, even those that promised to be responsive to the consent of the governed, would fall victim to capitalist corruption. As government became less transparent and less responsive to the citizenry, it would be transformed into an authoritarian state, in effect a plutocracy. Debs campaigned repeatedly for the presidency to call attention to the plight of the working man and the dangers of unfettered capitalism. His antagonistic message and charismatic delivery tested the boundaries of the First Amendment and the flexibility of the American political system.[5]

A group of younger socialists—Debs's successors in the American socialist movement—founded the League for Industrial Democracy (LID). LID's collegiate branch went through a series of name changes—the Student League for Industrial Democracy (SLID), which merged with the communist National Student League in the 1930s to become the American Student Union, and after a long dormant period morphed into the SDS in 1960. This evolution was by no means straightforward or without conflict, but the line of progression from blue-collar workers who felt exploited during the 1930s to relatively affluent, middle-class college students during the 1960s clearly existed.[6]

Social movements that garnered attention during the 1930s had waned by the 1960s. New strategies and tactics were required. Committed socialists and communists in the United States were frustrated by repeated failures to establish an effective third-party system that could compete against the Democratic and Republican political parties. A group of artists and liberals a decade earlier, usually referred to as the "Beats," initially offered promising grounds for creating a grassroots movement in line with socialist tendencies. Unfortunately for those activists with a political bent, the Beat Generation, with some exceptions, tended to be apolitical, preferring to express general discontent with society and its norms without offering practical alternatives to the *status quo ante*. Having resisted the communist witch hunts and blacklisting of the 1950s, dedicated socialists turned away from the Beats and resolved to work outside of the existing political system to use whatever means were necessary to influence American policy.[7]

If the Beat Generation could trigger discontent among young people during the Eisenhower era, something more was needed at decade's end. Two emerging issues galvanized college-age students during the early 1960s. First, an increasingly vocal group of activists began to protest nuclear weapons proliferation, especially in the wake of the October 1962 Cuban missile crisis. At approximately the same time, another group of activists demonstrated against racial segregation, especially in the Southern United States. It was only a matter of time before changing mores, as reflected in dance, film, drama, and music, triggered changes in America's slumbering youth, although even now it is difficult to say whether such changes were the cause or the effect of all that followed.[8]

Many historians sympathetic to the Left date the beginning of the 1960s protest movement to the first meeting of the SDS on the University of Michigan campus at Ann Arbor in 1960. Alan Haber, the first SDS president, issued a political manifesto thereafter known as the Port Huron Statement (PHS). Adopted at the first SDS convention in 1962, the PHS was the brainchild of a young student named Tom Hayden. In a conscious effort to unite the disparate protest movements throughout the country, Hayden and his cohorts bitterly criticized U.S. Cold War foreign policy, denouncing it as an utter failure that potentially would lead to, at best, a devastating arms race and, at worst, general nuclear war. The PHS also attacked continued racial discrimination and economic inequality perpetuated by longstanding American institutions. If societal ills were to be overcome, drastic reforms would be necessary. Owing to the rise of elitism throughout the entire American political system, including the major political parties, American corporations, and labor unions that were increasingly disconnected from the rank and file, the voices of average citizens had been muted, and government was no longer responsive to the will of the people. The PHS represented the rise of the "New Left." No longer satisfied to embrace the 1930s version of leftist policies and frustrated by the incremental nature of typical political reform, SDS members announced their willingness to embrace any group or cause to spread political power among the citizenry.[9]

If the PHS succeeded in bringing together disparate elements among young people on the left of the political spectrum, it also exposed tensions between the young Turks in the SDS and the old guard from LID. LID members were grounded in the anti-communism of earlier years as well as a concern for working men and women engaged in industrial trades. They worried that the overheated SDS rhetoric would trigger a backlash among reactionary forces within and without government. For their part, PHS proponents focused on capturing the attention of young people, especially liberal college students anxious to embrace a cause. To their way of thinking, appeals to the industrial classes were no longer effective. New strategies and tactics were needed to appeal to a new generation. This fissure between SDS and LID members ultimately led to a public split in 1965.[10]

Although one historian characterized the PHS as the "most comprehensive critique of American society that came out of the student movement," the early years of the SDS found the group marginalized, with few active members. During the 1962–1963 school year, the organization boasted nine chapters with approximately 1,000 members. Whatever else could be said about the SDS, its leadership had not yet found the formula to unite the "political moralism and cultural alienation" of leftist students. Little did anyone realize at the time that a costly war in a small country in Indochina would soon change the fortunes of the SDS.[11]

Throughout 1963 and 1964, the organization slowly added new members and chapters at universities across the nation. Eventually the group reached out to white unemployed youth through a program known as the Economic Research and Action Project (ERAP). While young, activist black men supported the nascent Black Power movement or accepted more formal roles in organizations such as the Student Nonviolent Coordinating Committee (SNCC), non-college-bound young white men found few outlets through which to express their disaffection. With the creation of ERAP, enterprising leaders at the SDS reached out to a great untapped resource to recruit a new class of political protesters.[12]

As promising as this movement "into the ghetto" appeared to be, by the summer of 1964, campus-centered SDS members began to split from their ERAP counterparts. The entire organization might have imploded that same year but for a fortuitous event that occurred at the University of California, Berkeley, on October 1. A charismatic student activist, Mario Savio, led a crowd of 3,000 students in a dramatic demonstration that became known as the "free speech movement." The SDS-led student protest movement, which had seemed on the verge of atrophy, suddenly gained new life.[13]

In the spring of 1965, as president Lyndon B. Johnson committed ground troops into South Vietnam, student protesters suddenly found a new raison d'être. During the next three years, the SDS led a series of anti-war demonstrations, predominantly on college campuses. When the group's leaders were not raging against the military-industrial complex or lamenting the innumerable failures of American institutions, they were championing a variety of campus issues such as the lack of power among student government associations, the need to prohibit military recruiting on college campuses, and even students' desires to force their institutions to serve better food in the campus dining hall. By the mid-1960s, it seemed that no issue was too large or small to fall beneath the umbrella of either the SDS or a companion activist group.[14]

While this evolution from a small, essentially unknown organization limited to a few tiny colleges to a ubiquitous presence on numerous campuses throughout the United States increased SDS clout among young people, some radical members grew dissatisfied with the "watered-down" demonstrations that occurred as a result. Matters came to a head during the spring of 1968, when SDS leaders organized "Ten Days of Resistance," a coordinated series of rallies, marches, sit-ins, and teach-ins designed to call attention to American hypocrisy in the Vietnam War. On April 26, 1968, approximately one million students skipped classes to show solidarity with the anti-war movement. It was, and remains, the largest student strike in American history. Some colleges, especially Columbia University in New York City, captured national attention when their students revolted against what they saw as an oppressive administration. SDS spokesperson Mark Rudd emerged from the Columbia student revolt as a household name. By 1969, even persons who did not follow the student protest movement in the mainstream media had become aware of the power and might of the SDS.[15]

Therein lay the problem. When a small, radical activist organization becomes chic and its cachet appeals to a large mass of mostly middle-class do-gooders, the organization may be forced to make compromises. In short, its breadth limits its depth. The 1968–1969 academic year was the highwater mark for the SDS. As the group spread across college campuses, local chapters chipped away at the group's core functions and sought to modify its goals. Some chapter presidents argued that the group had taken on too many activities and therefore needed to focus on a few key issues. Other local members contended that the SDS had been co-opted by other, more radical groups and must change its tactics if it hoped to remain relevant.

The University of Texas chapter of the Students for a Democratic Society (SDS) demonstrates against the Vietnam War. Courtesy of the Library of Congress.

Ironically, by enjoying runaway success throughout the country, the SDS had sown the seeds of its own demise. In attempting to unite disparate factions, the group collapsed into a series of ever-increasing factions.[16]

WEATHERMAN IS BORN

During the summer of 1969, factions formed inside the SDS, each claiming to be the real voice of the group, thereby leading to the demise of the national organization. One SDS member, Mike Klonsky, emerged as a spokesman for the conservative faction, the "National Office." Klonsky prepared a manifesto titled "Toward a Revolutionary Youth Movement" (RYM) outlining a plan for young workers to overthrow capitalism through violent means, if necessary, although the document refrained from advocating direct action. A group of more militant SDS activists argued that aggressive tactics were imperative if the youth movement hoped to effect positive change in public policy. At the SDS convention in Chicago in June 1969, two position papers circulated among attendees. A revised version of Klonsky's statement, supported by a group dubbed RYM II, called for a measured approach to social change.[17]

The militant faction, labeled RYM I, issued a competing manifesto titled "You Don't Need a Weatherman to Know Which Way the Wind Blows." The manifesto argued that North Vietnamese leader Ho Chi Minh was justified in fighting American imperialism in Southeast Asia because he was a liberator in the great struggle against a corrupt superpower. The appropriate response for anti-war activists in the United States was to throw their support to the North Vietnamese communists even if this position initially seemed audacious. The only effective means of opposing a tyrant is to support the tyrant's enemy. As for the bitterly divisive issue of race inside the country, RYM I supporters expressed unconditional support for a radical African-American organization, the Black Panthers, in the ongoing battle against white supremacists. When white police officers killed Black Panther Fred Hampton in Illinois in December 1969, RYM I supporters declared war on the U.S. government in direct response.[18]

Additional factions and splinter groups formed from these initial SDS factions. For the purposes of this chapter, however, it is instructive to focus on the more radical of the two major factions that arose in 1969. The radical RYM I group occasionally used the SDS name in communications, but members eventually began using the name "Weatherman," or, colloquially, "the Weathermen."[19]

Weatherman's founding manifesto, "You Don't Need a Weatherman to Know Which Way the Wind Blows," was a provocative document in many respects. Signed by SDS activists Karen Ashley, Bill Ayers, Bernadine Dohrn, John "J. J." Jacobs, Jeff Jones, Gerry Long, Howie Machtinger, Jim Mellon, Terry Robbins, Mark Rudd, and Steve Tappis, the manifesto announced that "the main struggle going on in the world today is between U.S. imperialism and the national liberation struggles against it." To fight against such a strong "oppressor nation," young people must mobilize to "make a revolution." As part of this mobilization, the activists vowed to "transform people's everyday problems, and the issues and struggles growing out of them, into revolutionary consciousness, active and conscious opposition to racism and imperialism." Specifically, "we can effect consciousness and pick up people through agitational work at plants, train shops, etc., selling Movements, handing out leaflets about the war, the Panthers, the companies' holdings overseas or relations to defense industry, etc."[20]

It was clear from the moment of inception that Weatherman believed the nonviolent protests of the early 1960s were no longer effective. American society and government had become so corrupted that only violent, revolutionary change could force the powers that be to change. Aside from

Prominent Weather Underground Organization activists march during the "Days of Rage" on October 11, 1969, to protest among other things, the trial of the Chicago Seven. Courtesy of Getty Images.

demonstrations on college campuses, during the June convention Weatherman called for "urban guerilla actions" that would draw attention to their cause and assist in triggering a worldwide revolution. Thus did the "Days of Rage" originate to "bring the war home," in John Jacobs's words. Scheduled to last for days in October 1969, the opening salvo occurred on October 8 when a small group destroyed a famous statue in Chicago commemorating the 1886 Haymarket riot. The bomb that toppled the statue blew out one hundred windows and sent pieces of the monument onto the nearby Kennedy Expressway. A year later, after the monument had been repaired, Weatherman blew it up again.[21]

The group held a series of rallies specifically designed to inflame the crowd. During those four days in October, Weatherman led hundreds of protesters in riots in several areas of Chicago, including the affluent Gold Coast neighborhood. When the smoke cleared, the Days of Rage cost Chicago and the state of Illinois $183,000 ($100,000 for National Guard expenses, $35,000 in damages, and $20,000 for one injured bystander's medical expenses). In the aftermath, many Weatherman and SDS leaders were jailed in lieu of $243,000 bail.[22]

Coupled with a July 1969 visit to Cuba by thirty Weatherman leaders, the group's activities during the Days of Rage captured headlines and called attention to a new, far more aggressive faction in the anti-war movement. During a series of meetings in Flint, Michigan, late in December 1969, the self-proclaimed "war council" of three hundred die-hard revolutionaries set forth an increasingly violent agenda. Bernadine Dohrn captured the spirit of those sessions when she urged participants to set aside their fear and commence with the inevitable "armed struggle." For his part, John Jacobs launched into a harangue denouncing the "pacifism" of conservative, bourgeois white youth. Perhaps the highlight of the convention was the mass "wargasm" where conference participants practiced karate and warbled through a series of revolutionary songs.[23]

The affair could be dismissed as another episode in the silliness that became the 1960s were it not for Weatherman's subsequent activities. The war council resolved to "go underground" and fight the U.S. government through violent actions practiced by a small, dedicated group of revolutionaries instead of reaching out to the masses. This decision necessitated the dissolution of the SDS. At its height, SDS chapters on college campuses throughout the United States boasted 100,000 members. In its new, more violent phase, Weatherman did not require grassroots appeal. The time for joining hands and recruiting well-meaning, white, liberal, middle-class college students had ended. The only effective means to combat the destructive power of the U.S. military and its corrupted government was to "engage in guerrilla warfare."[24]

And so it began.

Weatherman commenced a bombing campaign in February 1970. On February 16, an unknown assailant placed a nail bomb on a window ledge in a police substation in San Francisco. The resultant blast killed one police sergeant and wounded a second officer. Investigators believed that Weatherman was responsible, but they could never conclusively prove the case. Five days later, marauders tossed three Molotov cocktails at the home of New York State Supreme Court justice John Murtagh, who was then presiding over the criminal trial of a notorious gang known as "Panther 21," members of the Black Panther Party accused of plotting to bomb New York landmarks and department stores. Once again, police failed to apprehend the responsible parties, but no one doubted Weatherman involvement.[25]

Group members hatched plans to attack the Fort Dix army base as well as Columbia University, but an accident put an end to their initial schemes. On March 6, 1970, a small faction of Weatherman convened in a Greenwich Village safe house owned by the father of member Cathy Wilkerson to construct a nail bomb in preparation for the next wave of violence. The device, encompassing electric fuses and dynamite, was much more complex and elaborate than earlier bombs. To complicate matters, no one working on the device had experience with explosives. Consequently, the bomb prematurely detonated. Three group leaders—Ted Gold, Diana Oughton, and Terry Robbins—died. Two activists inside the townhouse, Kathy Boudin and Cathy Wilkerson, were upstairs at the time and thereby survived the blast. The women emerged from the building, dazed and shaken, as smoke billowed from a hole where the front door had been blown away.[26]

"I felt my house tremble," a neighbor, Susan Wager, later recalled. "It was like an earthquake." She rushed outside in time to see Cathy Wilkerson, naked, and Kathy Boudin, partially clad in jeans, emerge from the inferno. Presumably, the force of the explosion ripped the clothes from their bodies. Ms. Wager ushered the young women into her house, allowed them to take a shower, and supplied them with fresh clothes. Afterward, she rushed back outside to see if anyone else needed help and to try and learn what had happened. Later, when she returned to her house, she discovered that the two women had fled the scene. One of the young ladies was still wearing Ms. Wager's favorite coat and boots. "I thought they were in an accident," she explained. "I never thought they could have been responsible." Both Kathy Boudin and Cathy Wilkerson slipped underground for more than a decade.[27]

More than anything else Weatherman had attempted until that time, the March 1970 explosion garnered a frenzy of media attention. Police officers and firefighters converged on the scene, desperate to determine whether the blast was the result of a horrible accident or a purposive act of violence. Evening news broadcasts emphasized the powerful nature of the destruction, which was all the more sensational when journalists discovered that motion picture actor Dustin Hoffman lived next door to the Number 18 townhouse. Photographers captured shots of the famous actor, obviously shaken, as he surveyed the damage to his home and learned that he could not reenter the building until investigators gauged the level of damage.[28]

The townhouse destroyed by the bomb, formerly the residence of Merrill Lynch brokerage firm founder Charles Merrill and his son, a poet named James, was obliterated. James Merrill later penned one of his most famous poems, "18 West 11th Street," about the incident. Although the young poet no longer lived in the townhouse when the incident occurred, he imagined the destruction wrought by the tremendous blast: "Shards of a blackened witness still in place. The charred ice-sculpture garden / Beams fell upon. The cold blue searching beams." Investigators marveled at the force of the destruction, but they were thankful that not all of the dynamite ignited. If it had done so, according to a later report produced by the Federal Bureau of Investigation (FBI), the devastation probably would have been far worse since Weatherman possessed enough explosives to "level . . . both sides of the street."[29]

Not long after this high-profile episode, surviving members truly "went underground," changing their name to the Weather Underground Organization (WUO). What had started out as an idealistic movement comprised of anti-war youth had become a violent, revolutionary faction. Gone were the days of the SDS members picketing college campuses to provide more amenities and better food in the dining hall. WUO activists soon found themselves pursued vigorously by the FBI and other law enforcement personnel. Membership shrank precipitously, but the group's proponents remained convinced that their government's actions in Vietnam were morally unjustified and must be resisted.[30]

WUO apologists have always contended that the activists were not terrorists. They never sought to take human life or strike terror into the hearts of innocent bystanders. Their goal was to capture the attention of policy makers and bring pressure to bear on elected officials to democratize U.S. government decision-making processes. Rather than escalate the violence and risk harming civilians, the WUO initiated a campaign of bombing empty offices at night so no one would be injured or killed in the blast. If the WUO was going to claim the high moral ground, it was important to damage property without harming human life. The question of whether WUO participants were terrorists remains a point of no small contention.[31]

However the group might be characterized, the March 1970 explosion triggered a major reassessment of objectives. On May 21, the WUO issued a communiqué promising to assail a "symbol or institution of American injustice" within two weeks. Two weeks came and went, and no incidents occurred. On June 9, the group attempted to make good on its promise by planting ten sticks of dynamite in the New York City police headquarters. In keeping with the self-professed philosophy of avoiding casualties, someone telephoned a warning to the precinct approximately six minutes before the bomb exploded. A month later, a grand jury in Detroit indicted thirteen WUO participants for conspiracy to bomb and kill. Later in the year, the FBI placed prominent members of the group on the Ten Most-Wanted List.[32]

During the next two years, the Weather Underground engaged in highly visible insurrectionary activities. Perhaps the two most notable endeavors were the group's successful plan to engineer LSD champion Timothy Leary's prison escape in September 1970 and the May 1972 bombing of the women's bathroom in the Air Force wing of the Pentagon. In the former case, Leary, a former Harvard University psychologist who had become a vocal proponent of using hallucinogenic drugs, had been arrested in California in February 1970 for possessing a small amount of marijuana. Owing to a previous conviction for marijuana possession in Texas, Leary was characterized as a habitual offender. In the hysterical tenor of the times, he received a ten-year prison sentence for what otherwise would have been a misdemeanor case. Incarcerated at the California Men's Colony at San Luis Obispo, the self-confessed "high priest" of the drug culture reached out to his followers to help him escape.[33]

One group, a drug-trafficking organization known as the Brotherhood of Eternal Love, answered the call. The brotherhood contacted WUO members and requested assistance in carrying out the scheme. Anxious to prove their bona fides among counterculture organizations, Weather Underground participants agreed to assist. The WUO may have received $20,000 or $25,000 in return, although the point has been disputed. In any case, on the evening of September 13, 1970, Leary climbed onto a prison wall and, placing one hand over another, slowly shimmied along a cable that extended across the courtyard. After he was free from the walls, he released from the cable, dropped to the ground, and dashed toward a local highway. He waited in a ditch at a prearranged location until a car pulled to the shoulder of the road, signaled to the escapee, and drove him to safety.[34]

The WUO had meticulously planned the prison break. Driving north away from the men's colony, Leary's rescuers provided him with false identification papers and new clothing. They also insisted that he dye his hair a different color. After the first group left Leary's prison garb at one rest stop, another group retrieved the clothing and deposited it at a rest stop one hundred miles south of the prison to confuse the authorities investigating the episode. Finding the discarded rags south of the prison, police would assume that Leary was headed for Mexico and therefore would focus their efforts on securing the southern border. In the meantime, the WUO transported the good doctor to a safe house in North Oakland, California. He eventually hid in a series of Northern California locations before he was smuggled out of the country. Landing in Algeria, he took up residence with a separatist sect of the American Black Panther Party. Two years later, after seeking refuge in several countries, Leary was arrested and extradited to the United States. He offered to assist the FBI in obtaining information about the Weather Underground in exchange for leniency, although Leary later claimed that nothing he told federal investigators could be used to undermine WUO activities.[35]

The second major activity occurred on May 19, 1972—a date chosen because it was the late Ho Chi Minh's birthday. A WUO operative placed a bomb in the women's bathroom on the fourth floor of the U.S. Defense Department Pentagon office building near Washington, D.C. The blast tore out a thirty-foot section of the wall, destroying windows and damaging a computer on the first floor. Although the destruction was minimal—nothing to compare with the damage inflicted on September 11, 2001, from the terrorist attack on the Pentagon—the symbolic value of targeting the heart of the American military-industrial complex once again buttressed the WUO's credibility inside the counterculture movement.[36]

In many ways, the 1972 attack on the Pentagon represented the highwater mark of the Weather Underground. As the Vietnam War wound to an end, the mood of the country changed. The revolutionary movement among the nation's young people lost its momentum. WUO members had reveled in their martyrdom and dedication to the cause, but in 1973 things changed. First, with the end of the Vietnam War, anti-war activists lost the main source of their righteous indignation. In addition, the U.S. government dropped criminal charges against most WUO activists. Owing to recent court decisions barring electronic surveillance absent a court order, the FBI realized that prosecuting violent anti-war activists would be extremely difficult because much of the assembled evidence would be inadmissible. Moreover, U.S. intelligence agencies had used surveillance methods against domestic activists that would have to be detailed in court if members of the Weather Underground were prosecuted. Rather than risk revealing top-secret methods and operations, federal officials preferred to let the matter drop.[37]

It was not surprising that the FBI declined to prosecute the Weather Underground. During the early 1970s, the bureau increasingly came under attack for its counterintelligence program, known by the code name COINTELPRO. The program originated in 1956 in response to FBI director J. Edgar Hoover's concerns about the pervasive activities of subversive groups, primarily the U.S. Communist Party. During the ensuing years, COINTELPRO expanded to include surveillance on a variety of groups deemed a security risk to the U.S. government, including the Ku Klux Klan, the Nation of Islam, the Black Panther Party, nonviolent civil rights groups, and leftist organizations such as Weatherman. Ignoring constitutional requirements and other legal niceties, investigators frequently employed electronic surveillance without a warrant or effective judicial oversight. Aside from employing surveillance activities in clear violation of the Fourth Amendment to the U.S. Constitution, the bureau used a campaign of "dirty tricks" to browbeat suspects and persons of interest into curtailing their activities. Sometimes FBI agents sent anonymous letters to group members threatening to expose a compromising secret or publish a salacious photograph if the subject did not cease and desist in his or her activities. No manner of blackmail or innuendo was beyond the pale.[38]

COINTELPRO might have continued indefinitely were it not for a breach of security. A group calling itself "Citizens' Commission to Investigate the FBI" burglarized an FBI office in Media, Pennsylvania, in April 1971. Thieves absconded with hundreds of pages of confidential COINTELPRO files clearly showing the bureau's interest in radical groups such as the WUO. To minimize the resultant backlash, Hoover formally dissolved COINTELPRO in 1971. Nonetheless, the agency continued to keep a watchful eye on Weatherman even after Hoover died in 1972. In fact, the bureau's Special Target Information Development program sent agents undercover to infiltrate the organization and conduct "black-bag jobs," that is, illegal searches inside the homes of suspected WUO members, their families, and their associates.[39]

Congress subsequently investigated COINTELPRO and other FBI tactics employed in the 1950s and 1960s. In 1978, during the Carter administration, U.S. attorney general Griffin Bell launched an investigation that resulted in criminal indictments brought against several high-ranking FBI officials. The negative publicity and intense public scrutiny of the post–Hoover era FBI ensured that much of the information collected against groups such as the WUO could not be used to prosecute suspected offenders. Consequently, Weatherman activists who saw fit to renounce their ways and return to the mainstream generally faced few, if any, serious criminal charges.[40]

After the end of the Vietnam War, WUO members found themselves at a crossroads. To recapture the waning momentum, in 1974 movement leaders, principally Bill Ayers, Bernadine Dohrn, Jeff Jones, and Celia Sojourn, issued a new manifesto, *Prairie Fire: The Politics of Revolutionary Anti-Imperialism*. The manifesto began by remembering the three Weatherman members who perished in the March 1970 Greenwich Village bomb snafu. Afterward, the authors explained that their purpose was "to explain the changes in U.S. and world conditions since the Vietnam ceasefire and to evaluate the consequences of the Vietnamese victory." In their view, the end of the Vietnam War did not signal the end of American imperialism. "The only path to the final defeat of imperialism and the building of socialism is Revolutionary war," the manifesto boldly proclaimed. "Revolutionary war will be complicated and protracted. . . . Revolution is a fight by the people for power. It is a changing of power in which existing social and economic relations are turned upside down."[41]

Most of *Prairie Fire* attempted to explain why the first stages of the revolution had been successful but why the fight had to continue unabated. The authors recognized that the "U.S. people entered the '70s weary of war, skeptical of government leaders, uncertain about the future." Moreover, the "'70s bring inflation, recession, unemployment, the chance of war, in crisis after crisis in the lives of millions here." In the post-Vietnam era, citizens must rise up and take control of their government through whatever means are necessary to ensure success. As with most manifestoes dealing with broad social movements, *Prairie Fire* was short on specific recommendations apart from calling for improved organization among workers, radical teachers, and young people. At its conclusion, the manifesto urged sympathizers within the educational establishment to "radicalize other teachers, organize the parents, teach and encourage your students. Health workers can choose hospitals and clinics in poor communities. Cultural activists, street players, artists, writers should propagandize and relate to poor and working people." Recognizing that the current presidential administration was reeling from new revelations involving the Watergate break-in, *Prairie Fire* offered one bit of concrete political advice: "Impeach Nixon and jail him for his major crimes. He is one of the top criminals of the century, a war maker, a life taker. His isolation and exposed condition is the mirror image of U.S. defeat in Vietnam. Nixon merits the people's justice."[42]

They were stirring words, indicating that the WUO was as strident and unrepentant as ever. For all the fiery rhetoric, however, the group had already lost its grassroots base of support. The masses simply were unable or unwilling to engage in violent insurrectionary activities. To some extent *Prairie Fire*, with its emphasis on organizing sympathizers to work within the existing political system in hopes of achieving "consciousness of action," tacitly recognized that the time for armed resistance, like the Vietnam War, had ended. For that reason, during the ensuing years, WUO leaders would be drawn to community action projects, especially in urban areas.[43]

THE DEMISE OF THE WUO

By the mid-1970s, the times they were a-changin', and the Vietnam era was fading away rapidly. The war had ended several years earlier, Richard Nixon was no longer president, and the activist movement among college aged youth had all but dissolved. The public protests and landmark legislation enacted during the 1960s civil rights movement had led to marked improvements in race relations. The anger and frustration that had boiled over on college campuses half a dozen years earlier seemed somehow silly and antiquated. Americans of all ages seemed far more interested in securing gainful employment, coping with energy shortages amidst increasing petroleum prices, and competing with the USSR in democratizing the developing world. With the collapse of the FBI's COINTELPRO surveillance, Weatherman criminal prosecutions were not a realistic threat. The group's fifteen minutes of fame had passed.[44]

WUO activists understood that something needed to be done if the organization was to survive, but no one had a workable plan in mind. In 1975, the group launched a magazine titled *Osawatomie*, named for the Kansas town where messianic abolitionist John Brown led a guerrilla raid against pro-slavery partisans in 1856. Promising to publish the rag four times a year, the editors plainly stated their objective: "If everyone who has a copy shows it to at least 10 coworkers, friends, or people living in the same building, passing it hand-to-hand, tens of thousands of people can read it." Presumably, if enough people understood the group's central message, words could accomplish what violence thus far had not, namely a change in American consciousness. The authors stated "the certainty that we will see revolution in our lifetime, and a spirit of love for the exploited people of the world."

Acknowledging that such a small group faced almost insurmountable odds in fighting the Leviathan of American government, the writers character- ized their effort as "a bee sting": "This is a bee sting against such a powerful enemy, but a bee sting whose strength is multiplied many times by the fact that these actions represent the early stages of sustained armed struggle led by a political organization."[45]

They were powerful words, but the cause was already lost, and the Weather people knew it. Beginning in the mid-1970s, they gamely attempted to cre- ate an umbrella organization for activist groups, but the movement never got off the ground. The old schisms remained as potent as ever. Members debated whether to continue violent activities and, if so, how far to take the campaign. The Weather Underground dissolved into two new factions—the May 19 Communist Organization and the Prairie Fire Collective—a move that was the death knell for the original organization.[46]

In the meantime, in November 1977, police arrested five Weather Underground members for conspiring to bomb the offices of California state senator John Briggs, a conservative Republican who championed an increase in nuclear power production, wider application of the death pen- alty, and an ultimately unsuccessful measure to fire any teacher who was found to be "advocating, imposing, encouraging or promoting" homosexual activity. Two undercover FBI agents, Richard J. Gianotti and William D. Reagan, uncovered evidence of the conspiracy and compromised their identities to obtain arrest warrants for five radicals affiliated with Weather- man. Clayton Van Lydegraf, the mastermind of the plot, was a sixty-two- year-old longtime supporter of the U.S. Communist Party and cofounder of the Prairie Fire Organizing Committee. At the time, the FBI estimated that the WUO had only a few dozen hard-core members, but the zealots remained dedicated to disrupting government operations and perpetrating violent acts across the country. The presence of a dedicated activist such as Van Lydegraf was disquieting because it suggested that the Weather people had lost none of their appetite for violence.[47]

The other activists arrested along with Van Lydegraf included thirty- three-year-old Judith Bissell, married to Silas Bissell, descendant of a well-known carpet cleaner family. Bissell was a graduate of the University of Pennsylvania and was known in law enforcement circles for helping to plant a Molotov cocktail at the University of Washington Air Force ROTC building in 1970. Marc Curtis, aka Marc Perry, was a twenty-nine-year-old former prelaw student at the University of Washington who had been ar- rested at a Weatherman rally in Chicago in 1969 before going underground. Thomas "Michael" Justesen, aged twenty-seven, was a former student at

the University of Washington who had been arrested for destroying government property during a Seattle demonstration in 1970 but had gone
missing before trial. Leslie Anne "Esther" Mullin was a thirty-three-year-
old daughter of a retired Air Force colonel. She had been a Peace Corps
member in Africa prior to enrolling at the University of Washington and
joining the SDS. Each of the suspects, save Van Lydegraf, pleaded guilty to
the charges. Van Lydegraf chose to stand trial.[48]

The Briggs plot was the last major offensive planned by Weather people.
By the end of 1977, the WUO as a formal organization had ceased to exist.
The most radical members chose to remain underground and engage in
criminal enterprises of one sort or another while others searched for an opportunity to rejoin mainstream society. Within a few years, members in the
latter camp surrendered to authorities after availing themselves of President Ford's amnesty program for draft dodgers. WUO leader Mark Rudd
came forward on January 20, 1978, was fined $4,000, and received two
years probation, a relatively light punishment reflecting the changing tenor
of the times. Two of the most prominent Weatherman leaders, Bernadine
Dohrn and Bill Ayers, surrendered to authorities in New York on December 3, 1980. The charges against Ayers were dropped. Dohrn received
three years of probation and paid a $15,000 fine. During their years on the
lam, Dohrn and Ayers had married each other. After 1980, they settled in
the Chicago area, and as they aged, the couple settled into the comfortable,
middle-class existence they had railed against in their salad days. It was all
so normal, so mainstream, and so bourgeois.[49]

A handful of unreconstructed WUO radicals remained at large, but their
increasingly violent activities ensured that they could not stay underground
indefinitely. The most notorious holdouts were Kathy Boudin, Judith Alice
Clark, and David Gilbert, all of whom joined the Black Liberation Army
(BLA), a militant, pro-Marxist radical successor to the Black Panther Party.
The BLA robbed a Brinks armored truck and killed two police officers and
a security guard in October 1981. After their capture, trial, and conviction,
the trio were sent to prison for lengthy sentences. As for the BLA, the
group essentially dissolved after 1981.[50]

As terrorist groups go, the WUO was not prolific or especially violent.
Because they did not advocate violence against people and focused on symbolic property crimes, the surviving members rejoined mainstream society
with relatively little difficulty. Dohrn, originally trained as a lawyer, joined
the prestigious Chicago law firm of Sidley Austin before serving as a law
professor at Northwestern University. Her husband, Bill Ayers, became a
professor in the college of education at the University of Illinois at Chicago.

For close to three decades, the couple worked in a variety of community projects with very little fanfare. Occasionally, someone would dredge up the past and ask about their radical activities, but Dohrn and Ayers mostly slipped into obscurity.[51]

Suddenly, during the 2008 presidential campaign, Bill Ayers found himself thrust back into the limelight as news reporters and conservative political figures questioned his association with Democratic presidential nominee Barack H. Obama. As a rising political figure in Illinois politics, Obama had attended government and business meetings as well as social receptions where Ayers was present. It would have been a stretch to call the men friends, although clearly they knew each other and were associates. "I think my relationship with Obama was probably like that of thousands of others in Chicago and, like millions and millions of others," Ayers told two reporters in a 2008 interview, "I wished I knew him better." Aside from encountering Obama during an occasional Chicagoland business or political meeting, Ayers simply did not know the man well and could not claim to be part of the candidate's inner circle.[52]

Despite the tenuous connection, conservative politicians and anti-government bloggers could not resist the chance to wallow in demagoguery. It was a classic case of guilt by association, and enthusiastic Obama opponents played the supposedly nefarious relationship to the hilt. No opportunist was more zealous in denouncing the "Obama threat" than Sarah Palin, the Republican vice presidential nominee who repeatedly touted the Obama-Ayers "relationship" as potentially destructive to the American republic. If a youthful Bill Ayers had been a bomb-throwing radical hell-bent on subverting the U.S. government during the 1960s and 1970s, surely this strange, skinny mulatto with the funny, vaguely Arab-sounding name who had met Ayers on several occasions must be in cahoots with the unreconstructed terrorist. After all, once a terrorist, always a terrorist; and anyone a terrorist comes into contact with is, by definition, at least worthy of suspicion. It was a brilliant smear tactic that generated headlines and sensationalistic media attention for a brief period in the fall of 2008.[53]

After it became clear that the chicanery had failed to resonate beyond those Americans already predisposed to embrace wild conspiracy theories, an increasingly desperate Palin, her poll numbers fading, tried to whip Republican crowds into a frenzy of hysteria during several campaign rallies. "Our opponent is someone who sees America as imperfect enough to pal around with terrorists who targeted their own country," she said to enormous crowd approval on more than one occasion. By citing "terrorists" in the plural and deliberately withholding the context, the would-be vice president intended to stoke the fires of fear over terrorism by appealing to the baser instincts of U.S. voters. Some commentators suspected that race and xenophobia played a part as well, although Palin and her running mate, presidential candidate John McCain, vehemently denied the charge they were deliberately pandering to the dark side of American politics. Despite this attempt to resurrect the specter of proto-terrorists seizing control of the executive branch of government, the Republicans lost the 2008 presidential election.[54]

For all of the demagoguery surrounding the Ayers-Obama controversy, it raised an important underlying point. What constitutes a "terrorist," and did Weatherman meet that definition? The FBI labeled the organization a "domestic terrorist group," but Ayers took issue with the characterization. As he wrote in a memoir of his underground experiences, "Terrorists terrorize, they kill innocent civilians, while we organized and agitated. Terrorists destroy randomly, while our actions bore, we hoped, the precise stamp of a cut diamond. Terrorists intimidate, while we aimed only to educate. No, we're not terrorists." Dan Berger, author of *Outlaws in America* and an apologist for Weatherman, echoed Ayers's main argument, namely that Weatherman "purposefully and successfully avoided injuring anyone. . . . Its war against property by definition means that the WUO was not a terrorist organization."[55]

CONCLUSION

Weatherman presents a difficult case study in the history of American terrorism. Because the group was not the only counterculture organization to protest government action through violent means, the question naturally arises as to why this group, as opposed to others, should serve as emblematic. In addition, Bill Ayers's contention that the WUO was not dedicated to terrorist attacks suggests that the group does not meet this book's definition of terrorism, namely violence or the threat thereof that violates the law, targets civilians, and is dedicated to a broader goal than the attack itself.

The prominence of WUO members Bernadine Dohrn and Bill Ayers after they rejoined mainstream society and the latter's connection with Barack Obama provide ample justification for studying Weatherman. Other groups may have been more violent or they may have articulated a more coherent anti-war message, but for better or worse, Weatherman has become a symbol of the 1960s counterculture. The group's continued vitality in popular culture makes it a compelling candidate for a case study on terrorism.

The question of whether the group engaged in terrorist activities is more problematic. It is tempting to dismiss Weatherman's activities as simply the misguided shenanigans of naive, rogue idealists who, having grown frustrated and disillusioned with the slow nature of normal discourse and public policy development in the American political system, unapologetically employed violence to express their grievances. The source of the frustration and disillusionment is difficult to pinpoint precisely, for group members generally were not working class, nor were they directly affected by the social welfare policies of the state. Many leaders who broke away from the SDS were privileged, white, middle-class young people with leisure time on their hands and an exalted sense of their place in the American political landscape. If they had been called upon to make sacrifices for the polity in the same manner that their parents and grandparents of the Greatest Generation had sacrificed during the Great Depression and World War II, their sense of civic virtue might not have been warped by the confused, and confusing, developments in the Cold War and the nuclear age. Yes, the United States in the 1960s appeared to confront enormous, dispiriting problems—fears of creeping communist influence around the world, the quagmire of a disastrous ground war in Southeast Asia, a loss of confidence in Americans' values and sense of purpose—but the question remains as to whether engaging in violence was a suitable response. From the perspective of a later time, Weatherman is what happens "when good kids go bad."[56]

To an extent, this interpretation is persuasive. Some scholars have argued that a youth revolution was overdue in light of the societal rigidity and bland conformity of 1950s America as well as the deference to large institutions that occurred during the Eisenhower era when citizens were expected to "get with the program" and not question, much less criticize, their institutions of government or their political leaders. Following a long period of placid conformity, it was natural that socially conscious Americans, especially young people enrolled in elite universities, would feel compelled to express their dissatisfaction. As it became clear that the country's leaders were not the wise, benevolent figures of popular portrayal, citizens lost faith in the efficacy and good faith of government. A series of frightening, seemingly inexplicable developments—the formation of the Warsaw Pact, the launching of the Soviet satellite Sputnik, the humiliating failure of the Bay of Pigs invasion, the construction of the Berlin Wall, and the Cuban missile crisis, among other events occurring against the backdrop of the Cold War—convinced people who otherwise probably would have supported government that new solutions and ways of acting were necessary. The world was a scary place, far too scary to be left to the slipshod machinations of inept, secretive leaders. Across the globe, not just in the United States, the 1960s witnessed emerging conflicts over war, peace, race, class, and political power. Young people in that decade were poised to assail the *status quo ante*, whatever it might be. If the Vietnam War had not existed, it would have been necessary to create it. This insight recalls a well-known 1953 Marlon Brando film, *The Wild One*. In one scene, a character asks Brando's character, "What're you rebelling against, Johnny?" The response is classic: "Whaddya got?"[57]

For all its explanatory power, this neat and tidy interpretation seals off the WUO as yet another anomaly in that crazy, turbulent decade of the 1960s. It affords the facile student of history a means of glossing over the more important questions, especially whether a violent activist group, no matter how well meaning its proponents were in the beginning and no matter what the historical circumstances, can be considered a "terrorist" group. Addressing the question of whether the Weather people were terrorists requires an assessment of the case for and against such a conclusion.

Let us initially consider the case against characterizing Weatherman as a terrorist organization. As Bill Ayers claimed in his memoirs, most WUO activists deliberately sought to avoid human casualties, although whenever violence is employed, unintended consequences are possible. The "cut of diamond" argument suggests that violence can be an acceptable form of social and political protest if it is used with precision and accuracy. Destroying the property of a corrupted government, which had stolen the money and faith of its people in the first place, would not be a terroristic act in Ayers's way of thinking. Because the Weather people theoretically acted on behalf of the masses—however the "masses" might be defined—they were stewards of the people and not the vigilantes that conservative American political leaders claimed. The ultimate objective of their activities was to call attention to endemic flaws in the political system and thereby create a groundswell for reform. Unlike classic terrorist organizations that seek to horrify, maim, and kill innocent victims, Weather people carefully and methodically planned their operations. They were builders, not destroyers. Motivated by their desire to return the United States to its founding creed—namely, that all men are created equal and that all persons deserve equal justice under law—they acted as they did not because they hated their country, but because they loved it. According to this view, criticism, even expressed in violent ways, is directed toward the eventual salvation of a society, and its government.[58]

Weather people compared and contrasted their actions with the actions of the corrupted government they opposed. Ayers and his brethren contended that they adhered to a strict notion of right and wrong that, however much it might resemble the ends justifying the means, was at least based on pure motives. By contrast, the U.S. government employed all manner of subterfuge in hoodwinking the American public and in persecuting activist groups. As an example, the FBI's own campaign of illegal "dirty tricks," COINTELPRO, demonstrated that the U.S. government would stop at nothing to undermine the actions of a determined group of activists who resisted an imperialistic, authoritarian power. If the WUO fell short of their high ideals, at least they were ideologically committed to a noble cause, unlike the FBI, which sought to acquire and exploit power for power's sake.[59]

Ayers's argument, despite his protestations, can be used to justify any behavior that a small, determined group of people wishes to rationalize. Ayers assumes that violence, when used with precision, can educate instead of intimidate. Somehow violent acts, when directed by the pure of heart, can uplift the masses, allowing them to see the hypocrisy and dastardly behavior of an oppressive government. What does Ayers make of the March 1970 Greenwich Village explosion that, but for the grace of God, killed only the participants and not innocent bystanders? History suggests that violent acts by their very nature strike terror into the hearts of citizens. Terrorized people act emotionally, often at the expense of reflection. Any group that wishes to call attention to a political issue in hopes of triggering rational, calm, deliberative decision making would be well advised to soothe the passions of people rather than stoke the fires of fear and hysteria.[60]

Even when activists intend to minimize or avoid harm to innocents, violence can lead to unintended consequences. The self-righteous activist who employs violence and claims to value human life frequently attempts to rationalize injury or death to a bystander. The trite excuse typically is to conclude that an unintended injury, while regrettable, is a price that must be paid in furtherance of an overarching goal. "Collateral damage," the apologist argues, is inevitable when extremists are forced to confront a corrupted political system. Aside from the Greenwich Village explosion that killed several WUO members, the Sterling Hall incident, which occurred on August 24, 1970, when four young anti-war activists detonated a bomb on the University of Wisconsin–Madison campus to protest the university's research on behalf of the U.S. military, publicized the collateral damage that can occur when protesters use violence to achieve their goals but claim to avoid inflicting casualties. A university physics researcher was inadvertently killed, and three innocent bystanders were injured in the blast.[61]

The "price that must be paid" argument becomes a slippery slope; as the casualties mount, the rationalizations become ever more hollow and self-serving. The defense of the purity of violence sounds reasonable when considered as a bumper-sticker slogan, but these sentiments do not withstand close analysis or logical scrutiny. Violence, once employed, cannot be contained with certainty or precision. The notion that a terrorist indiscriminately employs violence while a committed activist acts violently in a calculated, deliberative manner appears to be a distinction without a difference.[62]

Moreover, it is one thing to criticize government's policies as misguided and in desperate need of reform; it is altogether another matter to embrace that government's enemies as morally righteous. Weatherman failed to recognize that while the policies of the U.S. government undoubtedly harmed the landed masses of Southeast Asia, the policies of America's enemies also achieved the same result—often at a much higher order of magnitude. By embracing Ho Chi Minh and the communist forces struggling for an end to imperialism in Indochina, WUO members conveniently overlooked the atrocities perpetrated by communist leaders against their own people. Totalitarianism can assume many guises, whether as U.S.-backed support for a corrupted, authoritarian regime, or an anti-imperialist, nationalistic insurgency. The old adage "the enemy of my enemy is my friend" is a useful insight into realpolitik, but it cannot serve as the basis for claiming the moral high ground. Weatherman, in denouncing the U.S. government as butchers of the people, naively embraced foreign butchers who could boast an infinitely higher body count than the soldiers and peasants killed by U.S. troops during the Vietnam War. In short, in any struggle between two opposing forces, it is entirely possible that both sides share some measure of blame, and no one comes to the struggle with clean hands. Unfortunately, when young people who lack experience in the murkiness of international diplomacy and power politics engage in violent acts, they can find themselves lost in the reeds.

Ayers's argument, at its core, is a claim that pure motives and narrowly tailored methods can be justified, in some instances. This convenient rationalization fails to acknowledge that virtually all persons and organizations classified as "terrorist" claim some overriding moral justification for their deeds. To address this point, the FBI has developed a simple definition of terrorism. The bureau's definition is "the unlawful use of force or violence against persons or property to intimidate or coerce a government, the civilian population or any segment thereof, in furtherance of political or social objectives." According to this definition, Weather people, in seeking to influence government policy through violence, were terrorists. As another commentator has observed, "terrorists are extremist groups with political agendas; their goal is to impose their views on others." They do not seek to accomplish this agenda through normal channels of political communication and participation. Instead, they use violence, which strikes fear into the hearts of both the targets of the violence and those who fear its random nature. To argue, as Bill Ayers does, that violence can be used to educate people is absurd. Education occurs with calm, deliberative, reasoned reflection and discourse, which is seldom possible when individuals fear for their safety or their lives. Ayers also assumes that terrorism only involves attacks against people, but the FBI definition makes it clear that deliberately destroying property can be a terrorist act.[63]

As discussed elsewhere in this book, all terrorist organizations share certain basic characteristics. First, they have given up on the possibility of using the existing political structure to express their discontent. In their view, seeking a moderate position or compromising to achieve at least some of their goals is anathema. Therefore, because the existing system is so corrupted that reform is impossible, the *status quo ante* cannot stand. They must destroy the existing world order if meaningful change is to occur.[64]

Terrorist groups also agree that change must occur quickly. Incremental reform typically favors those persons and organizations already in power; consequently, a root-and-branch overhaul is the only feasible alternative. Throughout history, radical reformers have urged their followers to reject moderate change. In the American experience, radicalism was most visible during the nineteenth-century anti-slavery debate. William Lloyd Garrison, the most famous opponent of gradualism with respect to the abolition of slavery, famously wrote, "On this subject, I do not wish to think, or to speak, or write, with moderation. No! no! Tell a man whose house is on fire to give a moderate alarm; tell him to moderately rescue his wife from the hands of the ravisher; tell the mother to gradually extricate her babe from the fire into which it has fallen;—but urge me not to use moderation in a cause like the present." The difference between Garrison, he of the fiery rhetoric, and John Brown, the anti-slavery advocate who led an armed insurrection against slavery twenty-eight years after Garrison penned his famous words and was cited by the WUO as a source of inspiration, was that the former talked the talk and the latter walked the walk. In the final analysis, however, it is difficult to conclude that John Brown was more successful in achieving his goals than was Garrison.[65]

The point is that Garrison can be labeled an extremist in his rhetoric, but Brown was a terrorist. Garrison exercised free speech, which, depending on the circumstances, can be seen as striking the match that leads to the conflagration, but he did not take up arms (setting aside, *arguendo*, the question of whether he provided funding for anti-slavery campaigns such as Brown's raid). This fine distinction does little to resolve the seminal quandary that one person's terrorist is another person's freedom fighter.

For all of Bill Ayers's rationalizations, the fact is that Weatherman employed violence against property to coerce the U.S. government into changing its political and social policies. Talk of acting on behalf of the masses and liberating the citizenry from totalitarian oppression was exactly that: talk. As the WUO turned its back on the SDS and became increasingly violent, its membership ranks dwindled. The idea that this small group of young people spoke for anyone other than themselves is patently absurd.[66]

In fact, the prospect of employing violence has its own appeal, especially to frustrated, alienated youth. Just as the Rolling Stones could sing of "the special pleasures of doing something wrong," the committed extremist could revel in disrupting social institutions, destroying government property, following news coverage of his exploits, and striking terror into the hearts of his fellow citizens. Weather people were young, idealistic, frustrated, angry, passionate, and caught up in the turbulent times in which they lived. These factors, and perhaps some internal psychology that will never be fully understood, compelled them to engage in violence. Whatever justifications they would later cite to explain their actions, Weatherman constituted an emblematic and important chapter in the history of domestic terrorism in the United States.[67]

NOTES

1. Sinker, "Catcalling," 62–63; Slonecker, "The Columbia Coalition," 969–78; Smith, "Present at the Creation and Other Myths," 3–5.

2. Ayers, *Fugitive Days*, 145; Franks, "From the Underground, a New Magazine," 24; Franks, "U.S. Inquiry Finds 37 in Weather Underground," 38; Miller, "A Change in the Weather," B31; "Underground on West Side," B4.

3. Berger, *Outlaws of America*, 162–65; Jacobs, "The New History of the Weather Underground," 59–60; Slonecker, "The Columbia Coalition," 967–69; Smith, "Present at the Creation and Other Myths," 1–2.

4. Ayers, *Fugitive Days*, 144; Berger, *Outlaws of America*, 91–94; Jacobs, "The New History of the Weather Underground," 59–61.

5. Cohen, "'Cartooning Capitalism,'" 36–38; Van Elteren, "Workers' Control and the Struggles against 'Wage Slavery' in the Gilded Age and After," 188–94.

6. Berger, *Outlaws of America*, 40–41; Sale, *SDS*, 687–90; Smith, "Present at the Creation and Other Myths," 2–4.

7. Ayers, *Fugitive Days*, 142; Smith, "Present at the Creation and Other Myths," 1–4.

8. Berger, *Outlaws of America*, 38–41; Miller, "A Change in the Weather," B31; Sinker, "Catcalling," 62–63.

9. Jacobs and Landau, *The New Radicals*, 3; Sale, *SDS*, 69; Smith, "Present at the Creation and Other Myths," 2–3.

10. Jacobs and Landau, *The New Radicals*, 26–29; Sale, *SDS*, 157–59, 678–87.

11. Sale, *SDS*, 97; Smith, "Present at the Creation and Other Myths," 4–5.

12. Berger, *Outlaws of America*, 41–42; Jacobs and Landau, *The New Radicals*, 33–40; Sale, *SDS*, 95–130.

13. Gitlin, *The Sixties*, 63–64; Jacobs and Landau, *The New Radicals*, 61; Sale, *SDS*, 301.

14. Berger, *Outlaws of America*, 89–80; Gitlin, *The Sixties*, 177; Lewy, *America in Vietnam*, 42–43.

15. Berger, *Outlaws of America*, 48–50; Gitlin, *The Sixties*, 306; Rudd, *Underground*, viii; Sale, *SDS*, 400–402.

16. Ayers, *Fugitive Days*, 140–44; Berger, *Outlaws of America*, 102–3.

17. Barber, *A Hard Rain Fell*, 157–58; Berger, *Outlaws of America*, 99–100; Gitlin, *The Sixties*, 387; Jacobs, *The Way the Wind Blew*, 39–40.

18. Ayers, *Fugitive Days*, 145; Barber, *A Hard Rain Fell*, 159–60, 208–9; Berger, *Outlaws of America*, 100–102; Franks, "U.S. Inquiry Finds 37 in Weather Underground," 38; Sinker, "Catcalling," 62.

19. Ayers, *Fugitive Days*, 145–46; Berger, *Outlaws of America*, 101–2.

20. Berger, *Outlaws of America*, 94–95; Jacobs, *The Way the Wind Blew*, 24–25; Rudd, *Underground*, 146; Students for a Democratic Society, *SDS New Left Notes—National Convention Proposals*, 3, 6.

21. Ayers, *Fugitive Days*, 158; Barber, *A Hard Rain Fell*, 183–85; Rudd, *Underground*, 171–73; Sale, *SDS*, 375.

22. Barber, *A Hard Rain Fell*, 183–86; Gitlin, *The Sixties*, 394; Sale, *SDS*, 375.

23. Barber, *A Hard Rain Fell*, 211–13; Berger, *Outlaws of America*, 94–103; Franks, "U.S. Inquiry Finds 37 in Weather Underground," 38; Sinker, "Catcalling," 62.

24. Jacobs, *The Way the Wind Blew*, 39; Sale, *SDS*, 479, 623; Students for a Democratic Society, *SDS New Left Notes—National Convention Proposals*, 3–6.

25. Barber, *A Hard Rain Fell*, 216; Berger, *Outlaws of America*, 340; Sale, *SDS*, 648; Wilkerson, *Flying Close to the Sun*, 325.

26. Ayers, *Fugitive Days*, 286; Barber, *A Hard Rain Fell*, 216–17; Franks, "From the Underground, a New Magazine," 24; Gussow, "The House on West 11th Street," 7–8; Sale, *SDS*, 3–5; Wilkerson, *Flying Close to the Sun*, 1–3.

27. Quoted in Gussow, "The House on West 11th Street," 9.

28. Gussow, "The House on West 11th Street," 9–10; Rudd, *Underground*, 195; Sale, *SDS*, 4.

29. Quoted in Gussow, "The House on West 11th Street," 14–15. See also Rudd, *Underground*, 274.

30. Ayers, *Fugitive Days*, 232; Franks, "From the Underground, a New Magazine," 24; Franks, "U.S. Inquiry Finds 37 in Weather Underground," 38; Miller, "A Change in the Weather," B31; Sale, *SDS*, 558; "Underground on West Side," B4.

31. Ayers, *Fugitive Days*, 271; Sale, *SDS*, 504.

32. Ayers, *Fugitive Days*, 302; Berger, *Outlaws of America*, 170; Sale, *SDS*, 611; Wilkerson, *Flying Close to the Sun*, 357–58, 395.

33. Ayers, *Fugitive Days*, 250–55; Berger, *Outlaws of America*, 152–53; Jacobs, *The Way the Wind Blew*, 117; Rudd, *Underground*, 226–31; Wilkerson, *Flying Close to the Sun*, 359.

34. Berger, *Outlaws of America*, 152–53; Jacobs, *The Way the Wind Blew*, 117–18; Rudd, *Underground*, 226.

35. Berger, *Outlaws of America*, 152; Jacobs, *The Way the Wind Blew*, 118–19; Rudd, *Underground*, 226–31.

36. Berger, *Outlaws of America*, 330; Jacobs, *The Way the Wind Blew*, 142; Wilkerson, *Flying Close to the Sun*, 395.

37. Berger, *Outlaws of America*, 76–78; Franks, "From the Underground, a New Magazine," 24; Miller, "A Change in the Weather," B31; "Underground on West Side," B4.

38. Barber, *A Hard Rain Fell*, 39; Chalmers, *Hooded Americanism*, 398–99; Cunningham, *There's Something Happening Here*, 27, 181–85; Gitlin, *The Sixties*, 413; Jacobs, *The Way the Wind Blew*, 74; Kessler, *The FBI*, 80; Wade, *The Fiery Cross*, 361–63.

39. Cunningham, *There's Something Happening Here*, 77–78, 181; Kessler, *The FBI*, 410; Wade, *The Fiery Cross*, 363.

40. Cunningham, *There's Something Happening Here*, 333; Kessler, *The FBI*, 410, 440.

41. Weather Underground, *Prairie Fire*, 2. See also Ayers, *Fugitive Days*, 240; Franks, "From the Underground, a New Magazine," 24; Rudd, *Underground*, 272–76.

42. Weather Underground, *Prairie Fire*, 140. See also Berger, *Outlaws of America*, 206–7; Rudd, *Underground*, 263, 272–76; Wilkerson, *Flying Close to the Sun*, 371–72.

43. Weather Underground, *Prairie Fire*, 144. See also Jacobs, *The Way the Wind Blew*, 157–70; Wilkerson, *Flying Close to the Sun*, 371–72.

44. Ayers, *Fugitive Days*, 302; Franks, "From the Underground, a New Magazine," 24; Miller, "A Change in the Weather," B31; "Underground on West Side," B4; Wilkerson, *Flying Close to the Sun*, 386.

45. Quoted in Franks, "From the Underground, a New Magazine," 24. See also Ayers, *Fugitive Days*, 240.

46. Jacobs, *The Way the Wind Blew*, 183–85; Rudd, *Underground*, 298.

47. Franks, "U.S. Inquiry Finds 37 in Weather Underground," 38; Jacobs, *The Way the Wind Blew*, 146.

48. "Infiltrating the Underground," n.p.; Jacobs, *The Way the Wind Blew*, 179.

49. Ayers, *Fugitive Days*, 219; Miller, "A Change in the Weather," B31; Rudd, *Underground*, 300.

50. Ayers, *Fugitive Days*, 317; Berger, *Outlaws of America*, 6; Gussow, "The House on West 11th Street," 8; Jacobs, *The Way the Wind Blew*, 184–86; "Underground on West Side," B4.

51. Ayers, *Fugitive Days*, 317; Rudd, *Underground*, 306; "Terrorist Bill Ayers Misrepresents His Past," 8.

52. Quoted in Remnick, *The Bridge*, 547. See also Hertzberg, "Beyond the Palin," 29; Lempert, "The Unmentionable," 188; Remnick, "Mr. Ayers's Neighborhood," n.p.; Weigel, "A Campaign of Narratives," 24; Wolffe, *Renegade*, 6–7, 181.

53. Hertzberg, "Beyond the Palin," 29–30; Remnick, *The Bridge*, 545–46; Remnick, "Mr. Ayers's Neighborhood," n.p.; "Terrorist Bill Ayers Misrepresents His Past," 8.

54. Ayers and Dohrn, "What Race Has to Do with It," 50–55; Hertzberg, "Beyond the Palin," 29–30; Lempert, "The Unmentionable," 188; Malik, "The Obama Campaign 2008," 190; Remnick, *The Bridge*, 545–48; Remnick, "Mr. Ayers's Neighborhood," n.p.; "Terrorist Bill Ayers Misrepresents His Past," 8; Weigel, "A Campaign of Narratives," 24.

55. Quoted in Ayers, *Fugitive Days*, 271; Berger, *Outlaws of America*, 286.

56. Barber, *A Hard Rain Fell*, 157–58; Berger, *Outlaws of America*, 99–100; Gitlin, *The Sixties*, 387; Jacobs, *The Way the Wind Blew*, 39–40; Leebaert, *The Fifty-Year Wound*, 354–60; Sale, *SDS*, 567–76.

57. Ayers, *Fugitive Days*, 151; Gitlin, *The Sixties*, 32; Leebaert, *The Fifty-Year Wound*, 354–57; Rudd, *Underground*, 12–17; Smith, "Present at the Creation and Other Myths," 22–23.

58. Ayers, *Fugitive Days*, 271; Berger, *Outlaws of America*, 286; Flaherty, "Youth, Ideology, and Terrorism," 29–58.

59. Cunningham, *There's Something Happening Here*, 77–78, 181; Jacobs, *The Way the Wind Blew*, 74; Kessler, *The FBI*, 410; Wade, *The Fiery Cross*, 363; Wilkerson, *Flying Close to the Sun*, 242–44.

60. Ayers, *Fugitive Days*, 279; Flaherty, "Youth, Ideology, and Terrorism," 32–33; Gussow, "The House on West 11th Street," 13–15; Weather Underground, *Prairie Fire*, 154.

61. See, for example, Bates, *RADS*, and Morris, *The Madison Bombings*.

62. Flaherty, "Youth, Ideology, and Terrorism," 29–58; McCann, *Terrorism on American Soil*, 288–91.

63. Ayers, *Fugitive Days*, 122–23; Barber, *A Hard Rain Fell*, 66–67; Berger, *Outlaws of America*, 17–18; Flaherty, "Youth, Ideology, and Terrorism," 29–30; McCann, *Terrorism on American Soil*, 7–8; Weather Underground, *Prairie Fire*, 41.

64. Flaherty, "Youth, Ideology, and Terrorism," 29–58; Khan and Azam, "Root Causes of Terrorism," 65–86; McCann, *Terrorism on American Soil*, 7–8.

65. Quoted in Howe, *What Hath God Wrought*, 425. See also Horwitz, *Midnight Rising*, 1–5; Kraditor, *Means and Ends in American Abolitionism*, 7–10; Oates, *To*

Purge This Land with Blood, 26–33; Rohrbach, "'Truth Stronger and Stranger Than Fiction,'" 727–55; Rowland, "John Brown's Moonlight March," 32.

66. Ayers, *Fugitive Days*, 140–44; Berger, *Outlaws of America*, 102–3; Franks, "From the Underground, a New Magazine," 24; Franks, "U.S. Inquiry Finds 37 in Weather Underground," 38; Miller, "A Change in the Weather," B31; "Underground on West Side," B4.

67. Ayers, *Fugitive Days*, 65–66; Flaherty, "Youth, Ideology, and Terrorism," 29–58; Khan and Azam, "Roots Causes of Terrorism," 65–86; McCann, *Terrorism on American Soil*, 7–8; Remnick, "Mr. Ayers's Neighborhood," n.p.; Rudd, *Underground*, 18–20; "Terrorist Bill Ayers Misrepresents His Past," 8; Wilkerson, *Flying Close to the Sun*, 60–64.

III

POSTMODERN TERROR

9

"A REVOLUTION AGAINST THE INDUSTRIAL SYSTEM"

The Unabomber (1970s–1990s)

Woe to the hand that shed this costly blood!

—William Shakespeare, *Julius Caesar*, Act III, Scene i

The story of Theodore John Kaczynski—the Unabomber—has become familiar to many Americans, but there is much subtext that is not as well known. The brilliant mathematician turned violent Luddite and social critic represents a domestic terrorist who suffered at the hands of society long before he pursued a career of mayhem and destruction. His story is a genuine tragedy on multiple levels. Yet nothing in his background justified his long campaign of terrorism aimed at what he believed to be the symbols of industrial society.

Kaczynski later claimed he would never have commenced his infamous bombing campaign had developers not encroached on the woods surrounding his ramshackle cabin on the outskirts of Lincoln, Montana. The veracity of this claim remains a subject of no small debate. Assuming the claim is accurate, the Unabomber both his life of crime from this simple beginning. Ted Kaczynski engaged in a series of bombing attacks on universities and airlines between 1978 and 1995, eventually killing three people and injuring twenty-three others. Before they apprehended the unknown assailant, the FBI identified him as the UNABOM (UNiversity and Airline BOMber), which the news media fashioned into the "Unabomber." When he was arrested in 1996 and paraded before the news media, the Unabomber was transformed into a celebrity in a culture that celebrates celebrity for the sake of celebrity.[1]

Kaczynski's story raises a plethora of ancillary issues aside from the historical facts surrounding the origins of his terrorist career. Because his mental capacity became an issue during the judicial proceedings, lawyers and criminologists continue to debate whether Kaczynski was denied his Sixth Amendment right to effective assistance of counsel. The defendant was so upset that his court-appointed attorneys were considering an insanity plea that he petitioned the court to allow him to defend himself. The judge found, however, that Kaczynski, although not legally insane, could not represent himself. If, in fact, Kaczynski was mentally impaired, his ability to act as a purposive terrorist becomes problematic. Can a mentally impaired person possess clearly articulated "political or social objectives," part of the FBI's definition of a "terrorist"? An even more fundamental question is whether degrees of mental illness exist so that an offender can knowingly and willingly engage in terroristic acts and yet not fully comprehend the nature of the legal charges filed against him. Because he acted alone and was not part of a larger conspiracy, some commentators question whether Kaczynski was merely an angry loner, a garden-variety serial criminal best handled through the normal channels of the American judicial system absent a "terrorist" label or designation. To this day, questions remain about whether he was a terrorist; a mentally ill, deranged man; a career criminal; or something else.[2]

THE LIFE AND CAREER OF A TERRORIST

Kaczynski's life and career started with much promise. Born into an affluent family of second-generation Polish Americans in Chicago on May 22, 1942, he seemed to have everything he needed to succeed in a conventional career. His parents were the epitome of the American dream: hardworking, resourceful citizens, devoted to their children, and dedicated to building a stable, materially comfortable, well-adjusted family unit. Ted's brother, David, was born seven years later, and he too enjoyed the advantages of membership in an ambitious, upper-middle-class American family.

It is no exaggeration to say that Ted was a child prodigy. The term "prodigy" is sometimes overused, but not in this case. When his IQ was tested in the fifth grade, young Ted scored 167, a figure sufficiently impressive to allow him to skip the sixth grade. In one sense, this recognition of his intellectual prowess confirmed what a proud family had long known. Their son was special, a gifted student with a bright, almost limitless future ahead of him. In another sense, a young, socially awkward child was propelled into a higher grade before he was sufficiently mature enough to handle the increasingly complicated interactions among his peers. Kaczynski later characterized the situation as a crucial moment in his life. Because he had difficulty identifying with his classmates and was bullied by some of the larger children, young Ted became increasingly alienated from people. In fact, his mother was so worried about his odd behavior that she seriously considered enrolling him in a medical study gauging the behavior of autistic children.[3]

In high school, Kaczynski settled into a now familiar pattern; he excelled academically but experienced difficulty adapting to social situations. Somehow, he persevered. By the time he was fifteen years old, he had completed all of the coursework necessary to graduate from high school. His teachers were so impressed that they urged the gifted young man to apply to Harvard University, the bastion of educational achievement in the United States. He was accepted as a student and subsequently enrolled in classes in 1958, when he was sixteen years old. Despite this difficult feat, the young man continued to accumulate accolades. Although his grades were hardly stellar during his first year of college—Ted was not enamored with several required courses—as he moved into his field of interest, his extraordinary knowledge of mathematics could not be denied. His final performance at Harvard indicated that his high school achievements were no fluke; Ted Kaczynski possessed a brilliant mind.[4]

Yet a brilliant mind did not equal a stable personality. To students who knew him, something was not quite right about Ted Kaczynski. He was so antisocial and reserved that he seemed to suffer physical pain when he was forced to deal with people one on one. Perhaps this insight into his bizarre behavior has been colored by the knowledge of his subsequent criminal career, but acquaintances of the young Ted Kaczynski nonetheless swear that his strange personality was on display as far back as his adolescence.

To add insult to the injury of his awkward personality, young Ted enrolled in a "purposefully brutalizing psychological experiment" while he was a student at the renowned university. Dr. Henry Murray, a Harvard psychology professor and former lieutenant colonel in the Office of Strategic Services (OSS), the forerunner of the Central Intelligence Agency (CIA), was an expert on psychologically induced stress. During his three decades as a Harvard researcher, Murray conducted numerous psychological experiments on students, including a series of multiyear personality studies to test student responses to stressful situations. By the standards of a later age, these highly suspect tests were at best unethical and possibly illegal. During the experiment, researchers ushered students into a room, strapped them into a chair, and connected electrodes to their bodies to monitor their physiological reactions as they faced bright lights and a two-way mirror. Prior to entering the room, each student had been required to write an essay explaining his or her personal beliefs and goals for the future. As soon as the subject was strapped into the chair, an anonymous third party, posing as an attorney, officiously entered the room and deliberately attacked the students' beliefs based on their disclosures in the essay. The students quickly became flustered and frustrated as they responded to the unprovoked, ad hominem attacks. For an emotionally unstable personality such as Ted Kaczynski, the rage he felt under these extreme conditions may have contributed to his later mental illness. Although all of his subsequent criminal activity cannot be laid at the feet of Dr. Murray and his colleagues, Kaczynski undoubtedly suffered owing to these experiments; they probably contributed to the feelings of outrage he expressed in the Unabomber manifesto.[5]

Kaczynski graduated from Harvard University in 1962. The twenty-year-old student immediately enrolled in a doctoral program in mathematics at the University of Michigan. At the time, Michigan's program was well known for its cutting-edge mathematics department. As he had done throughout his academic career, young Ted impressed his professors with his intellectual sophistication, his drive, and his focus. His dissertation was so impressive that one of his professors noted that "maybe 10 or 12 men in the country understood or appreciated it." Kaczynski earned Michigan's Sumner B. Myers Prize for the best mathematics dissertation produced at the university in 1967. He also held the National Science Foundation Fellowship and published more than a half dozen articles in academic journals during his tenure as a graduate student. He had done everything right to enter the professorate; by all accounts, Kaczynski seemed destined for a stellar career in academe.[6]

After earning his PhD in mathematics, the twenty-five-year-old scholar accepted a position as an assistant professor at the University of California at Berkeley. He was the youngest assistant professor ever hired to teach math at Berkeley. As part of his teaching load, the new faculty member taught undergraduate courses in geometry and calculus. For all of his brilliance as a researcher, Kaczynski could not hide his awkwardness in the classroom. Numerous students complained about their professor's ineffective teaching skills. As he stood in front of the class, Kaczynski either mumbled or stuttered so severely that almost no one understood him. He also failed to meet with students during office hours, thereby ensuring that he received low student ratings. Within less than two years, Kaczynski resigned his position and left the university. His colleagues were stunned by this unexpected development. Despite his inability to teach undergraduate students effectively, he could have carved out a respectable academic career as a researcher based on his record of publications and his groundbreaking work.[7]

Disgusted with the scholarly world, Kaczynski returned to live with his family in Lombard, Illinois. For two years, he languished in his parents' home as signs of mental illness began to surface. In 1971, when he was twenty-nine, he moved into a remote shack with no electricity or running water near Lincoln, Montana. Occasionally, he worked odd jobs to earn spending money. His family also provided financial support, which enabled Kaczynski to purchase land in Lincoln and, as subsequently became clear, fund his terrorist activities.[8]

In moving to Lincoln, Kaczynski deliberately chose to drop out of society and live a self-sufficient existence close to nature. This decision to exist autonomously, free from the trappings of civilized society, was in line with hallowed American tradition, most notably favored by the nineteenth-century writer Henry David Thoreau. Much as Thoreau had chosen to live a life of solitude away from the corruption and degradation of modern society, Kaczynski sought to enjoy a life of pristine simplicity. At least that was the way Kaczynski viewed it. In light of his fragile emotional state, it is unclear whether his withdrawal from society was a symptom of an underlying mental illness or the cause of his later terrorist campaign. In any case, he might have continued this way indefinitely but for a series of events that enraged him throughout the years.[9]

Kaczynski's family was deeply worried about Ted. In 1978, his father and brother, David, briefly intervened, finding work for him at a foam rubber factory where David was a supervisor. Unfortunately, David was forced to fire Ted for harassing a female co-worker. Once again, Ted Kaczynski had failed to find his place in organized society despite his family's attempts to shelter him from the world's vicissitudes.[10]

Returning to Montana to live in a remote cabin he had built in 1973, Kaczynski became the quintessential recluse, teaching himself survival skills such as tracking animals, planting crops, and identifying edible types of plants. To hear him tell it, his vision of an idyllic life was shattered when he found evidence that developers were encroaching on nearby forest land. Walking through his favorite spots in the woods one day, Kaczynski stumbled upon earth-moving equipment, clear evidence that civilization was intruding on his world. The breaking point came when he discovered a road had been built through a plateau where he often traveled to commune with nature. "You can't imagine how upset I was," he later remarked. "It was from that point on I decided that, rather than trying to acquire further wilderness skills, I would work on getting back at the system. Revenge."[11]

Whether this thirst for revenge against vague, unknown enemies would have occurred absent the episode Kaczynski reported is open to debate. Whatever the trigger, Kaczynski's first documented terrorist act occurred in May 1978, when he attacked a Northwestern University engineering professor, Buckley Crist, although Crist apparently was not the intended target. This was around the same time that Kaczynski was working with his father and brother at the foam rubber factory. Many years would pass before anyone made the connection between Kaczynski's work in the Chicago area and the May 1978 bombing at Northwestern University.

The incident was odd. On May 25, a woman named Mary Gutierrez found a brown package apparently lying abandoned in a parking lot next to the science and engineering building at the University of Illinois at Chicago. E. J. Smith, a rocket science professor at Rensselaer Polytechnic Institute in Troy, New York, was the intended recipient. The package bore Professor Crist's return address. Since the package contained ten $1.00 Eugene O'Neill stamps and was ready for delivery, Gutierrez retrieved the parcel and tried to slip it into a mailbox. It would not fit into the mail slot. Attempting to be a Good Samaritan, Gutierrez, who lived near Evanston, Illinois, resolved to return it to the apparent sender. She called Crist on the telephone the next day, and he sent a messenger to retrieve the package. After the messenger "returned" the package to the befuddled professor, he became suspicious when he noticed that the handwriting on the address label was not his. Because he did not recall sending a package to Professor Smith in the first place, Crist asked a Northwestern University campus policeman, Terry Marker, to investigate. Marker tried to open the package, but it exploded as soon as he did so. He received only minimal injuries, but the primitive explosive device clearly indicated that a terrorist was at work. University officials immediately notified the Bureau of Alcohol, Tobacco, Firearms and Explosives (ATF). ATF followed its normal procedures; agency officials recovered the bomb debris, cataloged the contents, disposed of the evidence, filed a report, and assumed it was a singular episode.[12]

Before closing the file, bomb squad investigators found that the device had been fashioned in a home workshop using a rudimentary trigger. Whoever had constructed the bomb had relied on wooden parts for the interior when threaded metal ends would have been the preferred material to inflict maximum damage. This was the handiwork of a novice terrorist; but, as subsequent events would demonstrate, he was capable of learning from his mistakes and improving on his technique.[13]

Slightly less than a year later, on May 9, 1979, someone left an explosive device on a table between two study carrels in a commons area at Northwestern University's Technological Institute. A young graduate student originally from Canada, John G. Harris, attempted to open the package, which was shaped like a "Phillies" cigar box. As soon as he pried it open, the device exploded, setting fire to the room, hurling the eyeglasses off his face, and singeing his eyebrows. He also suffered cuts and burns on his arms and around his eyes. Although he was unnerved by the explosion, Harris was not badly injured. "From my perspective," he later recalled, "it was a random event, nothing different than being hit by a car. I think the big impact has been all the interest from the press."[14]

Later that year, Kaczynski was ready to try again. Instead of planting another bomb at Northwestern University or focusing on another college, he targeted an airline. On November 15, 1979, a bomb placed in the cargo hold of American Airlines flight 444, a Boeing 727 headed from Chicago to Washington National Airport in Washington, D.C., failed to detonate owing to a faulty timing mechanism. Nonetheless, the device sent smoke billowing throughout the plane, forcing the pilot to make an emergency landing at Dulles International Airport. The pilot and co-pilot later recounted hearing a muffled sound and noticing that the cabin pressure had dropped. After inspecting the device, investigators concluded that if the bomb had exploded as the attacker intended, it was powerful enough to "obliterate the plane." U.S. postal inspectors who initially exercised jurisdiction over the case labeled the unknown assailant the "Junkyard Bomber" because he assembled his explosive devices using household materials that could be found discarded in any junkyard.[15]

Although this was the pre–September 11 era, authorities were so concerned about the possibility of a bomb being placed on an airplane that the Federal Bureau of Investigation (FBI) interceded and assigned the case a code name, UNABOM. Special Agent James C. "Chris" Ronay, the bureau's leading explosives expert, received a telephone call from his boss, Stewart Case, with the instructions, "Get to Dulles Airport right away. A plane's about to land there with a bomb on board." Ronay did as he was instructed.

When he arrived and inspected the device, Ronay was impressed with the bomber's ingenuity. The offender had assembled common, ordinary materials that could be purchased in any hardware store and crafted them into an elaborate bomb. Using an inexpensive barometer to measure air pressure changes in the aircraft, the bomb was designed to detonate when the airplane ascended past 2,000 feet in elevation. In the event that the primary mechanism failed to work or if the device was intercepted before the airplane departed, a second system would trigger the bomb as soon as the package was opened. The bomber had used a juice can to hold the explosive charge, which was derived from fireworks chemicals. The device was powered by four C batteries wired to the barometer and housed in a homemade wooden box. The device had been lovingly made, as if by a master craftsman.[16]

The bomber's signature was so distinctive that Ronay decided, on a hunch, to ask the FBI's Chicago office to query local law enforcement personnel about similar bombs planted in the area. His hunch paid off; the May 1979 incident immediately came to light. Along with ATF agents, FBI agents assembled a task force to investigate the matter. Eventually numbering more than 150 people, the task force painstakingly combed through forensic evidence from the bomb fragments and assiduously investigated the lives of victims in hopes of discovering clues as to the motives of the unknown bomber as well as the reasons he selected particular victims or sites. Investigators did not know it at the time, but traditional law enforcement practices would prove to be useless against Ted Kaczynski. Typically, law enforcement officials track criminals and terrorists through the trails they leave when they use credit cards, associate with other known criminals or terrorists, or attract attention to unusual, sometimes puzzling activities. Because he was a recluse who sometimes waited for years between his attacks, Kaczynski was virtually impossible to track. For almost seventeen years, the Unabomber eluded capture precisely because he "stayed off the grid" and deliberately avoided leaving a forensics or paper trail. It was only in 1995, after he mailed a letter to the *New York Times* vowing to "desist from terrorism" if the newspaper published his anti-technology manifesto, that the police captured the elusive fugitive.[17]

As months and years passed with no leads, task force members grew increasingly frustrated. In 1980, John Douglas, the legendary chief agent of the FBI's Behavioral Sciences Unit, developed a psychological profile of the Unabomber. According to Douglas, the unknown subject was an intelligent man with connections to academe. In a subsequent revision of the profile, the FBI characterized the bomber as a neo-Luddite, that is, someone harboring anti-technology tendencies. This iteration of the profile also indicated that the assailant had earned an advanced academic degree in the hard sciences. It was an uncanny and accurate portrayal, but not everyone agreed with the assessment. By 1983, a competing profile suggested that the bomber might be a blue-collar airplane mechanic owing to his fixation on airline destruction. No one in that era could quite understand the demons that drove Ted Kaczynski to act as a terrorist, so they could not figure out how to characterize him.[18]

From 1980 to 1985, the Unabomber struck, seemingly with impunity, seven times. On one occasion, he targeted the president of United Airlines, Percy Wood, but the resultant injuries were relatively minor. The episode occurred on June 10, 1980, which also happened to be Wood's birthday. He received a package from Chicago containing a copy of Sloan Wilson's novel *Ice Brothers*. In a separate letter that Wood received from someone named Enoch Fischer a few days earlier, the correspondent indicated that he would soon send "a book that should be read by all who make important decisions affecting the public welfare." Unbeknownst to Wood, the sender had hollowed out the pages following the title page and inserted a bomb. When Wood opened the book, the device exploded, inflicting cuts on his face as well as his left leg.[19]

A pattern emerged during the bombings of the 1980s. In sending a Sloan Wilson novel to an intended victim and in targeting universities and airlines, the assailant was telegraphing his anger and disaffection with society and technology. When he dispatched bombs to universities, he almost always targeted a professor or department involved in some manner with engineering or technology. For example, on May 5, 1982, the bomber sent a package to Professor Patrick Fischer, a computer scientist at Vanderbilt University in Nashville, Tennessee. As in his previous bombings, the offender included a clever return address, in this case indicating that Professor Leroy Wood Bearnson of Brigham Young University had mailed the box. He also used the same type of Eugene O'Neill stamps he had included with a previous mailing. Originally, the bomber had sent the device to Pennsylvania State University, where Fischer had worked prior to moving to Vanderbilt. In an attempt to be helpful, Penn State officials had forwarded the package to Fischer at his new university. Fischer was not even in the office when his secretary, Janet Smith, opened the package. The bomb blew up in her face, sending her to the hospital with severe eye injuries and burns. In his diary, Ted Kaczynski commented on the incident dispassionately: "Frustrating that I can't seem to make lethal bomb."[20]

Also in 1982, on July 2, Diogenes J. Angelakos, director of the Electronics Research Laboratory at the University of California, Berkeley, noticed a strange package bearing a lift-handle sitting next to Room 411 in the Cory Hall Mathematics Building. Assuming that a student had carelessly left the package in the hallway, Angelakos grabbed the handle and hoisted the device from the floor. He suffered damage to his right hand when the bomb exploded, although the injuries could have been far worse if a gasoline can attached to the pipe bomb had ignited. The modified Molotov cocktail was designed to inflict maximum damage if it ignited properly. Once again, Kaczynski confided to his diary that he was upset with his failure to craft a lethal weapon. "Apparently pipe bomb went off but did not ignite gasoline," he wrote of the event. "I don't understand. Frustrated. Traveling expenses for parades such as the foregoing are very hard on my slender financial resources."[21]

As fate would have it, Angelakos was present when another bomb exploded in the same building at Berkeley three years later. Reflecting on the Unabomber's criminal career after Kaczynski was arrested in 1996, Angelakos said, "If he believes in making changes for the good, why would he be hurting people? That's the only thing I'd like to know." It was a question never satisfactorily answered.[22]

Kaczynski spent the next three years without calling attention to himself, existing underground, perfecting his skills as a bomb maker. The respite could not last. When next he struck, Berkeley engineering student John Hauser was his victim. An air force pilot and would-be astronaut, Hauser walked into a computer room in Cory Hall on the Berkeley campus—the site of the Unabomber's previous attack—on May 15, 1985, and discovered a three-ring binder attached to a small box by a rubber band lying unattended on a table. Since no one else was around, Hauser was curious as to why the notebook had been left behind. He lifted the binder to see if he could find a name or other identification. In doing so, he inadvertently triggered an explosion. As he later recalled, "I was standing at the table and there was a chair between me and the bomb. I think that caught a lot of the blast. It could easily have killed me, given the force of the explosion." As it was, the force was powerful enough to cause partial vision loss in his left eye. In addition, the blast blew off four fingers from his right hand. His Air Force Academy ring was propelled into a nearby wall, leaving an indelible impression.[23]

Despite grave injuries, Hauser possessed the presence of mind to recognize the severity of his injury. Worried that he would bleed to death, he frantically rushed into the hall. The first people he encountered, two graduate students, saw the blood and Hauser's hysteria, and fled the scene. Fortunately, Diogenes Angelakos, all too familiar with a Unabomber attack, was present, realized that the injuries were severe, and applied a tourniquet to Hauser's arm. This quick-thinking action undoubtedly saved the student's life.[24]

After learning the details, Kaczynski recorded his disparate reactions in his diary. On one hand, he wrote, "Must admit I feel badly about having crippled this [man's] arm. It has been bothering me a good deal. This is embarrassing because while my feelings are partly from pity, I'm sure they come largely from the training, propaganda, brainwashing we all get, conditioning us to be scared by the idea of doing certain things. It is shameful to be under the sway of this brainwashing." On the other hand, he was pleased with the success of his effort. "I would do it all over again," he explained to his diary. "So many failures with feeble ineffective bombs was [sic] driving me desperate with frustration. Have to get revenge for all the wild country being fucked up by the system."[25]

Although the Unabomber sometimes waited more than a year between attacks, 1985 proved to be a prolific period in the terrorist's career. In November, a bomb disguised as a manuscript appeared at the home of James V. McConnell, a psychology professor at the University of Michigan. To ensure that the package would be opened with dispatch, the bomber had included a letter on the exterior. Purporting to be from a student named Ralph C. Kloppenburg, the letter explained that the student was enclosing his doctoral dissertation and eagerly desired feedback on the manuscript. The device exploded when McConnell's research assistant, Nicklaus Suino, attempted to open the package. Suino suffered shrapnel wounds and powder burns, while McConnell, standing about eight feet from the explosion, suffered hearing loss. Investigators took note of the presence of the ubiquitous $1.00 Eugene O'Neill stamps, by now a Unabomber signature.[26]

In December, less than a month later, the Unabomber recorded his first fatality. A thirty-eight-year-old California computer store owner, Hugh Scrutton of Sacramento, discovered a nail-and-splinter-loaded bomb in the parking lot of his store, a small, failing computer rental shop called Rentech, around lunchtime on December 11. He had just told his assistant, Dick Knight, that he was on his way to an appointment. When he noticed an odd block of wood next to the door, he stooped to pick up the strange object. As he lifted the package, he ignited the bomb.[27]

Knight recalled hearing a loud pop, followed by Scrutton's screams: "Oh my God! Help me!" Much to his horror, when Knight stepped out of the back door, he found his boss drenched in blood, his right hand missing, and his heart exposed from his chest cavity. Scrutton immediately collapsed. Nadia Bridson, from Nadia's Fashions next door, heard the commotion and came outside to investigate. As she ran back inside to call an ambulance, Dick Knight vainly administered CPR. Despite these heroic efforts, Hugh

Scrutton, a mathematics graduate from the University of California, Berkeley, died within half an hour.[28]

Chris Ronay's task force discovered telltale signs of the serial bomber who had eluded police for more than seven years: a homemade wooden box, a unique triggering system, batteries, and the distinctive "FC" (an acronym that stood for "Freedom Club," a nonexistent terrorist organization) initials. Despite the leads, Ronay recognized that he and his colleagues were no closer to capturing the assailant than they had been in previous years. The bomber was adept at changing his targets, waiting for long periods between attacks, and leaving no trail except the one he intended for police to find. Even as police investigators felt their frustration growing, the Unabomber was euphoric. "Excellent. Humane way to eliminate somebody," an ebullient Ted Kaczynski scribbled in his diary. "He probably never felt a thing. $25,000 award offered. Rather flattering."[29]

Recognizing that his accelerating pattern of attacks would generate additional law enforcement scrutiny, the bomber waited more than a year before executing his next attack. On February 20, 1987, another computer store owner, Gary Wright of Salt Lake City, Utah, drove into the parking lot in front of his store and found what appeared to be a piece of lumber lying there unattended. When Wright attempted to lift the object, the bomb exploded, severing nerves in Wright's left arm and sending more than two hundred pieces of shrapnel into his body. Task force investigators subsequently concluded that this device was identical to the bomb that killed Hugh Scrutton, although Gary Wright survived the episode. Years later, David Kaczynski, Ted's brother, became friends with Wright after the Unabomber's identity became public.[30]

The Salt Lake City bombing was the first time the Unabomber seemed to have made a mistake. An employee in a neighboring office later recounted that she had peered through the blinds covering a rear window just in time to see a man removing two-by-four pieces of wood nailed together from a cloth bag. To her surprise, he placed the device beneath the wheel of her car. No sooner had the employee called a co-worker to look through the blinds than the man looked in at her. He was approximately twenty feet away and wearing sunglasses. After quickly glancing back at the package, the man walked away casually. The eyewitness, now joined by her colleague, laughed at the man's odd behavior. She later recalled that she and her co-worker had commented on the fellow's "cute ass." Although she was curious about the package and had resolved to move it later, she promptly forgot about the episode when she was distracted by a ringing telephone. Shortly after the accidental encounter, Gary Wright drove into the parking lot and attempted to pick up the wooden box.[31]

Jeanne Boylan's composite sketch of the Unabomber. Courtesy of AP Images, the Associated Press.

An FBI artist hastily produced a drawing of the suspect based on the eyewitness account, although no one thought the composite sketch was especially accurate. Nonetheless, the bureau released the drawing to the public on March 10, 1987, over the witness's stringent objection that the drawing was "wrong." Seven and a half years later, the task force persuaded a well-known forensics artist, Jeanne Boylan, to "correct" the original sketch. Boylan's enhanced drawing, widely circulated following the reappearance of the Unabomber in the 1990s, proved to be little better than its predecessor. In this case, however, the inaccuracies were somewhat excusable since they were based on memories that were more than seven years old.[32]

For a time, police hoped that something had happened to the serial bomber. For more than six years, no additional attacks occurred. It seemed as though the assailant had moved on or died. Police had no way of knowing that Kaczynski, ever the faithful researcher, used the intervening years to research "the perfect detonator." Because he was continually disappointed in the results of his bomb making, the former professor decided to reeducate himself on the intricacies and niceties of fashioning explosive devices. He was confident that if he devoted enough time and energy to the project, he could significantly increase the lethality of his bombs.[33]

By June 1993, the sabbatical was at an end. Ted Kaczynski was ready to resume his career as a serial bomber. His previous targets had labored largely in obscurity, but the Unabomber now found a well-known scientist, a man practicing at the cutting edge of technology. It was an exciting era for scientists working on the West Coast of the United States, especially those engaged in medical research involving genetics. Scientific breakthroughs seemed to occur at a dizzying pace; it was only a matter of time, many researchers felt, before they discovered the answers to the mysteries of Alzheimer's disease and Down's syndrome as well as other dread maladies. Dr. Charles Epstein, a renowned geneticist at the University of California, San Francisco, was among the most prominent scientists working in the field. As a consequence, he had inadvertently become a target of an anti-technology zealot.[34]

On June 22, 1993, Dr. Epstein left his office ahead of schedule so he could go home and work on a grant proposal. It seemed to be just another ordinary day. The doctor stopped at a shopping center to pick up his laundry and some fish from the supermarket. When he arrived home, he found the place empty. His wife was out of town, and his daughter was not there. Dr. Epstein noticed that his daughter had left a pile of mail on the kitchen table. Among the letters and bills, he saw that he had received a package with a return address from James Hill, chairman of the chemistry department at California State University, Sacramento. As he lifted the unexpected parcel, it felt like a cassette tape, but heavier. Nonetheless, the package did not seem to be especially suspicious. When Epstein attempted to open the envelope, it exploded and blew off several fingers on his right hand, destroying both of his eardrums. He also suffered a broken arm and extensive abdominal injuries.

He remained conscious, but his right hand caused him indescribable agony. Realizing that he needed immediate medical attention, he reached for the telephone to call for help, but it had been ripped from the wall. Frantic with fear and pain, he ran from his home screaming. Two neighbors responding to his screams quickly called the police. Minutes later, an ambulance arrived to transport Dr. Epstein to the hospital. As for the bomb itself, it had mostly been obliterated except for batteries, wires, and wood debris.[35]

After lying dormant for so long, the Unabomber was not satisfied with one assault. Two days later, Yale University computer scientist David Gelernter, returning from vacation, found a package mailed to his office apparently from Mary Jane Lee, a computer science professor at California State University, Sacramento. For all intents and purposes, the package appeared to be a dissertation awaiting his review. Gelernter shared one common characteristic with Charles Epstein; they both had been featured in the news recently. For his part, Gelernter had helped to develop a software program known as "Linda" to link computers together in a larger network. Ironically, Gelernter was no mere technophile; he was a thoughtful author of books about the potentially corrosive effects of technology on culture. In 1991, the ambivalent Gelernter had authored a book of musings on whether technology was a benefit or detriment to human life.[36]

In an all-too-familiar pattern, when Gelernter opened the package, the bomb blew up in his face. He remembered hearing a hissing sound accompanied by pale gray smoke and, an instant later, a bright flash. Following the initial shock, Gelernter realized that he had been grievously injured. No one else was around, and he desperately needed help. Thus, Gelernter stumbled down five flights of stairs to the ground level, ran across the street, and entered the university health clinic. The proximity of the health clinic to his office may well have saved Gelernter's life. Clinic personnel discovered that his blood pressure was zero, and he needed more assistance than they could provide. Doctors rushed him to the surgical intensive care unit at the Yale–New Haven Hospital. As the result of quick action, Gelernter survived his encounter with the Unabomber. Nonetheless, he lost vision in his left eye, hearing in one ear, part of his right hand, and suffered serious wounds to his chest and abdomen.[37]

Investigators discovered that the bomber had greatly improved his technique. Finding no physical evidence, which they usually did with a Unabomber explosion, they understood that he had used his hiatus to enhance his skills as a terrorist. In another surprising new development, a letter mailed to the *New York Times* from the same location in Sacramento and around the same time as the Epstein and Gelernter bombs exploded urged the recipients to take note of "a newsworthy event" somewhere near the postmark location. The letter appeared to contain a notation with the words "Call Nathan R—Wed 7 pm." Assuming the inclusion of this information was an inadvertent error—perhaps made when the bomber penned a note on another piece of paper and accidentally made an imprint on the sheet beneath it—the FBI scoured the country for men with the first name "Nathan" and a last name beginning with an "R." Investigators subsequently learned that this was a red herring, a joke deliberately played on investigators by the incredibly canny Unabomber. Ted Kaczynski was nothing if not brilliant.[38]

These two new attacks, coming so long after the original bombings, confounded investigators. They thought perhaps a copycat was at work or someone was upset by a recent hit film, *Jurassic Park*. In that movie, genetics researchers from Yale University and San Francisco attempted to clone long-extinct dinosaurs with predictably disastrous results. The 1993 bomber might have been reacting to the film or he might be the crafty and patient Unabomber resuming his terrorist career. Subsequent events would make it clear that Kaczynski was back at work.[39]

The rest of 1993 and most of 1994 would pass before the Unabomber showed himself again. During this time, Kaczynski was busy preparing for his next attack. Apparently he read an article in the June 21, 1993, edition of *Earth First! Journal* blaming a public relations firm, "Burston Marsteller," for all manner of environmental mischief, especially the devastating oil spill in Prince William Sound, Alaska, in 1989. In November 1994, a small environmental group called the Native Forest Network promoted a pamphlet known as the "Eco-Fucker Hit List." According to the list, the Timber Association of California and its communications officer, Roberta Anderson, were environmental enemies in California. Exxon Corporation made the list at number three owing to the oil spill in Alaska. These materials contained numerous inaccuracies—for example, the Timber Association of California had changed its name to the California Forestry Association (CFA), Roberta Anderson had died several years earlier, and the name of the public relations firm was Burson Marsteller—but they were minor details. The environmentalists were far more interested in evoking feelings of outrage than they were in presenting logical, well-researched, factually accurate arguments. Investigators later discovered that Kaczynski was familiar with the *Earth First! Journal* article as well as the "Eco-Fucker Hit List." Moreover, he shared the Native Forest Network's outrage over real and perceived environmental transgressions. Unlike the environmental group, however, Kaczynski was not satisfied merely to hurl epithets at his enemies. In lieu of hiding behind a well-timed invective, he resolved to employ violence against his transgressors.[40]

On December 10, 1994, a New York City advertising executive with Burson Marsteller, Thomas J. Mosser, found a package mailed to his home in suburban North Caldwell, New Jersey. The package contained a San Francisco postmark. Until that moment, it had been an ordinary morning filled with the conviviality of friends and family. Mosser and his wife, Susan, had planned to spend the day with their children, aged fifteen months and thirteen years old, as well as a friend. They had also decided to pick out a Christmas tree that same afternoon.[41]

Mosser had returned from a business trip the preceding day, and a pile of mail was stacked on a foyer table awaiting his attention. After eating breakfast and playing with his toddler, he meandered into the hallway to sift through his correspondence. His wife recalled that she and their daughter Kelly, the fifteen-month-old, had been standing next to Tom a moment before he reached for the mail. As the child lumbered from the hallway, Susan followed behind. No sooner had they entered the living room than Susan heard "a thunderous noise" that reverberated throughout the house. "Stunned, I scooped Kelly up and put her near the front door," she later recalled. "A white mist was pouring from the kitchen doorway. I raced through it to find out what happened."[42]

What had happened was that Mosser had attempted to open the package from the Unabomber. Kaczynski's new and improved detonator performed its work with deadly efficiency. When Mosser tore into the package, it nearly decapitated him. He proved to be the Unabomber's second fatality. Susan Mosser remembered the horror of seeing her husband lying on his back, his face blackened and ripped open. She screamed for her children to get out of the house, relying on Kim, her thirteen-year-old, to lead Kelly away from the scene of destruction. After dialing 911 and retrieving towels and the baby's blanket, she returned to the hallway. She thought she heard her husband moaning, and so she told him that everything would be okay, and that she loved him. After the police and ambulance arrived, a fireman reluctantly told her the bad news. In response to her query —"He's dead, isn't he?"—the fireman nodded his head. "I'm sorry. He didn't make it."[43]

If this sad, dramatic death of Thomas Mosser was traumatic for his wife and children and a scene of incredible pathos for anyone empathetic to a fellow human being, it caused a different reaction for Ted Kaczynski. In his diary, he matter-of-factly observed that the blast "gave a totally satisfactory result." In an April 24, 1995, letter to the New York Times sent under the pseudonym "FC," he explained, "We blew up Thomas Mosser last December because he was a Burston-Marsteller executive. Among other misdeeds, Burston-Marsteller helped Exxon clean up its public image after the Exxon Valdez incident. But we attacked Burston-Marsteller less for its specific misdeeds than on general principles." Specifically, FC could not tolerate "the development of techniques for manipulating people's attitudes."[44]

The letter sought to explain the Unabomber's long campaign of violence by stating his anti-technology principles, a significant departure from his normal operating procedure, which was to allow the bomb to speak for itself. Using plural pronouns in a deliberate ploy to confuse investigators, Kaczynski explained, "Through our bombings we hope to promote social instability in industrial society, propagate anti-industrial ideas and give encouragement to those who hate the industrial system." To address the question of why the public pronouncement of goals was so long in coming, Kaczynski stated, "Why do we announce our goals only now though we made our first bomb some 17 years ago? Our early bombs were too ineffectual to attract much public attention or give encouragement to those who hate the system. . . . So we went back to work, and after a long period of experimentation we developed a type of bomb that does not require the pipe." Owing to these improved methods, "Clearly we're in a position to do a great deal of damage. And it doesn't appear that the FBI is going to catch us any time soon. The FBI is a joke." Toward the end of the letter, the Unabomber engaged in the age-old practice of blaming the victim. He portrayed himself—or rather his nonexistent group—as reluctant terrorists. "The people who were pushing all this growth and progress garbage deserve to be severely punished. But our goal is less to punish them than to propagate ideas. Anyhow we are getting tired of making bombs. It's no fun having to spend all your evenings and weekends preparing dangerous mixtures, filing trigger mechanisms out of scraps of metal while searching the Sierras for a place isolated enough to test a bomb."[45]

The reference to the Sierras and the misspelling of "Burson-Marsteller" as "Burston" suggested that the bomber had ties to the radical environmental community in California. Although this was a promising avenue of investigation, the FBI mistakenly focused on the environmental group Earth First! that had denounced "Burston-Marsteller" in the June 1993 issue of its magazine. Strengthening its case, the FBI recalled that two Earth First! activists, Judi Bari and Darryl Cherney, had been victims of a May 1990 car bomb. The bureau had long suspected that Bari and Cherney had constructed the bomb themselves and had been hurt when it prematurely exploded. As a result of the connection between the 1990 car bomb and the misspelling of "Burson-Marsteller," investigators spent innumerable hours following up on leads that proved fruitless in the long run.[46]

The terrorist's final victim, timber lobbyist Gilbert B. Murray, worked with the California Forestry Association. The date was April 24, 1995. A package mailed to the CFA offices was addressed to Bill Dennison, Murray's predecessor, who had retired a year earlier. Typically, the office receptionist opened the mail, but she had a doctor's appointment and was not in the office that day. Bob Taylor, the staff biologist, Jeanette Grimm, the controller, and Eleanor Anderson, the executive secretary, pitched in to sort through the mail. The package was wrapped so tightly that Grimm could not open it. "Maybe it's a bomb," she joked. "Perhaps we should forward it to Bill," meaning, of course, Bill Dennison.[47]

Gilbert Murray had just entered the office and happened upon the conversation. "Let's open it first, to see what it is," he said, ignoring Grimm's joke. Bob Taylor, recalling the Oklahoma City bombing that had occurred just five days earlier, told Murray that he should be careful. Nonetheless, the CFA president was an easygoing nature lover who did not believe in conspiracy theories. As far as he knew, he had no enemies and could not possibly be the target of a terrorist. He grabbed the package and without hesitation tried to open it.[48]

As he struggled with the wrapping, he experienced difficulty. He asked Eleanor Anderson to find a pair of scissors so he could cut through the nylon packing tape on the package exterior. In the meantime, Jeanette Grimm went to answer a ringing telephone. Bob Taylor, too, left the room, offering what he thought was a joke: "I'm getting out of here before the bomb goes off."[49]

Eleanor Anderson was walking down the hallway to her own office when the device exploded. The blast ripped the doors off their hinges, and the suspended ceiling collapsed, causing tiles and insulation to fall to the floor. The carpet was incinerated. In fact, the bomb was so powerful that it propelled nails into the walls of other offices located in the same building.[50]

Bob Taylor had just reached his desk when he heard a boom and felt the pressure of the bomb. Panicked, he rushed down the hallway and immediately encountered Eleanor Anderson and Jeanette Grimm. They were both shaken but essentially unharmed. Frantic with worry, Taylor searched for his boss. He could not find him. He rushed down the street to a fire station but found that all the trucks were out on assignment. As he returned to the office, Taylor arrived just as firemen and police officers converged on the scene. Only later did he learn that Gilbert Murray had been torn to pieces by the explosive device. According to the coroner, Murray's "face was ripped off; his arm was ripped off. There were parts of his body all over the room."[51]

Two months later, on June 24, "FC," having become a loquacious correspondent, addressed yet another letter to the *New York Times* to explain his actions. "We have no regret about the fact that our bomb blew up the wrong man, Gilbert Murray, instead of William Dennison, to whom it was addressed. Though Murray did not have Dennison's inflammatory style, he was pursuing the same goals, and he was probably pursuing them more effectively because of the very fact that he was not inflammatory." Any destruction, no matter how indiscriminate or seemingly unjustified, could be rationalized in the skewed world of the Unabomber.[52]

During the course of his career, Ted Kaczynski had created sixteen bombs over a seventeen-year period. He injured twenty-three people and killed three. In addition to changing his targets and waiting for long periods of time between attacks, he also left false clues to throw investigators off his trail. He left a metal plate stamped with the initials "FC" on some bombs. A note found with the bomb that injured Diogenes Angelakos read, "Wu—It works! I told you it would—RV." He also ensured that latent fingerprints found on some of the bombs did not match his own fingerprints. He sometimes included bits of bark and tree branches in his bombs, and once, in the case of Percy Wood, he even included a novel embedded in the bomb. Kaczynski later admitted that he intentionally sought to confuse the police through deliberate subterfuge, what police call "anti-forensic countermeasures."[53]

A TERRORIST IS APPREHENDED

By 1995, the Unabomber seemed anxious to tell the world about his cause. No longer satisfied to send piecemeal letters to the *New York Times*, late in June 1995, the fictional FC mailed a 35,000-word manuscript titled "Industrial Society and Its Future, by FC," to the *New York Times*, the *Washington Post*, and *Penthouse* magazine. The submissions to the *New York Times* and the *Washington Post* were accompanied by a promise: "If the enclosed manuscript is published reasonably soon and receives wide public exposure, we will permanently desist from terrorism." Perhaps because it was not considered a prestigious publication, *Penthouse* received a somewhat less favorable offer. "We promise to desist permanently from terrorism, except that we reserve the right to plant one (and only one) bomb intended to kill, after our manuscript has been published." News organizations, fearful of setting a dangerous precedent, vigorously debated the ethics of publishing a manuscript under threat, but they eventually relented after U.S. attorney general Janet Reno requested publication in the hopes that someone might recognize the author's distinctive style of thinking and writing.[54]

Although *Penthouse* never published the manifesto, on September 19, 1995, the *Washington Post* collaborated with the *New York Times* to publish the entire document as a special supplement. It ran to fifty-six pages. As soon as the screed appeared in print, numerous newspapers and journals republished it. Time Warner even placed it on Pathfinder, a free Internet site. Although a large percentage of Americans remain horrified by the Unabomber and his actions, a surprising number of fan sites multiplied on the World Wide Web.[55]

The manifesto's anti-government, anti-technology ideas struck a responsive chord with many Americans who believed that their government was out of control and that modern society was undermining human freedom. "The Industrial Revolution and its consequences have been a disaster for the human race," it began. "They have greatly increased the life-expectancy of those of us who live in 'advanced' countries, but they have destabilized society, have made life unfulfilling, have subjected human beings to indignities, have led to widespread psychological suffering (in the Third World to physical suffering as well) and have inflicted severe damage on the natural world. The continued development of technology will worsen the situation."[56]

In some places, the text was eerily reminiscent of the Weather Underground in its condemnation of life in postmodern America: "We therefore advocate a revolution against the industrial system. This revolution may or may not make use of violence. it may be sudden or it may be a relatively gradual process spanning a few decades. We can't predict any of that. But we do outline in a very general way the measures that those who hate the industrial system should take in order to prepare the way for a revolution against that form of society." Unlike the Weather people, however, the Unabomber criticized leftists as "mainly socialists, collectivists, 'politically correct' types, feminists, gay and disability activists, animal rights activists and the like."[57]

Toward the end of the document, the author stated his central thesis: "It is not possible to make a LASTING compromise between technology and freedom, because technology is by far the more powerful social force and continually encroaches on freedom through REPEATED compromises." By employing violence against the symbols of industrial society, FC claimed to champion human freedom over the totalitarianism inherent in a society that embraced ever-increasing technological advances.[58]

Despite praise from some sources, many commentators denounced the manifesto as a cliché-ridden screed, a confused jumble of turgid prose that was difficult to slog through from beginning to end. Whatever marginal merits the manuscript possessed as a philosophical work were lost in bombastic messages, repetitive phrases, and lengthy digressions that left the reader confused and exhausted. Ted Kaczynski's brilliance was evident, as were his difficult personality and skewed view of the world.[59]

Aside from the debate over the ethics of whether it should have been published and its qualities, or lack thereof, as a scholarly work, one important result of the publication, just as Janet Reno had hoped, was that it finally provided a clue as to the identity of the Unabomber. When it appeared in the newspapers, the anti-industrial diatribe caught the attention of Linda Patrik, a woman who had married David Kaczynski, Ted's younger brother. She had known that her brother-in-law was a strange man. Now Linda Patrik was convinced that Ted was the serial bomber who had eluded authorities for decades. Her husband, David, initially disagreed, but as he searched through old papers and letters, he recognized Ted's unusual style of writing and inimitable "voice" throughout the pages of the manifesto.[60]

As a child, David Kaczynski had looked up to his older brother, admiring his intellect and idealism. All through his young life, David had envied his brilliant sibling's academic accomplishments, especially when their parents touted Ted's intellectual prowess. David was no dummy—after all, he had graduated from Columbia University with a degree in English literature in 1970—but it was clear that the younger Kaczynski son was no match for the mathematics genius in their household. Despite the sibling rivalry, David always insisted that he harbored no ill will, only love and affection for his brother. Their temperaments were different, but the brothers were both socially awkward and lived strong interior lives. As he grew to adulthood, David also shared Ted's love of the outdoors.[61]

David later admitted that to some extent he felt alienated from modern society. He went through a period of following a primitive lifestyle, although it did not last. By 1989, young David had moved to Schenectady, New York, to live with an old girlfriend, Linda Patrik, a philosophy professor at Union College. In 1990, he and Linda married in a Buddhist ceremony. The marriage drove a wedge between the two brothers. As far as Ted was concerned, David had turned his back on the search for a pure, simple lifestyle. In marrying a woman and settling down in an urban area, David had committed the ultimate sin of embracing industrial society. By the early 1990s, Ted and David Kaczynski had become estranged.[62]

Linda Patrik opened her husband's eyes to Ted's obvious eccentricities. On more than one occasion, she remarked, "You've got a screwy brother. Maybe he's the Unabomber." Although she uttered these remarks half in jest, Linda impressed upon her husband that Ted was more than simply an odd character. After she read the manifesto in the newspaper, she persuaded David to read the Unabomber's text and compare it with essays and letters that Ted had written earlier in his life. As David later recalled, the similarities were eerie. "After I read the first few pages, my jaw literally dropped." One passage, in particular, caught his attention. The Unabomber wrote, "It is obvious that modern leftist philosophers are not simply cool-headed logicians systematically analyzing the foundation of knowledge." David remembered Ted employing the phrase "cool-headed logicians" in other writings. As he made his way through the text, the similarities between the manifesto and Ted's writings were unmistakable. In spelling, word choice, syntax, and turns of phrase, the words of the Unabomber and the words of Ted Kaczynski were often identical.[63]

This realization presented David Kaczynski with the most pressing ethical dilemma of his life. On one hand, Ted was his brother, the one individual he knew better than any other with the exception of his wife, Linda. On the other hand, if Ted really was the Unabomber, he had engaged in despicable, criminal acts—acts that would likely continue until he was apprehended. If David Kaczynski had a reasonable belief that his brother was a serial killer, did he not have an ethical and legal duty to inform the police?

Eventually, David and Linda sent a copy of the manifesto, along with five letters that Ted had written, to Susan Swanson, an old friend of Linda's and now a private investigator in Chicago. They asked her opinion. Swanson reviewed the material and also consulted a former FBI analyst working as a private consultant. Based on this diligent review, Swanson's best guess was that there was a 60 to 80 percent chance of a match. This conclusion reinforced David Kaczynski's opinion and confirmed his deepest fears. Recognizing that they could no longer remain silent, David and Linda contacted Anthony Bisceglie, a Washington, D.C., attorney and former law school classmate of Susan Swanson's. David explained that he wanted to shield Ted's identity until the FBI could positively determine that the author of the manifesto and the letters were the same person. At David Kaczynski's behest, Bisceglie contacted FBI special agent John Flynn and handed over five of Ted's letters to the bureau with all identifying markers redacted. Bisceglie told Flynn, "Either this is a historic moment, or the beginning of a wild goose chase."[64]

Thus began a delicate dance, a series of maneuvers between David Kaczynski, his attorney, and FBI agents. When David met investigators for the first time in February 1996, they attempted to bully him, demanding to know who wrote the letters and how they could find the author. He and Bisceglie held firm. Before he revealed additional information, David Kaczynski wanted assurances that the suspect would be treated as innocent until proven guilty and that no trigger-happy policemen would harass or harm the suspected offender. It was a valiant effort, but the bureau had employed its own considerable resources to investigate David's background. Despite his careful entreaties, after David Kaczynski had approached the FBI, it did not take much digging to discern that his older brother, Ted, was the probable author of the letters. Agents immediately staked out Ted's homemade shack in Lincoln, Montana.[65]

It was one thing to identify a reasonable suspect; it was another matter to build a legal case and apprehend the man with minimal bloodshed or destruction of evidence. The bureau still needed David Kaczynski's cooperation if they hoped to resolve the matter satisfactorily. Because they did not know what, if anything, Ted Kaczynski was planning to do in the future and whether he had booby-trapped his home, investigators recognized the value of working with the Kaczynski family. David's mother, Wanda, recalled the intense pressure that federal agents placed on her and David to cooperate.[66]

It was a difficult time for the family. Wanda vividly recalled David's anguish when he told her of his suspicions. "He was walking back and forth and the tears started raining down his face and I sort of sat there in shock," she said. "I thought it, it, it couldn't be Ted. It, it, it just couldn't. It must be a mistake. And I said, I'm, I'm sure the investigation will rule him out."[67]

Unfortunately for the family, the more they reviewed Ted's old writings and compared them with the Unabomber's manifesto, the more they realized that the FBI had its man. Finally, in exchange for a guarantee that Ted would not receive the death penalty, David Kaczynski assisted the bureau in apprehending his brother without incident.[68]

The raid on Ted's cabin in Lincoln occurred on April 3, 1996. Jerry Burns, a Forest Service ranger, approached the cabin in the company of Tom McDaniel from the FBI's Helena, Montana, office. Realizing that Ted was often prickly when people trespassed on his property, the two men feigned a loud argument over the proper boundary line for the property. "Hey Ted," Burns called, "can you come out here and show us where it is?"

A moment later, Ted Kaczynski looked outside his door. "Sure, just let me go back in and get my jacket," he said.

Before he could disappear inside the shack, Special Agent "Mad Max" Noel stepped forward, grabbed Kaczynski, slapped handcuffs on him, and pushed him away from the shack. Just like that, it was over. The decades-long search for the Unabomber had ended, although authorities still had to determine if their suspect acted alone. A team of FBI agents immediately rushed into the cabin, careful to search for booby-traps and explosives.[69]

The agents led Kaczynski to a nearby house for a preliminary interrogation. Several FBI agents on the Unabomber task force were initially skeptical that Ted Kaczynski was the right person, but the mountain of evidence recovered from the scene was eventually persuasive. Investigators uncovered a virtual bomb-making factory as well as reams of notebooks, some of which were written in Spanish, outlining Kaczynski's "experiments." Even as overwhelming evidence accumulated, a nagging question existed about whether all the acts attributed to this demented, modern Luddite were the

U.S. Marshals escort the Unabomber, Ted Kaczynski, to the federal courthouse in Helena, Montana. Courtesy of Corbis.

work of a lone individual. The lingering ambiguity was exactly what Kaczynski had hoped to create when he had occasionally written of "we" and mentioned other names in his writings. He was a crafty terrorist, deliberately attempting to confuse investigators with mind games such as the fictional organization known as "FC." Despite remaining doubts, by the time FBI agents had combed through the recluse's possessions; cataloged the books, chemicals, and weaponry on the premises; and performed a forensic analysis, they were satisfied that Ted Kaczynski was, in fact, the infamous and heretofore elusive Unabomber.[70]

THE UNITED STATES V. THEODORE JOHN KACZYNSKI

On June 18, 1996, a federal grand jury in Sacramento, California, indicted Theodore John Kaczynski on ten counts for bombing Hugh Scrutton,

Charles Epstein, David Gelernter, and Gilbert Murray. New Jersey prosecutors announced they were prepared to file charges against Kaczynski for Thomas Mosser's murder. Five days after the California indictment, authorities transported their suspect on a government jet to the Sacramento jail under heavy guard. On June 25, the court appointed well-known Sacramento public defender Quin Denvir to represent Kaczynski. To assist in preparing the case, Denvir added Judy Clarke, a prominent anti–death penalty attorney from Spokane, Washington, to his team.[71]

Despite the overwhelming evidence that had been amassed against their client, Denvir and Clarke valiantly attacked the prosecution's case. They filed a motion before the presiding federal district court judge, Garland E. Burrell Jr., seeking to exclude evidence taken from Kaczynski's Montana cabin, arguing that it had been illegally obtained based on a flawed search warrant. After Judge Burrell denied their motion, the defense attorneys switched tactics. As required by the Federal Rules of Criminal Procedure in cases where a defendant will argue that a "mental defect" drove him to commit the crime, Denvir and Clarke filed a Section 12.2(b) motion. The relevant section reads, "If a defendant intends to introduce expert evidence relating to a mental disease or defect or any other mental condition of the defendant bearing on either (1) the issue of guilt or (2) the issue of punishment in a capital case, the defendant must—within the time provided for filing a pretrial motion or at any later time the court sets—notify an attorney for the government in writing of this intention and file a copy of the notice with the clerk." To most criminal defense attorneys, this strategy seemed prudent in the wake of U.S. attorney general Janet Reno's May 15, 1997, announcement that prosecutors would seek the death penalty for the Unabomber.[72]

However prudent this course of action appeared to the defense attorneys, their client was dismayed when he learned of the strategy. "I categorically refuse to use a mental status defense," he wrote to them shortly after they counseled him to support a 12.2(b) filing. Under their relentless pressure, Kaczynski acquiesced in the filing. Nonetheless, he continued to harbor strong reservations. To his way of thinking, an admission of a "mental defect," even as a cynical legal strategy, suggested that his campaign of violence against technology run amok was the product of a diseased mind, not a rational choice by which a lone, heroic individual could arrest the gradual, sustained loss of personal liberty.[73]

As Kaczynski's legal maneuvering was transformed into a cause célèbre, numerous prominent criminal defense attorneys emerged out of the woodwork offering all manner of novel defense strategies. Psychologists and psychiatrists freely pontificated on possible causes and motives in the pages of national newspapers anxious to spread as much conjecture as their readers would purchase. For their part, the family, in an effort to help Ted avoid death by lethal injection, repeatedly spoke to reporters and appeared on television shows. Always they portrayed him as a brilliant but misguided man, a sympathetic victim of society who, for all of his dastardly deeds, did not deserve to die at the hands of the state.[74]

Ted Kaczynski did not believe he was insane. Years earlier, he had confided to his diary that he acted deliberately and without mental disease. "I intend to start killing people," he wrote. "If I am successful at this, it is possible that, when I am caught (not alive, I fervently hope!) there will be some speculation in the news media as to my motives for killing. . . . If some speculation occurs, they are bound to make me out to be a sickie, and to ascribe to me motives of a sordid or 'sick' type." In this judgment, at least, his words proved to be prescient.[75]

Understanding Ted Kaczynski's mental health was exceedingly difficult, especially after his participation in Dr. Murray's psychological experiments at Harvard University came to light. Perhaps the fragile young man had been driven to engage in heinous crimes owing to sadistic, unethical, possibly torturous experiments practiced on him decades earlier. For persons who struggled to understand the cause and effect between Ted Kaczynski's young life and the subsequent creation of the Unabomber persona, this new information conveniently suggested that the brilliant but socially awkward young man had not been born a monster; a monster had been created.[76]

During the jury selection phase of his trial in November 1997, Kaczynski was livid when he overheard a conversation between prosecutors and defense attorneys as well as Judge Burrell concerning "neuropsychological testing" of the defendant. On December 1, the angry suspect penned a letter to the judge complaining that defense attorneys were going to present him to jurors as "mentally ill without my consent." In a subsequent note, Kaczynski told the judge that he had been "tricked and humiliated by people for whom I'd had warm affection." He assured the judge that "I would rather die, or suffer prolonged physical torture, than have the 12.2(b) defense imposed on me in this way by my present attorneys." As someone deeply mistrustful of industrial society, Kaczynski argued that "I do not believe that science has any business probing the workings of the human mind, and that my personal ideology and that of the mental-health professions are mutually antagonistic."[77]

Matters came to a head on January 5, 1998, the day Judge Burrell had scheduled for opening arguments in the case. The defendant spoke up:

"Your Honor," he said, "before these proceedings begin I would like to revisit the issue of my relations with my attorneys. It's very important." The judge undoubtedly knew what was coming, yet he had no choice. He had to allow Kaczynski to reiterate his objection to pleading insanity. In addition, the defendant requested that he be allowed to fire his attorneys and replace them with an advocate who would not pursue a strategy the defendant deemed objectionable.[78]

Judge Burrell had previously ruled that Kaczynski could not switch attorneys, but the defendant could insist that the defense team forgo a Section 12.2(b) defense. Rejecting an insanity defense, however, did not mean that defense attorneys would eschew psychological testimony. For Ted Kaczynski, the committed ideologue who desperately wanted to alert the world to his ideas about the decay of industrial society, any discussion of his deteriorating psychological state must be avoided. His anti-technology, anti-society rants, while outside the mainstream, were not insane. In an act of desperation, the defendant asked that he be allowed to represent himself in court.[79]

After yet another examination by a psychiatrist, the court had to decide whether Kaczynski could handle the case himself. Ultimately, the judge ruled that he could not. A writer for the *New Yorker* magazine mused on the judge's wisdom in "flying a psychiatrist in from North Carolina for a week to determine the defendant's competency to represent himself and then, when she found him competent, ruling that he could not represent himself." Judge Burrell contended that Kaczynski's request was merely a tactic to delay the trial and transform it into a media circus.[80]

Although many lawyers and professors questioned the constitutionality of the judge's decision, the denial of Kaczynski's right to self-representation at trial led to a speedy conclusion. Defense attorneys, recognizing that their continued estrangement from their client would not be resolved in the foreseeable future, were anxious to find a resolution that would allow Kaczynski to avoid the death penalty. Prosecutors were concerned that the judge's decision might lead to a guilty verdict being overturned on appeal. They, too, sought a quick end to the proceedings. As for the defendant, he knew his options were limited. Because he could not replace his defense counsel and could not represent himself, he would be forced to go along with his attorneys' insanity defense. To avoid such a distasteful result, on May 4, 1998, Theodore John Kaczynski pleaded guilty to ten counts involving various terrorist acts and was sentenced to life in prison without the possibility of parole. He later tried to change his plea, but to no avail. The court refused to grant his request, and Kaczynski's appeal was unsuccessful. For all intents and purposes, the Unabomber had had his day in court.[81]

CONCLUSION

The Unabomber case is difficult to assess. Ted Kaczynski seemed to "psychologically shut down," in his brother David's words, when confronted with uncomfortable or stressful situations. He was a man so socially awkward and alienated from society, and so completely unable to empathize with his fellow human beings, that he could rationalize any act, no matter how repulsive, as necessary and righteous.

Lawyers and health care professionals often debate a defendant's state of mind. First, is the person so delusional and separated from reality that he or she simply cannot comprehend the nature of the legal proceedings? Second, even if the person is not delusional, is he or she healthy enough to understand the nature of the charges and actively participate in his or her own defense? Third, assuming the defendant is not delusional and is able to participate in a defense, can the person defend himself or herself in a court of law if the defendant seeks to exercise the right to self-representation? These issues arising from the Unabomber case continue to be debated.

The definition of terrorism employed throughout this book requires a perpetrator to be willing and able to initiate violence or the threat of violence that breaks the law, is aimed at civilians, and supports a broader social, moral, political, religious, or ethnic cause. A mentally ill person cannot meet this definition because his ability to form the requisite intent is compromised. The question is whether Kaczynski's mental defects disqualified him from the definition of a terrorist.

He certainly did not believe he was mentally ill. He understood that characterizing his actions as the consequence of derangement would refocus the debate away from his gripes against industrial society onto a discussion about the signs of mental illness. In his view, American life was threatened by rapidly developing technology, which eroded traditional values and mores. The only effective means to rage against the dying of the light was to undertake a campaign of violence against symbolic targets. He understood that actions have consequences. He was able to plan his attacks rationally, implement them effectively, and repeatedly elude detection by employing a series of countermeasures.

Whatever his mind-set, he shared with other terrorists a conviction that mainstream society was corrupted and could not be reformed through conventional means of redressing grievances. Violence became an acceptable form of protest for someone who viewed technological progress and societal change as destructive to human freedom. He also shared with many other terrorists an inability to see beyond his own pain, a narcissistic emphasis on his hopes and desires to the exclusion of all else.[82]

Assume, for the sake of argument, that Ted Kaczynski was exactly what he claimed to be, namely a combination separatist and ideologue who freely and knowingly engaged in acts of terrorism absent a mental defect. Perhaps he would have undertaken his life of crime even if he had not been subjected to the Harvard psychological experiments. He was not engaged in a conspiracy, but he had a clear, well-defined, premeditated vendetta against the agents of technological progress in American society. In his view, leftists and agents of industrial change were creating an Orwellian world that threatened to dehumanize the individual and undermine human freedom. To protest the loss of human individuality, the Unabomber deliberately designed a campaign of violence against what he perceived to be symbols of dehumanizing technology. Although this level of alienation and the nature of such an extreme form of protest may be very distasteful to mainstream Americans, they are not necessarily insane acts. In fact, the terrorist, by definition, is the person who strikes out at perceived enemies in a calculated way and deliberately steps outside of the existing social structure and political system while engaging in acts of often indiscriminate violence.[83]

When historians review the history of violence, terrorism, and mass murder, they often find the perpetrators to be persons of high intelligence. The level of advance planning and organization necessary to carry out systematic, ongoing violent acts while escaping detection and capture requires a superior intellect. Luke Pryor Blackburn, the infamous "Dr. Black Vomit" discussed earlier in this book, was a prominent physician in an era when few Americans could attain such lofty status. Vladimir Lenin, the revolutionary lawyer, economist, and political philosopher who helped to create the Soviet Communist Party that founded the USSR, was a talented intellectual known for his uncommon intelligence. Nathan Leopold and Richard Loeb, the two infamous Chicago "thrill killers" of the 1920s who believed they were Nietzschean supermen capable of pulling off the perfect crime, were gifted prodigies. Many high-ranking members of the Nazi Party during the 1930s and 1940s, especially the medical doctors who carried out grisly "scientific" experiments in the death camps, were intellectually advanced. Hideki Tojo, the Japanese general who led his nation's armed forces during the 1930s and 1940s, when some fifteen million people died, was a top graduate of the Imperial Army Staff College. The list of gifted terrorist candidates continues virtually *ad infinitum*.[84]

Yet superior intellect neither explains nor excuses the acts of a serial bomber. In the final analysis, Ted Kaczynski may have been an emotionally fragile, mentally disturbed man who, at a critical point in his young life, endured a brutal, devastating psychological experiment, but he seems to have understood right from wrong. In recognizing the boundaries of society and choosing deliberately to step beyond them, he fashioned himself into a separate being, the committed terrorist. To the extent that he reveled in any action he undertook or displayed any emotion apart from anger, he was happiest when his explosive devices were the deadliest. He serves as a shining example of the modern separatist, a human being who is willing and able to step beyond the boundaries of social convention to inflict pain and suffering on others in the name of a supposedly higher cause. Whether he was mentally ill or an opportunistic, ruthless terrorist will remain a matter of fierce debate.[85]

NOTES

1. Boylan, *Portraits of Guilt*, 7; Brooke, "New Portrait of Unabomber," A20; Egan, "Hiding Out Underneath the Big Sky," E1, E4; Guimond and Maynard, "Kaczynski, Conrad, and Terrorism," 3–4; Johnston, "Go-Between for Family Was in Dark," B8; Kifner, "Swirling around Unabom Suspect, an Environmental Dispute," A27; Oleson, "'Evil the Natural Way,'" 212.

2. Booth, "Kaczynski Resists the Insanity Defense," A1; Leeper, "An Adlerian Analysis of the Unabomber," 169–70; McFadden, "From a Child of Promise to the Unabom Suspect," A22.

3. Chase, *Harvard and the Unabomber*, 158–74; Leeper, "An Adlerian Analysis of the Unabomber," 173; McFadden, "From a Child of Promise to the Unabom Suspect," A22; Springer, "Patterns of Radicalization," 35.

4. Broad, "Unabom Manifesto Echoes 60's Tumult," A8; Chase, *Harvard and the Unabomber*, 181–84, 298–99; Leeper, "An Adlerian Analysis of the Unabomber," 170; McFadden, "From a Child of Promise to the Unabom Suspect," A22.

5. Chase, *Harvard and the Unabomber*, 228–39; Springer, "Patterns of Radicalization," 36–37.

6. Broad, "Unabom Manifesto Echoes 60's Tumult," A8; Chase, *Harvard and the Unabomber*, 299–306; Graysmith, *Unabomber*, 5, 56; McFadden, "From a Child of Promise to the Unabom Suspect," A1; Springer, "Patterns of Radicalization," 37–38.

7. Broad, "Unabom Manifesto Echoes 60's Tumult," A8; Chase, *Harvard and the Unabomber*, 309–11; Guimond and Maynard, "Kaczynski, Conrad, and Terrorism," 3; Springer, "Patterns of Radicalization," 39; Waits and Shors, *Unabomber*, 7.

8. Broad, "Unabom Manifesto Echoes 60's Tumult," A8; Chase, *Harvard and the Unabomber*, 21; Leeper, "An Adlerian Analysis of the Unabomber," 172; McFadden, "From a Child of Promise to the Unabom Suspect," A22; Oleson, "'Evil the Natural Way,'" 212; Waits and Shors, *Unabomber*, 13.

9. Egan, "Hiding Out Underneath the Big Sky," E1, E4; Oleson, "'Evil the Natural Way,'" 211–13.

10. Chase, *Harvard and the Unabomber*, 343; Oswell, *The Unabomber and the Zodiac*, 31–32.

11. Brooke, "New Portrait of Unabomber," A20; Chase, *Harvard and the Unabomber*, 339–42; Kifner, "Swirling around Unabom Suspect, an Environmental Dispute," A27.

12. Chase, *Harvard and the Unabomber*, 48–50; Douglas and Olshaker, *Unabomber*, 31; Graysmith, *Unabomber*, 60–61; McCann, *Terrorism on American Soil*, 221; Oswell, *The Unabomber and the Zodiac*, 6; Springer, "Patterns of Radicalization," 43.

13. Chase, *Harvard and the Unabomber*, 49–50; Douglas and Olshaker, *Unabomber*, 31–32.

14. Chase, *Harvard and the Unabomber*, 48–49; Douglas and Olshaker, *Unabomber*, 32; McCann, *Terrorism on American Soil*, 221; Oswell, *The Unabomber and the Zodiac*, 7.

15. Boylan, *Portraits of Guilt*, 7; Chase, *Harvard and the Unabomber*, 47–49; Douglas and Olshaker, *Unabomber*, 32–33; Graysmith, *Unabomber*, xx, 189; Oswell, *The Unabomber and the Zodiac*, 7.

16. Boylan, *Portraits of Guilt*, 7; Chase, *Harvard and the Unabomber*, 47–48; Douglas and Olshaker, *Unabomber*, 32–33; Graysmith, *Unabomber*, xxiii; Kifner, "Swirling around Unabom Suspect, an Environmental Dispute," A27.

17. Belluck, "A Brother's Anguish," A14; Booth, "Kaczynski Resists the Insanity Defense," A1; Chase, *Harvard and the Unabomber*, 48–50; Guimond and Maynard, "Kaczynski, Conrad, and Terrorism," 3–4; Kifner, "Swirling around Unabom Suspect, an Environmental Dispute," A27; Leeper, "An Adlerian Analysis of the Unabomber," 169–70.

18. Douglas and Olshaker, *Unabomber*, 42; Graysmith, *Unabomber*, 171–74.

19. Boylan, *Portraits of Guilt*, 7; Chase, *Harvard and the Unabomber*, 53–55; Douglas and Olshaker, *Unabomber*, 33; Graysmith, *Unabomber*, 77–78; McCann, *Terrorism on American Soil*, 222.

20. Chase, *Harvard and the Unabomber*, 56–57; Douglas and Olshaker, *Unabomber*, 43; Graysmith, *Unabomber*, 85; Oswell, *The Unabomber and the Zodiac*, 7.

21. Chase, *Harvard and the Unabomber*, 57–59; Douglas and Olshaker, *Unabomber*, 44; Oswell, *The Unabomber and the Zodiac*, 7–8.

22. Unabomber Pages, n.p.

23. Chase, *Harvard and the Unabomber*, 58; Douglas and Olshaker, *Unabomber*, 45; Oswell, *The Unabomber and the Zodiac*, 8.

24. Chase, *Harvard and the Unabomber*, 58; Unabomber Pages, n.p.

25. Quoted in the Unabomber Pages, n.p. See also Chase, *Harvard and the Unabomber*, 60–61; Douglas and Olshaker, *Unabomber*, 44.

26. Chase, *Harvard and the Unabomber*, 60–61; Oswell, *The Unabomber and the Zodiac*, 8.

27. Chase, *Harvard and the Unabomber*, 65–66; Douglas and Olshaker, *Unabomber*, 47; Graysmith, *Unabomber*, 183–85; Guimond and Maynard, "Kaczynski, Conrad, and Terrorism," 3; Oswell, *The Unabomber and the Zodiac*, 8.

28. Boylan, *Portraits of Guilt*, 7; Chase, *Harvard and the Unabomber*, 65–66; Graysmith, *Unabomber*, 183–85; Johnston, "A Device in Cabin Is Said to Match the Unabomber's," A1, A18; Unabomber Pages, n.p.

29. Quoted in the Unabomber Pages, n.p. See also Chase, *Harvard and the Unabomber*, 66; Douglas and Olshaker, *Unabomber*, 47.

30. Chase, *Harvard and the Unabomber*, 66–67; Douglas and Olshaker, *Unabomber*, 48; Oswell, *The Unabomber and the Zodiac*, 9; Unabomber Pages, n.p.

31. Chase, *Harvard and the Unabomber*, 66–67; Douglas and Olshaker, *Unabomber*, 48; Springer, "Patterns of Radicalization," 44.

32. Barnard, "Artist Has Portfolio of Crimes," A7; Boylan, *Portraits of Guilt*, 8–11.

33. Boylan, *Portraits of Guilt*, 8; Chase, *Harvard and the Unabomber*, 67–68.

34. Chase, *Harvard and the Unabomber*, 68; Douglas and Olshaker, *Unabomber*, 55; Graysmith, *Unabomber*, 240; Oswell, *The Unabomber and the Zodiac*, 9.

35. Chase, *Harvard and the Unabomber*, 68–69; Douglas and Olshaker, *Unabomber*, 55; Graysmith, *Unabomber*, 240–41; Oswell, *The Unabomber and the Zodiac*, 9; Unabomber Pages, n.p.

36. Chase, *Harvard and the Unabomber*, 69–71; Douglas and Olshaker, *Unabomber*, 55; Graysmith, *Unabomber*, 246–48; Unabomber Pages, n.p.

37. Chase, *Harvard and the Unabomber*, 70–71; Graysmith, *Unabomber*, 246–48; Unabomber Pages, n.p.

38. Chase, *Harvard and the Unabomber*, 72; Douglas and Olshaker, *Unabomber*, 55; Graysmith, *Unabomber*, 246–48; Unabomber Pages, n.p.

39. Chase, *Harvard and the Unabomber*, 72; Unabomber Pages, n.p.

40. Chase, *Harvard and the Unabomber*, 73; Douglas and Olshaker, *Unabomber*, 182; Oswell, *The Unabomber and the Zodiac*, 9.

41. Chase, *Harvard and the Unabomber*, 73–74; Douglas and Olshaker, *Unabomber*, 68; Graysmith, *Unabomber*, 279–80; Unabomber Pages, n.p.

42. Chase, *Harvard and the Unabomber*, 74; Unabomber Pages, n.p.

43. Chase, *Harvard and the Unabomber*, 74; Douglas and Olshaker, *Unabomber*, 68; Graysmith, *Unabomber*, 279–80; Guimond and Maynard, "Kaczynski, Conrad, and Terrorism," 3; Johnston, "A Device in Cabin Is Said to Match the Unabomber's," A1, A18; Oswell, *The Unabomber and the Zodiac*, 9; Unabomber Pages, n.p.

44. Quoted in the Unabomber Pages, n.p. See also Chase, *Harvard and the Unabomber*, 75.

45. Quoted in Chase, *Harvard and the Unabomber*, 75–76. See also Douglas and Olshaker, *Unabomber*, 68–69.

46. Chase, *Harvard and the Unabomber*, 76–78; Douglas and Olshaker, *Unabomber*, 182; Unabomber Pages, n.p.

47. Chase, *Harvard and the Unabomber*, 78; Douglas and Olshaker, *Unabomber*, 69; Graysmith, *Unabomber*, 306; Oswell, *The Unabomber and the Zodiac*, 9–10.

48. Chase, *Harvard and the Unabomber*, 78–79; Unabomber Pages, n.p.

49. Chase, *Harvard and the Unabomber*, 79; Douglas and Olshaker, *Unabomber*, 69; Oswell, *The Unabomber and the Zodiac*, 10.

50. Chase, *Harvard and the Unabomber*, 79; Unabomber Pages, n.p.

51. Chase, *Harvard and the Unabomber*, 79; Douglas and Olshaker, *Unabomber*, 69; Guimond and Maynard, "Kaczynski, Conrad, and Terrorism," 3; Johnston, "A Device in Cabin Is Said to Match the Unabomber's," A1, A18; Kifner, "Swirling around Unabom Suspect, an Environmental Dispute," A27; Oswell, *The Unabomber and the Zodiac*, 10.

52. Chase, *Harvard and the Unabomber*, 79; Douglas and Olshaker, *Unabomber*, 69–70.

53. Chase, *Harvard and the Unabomber*, 57–59; Douglas and Olshaker, *Unabomber*, 44; Graysmith, *Unabomber*, 100; Oswell, *The Unabomber and the Zodiac*, 7–8.

54. Boylan, *Portraits of Guilt*, 8; Chase, *Harvard and the Unabomber*, 83–87; Guimond and Maynard, "Kaczynski, Conrad, and Terrorism," 3.

55. Belluck, "A Brother's Anguish," A14; Broad, "Unabom Manifesto Echoes 60's Tumult," A8; Chase, *Harvard and the Unabomber*, 87–93; Dowd, "His Brother's Keeper," A25; Guimond and Maynard, "Kaczynski, Conrad, and Terrorism," 3–4.

56. Kaczynski, "Industrial Society and Its Future, by FC," 5.

57. Kaczynski, "Industrial Society and Its Future, by FC," 6–7. See also Chase, *Harvard and the Unabomber*, 84–87; Graysmith, *Unabomber*, 485; Oleson, "'Evil the Natural Way,'" 220.

58. Kaczynski, "Industrial Society and Its Future, by FC," 55.

59. Broad, "Unabom Manifesto Echoes 60's Tumult," A8; Chase, *Harvard and the Unabomber*, 87–89; Guimond and Maynard, "Kaczynski, Conrad, and Terrorism," 7–9; Oleson, "'Evil the Natural Way,'" 218–21.

60. Belluck, "A Brother's Anguish," A14; Douglas and Olshaker, *Unabomber*, 102; Graysmith, *Unabomber*, 113; Johnston, "Go-Between for Family Was in Dark," B8; McFadden, "From a Child of Promise to the Unabom Suspect," A1, A22.

61. Belluck, "A Brother's Anguish," A14; Chase, *Harvard and the Unabomber*, 106–9; Dowd, "His Brother's Keeper," A25; Hernandez, "Brother Who Tipped Off the Authorities Leads a Quiet, Simple Life," A25.

62. Belluck, "A Brother's Anguish," A14; Hernandez, "Brother Who Tipped Off the Authorities Leads a Quiet, Simple Life," A25; Johnston, "Go-Between for Family Was in Dark," B8; McFadden, "From a Child of Promise to the Unabom Suspect," A1, A22.

63. Belluck, "A Brother's Anguish," A14; Chase, *Harvard and the Unabomber*, 110–13; Douglas and Olshaker, *Unabomber*, 102; Dowd, "His Brother's Keeper," A25; Graysmith, *Unabomber*, 113; Hernandez, "Brother Who Tipped Off the Authorities Leads a Quiet, Simple Life," A25; Springer, "Patterns of Radicalization," 45.

64. Belluck, "A Brother's Anguish," A14; Chase, *Harvard and the Unabomber*, 112–13; Douglas and Olshaker, *Unabomber*, 107; Graysmith, *Unabomber*, 374; Johnston, "A Device in Cabin Is Said to Match the Unabomber's," A1, A18; Johnston, "Go-Between for Family Was in Dark," B8.

65. Belluck, "A Brother's Anguish," A14; Chase, *Harvard and the Unabomber*, 113–14; Hernandez, "Brother Who Tipped Off the Authorities Leads a Quiet, Simple Life," A25.

66. Chase, *Harvard and the Unabomber*, 113–14; Hernandez, "Brother Who Tipped Off the Authorities Leads a Quiet, Simple Life," A25; Johnston, "Go-Between for Family Was in Dark," B8; McFadden, "From a Child of Promise to the Unabom Suspect," A1, A22.

67. Belluck, "A Brother's Anguish," A14; Chase, *Harvard and the Unabomber*, 113–14; McFadden, "From a Child of Promise to the Unabom Suspect," A1, A22.

68. Belluck, "A Brother's Anguish," A14; Douglas and Olshaker, *Unabomber*, 107; Hernandez, "Brother Who Tipped Off the Authorities Leads a Quiet, Simple Life," A25, McFadden, "From a Child of Promise to the Unabom Suspect," A1, A22.

69. Brooke, "New Portrait of Unabomber," A20; Chase, *Harvard and the Unabomber*, 114–15; Egan, "Hiding Out Underneath the Big Sky," E1, E4; Ferkiss, "The FBI Comes Calling," 9–10; Kifner, "Swirling around Unabom Suspect, an Environmental Dispute," A27; Oleson, "'Evil the Natural Way,'" 218; Springer, "Patterns of Radicalization," 45.

70. Belluck, "A Brother's Anguish," A14; Brooke, "New Portrait of Unabomber," A20; Chase, *Harvard and the Unabomber*, 114–19; Douglas and Olshaker, *Unabomber*, 107; Ferkiss, "The FBI Comes Calling," 9–10; Hernandez, "Brother Who Tipped Off the Authorities Leads a Quiet, Simple Life," A25; Johnston, "A Device in Cabin Is Said to Match the Unabomber's," A1, A18; Kifner, "Swirling around Unabom Suspect, an Environmental Dispute," A27; McFadden, "From a Child of Promise to the Unabom Suspect," A1, A22; Waits and Shors, *Unabomber*, 8.

71. Booth, "Kaczynski Resists the Insanity Defense," A1; Chase, *Harvard and the Unabomber*, 133; Glaberson, "Accepts Life Term without Parole and Forgoes Right to Appeal," A1, A18; Mello, *The United States of America versus Theodore John Kaczynski*, 61.

72. Booth, "Kaczynski Resists the Insanity Defense," A1; Chase, *Harvard and the Unabomber*, 133–34; Mello, *The United States of America versus Theodore John Kaczynski*, 61–65.

73. Booth, "Kaczynski Resists the Insanity Defense," A1; Chase, *Harvard and the Unabomber*, 134–35; Mello, *The United States of America versus Theodore John Kaczynski*, 65–66.

74. Chase, *Harvard and the Unabomber*, 134–35; Glaberson, "Accepts Life Term without Parole and Forgoes Right to Appeal," A1, A18; Higgins, "A Difficult Client," 18.

75. Quoted in Chase, *Harvard and the Unabomber*, 137–38. See also Guimond and Maynard, "Kaczynski, Conrad, and Terrorism," 4–5; Higgins, "A Difficult Client," 18.

76. Akhtar, "The Psychodynamic Dimension of Terrorism," 351; Chase, *Harvard and the Unabomber*, 140–43; Leeper, "An Adlerian Analysis of the Unabomber," 169–75; Oleson, "'Evil the Natural Way,'" 212–21.

77. *United States Court of Appeals for the Ninth Circuit, United States of America v. Theodore John Kaczynski*, 239 F.3d 1108 at 1108–11. See also Chase, *Harvard and the Unabomber*, 143; Higgins, "A Difficult Client," 18.

78. *United States Court of Appeals for the Ninth Circuit, United States of America v. Theodore John Kaczynski*, 239 F.3d 1108 at 1108–13. See also Chase, *Harvard and the Unabomber*, 144–45; Higgins, "A Difficult Client," 18; Glaberson, "Accepts Life Term without Parole and Forgoes Right to Appeal," A1, A18.

79. Chase, *Harvard and the Unabomber*, 144–45; Higgins, "A Difficult Client," 18; Glaberson, "Accepts Life Term without Parole and Forgoes Right to Appeal," A1, A18; Mello, *The United States of America versus Theodore John Kaczynski*, 112.

80. Quoted in Chase, *Harvard and the Unabomber*, 147. See also Booth, "Kaczynski Resists the Insanity Defense," A1; Higgins, "A Difficult Client," 18; Glaberson, "Accepts Life Term without Parole and Forgoes Right to Appeal," A1, A18; Mello, *The United States of America versus Theodore John Kaczynski*, 112.

81. *United States of America v. Theodore John Kaczynski*, 262 F.3d 1034 (9th Cir. 2001). See also Chase, *Harvard and the Unabomber*, 147–49; McCann, *Terrorism on American Soil*, 228; Guimond and Maynard, "Kaczynski, Conrad, and Terrorism," 19–20; Mello, *The United States of America versus Theodore John Kaczynski*, 116.

82. Higgins, "A Difficult Client," 18; Glaberson, "Accepts Life Term without Parole and Forgoes Right to Appeal," A1, A18; Iftikhar, "Letter to the Editor: Home-Grown Terrorists," A28; Leeper, "An Adlerian Analysis of the Unabomber," 169–75; McCann, *Terrorism on American Soil*, 228–30.

83. Chase, *Harvard and the Unabomber*, 133–40; Higgins, "A Difficult Client," 18; Glaberson, "Accepts Life Term without Parole and Forgoes Right to Appeal," A1, A18; McCann, *Terrorism on American Soil*, 228–30.

84. Chase, *Harvard and the Unabomber*, 369–72; Khan and Azam, "Root Causes of Terrorism," 84–85; Leeper, "An Adlerian Analysis of the Unabomber," 173.

85. Akhtar, "The Psychodynamic Dimension of Terrorism," 351–53; Chase, *Harvard and the Unabomber*, 369–72; Guimond and Maynard, "Kaczynski, Conrad, and Terrorism," 3–5; Leeper, "An Adlerian Analysis of the Unabomber," 169–75; Oleson, "'Evil the Natural Way,'" 212–21.

10

"HOW CHARGED WITH PUNISHMENTS THE SCROLL"

The Oklahoma City Bombing (1995)

How shall your ancient warnings work for good
In the full might they hitherto have shown,
If for deliberate shedder of man's blood
Survive not Judgment that requires his own?

—William Wordsworth, "Upon the Punishment of Death"

By the end of the twentieth century, Oklahoma City, the county seat, state capital, and largest city in the Sooner State, contained a population of half a million people. Many citizens considered it an almost idyllic locale, a great place to work and raise a family. Although its economy originally depended on the stockyards and oil exploration, by the time the city celebrated its centennial, a slew of diverse businesses had set up shop, especially in the fields of information technology, health services administration, and education. *Forbes* magazine once characterized it as the most "recession-proof city in America."

Carved from the "unassigned lands" in the southwest territory in 1889, the city quickly rose to prominence as more than 10,000 homesteaders flooded into the area to take advantage of the federal government's "Land Run" incentives designed to boost the free white population in the Oklahoma Territory. Between 1890 and 1900, the town's population more than doubled. In 1907, Oklahoma became the forty-sixth state admitted to the Union, and the state's largest city came to know sustained growth and prosperity.[1]

In 1995, an Oklahoma City resident, if asked, probably would have identified extreme weather as the most dangerous aspect of living in the city. Owing to its location within the legendary "Tornado Alley"—a large swath of land extending from the Colorado Eastern Plains, eastern South Dakota, and down through Nebraska, Kansas, the Texas Panhandle, and Oklahoma—Oklahoma City suffers a disproportionate share of tornadoes compared with many other U.S. cities. No one would have guessed that one of the largest terrorist attacks on American soil would occur in this unlikely place. Yet that is exactly what happened.[2]

At 9:02 a.m. on April 19, 1995, the Alfred P. Murrah Federal Building, located in downtown Oklahoma City, exploded violently, killing 168 people, including nineteen infants and children in a day-care center on the second floor, and injuring hundreds of other people. In time, stunned Americans would learn that a domestic terrorist had attacked Oklahoma City. A young, alienated U.S. Army veteran, Timothy McVeigh, soon emerged as the leader of a terrorist cabal focused on assailing the federal government. To understand what happened in Oklahoma City on April 19, 1995, it is necessary to understand what happened in the life of this strange, troubled young man.[3]

LIFE AND TIMES

Born into a middle-class family in Lockport, New York, on April 23, 1968, Timothy James McVeigh was the second of three children, and the only boy, born to William and Mildred "Mickey" McVeigh. Searching for signs of things to come in his early childhood proves fruitless. Young Timothy exhibited no outwardly aberrant behavior. He was kind to animals. His boyhood was filled with friends and family, especially a doting grandparent who lived less than a mile away. Ed McVeigh, Tim's paternal grandfather, was retired. He had lost his wife, so he had ample time to spend with grandchildren. By all accounts, his bond with his grandson was especially strong.[4]

If trauma was to be found during the young man's early years, it occurred when the McVeighs divorced. Tim was ten years old, and although he later denied that the split had affected him negatively, his father was always convinced the boy had taken it hard. Mickey and Bill had endured trial separations in the past, so perhaps the final divorce was a welcomed end to overly dramatic household strife. Complicating matters in the final split was the child custody arrangement. Tim's sisters elected to remain with their mother while the boy's father took him to live in Pendleton, New York.[5]

Tim McVeigh shared some of Ted Kaczynski's attributes; he was an intelligent young man who displayed an aptitude for mathematics. He was uncomfortable around his peers; he often kept to himself and mistrusted conventional society. He longed for a simpler time when the government was far less intrusive in the life of the individual. He worried that individual liberty was increasingly under attack and that he must take action to counteract the corrosive effects of a mechanized, dehumanizing age.

During his adolescence, he was socially awkward, especially around girls. Friends recalled that he was playful and fully engaged as a young child but later became moody and withdrawn. In subsequent interviews, McVeigh admitted to retreating into a fantasy world when life became too difficult or complicated. He also claimed to have been bullied incessantly throughout his school years, although what effect, if any, this had on his life was never clear.[6]

Unlike Kaczynski, though, McVeigh was a classic underachiever in school. He simply did not see the value in pursuing higher education or in developing whatever intellectual gifts he possessed. He displayed a genuine aptitude in computer science, but he was never able to use his skills effectively. According to one account, the adolescent McVeigh hacked into a government computer system using a primitive Commodore 64 computer, which he had nicknamed "the Wanderer," after a song by the rock-and-roll singer Dion DiMucci. During his senior year in high school, McVeigh was named the school's "most promising computer programmer." Despite this flattering appellation, nothing else about the young man's academic record was noteworthy. He attended Starpoint Central High School, graduating along with 179 other students on June 29, 1986.[7]

Nothing in young Timothy McVeigh's first eighteen years of life suggested that he would become a notorious criminal, much less a mass murderer. That he was moody, withdrawn, and alienated cannot be denied. Yet many adolescents share these attributes. Perhaps the answers to his later behavior, if any are to be found, lie in his interest in guns as well as survivalist literature and tactics.

Ed McVeigh's advice cannot be underestimated. The old man taught Tim to use firearms, but he did much more. He was warm and nurturing whereas the boy's parents seemed to be preoccupied with their own tumultuous relationship or with eking out a living. Ed McVeigh had always enjoyed guns—owning them, buying them, talking about them, and shooting them. Aside from teaching the boy about proper gun care and safety, he waxed eloquent on the virtues of good citizenship and the need for self-defense and eternal vigilance against all enemies, foreign and domestic.

After grandfather and grandson shot their rifles at soft drink cans, they were always careful to remove the debris and avoid littering the community. They could exercise their right to discharge firearms, but they must also clean up after themselves.[8]

This one-on-one time with his grandfather did wonders for Timothy McVeigh's self-esteem. He became confident in his ability to stand up for himself and his rights. He had been bullied at school, but he would no longer tolerate such abuse. Gradually, the young man became obsessed with guns and all things gun related. If he felt powerless and out of control during his school day, he could take refuge in handling guns when he returned home in the afternoon.[9]

McVeigh briefly attended Bryant & Stratton College, a for-profit educational institution with campuses in several locations throughout the United States, including New York State. He sat through computer programming courses, but he was never engaged with the course of study. He also felt misled by the college because he assumed that he would devote all of his time and attention to computers. The school, however, had recently changed its academic requirements to make them more stringent for incoming students. They expected freshmen such as Tim McVeigh to complete a standard core curriculum of English, mathematics, sciences, and other classes offered by traditional colleges and universities. From McVeigh's perspective, these were the subjects that had bored him in high school. He simply saw no purpose in continuing his studies only to prepare for a middle-class, traditional career filled with drudgery. Dissatisfied with his educational experiences, he dropped out and led a rudderless existence for several years. Among the places he worked during this time in his life was a Burger King restaurant. He was under no illusions; his life had reached a dead end.[10]

Drifting from one odd job to another provided him with spending money, but not much else. During this time, he immersed himself in literature about gun ownership as well as the Second Amendment to the U.S. Constitution. He especially enjoyed *Soldier of Fortune*, a monthly magazine that reports on worldwide armed conflict and new weapons. After reading an advertisement in *Soldier of Fortune*, McVeigh ordered a book titled *The Turner Diaries*, a well-known anti-government diatribe popular among members of the U.S. militia movement. Written in 1978 by white supremacist William Luther Pierce under the pseudonym Andrew MacDonald, the apocalyptic novel followed the adventures of a gun-toting white supremacist as he joined with other white heroes to launch a "Great Revolution" to stop an obdurate federal government from destroying individuals' civil liberties and to prevent the amalgamation of the races.

The narrative commences with an act that horrifies every proponent of a strict interpretation of the Second Amendment—the federal government confiscates all civilian firearms. This outrageous act compels the novel's protagonist, Earl Turner, to join together with a brave band of brothers dedicated to resisting federal tyranny. At one point in the novel, the heroic freedom fighters deploy a powerful truck bomb to destroy the headquarters of the Federal Bureau of Investigation (FBI) in Washington, D.C. This scene impressed Timothy McVeigh. He had nursed anti-government sentiments throughout his adolescent years, but until he read *The Turner Diaries*, he was unable to articulate his growing feelings of rage and alienation. Finally, he had discovered a text that spoke to him like no other. The young man eventually bought multiple copies of the book to distribute to friends and to sell from his car to like-minded strangers.[11]

McVeigh became enamored of a fringe movement existing on the margins of American political culture. This movement has attracted, and continues to attract, discontented souls from across the nation; they live in households from Idaho and Montana, through the Midwest and the southwestern United States, and in many small southern towns. They are the inheritors of a nativist strain in popular culture that stretches back to the Founding period. "Don't tread on me" served as their slogan during the era of the American Revolution. They populated the American Party, sometimes called the "Know Nothings," during the antebellum years leading to the U.S. Civil War. Their extremist messages could be heard in the radical populism of Tom Watson and "Pitchfork Ben" Tillman at the turn of the twentieth century. They led the clarion call to root out the communist menace during the "red scares" of the Cold War. During the postmodern era, they often pleaded for Armageddon, anxiously awaiting the Rapture and apocalypse.[12]

The movement has never been well organized. It exists as a loose amalgamation of religious fundamentalists, xenophobic doomsayers, pseudoscientific anti-Semites, virulent racists, homophobes, and mentally ill crackpots. In most cases, though not all, they are embittered white men eking out a subsistence-level existence at the lower end of the socioeconomic spectrum. Often they are undereducated and dispossessed blue-collar workers who have lost their manufacturing jobs, or poor farmers who could not hold on to the family acreage. They burn with anger and humiliation at the series of real or perceived wrongs perpetrated by the ruling class against the interests of the common man. They long for a return to the halcyon days of small-town American life with its emphasis on the virtues of hard work, dedication to one's family, and the certainty that outsiders, including darker-hued peoples, are kept in their place. For these people, their sordid circumstances cannot be laid at their own feet. Outside forces working deep within the shadows and fueled by an insidious government conspiracy must be the root cause of their misfortunes. In seeking a scapegoat, these displaced persons hope to defeat the external forces that have caused their misery and thereby return themselves and their families to their rightful place at the vanguard of the American republic.[13]

Timothy McVeigh felt right at home in this world, for their seething resentment was his seething resentment. He, too, felt that all the vicissitudes of his life were caused by exterior, hidden forces beyond his control. Although he later claimed to admire the William Ernest Henley poem "Invictus," with its bold declaration that "I am the master of my fate / I am the captain of my soul," in reality he believed that the federal government was undermining his captaincy. The only way he could feel powerful was to turn his anger toward tangible institutions and, by opposing them, restore his own individual autonomy. If he had been forced to take stock of his life without blaming external forces for his failures, all that was yet to come might have changed.[14]

After obtaining a gun permit, McVeigh found a job at the Burke Armored Car Service in Buffalo, New York, in the fall of 1987. He was nineteen years old. His armored car route snaked through many poor, black neighborhoods. Listening to the more experienced, hardened security officers grouse about their misfortunes, McVeigh was exposed to a constant, unrelenting tirade of racial epithets. He recalled a co-worker angrily pointing at the "porch monkeys" who sat in front of their homes and watched the armored car pass by each day. The armored car employees worked long hours for little pay, inhaled noxious exhaust fumes, and constantly worried about potential armored car robberies; all the while, they resented the idle ne'er-do-wells who were "waiting for the welfare checks to come in." Gradually, McVeigh adopted the same attitude. It was grossly unfair that he worked so hard while others were unapologetically indolent.[15]

When he was twenty years old, McVeigh moved on to a more promising career. He needed direction in his life. As had so many young men before him, he enlisted in the U.S. Army. A friend, recognizing some of his own restlessness, had advised McVeigh that the army would provide him with opportunities sorely missing in the civilian world. In light of his interests in weaponry and military tactics, it seemed to be a suitable match.[16]

Something happened to Timothy McVeigh after he joined the army. He started with great promise, but gradually he soured on his choice. His first two years were rewarding as he found discipline and structure in his life. New recruits frequently complain about the physical challenges of basic training and the difficulties involved in learning to use new types of weapons. In contrast to many of his peers, Tim McVeigh enjoyed those experiences. They were tailor made for his increasingly skewed worldview. He remained convinced that an apocalyptic war was on the horizon and that only disciplined soldiers with strong survivalist skills would find a place in the brave new world. His goal, therefore, was to learn everything he could about military weapons and tactics so he would be prepared for whatever apocalypse the future held. He set his sights on joining an elite unit, perhaps the Special Forces or the Army Rangers. If Timothy McVeigh could earn a spot in one of these renowned groups of fighting men, he would earn the respect he felt had always been denied him. Even after he was deployed to Saudi Arabia during the Gulf War in 1991, he seemed to thrive on army life. No challenge was too great; no burden was too heavy. He later characterized those years as the finest of his life.[17]

He was stationed at Fort Benning, Georgia, for three months of basic training. One of 112 new recruits assigned to Company E, Fourth Battalion, he arrived on May 30, 1988. Despite the rigors of training and learning the army routine, Tim McVeigh thrived even as many fellow soldiers grumbled about the difficulties of the training regimen. When he left Fort Benning for Fort Riley, Kansas, in August 1988, McVeigh earned the maximum test score for an infantry trainee. Later, during his stint in Kansas, he impressed everyone with his superior marksmanship and his dedication to army life. To all outward appearances, he had found his ideal career path.[18]

Yet dark forces were at work. McVeigh's deepening obsession with racist, anti-government literature led him to harangue fellow servicemen incessantly. Whether it was offering to sell copies of *The Turner Diaries* or spreading tales of a postapocalyptic society, he presented himself as a violence-obsessed, gun-fixated zealot who might or might not be dangerous depending on his mood. It was as though there were two Timothy McVeighs. The first was a polite, well-scrubbed, upright model soldier who excelled in weaponry and tactics, constantly impressing peers and superiors with his unrivaled skill. The other was a deeply disturbed, angry, potentially explosive survivalist who thought nothing of hurling racial invectives against servicemen of color.[19]

Although most soldiers found the young man's rants off-putting, McVeigh met one sympathetic soul, Terry Lynn Nichols, who agreed with much of what he said. Nichols, thirteen years McVeigh's senior, was nicknamed "grandpa" by members of his platoon because he was so much older than the other soldiers. Nichols and McVeigh became friends after they discovered a shared antipathy toward blacks and an ardent mistrust of oppressive government. It was a friendship that eventually evolved into a criminal conspiracy.[20]

Nichols eventually received a hardship discharge from the U.S. Army after his wife divorced him and left him with sole custody of his son. Because he left the service in 1989, Nichols missed the Gulf War two years later. His friend, however, was deployed overseas and participated in the fighting. The first Persian Gulf war against Iraqi forces, codenamed Operation Desert Storm, would prove to be a defining experience in Tim McVeigh's life.[21]

He approached his mission with mixed feelings about U.S. involvement in the Middle East. Owing to his disdain for the abuse of power he attributed to the federal government, McVeigh viewed his country's role in confronting Iraqi dictator Saddam Hussein with suspicion. It was one thing for a nation to defend itself against the armed aggression of foreign powers, but deploying troops overseas to launch a military campaign when U.S. interests were not directly threatened seemed an illegitimate, unconscionable use of American force. Despite his misgivings, McVeigh was satisfied to play the part of the good soldier—for now.[22]

Company C, Second Battalion, Sixteenth Regiment of the First Infantry Division—famous as the Big Red One—arrived in Saudi Arabia early in January 1991. Within the company, McVeigh's platoon consisted of thirty-seven men and formed part of the Allied ground troops that would assault Iraqi strongholds. Although he was anxious to prove himself under fire, McVeigh confided his fears to more than one friend that "I'm coming home in a body bag." Such sentiments expressed by soldiers on the eve of battle are hardly unique. It is a human impulse to reflect on one's mortality before facing combat. In the case of Timothy McVeigh, he not only feared being killed by enemy soldiers, but he believed that the large number of coalition forces on the ground, at sea, and in the air increased the possibility of "friendly fire" mishaps. His concerns about accidental shootings proved to be well founded, although he was not injured.[23]

Along with seven other soldiers, McVeigh was assigned to a Bradley fighting vehicle. Under the command of Second Lieutenant Jesús Rodriguez, McVeigh and a detachment from the platoon were ordered to ride into battle as escorts for eight M-1 tanks. This dangerous assignment ensured that the men riding inside the Bradley vehicles would be subjected to the first wave of enemy artillery. Tim McVeigh questioned the wisdom of this decision. Bradleys were designed to be fast-moving, light-armored personnel carriers, far more nimble and mobile than most lumbering tanks. In his view, tanks were better equipped to absorb enemy fire than Bradley fighting vehicles; therefore, the tanks should precede the Bradleys, which could then be used to greater advantage maneuvering around the battle-field. The army's plan, by contrast, was to use the Bradleys as reconnais-sance vehicles to escort the tanks and provide much-needed intelligence on fluid battlefield conditions. As the plan evolved, at least the men in the Bradleys would not be the very first soldiers on the front lines. The army decided the Bradleys would follow a heavily armored vehicle designed to sweep the sand and locate hidden land mines. After the armored vehicle swept the mines from their path, the Bradley fighting vehicles would charge ahead with the tanks following behind.[24]

Tim McVeigh was the Bradley gunner. Owing to his skills as a sharp-shooter, the assignment fit him perfectly. His job was to command the gun mounted on top of the fighting vehicle. If he spotted an enemy missile fired toward Allied forces, he was instructed to estimate the range of the missile launcher and destroy the site. He also would need to lay down a wall of fire against any hostile forces that targeted the Bradley. If McVeigh failed to protect the vehicle, he and all of the men could be killed.[25]

Rodriguez's detached platoon moved into position near the southern border of Iraq early in February 1991. As the weeks dragged on and the men waited for action, they grew ever more restless. Someone later recalled that McVeigh coined the nickname "Bad Company" for their unit after a 1970s rock song. He also told his fellow soldiers of his premonition they would all die when they eventually confronted the enemy. His morbid sen-timents, while understandable under the circumstances, unnerved many of the men.[26]

Their test came on February 21, 1991, when the ground war for op-eration Desert Storm officially commenced. "This is it, guys," McVeigh called out to his fellow soldiers. "Get ready. We're going today." He was correct. Charlie Company came under fire both from the enemy and from overly anxious Allied forces. Lieutenant Rodriguez later reported that Tim McVeigh helped to save a soldier's life when the man lay prostrate in the sand, bleeding profusely from shrapnel wounds. Trained in combat lifesaving techniques, McVeigh calmly dressed the injured man's wounds and stanched the bleeding until an army surgeon could provide assistance. Rodriguez had initially ordered McVeigh to remove the shrapnel from the wounded soldier's hand, but McVeigh, fearing that this action might lead to greater blood loss, refused. The lieutenant was incensed, but subsequently he wrote up a commendation of McVeigh's actions that day.[27]

On the second day of the fighting, Tim McVeigh amazed his comrades when he took out two men in a machine-gun nest from nineteen football fields away with a single shot. Discussing the incident years later, McVeigh recalled seeing a white flag immediately after he killed the two enemy combatants. "They all surrendered. There was an Iraqi officer there. He later told one of our interpreters that when they first saw us coming, they thought we were either British or Egyptians. They don't like Egyptians. They fired on us, thinking they could engage us. When a single shot took out their main gun, they just gave up." He was justifiably proud of his actions, and he received the Army Commendation Medal as a result. During his service, McVeigh earned four additional medals.[28]

Despite his pride at having performed well under fire, Tim McVeigh reconsidered his role in Operation Desert Storm; he remained skeptical about the need for U.S. military action against Saddam Hussein. He also was upset by friendly fire episodes reported in the press as well as highly publicized incidents where Iraqi civilians, especially children, fell victim to Allied artillery. He later justified the "collateral damage" inflicted on children in the Oklahoma City bombing by citing the U.S. military's propensity to shoot first and ask questions later. He was paying forward the lessons he learned in the Iraqi desert.[29]

The war ended on February 28, much sooner than almost anyone could have predicted. Fewer than four hundred Americans died during the conflict, and many of those deaths occurred owing to accidents and friendly fire. Saddam Hussein's forces had been crushed in one of the most lopsided military victories in history. All that remained was a cleanup operation—no easy matter, to be sure, but not as arduous as engaging in active military operations. During this brief intersession, McVeigh and his fellow soldiers found themselves working security near Iraqi towns and villages that had been hard hit by war.[30]

For all of his stoic resolve and lack of empathy following the Oklahoma City bombing, Tim McVeigh was deeply disturbed by what he saw at the conclusion of the first Gulf War. Many Iraqis were destitute and forced to beg for basic necessities as Allied forces passed through their communities. It was difficult for McVeigh to watch a once proud people humbled by circumstances beyond their control. He was especially upset when he saw American soldiers, anxious to procure the spoils of war, looting the homes of impoverished Iraqis. Much of his bitterness toward the U.S. government stemmed from these experiences in postwar Iraq.[31]

Having distinguished himself under fire, Tim McVeigh returned to the States feeling reinvigorated despite his growing anger at his government. Moreover, for all of his disgust with the military brass, he still desired a career in uniform. He seemed close to fulfilling a long-held dream. Owing to his battlefield prowess, he was accepted into the U.S. Army Special Forces training program, a prestigious position for anyone considering a long-term military career.[32]

His career trajectory fell short of the goal, for he failed to complete the training. Perhaps if he had reported for his Special Forces audition at some other time in his life, McVeigh might have made the cut. When he reported for duty, however, he had only recently returned from Iraq. He was mentally, emotionally, and physically worn out. As he progressed through the twenty-four-day program, which was designed to tear down and root out all but the toughest, fittest soldiers, he simply could not keep up. After only a few days, McVeigh voluntarily withdrew from the program. He might have been given a second chance if he had stayed in the military long enough. It was not to be. For a deeply alienated individual who sought only to live a life in the military, this failure was devastating. After turning his back on many other institutions in American life, McVeigh now became disillusioned with the U.S. Army. His failure to join the Special Forces accelerated his descent into despair.[33]

As his disenchantment grew, he reverted back to his pre–Desert Storm behavior. Growing up as a child, he had not been a racist, but he recalled his days working on the armored car when his co-workers had bemoaned the sorry state of the black race. He subsequently claimed that he had known next to nothing about the Ku Klux Klan before this time. After reading KKK literature, however, he found the group's concern about the loss of individual rights compelling. Thereafter, he sent twenty dollars to Klan headquarters in North Carolina for a trial membership. With his membership, McVeigh received a "White Power" T-shirt, which he wore to protest against black soldiers who wore "Black Power" T-shirts on the army base. As someone who never wholeheartedly embraced the KKK ethos, Tim McVeigh's provocative act apparently was designed as a contrarian measure more than as a full-fledged embrace of the racist subculture. He would later align himself with the Patriot Movement, but he was not the virulent racist who typically populated white supremacist groups. Whatever his motivations, he soon found himself in trouble with his superiors. He was reprimanded for causing dissension in the ranks, an action he viewed as unwarranted. For a young man already suspicious of authority, McVeigh did not respond well to disciplinary action. The military's willingness to curb a soldier's militant, right-wing tendencies solidified his mistrust of centralized authority.[34]

By the end of 1991, he left the service. He had no clear plans for the future, but he knew he could not stay in the army when he no longer believed in its mission or its methods. His battalion commander, cognizant of McVeigh's heroism under fire in Iraq as well as his commendations and skill as a marksman, had assumed the young man would make his career in uniform. When the commander offered McVeigh the great honor of serving as his personal gunner, the senior officer was genuinely surprised when this young expert marksman announced he was leaving the service. The commander asked why. McVeigh had difficulty articulating his reasons, but apparently he could no longer serve a government he believed to be thoroughly corrupt.[35]

The dispirited twenty-three-year-old decorated combat veteran returned to his father's house in Pendleton, New York, and reverted to his prewar day-to-day existence without overt direction or visible ambition. Perhaps he suffered from undiagnosed posttraumatic stress disorder, or perhaps he finally succumbed to the alienation and narcissistic delusions he had flirted with on and off since puberty. He did not yet know how to express his rage and frustration to an indifferent world. Consequently, he listlessly lounged around the house, occasionally working odd jobs when he needed spending money. He later told interviewers he had expected to return, if not to a hero's welcome, certainly to find employers who would be pleased to have a combat veteran on the payroll. Unfortunately for McVeigh, the economy was struggling and many businesses were not hiring in late 1991 and early 1992. Jobs were few and far between even for skilled workers. Eventually, he secured a position supervising security guards at the Buffalo, New York, zoo. He also found part-time employment at a gun store. They were good, honest jobs, but far below the station he thought he had earned in life as a result of his combat experiences. Nothing seemed to work for Timothy McVeigh. With each passing day, week, and month, he became angrier and more frustrated with his situation. He reached out to his old friend, Terry Nichols, and eventually spent time living at the Nichols homestead in Michigan beginning in December 1991.[36]

McVeigh was not satisfied to seethe quietly; he wrote a series of increasingly angry letters to congressmen and newspapers expressing his outrage and alienation over the growth of federal power. In one typical tirade published in a local newspaper on February 11, 1992, McVeigh bemoaned the fact that "taxes are reaching cataclysmic levels, with no slowdown in sight" and "politicians are out of control." After asserting that "America is in serious decline," in questioning whether civil war was inevitable, he asked, "Do we have to shed blood to reform the current system? I hope it doesn't come to that, but it might."[37]

It is tempting in the light of subsequent events to read into McVeigh's incendiary rhetoric a fatal inevitability, a realization that the Oklahoma City bombing campaign had been conceived and was being quietly nurtured until the time was right. The truth is a bit more complicated. As deluded and confused as his thinking was in 1992, McVeigh was not yet ready to move beyond complaining about government mismanagement. It would take a series of personal and national events to convince him that violence was an appropriate solution to the ills of American society.

Personal events came to a head when McVeigh decided that Buffalo was far too liberal and tolerant for his tastes. After renewing his acquaintance with Nichols at the end of 1991, McVeigh decided not to return to upstate New York. Instead, he became a transient, moving from place to place in search of improved employment prospects and new friendships with like-minded, anti-government malcontents. During this time, he began to lose touch with reality, even suggesting that the army had implanted a microchip into his buttocks to keep track of him.[38]

To add insult to injury, the U.S. Army sent a letter indicating that McVeigh had been overpaid $1,058 while he served in uniform. After the letter demanded immediate repayment, McVeigh responded with an angry letter of his own. "I have received your notice informing me of my debt owed to you, as well as your threat of referring me to the Justice Department (Big Brother)," he stated. "In all honesty, I cannot even dream of repaying you the $1,000 which you say I owe. In fact, I can barely afford my monthly rent." Still upset with his army experiences and humiliated at the lack of gainful employment available to him, he blamed the federal government for his misfortunes. "Go ahead, take everything I own; take my dignity. Feel good as you grow fat and rich at my expense; sucking my tax dollars in property, tax dollars which justify your existence and pay your federal salary. Do you get it? By doing your evil job, you put me out of work." Tim McVeigh had noticed the overpayment at the time, but he had never reported it to his superiors. Now, being called to account for the error, he was incensed that an army bureaucrat would dare to challenge him in the midst of his misfortune.[39]

Although it did not seem possible that Timothy McVeigh could become any angrier at the U.S. government, incredibly he did. On April 19, 1993, as McVeigh watched television with his friend Terry Nichols in Michigan, the two men saw a live telecast of the FBI's standoff with cult leader David Koresh at the Branch Davidian compound in Waco, Texas. Seventy-four people, many of them women and children, died in a fiery blaze set by Koresh after federal agents forcibly attempted to remove him from the house. Right-wing survivalists already mistrustful of their government did not characterize Koresh as the villain in this set piece. Because the

FBI insisted on raiding private property during an armed confrontation, anti-government patriots viewed the resultant bloodshed as yet another example of the federal government's unremitting assault on civil liberties. For people who see government conspiracies around every bend, the Waco incident was proof positive that American life was under attack. *The Turner Diaries* seemed to be eerily prophetic.[40]

FROM CITIZEN TO TERRORIST

Brooding, angry, and alienated, Timothy McVeigh recalled the Waco incident as a turning point in his life. He had visited the site during the siege to distribute pro-gun-rights literature and bumper stickers, and clearly he empathized with the embattled Branch Davidians. During the days when he milled about outside the compound, McVeigh verbally assailed anyone who came within earshot. At one point, a student reporter approached to inquire about McVeigh's beliefs. The would-be rebel was only too happy to accommodate the budding journalist. "When guns are outlawed," McVeigh explained, reflecting the ideology he had gleaned from *The Turner Diaries*, "I will become an outlaw." He was not satisfied to limit his comments to self-dramatization. McVeigh the philosopher could not resist preaching his libertarian credo: "The government is afraid of the guns people have because they have to have control of the people at all times. Once you take away the guns, you can do anything to the people. You give them an inch and they take a mile." The Waco standoff proved that insidious forces were at work in the United States. "I believe we are slowly turning into a socialist government," he said. "The government is continually growing bigger and more powerful and the people need to prepare to defend themselves against government control."[41]

In the aftermath of the Waco episode, McVeigh was obsessed with Lon Horiuchi, an FBI sharpshooter who participated in controversial shootings in 1992 and 1993. Horiuchi was part of an FBI team that confronted white supremacist Randy Weaver in Ruby Ridge, Idaho, in August 1992 after members of Weaver's family discovered bureau agents reconnoitering the Weaver property on August 21. Although the sequence of events remains muddled, federal officials exchanged gunfire with members of the Weaver household. The next day, the FBI deployed sniper teams on the north ridge overlooking the cabin where Randy Weaver and his family, along with family friend Kevin Harris, were holed up. As Weaver stood outside his cabin, Horiuchi aimed at his back and, determined to kill the suspect, pulled the

trigger. At the last moment, Weaver moved, which sent the bullet career-
ing into his right shoulder and exiting through the armpit. Kevin Harris,
standing not far away, bolted for the house. Horiuchi aimed at the fleeing
suspect. Instead of hitting Harris, however, the sniper struck Weaver's wife,
Vicki, in the head as she stood in the doorway holding her ten-month-old
baby daughter. Vicki died instantly while Harris was struck in the chest by
the same bullet. A report subsequently prepared by the U.S. Department
of Justice determined that Horiuchi's first shot was justified by the circumstances, but his attempt to gun down the fleeing Kevin Harris was "inexcusable" owing to the possibility that he would strike an innocent bystander.[42]

A year after the Ruby Ridge incident, Horiuchi was again on duty, this
time stationed outside the Branch Davidian compound in Waco. Five
months later, during a follow-up investigation, another FBI sniper on the
scene recalled hearing Horiuchi fire at the compound, presumably triggering Koresh's violent actions, although eventually the officer retracted his
statement. To critics of the FBI in general, and Lon Horiuchi in particular,
this trigger-happy sharpshooter was part of a corrupt FBI culture that shot
first and asked questions later. As arguably the most visible representatives
of armed federal power, the FBI became the focal point for anti-government activists worried about the possibility of an out-of-control government
suppressing the liberty of its citizens.[43]

Timothy McVeigh shared these sentiments. No longer encumbered
by a job or other commitments, the increasingly peripatetic young man
hit the road. From May until September 1993, he traveled around to
gun shows handing out cards printed with Lon Horiuchi's name and address. McVeigh later explained that he did these things "in the hope that
somebody in the Patriot movement would assassinate the sharpshooter."
McVeigh himself seriously considered going after Horiuchi or the sniper's
family in lieu of targeting another person or a symbol of federal authority.
He also wrote hate mail to the agent, promising that "what goes around,
comes around."[44]

Ever the transient, McVeigh flittered from one gun show to another,
eventually visiting eighty gun shows in forty states. Throughout his travels,
he found a network of similarly disaffected persons. He eventually landed
in what he called the "People's Socialist Republic of California." Along the
way, he acquired a road atlas, which he used to designate places most sus-
ceptible to nuclear attack. In one entry, McVeigh indicated that Seligman,
Arizona, would be an ideal spot to own property because, in his view, it was
a "nuclear-free zone."[45]

In addition to honing his anti-government rhetoric, McVeigh experimented with pipe bombs and small explosive devices. Increasingly, he came to see himself as a defender of the U.S. Constitution from enemies such as the FBI, which subverted that precious document. His prose, always filled with talk of conspiracies and shadowy government alliances, now became more radical. He even wrote a letter to a boyhood friend, Steve Hodge, promising that "blood will flow in the streets" and that he envisioned a culmination to the struggle between good and evil.[46]

During his travels, McVeigh visited parts of the country where he was convinced nefarious government activities had occurred, including the infamous Area 51. According to widespread rumors, government agents were hiding evidence of extraterrestrial life on this remote section of Edwards Air Force Base in Nevada. He also visited Gulfport, Mississippi, to see for himself whether the United Nations was sponsoring military operations to bring about a new world order. These visits, suggestive of a deepening mental illness, would have been harmless enough had McVeigh not joined forces with his good friend Terry Nichols to purchase ammonium nitrate, an agricultural fertilizer, in bulk. McVeigh was convinced the government was preparing to ban sales of the fertilizer, along with its plans to prohibit individual gun ownership; therefore, he sought to acquire as much of the material as he could for resale to his fellow survivalists. The fertilizer was useful in making bombs.[47]

During his stint in Arizona, McVeigh reconnected with an old army buddy, Michael Fortier, who lived in Kingman, a small town on the edge of the Mojave Desert almost two hundred miles northwest of Phoenix. The two men had become friends during their training at Fort Benning, Georgia, in 1988, but they had lost touch in the intervening years. Fortier was deeply immersed in the drug culture, but, in a spirit of camaraderie, he freely shared his supply of cannabis and methamphetamine with his army pal. By all accounts, during their time together in Kingman, McVeigh and Fortier became thick as thieves. They grew so close that Fortier even asked his friend to serve as the best man in his wedding. The two fellows also discussed McVeigh's growing anger at the federal government and his plans to retaliate against federal authorities for the Waco episode. Ever the accommodating friend, Fortier assisted in stealing and selling guns to finance the criminal enterprise. Eventually, however, McVeigh realized that Fortier was too deeply involved in drugs and too ambivalent to serve as an active accomplice. Fortier discussed McVeigh's plans with his wife, Lori, but he repeatedly resisted entreaties to take a more active role in the conspiracy. Tim McVeigh and Michael Fortier parted on good terms, but McVeigh was more determined than ever to attack a symbol of federal authority—with or without help from his army friend.[48]

He followed a familiar pattern of behavior with one exception. Whenever Timothy McVeigh felt especially aggrieved, he wrote hostile letters expressing his outrage at perceived transgressions by his enemies. In typical fashion, he put pen to paper and spewed out his usual invective. An unmailed letter to agents of the Bureau of Alcohol, Tobacco, Firearms and Explosives (ATF) found in his car after the Oklahoma City bombing warned that "all you tyrannical motherfuckers will swing in the wind one day for your treasonous actions against the Constitution of the United States. Remember the Nuremberg War Trials." Unlike his previous tirades, however, McVeigh was no longer satisfied to denounce his enemies as "fascist tyrants" and "storm troopers." He was ready to move from a war of words to a war of action.[49]

As he searched for a suitable target for his rage, he contemplated "a campaign of individual assassination," focusing especially on high-profile targets such as Lon Horiuchi; Federal District Court judge Walter S. Smith Jr., who had handled the Branch Davidian trial; or U.S. attorney general Janet Reno. Reno had publicly accepted responsibility for the Waco debacle. McVeigh later said he considered assassinating her so that she would accept "full responsibility in deed, not just words." The logistics involved in assailing one of these targets, however, appeared daunting. In addition, McVeigh wanted to destroy an even larger target, a symbol of the tyrannical federal government that would be sure to capture headlines and shine a bright light on his cause. A single assassination was not loud enough to ensure that his voice was heard above the cacophony of public discourse. He needed a high body count to send exactly the right message.[50]

As he studied the conflict with David Koresh and the Branch Davidians, McVeigh was convinced that law enforcement officials operating out of the nine-story Alfred P. Murrah Federal Building in Oklahoma City had ordered the assault. An idea was born. A federal building was an appealing target because it was unequivocally a symbol of federal authority. A well-placed bomb would obliterate the building and, in the process, kill FBI and ATF agents, perhaps some of the same storm troopers who had assaulted the American patriots at Ruby Ridge and Waco. He knew that a large body count would increase press coverage and enshrine the bombing in the public imagination. Just as many terrorists before him had struck at large public symbols, so too did Timothy McVeigh seek to maximize the impact of his message. He would serve notice on the U.S. government that tyrannical power would not remain unchecked.[51]

Having found an appropriate target, McVeigh methodically planned the attack. Not only did he comb the pages of manuals that detailed how to maximize an explosive charge, but he experimented with bomb mixtures and devices for delivering a sufficient charge to kill scores of people. He placed telephone calls to barrel manufacturers, chemical companies, and demolition contractors to gather the necessary information for his plot.[52]

Working with assistance from Terry Nichols, McVeigh was almost ready to put his plan into action. During this time, his grandfather, Ed McVeigh, died. Tim had been traveling the country deliberately withholding information on his whereabouts. As a consequence, he missed his beloved grandfather's funeral, although he returned to Pendleton to assist his father in sifting through Ed McVeigh's possessions to prepare for an estate sale. It is difficult to know the psychological impact of his grandfather's death, but it may have convinced McVeigh that he had nothing to lose in moving forward with his scheme.[53]

Around the same time, in November 1994, Terry Nichols visited Arkansas. To implement McVeigh's plan, the conspirators needed money, and quickly. McVeigh had encountered a self-made millionaire ammunition dealer, Roger Moore, on the gun circuit. Although the two men initially got along well, their relationship eventually soured. McVeigh told Nichols that robbing Moore, who lived in Arkansas, would provide much-needed financing for the plan and, as a bonus, would exact revenge for real or imagined slights. Because Moore would recognize him, McVeigh did not participate in the robbery. Instead, he left it to Nichols, who confronted Moore inside the man's home and absconded with thousands of dollars of merchandise. The robbery succeeded, but Moore always suspected that McVeigh was behind the heist. For his part, McVeigh was pleased that Nichols had displayed the necessary intestinal fortitude to carry out the robbery. The only downside, as McVeigh saw it, was that Nichols had not killed the infuriating Roger Moore.[54]

After months of preparation, McVeigh was ready to act. He wrote a series of letters to family and friends that might be called "good-bye" correspondence. He had always enjoyed a close relationship with his younger sister, Jennifer, who had idolized her brother. In his last letter to her, Tim McVeigh explained that he would not "be back forever."[55]

Having made his peace with the past, on April 13, 1995, he initiated his plan. According to a later chronology developed by law enforcement authorities, McVeigh was busy during the five days leading up to the attack. He started with a trip to Oklahoma City to scout out the scene. Afterward, he traveled to Herington, Kansas, to inspect a storage shed where he and

Terry Nichols had stored the bombing-making chemicals. The following day, he purchased a 1977 Mercury Marquis in Junction City, Kansas, near his old army command post, to serve as his getaway car. Later that day, McVeigh called Ryder System Inc., a vehicle rental company, to reserve a moving truck. He also met with an increasingly reluctant Terry Nichols at Geary Lake, a fishing reservoir in Kansas adjacent to Junction City. That night, McVeigh checked into the Dreamland Motel near Junction City using his real name. He told the clerk, Lea McGown, he would stay a few days, and he negotiated a twenty-dollar-a-night rate, four dollars off the usual nightly charge.[56]

On April 15, McVeigh appeared at the Junction City Ryder office and deposited money on the moving truck using the alias "Robert Kling." The following day, he met Terry Nichols at a Herington Dairy Queen. The two men drove separate cars to Oklahoma City. McVeigh parked his newly purchased Marquis a few blocks away from the Murrah Building and returned to Junction City as a passenger in Nichols's car.[57]

On April 17, Robert Kling retrieved the Ryder truck and returned to the Dreamland Motel for the night. On the 18th, McVeigh met Nichols at the storage unit in Herington. They loaded 5,000 pounds of ammonium nitrate as well as nitromethane, a motor-racing fuel, into the truck and drove separately to Geary Lake. There, away from prying eyes, the conspirators mixed the materials into an explosive device. The recipe was similar to the bomb constructed in *The Turner Diaries*. It was a classic case of life imitating art, assuming that a screed such as *The Turner Diaries* could be considered "art." The two old army buddies parted company, and McVeigh drove south. He eventually pulled into a small gravel lot next to a roadside motel near Ponca City, Oklahoma, where he spent the night in the truck.[58]

On April 19, 1995—the second anniversary of the Waco attack as well as the 220th anniversary of the Battle of Lexington and Concord in the American Revolution—McVeigh got on the road around dawn. He had originally planned to arrive at the federal building around 11:00 a.m., but he was anxious to implement the plan and did not want to risk detection. Accordingly, he made a "command decision" to detonate the device ahead of schedule.[59]

He recognized that this day of all days would be a defining moment in his life. To celebrate the momentous occasion, he wore a treasured Patriot T-shirt. The front of the shirt sported a drawing of Abraham Lincoln above the words "Sic Semper Tyrannis," a Latin phrase that means "Thus always to tyrants," the state motto of Virginia and the words that John Wilkes Booth shouted immediately after he shot the sixteenth president of the United States in the head. The back of the shirt included Thomas

Jefferson's famous comment "The tree of liberty must be refreshed from time to time with the blood of patriots and tyrants."[60]

McVeigh deliberately drove the speed limit to avoid attracting undue attention. In keeping with his newly improvised plan, he timed his arrival in front of the federal building to miss the morning rush hour and also to ensure that employees inside the building would be at their desks and therefore the body count would be high. It was a warm spring day filled with blue skies and infinite promise. Passersby walked along the street as though it were just another average morning in Oklahoma City.[61]

He left the truck on the north side of the building. Despite his efforts to reconnoiter the scene, McVeigh did not realize he had parked adjacent to the America's Kids Day Care Center located on the second floor of the federal building. The center, which cared for the children of federal employees, had opened its doors minutes earlier.[62]

Everything proceeded according to plan. McVeigh inserted earplugs and quickly lit a five-minute fuse on the bomb. Attempting to appear nonchalant, he ambled toward the Mercury Marquis he and Terry Nichols had parked a few blocks away from the federal building. Half a dozen eyewitnesses later recalled seeing McVeigh walking away from the building. At the time, he wore a blue windbreaker over his Lincoln T-shirt, army boots, faded black jeans, and a black baseball cap. He never looked back. After he was safely away from the building and passed a police car he saw cruising by, he broke into a jog.[63]

At 9:02 a.m., the device exploded, ripping a gigantic hole in the northern facade of the Murrah Building and blowing out the windows in many downtown Oklahoma City structures. Investigators later estimated that more than three hundred buildings suffered damage from the bomb. McVeigh recalled that as he jogged away from the scene, the force of the blast propelled him nearly an inch off the ground. A vacuum created from the hot gas in the building lifted the structure, causing concrete slabs and metal beams to crack, and all nine floors on the northern end of the edifice collapsed. During a later interview, McVeigh remembered his first thoughts after the blast: "Just like at Waco. Reap what you sow."[64]

He did not stay at the scene to observe firsthand the carnage caused by his bomb. McVeigh was convinced, however, that the entire building must have collapsed. The damage was horrific, no doubt about it, but the building did not implode. Instead, the bomb tore a horseshoe-shaped hole in the northern half of the structure. Several floors destroyed by the explosion collapsed onto the floors immediately below, instantly crushing many occupants.[65]

The explosion killed 168 people, 163 of whom were inside the building. Four people standing in the parking lot died, and a nurse rushing to the scene to assist the victims perished as well. Some 509 others were injured. Nineteen children and infants under the age of five were among the dead. The ages of the victims ranged from three months to seventy-three years. To put the devastation into perspective, McVeigh's single act of terrorism killed more people than the number of American soldiers killed by enemy fire during Operation Desert Storm [66]

In targeting the Murrah Building, McVeigh had hoped to kill federal law enforcement personnel. McVeigh got his wish; eight federal agents died in the blast along with five law enforcement support staff. In addition, federal employees at the Department of Housing and Urban Development, the U.S. Department of Agriculture, the Federal Highway Administration, and the Social Security Administration met their deaths. When all was said and done, ninety-nine victims worked for the federal government in some capacity.[67]

When questioned about the murder of the children and infants after his capture, McVeigh referred to them as "collateral damage." He admitted that he had not known about the day-care center in the building. "It might have given me pause to switch targets," he said. "That's a large amount of collateral damage." Nonetheless, innocent bystanders could not expect to remain unscathed in the war against an oppressive government. "To these people in Oklahoma who have lost a loved one," he said, "I'm sorry but it happens every day. You're not the first mother to lose a kid, or the first grandparent to lose a grandson or granddaughter. It happens every day, somewhere in the world. I'm not going to go into that courtroom, curl into a fetal ball and cry just because the victims want me to do that."[68]

In the minutes following the blast, no one was sure what had happened. Was it a gas main rupture, a freak occurrence of some sort, or a terrorist attack? If it was the latter, would additional attacks follow? First responders finally arrived to sift through the wreckage and provide whatever assistance they could to the survivors. Ultimately, more than 12,000 volunteers and rescue workers assisted on-site.[69]

The medical examiner's office, struggling to preserve the bodies until they could be transported to the morgue, eventually brought two refrigerated trucks to the site. Because many corpses were mangled, crushed, or burned beyond recognition, identifying the remains proved to be challenging. Technicians painstakingly worked through a protocol of X-rays, dental examinations, fingerprinting, and blood testing. Because limbs and other body parts had been scattered throughout the building, investigators had to ensure that each specimen was catalogued properly and identified with a high degree of certainty so each part could be placed with the proper stack of remains. It was gruesome, grueling work.[70]

While first responders arrived to assess the situation and assist the wounded, McVeigh fled the city, driving north on Interstate 35. He felt the tremendous satisfaction of a mission accomplished. It was a job well planned and executed. He had sent a message that could not be ignored. McVeigh had been meticulous in his planning and careful to obey the speed limit and all traffic laws as he piloted the truck to Oklahoma City before the attack, but he was not as careful in his escape. He got sloppy. Sixty miles outside of the city, a state trooper stopped his car because a license plate was missing. This was a curious mistake. McVeigh later claimed that he knew the license plate was missing, but he simply left himself vulnerable to the whims of fate. Now that he had achieved his goal, he did not care whether he was apprehended. In the immediate aftermath of the bombing, he had entertained vague thoughts of harassing individual targets, perhaps using his sharpshooting skills to good effect, but he was ambivalent about future plans. If the authorities caught him, so be it.[71]

He might have avoided trouble, talking his way out of a relatively minor legal infraction, if he had applied himself to the task. In his usual melodramatic fashion, McVeigh also considered pulling out a Glock he had brought along and shooting the trooper dead. If the patrolman had been a federal authority instead of a state official, McVeigh probably would have shot him. As it was, he was satisfied to submit to routine questioning.[72]

As soon as he pulled his car to the shoulder of the road, he stepped from the vehicle. While McVeigh talked with the trooper, the officer noticed a bulge beneath the young man's windbreaker. When the officer asked about it, McVeigh mentioned that he had a gun. Although he had a permit to carry a concealed weapon, the permit was not legal in Oklahoma. The state trooper arrested him and escorted him to the Noble County jail in nearby Perry, Oklahoma. Local authorities booked him on misdemeanor charges: carrying a loaded firearm in a motor vehicle, unlawfully carrying a weapon, failing to display a current license plate, and failing to maintain proof of insurance.[73]

Back in Oklahoma City, the FBI sifted through the debris and discovered a vehicle identification number (VIN) on the rear axle of the demolished Ryder truck. Agents traced the VIN to the Ryder Center in Junction City, Kansas, where Robert Kling had rented the vehicle. Eyewitnesses supplied law enforcement with enough details for a sketch artist to produce two composite drawings of Robert Kling, which police began to circulate.

**FBI agents escort Timothy McVeigh from the courthouse in Perry, Okla-
homa. Courtesy of Corbis.**

Federal officials did not yet know whether Robert Kling had acted alone,
but they were fairly certain that he had not provided his real name when
he rented the truck.[74]

Their hunch proved to be accurate. Lea McGown, a manager at the
Dreamland Hotel in Junction City, identified the man in one drawing as
Timothy McVeigh. Using this newfound information, the FBI launched a
nationwide manhunt for the fugitive. A few days later, authorities seren-
dipitously discovered that McVeigh was already in custody in Oklahoma for
misdemeanor charges.[75]

Word spread quickly that the police had apprehended a suspect. Initial
reports had suggested that Middle Eastern extremists may have been involved, but with McVeigh in custody, it was clear that he was a homegrown
terrorist (although conspiracy theorists later suggested a Middle Eastern
connection). Media interest was intense. When authorities led the hand-
cuffed prisoner, clad in a bright orange jumpsuit, from the Perry jail on
April 21, a frenzied pack of journalists greeted them. FBI officials and
police vehemently denied that they had arranged McVeigh's transfer as
a deliberate "perp walk" for the benefit of a media circus. In fact, agents
were fearful of an assassination attempt. No one working in law enforcement could forget the dramatic scene when Lee Harvey Oswald, President

Kennedy's alleged assassin, was gunned down in cold blood before television cameras while he was escorted out of the Dallas, Texas, jail in 1963. The FBI was anxious to avoid a repeat shooting, especially since they had not gleaned much information from their suspect.[76]

Media representatives did not yet know the suspect's name—he was identified only as "John Doe #1"—but this did not stop them from firing questions as the young man calmly, stoically made his way through the crowd. McVeigh did his best not to acknowledge epithets and questions screamed in his direction. The world's first look at the mass murderer revealed a young man with a square jaw, a military-style crew cut, and the ordinary looks of the boy next door. Within a few minutes, McVeigh and his captors had maneuvered their way through the crowd and onto a waiting police helicopter.[77]

THE AFTERMATH

The world soon learned John Doe #1's name and story. Aside from the early, erroneous reports suggesting that Middle Eastern terrorists were responsible for the bombing, most news coverage focused on how and why a seemingly all-American young man could be filled with such rage that he deliberately executed innocent men, women, and children to satisfy his feelings of resentment. Images of the smoldering building, bloody survivors, and heroic rescuers flooded the airwaves. President Bill Clinton wrote in his memoirs that "America was riveted and heartbroken by the tragedy." As soon as the president learned of the attack, he "immediately declared a state of emergency and sent an investigative team to the site." During a memorial service in Oklahoma City not long after the explosion, he said, "You have lost too much, but you have not lost everything. And you have certainly not lost America, for we will stand with you for as many tomorrows as it takes." It was one of his finest moments as president. At the same service, the Reverend Billy Graham remarked, "The spirit of the city and of this nation will not be defeated." The renowned editorial cartoonist Herblock produced an iconic image featured in the *Washington Post* the day after the blast. The cartoon, which showed a large skull bearing the label "Terrorism" ascending from the rubble of the federal building, captured the anguish that many Americans felt when they learned of the attack.[78]

The bloodshed seemed senseless and inexplicable. While investigators asked how, citizens wanted to know why. As the public and journalists demanded answers, law enforcement personnel were eager to provide

OKLAHOMA CITY, U.S.A.

This iconic Herblock cartoon labeled "Oklahoma City U.S.A." vividly depicts the horrors of terrorism. Courtesy of the Library of Congress and the Herb Block Foundation.

them. Investigators delved into McVeigh's background, quickly uncovering his anti-government diatribes as well as his obsession with the 1993 Waco incident. They also followed the trail to two of McVeigh's army buddies, Terry Nichols and Michael Fortier. It soon became clear that the former assisted McVeigh in constructing the bomb while the latter helped to plan the assault.[79]

Nichols remained loyal to his friend and initially refused to cooperate when federal agents arrived on his doorstep. Fortier was an easier nut to crack; he expressed outrage that he had been implicated in the plot. Gradually, interrogators penetrated his belligerent facade and broke down his resistance. Fortier, a drug-addled, reluctant terrorist, had always been a sorry confederate. Recognizing that he could receive the death penalty if he did not cooperate with federal investigators, he agreed to a plea bargain and a reduced sentence in exchange for testifying against McVeigh and Nichols. The deal included a grant of immunity for Lori Fortier, Michael's wife, who confessed to providing McVeigh with a laminated fake driver's license using the name "Robert Kling." The Fortiers' testimony would prove crucial to placing Timothy McVeigh at the center of the conspiracy.[80]

During the ensuing months, federal prosecutors built a solid case against Timothy McVeigh for the Oklahoma City bombing. They also indicted Terry Nichols for conspiracy. In addition to the physical evidence recovered from the bomb site, they uncovered records of the purchases that McVeigh and Nichols had made to acquire the ammonium nitrate, nitromethane, the storage locker, and the Ryder truck. They also had Lea McGown's testimony linking McVeigh to the Dreamland Motel and the Ryder truck as well as testimony from Michael and Lori Fortier regarding the details of the plot. Armed with a mountain of corroborating evidence, on August 10, 1995, prosecutors indicted McVeigh on eleven federal counts, including conspiracy to use a weapon of mass instruction, use of a weapon of mass destruction, destruction by explosives, and eight counts of first-degree murder for the killing of federal officials inside the Murrah Building. If he somehow won an acquittal on the federal charges, he would face state murder charges as well.[81]

McVeigh's original court-appointed defense attorneys, John W. Coyle and Susan Otto, asked to be relieved from their assignment long before the expected indictment was announced. They both had known many Oklahoma City victims and did not feel they could adequately represent their client. To ensure a fair trial, the court relieved the attorneys from the case. Eventually, U.S. district judge David L. Russell appointed Stephen Jones, an Enid, Oklahoma, defense attorney to represent Tim McVeigh as lead counsel. Although Jones referred to himself as a "small-town, county-seat lawyer," he was anything but a naive rube. Because he had served as Richard Nixon's personal research assistant before Nixon became president, Jones was well connected in the Oklahoma Republican Party. Aside from his political affiliation, he had a great deal of experience representing unpopular defendants in high-profile civil and criminal cases, including radical leftist Abbie Hoffman when Oklahoma State University refused to allow Hoffman to speak on campus, and Keith Green, a student anti-war activist who had displayed a Vietcong flag during an anti-war demonstration at the University of Oklahoma. Jones had handled more than fifteen death penalty cases and was no stranger to the pressures that a high-profile criminal prosecution invariably places on defense counsel.[82]

McVeigh was impressed with his lawyer's credentials and experience, but he came to suspect that Jones cared more for the notoriety and national publicity that came from handling a highly publicized case than he cared for defending his client. McVeigh was especially upset to read information in the Oklahoma press about his confidential discussions with defense counsel. Although Jones adamantly denied leaking the information, McVeigh came to believe that his attorney, who was being paid by the government to handle the defense, was not looking out for him. Nonetheless, he had already lost two defense attorneys. It was time to move forward without the delay necessitated by finding another lawyer to represent him.[83]

The case came to trial in 1997 and lasted five months from the time of jury selection to the sentencing of the defendant. After the court granted a defense motion for a change of venue, the case moved to Denver, Colorado, to avoid the passions and prejudices associated with holding the trial in Oklahoma. Despite the change of location, McVeigh never doubted that he would be found guilty and sentenced to die by lethal injection. He had become the most hated man in America, and he knew jurors would want someone to pay the ultimate penalty. He tried to remain outwardly calm and stoic as he sat in the courtroom, but inside he was screaming, "Knock it off! Everyone here knows I'm guilty! Let's get on with it!"[84]

Initially, McVeigh had pressed his attorneys to present a defense of necessity. If he could demonstrate that attacking the Murrah Building had been necessary to prevent the federal government from enslaving the populace, McVeigh was convinced he could broadcast his message to a mass audience, which was even more important to him than winning an acquittal. Jones insisted that McVeigh's message was nothing more than political propaganda, and it would do nothing to assist the defense team at trial. Instead, the defense attorney argued that an effective strategy would be to poke holes in the government's case against McVeigh and thereby lay the groundwork for reasonable doubt. If prosecutors could not prove each element of the criminal case, the jury would have to return a verdict of not guilty.[85]

Reluctantly, the defendant acquiesced in approving the trial strategy. Yet throughout the proceedings, Tim McVeigh grew ever more disenchanted with his defense team. In his view, Stephen Jones and his associates were ineffective in picking jurors and interrogating key witnesses. He also found his attorneys' desire to present evidence of additional conspiracies to be perverse. Jones wanted to argue that Arab terrorists operating out of the Philippines, with support from American neo-Nazis and white supremacists from Elohim City, a private community in Adair County, Oklahoma, were involved in the Oklahoma City bombing. Much to McVeigh's relief, the presiding judge, Richard P. Matsch, refused to allow such unsubstantiated conjecture to be presented to the jury since there was no credible evidence of participation by any of those parties. If Jones hoped to demonstrate reasonable doubt, he would have to develop another strategy for doing so.[86]

During the trial, the prosecution presented 141 witnesses, while 27 came forth for the defense. Many prosecution witnesses were not paraded before the jury to testify about McVeigh's guilt or innocence. Instead, they told stories of their tragic personal circumstances or their experiences losing a loved one in the bombing. In the words of the old adage, their testimony did not shed much light, but it provided intense heat. The heart-wrenching tales of parents frantically searching for their toddlers amidst the ruins of the day-care center and distraught family members desperately seeking information about their loved ones in the minutes, hours, and days following the attack were difficult to hear.[87]

News commentators and victims' families were upset with the defendant's apparent lack of remorse. He sat stoically staring straight ahead or smiling as he joked with his attorneys and even flirted with attractive female reporters between court sessions. It was all too much. In a subsequent interview, McVeigh acknowledged his effect on bystanders. "The victims are looking for some show of remorse," he said. "I understand and empathize with the victims' losses, but at the same time, I'm a realist. Death and loss are an integral part of life everywhere. We have to accept it and move on."[88]

Michael and Lori Fortier took the stand and testified against their friend in exchange for a reduced sentence in the former case and a grant of immunity in the latter. Jennifer McVeigh, a reluctant prosecution witness, also took the stand. She still loved her brother, but nonetheless she spoke of his hostility toward the federal government and his determination to do "something big" after the debacles at Ruby Ridge and Waco. Her obvious discomfort and the believability of her testimony did much to convince the jury that Timothy McVeigh was the perpetrator.[89]

Lead defense counsel Stephen Jones used his closing statement to implore jurors not to allow their sympathy for the victims to overtake their sense of justice and fair play. Hammering on the gaps in the case, especially mistakes made by FBI agent David Williams, who supervised evidence gathering at the scene, Jones argued passionately that reasonable doubt existed. In the end, he simply could not overcome the massive body of evidence indicating that Timothy McVeigh had perpetrated one of the worst terrorist attacks in American history.[90]

The jury deliberated for four days. On June 2, 1997, the jurors delivered a guilty verdict against Timothy McVeigh on all eleven counts. The defendant sat expressionless, his hands clasped together tightly, as he listened to the verdict read aloud. Spectators burst into tears, hugging each other and expressing relief. Hundreds of people gathered near the site of the bombing cheered when they heard the announcement. Perhaps now, some observers mused, the families could feel a measure of closure. Justice had been served.[91]

For Tim McVeigh's family, there was no closure, and no justice. Eleven days later, the jury recommended he receive the death penalty. Bill McVeigh and his ex-wife, Mickey Hill, had not attended the original trial proceedings; however, they appeared during the sentencing phase. Although the announcement of the death penalty was not surprising, it left his family in a state of shock. According to onlookers, Bill McVeigh slumped in his seat, and Tim's sister, Jennifer, burst into tears.[92]

Tim McVeigh had not testified at his trial, but he chose to speak during the sentencing proceeding. Unrepentant and defiant to the end, he stepped to the podium and looked up at Judge Matsch. "I wish to use the words of Justice Brandeis. He wrote, 'Our government is the potent, the omnipresent teacher. For good or ill, it teaches the whole people by its example.' That's all I have."[93]

The rift between McVeigh and his lead defense attorney, Stephen Jones, widened after the conviction. McVeigh remained convinced that his attorney had not represented him well. Aside from rejecting the necessity defense, Jones seemed unwilling or unable to question witnesses effectively, and in McVeigh's view he apparently cared more for chatting up national media representatives than for zealously defending his client.

Jones was accustomed to criminal defendants blaming their attorneys for a guilty verdict. He took issue with McVeigh's uncharitable characterization of the defense. "It was the largest murder case in American history," he explained. "We read 30,000 witness statements, listened to 400 hours of audiotape, watched 500 hours of videotape and examined 150,000 photographs, 7,000 pounds of debris, over 15,000 pages of lab reports in the medical examiner's files of 168 deceased persons, about 1 million hotel registrations and 136 million telephone records." Jones also insisted that he and his team had borne considerable risk in representing such an unpopular defendant. "I owed Mr. McVeigh the duty of loyalty, and I discharged that duty," he concluded.[94]

On December 23, 1997, shortly after the McVeigh trial concluded, another federal jury returned a guilty verdict against Terry Nichols for conspiracy as well as eight counts of involuntary manslaughter, although he avoided a conviction on the more serious counts of conspiracy to use a weapon of mass destruction and first degree murder. Because he demonstrated remorse and requested leniency from the presiding judge, Terry Nichols received a sentence of life in prison without possibility of parole in lieu of the death penalty. The jurors' belief that Nichols never intended to kill anyone served as a strong mitigating factor.[95]

Michael Fortier, a crucial prosecution witness who did much to buttress the government's case, accepted a plea bargain in exchange for a twelve-year sentence and immunity for his wife, Lori, who had provided false identification cards to McVeigh. Prosecutors believed he knew more than he had told them; however, they granted leniency in recognition of his invaluable assistance in prosecuting McVeigh. Following his release from prison in 2006, Fortier entered the federal witness protection program.[96]

Many observers and conspiracy theorists believed, and continue to believe, that McVeigh worked with other co-conspirators to plan and carry out his crime. A major unresolved issue revolved around several eyewitness accounts of a John Doe #2 who accompanied McVeigh when he rented the Ryder truck. Crime scene investigators also found a severed leg in the debris of the federal building that could not be connected to the other known victims, leading some skeptics to question whether John Doe #2 had been killed in the blast. In the final analysis, however, testing revealed that the leg belonged to another victim, a woman, who had been buried without it. Nonetheless, the story of "others unknown" refuses to die.[97]

One astonishing story suggests that Terry Nichols met with Ramzi Yousef, the Islamic terrorist who masterminded the first World Trade Center attack in 1993, to seek assistance in constructing an explosive device. The tale, although far-fetched, seemed to have a plausible basis when federal officials discovered that Nichols had traveled to the Philippines between August 1990 and January 1995, when Yousef was thought to be there. As it turned out, Nichols was searching for a mail-order bride, which he eventually found. No evidence exists that he met with Yousef or anyone else regarding a terrorist plot.[98]

Even as investigators sifted through evidence and searched for additional accomplices, Timothy McVeigh remained an active, unrepentant hatemonger. He used his newfound infamy to spread his anti-government vitriol to a wider audience than he had ever enjoyed before. In his diatribe "An Essay on Hypocrisy," he self-righteously sought to justify his actions by cataloging past U.S. atrocities in a variety of armed conflicts, including the war in Iraq; the bombing of Dresden, Hiroshima, and Nagasaki during World War II; and the U.S. military involvement in Vietnam. Comparing Saddam Hussein's supposed war crimes with U.S. activities throughout history, he concluded that "the U.S. has set the standard when it comes to the stockpiling and use of weapons of mass destruction."

McVeigh recognized that even some Americans who were sympathetic to his libertarian mission were appalled at the deaths of innocent children inside the federal building. Therefore, he attempted to put the matter into perspective. "In Oklahoma City, it was family convenience that explained the presence of a day-care center placed between street level and the law enforcement agencies which occupied the upper floors of the building," he wrote. "Yet when discussion shifts to Iraq, any day-care center in a government building instantly becomes 'a shield.' Think about that."

At the conclusion of the essay, he explained that his actions, while condemned as morally reprehensible by some, were essentially no different than the actions undertaken by the U.S. government in foreign countries such as Iraq. "Whether you wish to admit it or not, when you approve, morally, of the bombing of foreign targets by the U.S. military, you are approving of acts morally equivalent to the bombing in Oklahoma City," he argued. "The only difference is that this nation is not going to see any foreign casualties appear on the cover of *Newsweek* magazine." In his view, persons who would condemn the Oklahoma City bombing must also condemn the actions of the U.S. government "It seems ironic and hypocritical that an act viciously condemned in Oklahoma City is now a 'justified' response to a problem in a foreign land. Then again, the history of United States policy over the last century, when examined fully, tends to exemplify hypocrisy."[99]

The essay was an amazingly articulate summary of the central tenets of the U.S. militia movement. By equating the actions of a terrorist acting out his own apocalyptic view of history with the actions of countries involved in global confrontations, McVeigh implicitly suggested that any act, no matter how repugnant to mainstream society, could be morally justified if it was at least no worse than the worst act of any government engaged in warfare. Assuming, for the sake of argument, that the actions of individuals and nations are equivalent—and this is by no means an unassailable proposition—McVeigh's point is diametrically opposed to, say, Martin Luther King Jr.'s position. In his famous "Letter from Birmingham Jail," King observed, "Injustice anywhere is a threat to justice everywhere." In Timothy McVeigh's world, the statement should read, "Injustice anywhere is an invitation for anyone to practice that same injustice with impunity." As a morally expedient justification for any manner of narcissistic self-indulgence, this concept has undeniable appeal. As the foundation for a coherent, workable system of ethics, it is terribly misguided and harmful to the body politic.[100]

In a similar vein, on April 26, 2001, McVeigh sent a letter to Fox News titled "I Explain Herein Why I Bombed the Murrah Federal Building in Oklahoma City." As was the case with Ted Kaczynski, McVeigh wanted the world to know he was a rational, purposive human being. "I explain this not for publicity, nor seeking to win an argument of right or wrong," he wrote. "I explain so that the record is clear as to my thinking and motivations in bombing a government installation." He began by arguing that he had considered competing options but ultimately concluded that bombing innocent civilians "served more purposes than other options." His rhetoric and tone certainly sounded reasonable as long as the reader did not dwell on the human carnage and extensive property damage associated with the option he selected.

"Foremost, the bombing was a retaliatory strike; a counter attack, for the cumulative raids (and subsequent violence and damage) that federal agents had participated in over the preceding years (including, but not limited to, Waco.)" In his view, as "federal actions grew increasingly militaristic and violent," patriotic citizens had to intervene to ensure that individual liberty was not destroyed. In effect, he was a citizen soldier preemptively striking against an enemy before the enemy could engage in additional mischief. According to McVeigh, "this bombing was also meant as a pre-emptive (or pro-active) strike against these forces and their command and control centers within the federal building. When an aggressor force continually launches attacks from a particular base of operation, it is sound military strategy to take the fight to the enemy."

Based on his evaluation of the circumstances and available options, "I viewed this action as an acceptable option." He never for a moment doubted that his actions were justified because, after all, his act of bombing a federal building on American soil was "morally and strategically equivalent to the U.S. hitting a government building in Serbia, Iraq, or other nations." He relied on the old adage of "an eye for an eye." Therefore, "borrowing a page from U.S. foreign policy, I decided to send a message to a government that was becoming increasingly hostile, by bombing a government building and the government employees within that building who represent that government." If children or innocent civilians were inside the symbol of American government at the time the blast occurred, such were the vicissitudes of life. "From this perspective, what occurred in Oklahoma City was no different than what Americans rain on the heads of others all the time, and subsequently, my mindset was and is one of clinical detachment," he concluded. "The bombing of the Murrah Building was not personal, no more than when Air Force, Army, Navy, or Marine personnel bomb or launch cruise missiles against government installations and their personnel."[101]

McVeigh's message was not new, but it indicated that even six years after the event, he felt no remorse. In establishing himself as judge, jury, and executioner, he saw no need for mercy and no grounds for apology. He later said his only regret was not completely destroying the building.[102]

The unrepentant inmate languished in federal prison for four years as he awaited lethal injection, spending much of the time in the Florence, Colorado, prison nicknamed the "Supermax." The prison, first opened in the mid-1990s, was designed to house the most violent, incorrigible inmates in the federal prison system. Over the years it has served as home to numerous high-profile villains, including Ted Kaczynski; Eric Rudolph; former civil-rights-activist-turned-killer H. Rap Brown; former FBI agent and Russian spy Robert Hanssen; al-Qaeda operative and unsuccessful "shoe bomber" Richard Reid; physician and serial killer Michael Swango; and contract killer Charles Harrelson, father of actor Woody Harrelson, among others. During his residency in the Supermax, McVeigh spent time in the disciplinary unit, where he encountered Ted Kaczynski; Ramzi Ahmed Yousef, mastermind of the 1993 World Trade Center bombing; and Luis Felipe, leader of the notorious gang the Latin Kings. One day, McVeigh received a newspaper clipping in the mail showing photographs of him, Kaczynski, Yousef, and Felipe. A fan who sent the article asked if McVeigh would autograph the clipping. The celebrity offender cheerfully signed the article "The A-Team! T.J.M."[103]

On July 13, 1999, the authorities transferred Tim McVeigh to the Federal Correctional Complex in Terre Haute, Indiana. He spent the next twenty-three months awaiting execution there. The Terre Haute prison was home to the "Special Confinement Unit" where lethal injections were administered. As he waited for the appointed rendezvous, his life was filled with the monotony of prison confinement, although from time to time his routine varied. In March 2000, journalist Ed Bradley interviewed him on the television program *60 Minutes*. As he had in the past, McVeigh remained surly and defiant, refusing to accept blame for the deaths he had caused in the Oklahoma City blast. He was nothing if not consistent and predictable.[104]

During his years of incarceration, McVeigh retained a series of attorneys to handle his court appeals. Eventually, after enduring the lengthy appeals process for years, McVeigh instructed his advocates to cease their efforts, although he never explained why he had changed his mind. In any case, the decision accelerated the schedule for execution. Early in 2001, the Federal Bureau of Prisons set May 16 as the date. After the FBI released additional documents to McVeigh's attorneys early in May, however, U.S. attorney general John Ashcroft stayed the execution until June.[105]

The end came at 7:14 a.m. on June 11, 2001. His only regret, McVeigh said, was failing to demolish the Murrah Building. As his final statement, he recited the famous William Ernest Henley poem "Invictus." This short verse appealed to the melodramatic, militaristic terrorist. In the first stanza, the narrator thanks "whatever gods may be for my unconquerable soul." He goes on to say, "My head is bloody, but unbowed." The final stanza captures McVeigh's defiant attitude:

> It matters not how strait the gate,
> How charged with punishments the scroll.
> I am the master of my fate:
> I am the captain of my soul.[106]

Through the years of Tim McVeigh's incarceration, the people of Oklahoma City struggled to come to terms with the tragedy. A thirty-five-foot American elm tree that stood 150 feet from the Murrah Building on the day of the explosion became known as the Survivor Tree because, aside from losing its leaves in the blast, it managed to live despite the trauma it had endured. For the people of Oklahoma City, it was a symbol of the tenacity of life. When the city unveiled a national memorial to honor the living and dead who had suffered through the devastation, the Survivor Tree became the centerpiece of the monument. Before the bombing, it had been just another tree growing in a parking lot. With the unveiling of the memorial on April 19, 2000—the fifth anniversary of the attack—the tree stood on an overlook adjacent to a stone wall containing these words: "The spirit of the city and this nation will not be defeated; our deeply rooted faith sustains us."

The Survivor Tree was but one part of the memorial. The Field of Empty Chairs stands on the exact spot where the federal building once stood. The 168 high-back bronze and stone chairs represent the number of people killed in the terrorist attack. Each chair contains the name of a victim and rests on a boxed glass pedestal that, when lighted at night, becomes a symbol of hope blazing out of darkness. The chairs form nine rows to represent the number of floors in the building. Nineteen chairs—15 of which are in the second row, representing the second floor of the building, where the day-care center was located—are smaller than the others, indicating that the victims were children. Visitors enter through bronze gates at the east and west ends of the site. The surrounding walls contain an inscription: "We come here to remember those who were killed, those who survived, and those changed forever. May all who leave here know the impact of violence. May this memorial offer comfort, strength, peace, hope and serenity." The east wall records the time as 9:01 while the west wall indicates 9:03—a minute immediately preceding the explosion, and a minute immediately follow-

The Oklahoma City Memorial honoring victims, survivors, and rescuers from the April 19, 1995, terrorist attack. Courtesy of the Granger Collection, New York.

ing the explosion. Pine trees surround the perimeter of the field and should one day reach ninety feet into the air, the height of the original Alfred P. Murrah Federal Building. Torrey and Hans Butcher, a young couple who won a competition to memorialize the tragedy, chose the deeply symbolic design to remind onlookers of the human cost of terrorism.[107]

CONCLUSION

Timothy McVeigh remains a fascinating character. A seemingly "normal," middle-class American with many prospects for a bright future somehow decided that violence was an appropriate form of protest. His case suggests that the conventional wisdom about why people choose terrorism—because they are poor and ignorant with few appealing prospects for a happy life—does not adequately explain the motivations of every perpetrator.

It is tempting to dismiss McVeigh as merely an alienated separatist existing on the margins of society, a young man so filled with hate and so warped by his immersion in the militia movement that he was deluded into committing one of the worst terrorist acts in American history. If this is the explanation for his behavior, McVeigh becomes a singular creature. If he was not mentally ill, according to this explanation, he exhibited some symptoms of mental illness. This interpretation certainly is reasonable, but it is only part of the story, and perhaps an overly simplified version at that. Just as some observers dismissed Ted Kaczynski as a deeply disturbed individual suffering from a mental defect, so too could Tim McVeigh be dismissed as a crank.

Setting aside the ongoing conspiracy controversies and focusing on Timothy McVeigh himself, he still seems emblematic of the societal condition that extends beyond the possibly mentally deranged actions of a nutcase. A nutcase holds no larger, generalizable lessons apart from the ubiquity of mental illness in some individuals. As this book discusses in many places, terrorists typically are motivated by many related factors, and generalizations sometimes can be made. Although they employ extreme measures, often terrorists reflect a strain of discontent that ripples throughout mainstream culture. Because these factors can be hidden, distorted, or intertwined with other factors, it is difficult to determine who will be a terrorist until after the fact. Some signs exist for those who know where to look.

Even as a child, something was not quite right with this young man. Perhaps his home life was not idyllic, but many, perhaps most, Americans could make a similar claim. No evidence exists that he was abandoned, tortured, or denied the basic necessities of life during his childhood. Yet, for whatever reason, he grew to adulthood with a skewed view of the world. His increasingly obsessive interest in the militia movement and survivalist tactics, considered with the benefit of hindsight, suggests a terrorist in the making, yet many young men are infatuated with military weapons and tactics. Few grow up to be terrorists. They generally become law-abiding, taxpaying, reasonably well-adjusted citizens.[108]

For whatever reasons, young men such as Tim McVeigh believe they are outsiders, constantly humiliated by insiders who deny them their rightful place in society. Over time, the outsiders become so alienated that they seek an outlet to express their frustration and relieve their powerlessness. Groups of like-minded individuals provide this outlet. This explanation does much to suggest why some young men join gangs while others willingly affiliate themselves with paramilitary organizations. Denied the company of like-minded individuals, outsiders such as Ted Kaczynski act on their own, but they are the exception that proves the rule. For the Timothy McVeighs of the world, the camaraderie of group membership is important—ironically, a necessary supplement to their essential narcissism.

McVeigh's case makes sense when viewed in the broader context of the militia movement, which has motivated many a discontented soul to rail against an oppressive government. McVeigh found kindred spirits who understood his anger against the "other" and nursed that anger. Perhaps he would have acted without the embrace of right-wing extremists, but his immersion in that culture exacerbated the young man's violent tendencies.[109]

NOTES

1. Greater Oklahoma City Chamber of Commerce website, "Oklahoma City Accolades," n.p.

2. Allen, "An Image from Oklahoma City," 172; Hefner, "Jesus Wept," 4; TornadoChaser.net, "Where Is Tornado Alley?" n.p.

3. Hefner, "Jesus Wept," 4; Jones and Israel, *Others Unknown*, 4–5; Rappoport, *Oklahoma City Bombing*, 3.

4. Michel and Herbeck, *American Terrorist*, 13–16; Russakoff and Kovaleski, "An Ordinary Boy's Extraordinary Rage," A1, A21.

5. Michel and Herbeck, *American Terrorist*, 23–29; Russakoff and Kovaleski, "An Ordinary Boy's Extraordinary Rage," A1, A21; Springer, "Patterns of Radicalization," 13–15.

6. Springer, "Patterns of Radicalization," 16–17; Stickney, *All-American Monster*," 47.

7. Michel and Herbeck, *American Terrorist*, 40–41; Springer, "Patterns of Radicalization," 17; Stickney, *All-American Monster*," 75–78.

8. Michel and Herbeck, *American Terrorist*, 26–28; Russakoff and Kovaleski, "An Ordinary Boy's Extraordinary Rage," A1, A21; Springer, "Patterns of Radicalization," 16.

9. Michel and Herbeck, *American Terrorist*, 27–28; Russakoff and Kovaleski, "An Ordinary Boy's Extraordinary Rage," A1, A21.

10. Michel and Herbeck, *American Terrorist*, 43–44; Springer, "Patterns of Radicalization," 17; Stickney, *All-American Monster*," 78–80.

11. Hamm, *Apocalypse on Oklahoma*, 4; Jones, *Others Unknown*, 78; McCann, *Terrorism on American Soil*, 211–12; Ridgeway, *Blood in the Face*, 109; Stickney, *All-American Monster*," 99–100; Wright, *Patriots, Politics, and the Oklahoma City Bombing*, 113.

12. Ridgeway, *Blood in the Face*, 9–10; Russakoff and Kovaleski, "An Ordinary Boy's Extraordinary Rage," A1, A21.

13. Crothers, "The Cultural Foundations of the Modern Militia Movement," 221–22; Michel and Herbeck, *American Terrorist*, 148–49; Ridgeway, *Blood in the Face*, 9–10; Springer, "Patterns of Radicalization," 16–18.

14. Michel and Herbeck, *American Terrorist*, 455; Russakoff and Kovaleski, "An Ordinary Boy's Extraordinary Rage," A1, A21.

15. Michel and Herbeck, *American Terrorist*, 51; Springer, "Patterns of Radicalization," 17–18.

16. Russakoff and Kovaleski, "An Ordinary Boy's Extraordinary Rage," A21; Springer, "Patterns of Radicalization," 18; Stickney, *"All-American Monster,"* 85–86.

17. Michel and Herbeck, *American Terrorist*, 63; Springer, "Patterns of Radicalization," 19–21; Stickney, *"All-American Monster,"* 85–86.

18. Michel and Herbeck, *American Terrorist*, 60–69; Russakoff and Kovaleski, "An Ordinary Boy's Extraordinary Rage," A4; Springer, "Patterns of Radicalization," 19.

19. McCann, *Terrorism on American Soil*, 212; Russakoff and Kovaleski, "An Ordinary Boy's Extraordinary Rage," A1, A21.

20. Hamm, *Apocalypse on Oklahoma*, 134; Springer, "Patterns of Radicalization," 19; Stickney, *"All-American Monster,"* 92–93.

21. McCann, *Terrorism on American Soil*, 212; Michel and Herbeck, *American Terrorist*, 78–96; Russakoff and Kovaleski, "An Ordinary Boy's Extraordinary Rage," A1, A21; Springer, "Patterns of Radicalization," 19–20.

22. Michel and Herbeck, *American Terrorist*, 77–78; Russakoff and Kovaleski, "An Ordinary Boy's Extraordinary Rage," A1, A21.

23. McCann, *Terrorism on American Soil*, 212; Michel and Herbeck, *American Terrorist*, 78–79; Springer, "Patterns of Radicalization," 20.

24. Michel and Herbeck, *American Terrorist*, 78–80; Springer, "Patterns of Radicalization," 20.

25. McCann, *Terrorism on American Soil*, 212; Michel and Herbeck, *American Terrorist*, 80; Russakoff and Kovaleski, "An Ordinary Boy's Extraordinary Rage," A1, A21.

26. Michel and Herbeck, *American Terrorist*, 80–84; Russakoff and Kovaleski, "An Ordinary Boy's Extraordinary Rage," A1, A21; Stickney, *"All-American Monster,"* 113.

27. Michel and Herbeck, *American Terrorist*, 87; Springer, "Patterns of Radicalization," 20.

28. Hamm, *Apocalypse in Oklahoma*, 148; Michel and Herbeck, *American Terrorist*, 87–89; Springer, "Patterns of Radicalization," 20.

29. Derbyshire, "The Execution of Timothy McVeigh: Must See TV?" 1254; Michel and Herbeck, *American Terrorist*, 89–96; Russakoff and Kovaleski, "An Ordinary Boy's Extraordinary Rage," A1, A21; Springer, "Patterns of Radicalization," 20.

30. Michel and Herbeck, *American Terrorist*, 93–94; Russakoff and Kovaleski, "An Ordinary Boy's Extraordinary Rage," A1, A21.

31. Hamm, *Apocalypse in Oklahoma*, 148; Michel and Herbeck, *American Terrorist*, 93–94; Russakoff and Kovaleski, "An Ordinary Boy's Extraordinary Rage," A1, A21.

32. McCann, *Terrorism on American Soil*, 212; Michel and Herbeck, *American Terrorist*, 95–96; Springer, "Patterns of Radicalization," 20.

33. Hamm, *Apocalypse in Oklahoma*, 150; Jones and Israel, *Others Unknown*, 49; McCann, *Terrorism on American Soil*, 212; Michel and Herbeck, *American Terrorist*, 101–3; Russakoff and Kovaleski, "An Ordinary Boy's Extraordinary Rage," A1, A21; Springer, "Patterns of Radicalization," 20; Stickney, *"All-American Monster,"* 117.

34. Michel and Herbeck, *American Terrorist*, 104–6; Stickney, *"All-American Monster,"* 120–27.

35. Michel and Herbeck, *American Terrorist*, 108–10; Springer, "Patterns of Radicalization," 20; Stickney, *"All-American Monster,"* 125–27.

36. Michel and Herbeck, *American Terrorist*, 113–16; Stickney, *"All-American Monster,"* 117–18, 135.

37. Quoted in Michel and Herbeck, *American Terrorist*, 116–18. See also Springer, "Patterns of Radicalization," 22; Stickney, *"All-American Monster,"* 197.

38. Michel and Herbeck, *American Terrorist*, 135–38; Russakoff and Kovaleski, "An Ordinary Boy's Extraordinary Rage," A1, A21; Stickney, *"All-American Monster,"* 135.

39. Quoted in Michel and Herbeck, *American Terrorist*, 139–40.

40. Hamm, *Apocalypse in Oklahoma*, 28; Michel and Herbeck, *American Terrorist*, 141–43, 159–67; Ridgeway, *Blood in the Face*, 10; Springer, "Patterns of Radicalization," 24–25; Stickney, *"All-American Monster,"* 153–55; Wright, *Patriots, Politics, and the Oklahoma City Bombing*, 5.

41. Quoted in Michel and Herbeck, *American Terrorist*, 142–43. See also Springer, "Patterns of Radicalization," 24–25; Stickney, *"All-American Monster,"* 155.

42. Michel and Herbeck, *American Terrorist*, 164, 200; Stickney, *"All-American Monster,"* 148–49.

43. Michel and Herbeck, *American Terrorist*, 160–62; Springer, "Patterns of Radicalization," 24–25; Stickney, *"All-American Monster,"* 148–55.

44. Michel and Herbeck, *American Terrorist*, 200; Springer, "Patterns of Radicalization," 22–23.

45. Michel and Herbeck, *American Terrorist*, 144; Springer, "Patterns of Radicalization," 22–23; Stickney, *"All-American Monster,"* 152–60.

46. Michel and Herbeck, *American Terrorist*, 182–83; Springer, "Patterns of Radicalization," 27.

47. Michel and Herbeck, *American Terrorist*, 184; Springer, "Patterns of Radicalization," 26; Stickney, *"All-American Monster,"* 147, 210, 216.

48. Jones and Israel, *Others Unknown*, 55–56; Springer, "Patterns of Radicalization," 23; Stickney, *"All-American Monster,"* 95; Wright, *Patriots, Politics, and the Oklahoma City Bombing*, 189.

49. Quoted in Coulson and Shannon, *No Heroes*, 521. See also Michel and Herbeck, *American Terrorist*, 200–201.

50. Michel and Herbeck, *American Terrorist*, 197–201; Springer, "Patterns of Radicalization," 26; Wright, *Patriots, Politics, and the Oklahoma City Bombing*, 4–5.

51. Jones and Israel, *Others Unknown*, 74; McCann, *Terrorism on American Soil*, 213–14; Springer, "Patterns of Radicalization," 26–27; Wright, *Patriots, Politics, and the Oklahoma City Bombing*, 4–5.

52. McCann, *Terrorism on American Soil*, 214; Michel and Herbeck, *American Terrorist*, 201–3.

53. Michel and Herbeck, *American Terrorist*, 204–5; Stickney, *"All-American Monster,"* 166.

54. Michel and Herbeck, *American Terrorist*, 205–9; Springer, "Patterns of Radicalization," 26; Stickney, *"All-American Monster,"* 190.

55. Michel and Herbeck, *American Terrorist*, 217–18, 232–35; Springer, "Patterns of Radicalization," 27.

56. Michel and Herbeck, *American Terrorist*, 248; Rappoport, *Oklahoma City Bombing*, 3; Stickney, *"All-American Monster,"* 172.

57. Jones and Israel, *Others Unknown*, 7; Michel and Herbeck, *American Terrorist*, 237, 247–50; Stickney, *"All-American Monster,"* 190–91.

58. Hamm, *Apocalypse on Oklahoma*, 148; Michel and Herbeck, *American Terrorist*, 251–62; Ridgeway, *Blood in the Face*, 9–10.

59. Michel and Herbeck, *American Terrorist*, 262, 269; Stickney, *"All-American Monster,"* 25.

60. McCann, *Terrorism on American Soil*, 215; Michel and Herbeck, *American Terrorist*, 269; Stickney, *"All-American Monster,"* 25–32.

61. McCann, *Terrorism on American Soil*, 214; Michel and Herbeck, *American Terrorist*, 267–68.

62. Hefner, "Jesus Wept," 5; Krug et al., "Psychological Response to the Oklahoma City Bombing," 103; Michel and Herbeck, *American Terrorist*, 278–79.

63. Michel and Herbeck, *American Terrorist*, 273–75; Stickney, *"All-American Monster,"* 25–32.

64. Allen, "An Image from Oklahoma City," 172; Hefner, "Jesus Wept," 4; Jones and Israel, *Others Unknown*, 6; Krug et al., "Psychological Response to the Oklahoma City Bombing," 103–4; Michel and Herbeck, *American Terrorist*, 274.

65. Krug et al., "Psychological Response to the Oklahoma City Bombing," 103–4; McCann, *Terrorism on American Soil*, 215; Michel and Herbeck, *American Terrorist*, 274.

66. Allen, "An Image from Oklahoma City," 172; Caeti et al., "Police-Media Relations at Critical Incidents: Interviews from Oklahoma City," 87; Derbyshire, "The Execution of Timothy McVeigh: Must See TV?" 1254; Jones and Israel, *Others Unknown*, 4–5; Krug et al., "Psychological Response to the Oklahoma City Bombing," 103; McCann, *Terrorism on American Soil*, 215; Memon and Wright, "Eyewitness

Testimony and the Oklahoma City Bombing," 292; Springer, "Patterns of Radicalization," 28; Wright, *Patriots, Politics, and the Oklahoma City Bombing*, 6.

67. Hamm, *Apocalypse in Oklahoma*, 40–41; Michel and Herbeck, *American Terrorist*, 385–86.

68. Quoted in Michel and Herbeck, *American Terrorist*, 386. See also Derbyshire, "The Execution of Timothy McVeigh: Must See TV?" 1254.

69. Hefner, "Jesus Wept," 4–5; Jones and Israel, *Others Unknown*, 4–8; Michel and Herbeck, *American Terrorist*, 277–81.

70. Fernandez, "Remembering the Oklahoma City Bombing," 179–81; Krug et al., "Psychological Response to the Oklahoma City Bombing," 103–4; Michel and Herbeck, *American Terrorist*, 278–79.

71. Johnston, "Terror in Oklahoma," A1; Michel and Herbeck, *American Terrorist*, 282–85; Ridgeway, *Blood in the Face*, 9–10; Stickney, "All-American Monster," 32; Wright, *Patriots, Politics, and the Oklahoma City Bombing*, 6.

72. Michel and Herbeck, *American Terrorist*, 284–88; Springer, "Patterns of Radicalization," 28; Stickney, "All-American Monster," 32.

73. Michel and Herbeck, *American Terrorist*, 288–90; Springer, "Patterns of Radicalization," 28; Wright, *Patriots, Politics, and the Oklahoma City Bombing*, 6.

74. Jones and Israel, *Others Unknown*, 7; McCann, *Terrorism on American Soil*, 216; Michel and Herbeck, *American Terrorist*, 296; Rappoport, *Oklahoma City Bombing*, 3.

75. Jones and Israel, *Others Unknown*, 7–8, 315; McCann, *Terrorism on American Soil*, 216; Michel and Herbeck, *American Terrorist*, 297; Rappoport, *Oklahoma City Bombing*, 3; Stickney, "All-American Monster," 175.

76. Jones and Israel, *Others Unknown*, 9; McCann, *Terrorism on American Soil*, 216; Memon and Wright, "Eyewitness Testimony and the Oklahoma City Bombing," 292–94; Michel and Herbeck, *American Terrorist*, 296–97.

77. Jones and Israel, *Others Unknown*, 9; McCann, *Terrorism on American Soil*, 216; Michel and Herbeck, *American Terrorist*, 303–7.

78. Clinton, *My Life*, 650–52; Jones and Israel, *Others Unknown*, 8; Michel and Herbeck, *American Terrorist*, 295–96; Ridgeway, *Blood in the Face*, 9–10.

79. Coulson and Shannon, *No Heroes*, 523; Crothers, "The Cultural Foundations of the Modern Militia Movement," 221–22; McCann, *Terrorism on American Soil*, 216–17.

80. Coulson and Shannon, *No Heroes*, 523–24; McCann, *Terrorism on American Soil*, 217; Michel and Herbeck, *American Terrorist*, 320–25, 348; Wright, *Patriots, Politics, and the Oklahoma City Bombing*, 10–11.

81. Jones and Israel, *Others Unknown*, 111; Michel and Herbeck, *American Terrorist*, 347–48.

82. Jones and Israel, *Others Unknown*, 29; Michel and Herbeck, *American Terrorist*, 307–8, 327–30, 334–35; Stickney, "All-American Monster," 233.

83. Michel and Herbeck, *American Terrorist*, 336–43; Stickney, "All-American Monster," 303.

84. Jones and Israel, *Others Unknown*, 139–44; Michel and Herbeck, *American Terrorist*, 362, 365; Stickney, *"All-American Monster,"* 302–5; Wright, *Patriots, Politics, and the Oklahoma City Bombing*, 7.

85. Jones and Israel, *Others Unknown*, 51, 366; Michel and Herbeck, *American Terrorist*, 365–67; Wright, *Patriots, Politics, and the Oklahoma City Bombing*, 14.

86. Jones and Israel, *Others Unknown*, 184; Michel and Herbeck, *American Terrorist*, 376–77.

87. Jones and Israel, *Others Unknown*, 315; Memon and Wright, "Eyewitness Testimony and the Oklahoma City Bombing," 292–95; Michel and Herbeck, *American Terrorist*, 383–84, 420.

88. Derbyshire, "The Execution of Timothy McVeigh: Must See TV?" 1254; Michel and Herbeck, *American Terrorist*, 385–86.

89. Jones and Israel, *Others Unknown*, 283; Michel and Herbeck, *American Terrorist*, 390–93.

90. McCann, *Terrorism on American Soil*, 217; Memon and Wright, "Eyewitness Testimony and the Oklahoma City Bombing," 292; Springer, "Patterns of Radicalization," 28.

91. Michel and Herbeck, *American Terrorist*, 405–6; Springer, "Patterns of Radicalization," 28.

92. Derbyshire, "The Execution of Timothy McVeigh: Must See TV?" 1254; McCann, *Terrorism on American Soil*, 217; Michel and Herbeck, *American Terrorist*, 415–16; Valentine, "The Execution of Timothy McVeigh as Religious Sacrifice," 531–36.

93. Quoted in Michel and Herbeck, *American Terrorist*, 418.

94. Quoted in Michel and Herbeck, *American Terrorist*, 420. See also Stickney, *"All-American Monster,"* 303.

95. McCann, *Terrorism on American Soil*, 217; Michel and Herbeck, *American Terrorist*, 435.

96. Jones and Israel, *Others Unknown*, 114–16; McCann, *Terrorism on American Soil*, 217; Michel and Herbeck, *American Terrorist*, 439.

97. Jones and Israel, *Others Unknown*, xv; McCann, *Terrorism on American Soil*, 217–19.

98. Jones and Israel, *Others Unknown*, 142; McCann, *Terrorism on American Soil*, 219; Michel and Herbeck, *American Terrorist*, 340.

99. McVeigh, "An Essay on Hypocrisy," n.p.; Michel and Herbeck, *American Terrorist*, 437–38.

100. King, "Letter from Birmingham Jail," 85; McVeigh, "An Essay on Hypocrisy," n.p.

101. McVeigh, "I Explain Herein Why I Bombed the Murrah Federal Building in Oklahoma City," n.p.

102. McVeigh, "I Explain Herein Why I Bombed the Murrah Federal Building in Oklahoma City," n.p.; Michel and Herbeck, *American Terrorist*, 291.

103. Jones and Israel, *Others Unknown*, xi; Michel and Herbeck, *American Terrorist*, 424–40.

104. Michel and Herbeck, *American Terrorist*, 429.

105. Michel and Herbeck, *American Terrorist*, 465–66; Wright, *Patriots, Politics, and the Oklahoma City Bombing*, 16.

106. Henley, "Invictus," *Poems*, 119.

107. Hefner, "Jesus Wept," 4–7; Michel and Herbeck, *American Terrorist*, 456–59; Pridemore et al., "A Test of Competing Hypotheses about Homicide Following Terrorist Attacks: An Interrupted Time Series Analysis of September 11 and Oklahoma City," 391–93.

108. McCann, *Terrorism on American Soil*, 211, 220; Michel and Herbeck, *American Terrorist*, 473–75; Ridgeway, *Blood in the Face*, 9–10.

109. Crothers, "The Cultural Foundations of the Modern Militia Movement," 221–34; Ridgeway, *Blood in the Face*, 9–10; Russakoff and Kovaleski, "An Ordinary Boy's Extraordinary Rage," A1, A21; Springer, "Patterns of Radicalization," 30–32.

"THERE IS A BOMB IN CENTENNIAL PARK; YOU HAVE THIRTY MINUTES"

Eric Robert Rudolph (Late 1990s)

That's why Monday, when it sees me coming
with my convict face, blazes up like gasoline,
and it howls on its way like a wounded wheel,
and leaves tracks full of warm blood leading toward the
night.

—Pablo Neruda, "Walking Around"

Eric Rudolph, a young man disillusioned with life in the United States after a stint in the armed forces, resembles Timothy McVeigh and other disaffected homegrown terrorists in the United States. He became a serial bomber following a period when his behavior became unstable and erratic. His anti-government philosophy sprang from his sense that white fundamentalist Christian values were threatened by changes in modern lifestyles as homosexuality, abortion, and centralized government authority were on the rise.

Rudolph chose one of the most high-profile venues of the 1990s, the 1996 Summer Olympic Games in Atlanta, Georgia, as the site of his first major terrorist act. Recalling the terrorist attacks on Israeli athletes at the 1972 Olympic Games in Munich, Germany, the Atlanta Committee for the Olympic Games (ACOG) took special care to ensure that security forces were out in full force and alert for any danger. Law enforcement personnel conspicuously patrolled each venue in the downtown Atlanta corridor.

Despite their presence, a bomber struck with deadly precision, demonstrating how difficult it is to thwart the malicious intentions of a dedicated zealot.[1]

Early on the morning of July 27, 1996, Tom Davis, an officer with the Georgia Bureau of Investigation (GBI), was patrolling near a lighting tower in Centennial Olympic Park, a large open area in the heart of Atlanta designed for tourists and athletes to socialize between sporting events. As Officer Davis surveyed the crowded scene, a private security guard, Richard Jewell, approached and told him that several apparently intoxicated men were causing a commotion. Davis and Jewell decided to investigate, but the men ran away when they saw the officers headed toward them.

Until that moment, the episode had appeared to be an ordinary occurrence on an ordinary evening. Rowdy, inebriated crowds were not unusual when a large street party erupted. After the men disappeared, Davis observed a green military-style backpack lying unattended near a bench. Davis and Jewell initially considered the possibility that the intoxicated men had left it behind. The backpack lay not far from the makeshift lighting tower. Davis and Jewell searched for the owner by questioning bystanders, but when that person was nowhere to be found they discussed the possibility that the backpack contained a bomb. It was an unlikely scenario, but a security officer was trained to investigate unlikely scenarios.

Davis and Jewell examined the package and spied wires and a pipe inside. While Davis alerted the bomb squad, Jewell quietly cleared the area, careful not to create panic. The ordinary evening suddenly had become extraordinary.[2]

Davis and Jewell did not know that a 911 emergency telephone operator had received a bomb threat at approximately the same time the officers discovered the backpack. A man's voice said, "There is a bomb in Centennial Park; you have thirty minutes." This warning might have been sufficient to ensure that the park was cleared in time, but a series of communications errors, including confusion about the Centennial Park address, meant that Davis, Jewell, and other officers in the park were unaware of the 911 call and did not recognize the urgency of the situation.[3]

At 1:18 a.m., approximately twenty minutes after the 911 call was recorded, the homemade device exploded, killing one woman instantly and triggering a fatal heart attack for a Turkish cameraman who was present. One hundred and eleven other people were injured in the blast. Had Davis and Jewell not acted with as much dispatch as they did, the destruction and death toll probably would have been higher.[4]

As agents of the Federal Bureau of Investigation (FBI) and the Bureau of Alcohol, Tobacco, Firearms and Explosives (ATF) poured onto the scene, no suspects were immediately apparent. The FBI assembled a profile of the probable offender, determining him to be a white American male who operated on the "fringes of law enforcement [and] who would plant a bomb so he could come to the rescue." Richard Jewell seemed to fit the profile. Consequently, the FBI focused their investigation on him. Fearful that he would be framed for a crime he did not commit, Jewell hired an attorney and spent almost three months clearing his name. When authorities eventually ruled him out as a suspect, precious time had been lost and the case had grown cold.[5]

In the months and years to come, other bombings similar to the Centennial Park incident occurred. On January 16, 1997, a device exploded at a suburban Atlanta family planning clinic that performed abortions for pregnant women. A second device exploded about forty-five minutes later in a trash bin as emergency response personnel arrived to assist victims from the initial blast. A month later, a bomb detonated at a popular Atlanta gay and lesbian nightclub. Authorities disabled a second bomb before it could explode. Within a few days of the nightclub bombing, several media outlets received anonymous notes purporting to be from the bomber. He claimed that abortion and homosexuality were destroying America and he was doing what was necessary to save the country from these insidious forces.[6]

The police believed these bombings were tied to the Centennial Park blast, but they still did not have a suspect in custody. The first major break in the case would not come for another year. On January 29, 1998, a bomb planted at an abortion clinic in Birmingham, Alabama, exploded, killing a security guard and severely injuring a nurse. The bomber might have escaped once again had an alert university student not noticed a strange man walking away from the scene while everyone else was walking toward the source of the disturbance. Along with assistance from another man, the student followed the strange fellow and copied down the license tag number of the man's pickup truck. It was registered to Eric Robert Rudolph of North Carolina.[7]

Rudolph fit the FBI profile especially well. He had been a member of the U.S. Army and had received training in explosives and demolitions. After he failed to qualify for the Army Rangers Special Forces unit, he became disillusioned with a life in uniform. His behavior worsened after he left the service. Rudolph's family was affiliated with the Christian Identity movement, a militant white supremacist organization that fostered anti-government messages and railed against sins such as homosexuality and abortion.[8]

THE LIFE AND TIMES OF A SERIAL BOMBER

He was born Eric Robert Rudolph on September 19, 1966, in Merritt Island, Florida. The fifth of six children born to Robert Thomas and Patricia Rudolph, Eric later told an interviewer that he enjoyed "a typical middle-class family" upbringing. His father had served both in the army and the navy, a veteran of the Korea and Vietnam conflicts. After his discharge, Robert Rudolph went to work as an aircraft mechanic at McDonnell Douglas, a job that took him to Cape Canaveral. The Rudolph family lived in nearby Merritt Island when Eric was born. Later, Robert worked for TWA airlines in the Miami International Airport, which necessitated a move to South Florida.[9]

Religion played an important, albeit convoluted, role in the family dynamics. Robert and Patricia at one time were devout practicing Catholics, although Eric was not baptized as such. During her adolescence, Patricia Murphy had become a novice, the first step toward becoming a nun. Ultimately, she refused to take her vows. Throughout much of her life, she struggled to find religious guidance through an amalgamation of religious beliefs that often ignored strict doctrinal lines.[10]

When she married Robert in 1956, Patricia was active in the Catholic Worker movement, an effort dedicated to nonviolence, voluntary poverty, prayer, and hospitality directed toward the poor and downtrodden. She was so committed to the group's activist agenda that she even moved to Washington, D.C., for a brief time to protest the use of nuclear weapons by the United States. During those fearful days of the 1950s, when the FBI thought communists lurked around every corner and in every nook and cranny of the American bureaucracy, the Catholic Worker movement was considered a subversive organization hell-bent on undermining the safety and security of the U.S. government. A self-proclaimed anarchist, pacifist, and "anti-government Christian," Patricia Murphy later remarked, "Those were exciting days." Her son's antipathy toward government can be traced to an era long before his birth. By the time the boy was three years old, the family had abandoned the Catholic Church and become active Baptists in Fort Lauderdale, Florida.[11]

Sometime during the 1970s, the Rudolphs encountered a man named Thomas Wayne Branham, a sawmill operator from Topton, North Carolina, a small town nestled in the western part of the state. Branham was a survivalist who was convinced that the apocalypse would occur during his lifetime. Deeply suspicious of centralized authority and worried that the federal government was encroaching on human freedom, Branham proclaimed himself a sovereign citizen, which meant that he recognized no legal authority over his person or property. Topton was the ideal community for a man who believed he had been called by God to go "back to the land." It is a tiny, isolated hamlet situated between Andrews and Nantahala Gorge and barely large enough to contain the filling station and a post office. For a person anxious to avoid contact with government agents and modern, newfangled ways, this isolated hamlet was ideal.[12]

The newfound friend informed the Rudolph family that some property adjacent to his home was for sale. He encouraged them to purchase the land, which they did. While the family was constructing a home, however, Robert Rudolph died of cancer. He had been diagnosed with a malignant melanoma in 1980. Deeply suspicious of modern medicine, Robert sought alternative treatments for his disease. During this turbulent period in the family's life, young Eric lived with Tom Branham on the adjacent property. From afar, the boy watched as his father grew ever sicker and sought progressively more desperate treatment options. Robert Rudolph drank glasses of wheatgrass juice, choked down doses of potassium, and, along with his wife, Patricia, researched promising cancer treatments. In a last-ditch effort to save his life, Robert even traveled to Tijuana, Mexico, for treatment using an experimental drug, laetrile. During the early 1980s, laetrile, a substance made using poisonous apricot pits, seemed to be a promising cancer drug. Although it was never licensed in the United States, many American citizens traveled to Mexico to partake of the experimental treatment. Whatever its ultimate medicinal value, it did not save Robert Rudolph's life. He died in 1981.[13]

With the loss of the family patriarch, it was natural that the adolescent Eric Rudolph would regard Thomas Branham as a father figure and mentor. In a letter he wrote years later to author Maryanne Vollers, Eric recalled his affinity for Tom Branham. "Tom taught me rudimentary construction and mechanical skills, basic farming and wilderness survival techniques," he wrote. "He was notorious for finding an alternative method for doing things. This is the only real influence he has had on me or the other boys. He prided himself on being self-sufficient where others were dependent."[14]

Branham was an attractive figure for local adolescents. Teenage boys always seemed to hang out near his house. Sometimes they shot targets with a .22 rifle. Often they listened to stories about the importance of self-reliance, independence, and pride. Tom Branham regaled his friends and sycophants with tales of his ingenuity in scratching out a living from the soil, hauling scrap metal, selling coupons, and rooting around in the Dumpsters of grocery stores for items of value. These were lessons Eric Rudolph would take to heart.[15]

And, of course, this charismatic, self-made man could not resist haranguing his audience on his favorite subject, politics. Branham was friends with Nord Davis Jr., an important figure in the Christian Identity movement. The movement has had a long, tortuous evolution with many offshoots. Gerald L. K. Smith, a fundamentalist minister active shortly after World War II, is credited, along with his friend Wesley Swift, as the father of the American version of Christian Identity. Originally known under various names—Kingdom Message, British Israelism, and Israel Identity among them—the movement originated in Great Britain in the middle of the nineteenth century. Christian Identity is hardly a model of doctrinal consistency, but its adherents seem to agree that white Christians are the true Israelites of the Old Testament. Accordingly, they are God's chosen people. This teaching conflicts with the traditional assumption that Jews are descendants of the Israelites.[16]

Christian Identity mythology posits that the ten lost tribes of Israel were ancestors of modern Nordic, British, and American white people. According to this version of history, Jews comprise a separate kingdom of Judah. In fact, Jews are a villainous tribe, the spawn of Satan and behind virtually all of the great conspiracies in world history. Christian Identity believers contend that the United States is God's Promised Land; therefore, Jewish claims to special status and a special land in the Middle East are false and potentially dangerous.

Some members, especially those in England, are overtly anti-Semitic, while many American Identity members subscribe to the "two seed" theory. This bizarre corollary suggests that nonwhites are "pre-Adamic." God created these races before he created Adam in the Bible. Consequently, "pre-Adamic" races are subhuman and were banished from the Garden of Eden before God created Adam and Eve. After Eve broke God's commandment and was banished, along with Adam, from the garden in the land of Nod, east of Eden, God implanted her with two seeds. Abel, her good child, sprang from Adam's seed and gave birth to the white race. Satan's seed produced the wicked Cain, father to nonwhite races and the cause of much mischief in the world.

The true lost tribes migrated to Great Britain throughout the centuries across two separate paths. One route traveled through Spain, Scotland, and Ireland, which explains why the British royal family is descended from the lost Israelites. The other tribes of Israel scattered throughout the world, including the United States. For example, the Manasseh was the thirteenth tribe. The number thirteen is especially important to Christian Identity affiliates. The United States was comprised of thirteen original colonies, and the first flag contained thirteen stars. Even the nation's motto, *E pluribus Unum*, contains thirteen letters.

Christian Identity members are fascinated with Native Americans, believing them to be genuine descendants of the lost tribes. Because Native Americans historically lived off the land, Christian Identity followers pride themselves on their ability to survive in the wilderness. Members also help fellow members whenever they can. According to a survivalist and former American Nazi, Kurt Saxon, "it is like one great big club, and if you are on the run, a believer will shelter you regardless if he wears overt labels or not."[17]

Enter Nord Davis, a right-winger from New York State. In 1966, Davis resigned from a position working at International Business Machines (IBM) when he learned that the company intended to sell computers to communist countries. A member of the fiercely anti-communist John Birch Society, Davis was livid that IBM would give aid and comfort to the enemy. Even the radically right-wing John Birch Society eventually seemed too mainstream and reasonable for Davis's tastes. After breaking away from the group and drifting through New Hampshire and Massachusetts, he eventually settled on two hundred acres of land outside of Andrews, North Carolina. There, he founded the Northpoint Tactical Teams as well as other white supremacist groups. Davis could never quite pin his delusions on one particular school of white supremacy; he borrowed tenets from a variety of fanatical groups, including Christian Identity.[18]

When the Rudolph family befriended Tom Branham and moved near his Topton home in western North Carolina, they tapped into a rich vein of right-wing lunacy. Eric, in particular, found himself attracted to Branham and the Christian Identity brand of zealotry. The young man had not seemed especially troubled or freakish before 1981. In the years that followed, however, his outlook became increasingly bizarre.[19]

Eric attended Nantahala High School briefly. Test scores suggested that the boy possessed average intelligence, albeit his math skills were poor. Interviewed years later, his teachers recalled a strange, stubborn boy who, when he tried, displayed a modicum of wit. He deliberately set himself apart from other students with his odd views and strident, ultraconservative politics. He once wrote a term paper denying that the Holocaust had ever occurred. He peppered his speech with angry comments about how "queers," "dykes," and "niggers" were destroying America. Some accounts indicate that he decorated his body with swastikas and other offensive symbols.[20]

He was painfully shy around girls, although in the eighth and ninth grades he occasionally dated one young lady. She remembered going home to meet Eric's mother, Patricia, who informed the startled girl that if she and Eric had a baby, they should not worry. Patricia had completed mid-wife training and would be able to deliver the baby without having to go to the hospital, provide a record of the birth, or procure a Social Security number. This paranoia and anti-government sentiment extended across all of Eric's activities. Former classmates recall that Eric never liked to have his picture taken because he was worried the government might use it to identify him. He refused to sign anyone's yearbook for fear that his hand-writing would be on file and potentially used against him in the future. He preferred traveling along trails and in ravines rather than walking along a highway in case he needed to escape quickly. Sometimes after school re-cessed on Fridays, he would disappear in the woods and live off the land for the entire weekend. When he returned to school on Monday, he wore the same soiled clothes he had worn on Friday. After he finished the ninth grade, Eric never returned to the school. His mother homeschooled him.[21]

The family's behavior further degenerated after Tom Branham had a falling out with the Rudolphs. Branham was upset when the family re-fused to come to his aid after the ATF arrested him. With the dissolution of this friendship, the Rudolph family departed on an extended journey to Schell City, Missouri, where they joined up with a Christian Identity preacher named Dan Gayman, leader of the Church of Israel. The FBI had been keeping track of Gayman after the man was indicted in 1987 for receiving $10,000 in illegally seized money from a right-wing paramili-tary group called the Order. In exchange for leniency, Gayman turned state's evidence against members of the Order. How long the Rudolph family stayed in Missouri with this character is unknown. Some family members later recollected six months while others were convinced they stayed for two and a half years. As with so much about the Rudolph clan, it was difficult to ferret out the truth from the lies they intentionally dis-seminated.[22]

Eric later earned his general equivalency diploma (GED) and enrolled in Western Carolina University in Cullowhee, North Carolina. A lackadaisical student, he quit the university after two semesters. He left few impressions among the students, faculty, or staff.

On August 4, 1987, Eric Rudolph enlisted in the U.S. Army. It was a curious choice for a young man who was so distrustful of the U.S. govern-ment and its control over the individual. Apparently, Eric's desire to be a part of a prestigious military unit such as the Rangers or the Special Forces outweighed his disdain for governmental control.[23]

He was sent to Fort Benning, Georgia, for basic training. Following that initial stint, he was assigned to Company A, Second Battalion, 327th Infantry Regiment of the legendary 101st Airborne based in Fort Campbell, Kentucky. As part of his training, Rudolph learned survival skills, enabling him to live off the land if he were ever marooned behind enemy lines. He also learned the fine art of constructing booby traps. One exercise required soldiers to fashion improvised explosive devices (IEDs) from an ammunition can filled with half sticks of dynamite, nails, rocks, and other readily available items.[24]

Rudolph thrived in the survivalist atmosphere, but gradually his superiors noticed an "attitude problem" developing. Assigned a task to his liking, the young man performed competently enough, but on other occasions he was called to account for "mocking authority." The soldier was unwilling or unable to carry out arduous, distasteful tasks without demonstrating insubordination and open defiance of authority.[25]

His fellow soldiers observed that "Rudy," as they called him, possessed an almost encyclopedic knowledge of the Bible. At the same time, he did not proselytize his colleagues on religious subjects or display a pious attitude. He was satisfied to chew tobacco, drink beer, and smoke marijuana. When he discussed non-army-related topics, typically he revisited his well-worn diatribes against government power; high taxes; the problem with Jews, blacks, and women in positions of authority, and the absurdity of the army bureaucracy.[26]

Within fifteen months of his enlistment, Eric Rudolph decided he no longer desired a career in uniform. Although he had agreed to a four-year term, he knew how to get out of his commitment. In November 1988, he tested positive for marijuana usage during a routine urinalysis. The army offered a general discharge, and Rudolph agreed. In January 1989, he left the army for civilian life. As he later wrote to an army friend, "Surprise, surprise! I am out of the Army since 25 January. No more slavery, no more neighbors standing over me in the morning."[27]

Now that he was on his own, Rudolph had to support himself. He had discovered an ideal, lucrative trade: marijuana cultivation. Having found his calling, Eric Rudolph threw himself into the venture with energy and zeal. He assiduously combed through the pages of *High Times* magazine in search of tips for planting, harvesting, and selling his crop. He traveled to Amsterdam in search of perfect seeds. Ever mindful of the risks of detection by law enforcement authorities, he purchased a generator so he could power the lights necessary to nurture his hydroponic plants. The U.S. Drug Enforcement Agency (DEA) considered large spikes in electric energy usage as a strong indicator of illegal marijuana cultivation. Rudolph was pleased to have outfoxed the DEA.[28]

Investigators later noted the irony of Eric Rudolph, the proverbial "lone wolf" terrorist, working in the drug trade, a business generally reliant on the social skills necessary to move the product. No one would characterize the young man as convivial. Rudolph himself recognized his limitations as a supplier; consequently, he identified a small group of distributors and worked almost exclusively within that network. Accounts of his success vary. Questioned later by authorities, several friends estimated Rudolph's annual income at $70,000 during that phase of his life. Others suggested a more modest figure. In any case, it was enough money to sustain his ascetic lifestyle.[29]

Neighbors and acquaintances witnessed changes in Eric Rudolph's behavior from the early to mid-1990s. To many observers, the young man, always volatile and opinionated, somehow grew more radical, bitter, secretive, and paranoid. He was careful to hide evidence of his marijuana business, but he lived in perpetual fear of being apprehended by law enforcement. Because knowledge of his illicit activities was an open secret in the community, Rudolph vowed to exact vengeance on anyone who exposed his enterprise.[30]

Eric had been living in his family's house, but in 1996 he sold the property for $65,000 and split the proceeds with his mother, Patricia, and siblings Dan and Joel. Shortly afterward, Eric told his family he was taking a trip out West, but apparently he never made it. He was seen walking around Murphy, North Carolina, a week before the Centennial Olympic Park bombing in Atlanta. Investigators surmised he was planning the attack that would initiate his terrorist career.[31]

In fact, Eric had resided on and off in Murphy for a year and a half. He deliberately lived off the grid, avoiding his family, always careful to pay in cash and move frequently lest he be identified. On one memorable occasion, he accompanied his mother on a visit to Civil War battlefields, but he soon vanished again. Although this was undeniably eccentric behavior, it was fairly common in Eric Rudolph's world. Family members did not sense anything amiss apart from the young man's usual idiosyncrasies.[32]

THE 1996 SUMMER OLYMPIC GAMES

Atlanta, Georgia, an up-and-coming southern city of almost three million people (according to the 1990 census of metropolitan residents) was selected to host the 1996 summer Olympic Games. The "city too busy to hate" was anxious to show the world that this progressive, cosmopolitan destination was finally, irrevocably poised to take its place among the great cities of the world. The Olympic Games, with their virtually nonstop news coverage and worldwide audience, were an ideal vehicle to promote Atlanta's new image.[33]

Centennial Olympic Park was ground zero for the festivities. Specially constructed as a central gathering point for athletes and visitors, the twenty one-acre park was surrounded by the city's landmark structures: the Georgia World Congress Center, the Georgia Dome, the CNN Center, and Philips Arena. During the summer of 1996, the Atlanta Committee for the Olympic Games used the park for a variety of activities, including the medal awards ceremonies, a sponsors' pavilion, an entertainment venue for musical groups, and a central meeting place. The park became a symbol of the Olympic Games in the city of Atlanta.[34]

On the evening of July 26, 1996, the park was jammed full of people enjoying a pleasant, albeit humid summer evening, the capstone to a long day of Olympic activities. No one paid attention to a lone figure, a young man wearing a hooded sweatshirt and a cap, and sporting a goatee. He appeared to be no different from anyone else visiting downtown Atlanta that evening. The block party was in full swing, and individuals were lost in the collective mass.

This lone, unheralded figure approached a pay telephone on a street corner next to the entrance of a Days Inn motel. The laughing, shouting, and music all around him made his voice difficult to hear over the din. Nonetheless, at 12:58 a.m., not long after Friday night became Saturday morning, he dialed three digits.

"Atlanta 911," a voice on the other end of the phone said.

"There is a bomb in Centennial Park," the man calmly told the operator. "You have thirty minutes." The call lasted a mere fifteen seconds.

What happened next was a monument to bureaucratic incompetence. It was difficult to know if the call was a bad joke, but it had to be treated as genuine. When the 911 operator tried to call the Atlanta Police Department Command Center, she received a busy signal. Three precious minutes passed before she found someone on the other end of the line.

"You know the address to Centennial Park?" she asked. Until she had a complete address, the computer system would not allow her to input data that would generate a message for the Atlanta Police Department to send a patrol car to investigate. The most famous park in the world at that moment, eagerly watched by billions of people around the globe, could not be protected from mayhem without a complete street address.

The police dispatcher laughed. "Girl," she said, "don't ask me to lie to you."

The operator explained what the caller had said. The gravity of the threat quickly changed the dispatcher's tone. "Oh Lord, child. One minute, one minute." The correspondents spent that minute debating the spelling of the word "centennial" in case that was the reason the computer system would not allow the operator to input the data. Eventually they realized that the word was spelled correctly.

With one problem resolved, they moved to the next one. Eventually they found a street address for the park. A message went to the Atlanta Police Department to investigate. Unfortunately, the state of Georgia, not the city of Atlanta, was responsible for security during the Olympic Games. No one acted on the information.[35]

In the meantime, GBI officer Tom Davis had discovered a suspicious backpack and, with security guard Richard Jewell's help, was taking steps to brief his superiors on the situation. Regrettably, he was unaware that an anonymous caller had announced a thirty-minute deadline. Careful to avoid triggering panic, he and other police officials were slowly, methodically establishing a perimeter away from the backpack as they weighed the pros and cons of a general evacuation. A camera crew from KNBC, Los Angeles, had gotten wind of a potential story and was zeroing in on the backpack with a video camera. It was only a matter of time before a story broke.[36]

At Davis's request, a bomb assessment team arrived on the scene shortly after 1:00 a.m. Technicians Steve Zoeller and Bill Forsyth discussed the situation with Davis before approaching the backpack. Carefully opening the pack, a technician recognized wires and a pipe. What he saw heightened everyone's suspicions; it was time to alert the bomb disposal unit.[37]

Tom Davis still considered the possibility of a hoax, but he could not take chances. He would recommend a general evacuation. As he stood approximately twenty paces from the backpack, with his back turned, Davis talked with his commanding officer about the sequence of events. He had no sooner mentioned the time necessary for the bomb disposal crew to arrive than he felt a flash of heat as though the air had been sucked out of the park. His body flew forward; it felt as if someone standing behind him had reached out and shoved him with both hands to the ground.

His ears were ringing, producing a muffled, muted sound. Despite his momentary partial deafness, Davis recalled the noise of the crowd. All around he heard screams and moans as people struggled to make sense of what had happened. Most people remained calm. Perhaps they thought it was a fireworks display or a stunt. Several minutes passed before it was clear what had occurred on that early summer morning. Somehow, in the seconds following the blast, Davis found his radio and sent a frantic message to the command post. The call went out at 1:18 a.m.[38]

Fallon Stubbs of Albany, Georgia, was celebrating her fourteenth birthday with her mother, Alice Hawthorne. Much to Fallon's delight, her mom had bought tickets to the next day's Dream Team basketball game. The young girl was thrilled at the prospect of watching famous U.S. athletes take to the court against an outclassed opponent from some foreign country no one had heard of before. It was all so exciting, a perfect way to celebrate a memorable birthday.

Mother and daughter arrived in Atlanta late that evening. Parking had been difficult owing to the throngs of people threading their way through the downtown streets. Fortunately, they found a place with plenty of time to enjoy the crowds and even explore the Planet Hollywood restaurant. For a girl from South Georgia, Atlanta represented a big city filled with people and promises of a good time.

Always thinking ahead, Alice had brought a disposable camera. They snapped numerous pictures as they made their way toward the central meeting site in Centennial Olympic Park. They could hear music wafting toward them. Perhaps they would arrive in time to hear Black Uhuru, a well-known reggae band from Jamaica.

The duo enjoyed a magical night meandering through the park, mingling with the crowd, taking in the sights of the big city and the extraordinary celebration. To Fallon, it was a dream come true, but all dreams must end, as she learned. Around 1:00 a.m., Fallon and Alice decided to leave the park. They were tired. The block party was still going strong, but most of the people involved were teenagers and young adults whose stamina seemed never ending.

Finding their way to the car would prove challenging. As they struggled toward the park exit, fighting their way through the multitudes, they lingered to capture a few final shots on the disposable camera. Fallon snapped a photograph of her mother as Alice posed in front of a large brass statue honoring the spirit of the Olympics. They did not notice the men of the bomb squad huddled around the base of the nearby sound tower. Even if they had, the nature and purpose of the group's activities were unclear.

They briefly discussed who should be pictured in the photograph and who should take the shot. Fallon, the birthday girl, won the good-natured argument. She wanted one final photograph of Alice standing in the historic arena. Seconds later, Fallon aimed her camera, framed her mother's face in the viewfinder, and depressed the button.

A flash of light blinded her. It was far too bright to have come from the camera. Almost immediately, a large explosion propelled her to the ground as she saw her mother swing around in a complete 360 before also falling. It was like watching a scene from a horror movie.[39]

Several people in the park were recording the event with video cameras. The footage captured the moment of the explosion, which sounded more like a heavy rifle shot, a crack rather than a boom. White smoke and dust coated nearby people and property. Bystanders closest to the bomb were sprayed with shrapnel. Of the approximately 100,000 park visitors, 110 suffered injuries, although most were minor gashes and lacerations. One man found a backpack buckle lodged in his jaw. A forty-year-old Turkish cameraman, Melih Uzunyol, suffered a fatal heart attack as he rushed to the scene.[40]

Fallon was dazed and bleeding with a shrapnel wound to her leg. One of her fingers was nearly torn from her hand. Despite her injuries, she struggled to her feet and ran to her mother's side. Alice Hawthorne was lying on the ground, bleeding and quiet. Fallon called her name as onlookers tried to keep her away from her mother's prostrate body.[41]

Paramedics and emergency responders arrived within minutes. Soon adjacent streets were clogged with police cars, fire engines, and ambulances. Emergency medical technicians immediately recognized the severity of Fallon's wounded hand. They must get her into surgery quickly; otherwise, she might lose her finger. As they loaded her onto a stretcher, the young girl kept calling for her mother. No one seemed to listen. It was only later, after she woke up in the hospital with her stepfather, John, and the rest of her family at her bedside that she learned her mother had died. Alice Hawthorne, aged forty-four, was killed when a piece of masonry nail struck her skull at the temple, penetrating her brain. She and the Turkish cameraman were the only people to perish as a result of the Centennial Olympic Park bombing.[42]

For all of the millions of dollars spent on security and the thousands upon thousands of man-hours spent training agents to prevent acts of terrorism, a lone individual had managed to place a pipe bomb in the heart of Atlanta while the whole world watched the festivities. Investigators felt an immediate, unrelenting pressure to apprehend a suspect and solve the case as soon as possible. FBI director Louis Freeh, a former federal prosecutor known for his hands-on style of management, made it known that he was outraged and expected immediate results.[43]

In the wake of the bombing, the games moved forward. Citizens and visitors, as illustrated in a defiant image penned by editorial cartoonist Mike Luckovich in the *Atlanta Journal-Constitution*, remained steadfastly com-

A Mike Luckovich cartoon depicts the defiant attitude of Olympic organizers and athletes following the Centennial Olympic Park bombing. Courtesy of the _Atlanta Journal-Constitution_, Mike Luckovich, and Creators Syndicate.

mitted to the events even as law enforcement officers were deeply embarrassed. Before the games began, ACOG's security chief, Bill Rathburn, had boasted that surveillance cameras were located strategically around Centennial Olympic Park, in many cases disguised, so that would-be marauders could not easily elude detection. This tough talk, unfortunately, was only that—tough talk. The cameras often did not operate properly. No one had thought to provide a budget for VHS tapes; a supervisor had to buy them out of his own pocket. Even when the cameras managed to capture crowd scenes, soldiers who were brought in to assist in security usually aimed them at attractive women rather than at suspicious characters.[44]

The security snafus were part of a larger problem with the Atlanta games. Numerous attendees were unimpressed with the poor logistics, overwhelming traffic, tacky and aggressive vendors, and poor computer systems that delayed notification of results at the conclusion of various sporting events. Atlanta had hoped to showcase itself as a cosmopolitan city, but for many critics, the games illustrated the opposite. International Olympic Committee president Juan Antonio Samaranch apparently agreed with the poor assessment. Normally, the coded language in the president's closing remarks was phrased to acknowledge the host city for providing the "greatest games ever." When he spoke of the 1996 summer games, however, Samaranch damned with faint praise as he thanked Atlanta for hosting a "most exceptional" event.[45]

With the games continuing after the bombing, investigators were under enormous pressure to arrest a suspect. They recalled the 1984 Olympic Games in Los Angeles when a police officer, Jimmy Pearson, claimed to have discovered a pipe bomb on a bus transporting athletes to and from the venues. Initially, Pearson received widespread praise as a hero for his quick-thinking action in dismantling the bomb. Later, law enforcement personnel discovered that the officer had planted the device himself. This type of "hero bomber" who created an emergency so he could save the day, while rare, was not unprecedented. Therefore, federal agents searched for a similar personality in considering suspects for the Atlanta bombing.[46]

Richard Jewell, the security guard who had first approached Tom Davis that evening in the park, fit the profile. FBI agents watched Jewell grant a television interview shortly after the bombing. Something in his demeanor did not seem quite right. His monotone answers to questions, his frequent use of police jargon, and his willingness to discuss possible job opportunities in law enforcement as a result of his actions in the park suggested that Jewell could be a hero bomber. A background check confirmed that Jewell was an odd character. He had worked in security at Piedmont College, a small liberal arts institution in the North Georgia mountains, where some members of the community complained that he was overzealous in discharging his duties. He lived with his mother at the age of thirty-three, had no girlfriend, and seemed far too interested in inserting himself into the investigation. He quickly became a person of interest.[47]

Jewell knew enough about FBI tactics and standard operating procedures not to be alarmed when two agents showed up at his mother's apartment. Interviewing everyone at the scene was a necessary part of investigating the crime. Eager to be helpful, he readily agreed to accompany the agents to the FBI Atlanta headquarters to be interviewed. The first clue that something was amiss was the presence of a dozen television crews camped outside his mother's place. When Jewell arrived at FBI headquarters, the agents told him they wanted to film him for a "training video" about interviewing first responders. The ruse appeared to succeed until the agents, at Director Freeh's insistence, informed Jewell of his *Miranda* rights. The agents tried to pretend the warning about his rights was merely part of the exercise, but Jewell finally understood that the bureau was interested in him for more than a mere interview. He invoked his right to remain silent and requested a lawyer.[48]

For the next three months, the FBI focused its investigation on Richard Jewell. After obtaining a search warrant for his mother's apartment, they tore the place apart. Although the agents seized a variety of items, including videos, a roll of black electrical tape, and a box of nails, they found nothing tying Richard Jewell to the bombing. Jewell withered under the intense media scrutiny. His life became a media feeding frenzy with neighbors selling location rights for cameramen who wanted to park on the lawn. News helicopters flew over his mother's apartment as breathless anchormen provided a minute-by-minute recap on the whereabouts of the probable Olympic Park bomber. Whenever Jewell left the apartment, federal agents in at least one vehicle kept him under constant surveillance. On several occasions, an FBI airplane flew overhead, presumably to ensure that Jewell did not escape the convoy of automobiles trailing behind.[49]

No stone was left unturned. Although Jewell was later cleared of wrongdoing, every foible and eccentricity in his life was exposed to the glaring lights of the international news media. Ray Cleere, president of Piedmont College, told FBI agents that Jewell had engaged in "improper conduct" on the campus, and therefore Cleere would not be surprised if Jewell was involved in the bombing. A story circulated that Jewell had been arrested for impersonating a police officer in 1990. He had also suffered through numerous bouts of unemployment and difficulties in securing a law enforcement position, and these facts quickly surfaced.[50]

As the months dragged on, investigators found no credible evidence that Richard Jewell was involved in the episode. Recognizing that he must fight to restore his good name, Jewell pursued legal action against law enforcement personnel and the overzealous news media. Originally, he had contacted an attorney named Watson Bryant, whom he had known years earlier when they had played video games together during breaks at the federal courthouse in Atlanta. Bryant instinctively understood that because his client was being tried by the media, it was best to fight back by using the media. He became a familiar face on television as he argued Jewell's case in the court of public opinion.[51]

Bryant also enlisted a crackerjack team of attorneys, including well-known criminal lawyer Jack Martin and civil rights attorneys Lin Wood and Wade Grant. These men were aggressive advocates who understood the importance of rehabilitating their client's good name in the press as much as in a court of law. Lin Wood, in particular, was well known for his propensity to try cases in the press. He immediately took to the airwaves, frequenting news shows on NBC and CNN as well as granting interviews to the *Atlanta Journal-Constitution*. In the fall of 1996, Wood's high-profile appearance on *60 Minutes* provided a visible public forum to question not only authorities' handling of the case, but the biased news reporting that convicted Richard Jewell without the benefit of a fair trial.[52]

The months passed, and it became increasingly clear that Jewell may have been a strange man, but he was not the Centennial Park bomber. Investigators were so heavily invested in implicating their suspect that they simply refused to consider the mounting contrary evidence. The FBI agents who had used the video ruse on Jewell were especially interested in demonstrating their investigatory prowess. It was not to be.[53]

U.S. attorney Kent Alexander finally cut the Gordian knot; he agreed to issue a letter indicating that Jewell was not a target of investigation if the man would come in and submit to an informational interview to tell law enforcement personnel whatever he knew about the events of that night. Although the letter was hardly an apology or a resounding exoneration, Jewell agreed. The interview went off without a hitch. True to his word, Alexander issued a letter, which Jewell's attorneys released to the media during a news conference.[54]

Richard Jewell later filed defamation lawsuits against media outlets that had run the most outrageous stories. He received a $500,000 settlement from NBC and an undisclosed sum from the *New York Post* and CNN. Jewell went on to work again in law enforcement when it was clear that he was not involved in the bombing. His story did not end well. He died suddenly on August 29, 2007, at the age of forty-four from health problems associated with heart disease, kidney disease, diabetes, and obesity.[55]

With the most promising person of interest removed from the case, the investigation was back to square one. In devoting so much time and attention to pursuing Richard Jewell as the most likely suspect, federal agents had allowed the trail to grow cold on other possible suspects. Despite the dearth of viable perpetrators to pursue, ATF bomb technicians had reconstructed the device and marveled at its sophistication. Whoever built the bomb clearly had experience with military weaponry. Moreover, it was obvious the culprit intended to kill and maim numerous people.[56]

Agents reviewed the events in the moments before the explosion, and they recalled that Davis and Jewell had encountered a group of rowdy men that had dispersed quickly. Investigators informally referred to the three fellows as the "Speedo Boys." When they interviewed the trio—Jason Fishburn, Steve Schmidt, and David Szabo—they learned that the men had spotted a lone figure sitting on a bench near the backpack. He seemed aggravated when the Speedo boys spoke to him. As they recalled, he wore a dark cap and a hooded sweatshirt. He may have sported a goatee.[57]

The three young men noticed the backpack after the goateed man left. Another friend, Larry Coune, walked over, pushed the pack, and asked if it belonged to anyone in their group. Someone tipped it over on its back, which turned out to be fortuitous. When the bomb later exploded, much of the blast was aimed upward instead of out at the crowd. If the bomb had exploded outward, as the perpetrator intended, the casualty rate probably would have been higher.[58]

Investigators built a new profile of the bomber, but after the Richard Jewell debacle, they were uncertain of how far to take their efforts. In a frantic effort to generate new leads, they also issued a public plea for information. Perhaps someone had seen something or inadvertently recorded a photo of the goateed man without realizing it. Eventually, they added a $500,000 reward. Despite several initially promising leads, the investigation came to a standstill. By the end of 1996, police were no closer to solving the case than they had been before they wasted so much time pursuing Richard Jewell.[59]

SUBSEQUENT BOMBINGS

By early 1997, the Olympic Park bomber seemed to have disappeared. As with Ted Kaczynski, however, he was not retired or dead. He was biding his time and planning his next attack. He no longer sported a goatee. He changed his tactics and his location. Rather than focusing on a high-profile target while the world watched, he aimed to send a message at a controversial, less noticeable target.[60]

Northside Family Planning Services was an abortion clinic housed in a nondescript building in Sandy Springs, a quiet Atlanta suburb. The clinic was not an attractive or high-profile target. When radical anti-abortion groups such as Operation Rescue demonstrated against abortions, they typically chose a clinic in Midtown Atlanta. Northside mostly operated under the radar in a quiet neighborhood far from the hustle and bustle of the downtown or midtown crowd.[61]

The situation changed at 9:30 a.m. on January 16, 1997. At that instant, a flash of light and a sharp blast ripped through the peaceful neighborhood. Fortunately, the building was sturdy and constructed from reinforced concrete. The blast ripped down drywall, blew out sixty windows, and hurled shrapnel into the side of the structure, but no one died. Northside Family Planning had survived the assault.[62]

Police officers arrived on the scene quickly, with the media not far behind. As investigators sifted through the debris and assessed the evidence, news crews set up shop. No one paid attention to a trash Dumpster at the other end of the building. Cars piled up in the nearby parking lot, including a Nissan parked near the receptacle.[63]

An hour had elapsed since the initial blast had occurred. As the agents and media representatives went about their chores, another flash shot through the parking lot. Eyewitnesses recalled seeing a car near the Dumpster rise up amidst a plume of dirt. Many people fell to the ground from the concussive blast. Still others hurled themselves to the pavement in the excitement of the moment. No one knew quite what was happening. Was the explosion the result of a car bomb? Were the people in the area under attack? No one died, but six onlookers were wounded badly enough to require hospitalization.[64]

In retrospect, ATF and FBI agents understood the significance of the event. It was a well-known ruse perpetrated by serial bombers to maximize the terroristic effect of their handiwork. They planted a bomb, set it to explode, and included a secondary device triggered to explode either when it was moved or set to a timer. This one-two punch ensured that the first device would inflict harm and the secondary bomb would target first responders and other emergency personnel arriving on the scene. Whoever had set the bomb had carefully and methodically planned the crime. He had chosen the location, selecting high ground in a relatively quiet neighborhood, and placed the charges to ensure maximum damage. It was only a fluke that no one was killed. Investigators entertained little doubt it was the same person who had planted the Centennial Park device.[65]

The potential problem with this reasoning was that the two bombs were configured differently. The abortion clinic bomber used dynamite while the Olympic Park bomber did not. The type of clock and the nails used were also dissimilar. Bomb squad experts recognized, of course, that a serial bomber can change his methods over time—either as a deliberate ploy to confuse investigators or because he finds more destructive methods for inflicting damage. Atlanta had not been a hotbed of bombing activity before the Olympic Park episode; it seemed unlikely that another assailant would surface less than a year after the initial bombing unless the person was a copycat. Still, it was dangerous and foolhardy to make too many assumptions until the agents knew more about the circumstances surrounding the two incidents.[66]

On February 21, a Friday night a little more than a month after the Northside Family Planning bombing, the Otherside Lounge, a nightclub on busy Piedmont Road in Midtown Atlanta, became the scene of an attack. The Otherside was housed in a mock Tudor building with a green-shingled roof. What it lacked in splendor it compensated for in tolerance and a certain chic ambience. Catering to Atlanta's vibrant gay community, the nightclub was a prominent gathering place for lesbians. The club was filled with patrons when the device exploded. To some witnesses, it sounded as though someone had fired a shotgun at close range. A woman staggered around with a nail in her arm. Other people realized that they, too, had been injured in the blast. Fortunately, no one was killed.[67]

Law enforcement officials arriving on the scene were immediately suspicious. Recalling the second bomb placed at the abortion clinic, they carefully searched outside the lounge. Sure enough, they spotted a device sitting on a retaining wall near a covered outdoor patio behind the club. It was tucked inside a green backpack. After a series of frenzied discussions among the investigators, they decided to deploy a GBI bomb-handling robot. If they could disarm the device and preserve it, the intact bomb might yield a treasure trove of information. Up until this point, ATF and FBI agents had been forced to sift through bomb fragments. Having an entire device in one piece would greatly simplify and perhaps speed up the investigation.[68]

GBI agents carefully maneuvered the robot next to the backpack and for forty-five minutes attempted to disarm the bomb. When this approach proved to be unsuccessful, the robot doused the backpack with water, causing it to ignite. In addition to shaking cars and rattling windows throughout the neighborhood, the explosion hurled a chunk of metal almost a quarter mile. It shot through the roof of a vacant house and landed in the living room. The metal, a quarter of an inch thick and approximately the size of a CD, was remarkably similar to metal plates found in both the Centennial Olympic Park bomb and the Northside Family Planning Services bomb. If they had harbored any doubts that a single perpetrator was involved, this key piece of evidence resolved those doubts.[69]

A few days later, as federal and state authorities combed through the debris, the bomber decided to explain his actions to the world. He sent envelopes postmarked February 23 to four Atlanta media outlets: the Reuters news service, NBC News, the local CBS affiliate, and the *Atlanta Journal-Constitution* newspaper. Written with a felt-tipped pen in all capital letters and containing virtually identical messages, the communiqués obviously emanated from the same person. The bomber explained:

THE BOMBING'S IN SANDY SPRING'S AND MIDTOWN WERE CARRIED-OUT BY UNITS OF THE <u>ARMY OF GOD</u>. . . .

THE ABORTION WAS THE TARGET OF THE FIRST DEVICE. THE MURDER OF 3.5 MILLION CHILDREN EVERY YEAR WILL NOT BE "TOLERATED." THOSE WHO PARTICIPATE IN <u>ANYWAY</u> IN THE MURDER OF CHILDREN MAY BE TARGETED FOR ATTACK. THE ATTACK THEREFORE SERVES AS A WARNING: <u>ANYONE</u> IN OR AROUND FACILITIES THAT MURDER CHILDREN MAY BECOME VICTIMS OF RETRIBUTION. THE NEXT FACILITY TARGETED <u>MAY NOT BE EMPTY</u>.

THE SECOND DEVICE WAS AIMED AT AGENT OF THE SO-CALLED FEDERAL GOVERNMENT I.E. A.T.F. F.B.I. MARSHALL'S E.T.C. WE DECLARE AND WILL WAGE <u>TOTAL WAR</u> ON THE UNGODLY COMMUNIST REGIME IN NEW YORK AND YOUR LEGASLATIVE-BUREAUCRATIC LACKEY'S IN WASHINGTON. IT IS YOU WHO ARE RESPOSIBLE AND PRESIDE OVER THE MURDER OF CHILDREN AND ISSUE THE POLUCY ON UNGODLY PREVERSION THAT'S DESTROYING OUR PEOPLE. WE ILL TARGET ALL FACILITIES AND PERSONELL OF THE FEDERAL GOVERNMENT.

THE ATTACK ON MIDTOWN WAS AIMED AT THE SODOMITE BAR (THE OTHERSIDE). WE WILL TARGET SODOMITES, THERE ORGANIZATIONS, AND ALL THOSE WHO PUSH THERE AGENDA.

IN THE FUTURE WHERE INNOCENT PEOPLE MAY BECOME THE PRIMARY CASUALTIES, A WARNING PHONE CALL WILL BE PLACED TO ONE OF THE NEWS BUREAU'S OR 911. GENERALLY A 40 MINUTE WARNING WILL BE GIVEN. TO CONFIRM THE AUTHENTICITY OF THE WARNING A CODE WILL BE GIVEN WITH THE WARN AND STATEMENT.

THE CODE FOR OUR UNIT IS 4–1–9–9–3.

"DEATH TO THE NEW WORLD ORDER"[70]

The letter also contained details about the components of the bombs, details that would only be known to the perpetrator himself. Despite the claim that the bomber was working with units of people, analysts predicted he was a lone wolf acting on paranoid tendencies. The Army of God referenced in the letter sounded ominous, but investigators knew it was a loose amalgamation of anti-abortion extremists that first surfaced in the mid-

1980s. Although the group was known to commit violent acts, the bombings did not fit their standard operating procedure. In all likelihood, the terrorist who was engaged in bombing Atlanta-area targets was acting alone.[71]

The unit code was significant because it suggested that the bomber was angry with the government. Everyone in law enforcement knew that April 19, 1993, was the date of the Waco incident involving the Branch Davidians. This was the incident that drove Timothy McVeigh to a life of crime and continued to incense white supremacists and other members of the radical right. Assuming he was not deliberately trying to confuse the police, including the 4–1–9–9–3 reference was extremely helpful to investigators who wanted to understand the assailant.[72]

With relatively clear evidence that all the bombings had been masterminded by the same individual, the ATF, GBI, and FBI consolidated their forces into the Atlanta Bomb Task Force under the command of FBI inspector Woody Enderson. Enderson decided it was again time to ask the public for assistance. Perhaps someone at one of the sites had witnessed a key event and had yet to come forth either because the person was frightened or simply did not know the significance of what he or she had seen. In November 1997, task force members scheduled a press conference to show the public components of the bomb and offer a $100,000 reward for information leading to the arrest and conviction of the perpetrator.[73]

Going public with the investigation had led to crucial evidence in the Ted Kaczynski case, but this time the news conference did not uncover new leads. Despite the extraordinary number of resources dedicated to the case, the large expenditures involved, and the dedication of law enforcement personnel, investigators simply had encountered a dead end. Although they were loath to admit it to people outside the office, their best bet for capturing the bomber was to wait for him to plant another device and, hopefully, make a mistake in the process.[74]

A mistake in planting the next bomb was exactly what happened. Eleven months later, the bomber struck again, this time in Birmingham, Alabama. As discussed earlier in this book, Birmingham had earned the nickname "Bombingham" during the dark days of the 1960s civil rights movement. Since that time, city fathers had worked hard to rehabilitate the area's reputation. It remained a blue-collar, working-class town lacking the chic and prestige of other large southern cities, but Birmingham nonetheless seemed to be on the upswing. As the city's steel mills closed in the 1970s, the local economy came more and more to focus on new industries, especially a health-care service-based economy and a large expansion by the University of Alabama at Birmingham (UAB).[75]

The New Woman, All Women Health Care Clinic on the city's south side normally opened for business shortly after a nurse arrived around 7:30 a.m. to prepare for the day. The clinic was located just off Tenth Avenue South at the edge of the UAB medical complex. It was housed in a white two-story building sporting a burgundy awning hanging over the front door. Having been in business for a decade, the clinic generally did not engender much protest. A week earlier, however, several hundred anti-abortion demonstrators had marched past the building to mark the twenty-fifth anniversary of the *Roe v. Wade* U.S. Supreme Court opinion that legalized abortion in the United States. Other than that milestone, which had not triggered violence, nothing unusual had occurred in recent days.[76]

Emily Lyons, a nurse who worked at the abortion clinic, almost always arrived after the doors opened. It was unusual for her to arrive so early, but on the morning of January 29, 1998, Lyons was filling in for another nurse on maternity leave. Although New Woman, All Women had not been subjected to high-profile protests, employees were always cognizant of the potential for violence at abortion clinics, especially in the Bible Belt. An abortion clinic in Tuscaloosa, Alabama, had been firebombed six months earlier, and of course everyone was familiar with the Sandy Springs bombing from the previous year. Abortion doctors had been murdered in 1993 and 1994 in Pensacola, Florida, not far away from Birmingham. Owing to the potential for violence, the clinic employed security guards to ensure their employees' and patients' safety.[77]

Thirty-four-year-old Robert "Sande" Sanderson was the security guard on duty on January 29. He had just finished the night shift with the Birmingham Police Department when he arrived that morning. He was working at the clinic to earn extra money so he could buy his stepson a car. Everyone who knew him agreed he was the kind of policeman who enriched his community, always going above and beyond the call of duty. In fact, he was known for his love of volunteer work. He had carried the Olympic torch through Birmingham, Alabama, on its journey to the Centennial Games in Atlanta in 1996. He was once injured when he tried to catch a woman who had jumped from the second story of a burning building. Ironically, Sanderson did not approve of abortion; however, his job was to set aside his personal feelings and provide security regardless of what went on inside the building.[78]

He arrived shortly before Emily Lyons drove her car into the parking lot at 7:30. A family also arrived in an SUV shortly before the clinic was scheduled to open. They encountered Minzor Chadwick, a regular anti-abortion protester, who yelled at them not to enter the clinic. The father, apparently visiting the clinic with his wife and adolescent daughter, stepped out of the SUV to speak with officer Sanderson. While the two men spoke, Emily Lyons arrived to start the day.[79]

As she stepped from her vehicle and crossed the parking lot toward the front of the building, Lyons noticed Sanderson standing near the entrance. She remembered the father passing her as he marched back to his SUV. Although she experienced difficulty remembering details later, Lyons vaguely recalled Sanderson walking toward an object positioned on the front steps. He removed a retractable police baton and used it to poke at the object, which sat next to a flowerpot.[80]

The object, a bomb, exploded. Minzor Chadwick recalled feeling a wave of hot air envelop him, slamming bits of concrete and grit into his face. His initial reaction was that someone affiliated with the clinic was trying to kill him. He ducked behind a parked car out of what he thought was a line of fire. Chadwick was legally blind; accordingly, he had difficulty making out details, although he thought he saw the crumpled body of the policeman lying near a fence. As far as anyone knew, the frightened family in the SUV was uninjured. Witnesses recall seeing the father back up his vehicle and peel out of the parking lot in a panic.[81]

Owing to his proximity to the explosive device, Sande Sanderson had no chance to survive the force of the blast. Metal shards struck him in the head. It tore away part of his skull, exposing brain matter. The device ripped his arm from his body and knocked his legs out from under him, almost amputating one of them. The explosion also vaporized his uniform and tossed him away from the building as though he were a rag doll rudely deposited into a trashcan. When the first responders found his body, he was almost unrecognizable. Only his service belt remained fastened around his waist.[82]

Emily Lyons also suffered grievously, although Sanderson's body, which was initially positioned between her and the bomb, absorbed much of the blast. The explosion ripped off her eyelids and shredded her lip; drove hundreds of nails into her face, torso, and legs; and tore a hole in her abdomen, depositing a piece of circuit board in the top of her liver. A piece of metal pierced her right eye, blinding her, and a tooth was broken off. Despite such massive trauma, she survived the blast.[83]

Several eyewitnesses recalled seeing a long-haired man wearing a backpack scurrying away from the scene. The normal reaction when an unexplained, exciting event occurs is for spectators to rush toward the site. This man's behavior seemed odd, but most witnesses, focused on the source of the mayhem, quickly dismissed his presence.[84]

Emergency personnel arriving on the scene recalled an ATF videotape distributed to fire and police departments throughout the southeastern United States warning them to beware of secondary explosive devices. Although emergency personnel did not know whether this was the work of the same bomber who attacked the Olympic Games and the Otherside Lounge in Atlanta, they had to assume it was a strong possibility. Even as the victims were treated at the scene and transported to local hospitals, investigators carefully combed the site for additional explosive devices. A bomb-sniffing dog initially indicated that another device might be hidden in a shrub, but the police never found another bomb at the site.[85]

Minzor Chadwick immediately came under suspicion. He may have been legally blind, but he was on the scene and certainly had an ax to grind. During his six-hour interrogation, Chadwick explained that he knew Officer Sanderson from their many encounters and actually considered the man his friend. It was true that Chadwick considered abortion to be murder, but he saw a brazen attack on the clinic to be equally unjustified. In fact, Chadwick was distraught when he learned that Sande Sanderson had died in the explosion. The police quickly cleared him as a suspect. No one had the stomach to transform this sympathetic figure into another Richard Jewell.[86]

The New Woman, All Women Health Care Clinic might have been yet another bombing that failed to produce investigative leads were it not for a young UAB premed student initially called WN-1 (witness one). Investigators eventually identified him as Jermaine Jerome Hughes. Hughes later attended Harvard Law School. On the morning of the Birmingham incident, he was an undergraduate student struggling to finish his classes.

For Hughes, the morning started off as simply another average day. He was washing his clothes in a laundry room on the ground floor of his dormitory when he felt the windows shake. Although the glass did not shatter in his dormitory as it did in other buildings, he could tell that something was wrong.[87]

Looking out the window and spying a plume of white smoke rising from the Domino's Pizza restaurant a block away, Hughes raced from the building. That was when he spotted a man hurrying away from the scene. Apparently it was the same fellow that other eyewitnesses had seen. Unlike other witnesses, Hughes took more than a passing notice of the man. "That guy ain't right," he thought. Anticipating the importance of his account, Hughes struggled to recall distinguishing characteristics: the man was about six feet one inch tall, approximately 175 pounds, between thirty-two and forty-two years of age, sporting long brown hair and wearing a black baseball cap.

He carried an empty black backpack. As the man crossed a park between Sixteenth and Seventeenth streets, he started running away from the area.[88]

If Jermaine Hughes had dialed 911 and reported his suspicions, he already would have performed his civic duty, but what he did next was astonishing, earning him the sobriquet "hero." Instead of calling 911, he gave chase. When he came to the parking lot in front of his dormitory, Hughes slid behind the wheel of his car, started the engine—no mean feat because the transmission was damaged—and followed the strange man. He saw the guy cut to a side street between two buildings. Hughes's instincts proved to be excellent. When the man emerged from between the buildings, he had changed his look. He had discarded his jacket, pulled off his cap, and rearranged his hair. Donning a pair of large sunglasses, the man clearly had made an effort to disguise his identity. These were not the actions of an innocent passerby.

Anxious to avoid detection, the young student drove around the building, parked, popped the hood, and pretended to be another frustrated motorist experiencing car trouble. The ruse apparently worked. The suspicious gentleman glanced at Hughes but did not seem to register his face.

Unfortunately, Hughes did not have a cell phone to call for help. He tried to flag down a nearby student for assistance, but the guy begged off with the excuse that he was late for class. Afraid that the suspect would escape, Hughes jumped back into his car and slowly patrolled the street. Realizing that he would not be able to follow the man indefinitely without arousing suspicion, he attempted to stop a woman for help. Although she later reported the exchange, Hughes was not certain he had communicated the urgency of the situation. To make matters worse, he lost sight of the man.

Rushing into a McDonald's restaurant, he persuaded the manager to let him use the telephone to call 911. Tape recordings indicate a flustered young man trying to recall the details of what he had seen. At one point, he lost the connection and had to call back.

Suddenly, in an incredibly serendipitous event, Hughes spotted the fellow walking across from the restaurant even as he spoke to the 911 operator.

"I got him—I got him," Hughes exclaimed.

"Where is he?" the operator asked.

"I got him. I think this is him."

"Is he on foot?"

As Hughes struggled to explain this new development, another man, a lawyer later identified as WN-2, Jeff Tickal, approached to see if he could help.

"I can't see him now," Jermaine Hughes told the operator. "I can't believe I'm standing here and there's not a cop here by now!"

The 911 operator told him that a police car had been dispatched. In the meantime, Tickal decided he would go to his car and see if he could locate the suspect. The strange man had entered a wooded area, but he might emerge somewhere else.

Tickal had already departed when the police arrived at the McDonald's restaurant. The officers initially investigated on foot before they too jumped in their car and circled the area.

As luck or fate would have it, Tickal spotted the man putting something inside a gray Nissan pickup truck. When the truck pulled out of its parking space and left, Tickal swung his car around and followed. He jotted down a North Carolina license plate number: KND 1117. Tickal stopped to tell the officers what he had seen.

Jermaine Hughes was in his car when he spotted Tickal tailing a gray pickup truck. Pulling beside the truck, Hughes was reasonably sure it was the same man he had seen earlier. Although the truck eluded him in traffic, Hughes managed to write down the license tag. It was a North Carolina plate: KND 1117.

With two eyewitnesses providing similar physical descriptions of the suspect and recording the same tag number, for the first time investigators had found a promising lead. After the two witnesses repeated their stories to myriad law enforcement personnel, the Alabama State Police and the Birmingham authorities issued a be-on-the-lookout (BOLO) for the Nissan truck with North Carolina plate KND 1117.[89]

The truck was registered to a North Carolina resident named Eric Robert Rudolph. Alabama authorities contacted the Asheville, North Carolina, police and asked that the North Carolina authorities follow up with a face-to-face interview. Although his driver's license photograph was similar to the eyewitness descriptions, early in the investigation the only evidence linking Rudolph to the bombing was that he owned the gray Nissan truck. Before officials charged him with a crime, they wanted to be sure their case was strong. An initial interview would determine whether they had their man or should search for a different suspect.[90]

In the meantime, Doug Jones, the U.S. attorney for northern Alabama, which included Birmingham, decided to go public with the description. He had few options. The press corps already knew about the BOLO and had discovered Rudolph's identity. The story would break any minute. Jones wanted to get out in front and emphasize that Eric Rudolph was only a material witness at this stage of the investigation. If they could interview

Rudolph and assess the strength of any alibi he offered, the case might yet take a different turn. The Richard Jewell fiasco had taught everyone the value of thoroughly investigating a lead before charging in without sufficient credible evidence to sustain a solid criminal case.[91]

NOTES FROM UNDERGROUND

When Rudolph learned that the authorities wanted to question him about the Birmingham bombing, he disappeared into the forests of North Carolina. The precise time he learned of the authorities' interest is unclear. Nine hours after the device exploded, he entered a Plaza Video store in Murphy, North Carolina, 240 miles from Birmingham, and rented a video. He returned the next morning, returned the video he had rented the preceding evening, and rented another one. This sequence of events suggests he either knew nothing of the BOLO or he was an incredibly calm, unruffled man.[92]

The last time anyone reported seeing Rudolph as the authorities closed in on him was on the evening of January 30. At 6:56 p.m., he bought a double Whopper, fries, and a Coke at a Burger King restaurant. After he ate, Rudolph shopped for supplies at a BI-LO store across the street. He paid $109.06 in cash for a variety of items such as batteries, canned food, soap, and oatmeal. The cash register noted the time as 7:11 p.m. Law enforcement officials approached Rudolph's trailer a little more than an hour later, but he had already fled, disappearing into the rugged wilderness of western North Carolina.[93]

The police interviewed Cal Stiles, a local businessman who had rented a storage unit to Eric Rudolph in the nearby town of Marble. Stiles contacted police and positively identified the man—Rudolph had used his real name when he rented the unit—so investigators brought in a canine named Garrett, a yellow Labrador retriever trained to sniff out bomb-making residue. After determining that the storage unit was not booby-trapped, the police released Garrett and he immediately fixed on a wooden box. Forensic chemists discovered spent bullet shells and explosives residue, which gave them enough evidence to secure a search warrant. The warrant allowed investigators to inventory the unit contents, revealing a great deal of insight into Rudolph's life, including a series of racist tracts as well as a book on Oklahoma City bomber Timothy McVeigh's life. After sifting through the storage unit as well as Rudolph's trailer, local police and FBI agents were certain they had identified the bomber.[94]

Identifying their man and finding him were two different tasks. Trained as a survivalist, Eric Rudolph possessed the skills and wherewithal to live off the land, which he did for an incredible five-year period. Police investigators suspected he was receiving assistance from friends and family, but they could not prove it. They scoured the hills of western North Carolina in search of hiding places Rudolph was known to frequent, but to no avail. Earlier in his life, he had talked about his ability to go underground and live off the land, and his actions beginning late in the 1990s confirmed that it was no idle boast.[95]

During those years between 1998 and 2003, investigators occasionally heard rumors of Eric Rudolph sightings. He was said to be hiding in Mexico. From time to time, residents living near Murphy told stories of seeing him near their property or finding that supplies had been stolen from their homes or outlying buildings. George Nordmann claimed that Rudolph had poisoned his dog, a collie-chow mix named Bobo, probably so that Bobo would not alert anyone to Rudolph's presence in the nearby woods. On one occasion, Nordmann claimed to have seen Rudolph and briefly spoken with him.[96]

For anti-government residents of the North Carolina mountains, Eric Rudolph was transformed into a folk hero in the vein of Billy the Kid, Robin Hood, or airline hijacker D. B. Cooper. As the weeks and months passed and he eluded police squads and search dogs, they celebrated his outlaw status. "Run, Rudolph, Run!" one set of bumper stickers and T-shirts proclaimed. Another souvenir slogan read, "Eric Rudolph: Hide and Seek Champion 1998." A sign in front of a Nantahala Lake restaurant announced, "Eric Rudolph Eats Here."[97]

One of the strangest episodes in the Eric Rudolph saga involved the fugitive's brother, Daniel. After Eric's name appeared in the press, the intensely private Rudolph family was subjected to an avalanche of media scrutiny. They became virtual prisoners inside their homes. On the afternoon of March 10, 1998, Daniel turned on his video cassette recorder and captured himself on tape in his garage. Appearing gaunt and wearing a tie and jacket, he removed his jacket, sat down, and rolled up his sleeve. "This is for the FBI and the media," he said. With that, he pushed his arm into the path of a circular saw, severing his left hand above the wrist. Wrapping his arm in a towel, he disappeared from the frame. Paramedics arrived to transport Daniel to the hospital where surgeons reattached the hand.[98]

Eric Rudolph appeared on an episode of the popular television show *America's Most Wanted*. During its eighteen-year run, the program had assisted in capturing nine hundred fugitives, and law enforcement personnel hoped for similar good fortune. Unfortunately, the episode generated only a few tips, none of which led to new information. The fugitive remained on the lam.[99]

As the years passed, the case grew cold. Occasionally, a new set of investigators resumed the search and reinterviewed old witnesses. They sifted through tattered old files or followed up on rumors. Despite these efforts, Eric Rudolph seemed to have disappeared as though he were a ghost. Perhaps he had fled the country or died. No one knew what to think.[100]

Finally, in the early morning hours of May 31, 2003, the case came to an unlikely conclusion. A rookie police officer, Jeff Postell, in Murphy, North Carolina, spotted a man lurking in an alley behind downtown businesses around 3:00 a.m. Thinking a burglary was taking place, the officer pulled his car to a stop behind the Save-a-Lot store and called for backup. The man may have been carrying something in his hand, perhaps a gun, but it was too dark to tell.

"Drop anything in your hands," Postell called out in his most commanding voice. "Come out with your hands up. Get on the ground, face down. Put your hands behind you."

Backup officers Charles Kilby from the Murphy Police Department, Sean Matthews of the Cherokee County Police Department, and Jody Bandy from the Tennessee Valley Authority police arrived to assist Postell. When they had the suspected thief in custody, Postell asked who he was. The man claimed his name was Jerry Wilson, he originally came from Ohio, he was homeless, and he was searching for food. He carried no identification.[101]

The story initially sounded plausible. The man appeared gaunt and in need of food. Yet something about the situation seemed odd. Even as Postell was checking on the man's story, Sean Matthews kept staring at the suspect. He was not certain, but the thief resembled a Most Wanted poster that Matthews had seen for Eric Robert Rudolph. They transported the individual to the Cherokee County Jail, and Jody Bandy searched the Internet.

Finally, Bandy confronted the man. "You aren't Jerry Wilson," he said. "Just who the hell are you?"

The man laughed and said, "Eric Rudolph. I'm relieved."[102]

The thief had finally spoken the truth. The officer had arrested a man who was on the FBI's Most Wanted list. To verify this, local officers fed the suspect's fingerprints into the Automated Fingerprint Identification System (AFIS) database. They also alerted the FBI regional office in Asheville, North Carolina. Within hours, representatives of CNN were calling to confirm that Eric Rudolph had been captured.[103]

Bombing suspect Eric Rudolph takes a "perp walk" from the Cherokee County jail in Murphy, North Carolina. Courtesy of Corbis.

He had said he was relieved, and it seemed to be the truth. The prisoner became talkative and convivial. He joked with his jailers, asked about their families, and even agreed to sign their Wanted posters. Although he was thinner than he had been when his earlier photographs were snapped, Rudolph seemed to be in good health and fine spirits.

He did not ask about his family the way a man would if he had been hiding in the forest sequestered from the outside world. In addition, as he talked about current events with the deputy sheriffs in the jail, he seemed to be remarkably well informed about news of the day. All of these facts suggested that Rudolph had been moving in and out of the woods, probably with assistance from friends and family.[104]

After two days, the jailers moved Rudolph from the county jail. The press had been alerted and were on hand for the customary "perp walk" as the suspect was herded to a waiting vehicle. Just as Timothy McVeigh had done, Eric Rudolph attempted to look cool and a bit menacing as he sported his orange jumpsuit and ambled through the crowd. One journalist labeled his expression "a mixture of contempt, disdain, and disinterest." It was over in a matter of minutes. From there, authorities directed their man to a waiting car and a helicopter at the Asheville airport.[105]

CONCLUSION

Federal district court judge C. Lynwood Smith appointed Richard Jaffe, a prominent Alabama criminal defense attorney with the Birmingham firm of Jaffe, Strickland, and Drennan, to represent Eric Rudolph in the case involving the New Woman, All Women Health Care Clinic bombing. At the June 3, 2003, arraignment in a Birmingham courtroom, Jaffe stood with his new client, whom he had met that morning for the first time, as Rudolph entered a not guilty plea in open court. After hearing the plea, chief U.S. magistrate Michael T. Putnam set August 4 as the trial date, although everyone knew it would probably be continued into 2004 or beyond.[106]

Another defense attorney, Bill Bowen, had also been appointed to represent Rudolph. Bowen was a former assistant state attorney general as well as a former state appellate court judge. Along with Jaffe, he would add a third defense attorney, Judy Clarke, the federal public defender from San Diego who had represented Unabomber Ted Kaczynski. This trio of experienced advocates would ensure that their client received a fair trial in the grueling legal maneuvering that was sure to follow. They would have a lot of work to do: prosecutors had provided 17,000 documents, the first batch of more than 700,000 (along with 20,000 photographs) that would be produced in the case.[107]

Jaffe and his team reached out to the Federal Public Defender Program, a group of attorneys that provides services to indigent criminal defendants. The Atlanta office agreed to assist Rudolph's defense team in reviewing the discovery materials. As time progressed, however, fissures developed among team members, and Jaffe eventually departed. Jaffe cited client confidentiality in refusing to discuss the case, but Rudolph later acknowledged that the lawyers bickered among themselves about the best means of presenting a defense, and Jaffe simply felt he could no longer provide adequate representation in such a contentious atmosphere.[108]

While the defense attorneys went through their tribulations, prosecutors developed their case and assembled the evidence to convict their man. Experienced attorneys recognize that juries can act in unexpected ways even when evidence of criminality is strong. The Eric Rudolph matter was a death penalty case, but both sides remained open to a possible plea bargain. Rudolph subsequently agreed to plead guilty in exchange for a life sentence in prison without the possibility of parole in lieu of the death penalty. As part of this arrangement, Rudolph disclosed the location of 250 pounds of explosives. He also put to rest any lingering doubts about Richard Jewell's involvement in the Centennial Park bombing when he indicated that he and Jewell did not know each other and had no connection.[109]

In an eleven-page document, "Statement of Eric Robert Rudolph April 13, 2005," the defendant publicly admitted his involvement in the four bombings. He also explained his motives. "Abortion is murder," he wrote. "And when the regime in Washington legalized, sanctioned and legitimized this practice, they forfeited their legitimacy and moral authority to govern. At various times in history men and women of good conscience have had to decide when the lawfully constituted authorities have overstepped their moral bounds and forfeited their right to rule." According to Rudolph, he was acting in accordance with the principles espoused by the Founders, who broke away from Great Britain owing to the illegitimacy of a corrupt regime. He was a patriot acting on behalf of fifty million unborn children. "Because this government is committed to maintaining the policy of abortion, the agents of this government are the agents of mass murder, whether knowingly or unknowingly." This bizarre logic required someone to resist "this holocaust." That someone was Eric Robert Rudolph, not a villain but a hero to millions of unborn human beings.

Rudolph also explained that he felt compelled to resist the "homosexual agenda" in the United States. Although he understood that consenting adults could maintain their private lives behind closed doors as they saw fit, "when the attempt is made to drag this practice out of the closet and into the public square in an 'in-your-face' attempt to force society to accept and recognize this behavior as being just as legitimate and normal as the natural man/woman relationship, every effort should be made, including force if necessary, to halt this effort."

In Rudolph's opinion, the 1996 Olympic Games in Atlanta served as an ideal target for his bombing because the venue was "under the protection and auspices of the regime in Washington" and was specifically designed "to celebrate the ideals of global socialism." Therefore, "the purpose of the attack on July 27 was to confound, anger and embarrass the Washington government in the eyes of the world for its abominable sanctioning of abortion on demand." Rudolph intended "to force the cancellation of the Games, or at least create a state of insecurity to empty the streets around the venues and thereby eat into the vast amounts of money invested." He also explained that he had called 911 to ensure that ample opportunity was available to minimize the carnage among innocent civilians.

As for the next two targets, "I resolved to improve my devices and focus the blasts upon a very narrow target." He waited until 1997. "The first in January was an abortion mill (Northside Family Planning). The second was a homosexual establishment (the Otherside Lounge)." He chose these targets specifically because they promoted abortion and the homosexual agenda. "Despite the inherent dangers involved in time devices, all of these devices used in both of these assaults functioned within the parameters of the plan, and I make no apologies."

As for his Birmingham bombing, that city and "that particular abortion mill were chosen purely for tactical reasons. The city was a sufficient distance away from any location I was known to have frequented. Three abortion mills were looked at in Birmingham, none of which I actually liked for a target. New Woman All Women was tactically the least objectionable." Focusing on the victims, Rudolph admitted that he felt "nothing personal against Lyons and Sanderson. They were targeted for what they did, not who they were as individuals."[110]

Pursuant to the terms of his plea agreement, on July 18, 2005, Eric Robert Rudolph was sentenced to two consecutive life terms without the possibility of parole for the January 1998 death of Officer Robert "Sande" Sanderson in Birmingham, Alabama. On August 22, 2005, he was sentenced to three consecutive life terms for the Atlanta bombings. That same month, federal authorities transported Rudolph to the Florence, Colorado, ADX prison nicknamed the "Supermax," which had once been home to Timothy McVeigh and remained Ted Kaczynski's permanent residence. Since 2005, Rudolph has lived in a tiny concrete cell, occasionally issuing manifestos justifying his actions during the bombing spree of the late 1990s.[111]

Once again, as with Timothy McVeigh and Ted Kaczynski, the Eric Rudolph case shows what can happen when a disillusioned individual believes that his failures are caused by an outside force, in this case imperial, oppressive federal authorities. Moreover, because Rudolph wanted to fight threats to fundamentalist Christian values, especially abortion and homosexuality, he thought he was justified in undertaking acts of violence. He escaped detection for as long as he did because he was prepared to "go off the grid" and not leave a paper trail.

Rudolph shared another common characteristic with Timothy McVeigh. Both young men tapped into the hostility that right-wing extremist groups propagate in numerous speeches, pamphlets, books, and websites. Rage against an objectified foe—the government, homosexuals, certain racial and ethnic groups, and abortionists—fueled acts of hatred. Eric Rudolph seemed to be a walking contradiction: he was a separatist as well as an ideologue, a lone wolf as well as a quasi-member of the right-wing resistance movement, an individual carrying out a singular mission as well as a warrior in the Army of God.[112]

NOTES

1. McCann, *Terrorism on American Soil*, 231–38; Springer, "Patterns of Radicalization," 51.

2. McCann, *Terrorism on American Soil*, 231–32; Schuster and Stone, *Hunting Eric Rudolph*, 12–14; Vollers, *Lone Wolf*, 20–23.

3. Schuster and Stone, *Hunting Eric Rudolph*, 1–2, 14–15; Vollers, *Lone Wolf*, 22–23.

4. McCann, *Terrorism on American Soil*, 232; Schuster and Stone, *Hunting Eric Rudolph*, 16–17; Springer, "Patterns of Radicalization," 61–62; Vollers, *Lone Wolf*, 24–25.

5. McCann, *Terrorism on American Soil*, 233; Schuster and Stone, *Hunting Eric Rudolph*, 27–33; Stephen, "America: Eric Rudolph Is Alleged to Have Bombed Abortion Clinics, a Gay Club and the Olympic Games," 9; Vollers, *Lone Wolf*, 27–34.

6. McCann, *Terrorism on American Soil*, 234–35; Springer, "Patterns of Radicalization," 62; Stephen, "America: Eric Rudolph Is Alleged to Have Bombed Abortion Clinics, a Gay Club and the Olympic Games," 9; Vollers, *Lone Wolf*, 35–36, 42–43; Wilkinson, "The Making of a Maniac," 31–34.

7. McCann, *Terrorism on American Soil*, 236; Schuster and Stone, *Hunting Eric Rudolph*, 73–78; Vollers, *Lone Wolf*, 55–61.

8. McCann, *Terrorism on American Soil*, 236–37; Stephen, "America: Eric Rudolph Is Alleged to Have Bombed Abortion Clinics, a Gay Club and the Olympic Games," 9–10; Wilkinson, "The Making of a Maniac," 31–34.

9. Schuster and Stone, *Hunting Eric Rudolph*, 111; Springer, "Patterns of Radicalization," 51–52; Vollers, *Lone Wolf*, 63.

10. Morrison, "Special Report: 'Your Wayward Son, Eric Rudolph,'" 1A; Schuster and Stone, *Hunting Eric Rudolph*, 111–12; Springer, "Patterns of Radicalization," 51–52; Wilkinson, "The Making of a Maniac," 31–34.

11. Morrison, "Special Report: 'Your Wayward Son, Eric Rudolph,'" 1A; Springer, "Patterns of Radicalization," 51–52; Vollers, *Lone Wolf*, 243–46; Wilkinson, "The Making of a Maniac," 31–34.

12. Schuster and Stone, *Hunting Eric Rudolph*, 112, 122–24; Vollers, *Lone Wolf*, 88–89; Wilkinson, "The Making of a Maniac," 31–32.

13. Fonda et al., "How Luck Ran Out for a Most Wanted Fugitive," 8; Schuster and Stone, *Hunting Eric Rudolph*, 112; Vollers, *Lone Wolf*, 94–95; Wilkinson, "The Making of a Maniac," 31–32.

14. Quoted in Vollers, *Lone Wolf*, 94–97. See also Schuster and Stone, *Hunting Eric Rudolph*, 112; Springer, "Patterns of Radicalization," 54–55; Wilkinson, "The Making of a Maniac," 31–33.

15. Schuster and Stone, *Hunting Eric Rudolph*, 112; Springer, "Patterns of Radicalization," 55; Vollers, *Lone Wolf*, 95–97.

16. Borgeson and Valeri, *Terrorism in America*, 47–48; Jonsson, "How Did Eric Rudolph Survive?" 1; Ridgeway, *Blood in the Face*, 71; Vollers, *Lone Wolf*, 97–98.

17. Quoted in Ridgeway, *Blood in the Face*, 72. See also Barkun, *Religion and the Racist Right*, 173–74; Borgeson and Valeri, *Terrorism in America*, 47–71; Jonsson, "How Did Eric Rudolph Survive?" 1; Stephen, "America: Eric Rudolph Is Alleged to Have Bombed Abortion Clinics, a Gay Club and the Olympic Games," 9; Vollers, *Lone Wolf*, 97–99.

18. Schuster and Stone, *Hunting Eric Rudolph*, 194–96; Vollers, *Lone Wolf*, 97–98.

19. Schuster and Stone, *Hunting Eric Rudolph*, 112; Springer, "Patterns of Radicalization," 55–56; Vollers, *Lone Wolf*, 100–101.

20. Schuster and Stone, *Hunting Eric Rudolph*, 112; Springer, "Patterns of Radicalization," 55–56; Tharp, "Where Is Eric Rudolph?" 26; Vollers, *Lone Wolf*, 100–101; Wilkinson, "The Making of a Maniac," 31–33.

21. Schuster and Stone, *Hunting Eric Rudolph*, 112; Vollers, *Lone Wolf*, 101.

22. Schuster and Stone, *Hunting Eric Rudolph*, 112–13; Springer, "Patterns of Radicalization," 56–57; Vollers, *Lone Wolf*, 103–5; Wilkinson, "The Making of a Maniac," 31–33.

23. Schuster and Stone, *Hunting Eric Rudolph*, 113; Springer, "Patterns of Radicalization," 58; Stephen, "America: Eric Rudolph Is Alleged to Have Bombed Abortion Clinics, a Gay Club and the Olympic Games," 9–10; Vollers, *Lone Wolf*, 105–7; Wilkinson, "The Making of a Maniac," 31–33.

24. McCann, *Terrorism on American Soil*, 237; Schuster and Stone, *Hunting Eric Rudolph*, 113; Springer, "Patterns of Radicalization," 59; Vollers, *Lone Wolf*, 106–7; Wilkinson, "The Making of a Maniac," 31–33.

25. Schuster and Stone, *Hunting Eric Rudolph*, 113; Stephen, "America: Eric Rudolph Is Alleged to Have Bombed Abortion Clinics, a Gay Club and the Olympic Games," 9–10; Vollers, *Lone Wolf*, 107.

26. Schuster and Stone, *Hunting Eric Rudolph*, 113; Springer, "Patterns of Radicalization," 59; Vollers, *Lone Wolf*, 106–7; Wilkinson, "The Making of a Maniac," 31–33.

27. Quoted in Vollers, *Lone Wolf*, 108. See also McCann, *Terrorism on American Soil*, 237; Schuster and Stone, *Hunting Eric Rudolph*, 113; Stephen, "America: Eric Rudolph Is Alleged to Have Bombed Abortion Clinics, a Gay Club and the Olympic Games," 9–10.

28. Schuster and Stone, *Hunting Eric Rudolph*, 135–43; Springer, "Patterns of Radicalization," 59; Vollers, *Lone Wolf*, 108–9.

29. Schuster and Stone, *Hunting Eric Rudolph*, 140–41; Springer, "Patterns of Radicalization," 59; Vollers, *Lone Wolf*, 109; Wilkinson, "The Making of a Maniac," 32–33.

30. McCann, *Terrorism on American Soil*, 237; Schuster and Stone, *Hunting Eric Rudolph*, 141; Springer, "Patterns of Radicalization," 60; Vollers, *Lone Wolf*, 111–12; Wilkinson, "The Making of a Maniac," 32–33.

31. Springer, "Patterns of Radicalization," 61; Vollers, *Lone Wolf*, 113; Wilkinson, "The Making of a Maniac," 32–33.

32. Vollers, *Lone Wolf*, 113–14; Wilkinson, "The Making of a Maniac," 32–33.

33. McCann, *Terrorism on American Soil*, 231; Schuster and Stone, *Hunting Eric Rudolph*, 4–5; Vollers, *Lone Wolf*, 20–21.

34. Schuster and Stone, *Hunting Eric Rudolph*, 4–5; Vollers, *Lone Wolf*, 21.

35. McCann, *Terrorism on American Soil*, 232; Schuster and Stone, *Hunting Eric Rudolph*, 2, 14–15, 21; Vollers, *Lone Wolf*, 22–23.

36. Schuster and Stone, *Hunting Eric Rudolph*, 12–14; Vollers, *Lone Wolf*, 22–25.

37. McCann, *Terrorism on American Soil*, 232; Schuster and Stone, *Hunting Eric Rudolph*, 12–14; Vollers, *Lone Wolf*, 23–24.

38. McCann, *Terrorism on American Soil*, 232; Schuster and Stone, *Hunting Eric Rudolph*, 16–17; Vollers, *Lone Wolf*, 24; Wilkinson, "The Making of a Maniac," 33–34.

39. Copeland, "Olympics Bomber Apologizes, but Not to All Victims," 3A; Schuster and Stone, *Hunting Eric Rudolph*, 2–3, 12, 15, 16–17; Vollers, *Lone Wolf*, 23–25.

40. Copeland, "Olympics Bomber Apologizes, but Not to All Victims," 3A; McCann, *Terrorism on American Soil*, 232–33; Schuster and Stone, *Hunting Eric Rudolph*, 17–21; Stephen, "America: Eric Rudolph Is Alleged to Have Bombed Abortion Clinics, a Gay Club and the Olympic Games," 9–10; Vollers, *Lone Wolf*, 24–25.

41. Copeland, "Olympics Bomber Apologizes, but Not to All Victims," 3A; Schuster and Stone, *Hunting Eric Rudolph*, 18; Vollers, *Lone Wolf*, 24–25.

42. Copeland, "Olympics Bomber Apologizes, but Not to All Victims," 3A; McCann, *Terrorism on American Soil*, 232–33; Schuster and Stone, *Hunting Eric Rudolph*, 21; Stephen, "America: Eric Rudolph Is Alleged to Have Bombed Abor-

tion Clinics, a Gay Club and the Olympic Games," 9–10; Tharp, "Where Is Eric Rudolph?" 26; Vollers, *Lone Wolf*, 24–25.

43. Schuster and Stone, *Hunting Eric Rudolph*, 24–27; Vollers, *Lone Wolf*, 30–31.

44. Luckovich, "I Couldn't Let an Injury Stop Me" [editorial cartoon], SS25; Schuster and Stone, *Hunting Eric Rudolph*, 34–35; Vollers, *Lone Wolf*, 47–48.

45. McCann, *Terrorism on American Soil*, 231–32; Schuster and Stone, *Hunting Eric Rudolph*, 33–34; Vollers, *Lone Wolf*, 21.

46. Schuster and Stone, *Hunting Eric Rudolph*, 28; Vollers, *Lone Wolf*, 27–28.

47. McCann, *Terrorism on American Soil*, 232–33; Schuster and Stone, *Hunting Eric Rudolph*, 27–29; Stephen, "America: Eric Rudolph Is Alleged to Have Bombed Abortion Clinics, a Gay Club and the Olympic Games," 9–10; Vollers, *Lone Wolf*, 31–32.

48. McCann, *Terrorism on American Soil*, 233–34; Schuster and Stone, *Hunting Eric Rudolph*, 29–31; Vollers, *Lone Wolf*, 31–32.

49. Curriden, "Rebuilding a Reputation," 20; Goodman, "Falsely Accused Suspect Pursues Libel Case," A11; Lopresti, "Unfounded Suspicion Took Cruel Toll on Atlanta Olympic Hero Jewell," C8; Schuster and Stone, *Hunting Eric Rudolph*, 29–32; Vollers, *Lone Wolf*, 31–32.

50. Curriden, "Rebuilding a Reputation," 20; Goodman, "Falsely Accused Suspect Pursues Libel Case," A11; Lopresti, "Unfounded Suspicion Took Cruel Toll on Atlanta Olympic Hero Jewell," C8.

51. Goodman, "Falsely Accused Suspect Pursues Libel Case," A11; Lopresti, "Unfounded Suspicion Took Cruel Toll on Atlanta Olympic Hero Jewell," C8; Schuster and Stone, *Hunting Eric Rudolph*, 32–33.

52. Goodman, "Falsely Accused Suspect Pursues Libel Case," A11; Schuster and Stone, *Hunting Eric Rudolph*, 32–34.

53. Curriden, "Rebuilding a Reputation," 20; Goodman, "Falsely Accused Suspect Pursues Libel Case," A11; Lopresti, "Unfounded Suspicion Took Cruel Toll on Atlanta Olympic Hero Jewell," C8; McCann, *Terrorism on American Soil*, 233–34; Schuster and Stone, *Hunting Eric Rudolph*, 32–33; Vollers, *Lone Wolf*, 33–34.

54. McCann, *Terrorism on American Soil*, 233–34; Schuster and Stone, *Hunting Eric Rudolph*, 33–34; Vollers, *Lone Wolf*, 32.

55. Lopresti, "Unfounded Suspicion Took Cruel Toll on Atlanta Olympic Hero Jewell," C8.

56. Schuster and Stone, *Hunting Eric Rudolph*, 36–37; Vollers, *Lone Wolf*, 33–34.

57. McCann, *Terrorism on American Soil*, 234; Schuster and Stone, *Hunting Eric Rudolph*, 36–40.

58. Schuster and Stone, *Hunting Eric Rudolph*, 36–37; Vollers, *Lone Wolf*, 234–35.

59. McCann, *Terrorism on American Soil*, 234; Schuster and Stone, *Hunting Eric Rudolph*, 38–40; Vollers, *Lone Wolf*, 233–35.

60. McCann, *Terrorism on American Soil*, 234–35; Schuster and Stone, *Hunting Eric Rudolph*, 41–43; Vollers, *Lone Wolf*, 35–37; Wilkinson, "The Making of a Maniac," 33–34.

61. Schuster and Stone, *Hunting Eric Rudolph*, 42–43; Vollers, *Lone Wolf*, 35–36.

62. McCann, *Terrorism on American Soil*, 234–35; Schuster and Stone, *Hunting Eric Rudolph*, 43; Vollers, *Lone Wolf*, 35–36; Wilkinson, "The Making of a Maniac," 33–34.

63. Schuster and Stone, *Hunting Eric Rudolph*, 42–43; Vollers, *Lone Wolf*, 35–36.

64. McCann, *Terrorism on American Soil*, 234–35; Schuster and Stone, *Hunting Eric Rudolph*, 41–46; Vollers, *Lone Wolf*, 35–37; Wilkinson, "The Making of a Maniac," 33–34.

65. Schuster and Stone, *Hunting Eric Rudolph*, 45–46; Vollers, *Lone Wolf*, 36–37.

66. McCann, *Terrorism on American Soil*, 234; Schuster and Stone, *Hunting Eric Rudolph*, 47–49.

67. McCann, *Terrorism on American Soil*, 235; Schuster and Stone, *Hunting Eric Rudolph*, 49–50; Springer, "Patterns of Radicalization," 62–63; Stephen, "America: Eric Rudolph Is Alleged to Have Bombed Abortion Clinics, a Gay Club and the Olympic Games," 9–10; Vollers, *Lone Wolf*, 42–43.

68. Schuster and Stone, *Hunting Eric Rudolph*, 50–52; Vollers, *Lone Wolf*, 43.

69. Howard and Gajilan, "A New Link," 4; McCann, *Terrorism on American Soil*, 235; Schuster and Stone, *Hunting Eric Rudolph*, 50–52; Vollers, *Lone Wolf*, 43.

70. Quoted in Vollers, *Lone Wolf*, 44–45. See also McCann, *Terrorism on American Soil*, 235–36; Schuster and Stone, *Hunting Eric Rudolph*, 54–55; Stephen, "America: Eric Rudolph Is Alleged to Have Bombed Abortion Clinics, a Gay Club and the Olympic Games," 9.

71. Schuster and Stone, *Hunting Eric Rudolph*, 55–58; Vollers, *Lone Wolf*, 44–48.

72. McCann, *Terrorism on American Soil*, 236; Schuster and Stone, *Hunting Eric Rudolph*, 57–58; Vollers, *Lone Wolf*, 46.

73. Schuster and Stone, *Hunting Eric Rudolph*, 60–61; Vollers, *Lone Wolf*, 48.

74. McCann, *Terrorism on American Soil*, 236; Schuster and Stone, *Hunting Eric Rudolph*, 63; Vollers, *Lone Wolf*, 47–48; Wilkinson, "The Making of a Maniac," 33–34.

75. Schuster and Stone, *Hunting Eric Rudolph*, 63–64; Springer, "Patterns of Radicalization," 63; Vollers, *Lone Wolf*, 49–50.

76. McCann, *Terrorism on American Soil*, 236; Schuster and Stone, *Hunting Eric Rudolph*, 64–65; Springer, "Patterns of Radicalization," 62–63; Stephen, "America: Eric Rudolph Is Alleged to Have Bombed Abortion Clinics, a Gay Club and the Olympic Games," 9–10; Vollers, *Lone Wolf*, 50–51; Wilkinson, "The Making of a Maniac," 33–34.

77. Schuster and Stone, *Hunting Eric Rudolph*, 64–67; Vollers, *Lone Wolf*, 50–51.

78. Schuster and Stone, *Hunting Eric Rudolph*, 67–68; Vollers, *Lone Wolf*, 51–52; Wilkinson, "The Making of a Maniac," 34.

79. Schuster and Stone, *Hunting Eric Rudolph*, 64–65; Vollers, *Lone Wolf*, 52.

80. McCann, *Terrorism on American Soil*, 236; Schuster and Stone, *Hunting Eric Rudolph*, 69–70; Vollers, *Lone Wolf*, 52.

81. Schuster and Stone, *Hunting Eric Rudolph*, 68–70; Vollers, *Lone Wolf*, 52–53.

82. McCann, *Terrorism on American Soil*, 236; Schuster and Stone, *Hunting Eric Rudolph*, 69–71; Springer, "Patterns of Radicalization," 63; Stephen, "America: Eric Rudolph Is Alleged to Have Bombed Abortion Clinics, a Gay Club and the Olympic Games," 9–10; Vollers, *Lone Wolf*, 52–55; Wilkinson, "The Making of a Maniac," 33–34.

83. Schuster and Stone, *Hunting Eric Rudolph*, 71; Vollers, *Lone Wolf*, 53–55.

84. McCann, *Terrorism on American Soil*, 236; Schuster and Stone, *Hunting Eric Rudolph*, 72–73; Vollers, *Lone Wolf*, 54–55.

85. Schuster and Stone, *Hunting Eric Rudolph*, 79–80; Vollers, *Lone Wolf*, 64–65.

86. McCann, *Terrorism on American Soil*, 236; Schuster and Stone, *Hunting Eric Rudolph*, 72–73; Vollers, *Lone Wolf*, 53–54, 309–10.

87. Schuster and Stone, *Hunting Eric Rudolph*, 73; Vollers, *Lone Wolf*, 55–56; Wilkinson, "The Making of a Maniac," 33–34.

88. Schuster and Stone, *Hunting Eric Rudolph*, 73–75; Vollers, *Lone Wolf*, 58–60.

89. McCann, *Terrorism on American Soil*, 236; Pedersen et al., "A Mountain Manhunt," 16–19; Schuster and Stone, *Hunting Eric Rudolph*, 73–78; Stephen, "America: Eric Rudolph Is Alleged to Have Bombed Abortion Clinics, a Gay Club and the Olympic Games," 9; Vollers, *Lone Wolf*, 55–61.

90. Schuster and Stone, *Hunting Eric Rudolph*, 81–83; Vollers, *Lone Wolf*, 60–61.

91. McCann, *Terrorism on American Soil*, 236–37; Schuster and Stone, *Hunting Eric Rudolph*, 83; Vollers, *Lone Wolf*, 68–69.

92. McCann, *Terrorism on American Soil*, 236–37; Schuster and Stone, *Hunting Eric Rudolph*, 85–87; Vollers, *Lone Wolf*, 83–85; Wilkinson, "The Making of a Maniac," 33–34.

93. Schuster and Stone, *Hunting Eric Rudolph*, 91–93; Vollers, *Lone Wolf*, 84–85.

94. McCann, *Terrorism on American Soil*, 236–37; Schuster and Stone, *Hunting Eric Rudolph*, 96; Vollers, *Lone Wolf*, 72–73.

95. McCann, *Terrorism on American Soil*, 237; Pedersen et al., "A Mountain Manhunt," 16–19; Schuster and Stone, *Hunting Eric Rudolph*, 213–18; Springer, "Patterns of Radicalization," 64; Stephen, "America: Eric Rudolph Is Alleged to Have Bombed Abortion Clinics, a Gay Club and the Olympic Games," 9; Wilkinson, "The Making of a Maniac," 33–34.

96. Monroe and Roche, "The Forest Is His Ally," 26–27; Schuster and Stone, *Hunting Eric Rudolph*, 153–75; Tharp, "Where Is Eric Rudolph?" 26; Vollers, *Lone Wolf*, 140–50.

97. Fonda et al., "How Luck Ran Out for a Most Wanted Fugitive," 8; McCann, *Terrorism on American Soil*, 237; Monroe and Roche, "The Forest Is His Ally," 26–27; "Out of the Woods," 26; Pedersen et al., "A Mountain Manhunt," 16–19; Schuster and Stone, *Hunting Eric Rudolph*, 218–19; Vollers, *Lone Wolf*, 158–59.

98. Schuster and Stone, *Hunting Eric Rudolph*, 126–28; Vollers, *Lone Wolf*, 91–92.

99. Schuster and Stone, *Hunting Eric Rudolph*, 271, 272; Stephen, "America: Eric Rudolph Is Alleged to Have Bombed Abortion Clinics, a Gay Club and the Olympic Games," 9; Vollers, *Lone Wolf*, 92, 162.

100. Campos-Flores et al., "How He Stayed Hidden," 36; Copeland, "Rudolph Ate Acorns, Lizards, Game," 1A; Jonsson, "How Did Eric Rudolph Survive?" 1; Monroe and Roche, "The Forest Is His Ally," 26–27; O'Donnell and Howard, "The Hunt Intensifies," 6; "Out of the Woods," 26; Pedersen et al., "A Mountain Manhunt," 16–19; Stephen, "America: Eric Rudolph Is Alleged to Have Bombed Abortion Clinics, a Gay Club and the Olympic Games," 9–10.

101. Campos-Flores et al., "How He Stayed Hidden," 36; Jonsson, "How Did Eric Rudolph Survive?" 1; McCann, *Terrorism on American Soil*, 237; Monroe and Roche, "The Forest Is His Ally," 26–27; Vollers, *Lone Wolf*, 1–6, 175–80.

102. Fonda et al., "How Luck Ran Out for a Most Wanted Fugitive," 8; Jonsson, "How Did Eric Rudolph Survive?" 1; McCann, *Terrorism on American Soil*, 237–38; "Out of the Woods," 26; Schuster and Stone, *Hunting Eric Rudolph*, 277–82; Stephen, "America: Eric Rudolph Is Alleged to Have Bombed Abortion Clinics, a Gay Club and the Olympic Games," 9; Wilkinson, "The Making of a Maniac," 31.

103. Campos-Flores et al., "How He Stayed Hidden," 36; Copeland, "Rudolph Ate Acorns, Lizards, Game," 1A; Jonsson, "How Did Eric Rudolph Survive?" 1; McCann, *Terrorism on American Soil*, 237; Monroe and Roche, "The Forest Is His Ally," 26–27; O'Donnell and Howard, "The Hunt Intensifies," 6; "Out of the Woods," 26; Pedersen et al., "A Mountain Manhunt," 16–19; Schuster and Stone, *Hunting Eric Rudolph*, 287; Stephen, "America: Eric Rudolph Is Alleged to Have Bombed Abortion Clinics, a Gay Club and the Olympic Games," 9–10.

104. Jonsson, "How Did Eric Rudolph Survive?" 1; "Out of the Woods," 26; Schuster and Stone, *Hunting Eric Rudolph*, 296–303; Vollers, *Lone Wolf*, 198–203.

105. Schuster and Stone, *Hunting Eric Rudolph*, 303–8; Vollers, *Lone Wolf*, 202–3.

106. Jonsson, "How Did Eric Rudolph Survive?" 1; "Out of the Woods," 26; Schuster and Stone, *Hunting Eric Rudolph*, 309–13; Vollers, *Lone Wolf*, 212–14.

107. Schuster and Stone, *Hunting Eric Rudolph*, 311, 312; Vollers, *Lone Wolf*, 214–16.

108. Vollers, *Lone Wolf*, 260–64.

12

"THE SYSTEM WAS BLINKING RED"

The Radical Islamic Movement and the September 11 Attacks

The rooted fibers rose, and from the wound
Black bloody drops distill'd upon the ground.
Mute and amaz'd, my hair with terror stood;
Fear shrunk my sinews, and congeal'd my blood.

—Virgil, *The Aeneid*, Book III

September 11, 2001, is a date that will forever resonate in American history. Just as the Japanese attack on Pearl Harbor on December 7, 1941, and the assassination of President John F. Kennedy in Dallas, Texas, on November 22, 1963, live on in public memory, so too will this horrific episode exist in perpetuity in the American collective consciousness. The events of that day were dramatic, but the root causes extended far earlier in history. Few people realized that a new chapter of terrorism had opened in the United States owing to decisions reached by a small group of discontented, marginalized people who nursed their grievances a world away. Islamic extremists, incensed at the corrupting influences of western culture, had deliberately plotted to attack the values of a society they believed was undermining all that was right and holy in the world. This chapter traces the events leading up to the September 11 attacks as well as the consequences that flowed from the episode.

RADICAL ISLAM AND THE RISE OF AL-QAEDA

The story of militant Islam can be traced back hundreds of years, but the limited purpose here is to review the radical ideology of Osama bin Laden, the intellectual mastermind behind the September 11 attacks on U.S. soil. He was born in Riyadh, Saudi Arabia, on March 10, 1957, to Mohammed bin Awad bin Laden, a billionaire construction tycoon with ties to the Saudi royal family. Osama was born of the magnate's tenth wife, Hamida al-Attas (called Alia Ghanem), the seventeenth child from a total of fifty-seven off-spring. Osama later inherited between $25 million and $30 million of his father's money.[1]

Details of his young life remain sketchy. His parents divorced when Osama was a small boy. His mother subsequently married Mohammed al-Attas, a family friend and associate. The new couple bore children; consequently, Osama grew up in a household with three half brothers and a half sister. He was raised as a devout Wahhabi Muslim, a fundamentalist branch that has become associated with militant, puritanical Islam.[2]

Although some commentators deride the use of the term "fundamentalist" with respect to extreme interpretations of Islam, the label is widely used nonetheless. Fundamentalists in any religious tradition believe there was a perfect moment in time, but the moment has come and gone. To again enjoy the apex of their influence that has vanished with this bygone time, fundamentalists strive to recover the moment. The effort occasionally requires them to confront threats to the ideal. Fundamentalists need not be extremists, but sometimes they embrace extreme views. Groups such as Hezbollah, Hamas, and Islamic Jihad believe the realization of their vision of an Islamic state is being undermined by corrupt leaders in predominantly Muslim countries. The dominance of external western powers, especially the United States, is also seen as both polluting and exploiting Islamic culture. Some groups have sought to work within particular political systems, but others have resorted to violent extremism.[3]

The fundamentalist sect of "Wahhabism," as it came to be called, compels true Muslims to return to the pure form of Islam by stripping away tenets added to the religion since the first generation of Islam. Developed during the eighteenth century by Muhammad ibn Abd al-Wahhab, Wahhabism was designed to counteract the general challenge of encroaching western civilization as well as the specific threats posed by Christian missionaries. Removing impurities from the true religion was a means of removing western contamination. Ironically, during the modern era, Wahhabism became largely associated with the Saudi version of Islam. With its frequent contacts with the West and its emphasis on economics and oil production, modern Saudi Arabia is more secularized than it was in Wahhab's day. Were he alive, no doubt Muhammad ibn Abd al-Wahhab would rail against the Saudi government.[4]

Bin Laden also fell under the influence of Abdullah Azzam, a charismatic Palestinian and a disciple of Sayyid Qutb. Qutb was an Egyptian Muslim who visited the United States during the late 1940s and found it to be an alien, corrupting place where materialism, sexual promiscuity, racism, and "bad haircuts" proliferated. In his work, Qutb explained the concept of Ma'alim fi-l-Tariq, a strong belief that anything non-Islamic is evil and corrupt. He called for a revolutionary form of "anarcho-Islam," where Muslims could peacefully coexist in accordance with divine law, free and unfettered, absent any government constraints. This idealistic Islamic utopia held great appeal for disenfranchised Muslims who were frustrated with all manner of oppressive political regimes. From these seeds would grow a bitter harvest as bin Laden came to see the corrupting West as a threat to the values he held dear.[5]

An organized, militant anti-western campaign was far in the future when Osama bin Laden grew to adulthood. As a boy and a young man, he enjoyed the advantages available to a male child born of privilege. He attended a prestigious secular school, the Al-Thager Model School, and from there matriculated to King Abdulaziz University in Jeddah, Saudi Arabia. His school records are difficult to locate, but he seems to have studied economics and business administration. He may have earned degrees in civil engineering and public administration, although some sources suggest that he left the university without completing his studies.[6]

By 1980, the twenty-three-year-old bin Laden had arrived in Afghanistan. He was an impressive physical specimen, towering over his colleagues at six feet, five inches in height. He was known as an accomplished horseman, runner, climber, and soccer player. When he was not competing in sporting events, he frequently listened to tape-recorded sermons of fiery Muslim clerics preaching militant Islamic tirades. The young man's religious fervor was not especially memorable—numerous Muslims of his era turned toward fundamentalism—but his enormous personal fortune, massive physical appearance, and natural charisma lent him an air of gravitas that caused Osama bin Laden to stand apart from the crowd.[7]

He had traveled to this far-off, physically isolated land to oppose the Soviet Union's invasion, which occurred in 1979. The large communist superpower had violated its southern neighbor's sovereignty to prop up an unstable communist government. During the next decade, the Soviets struggled in the inhospitable terrain against shadowy guerrilla forces to assert their military authority. Gleeful Americans watched the giant communist forces become ensnarled in an endless quagmire reminiscent of the U.S. debacle in Vietnam. The parallels were lost on no one.[8]

Many young men from the Arab world who traveled to Afghanistan during the 1980s took part in battles against the Soviets. Osama bin Laden was not one of them. Although he reportedly participated in one battle, for the most part this unusual young man was satisfied to work behind the scenes. With his financial resources and extensive contacts, he had developed a valuable skill set. The young operative assembled an intricate network of financiers who funneled money into the country to support guerrilla activities. Known as the "Golden Chain," the network allowed bin Laden and his associates to equip and train the Afghan mujahedeen (alternately spelled "mujahedin"), or "holy warriors."[9]

Bin Laden evolved into a master recruiter of soldiers, weaponry, and money. Instead of casting the struggle as a clash of nations and secular ideologies, he approached mosques and religious schools and told a tale of holy war. The fight was far more than a struggle between competing western ideologies; it was a crucial, acrimonious war against Islam. In such an effort, all resources must be brought to bear against those who would wipe out the sacred religion. Even nations that did not buy into bin Laden's religious dogma channeled resources into the financier's coffers based on the age-old principle that the enemy of my enemy is my friend. If bin Laden and the mujahedeen were willing to serve as proxies for an anti-Soviet war, countries such as the United States and Saudi Arabia were willing and eager to cough up monies. Although bin Laden received little or no direct assistance from the United States, funds that the U.S. government sent through the Pakistani military intelligence service helped to train and equip rebel forces, which freed up bin Laden's money to be used elsewhere. The tidy arrangement satisfied everyone during the struggle against Soviet hegemony.[10]

In April 1988, the Soviet government, already weakening internally and well on its way toward an epic implosion, announced that it would no longer support a war in Afghanistan. During the nine-month withdrawal that followed, the victorious mujahedeen discovered, in the triumphal hour, a fundamental problem facing any group that achieves its goal, namely a loss of purpose. If the evil Soviet empire pulled troops out of Afghanistan following a humiliating defeat, what would the future hold?[11]

Having earned a measure of respect, indeed admiration, for his work during the war, Osama bin Laden chose this moment to formalize his network. He and Abdullah Azzam had established an organization known as the Bureau of Services (Mektab al Khidmat, or MAK) to funnel matériel and personnel into Afghanistan during the fighting. Now they sought to create a base or foundation (known as al-Qaeda) for future jihads. Azzam had served as the principal in MAK, but bin Laden stepped into the paramount leadership role for al-Qaeda. It would become one of the most successful terrorist organizations of all time owing in no small part to bin Laden's superlative organizational skills. The group established an intelligence branch, a military committee, a financial committee, a political committee, and a propaganda committee. An advisory committee (Shura) comprised of bin Laden's closest confidants ensured that al-Qaeda stayed firmly under bin Laden's control.[12]

During the next year, a rift developed between bin Laden and Azzam about the purpose of the new organization. The wily and ambitious bin Laden wanted to transform al Qaeda into a global organization willing and able to assist a variety of causes around the world. By contrast, Azzam favored a more localized approach, focusing especially on Afghanistan, where unfinished work remained. Their differences threatened the stability of the new group.[13]

Bin Laden won absolute control over al-Qaeda when Abdullah Azzam died violently. On November 24, 1989, a remote-controlled bomb killed the Palestinian and two of his sons. Suspicion fell on competing Islamic factions as well as the Israeli Mossad and the U.S. Central Intelligence Agency (CIA). The responsible party has never been identified clearly, but one thing was clear in the aftermath of the explosion: Osama bin Laden became the undisputed leader of al-Qaeda.[14]

With his power consolidated, bin Laden assembled a team dedicated to spreading al-Qaeda's influence far and wide. An Egyptian surgeon, Ayman al-Zawahiri, became his most trusted adviser, eventually serving as al-Qaeda's chief deputy. The "Blind Sheikh," Omar Abdel-Rahman, spiritual guide for fundamentalist organizations such as the Islamic Group and the Egyptian Islamic Jihad, also influenced Osama bin Laden and his followers. Abdel-Rahman inspired the 1981 murder of Egyptian president Anwar Sadat, and his influence upon militants grew tremendously in the ensuing years. The sheikh later moved to the United States to establish a base of operations for disseminating ideas about killing infidels as enemies of Islam.[15]

In 1989, bin Laden moved to Sudan to forge an alliance with Hassan al Turabi, leader of the National Islamic Front. Turabi had recently seized power in Khartoum, and he needed assistance in fighting African separatists who challenged his authority. In exchange for assistance from al-Qaeda, Turabi allowed bin Laden to enjoy a safe haven in Sudan.[16]

A year later, bin Laden was back in Saudi Arabia. In August 1990, after Iraq invaded Kuwait, he approached the Saudi royal family with a proposal to reactivate the mujahedeen for a jihad to combat Iraq. The Saudis rejected the proposal. Afterward, bin Laden was outraged when the royal family joined forces with a coalition headed by the United States. To add insult to injury, the Saudis granted permission for U.S. armed forces to base soldiers in Saudi Arabia. Bin Laden spoke out publicly against this decision only to learn that the royals had revoked his passport. With assistance from a dissident member of the family, bin Laden slipped out of the country under the pretext of attending a meeting in Pakistan. By 1994, in retaliation for his disobedience, the Saudis stripped him of his citizenship and froze his domestic assets.[17]

This setback might have discouraged lesser men, but Osama bin Laden was emboldened by adversity. No manner of opposition would dissuade him from pressing forward in the global effort to eradicate unbelievers and enemies of Islam. During the ensuing years, he established an increasingly complex series of businesses that supported his worldwide terrorist network. He also traveled extensively to meet with key allies, establish training camps, acquire weapons, and position himself to conduct jihad at opportune times and places of his choosing.[18]

During the early 1990s, bin Laden publicly lauded efforts to attack western interests. In 1992, al-Qaeda issued a fatwa, or Islamic legal opinion, calling for jihad against the western "occupation" of Islamic lands. Around this same period, bin Laden spoke of striking against the United States and thereby severing "the head of the snake." Although he did not possess the resources to carry out his threat, and much of what he said during this period was empty rhetoric, it was clear that he looked to a future when al-Qaeda could strike at the enemy.[19]

Bin Laden and his terrorist network grew increasingly angry at the West throughout the 1990s. It started when U.S. troops landed in Somalia toward the end of 1992. Al-Qaeda and allied terrorist organizations issued a fatwa demanding that the interlopers be evicted. A series of violent attacks followed. In December 1992, a bomb exploded at two hotels in Aden, Yemen, known to be frequented by American military personnel. Although two people died, no Americans were killed. Al-Qaeda operatives stepped up their efforts to lash out at the snake by supplying arms to Somali warlords pledged to resist American advances. Later, Somalis trained and equipped by al-Qaeda bragged that they had shot down two U.S. Black Hawk helicopters in a widely publicized debacle for the U.S. military in October 1993.[20]

The terrorist incidents continued. A November 1995 car bomb exploded in Riyadh, Saudi Arabia, adjacent to a Saudi National Guard training facility and killed five Americans and two Indians. Although bin Laden was not directly involved, the four perpetrators who were caught and executed for the crime admitted that al-Qaeda had "inspired" their terrorist acts. Intelligence sources discovered that several bin Laden associates claimed credit for instigating the bombing. Taking credit and providing inspiration were not enough, though. Al-Qaeda assisted in an infamous bombing at the Khobar Towers building in Dhahran, Saudi Arabia, that killed nineteen Americans and wounded 372 people in June 1996. The Saudi branch of Hezbollah Al-Hejaz (Party of God in the Hijaz) planned and executed the attack. To this day, the nature extent of al-Qaeda's involvement remains murky.[21]

THE 1993 WORLD TRADE CENTER BOMBING: PRELUDE TO SEPTEMBER 11, 2001

Attacks on U.S. interests abroad garnered press coverage and spread fear among American intelligence planners, but bin Laden was anxious to demonstrate al-Qaeda's growing power and influence by striking closer to home. He finally found an opportunity. At 12:18 p.m. on February 26, 1993, a truck bomb exploded in the parking garage of Tower One of the World Trade Center in New York City. Six people died and more than 1,000 were injured. The blast ripped a hole in the building seven stories high. Eight and a half years later, a group of militant al-Qaeda suicide bombers would attack American targets with far greater results and casualties, but the first attack served as a crude dress rehearsal for what came later.[22]

A group of conspirators that included Ramzi Yousef, Mahmud Abouhalima, Mohammad Salameh, Nidal Ayyad, Abdul Rahman Yasin, and Ahmad Ajaj, with financing from Yousef's uncle, Khalid Sheikh Mohammed, planned and executed the 1993 attack. These men were not suicide bombers; they meticulously prepared for the assault, but they had no intention of sacrificing their own lives or the lives of their warriors. Yousef subsequently confessed that he had hoped to kill 250,000 people, but presumably he meant non-Muslims.[23]

Compared with the ambition and scale of the September 11 attacks, the 1993 operation was an amateur affair. According to evidence revealed at trial, Yousef and Eyad Ismoil, a Jordanian friend, drove a Ryder truck into the World Trade Center parking lot and left it there. Yousef lit a twenty-foot fuse and immediately fled from the premises. Twelve minutes later, the bomb detonated. Although the parking garage suffered extensive damage, Yousef had hoped that the towers would collapse. Had he parked the truck closer to the concrete building foundations, the plan might have succeeded.[24]

Investigators captured Yousef and his co-conspirators using the same techniques that led to Timothy McVeigh. Sifting through the wreckage, law enforcement officers discovered a truck axle containing a Vehicle Identification Number (VIN), which they traced to a Ryder truck rental outlet in Jersey City. They learned that Mohammad Salameh had rented the truck and subsequently reported it stolen.[25]

The plot unraveled after an unwitting Salameh called the rental office to report the truck stolen and requested that his four-hundred-dollar deposit be returned. When Salameh turned up on March 4, 1993, to retrieve his four hundred dollars, Federal Bureau of Investigation (FBI) officials arrested him. Shortly thereafter, they apprehended his confederates Ayyad and Abouhalima.[26]

The three men had ties to Brooklyn's Farouq mosque, which was associated with Blind Sheikh Omar Abdel-Rahman, the cleric who had done so much to influence Osama bin Laden and al-Qaeda. From his base in the United States, Abdel-Rahman preached a message of hatred, contending that his host country oppressed Muslims and was therefore an enemy of Islam. The Blind Sheikh was not the only shrill voice vehemently protesting the U.S. "war on Islam," but he was an influential and persistent critic, with adherents scattered across the globe. During the investigations conducted in the aftermath of the 1993 World Trade Center episode, the FBI learned of the sheikh's plan to bomb the United Nations, the Lincoln and Holland tunnels, the George Washington Bridge, and a New York federal building housing FBI offices. In 1995, Omar Abdel-Rahman stood trial and was convicted of seditious conspiracy. The following year, the court sentenced him to life in prison.[27]

As for Yousef's warriors, they paid a heavy price for their involvement in the 1993 World Trade Center incident. In March 1994, four men were convicted of carrying out the bombing: Abouhalima, Ajaj, Ayyad, and Salameh. The charges included conspiracy, explosive destruction of property, and interstate transportation of explosives. In November 1997, Yousef, the mastermind behind the bombings, and Eyad Ismoil, who drove the truck carrying the bomb, were convicted.[28]

The 9/11 Commission later concluded that the relative speed and efficiency with which federal officials resolved the 1993 case, ironically enough, was unfortunate because "it created an impression that the law enforcement was well-equipped to cope with terrorism." Because the existing criminal justice system apparently worked well, few if any investigators thought to delve into the reasons behind the attack or problems that the civilian criminal justice system might experience in prosecuting terrorists.

Had they posed hard questions about the timing and extent of the rising anger among fundamentalist Muslims, federal officials might have realized that the threat of additional terrorist threats was growing.[29]

PLANNING THE SEPTEMBER 11 ATTACKS

The next attack on the World Trade Center has become etched in the minds of virtually all Americans, indeed all world citizens, who were old enough to follow the sequence of events. On Tuesday, September 11, 2001, in a coordinated effort, nineteen hijackers seized control of four commercial airliners traveling to San Francisco and Los Angeles from Boston, Newark, and the Washington Dulles International airports. For most hijackers, escape presents an almost insurmountable obstacle, but in this case the hijackers had no intention of escaping. It was a suicide mission, and each hijacker understood that he would not return home.[30]

The September 11 attacks would transform Osama bin Laden into the most infamous terrorist in the world, but U.S. officials had known about him long before that time. He first came to their attention in the aftermath of the 1993 World Trade Center bombing when they found bin Laden's telephone number among the list of calls that Ramzi Yousef placed from New York safe houses. A CIA paper dated April 2, 1993, described the al-Qaeda leader as "an independent actor [who] sometimes works with other individuals and governments" to further "Islamic causes." The more the agency examined this heretofore shadowy figure, the more they learned of his nefarious activities. "Every time we turned over a rock," a CIA official later explained of that period, "there would be some sort of connection to bin Laden."[31]

They initially believed he was merely a financier—a gifted one, to be sure, but hardly an operational man willing to get his hands dirty in the nitty-gritty work of planning and executing terrorist operations. By the summer of 1993, that initial assessment began to evolve. The CIA Counterterrorist Center (CTC) started monitoring the man's activities, a rare acknowledgment that a single individual required intense CIA scrutiny.[32]

Interest in bin Laden increased significantly throughout the 1990s. In May 1996, he returned to Afghanistan after the Taliban, a group of Islamic religious fundamentalists, moved into a power vacuum in that war-torn nation. On August 23, he issued "The Declaration of Jihad on the Americans Occupying the Country of the Two Sacred Places," a reference to Mecca and Medina in Saudi Arabia. The declaration formalized what the CIA had come to recognize—al-Qaeda was at war with the United States. To drive home his message, bin Laden granted interviews with media outlets that included Al Jazeera, the Arab-language news network, as well as the Cable News Network (CNN) and ABC News.[33]

In retrospect, the U.S. military and intelligence community might have taken additional steps beyond merely monitoring the emerging terrorist threat from al-Qaeda and bin Laden. At the time, much of his militaristic rhetoric seemed to be the usual bluster of marginal, disaffected organizations around the world. Expending resources to pursue a small group of discontented souls half a world away seemed unwise in light of other pressing global concerns, notably state supporters of terrorism such as Saddam Hussein in Iraq, Muammar Muhammad Abu Minyar al-Gaddafi in Libya, and the always unpredictable Iranian regime. By the time the U.S. intelligence community elevated the threat that Osama bin Laden and his terrorist network posed, it was too late to intervene without committing substantial intelligence and military resources.[34]

On February 22, 1998, bin Laden stepped up his anti-American campaign when he announced that he had formed the International Islamic Front for Jihad against Jews and Crusaders. The group's intentions were unambiguous, as the accompanying fatwa made clear: "To kill the Americans and their allies—civilians and military—is the individual duty for every Muslim who can do it in any country in which it is possible." The campaign that followed proved that bin Laden was far more than the passive financier the CIA had once thought.[35]

The next few years revealed the extent of al-Qaeda's commitment to the jihad. On August 7, 1998, a suicide bomber detonated a bomb at the American embassy in Nairobi, Kenya, killing 12 Americans and 201 other people, mostly Kenyans who worked in the embassy offices. Four minutes later, a bomb erupted outside the American embassy in Dar es Salaam, Tanzania, killing 11 people and wounding 85 more.[36]

In a subsequent interview, bin Laden was evasive when asked whether he had directly participated in the bombings. Nonetheless, he defended the acts. In his view, "when it becomes apparent that it would be impossible to repeal these Americans without assaulting them, even if this involved the killing of Muslims, this is permissible under Islam." In other words, the ends justify the means. Islam can be used to excuse any actions the person searching for a rationalization deems to be necessary. Filled with the zeal of the truly self-righteous, bin Laden told his interviewer, "let history be a witness that I am a criminal."[37]

Reflecting on the East Africa bombings, President Bill Clinton recalled that by 1998, "we had been following bin Laden for years." The coordinated attacks in Africa woke the American intelligence to the need for more aggressive action. "By all accounts, bin Laden was poisoned by the conviction that he was in possession of absolute truth and therefore free to play God by killing innocent people," the former president wrote in his 2004 memoirs. "Since we had been going after his organization for several years, I had known for some time that he was a formidable adversary. After the African slaughter I became intently focused on capturing or killing him and with destroying al-Qaeda."[38]

Despite the enormous resources of the United States, rooting out the formidable adversary was no simple task. A report that bin Laden would attend a meeting at the Zawhar Kili camp complex later in August convinced the president that firing Tomahawk cruise missiles into the camp presented a prime opportunity to kill the elusive terrorist. On August 20, in an operation code-named "Operation Infinite Reach," five U.S. Navy destroyer ships stationed in the Arabian Sea launched seventy five missiles at the target. The attack killed at least twenty-one Pakistani jihadist volunteers and wounded dozens more. Bin Laden was not killed or injured. In fact, his ability to elude the U.S. attack transformed him into a folk hero among many in the Arab world who were aggrieved by the West. "Osama" became a common name for sons born in Pakistan in the ensuing years. By elevating bin Laden's stature with the failed attack, the U.S. had ensured that its nemesis was a bona fide celebrity.[39]

Days later, Clinton signed a Memorandum of Notification (MON), the first of several, authorizing the CIA to target bin Laden by using tribal resources in Afghanistan to capture or kill the fugitive. As the months passed, however, confusion reigned as to whether he should be killed or captured. For all its efforts to that point, the U.S. government had yet to appreciate how dangerous the adversary might become. The legend of Osama bin Laden grew as reports filtered in that he had escaped from ambushes time and again. It seemed almost as if the CIA were chasing a ghost. Reports of bin Laden sightings in the region spread far and wide, yet somehow he lived to fight another day. On several occasions, American intelligence authorities received reports of bin Laden's whereabouts, but in each instance no one was willing to risk an attack without verifiable evidence.[40]

Students of American foreign policy and the nation's security apparatus continue to debate how seriously the Clinton administration pursued al-Qaeda. At decade's end, the organization and its leader remained a worrisome problem for intelligence operatives, but the extent of the threat was a great unknown. In October 2000, the United States learned additional facts about the al-Qaeda agenda.[41]

Bin Laden and his associates had debated the possibility of attacking an American ship somewhere in the Middle East. Early discussions focused on a commercial vessel such as an oil tanker, but bin Laden understood the importance of symbolism. Nothing would demonstrate al-Qaeda's power and the vulnerability of the mighty United States as much as targeting an American naval vessel. After reviewing data on ships entering the port of Aden in the nation of Yemen, bin Laden decided on an American destroyer as his target.

On October 12, 2000, the USS *Cole* stopped to refuel in Aden. Two Arab men in a skiff approached the destroyer as they smiled and waved at the American sailors. In an instant, the small craft, loaded with explosives, erupted into a huge fireball, tearing a forty-foot gash in the side of the *Cole*, killing seventeen sailors and wounding more than forty. The desperate efforts of the crew barely saved the ship from sinking. Anticipating a violent backlash, al-Qaeda operatives melted into the hinterlands of Afghanistan. To the terrorists' astonishment, the U.S. military did not respond. The success of the attack on the USS *Cole* emboldened bin Laden. The giant Satan was strong, but also afraid to wield power aggressively. The episode also underscored the effectiveness of suicide bombers.[42]

Although it appeared to bin Laden and his confederates that the United States took no action in the wake of the *Cole* assault, behind the scenes military intelligence officers weighed their options. All evidence strongly indicated that bin Laden was behind the incident, but definitive evidence was not forthcoming. U.S. discussions with the Yemeni government, although not overtly hostile, proceeded in fits and starts. The tension was undeniable. Investigators sought permission to carry weapons and zealously pursue leads inside the country, but Yemeni officials balked at allowing a foreign government to exercise such aggressive authority inside their country. A frustrated President Clinton chided his advisers when they could not supply him with the credible information he felt he needed to pursue military operations against al-Qaeda. The U.S. government had asked the Taliban in Afghanistan to turn over bin Laden in the past, but after this latest episode, Clinton did not wish to reiterate the request without solid evidence. In his opinion, if he continued to push the Taliban and the group refused to cooperate, the United States would have to respond with force or risk appearing to be a paper tiger.[43]

Even before the *Cole* attack, al-Qaeda had considered a host of bold, ambitious operations. Khalid Sheikh Mohammed began planning attacks inside the United States after he witnessed the partial success of the 1993 episode. He was ready to take the next step, especially after the attack on the *Cole* suggested that the Americans were hesitant to retaliate. As he carefully worked through the logistics, the sheikh recognized that planting explosive devices was complicated and difficult to execute in urban areas where many impediments existed and alert eyewitnesses might spoil the plot before it could be implemented.[44]

He and Ramzi Yousef mulled over the possibility of blowing up commercial airliners in midflight on several occasions, most notably in January 1995. Although earlier plots had failed to come to fruition, the two men still considered the use of airplanes to be a viable plan. Because the airplanes contained large numbers of passengers, a great deal of jet fuel, and could be seized with little sophisticated weaponry, they offered an ideal method of killing multitudes of innocent people in a relatively short time.[45]

When Sheikh Mohammed first outlined his plan to the al Qaeda leadership during the spring of 1999, Osama bin Laden expressed skepticism. The original scheme was to coordinate attacks on ten separate airplanes, striking targets in Washington, D.C.; New York City; and California. Sheikh Mohammed was especially interested in striking at FBI and CIA headquarters. One version of the plot called for the sheikh to fly the tenth plane himself. He would land the aircraft at a U.S. airport, slaughter all the male passengers on board, and deliver an impassioned speech criticizing American support for Israel and oppressive anti-Arab regimes around the world.[46]

Although bin Laden initially balked at the concept, Sheikh Mohammed was not ready to abandon the idea. He refined the plan, simplifying the operational logistics. Eventually bin Laden came to appreciate the virtue of the "planes" concept. After he approved the operation, the al-Qaeda leader actively participated in drawing up a list of potential targets. Sheikh Mohammed later recalled that bin Laden was interested in destroying the White House and the Pentagon. Sheikh Mohammed favored striking at the World Trade Center. Everyone agreed that the U.S. Capitol building would be an ideal target. With the overall strategy in place, the conspirators focused on developing the tactics necessary to carry out the scheme.[47]

Two eager al-Qaeda members, Khalid al Mihdhar and Nawaf al Hazmi, signed on to participate in the early days, as did Walid Muhammad Salih bin Roshayed bin Attash, a Saudi-born bin Laden associate suspected of masterminding the *Cole* attack. Using the nom de guerre "Khallad," bin Attash and another associate, Abu Bara al Yemeni, initially intended to pilot the planes along with the other suicide bombers. When the two would-be operatives encountered difficulties obtaining travel visas, Sheikh

Mohammed decided to divide the "planes" operations into two components. The first phase would involve piloting airplanes into symbolic targets
inside the United States. The next phase would involve hijacking airplanes
traveling from East Asia over the Pacific Ocean to the United States and
blowing them up in midair, just as the sheikh had contemplated back
in 1995. Khallad and Abu Bara al Yemeni would take part in phase two,
thereby avoiding problems entering the United States in time for phase
one. Unlike Mihdhar and Hazmi, the phase-two suicide bombers would
not need flight training because their mission was to detonate an explosive
device while the jet was in the air.[48]

The four terrorists trained at al-Qaeda's Mes Aynak training camp in Afghanistan. Each man, excluding Mihdhar, immersed himself in the details
involved in navigating through American life and culture by reading a telephone book, surfing the Internet, making travel arrangements, and using
code words in routine communications to elude detection. They also played
video games that simulated airline flights and familiarized themselves with
aircraft models and principles of airplane transportation. Departing for
various destinations throughout Europe and Asia, the first group readied
for the arduous mission ahead. The operatives were directed to enter the
United States and complete lessons at flight training schools in preparation
for the planes operation. Sheikh Mohammed had asked bin Laden to unleash both phases one and two simultaneously to maximize the psychological effect, but by the spring of 2000, the al-Qaeda leader had canceled the
plan to explode the flights in midair. The logistics simply were too daunting.
Concentrating on the mission inside the United States would be al-Qaeda's
major priority.[49]

As part of the planning, al-Qaeda recruited another team of suicide terrorists. Members of the second team hailed from four different countries—
Egypt, the United Arab Emirates, Lebanon, and Yemen. The men knew
each other because they had lived and studied together as part of a cell in
Hamburg, Germany. Initially, the young men sought to undertake a mission
in Chechnya, but bin Laden had different plans. The men—Mohammed
Atta, Ramzi Binalshibh, Marwan al Shehhi, and Ziad Jarrah—would form
the nucleus of the terrorist leadership for the September 11, 2001, attacks.[50]

Mohammed Atta, an Egyptian-born Islamic fundamentalist, was thirty-
three years old in 2001, the product of a well-to-do family. Atta enjoyed
many privileges as a boy and excelled in his engineering studies at Cairo
University and later a graduate program in urban planning at the Technical
University of Hamburg, Germany. His introverted personality and his strict
Islamic practices were off-putting to many acquaintances. They described

the strange young man as alienated, depressed, and seething with hostility. He was especially upset with the Egyptian government for draconian measures undertaken to limit the power and influence of the Muslim Brotherhood, a radical Islamic group devoted to using the Koran, the Muslim holy book, as the basis for an Islamic government.[51]

Atta undertook a holy pilgrimage to Mecca during the fall of 1995. Afterward, his movements became difficult to track. His participation in formal graduate studies became spotty and inconsistent although he apparently attended classes at a Turkish mosque where he immersed himself in the tenets of radical Islam. Atta also fell in with other like-minded young men who discussed their rage at "the West" and what they believed to be a holy war aimed against Islam. He may have attended al-Qaeda training camps in Afghanistan and met Osama bin Laden late in 1999 or sometime in early 2000, although investigators continue to debate the timing of the encounter, or if it ever occurred.

The standard version of the story has it that Atta attended a preliminary training course at the Khaldan camp in November 1999 and first learned of the "planes" scheme. The plan was ingenious and immediately appealed to the alienated young man. It could be implemented with logistical simplicity because the operatives need not smuggle explosives or other complicated destructive devices onto the planes; the planes themselves would serve as the weapons. The attackers did not have to construct an elaborate escape plan because no escape was contemplated or necessary. All that was needed were dedicated warriors in the holy war who could wield a weapon deadly enough to take over the airplane controls and conversant enough with the mechanics of flying to pilot the beast into an appropriate target.[52]

Al-Qaeda found no lack of willing martyrs for the cause, but many were unschooled in western ways and lacked knowledge of airplanes. This is where Mohammed Atta proved to be a valuable addition to the team. He knew a great deal of the West from his days living in Hamburg. Moreover, he knew how to acquire the requisite skills to set the scheme into motion. By the spring of 2000, Atta was preparing to launch the attack. On March 22, 2000, he sent an e-mail to a flight school in Lakeland, Florida, asking if "a small group of young men from different Arab countries" could study flying "to start training for the career of airline professional pilots." He forwarded a similar message to between fifty and sixty flight schools throughout the United States.[53]

If not as accomplished as Atta, the other members of the new team nonetheless shared his zeal for the suicide mission. Ramzi Binalshibh was born in Yemen in 1972. As far as anyone recalls, his childhood was uneventful. He worked for the International Bank of Yemen before moving to Germany. There, he applied for asylum under a false name. When his application was denied, Binalshibh returned to Yemen. Eventually returning to Germany as a student, he soon flunked out of school. He met Mohammed Atta around 1995, and the two men became fast friends. Binalshibh embraced extremist views, occasionally denouncing the "Jewish world conspiracy" and professing his willingness to die during the jihad. For all of these outwardly radical sentiments, people who knew Binalshibh in Hamburg remembered him as polite, easygoing, and far more likable than the caustic Atta.[54]

Marwan al Shehhi was the youngest of the new al-Qaeda recruits. Born in the United Arab Emirates in 1978, Shehhi spent a year in the military after he completed high school. He turned up in Germany in 1996, shortly before his eighteenth birthday. Although he prayed frequently and impressed those who knew him as deeply religious, he also came across as "a regular guy" who wore western clothes and enjoyed a normal social life. It is unclear how he first met Binalshibh and Atta, but by April 1998 the three men were living together in Hamburg. Presumably at this point Shehhi came under the influence of his older and more radical associates and turned his back on his earlier, carefree lifestyle.[55]

Ziad Jarrah seemed an unlikely convert to radical Islam. Born into an affluent family in Lebanon in 1975, he moved to northeastern Germany at the age of twenty to attend junior college. He was an outgoing, convivial young man known for his ability to sniff out desirable discos and beach parties to attend with his friends. Jarrah originally intended to study dentistry, but by September 1997, he had changed course. He moved to Hamburg and began studying aircraft engineering. Whether he pursued this course of study and therefore became important to the other al-Qaeda operatives or embraced the radical cause and switched his course of study afterward is not clear. Aysel Senguen, the daughter of Turkish immigrants and Jarrah's girlfriend during his years in Germany, saw a change in the young man in any case. Jarrah had become increasingly religious. He and Aysel frequently fought, broke up, and reconciled. He grew a full beard, began criticizing her provocative dress, and even intimated that he was preparing to die for Allah in a mighty jihad.[56]

The exact timing is not altogether clear, but sometime late in 1999, Atta, Binalshibh, Shehhi, and Jarrah focused on attacking the United States. Visits to Afghanistan clarified the operational mission. They would enroll in flight schools and learn to pilot airliners. On a prearranged day, accompanied by a team of four other men—"muscle" hijackers who would keep passengers and the crew under control—the pilots would assume command of commercial passenger planes and, in a coordinated assault, deliberately crash the jets into symbolic targets.[57]

Khalid al Mihdhar and Nawaf al Hazmi arrived in the United States through California sometime in January 2000. The nature of their movements and their contacts during the first weeks remains unknown; they apparently hoped to learn English and complete flying lessons. They lived in the Los Angeles area before moving to San Diego. Investigators later surmised that their plans were to reach out to members of the dissident Muslim community. If the ultimate goal was to recruit al-Qaeda sleeper cells, they apparently did not succeed.[58]

Mihdhar and Hazmi sought out flight schools near San Diego. Apparently possessing neither the patience nor aptitude for the lessons, by May 2000 the two men had flunked out of the program. Mihdhar left the United States and traveled to Yemen. He would eventually return to take part in the September 11 assaults. In the meantime, Saudi-born Hani Hanjour, the only operative to have visited the United States previously, arrived and made contact with Hazmi.[59]

The Hamburg terrorists began arriving in mid-2000. Mohammed Atta entered the United States on June 3, 2000, through Newark International Airport, although at least one eyewitness later claimed to have met him in the country prior to that date. He is known to have visited at least one flight school, in Norman, Oklahoma, before enrolling in a program with Huffman Aviation in Venice, Florida. Marwan al-Shehhi arrived on May 29 and soon reconnected with Atta. They trained rigorously throughout July. Atta earned his private pilot license in September 2000. They later switched to the Jones Aviation School in Sarasota before returning to Huffman. By the end of the year, Atta had earned his instrument rating and commercial pilot's license. Ziad Jarrah earned a pilot's license at the Florida Flight Training Center in Venice.[60]

While the terrorists who would pilot the airplanes on September 11 patiently acquired the requisite skills, al-Qaeda leaders recruited the muscle hijackers who would protect the pilots until they could murder the passengers and crew. The plan originally was to include twenty men—four teams of five each—but one spot was never filled. Some reports later suggested that Ramzi Binalshibh of Yemen was the original twentieth man. For whatever reasons, he did not join his comrades in arms. Zacarias Moussaoui, a French citizen, may have been a replacement, but he was arrested for an immigration violation in August 2001 and was therefore unavailable at the time of the murders. Moussaoui undoubtedly was involved in the conspiracy, but the precise nature of his role remains a point of contention.[61]

Mohammed Atta traveled to Spain in July 2001 to meet with Ramzi Binalshibh and finalize the plot. Binalshibh had met with bin Laden and carried final instructions. The conspirators confirmed the targets—the Twin Towers, the Pentagon, and either the U.S. Capitol Building or the White House. Bin Laden preferred the White House, but Atta was worried that it was a more difficult target than the Capitol. The two men also discussed the steps the hijackers would take to seize control of the airplanes.[62]

Binalshibh told Atta that bin Laden was anxious to initiate the plan as soon as possible. The al-Qaeda leader was worried that the presence of so many terrorists in the country at one time would trigger scrutiny from U.S. authorities. Atta replied that he had not yet selected a date. He promised to alert Binalshibh a week before the attack so that Binalshibh could travel to Afghanistan and inform bin Laden personally.[63]

The plan was in its final stages during the early summer of 2001. Atta, Shehhi, and Jarrah flew on cross-country flights to observe the habits of airline crews. Jarrah took additional flying lessons to familiarize himself with the Hudson Corridor, a low-altitude route that passes along the Hudson River adjacent to New York landmarks such as the World Trade Center. The fourth pilot, Hanjour, took additional flying lessons on a route from Fairfield, New Jersey, to Gaithersburg, Maryland, so he could become acclimated to the area around Washington, D.C. Atta and Shehhi handled logistics as the last group of terrorists filtered into the country. Most of the conspirators settled in Florida.[64]

Sometime during the third week of August, Atta picked the date. The men purchased tickets on flights that departed at approximately the same time on the morning of September 11. As Atta coordinated with the pilots, the musclemen bought knives to use during the cockpit seizure. As the target date drew closer, al-Qaeda leaders admonished the suicide attackers not to contact family members directly for fear that the operation might be leaked, although at least a few disregarded instructions. Anticipating an angry backlash from the U.S. government, al-Qaeda leaders throughout Europe and Asia made plans to travel to Afghanistan.[65]

SEPTEMBER 11, 2001: IN THE AIR

September 11 was a mild, cloudless day in the northeastern United States. Onlookers recalled the stunningly blue sky that served as a backdrop to the horrific events. Checking in for a predawn flight from Portland, Maine, to Boston, Massachusetts, Mohammed Atta traveled that morning with his colleague and fellow terrorist Abdul Aziz al Omari. Their 6:00 a.m. flight was uneventful. During his initial check-in, Atta was selected by the Computer Assisted Passenger Prescreening System (CAPPS) for additional screening. The system only required security personnel to ensure that Atta was on board his flight before his checked luggage was loaded onto the plane. Three of his fellow hijackers later were selected for additional screening in Boston, but, as with Atta, the result was a cursory review of their checked bags.[66]

American Flight 11 departed from Boston bound for Los Angeles at 7:59 a.m. Captain John Ogonowski and First Officer Thomas McCuinness were at the controls of the Boeing 767. Nine flight attendants and eighty-one passengers, including the five terrorists, were on board. Within fifteen minutes of departure, American 11 ascended to 26,000 feet on its way to a cruising altitude of 29,000 feet. It would have been standard procedure for the captain to turn off the "Fasten Seatbelt" sign indicating that the passengers could leave their seats and the flight attendants should initiate cabin service. Communications and flight profile data indicated that everything was normal.

Shortly thereafter, something went wrong with American Flight 11. The last routine communication with ground control consisted of the flight crew's acknowledgment that they had received navigational instructions from the Federal Aviation Administration's (FAA's) air traffic control (ATC) center in Boston. Sixteen seconds after that acknowledgment, ATC instructed the pilot to climb to 35,000 feet. When air traffic controllers received no further acknowledgments, they recognized that Flight 11 was in trouble. They would receive no further communications from the pilot or first officer. Based on this information, investigators believe that American Airlines Flight 11 was hijacked at 8:14 a.m. or within minutes of that time.

Most credible information about what happened on Flight 11 following the hijacking came from two flight attendants in the coach cabin, Betty Ong and Madeline "Amy" Sweeney. Ong initiated contact by using an AT&T Airfone to call the American Airlines Southeastern Reservations Office in Cary, North Carolina, to report an emergency. Strictly speaking, Ong had violated airline protocol. Flight attendants are trained to communicate only with the cockpit crew during a hijacking. In this case, she explained that the hijackers had stabbed two flight attendants. Investigators have suggested that Wail al Shehri and Waleed al Shehri, who were seated in the second row of the first-class section of the airplane, probably carried out this part of the attack.

"The cockpit is not answering," Ong reported at 8:19 a.m. "Somebody's stabbed in business class—and I think there's Mace—that we can't breathe—I don't know; I think we're getting hijacked." Despite the urgency of the situation, everyone at American Airlines marveled at Ong's calm, professional demeanor. Her emergency call lasted approximately twenty-five minutes as she described the events unfolding on the airplane.

Within two minutes of receiving Ong's phone call, American Airlines personnel contacted their operations center in Fort Worth, Texas. Two minutes after that, the airline dispatcher repeatedly attempted to contact the flight crew. At 8:29, an American Airlines representative called the FAA ATC center in Boston. By that time, air traffic controllers were aware of the hijacking.

The Boston air traffic control center had learned of the hijacking at 8:25 when the terrorists apparently keyed the microphone inadvertently. As a result of this serendipitous event, air traffic controllers overheard a hijacker trying to address the passengers over the airplane intercom. "Nobody move," the man said. "Everything will be okay. If you try to make any moves, you'll endanger yourself and the airplane. Just stay quiet." Air traffic controllers heard the message while passengers and flight attendant Betty Ong did not. Apparently, the hijackers did not understand how to operate the radio communication system correctly. They accidentally broadcast the message meant for the passengers on the air traffic control channel instead of using the airplane's public address system.

As Betty Ong spoke with American Airlines employees, her fellow flight attendant, Amy Sweeney, telephoned the American Airlines Flight Services Office in Boston. After being disconnected, Sweeney called back and spoke with her manager, Michael Woodward. She confirmed much of what Betty Ong had already told ground personnel, although Sweeney added details. She explained that one flight attendant was seriously hurt in the stabbing while another flight attendant's wounds were minor. Sweeney believed the hijackers had taken a bomb into the cockpit. Both Ong and Sweeney relayed information about the hijackers' seat numbers. Sweeney told Michael Woodward she believed the hijackers were of Middle Eastern descent. She said that one man spoke little English but another man seemed well versed in the language.

At 8:26 and again at 8:38, Betty Ong reported that the airplane was "flying erratically." Air traffic controllers tracking the flight noticed that it had turned south, away from the initial flight path. During the 8:38 report, Ong explained that the airplane was descending rapidly.

Incredibly, as late as 8:41 a.m., some passengers in the coach section did not realize the airplane had been hijacked. They were under the impression that the aircraft had been diverted to another location because of a routine medical emergency in the first class section. Despite the "erratic" maneuvers, they remained calm.

Betty Ong lost telephone contact at 8:44. Amy Sweeney stayed on the line. Her last report to Woodward indicated that she knew the airplane was in trouble. "Something is wrong. We are in a rapid descent," she reported. "We are all over the place." When Woodward asked if she could look out the window and see where the airplane was flying, Sweeney's response was chilling. "We are flying too low. We are flying very, very low. We are flying way too low." Within a few seconds, she said, "Oh my God, we are way too low." The phone line went dead.

Fewer than three minutes later, at 8:46:40, American Airlines Flight 11 collided with the North Tower of the World Trade Center. Everyone on board died instantly along with an unknown number of persons inside the building.[67]

Shortly after Atta and his team boarded American Flight 11, Marwan al Shehhi and his colleagues Fayez Banihammad, Mohand al Sheri, Ahmed al Ghamdi, and Hamza al Ghamdi boarded United Airlines Flight 175 in a different terminal at Boston's Logan Airport. The flight was slated to fly to Los Angeles. A United Airlines ticket agent later recalled that the men seemed unaccustomed to airline travel. They were confused when asked to respond to the standard security questions. Accordingly, the hijackers had to be prompted for the appropriate response. In light of subsequent events, the utility of posing the questions in the first place was called into question.

The flight was scheduled to depart at 8:00 a.m. with Captain Victor Saracini at the helm. He was assisted by First Officer Michael Horrocks and seven flight attendants. Fifty-six passengers came on board.

As was the case with American Airlines Flight 11, United Flight 175 started as a routine cross-country trip. The airplane pushed back from the gate at 7:58 a.m. and took off sixteen minutes later. At 8:33, United Flight 175 reached its cruising altitude of 31,000 feet. The flight attendants began serving food and beverages to the passengers.

United 175 departed from Logan Airport at approximately the same time the hijackers took control of American Airlines Flight 11. Captain Sarachini and First Officer Horrocks reported overhearing a "suspicious transmission" from another airplane—investigators subsequently learned that the transmissions emanated from American Flight 11—at 8:42 a.m. It was the crew's last communication with air traffic control. Sometime between that transmission and 8:46 a.m., the hijackers seized United Flight 175. Passengers and a flight attendant in the rear of the plane placed phone calls to report that the terrorists had brandished knives to subdue the crew. Another passenger claimed the attackers used mace and threatened to detonate a bomb if anyone interfered. The attackers apparently stabbed the flight crew, killing both pilots.

For ground technicians, the first indication that the flight was unusual came at 8:47 when the airplane changed beacon codes twice in a minute. Four minutes later, the plane diverted from its assigned altitude. Air traffic controllers frantically tried to contact the pilots, but to no avail. United Flight 175 would not respond.

Lee Hanson of Easton, Connecticut, later reported that his son, Peter, a passenger on the flight, called at 8:52 a.m. Peter, a thirty-two-year-old software salesman from Massachusetts, was headed to Disneyland with his new wife, Sue, and their two-and-a-half-year-old daughter, Christine, before a planned visit to Sue's parents.

"I think they've taken over the cockpit," Peter told his worried father. "An attendant has been stabbed—and someone else up front may have been killed. The plane is making strange moves. Call United Airlines—tell them it's Flight 175, Boston to L.A." When the call ended, Lee Hanson alerted the Easton Police Department.

At 8:58 a.m., United Airlines Flight 175 turned toward New York City and a date with history.

No one either on the ground or inside the airplane knew what was happening. Although American Flight 11 had already collided with the North Tower of the World Trade Center when United 175 turned toward New York, the audacity of a coordinated series of terrorist attacks was not yet understood. Air traffic controllers did not recognize a pattern.

A minute after the airplane turned toward the city, passenger Brian David Sweeney called his wife. When she did not answer, he left a voice message and dialed his mother's number. Louise Sweeney reported that her son called, told her the flight had been hijacked, and the passengers were sensing something was terribly wrong. They were planning to storm the cockpit and forcibly thwart the hijackers.

In the meantime, Peter Hanson called his father a second time. "It's getting bad, Dad," he said. He repeated information about a flight attendant being stabbed. Whoever was at the controls was jerking the plane so much that passengers were vomiting. "I think they intend to go to Chicago or someplace and fly into a building," he said, although he did not explain why he had reached this conclusion. "Don't worry, Dad—if it happens, it'll be very fast." Lee Hanson heard a woman scream and his son's final comment—"My God, my God!"—before the call ended.

Louise Sweeney and Lee Hanson switched on their televisions in time to witness their children and other passengers and crew on board United

United Airlines Flight 175 moments before it crashed into the South Tower of the World Trade Center on September 11, 2001. Courtesy of Corbis.

Airlines Flight 175 slam into the South Tower of the World Trade Center. It was 9:03:11 a.m., and everyone on board died instantly. An unknown number of people inside the building perished in that moment as well.[68]

A few minutes after the first two groups of suicide bombers boarded their targeted flights in Boston, five men stepped onto American Airlines Flight 77 at Washington Dulles International Airport. Three of the five, Hani Hanjour, Khalid al Mihdhar, and Majed Moqed, were selected for CAPPS screening. Two brothers, Nawaf al Hazmi and Salem al Hazmi, attracted attention from a customer service representative at the check-in counter because they acted suspiciously. One of the brothers did not even carry photo identification, and he understood almost no English. Despite these unusual occurrences, all five hijackers eventually boarded the airplane.

Flight 77 was scheduled to take off at 8:10 a.m. under the command of Captain Charles F. Burlingame and assisted by First Officer David Charlebois. Four flight attendants and fifty-eight passengers were on board. A minute ahead of schedule, the airplane pushed back from the gate and was airborne eleven minutes later. By 8:46, the aircraft was cruising at 35,000 feet, and nothing seemed amiss. Five minutes later, the pilots transmitted a routine message. Sometime between 8:51 and 8:54, the hijackers seized control of the flight and herded everyone to the rear. A passenger reported that the men brandished box cutters, a detail that was missing from reports of the other hijackings.

At 8:54 a.m., Flight 77 veered south, far off its anticipated course. Someone turned off the flight transponder two minutes later so air traffic controllers could not directly track the flight path. American Airlines employees and the Indianapolis Air Traffic Control Center repeatedly attempted to initiate contact, but they received no response.

Alerted that the airplane was off course and unresponsive, American Airlines executive vice president Gerard Arpey realized he must act swiftly. Coming on the heels of the Flight 11 hijacking, he recognized that the airplane was in danger. No one knew whether other American Airlines flights might be seized at any moment. Accordingly, Arpey ordered all flights in the Northeast to remain on the ground. After learning that two aircraft had struck the World Trade Center and a United Airlines flight was missing, American Airlines ordered all company planes to remain on the ground until further notice.

Flight 77 passengers began calling loved ones. Barbara Olson, a prominent conservative lawyer, television commentator, and author, was en route to Los Angeles to tape an episode of the popular television program *Politically Incorrect*. Between 9:16 and 9:26 a.m., she called her husband, U.S. solicitor general Theodore Olson. She calmly informed him that hijackers had seized control of the aircraft using knives and box cutters. The call abruptly ended after a minute. Olson immediately tried to contact attorney general John Ashcroft but was unsuccessful.

Not long after their initial telephone conversation, Barbara Olson called again. Her husband told her the news about the other airplanes crashing into the World Trade Center. Barbara said she could look out the window and see houses beneath the aircraft. Moments later, the call went dead. They did not speak again.

The hijackers apparently disengaged the airplane autopilot at 9:29 a.m. while Flight 77 was flying at 7,000 feet approximately thirty-eight miles west of the Pentagon. Three minutes later, Dulles Airport controllers "observed a primary radar target tracking eastbound at a high rate of speed." Airport authorities contacted the Secret Service to alert them that an aircraft might be directed toward the White House. Flight 77 eventually turned toward the Pentagon, crashing into the building at 530 miles per hour. The time was 9:37:46.[69]

United Airlines Flight 93 was the last of the four aircraft hijacked that morning. Shortly after 7:00 a.m., Saeed al Ghamdi, Ahmed al Nami, Ahmad al Haznawi, and Ziad Jarrah checked in for the flight at Newark Airport in New Jersey. Between thirty and forty-five minutes later, they boarded the flight and took their assigned seats. On each of the other hijacked flights, the terrorists had operated in five-man teams, but only four men boarded Flight 93. An immigration officer at Orlando International Airport had denied Mohamed al Kahtani, a suspected team member and "muscle hijacker," entry into the United States. U.S. officials later transported al Kahtani to the U.S. base in Guantanamo Bay, Cuba. Similarly, because Ramzi Binalshibh and Zacarias Moussaoui could not participate, the team was down a man. This lack of muscle may have facilitated a subsequent passenger revolt.[70]

The four terrorists were among a total of thirty-seven passengers listed on the manifest for United 93. The flight, bound for San Francisco, departed at 8:42 a.m., four minutes before American Airlines Flight 11 crashed into the World Trade Center's North Tower and twenty-one minutes before United Airlines Flight 175 collided with the South Tower. The presence of a four-man team and the late timing for United Flight 93 would be crucial elements in the events that followed.

Military strategists observe that timing is everything in battle, and the fate of United Airlines Flight 93 demonstrated the wisdom of this observation. The hijackers' scheme was to board flights that took off within minutes of each other. According to the published schedules, American Airlines Flight 11 was slated to depart at 7:45 a.m., United Airlines Flight 175 and United Airlines Flight 93 at 8:00 a.m., and American Airlines Flight 77 at 8:10 a.m. As soon as air traffic controllers and government officials recognized that coordinated terrorist attacks were under way, they would react and the crucial element of surprise would be lost. United Flight 93 left the ground forty-two minutes behind schedule, a delay that led to a dramatic conclusion.

Jason Dahl, a diminutive forty-three-year-old pilot with sixteen years of experience as a United Airlines pilot, was at the controls. He had agreed to fly that day so he could earn time off to celebrate his fifth wedding anniversary on September 14. The plan was to fly with his wife, Sandy, to London on September 16 in recognition of the special day. First Officer Leroy Homer Jr., a thirty-six-year-old air force veteran with extensive flight experience, joined Captain Dahl in the cockpit for the early-morning cross-country flight.[71]

It began as an ordinary trip for the pilots and five flight attendants. Although thirty-seven passengers was a smaller number than usual, nothing else seemed unusual. Unbeknownst to the passengers and crew, during the first forty-six minutes of the flight, as information about multiple hijackings filtered through airline offices and the FAA, a debate raged about who should exercise responsibility for informing flight crews of potential danger. As this bureaucratic snafu occurred, an enterprising United Airlines flight dispatcher named Ed Ballinger seized the initiative and radioed a dire message to sixteen transcontinental flights. "Beware any cockpit intrusion," he warned. "Two a/c [aircraft] hit World Trade Center." Ballinger had to reach each airplane separately; his message to Flight 93 did not transmit until 9:23 a.m.

The warning message logged into the cockpit a minute later. Two minutes after that, Captain Dahl asked for clarification: "Ed, confirm last mssg plz—Jason." Before the message could be confirmed, the hijackers struck. The next transmission came from a crew member calling a "Mayday." Traveling at 35,000 feet, United Flight 93 suddenly dropped 700 feet. Apparently the pilots were locked in a struggle with the terrorists. A second radio transmission picked up someone crying out, "Hey, get out of here—get out of here—get out of here."

At 9:32, a voice believed to be Ziad Jarrah could be heard attempting to address the passengers over the intercom. "Ladies and gentlemen," it said in broken English. "Here the captain. Please sit down; keep remaining sitting. We have a bomb on board. So, sit." The cockpit voice recorder captured a woman's voice, most likely a flight attendant held captive. She was struggling with the terrorists. Her voice eventually fell silent, suggesting that she had been incapacitated or killed. The flight turned and headed east.

Huddled toward the rear of the plane, passengers and crew began calling friends, family, and authorities with information. At least twelve people, including two crew members, called from the airplane and shared vital details about the circumstances aboard the airplane. Almost everything investigators learned about the events that transpired on United Flight 93 came from these calls. Callers learned about the other hijacked flights and the collisions with the Twin Towers.

According to eyewitnesses, the terrorists sported red bandannas and brandished knives. They claimed to possess a bomb, although no one actually saw the device. One caller said he saw a gun, but no one else reported seeing it. At least one passenger was stabbed and two bodies were on the floor, possibly the captain and the first officer, although their identities were never verified. One caller was certain that a flight attendant had been killed.

The terrorists on the first three planes had enjoyed information asymmetry. They could assure the passengers and crew that all would be well if the group cooperated. By the time the hijackers seized United Flight 93, they could no longer credibly promise that their intentions were mostly benign.

This distinction was crucial. Whereas passengers on the first three flights remained calm and relatively placid in hopes of preventing a calamity, the men and women of Flight 93 harbored no illusions. This was a suicide mission, and they would certainly perish if they did not attempt to wrest control of the flight away from their tormentors.

At 9.57 a.m., the passengers revolted. Realizing they had little to lose, they launched themselves at the terrorists. A female caller told her correspondent on the telephone, "Everyone's running up to first class. I've got to go. Bye." The cockpit recorder captured muffled sounds that apparently indicated an assault. Family members who later heard the recordings claimed to recognize the voice of a loved one.

Ziad Jarrah was probably at the controls of Flight 93. When the passenger revolt began, he rolled the airplane left and right to knock the assailants off their feet. He also instructed a co-conspirator to bar the cockpit door. As the attack intensified, Jarrah pitched the nose of the plane up and down.

After the aircraft stabilized a few seconds later, he asked, "Is that it? Shall we finish it off?" Someone responded, "No. Not yet. When they all come, we finish it off."

Within seconds, Jarrah rolled the plane again. A passenger's voice cried out, "In the cockpit. If we don't, we'll die!"

Investigators believe that United Airlines Flight 93 was headed for the U.S. Capitol Building or the White House, but with a blitz attack from passengers under way, the terrorists would never make their target. "Allah is the greatest," a hijacker exclaimed. Immediately on the heels of that statement, he asked, "Is that it? I mean, shall we put it down?"

"Yes," came the chilling reply. "Put it in, and pull it down."

Within seconds, Jarrah pulled the controls hard right, causing the plane to roll onto its back and bullet toward the earth. It slammed into the ground at 580 miles per hour in an empty field near Shanksville, Pennsylvania, at 10:03 a.m. United Flight 93 was a twenty-minute flight away from Washington, D.C., when the heroic unarmed passengers and crew forced their murderers to abandon the original plan.

United 93 became an iconic symbol of ordinary Americans who refused to go gently into that good night. Books, magazines, and a major Hollywood film would speculate on the events aboard the doomed airliner. The drama was heightened when a passenger, Todd Beamer, tried to call his wife on a GTE air phone and instead ended up talking with Lisa Jefferson, a GTE supervisor. When Jefferson told Beamer about the fate of other hijacked planes, she said he dropped the phone, leaving the line open. She overheard him talking with fellow passengers about rushing the cockpit. "Let's roll," she heard him say. The defiant refusal to cower or passively accept his fate transformed Beamer and the other Flight 93 passengers into symbols of the resilient, tenacious American spirit. President George W. Bush later repeated the comment to a joint session of Congress as he sought to inspire the citizenry in the wake of the attacks.[72]

SEPTEMBER 11, 2001: ON THE GROUND

American Airlines Flight 11 slammed into the North Tower at 8:46:40 a.m. Within minutes, news reporters took to the airwaves. "It's 8:52 here in New York," CBS News correspondent Bryant Gumbel told his viewers. "I understand that there has been a plane crash on the southern tip of Manhattan." The initial reports were chaotic and confusing, but "we understand that a plane has crashed into the World Trade Center. We don't know any more than that. We don't know if it was a commercial aircraft. We don't know if it was a private aircraft." CBS News producers had found eyewitnesses who described what they had seen, but their accounts conflicted. Eleven minutes after Gumbel started his broadcast, United Flight 175 crashed into the South Tower, and it quickly became clear that these were not accidents.[73]

One hundred and two minutes after American Flight 11 crashed into the North Tower, the building collapsed to the ground. During those minutes, a human drama unfolded that will not be forgotten. It all happened so fast, and the scene was unimaginable before that day. The first impact was startling and inexplicable, but the true horror of September 11 became unequivocally clear seventeen minutes after the initial impact with the North Tower, when United Airlines Flight 175 struck the South Tower. Although it was damaged second, the South Tower imploded first, collapsing on its foundation at 9:59 a.m. after burning for fifty-six minutes in a fire caused by the impact. Twenty-nine minutes after the South Tower fell, the North Tower crumbled, sending heavy debris onto the nearby 7 World Trade Center, which eventually collapsed at 5:20 p.m. that same day. Some 2,973 people died as a result of these horrific events.[74]

When American Flight 11 struck the North Tower, the resultant explosion cut through floors 93 to 99, immediately killing untold numbers of people. All three stairwells suffered severe damage. A fireball of jet fuel blew into several floors, including the seventy-seventh, the twenty-second, the West Street lobby, and B4, four stories below ground, as well as through at least one bank of elevators. Thick black smoke poured out of the upper floors and drifted over to the South Tower next door. Anyone inside the North Tower on floors 100 to 110 was trapped.[75]

Security personnel had developed procedures for emergencies that occurred inside high-rise buildings. Persons inside the building were expected to contact authorities via the 911 telephone system and wait in their offices for further instructions delivered through the building public address system. This plan was adequate to meet the needs of occupants under reasonably foreseeable circumstances, but a large airliner filled with jet fuel slamming into the building was not reasonably foreseeable. The New York City 911 emergency telephone system was inundated with calls from eyewitnesses as well as people inside the North Tower. Callers trapped on the upper floors asked whether they should stay where they were, try to descend past the damaged stairwells, or head to the roof for a helicopter rescue. The 911 operators were unaware of the details of the attack, and they did not know that attempting a rooftop rescue was impossible owing to the lack of a suitable landing strip, the presence of blinding smoke billowing from the fire, and the fact that the doors leading to the roof were locked.[76]

Responding to multiple calls for assistance, the Fire Department of New York (FDNY) mobilized within seconds of the initial plane crash. By 9:00 a.m., 235 firefighters—twenty-one engine companies, nine ladder companies, four elite rescue teams, two elite squad companies, a hazardous materials (HazMat) team, and support staff—were en route or on the scene. In fact, during the seventeen minutes between the North Tower impact and the South Tower impact, New York City and the Port Authority of New York and New Jersey organized the largest rescue operation in the city's long history.[77]

Despite the impressive response time, the North Tower was a scene of enormous chaos. First responders struggled to understand the magnitude of the damage and determine the scope of the operation. Firefighters and rescue personnel encountered badly burned victims of the initial explosion as well as persons injured by debris that continued to fall from the floors above. A fire chief on the scene recalled that "we determined, very early on, that this was going to be strictly a rescue mission. We were going to vacate the building, get everybody out, and then we were going to get out." The assessment was based on several faulty assumptions. First, it was too soon to tell the nature and extent of the damage to the North Tower. It was inconceivable to most people that the building would collapse in fewer than two hours. In addition, no one could know that another jet was on its way toward the second tower of the World Trade Center and would significantly increase the complexity of rescue efforts. Finally, the realization that terrorists had deliberately murdered thousands of innocent people ensured that federal, state, and local authorities must consider the possibility of subsequent attacks even as they responded to the initial disaster.[78]

While first responders grappled with the challenges involved with handling the North Tower catastrophe, United Airlines Flight 175 appeared in the skies over Manhattan. Few people had witnessed American Airlines Flight 11 slam into the North Tower, but multiple camera crews and onlookers were watching as Flight 175 approached. While horrified onlookers helplessly watched, the airplane hit the South Tower between the seventy-seventh and eighty-fifth floors. As with the North Tower, most people unlucky enough to occupy the floors directly in the path of the jetliner were killed on impact or died shortly thereafter.[79]

Within minutes, survivors attempted to descend past portions of the damaged building, although in some cases occupants chose to wait for emergency responders to find them rather than venture into the smoky hallways. Most people knew that the explosions were not ordinary emergencies. Something unprecedented had happened, although the nature of the event was murky. Even if people inside the buildings did not fully comprehend that terrorism had triggered the horror, they knew their experience was unprecedented.[80]

Faced with an undeniable act of terrorism and multiple problems evacuating the buildings, FDNY and other emergency personnel huddled together to decide on a plan of action. Among the largest problems was the lack of a single communications network. "One of the most critical things in a major operation like this is to have information," a chief on the scene later explained. "We didn't have a lot of information coming in. We didn't receive any reports of what was seen from the [NYPD] helicopters. It was impossible to know how much damage was done on the upper floors, whether the stairwells were intact or not." Another chief agreed. "People watching on TV certainly had more knowledge of what was happening a hundred floors above us than we did in the lobby."[81]

At 9:07 a.m., fire companies gathered in Stairwell B of the North Tower with one hundred pounds of rescue equipment assigned to each fireman. They carried heavy protective clothing, tools, hoses, and self-contained breathing apparatuses. As the rescuers marched up the stairs, they encountered a stream of exhausted, frightened men and women descending from the upper floors. Survivors later testified that the sight of firemen climbing up to rescue wounded and trapped occupants calmed the people who saw them.[82]

Rescue personnel who were not occupied inside the North Tower assembled at the base of the South Tower. Commanders on the scene were concerned that they lacked the requisite personnel to mount a successful rescue operation because so many first responders were already working inside the North Tower. At 9:37 a.m., a call went out to send additional firefighters to the staging area. No one knew that the building was twenty-two minutes away from collapsing.[83]

The first recorded FDNY fatality of the morning occurred at 9:30 a.m. when a body falling from the South Tower landed on a fireman near the intersection of West and Liberty streets. No one was certain if the person had jumped from the building to avoid the fire or had fallen. Additional bodies landed in coming minutes, perhaps two hundred in all. An iconic photograph known as "the falling man" captured the horror of people raining from the sky. A man seemed to be falling to earth in a straight line, head first, although in reality he was tumbling through the air. Was he defiant in his last moments on earth? Was he frightened, resolute, disconsolate?[84]

The horror continued unabated. When the South Tower crumbled at 9:58:59, all people inside the building perished in seconds. It was as though an accordion folded in on itself. A top floor gave way and cascaded onto the floors below it, seemingly picking up speed as gravity dragged the entire structure to the ground. People unfortunate enough to be standing in the concourse, at the Marriott, and on neighboring streets died as well. Eyewitnesses inside the North Tower reported hearing a terrible roar as the South Tower disappeared from sight. A thick coat of dust and debris blanketed everything in the vicinity. If someone was close enough to a window, he or she could see the South Tower fold in on itself. For persons situated in the building interior, the source of the noise was unclear, but it sounded as if a freight train was charging through the neighborhood.[85]

The significance of the demolished building was not lost on first responders. FDNY officials issued the order to evacuate the North Tower within minutes of the South Tower collapse. The unthinkable had suddenly become more than thinkable; it had become probable. If one building could fold in on itself, the other building might follow suit. Owing to communications problems, some firefighters inside the building did not hear the order. Even those who heard the order and complied did not understand the reasons for evacuation. Several surviving first responders remarked that they would have moved with greater dispatch if they had been aware that the South Tower had collapsed. As it was, numerous firemen stopped to assist injured civilians or attend to the needs of frightened men and women as they made their way to the ground floor. Their humanity was noble and laudatory, but they lost precious time in evacuating the doomed structure.[86]

The North Tower collapsed at 10:28:25, killing many high-ranking officials, including the FDNY chief of department, the Port Authority Police Department superintendent, and numerous senior staff in the FDNY and police departments. Most people inside the building died as well, although, remarkably, twelve firefighters, one Port Authority police officer, and three civilians descending Stairwell B survived the collapse. When investigators subsequently tallied the final results, the FDNY had lost 343 people in both buildings while the Port Authority had lost 37 people and the New York Police Department had lost 23 people. It was the most costly day in New York history in terms of blood and treasure.[87]

Even as the drama unfolded in New York City that morning, the terrorists had not finished their assault on the American Leviathan. Two hundred and thirty miles to the south, at 9:37 a.m., American Airlines Flight 77 plowed into the west wall of the U.S. Defense Department's headquarters building, the Pentagon, located in Arlington County, Virginia, just outside of Washington, D.C. The impact killed all sixty-nine people on board the plane, including the terrorists, as well as seventy civilians and fifty-five military service members inside the Pentagon. In addition, 106 people suffered serious injuries. The Arlington County Fire Department served as the incident commander owing to the location of the building, but the Metropolitan Washington Airports Authority; the Ronald Reagan Washington National Airport Fire Department; the Fort Myer Fire Department; the Virginia State Police; the Virginia Department of Emergency Management; the FBI; the Federal Emergency Management Agency (FEMA); a National Medical Response Team; the Bureau of Alcohol, Tobacco and Firearms (ATF); and military personnel from surrounding areas also assisted.[88]

On any other day, the attack on the Pentagon would have captured major headlines and ricocheted around the world as front-page news. Because it lacked the drama and body count of the Twin Towers in New York, however, the story of the assault on the nation's symbol of military dominance generally receives short shrift in accounts of September 11, including this one. Few civilians were involved, the emergency response was well coordinated, a large number of trained emergency response personnel were readily available, and tall buildings with thousands of people trapped inside were absent; therefore, the attack lacked the pathos of the scene unfolding to the north. This assessment does not minimize the horrific events at the Pentagon. Rather, it underscores the professionalism of the emergency response and the comparatively small number of casualties.[89]

First responders were on the scene four minutes after the collision. At 9:55 a.m., the incident commander, recognizing that a partial collapse of the building could occur at any time, ordered a full evacuation of the area around the command post. When the collapse occurred two minutes later, no first responder was harmed. Although personnel on the scene experienced some of the same communications and coordination challenges that

The scene at the Pentagon following the September 11, 2001, terrorist attacks. Courtesy of the Library of Congress.

emergency responders experienced in New York, they were able to overcome the problems without the loss of life that occurred in the high-rise buildings.[90]

As first responders struggled to save lives in the Twin Towers and at the Pentagon, the last hijacked aircraft, United Flight 93, crashed into a reclaimed strip mine in Somerset County, near Shanksville, Pennsylvania. The time was 10:03:11 a.m. The explosion left a crater between eight and ten feet deep and thirty to fifty feet wide. Everyone on board died. Because the airplane came apart and the victims were ripped to pieces by the crash, it took weeks for investigators to identify remnants of the wreckage as well as the bodies of the passengers and crew. No one on the ground was killed or injured.[91]

Few people were present near the field to witness the crash, although one man, Eric Peterson, happened to look up as Flight 93 passed overhead. "It was low enough I thought you could probably count the rivets," he recalled later. "You could see more of the roof of the plane than you could the belly. It was on its side. There was a great explosion and you could see the flames. It was a massive, massive explosion—flames and then smoke and then a massive, massive mushroom cloud."[92]

Several people heard the collision. Val McClatchey remembered watching television coverage of the other attacks at the same time she heard the sound of an airplane passing close by. She felt a loud impact that knocked out telephone service as well as the electricity in her house. Uncertain about what had happened, she snatched up a camera and ran to the scene, managing to capture the only known photograph of a smoke cloud rising from Flight 93. Resident Kelly Leverknight remembered, "I heard the plane going over and I went out the front door and I saw the plane going down. It was headed toward the school, which panicked me, because all three of my kids were there. Then you heard the explosion and felt the blast and saw the fire and smoke."[93]

THE AFTERMATH

The nation, indeed the world, was stunned. What the 1993 bombing had failed to achieve, the 2001 attacks completed, namely the collapse of three buildings in the World Trade Center complex. The attacks also changed the way Americans and their government officials thought about terrorism. It had always been a possibility in the American landscape. High-profile terrorists such as the other men discussed throughout this book often captured headlines, but their work tended to be piecemeal, and their victim pool was small. The September 11 attacks were dramatic and on a scale heretofore unimaginable.[94]

Al-Qaeda had posed a threat to U.S. interests for years, but the idea that this loose network of alienated souls could implement destruction on such a large scale had been inconceivable. Therein lay the problem. What had been unimaginable to U.S. intelligence officials had been a distinct possibility to al-Qaeda terrorists.[95]

Investigators left no stone unturned in the quest to discover how the operation had been carried out. The FBI discovered the names and in many cases the personal details of the suspected pilots and hijackers within a short time. Fifteen were from Saudi Arabia, two from the United Arab Emirates, one from Egypt, and one from Lebanon. Mohammed Atta, generally regarded as the ringleader, owned luggage that did not make his connecting flight. Inside the luggage were papers identifying the terrorists and providing details about their motivations and plans. Intelligence data also revealed that Osama bin Laden was the mastermind of the plot along with Khalid Sheikh Mohammed. Unlike the confusion in the aftermath of the USS *Cole* bombing, no one doubted that al-Qaeda had engineered the attacks.[96]

The administration of U.S. president George W. Bush had received reports before September 11 that a large-scale terrorist operation potentially was brewing, but the nature of the operation was sketchy. The difficulty was that much of the "chatter" was incomplete, vague, ambiguous, or conflicting. In his President's Daily Brief (PDB), a series of six to eight short articles and briefings on sensitive intelligence matters, President Bush had read forty articles involving bin Laden and al-Qaeda between his inauguration on January 20 and September 10, 2001. The PDB is distributed to a limited number of parties. Other administration officials receive a Senior Executive Intelligence Brief (SEIB), which covered many of the same topics in the same format. It was clear from the PDBs and SEIBs produced during this period that al-Qaeda remained an ongoing, credible threat to U.S. interests. The challenge, as always, was how a country could and should respond to substate terrorism.[97]

In April and May 2001, intelligence officials reported that bin Laden's men seemed to be planning a major operation. By June, Director of Central Intelligence George Tenet asked that all U.S. ambassadors be briefed on the possibility of al-Qaeda attacks on foreign targets with U.S. interests. Throughout June and July, additional warnings indicated that "Bin Laden Attacks May Be Imminent." A truck bomb delivered to a U.S. embassy seemed to be the likely scenario. Tenet later commented that during the summer of 2001, "the system was blinking red."[98]

The difficulty was that a system "blinking red" is vague and does not provide actionable data about a credible, specific threat. It was not until August 6 that an intelligence report concluded "Bin Ladin [sic] Determined to Strike in US." Even after that assessment appeared, no one could assemble the pieces of an intricate intelligence puzzle. Top administration officials, including National Security Adviser Condoleezza Rice, were well aware of the threats, but, in the words of the 9/11 Commission Report, the "September 11 attacks fell in the void between the foreign and domestic threats." Foreign intelligence agencies were vigilant in searching for evidence of threats to overseas targets while domestic agencies searched for sleeper cells inside the United States. No one bridged the gap to consider the possibility of foreign sources coming into the United States to pose a threat to domestic targets. This statement may seem to be a game of semantics, but it illustrated a weakness in U.S. homeland security. Foreign and domestic agencies did not share intelligence information. The creation of a new cabinet-level agency, the U.S. Department of Homeland Security, was designed, at least in part, to correct the deficiency.[99]

In the immediate aftermath of the attacks, President Bush enjoyed what some commentators called a "rally 'round the flag" factor. Rather than blaming the administration for failing to stop the attacks, the citizenry set aside partisan bickering for a short time. Americans and indeed many people the world over expressed their support of the president's efforts to pursue and capture the terrorists responsible for the death and destruction of September 11. Bush's approval rating soared to 90 percent.[100]

The president was anxious to capitalize on this goodwill and bipartisan support. On September 20, 2001, he spoke before a joint session of Congress about the attacks and his planned response to those events, promising a quick, decisive, muscular response. In the months and years to come, American policy was driven by this new "war on terror." A variety of events, including the decision to send troops to Afghanistan and the enactment of the USA Patriot Act, were to have a lasting, and controversial, effect on American public policy. Bush also used the 9/11 attacks as partial justification for the decision to invade Iraq in 2003, although the linkage between al-Qaeda and Iraq generally has been dismissed as illusory.[101]

Members of the U.S. intelligence community were particularly upset. Having known about bin Laden and al-Qaeda for so long and yet having failed to react effectively enough to forestall a major attack was dismaying. The episode sent shock waves through the defense and military apparatus. Inside the government, personnel debated an appropriate response. Defense secretary Donald Rumsfeld posed the core question succinctly. "Do we focus on bin Laden and al-Qaeda or terrorism more broadly?" he asked. It was not a rhetorical question.

President Bush understood the need to put a human face on terrorism. "Start with bin Laden, which Americans expect," he said. "And then if we succeed we've struck a huge blow and can move forward."[102]

The mission was clear. The evil mastermind at the top of the al-Qaeda pyramid was the primary target, although that emphasis did not preclude chasing other targets. Cofer Black, head of the CTC, expressed the anger and frustration many Americans felt after September 11 when he spoke to a CIA paramilitary team being dispatched to Afghanistan. "Your mission is to exert all efforts to find Osama bin Laden and his senior lieutenants and kill them," he said. "I don't want bin Laden and his thugs captured; I want them dead. . . . They must be killed. I want to see photos of their heads on pikes. I want bin Laden's head shipped back in a box filled with dry ice." At the end of his tirade, Black paused. "Have I made myself clear?"[103]

The message was crystal clear. The problem, of course, was that killing the elusive terrorist was far easier said than done. First, U.S. forces had to find him.

Intelligence sources agreed that bin Laden was probably hiding in Afghanistan. Because the Taliban ruled the country, to the extent that anyone ruled it, and Americans recognized that the Taliban were not cooperating in handing over the target, CIA and military personnel began to work with the Northern Alliance, a group of anti-Taliban opposition forces. During the last months of 2001, elite American Special Forces soldiers pursued leads, always gaining ground but never quite locating the prey. After an American bomb obliterated an al Qaeda safe house in Kabul, Afghanistan, investigators discovered the body of Mohammed Atef, sometimes known by the alias Abu Hafs, a notorious former Egyptian policeman who had served as bin Laden's security chief. It was a promising lead. Other leads suggested that bin Laden was on the run toward a remote area of the White Mountains of Afghanistan known as Tora Bora.[104]

The retreat to Tora Bora made a great deal of strategic sense. Earlier in his career, bin Laden had spent time building a road through the rugged mountains. He had even lived in a house in the region. With its multiple, jagged peaks and deep, cavernous ravines, the White Mountains were hospitable terrain for al-Qaeda fighters. They could disappear into a series of

Osama bin Laden appears on the Al Jazeera television network on October 7, 2001. Courtesy of the Granger Collection, New York.

underground caves or plot an ambush for pursuing forces and escape in the aftermath of a quick and dirty firefight.[105]

And disappear is exactly what Osama bin Laden did during the waning days of 2001. Teams of American fighters followed a trail, sometimes only hours or minutes old, as al-Qaeda members fled through the mountains and valleys around Tora Bora. During pitched battles with the terrorists, Americans employed their superior resources effectively, invariably besting the enemy. Estimates placed the number of al-Qaeda foot soldiers killed in the last months of 2001 at between 220 and 500, although it was impossible to pinpoint precise figures after bombing raids blew bodies to pieces. This predicament raised the fear that bin Laden was dead, but his remains would never be found. If this scenario occurred, it would be fortunate that bin Laden was no longer in a position to wreak havoc on western forces, but his legend would grow. He would become a ghost, never seen yet never quite destroyed. Another fear was that he remained at large and would live to fight another day.[106]

Speaking to NBC News reporters, Secretary of State Colin Powell assured the public that the administration would follow every lead in the hunt for America's most wanted terrorist. "We'll get bin Laden," he promised. "Whether it's today, tomorrow, a year from now, two years from now, we will not rest until he is brought to justice or justice is brought to him."[107]

They were tough fighting words, exactly what an incensed American public wanted to hear spoken in December 2001. The problem was that no one knew where bin Laden had gone. He seemed to have dropped off the planet. Perhaps he really was dead, one of the innumerable pieces of human flesh strewn across a debris field in the wilds of Afghanistan.[108]

Suddenly, on December 27, 2001, a new videotape emerged showing a wan, haggard-looking Osama bin Laden. Although he appeared to be in poor health, he remained very much alive and hidden away from the U.S. military. Even if he was "marginalized," as President Bush contended in March 2002, bin Laden remained a symbol of defiance to U.S. military might. He had attacked the great Satan in the heart of its major cities and lived to tell the tale. He might be diminished, but he and al-Qaeda had not been obliterated. He became a hero to extremists the world over.[109]

New videotapes appeared from time to time in the ensuing years, but the man's whereabouts remained a mystery. As time passed and the trail grew cold, the Bush administration shifted its tone. Instead of focusing on Osama bin Laden, officials began to speak about a general "war on terror." Rather than targeting an individual, the U.S. military, in the words of Lieutenant

General Dan McNeil, decided to emphasize other targets. "I'm not solely fixated on Osama bin Laden," General McNeil explained during a briefing in the summer of 2002. The death of this individual, as symbolically valuable as it would be, "is incidental to our operations."[110]

Incidental or not, Americans never relinquished the goal of finding and either capturing or killing the September 11 mastermind. As the years passed, speculation increased that bin Laden was dead or incapacitated, hiding somewhere in a dirty cave near Tora Bora or among sympathetic terrorists in Pakistan. Occasional reports on his health and his future plots generated intense speculation and scrutiny, but for many years no usable intelligence information was forthcoming.[111]

Investigators later learned that bin Laden had escaped from Tora Bora late in 2001 and had hidden in the tribal regions of Pakistan. Although nominally a U.S. ally in the war on terror, Pakistan was always a troubling partner. Despite assurances that al-Qaeda and members of its network had been rooted out of the country, Pakistan was well known as a safe haven for all manner of extremist groups. Osama bin Laden apparently spent the next four years hiding there as he planned for more fortified accommodations to be constructed. His family's vast wealth made his exile possible.[112]

In 2003, bin Laden's supporters began building a reinforced compound in Abbottabad, Pakistan, a city of 100,000 residents situated in the Hazara region of the Khyber Pakhtunkhwa province approximately thirty-one miles northeast of the capital city of Islamabad. The edifice was not a normal construction project. The walls varied in size between twelve and eighteen feet, and razor wire surrounded the main building. The million-dollar structure was roughly eight times larger than the surrounding houses. Located adjacent to the prestigious Pakistan Military Academy, this new building was so expensive and unusual that it must have invited scrutiny from Pakistani officials. Whether anyone placed high in the military or political echelon knew of the purposes of the compound remains an open question, but it seems likely that someone either knew and remained silent or officials deliberately turned a blind eye to the construction.[113]

Sometime in 2005, Osama bin Laden quietly moved into the Abbottabad compound. A trusted courier, Abu Ahmed al-Kuwaiti, lived in an outbuilding and attended to the al-Qaeda leader's needs. Bin Laden remained engaged in the group's organizational goals and planning, but he was careful to shield his identity. While he stayed hidden behind the walls of his compound, he passed messages to his courier for delivery. He was careful to limit his telephone calls, Internet traffic, and sources that could be traced or compromised electronically.[114]

In the meantime, in 2003 Pakistani officials apprehended Khalid Sheikh Mohammed, the chief architect of the September 11 murders, and turned him over to the CIA. Transported to the Guantanamo Bay, Cuba, prison, the portly terrorist was among the detainees selected for the "enhanced" interrogations that ignited controversy among legal scholars and civil rights activists. It is unclear what information, if any, Sheikh Mohammed divulged, but it is clear that the CIA became increasingly interested in al-Kuwaiti, bin Laden's assistant, in the wake of those interrogations. As intelligence officers scoured the Pakistani landscape for the al-Qaeda courier, they wondered whether he might still be carrying messages for his former boss.[115]

In August 2010, U.S. intelligence officials informed President Bush's successor, Barack H. Obama, that the CIA had tracked al-Kuwaiti's movements and were reasonably sure he was assisting bin Laden at a compound in Abbottabad. President Obama could have ordered air strikes against the building, thereby decimating it and everyone inside. After initially considering this course of action, the president decided instead to authorize a commando raid using Sea, Air and Land teams, commonly called SEALs, the U.S. Navy's principal special operations force. SEALs are part of the Naval Special Warfare Command as well as the U.S. Special Operations Command, among the most effective elite units in the U.S. military. Although the raid was riskier than an air strike, in all likelihood it would allow the U.S. to determine definitively whether bin Laden was hiding inside the compound and, if so, whether he could be captured or killed. As an added bonus, if the commandos could secure the premises, they might discover evidence of pending terrorist plots.[116]

The president and his intelligence team were cognizant of precedents where a commando raid ended in disaster. No one could forget President Carter's failed attempt to send helicopter teams to rescue the Iranian hostages in 1980 or the loss of the Black Hawk helicopters in Somalia in 1993. The operation that Obama approved would involve seventy-nine commandos and four helicopters, and much could go wrong. They would be flying into unfamiliar terrain at night in hostile territory to neutralize a target they could not be certain was even present at the location. By violating the sovereignty of a nominal ally, they risked igniting an international incident, particularly if innocent civilians were injured or killed. The enterprise was fraught with danger and risk.[117]

Even a successful raid could invite reprisals from enraged terrorist organizations, as well as the Pakistani government, which would not be informed of the operation ahead of time lest leaks compromise the integrity of the mission. President Obama had done much to tell the Arab world that the United States was not hostile toward Islam generally, but a botched operation in the Middle East could undermine that message. Moreover, the capture or death of Osama bin Laden would not end terrorism. As this book discusses, terrorist threats always have been, and always will be, a part of life in an organized society. Terrorism is bigger than one man, no matter how notorious he becomes.[118]

Despite the enormous risks, the Obama administration, like the Bush administration before it, recognized the symbolic importance of taking Osama bin Laden out of commission. Feelings of outrage and injustice that lingered from the September 11 attacks might be relieved if the man who had caused so much destruction could be given his just deserts. A blitz attack on a legendary outlaw would also send a message to would-be terrorists that a similar fate awaited anyone audacious enough to perpetrate terrorism on American soil. It was a risk worth taking, but the Americans might have only one chance. They must plan the operation carefully.[119]

As months passed and intelligence officers struggled to validate their sources of information, the commandos rehearsed. By the spring of 2011, everyone was reasonably sure they had their man and their preparations were sufficient. Even if the intelligence was not indisputable, it was not likely to improve. With the two dozen members of SEAL Team Six trained and ready to go, President Obama issued the long-awaited order to capture or kill the world's most wanted fugitive.[120]

On May 1, 2011, five helicopters—two modified Black Hawks and three Chinooks—departed from an airfield in Jalalabad, Afghanistan, crossed the border into Pakistan, and headed for Abbottabad under cover of darkness. When they arrived at the compound, the Black Hawks hovered over the target. The lead helicopter was supposed to hold its position over the main house and allow commandos to appel onto the roof. Unfortunately for the soldiers, the aircraft became trapped in an air vortex that forced it to the ground, clipping the side of the compound as it descended. Despite what operatives called a "hard landing," the SEALs were not injured, although the helicopter was no longer operational. It had to be destroyed. As for the commandos inside the downed Black Hawk, they dashed into the courtyard and initiated a search.[121]

The second helicopter pilot, fearing the same problem with an air vortex, changed plans. Instead of disgorging his passengers inside the walls, he landed the SEALs outside the walls and they used explosives to gain entry. The plan was to stay on the ground as short a time as possible—ideally no more than half an hour.[122]

It was the stuff of Hollywood action films. The SEALs came under fire from the compound guesthouse. They killed a man and a woman in the ensuing firefight. Inside the house, the commandos ran from room to room, blowing doors open with explosive charges. They killed two more men before climbing to the third floor.

In the dim lighting of the main house they spied the elusive fugitive they had long sought. Tall and gaunt, diminished but not neutralized, Osama bin Laden could not escape. He took shots to the head and chest. When they were certain he was dead, the SEALs grabbed his body as well as a treasure trove of documents and equipment. They departed as quickly as possible. The entire operation had lasted just forty minutes, ten minutes longer than the ideal projection. Except for the loss of a helicopter, it had been a textbook operation. The SEALs suffered no casualties.[123]

President Obama and his national security team watched the operation on video in real time from the White House situation room. The tension was almost unbearable as they were forced to wait for twenty-five minutes while the commandos conducted a room-by-room search inside the main house. Finally, at 1:10 a.m. in Pakistan—4:10 p.m. Washington, D.C., time—Joint Chiefs of Staff commander Admiral William McRaven issued a welcomed message. "Geronimo," he said, meaning that the mission had succeeded. A few minutes later, he remarked, "Geronimo, EKIA [enemy killed in action]!"[124]

Thirteen long years after he first declared war on the United States, Osama bin Laden was dead. The SEALs transported his corpse to the Arabian Sea and dropped it in the water. They snapped photographs to record the death for posterity, although President Obama and his advisers have not released the photographs as of this writing.[125]

During the evening of May 2, 2011, as details of the successful mission became clear, President Obama decided he must not wait. He appeared on television to reveal the operation to the world for the first time. Coming late on a Sunday night, the address was dramatic and surprising. No word of the operation had leaked out during the long months leading up to the commando raid. "Tonight, I can report to the American people and to the world that the United States has conducted an operation that killed Osama bin Laden, the leader of al-Qaeda, and a terrorist who's responsible for the murder of thousands of innocent men, women, and children," the president reported on live television from the East Room of the White House. It was a satisfying moment, but not an occasion for gloating.

He reminded the world why the operation had been necessary. "It was nearly ten years ago that a bright September day was darkened by the worst attack on the American people in our history. The images of 9/11 are seared into our national memory—hijacked planes cutting through a cloudless September sky; the Twin Towers collapsing to the ground; black smoke billowing up from the Pentagon; the wreckage of Flight 93 in Shanksville, Pennsylvania, where the actions of heroic citizens saved even more heartbreak and destruction."

Somber and dignified, the president would not demonstrate joy or excess emotion on this important night. He could take pride in "the tireless and heroic work of our military and our counterterrorism professionals," but he would not appear gleeful at the thought of killing anyone, even an evil mastermind. "Today, at my direction," he continued, "the United States launched a targeted operation against that compound in Abbottabad, Pakistan. A small team of Americans carried out the operation with extraordinary courage and capability. No Americans were harmed. They took care to avoid civilian casualties. After a firefight, they killed Osama bin Laden and took custody of his body."

He spoke to "the families who lost loved ones on 9/11," assuring them "that we have never forgotten your loss, nor wavered in our commitment to see that we do whatever it takes to prevent another attack on our shores." As he concluded his remarks, he reminded Americans that the death of one man would not end terrorism or lessen the need for America's eternal vigilance. "The cause of securing our country is not complete. But tonight, we are once again reminded that America can do whatever we set our mind to. That is the story of our history, whether it's the pursuit of prosperity for our people, or the struggle for equality for all our citizens; our commitment to stand up for our values abroad, and our sacrifices to make the world a safer place."[126]

CONCLUSION

The terrorist attacks of September 11, 2001, will be studied and deconstructed for as long as terrorism remains an issue of concern for civilized people. In retrospect, many signs pointed to an imminent al-Qaeda attack on American soil in 2001. In the wake of the episode, students of terrorism have scrambled to learn the lessons of that terrible day. A major insight that students of history can glean from the attacks is that the lack of coordination among and between officials in different government agencies led to a systemic breakdown that allowed the nation's enemies to succeed in murdering innocent civilians. One agency possessed information that another agency lacked and vice versa. Had the agencies exchanged information in a timely fashion, persons responsible for monitoring terrorist activity might have been able to piece together the puzzle suggesting that airline hijackings were possible and even imminent. One reason the Bush administration created the U.S. Department of Homeland Security was precisely so that agencies involved in intelligence activities could share information to better understand and assess the nature of terrorist threats.[127]

Whatever agency they work for and however it is organized, intelligence officials must remain alert to emerging threats and never surrender to complacency. They must employ energy and imagination to appreciate the risks posed by terrorism. Time and again, officials gathered information about al-Qaeda's intentions and Osama bin Laden's efforts to attack U.S. interests. During the "summer of threat" in 2001, as George Tenet noted, "the system was blinking red." Yet intelligence officials failed to appreciate that an attack was imminent. Moreover, because counterterrorism officers did not consider the full range of possibilities, they failed to understand how aircraft could be used as weapons. Had they employed this kind of imagination in considering possible avenues of attack, they might have followed up to determine whether groups of young people enrolled in flight schools for suspicious reasons posed a genuine threat to national security.[128]

The U.S. government has sometimes turned a blind eye to governments that harbor known terrorists and terrorist cells because political leaders have deemed the relationships with such governments fragile and tenuous, and thus unable to withstand sustained critical evaluation. Countries such as Afghanistan, Pakistan, and Saudi Arabia have allowed al-Qaeda and other terrorist organizations to thrive without fearing negative repercussions from the United States. The 9/11 Commission recommended that these relationships be constantly reevaluated and hard choices made when terrorists who seek refuge in these nations continue to operate against U.S. interests. As uncomfortable as the conversations will be, U.S. officials must directly confront these issues instead of allowing them to fester. American political and military leaders must send a message to the world that terrorists will not be allowed to act with impunity. Punishment will be consistent and harsh.[129]

A message also must be sent to individuals that viable alternatives exist. Terrorism is not the answer. Although some alienated souls will always rely on violence to resolve long-simmering issues, marginal participants may be amenable to receiving a positive message. Cherished values such as the efficacy of participation in the political process, the virtues of pluralism, and exciting opportunities for economic advancement may yet convince marginalized persons that the promise of a new day is preferable to violent extremism and the certainty of an endless night.[130]

NOTES

1. As with so much of the information reported on Osama bin Laden, even the man's birth date and basic facts about this life are subject to uncertainty and controversy. Some sources place his birth date in 1957—March 10 and July 30 are the dates usually cited—and some sources prefer 1958, usually sometime in January. The number of bin Laden siblings is variously reported as between fifty-three and fifty-six. The inheritance is estimated in the range of $25 million to $30 million although even those figures are not certain. See, for example, Editors of *Life*, *Brought to Justice*, 19; Gunaratna, *Inside Al Qaeda*, 16; National Commission on Terrorist Attacks upon the United States, *The 9/11 Commission Report*, 55; Wright, *The Looming Tower*, 72.

2. Editors of *Life*, *Brought to Justice*, 19, 21; Gunaratna, *Inside Al Qaeda*, 17; Wright, *The Looming Tower*, 72–74.

3. Jansen, *Militant Islam*, 28, 46, 87–89; National Commission on Terrorist Attacks upon the United States, *The 9/11 Commission Report*, 49–54; Swazo, "My Brother Is My King,'" 9–13; Wright, "The Struggle within Islam," 104–14.

4. Abuza, "Tentacles of Terror," 432; Allen, "The Hidden Roots of Wahhabism in British India," 88; Coll, *Ghost Wars*, 75–76; Jansen, *Militant Islam*, 87–88.

5. Coll, *Ghost Wars*, 85; Doran, "The Pragmatic Fanaticism of al-Qaeda," 180–82; Gerges, *The Rise and Fall of Al-Qaeda*, 31–33, 40; Henzel, "The Origins of al-Qaeda's Ideology," 74–75; Wright, *The Looming Tower*, 7–31.

6. Coll, *Ghost Wars*, 85; Editors of *Life*, *Brought to Justice*, 21, 23; National Commission on Terrorist Attacks upon the United States, *The 9/11 Commission Report*, 55; Wright, *The Looming Tower*, 74–83.

7. Editors of *Life*, *Brought to Justice*, 23; Lesch, "Osama bin Laden," 82–83; Wright, *The Looming Tower*, 94–98.

8. Black, "1979," 5–6; Editors of *Life*, *Brought to Justice*, 21, 23; Gunaratna, *Inside Al Qaeda*, 17; Hoodbhoy, "Afghanistan and the Genesis of Global Jihad," 19–23; Lesch, "Osama bin Laden," 82–83; Nasir, "Al-Qaeda, Two Years On," 35; Oleinik, "Lessons of Russian in Afghanistan," 288–93; Wright, *The Looming Tower*, 74–83.

9. Editors of *Life*, *Brought to Justice*, 38; Hoodbhoy, "Afghanistan and the Genesis of Global Jihad," 27–29; National Commission on Terrorist Attacks upon the United States, *The 9/11 Commission Report*, 55; Wright, *The Looming Tower*, 95–96, 99–100; Wright, *Rock the Casbah*, 49–50.

10. Henzel, "The Origins of al-Qaeda's Ideology," 75–76; Hoodbhoy, "Afghanistan and the Genesis of Global Jihad," 25–26; Lesch, "Osama bin Laden," 82–84; Wright, *The Looming Tower*, 101–2.

11. Editors of *Life*, *Brought to Justice*, 38; Gunaratna, *Inside Al Qaeda*, 27; Hoodbhoy, "Afghanistan and the Genesis of Global Jihad," 24–26; Lesch, "Osama bin Laden," 82–84; National Commission on Terrorist Attacks upon the United States, *The 9/11 Commission Report*, 56; Oleinik, "Lessons of Russian in Afghanistan," 288–93; Wright, *The Looming Tower*, 110, 137.

12. Abuza, "Tentacles of Terror," 429; Coll, *Ghost Wars*, 17, 204; Editors of *Life*, *Brought to Justice*, 35, 37, 38, 43; Gunaratna, *Inside Al Qaeda*, 21–23; Nasir, "Al-Qaeda, Two Years On," 34; National Commission on Terrorist Attacks upon the United States, *The 9/11 Commission Report*, 56; Wright, *The Looming Tower*, 129–33.

13. Abuza, "Tentacles of Terror," 429–31; Gerges, *The Rise and Fall of Al-Qaeda*, 40–43; National Commission on Terrorist Attacks upon the United States, *The 9/11 Commission Report*, 56; Wright, *The Looming Tower*, 133–37.

14. Coll, *Ghost Wars*, 204; Editors of *Life*, *Brought to Justice*, 35; Gunaratna, *Inside Al Qaeda*, 25–26; Nasir, "Al-Qaeda, Two Years On," 34; National Commission on Terrorist Attacks upon the United States, *The 9/11 Commission Report*, 56; Wright, *The Looming Tower*, 141–44.

15. Coll, *Ghost Wars*, 203, Editors of *Life*, *Brought to Justice*, 35, 46; Hoffman, "The Global Terrorist Threat," 45–53; Hoodbhoy, "Afghanistan and the Genesis of Global Jihad," 26; Nasir, "Al-Qaeda, Two Years On," 32; National Commission on Terrorist Attacks upon the United States, *The 9/11 Commission Report*, 56–57; Wright, *The Looming Tower*, 32–59, 95, 124–26; Wright, *Rock the Casbah*, 6.

16. Coll, *Ghost Wars*, 267; Editors of *Life*, *Brought to Justice*, 43, 45; Lesch, "Osama bin Laden," 84–85; National Commission on Terrorist Attacks upon the United States, *The 9/11 Commission Report*, 57–58; Wright, *The Looming Tower*, 164–66.

17. Coll, *Ghost Wars*, 270–71; National Commission on Terrorist Attacks upon the United States, *The 9/11 Commission Report*, 57; Wright, *The Looming Tower*, 194–97; Wright, *Rock the Casbah*, 171.

18. Assadi and Lorunser, "Strategic Management Analysis of al-Qaeda," 65–67; Burke, "Al-Qaeda," 18–19; National Commission on Terrorist Attacks upon the United States, *The 9/11 Commission Report*, 57–59; Wright, *The Looming Tower*, 133–34, 168–69.

19. Lesch, "Osama bin Laden," 85; National Commission on Terrorist Attacks upon the United States, *The 9/11 Commission Report*, 59–60.

20. National Commission on Terrorist Attacks upon the United States, *The 9/11 Commission Report*, 59–60; Wright, *The Looming Tower*, 188–89.

21. Editors of *Life*, *Brought to Justice*, 45, 48–49; Lesch, "Osama bin Laden," 85; National Commission on Terrorist Attacks upon the United States, *The 9/11 Commission Report*, 60; Wright, *The Looming Tower*, 237–39.

22. Coll, *Ghost Wars*, 250–51; Editors of *Life*, *Brought to Justice*, 45; McCann, *Terrorism on American Soil*, 187–88; National Commission on Terrorist Attacks upon the United States, *The 9/11 Commission Report*, 71; Wright, *The Looming Tower*, 177–78.

23. Abuza, "Tentacles of Terror," 441–42; Coll, *Ghost Wars*, 249–51; McCann, *Terrorism on American Soil*, 188–91; National Commission on Terrorist Attacks upon the United States, *The 9/11 Commission Report*, 71–72; Wright, *The Looming Tower*, 177–78.

24. Editors of *Life*, *Brought to Justice*, 45; McCann, *Terrorism on American Soil*, 187–88; National Commission on Terrorist Attacks upon the United States, *The 9/11 Commission Report*, 71–72; Wright, *The Looming Tower*, 177–78.

25. McCann, *Terrorism on American Soil*, 189; National Commission on Terrorist Attacks upon the United States, *The 9/11 Commission Report*, 72.

26. McCann, *Terrorism on American Soil*, 189; National Commission on Terrorist Attacks upon the United States, *The 9/11 Commission Report*, 72; Wright, *The Looming Tower*, 177–78.

27. Editors of *Life*, *Brought to Justice*, 45, 46; McCann, *Terrorism on American Soil*, 190–92; National Commission on Terrorist Attacks upon the United States, *The 9/11 Commission Report*, 71–73.

28. McCann, *Terrorism on American Soil*, 190–92; National Commission on Terrorist Attacks upon the United States, *The 9/11 Commission Report*, 73.

29. National Commission on Terrorist Attacks upon the United States, *The 9/11 Commission Report*, 72–73.

30. CBS News, *What We Saw*, 9; Editors of *Life*, *Brought to Justice*, 9–10; McCann, *Terrorism on American Soil*, 274–75; National Commission on Terrorist Attacks upon the United States, *The 9/11 Commission Report*, 1–46.

31. Quoted in Runkle, *Wanted Dead or Alive*, 158. See also McCann, *Terrorism on American Soil*, 191–92; National Commission on Terrorist Attacks upon the United States, *The 9/11 Commission Report*, 108–9.

32. McCann, *Terrorism on American Soil*, 277; National Commission on Terrorist Attacks upon the United States, *The 9/11 Commission Report*, 126–34; Runkle, *Wanted Dead or Alive*, 158–59; Wright, *The Looming Tower*, 265–66.

33. Lesch, "Osama bin Laden," 86; Runkle, *Wanted Dead or Alive*, 158–59; Wright, *The Looming Tower*, 262–65; Wright, *Rock the Casbah*, 69.

34. McCann, *Terrorism on American Soil*, 276–77; National Commission on Terrorist Attacks upon the United States, *The 9/11 Commission Report*, 108–15; Runkle, *Wanted Dead or Alive*, 158–59.

35. Lesch, "Osama bin Laden," 87; McCann, *Terrorism on American Soil*, 276–77; National Commission on Terrorist Attacks upon the United States, *The 9/11 Commission Report*, 69; Runkle, *Wanted Dead or Alive*, 160; Sale, *Clinton's Secret Wars*, 295; Wright, *The Looming Tower*, 259–61.

36. Clinton, *My Life*, 797; Coll, *Ghost Wars*, 403–5; Doran, "The Pragmatic Fanaticism of al-Qaeda," 183; Editors of *Life*, *Brought to Justice*, 48–49; Lesch, "Osama bin Laden," 87; National Commission on Terrorist Attacks upon the United States, *The 9/11 Commission Report*, 70, 115–16; Runkle, *Wanted Dead or Alive*, 160–61; Sale, *Clinton's Secret Wars*, 295–96; Wright, *The Looming Tower*, 270–72.

37. Quoted in National Commission on Terrorist Attacks upon the United States, *The 9/11 Commission Report*, 70. See also Runkle, *Wanted Dead or Alive*, 161–62; Wright, *The Looming Tower*, 272.

38. Clinton, *My Life*, 797, 798.

39. National Commission on Terrorist Attacks upon the United States, *The 9/11 Commission Report*, 117–18; Runkle, *Wanted Dead or Alive*, 161–62; Wright, *The Looming Tower*, 283.

40. National Commission on Terrorist Attacks upon the United States, *The 9/11 Commission Report*, 115–19; Runkle, *Wanted Dead or Alive*, 162; Sale, *Clinton's Secret Wars*, 298–301.

41. Doran, "The Pragmatic Fanaticism of al-Qaeda," 183; Lesch, "Osama bin Laden," 87; National Commission on Terrorist Attacks upon the United States, *The 9/11 Commission Report*, 134–43; Runkle, *Wanted Dead or Alive*, 164–66.

42. Coll, *Ghost Wars*, 537; Doran, "The Pragmatic Fanaticism of al-Qaeda," 183; Editors of *Life, Brought to Justice*, 52; Gerges, *The Rise and Fall of Al-Qaeda*, 68; Lesch, "Osama bin Laden," 87; McCann, *Terrorism on American Soil*, 277; National Commission on Terrorist Attacks upon the United States, *The 9/11 Commission Report*, 190–91; Runkle, *Wanted Dead or Alive*, 166–67; Wright, *The Looming Tower*, 319–20.

43. Doran, "The Pragmatic Fanaticism of al-Qaeda," 183; National Commission on Terrorist Attacks upon the United States, *The 9/11 Commission Report*, 121–34, 192–97; Runkle, *Wanted Dead or Alive*, 167–70; Sale, *Clinton's Secret Wars*, 292–302; Wright, *The Looming Tower*, 324–32.

44. National Commission on Terrorist Attacks upon the United States, *The 9/11 Commission Report*, 145–49; Wright, *The Looming Tower*, 235–36.

45. Abuza, "Tentacles of Terror," 441–43; McCann, *Terrorism on American Soil*, 277–79; National Commission on Terrorist Attacks upon the United States, *The 9/11 Commission Report*, 153–54; Wright, *The Looming Tower*, 307–8.

46. Gerges, *The Rise and Fall of Al-Qaeda*, 84–85; National Commission on Terrorist Attacks upon the United States, *The 9/11 Commission Report*, 153–56.

47. National Commission on Terrorist Attacks upon the United States, *The 9/11 Commission Report*, 155; Wright, *The Looming Tower*, 308.

48. McCann, *Terrorism on American Soil*, 277–78; National Commission on Terrorist Attacks upon the United States, *The 9/11 Commission Report*, 153–56; Wright, *The Looming Tower*, 307–11.

49. Coll, *Ghost Wars*, 473–78; National Commission on Terrorist Attacks upon the United States, *The 9/11 Commission Report*, 155–56.

50. Coll, *Ghost Wars*, 473–78; Editors of *Life, Brought to Justice*, 58–59; McDermott, "A Perfect Soldier," A1; National Commission on Terrorist Attacks upon the United States, *The 9/11 Commission Report*, 160–63; Shenon, "Report Claims That 9/11 Terrorists Were Identified before Attacks," A15; Wright, *The Looming Tower*, 308–10.

51. Coll, *Ghost Wars*, 476; McDermott, "A Perfect Soldier," A1; McDermott, *Perfect Soldiers*, 2–3; National Commission on Terrorist Attacks upon the United States, *The 9/11 Commission Report*, 160–61; Shenon, "Report Claims That 9/11 Terrorists Were Identified before Attacks," A15.

52. McDermott, "A Perfect Soldier," A1; National Commission on Terrorist Attacks upon the United States, *The 9/11 Commission Report*, 165–67; Shenon,

"Report Claims That 9/11 Terrorists Were Identified before Attacks," A15; Wright, *The Looming Tower*, 307–8.

53. McDermott, "A Perfect Soldier," A1; National Commission on Terrorist Attacks upon the United States, *The 9/11 Commission Report*, 167–69; Shenon, "Report Claims That 9/11 Terrorists Were Identified before Attacks," A15.

54. Fouda and Fielding, *Masterminds of Terror*, 73, 100; McDermott, "A Perfect Soldier," A1; National Commission on Terrorist Attacks upon the United States, *The 9/11 Commission Report*, 161; Shenon, "Report Claims That 9/11 Terrorists Were Identified before Attacks," A15.

55. Fouda and Fielding, *Masterminds of Terror*, 86; McDermott, "A Perfect Soldier," A1; McDermott, *Perfect Soldiers*, 53; National Commission on Terrorist Attacks upon the United States, *The 9/11 Commission Report*, 162; Shenon, "Report Claims That 9/11 Terrorists Were Identified before Attacks," A15.

56. Fouda and Fielding, *Masterminds of Terror*, 85; McDermott, "A Perfect Soldier," A1; McDermott, *Perfect Soldiers*, 78; National Commission on Terrorist Attacks upon the United States, *The 9/11 Commission Report*, 160; Shenon, "Report Claims That 9/11 Terrorists Were Identified before Attacks," A15; Wright, *The Looming Tower*, 309–10.

57. McCann, *Terrorism on American Soil*, 278; National Commission on Terrorist Attacks upon the United States, *The 9/11 Commission Report*, 163–67; Shenon, "Report Claims That 9/11 Terrorists Were Identified before Attacks," A15.

58. McCann, *Terrorism on American Soil*, 277–78; National Commission on Terrorist Attacks upon the United States, *The 9/11 Commission Report*, 215–17; Wright, *The Looming Tower*, 312.

59. McDermott, "A Perfect Soldier," A1; National Commission on Terrorist Attacks upon the United States, *The 9/11 Commission Report*, 215–23; Wright, *The Looming Tower*, 314–15.

60. McDermott, "A Perfect Soldier," A1; McDermott, *Perfect Soldiers*, 53; National Commission on Terrorist Attacks upon the United States, *The 9/11 Commission Report*, 223–24; Shenon, "Report Claims That 9/11 Terrorists Were Identified before Attacks," A15.

61. Doran, "The Pragmatic Fanaticism of al-Qaeda," 183; Editors of *Life*, *Brought to Justice*, 9–10, 58–59; McCann, *Terrorism on American Soil*, 278; National Commission on Terrorist Attacks upon the United States, *The 9/11 Commission Report*, 231–41, 273–76; Rosenthal, "Doing Justice to Zacarias Moussaoui," 47–49.

62. Editors of *Life*, *Brought to Justice*, 15; National Commission on Terrorist Attacks upon the United States, *The 9/11 Commission Report*, 243–47.

63. McDermott, "A Perfect Soldier," A1; National Commission on Terrorist Attacks upon the United States, *The 9/11 Commission Report*, 248–50; Shenon, "Report Claims That 9/11 Terrorists Were Identified before Attacks," A15.

64. McDermott, *Perfect Soldiers*, 224; National Commission on Terrorist Attacks upon the United States, *The 9/11 Commission Report*, 248–53; Shenon, "Report Claims That 9/11 Terrorists Were Identified before Attacks," A15.

65. McDermott, "A Perfect Soldier," A1; National Commission on Terrorist Attacks upon the United States, *The 9/11 Commission Report*, 248–53; Shenon, "Report Claims That 9/11 Terrorists Were Identified before Attacks," A15.

66. Editors of *Life, Brought to Justice*, 58–59; Fouda and Fielding, *Masterminds of Terror*, 110. Most of the details for the descriptions of what happened on board the airplanes come from *The 9/11 Commission Report*. See, for example, National Commission on Terrorist Attacks upon the United States, *The 9/11 Commission Report*, 1–2.

67. National Commission on Terrorist Attacks upon the United States, *The 9/11 Commission Report*, 4–8.

68. National Commission on Terrorist Attacks upon the United States, *The 9/11 Commission Report*, 2, 7–8. See also Fouda and Fielding, *Masterminds of Terror*, 110–11.

69. National Commission on Terrorist Attacks upon the United States, *The 9/11 Commission Report*, 2–4, 8–10.

70. National Commission on Terrorist Attacks upon the United States, *The 9/11 Commission Report*, 4. See also Editors of *Life, Brought to Justice*, 58–59; Rosenthal, "Doing Justice to Zacarias Moussaoui," 47–57.

71. National Commission on Terrorist Attacks upon the United States, *The 9/11 Commission Report*, 10. See also Weber, "Popular Visual Language as Global Communication," 144.

72. National Commission on Terrorist Attacks upon the United States, *The 9/11 Commission Report*, 10–14. See also Editors of *Life, Brought to Justice*, 15; Fouda and Fielding, *Masterminds of Terror*, 144; Weber, "Popular Visual Language as Global Communication," 141–42.

73. CBS News, *What We Saw*, 16. See also Dwyer and Flynn, *102 Minutes*, 93; Nacos, "Terrorism as Breaking News," 23–27; National Commission on Terrorist Attacks upon the United States, *The 9/11 Commission Report*, 8.

74. CBS News, *What We Saw*, 14–15; Dwyer and Flynn, *102 Minutes*, xxi–xxiv; Editors of *Life, Brought to Justice*, 9–10; Nacos, "Terrorism as Breaking News," 45–52.

75. Dwyer and Flynn, *102 Minutes*, 19; National Commission on Terrorist Attacks upon the United States, *The 9/11 Commission Report*, 285–86.

76. Dwyer and Flynn, *102 Minutes*, 38–39; National Commission on Terrorist Attacks upon the United States, *The 9/11 Commission Report*, 285–87; Pryor, "The 2001 World Trade Center Disaster," 216–17.

77. National Commission on Terrorist Attacks upon the United States, *The 9/11 Commission Report*, 289; Pryor, "The 2001 World Trade Center Disaster," 213–14, 216–18.

78. Quoted in National Commission on Terrorist Attacks upon the United States, *The 9/11 Commission Report*, 291. See also Dwyer and Flynn, *102 Minutes*, 41–44; National Commission on Terrorist Attacks upon the United States, *The 9/11 Commission Report*, 290–91; Pryor, "The 2001 World Trade Center Disaster," 216–17.

79. CBS News, *What We Saw*, 23; Dwyer and Flynn, *102 Minutes*, 93–95; National Commission on Terrorist Attacks upon the United States, *The 9/11 Commission Report*, 293–94.

80. Dwyer and Flynn, *102 Minutes*, 101–12; National Commission on Terrorist Attacks upon the United States, *The 9/11 Commission Report*, 294–95; Pryor, "The 2001 World Trade Center Disaster," 216–18.

81. Quoted in National Commission on Terrorist Attacks upon the United States, *The 9/11 Commission Report*, 298. See also Dwyer and Flynn, *102 Minutes*, 60–62; Pryor, "The 2001 World Trade Center Disaster," 221–23.

82. Dwyer and Flynn, *102 Minutes*, 126–30; National Commission on Terrorist Attacks upon the United States, *The 9/11 Commission Report*, 297–304.

83. Dwyer and Flynn, *102 Minutes*, 120–25; National Commission on Terrorist Attacks upon the United States, *The 9/11 Commission Report*, 298–301; Pryor, "The 2001 World Trade Center Disaster," 221–22.

84. Caputi, "Guest Editor's Introduction," 2; Marshall and Suh, "Contextualizing Trauma," 411; Miles, "After 9/11," 250–51; National Commission on Terrorist Attacks upon the United States, *The 9/11 Commission Report*, 300.

85. Dwyer and Flynn, *102 Minutes*, 207–15; Mole, "9/11 Conspiracy Theories," 30–34; National Commission on Terrorist Attacks upon the United States, *The 9/11 Commission Report*, 305–7.

86. Mole, "9/11 Conspiracy Theories," 30–34; National Commission on Terrorist Attacks upon the United States, *The 9/11 Commission Report*, 306–11; Pryor, "The 2001 World Trade Center Disaster," 217–18.

87. Dwyer and Flynn, *102 Minutes*, 255–63; National Commission on Terrorist Attacks upon the United States, *The 9/11 Commission Report*, 311.

88. McCann, *Terrorism on American Soil*, 276; Mole, "9/11 Conspiracy Theories," 37–38; National Commission on Terrorist Attacks upon the United States, *The 9/11 Commission Report*, 314–15.

89. Mole, "9/11 Conspiracy Theories," 37–38; National Commission on Terrorist Attacks upon the United States, *The 9/11 Commission Report*, 314; Wright, *The Looming Tower*, 359.

90. Mole, "9/11 Conspiracy Theories," 37–38; National Commission on Terrorist Attacks upon the United States, *The 9/11 Commission Report*, 315.

91. Editors of *Life*, *Brought to Justice*, 15; McCann, *Terrorism on American Soil*, 276; National Commission on Terrorist Attacks upon the United States, *The 9/11 Commission Report*, 30, 313.

92. Sweeney, Solov, and Exner, "Pennsylvania Crash Carries Horror into Small Towns," A6.

93. Cleary, "Bloggers Smell Conspiracy with Flight 93 Photo," B1; Hamill, "A Sept. 11 Photo Brings Out the Conspiracy Theorists," A20.

94. Borradori, "Beyond the Culture of Terrorism," 397–98; Editors of *Life*, *Brought to Justice*, 6, 9–10; Kleinfield, "Getting Here from There," 1–2; Laqueur, "The Terrorism to Come," 49–51; McCann, *Terrorism on American Soil*, 275–75;

Merari, "Deterring Fear," 26; National Commission on Terrorist Attacks upon the United States, *The 9/11 Commission Report*, 339–60; Runkle, *Wanted Dead or Alive*, 2–4; Stephens, "9/11 and the Struggle for Meaning," A19; Swazo, "'My Brother Is My King,'" 9–13; "Ten Years On," 11–12.

95. Doran, "The Pragmatic Fanaticism of al-Qaeda," 183–85; Hoffman, "The Global Terrorist Threat," 55–57; Lesch, "Osama bin Laden," 86–88; McCann, *Terrorism on American Soil*, 278–79; Nasir, "Al-Qaeda, Two Years On," 32, 34–40; National Commission on Terrorist Attacks upon the United States, *The 9/11 Commission Report*, 361–63; Runkle, *Wanted Dead or Alive*, 1–6; Shenon, "Report Claims That 9/11 Terrorists Were Identified before Attacks," A15.

96. Clinton, *My Life*, 955–56; Editors of *Life*, *Brought to Justice*, 58–59, 63, 65; National Commission on Terrorist Attacks upon the United States, *The 9/11 Commission Report*, 325–28.

97. Assadi and Lorunser, "Strategic Management Analysis of al-Qaeda," 59–67; McDermott, "A Perfect Soldier," A1; National Commission on Terrorist Attacks upon the United States, *The 9/11 Commission Report*, 254–63; Runkle, *Wanted Dead or Alive*, 166–67; Shenon, "Report Claims That 9/11 Terrorists Were Identified before Attacks," A15.

98. McCann, *Terrorism on American Soil*, 278–81; National Commission on Terrorist Attacks upon the United States, *The 9/11 Commission Report*, 255–77.

99. Quoted in National Commission on Terrorist Attacks upon the United States, *The 9/11 Commission Report*, 263. See also McCann, *Terrorism on American Soil*, 278–81; Wright, *The Looming Tower*, 311–15.

100. Editors of *Life*, *Brought to Justice*, 63, 65; National Commission on Terrorist Attacks upon the United States, *The 9/11 Commission Report*, 330–34; Runkle, *Wanted Dead or Alive*, 1–6.

101. Brzezinski, "Right Cause, Wrong Response," A19; Helprin, "We Can't Reform the Arab World," A19; McFarlane, "Afghanistan Should Have Been the Focus," A19; National Commission on Terrorist Attacks upon the United States, *The 9/11 Commission Report*, 328, 330–38; Runkle, *Wanted Dead or Alive*, 167–70; Slaughter, "Resilience vs. Revenge," A19; Wieseltier, "Even Obama Embraces Drones," A19; Wolfowitz, "We Had to Address State Sponsors of Terror," A19; Yoo, "Ten Years without an Attack," A21.

102. Quoted in Runkle, *Wanted Dead or Alive*, 167. See also Editors of *Life*, *Brought to Justice*, 63; National Commission on Terrorist Attacks upon the United States, *The 9/11 Commission Report*, 330–34; Runkle, *Wanted Dead or Alive*, 167–70.

103. Quoted in Runkle, *Wanted Dead or Alive*, 167.

104. Editors of *Life*, *Brought to Justice*, 63, 65, 66; Runkle, *Wanted Dead or Alive*, 167–69.

105. Editors of *Life*, *Brought to Justice*, 63, 65, 71; Hoffman, "The Global Terrorist Threat," 55–57; Nasir, "Al-Qaeda, Two Years On," 41; National Commission on Terrorist Attacks upon the United States, *The 9/11 Commission Report*, 336–38; Runkle, *Wanted Dead or Alive*, 168–76.

106. Edwards, "Bin Laden's Last Stand," 181–83; National Commission on Terrorist Attacks upon the United States, *The 9/11 Commission Report*, 336–38; Runkle, *Wanted Dead or Alive*, 176–77, 205–6.

107. Quoted in Runkle, *Wanted Dead or Alive*, 177.

108. Editors of *Life, Brought to Justice*, 72, 78; Edwards, "Bin Laden's Last Stand," 178–85; Hoffman, "The Global Terrorist Threat," 55–57; Nasir, "Al-Qaeda, Two Years On," 41; Runkle, *Wanted Dead or Alive*, 176–77; Saleh, "Egypt," 40–44.

109. Editors of *Life, Brought to Justice*, 63; Runkle, *Wanted Dead or Alive*, 177.

110. Quoted in Runkle, *Wanted Dead or Alive*, 205. See also Wright, *Rock the Casbah*, 185.

111. Editors of *Life, Brought to Justice*, 78, 80, 83; Edwards, "Bin Laden's Last Stand," 178–85; Hoffman, "The Global Terrorist Threat," 55–57; Nasir, "Al-Qaeda, Two Years On," 41; Runkle, *Wanted Dead or Alive*, 205–6; Scherer, "Locating Bin Laden," 22–25.

112. Brzezinski, "Right Cause, Wrong Response," A19; Editors of *Life, Brought to Justice*, 78, 80, 83; Runkle, *Wanted Dead or Alive*, 205–6.

113. Editors of *Life, Brought to Justice*, 78; Runkle, *Wanted Dead or Alive*, 224.

114. Gerges, *The Rise and Fall of Al-Qaeda*, 15; Runkle, *Wanted Dead or Alive*, 224.

115. Editors of *Life, Brought to Justice*, 83–84; Gerges, *The Rise and Fall of Al-Qaeda*, 105; Runkle, *Wanted Dead or Alive*, 206.

116. Editors of *Life, Brought to Justice*, 84; Runkle, *Wanted Dead or Alive*, 222–25.

117. Berkowitz, "Assassinating Justly," 346–48; Crook, "U.S. Special Operations Personnel Raid Compound in Pakistan, Kill Osama bin Laden," 602–3; Editors of *Life, Brought to Justice*, 84; "The President Reports the Death of Osama bin Laden," 6–7; Runkle, *Wanted Dead or Alive*, 223–25.

118. Berkowitz, "Assassinating Justly," 347–48; Burke, "Al Qaeda," 19; "The President Reports the Death of Osama bin Laden," 6–7; Runkle, *Wanted Dead or Alive*, 224–25.

119. Blanche, "After Bin Laden," 23; Editors of *Life, Brought to Justice*, 84; Runkle, *Wanted Dead or Alive*, 226; Zarate and Gordon, "The Battle for Reform with Al-Qaeda," 104.

120. Berkowitz, "Assassinating Justly," 346; Blanche, "After Bin Laden," 20; Editors of *Life, Brought to Justice*, 84; "The President Reports the Death of Osama bin Laden," 6–7; Runkle, *Wanted Dead or Alive*, 206.

121. Crook, "U.S. Special Operations Personnel Raid Compound in Pakistan, Kill Osama bin Laden," 602–3; Editors of *Life, Brought to Justice*, 84; "The President Reports the Death of Osama bin Laden," 6–7; Runkle, *Wanted Dead or Alive*, 206–7.

122. Editors of *Life, Brought to Justice*, 84; "The President Reports the Death of Osama bin Laden," 6–7; Runkle, *Wanted Dead or Alive*, 206–7.

123. Berkowitz, "Assassinating Justly," 346–48; Crook, "U.S. Special Operations Personnel Raid Compound in Pakistan, Kill Osama bin Laden," 602–4; Editors

of *Life, Brought to Justice*, 84; "The President Reports the Death of Osama bin Laden," 6–7; Runkle, *Wanted Dead or Alive*, 206–7.

124. Editors of *Life, Brought to Justice*, 84, 86, 88; Runkle, *Wanted Dead or Alive*, 207.

125. Berkowitz, "Assassinating Justly," 346–47; Editors of *Life, Brought to Justice*, 84; "The President Reports the Death of Osama bin Laden," 6; Runkle, *Wanted Dead or Alive*, 207, 225–26.

126. Quoted in Obama, "Remarks by the President on Osama Bin Laden." See also Editors of *Life, Brought to Justice*, 91; President Reports the Death of Osama bin Laden," 6.

127. McCann, *Terrorism on American Soil*, 279–81; National Commission on Terrorist Attacks upon the United States, *The 9/11 Commission Report*, 339–60; Runkle, *Wanted Dead or Alive*, 233–38.

128. Blanche, "After Bin Laden," 20–23; McCann, *Terrorism on American Soil*, 278–81; National Commission on Terrorist Attacks upon the United States, *The 9/11 Commission Report*, 255–77; Zarate and Gordon, "The Battle for Reform with Al-Qaeda," 103–22.

129. Blanche, "After Bin Laden," 20–23; McCann, *Terrorism on American Soil*, 278–81; National Commission on Terrorist Attacks upon the United States, *The 9/11 Commission Report*, 365–74.

130. Blanche, "After Bin Laden," 20–23; Borradori, "Beyond the Culture of Terrorism," 397–407; Laqueur, "The Terrorism to Come," 49–64; McCann, *Terrorism on American Soil*, 278–81; Merari, "Deterring Fear," 26–31; National Commission on Terrorist Attacks upon the United States, *The 9/11 Commission Report*, 255–77, 365–74; Zarate and Gordon, "The Battle for Reform with Al-Qaeda," 103–22.

IV

CONCLUSION

THE LESSONS OF TERRORISM

Can I see another's woe,
And not be in sorrow too?
Can I see another's grief,
And not seek for kind relief?

—William Blake, "On Another's Sorrow"

September 11 begins and ends this book—a coincidence, to be sure, but no less unnerving. The final act in the Mountain Meadows Massacre, as detailed in chapter 1, occurred on September 11, 1857. The dramatic, horrific al-Qaeda-sponsored terrorist attacks in New York; Washington, D.C.; and Shanksville, Pennsylvania, occurred exactly 144 years later. These two episodes are neither the first nor the last terrorist incidents on American soil, but they are emblematic of attacks that have occurred in the United States over the course of the nation's history.

For peaceful, law-abiding citizens who seek to live and work free from harm or the fear of harm two questions invariably arise. First, why do individuals or groups of individuals feel compelled to engage in terrorism? Second, what, if any, steps can be taken to eliminate or, at the very least, mitigate terrorist actions?

Drawing lessons from infamous acts of terrorism is challenging because the causes of terrorism and the nature of the acts vary widely, as the cases discussed in this book illustrate. Attacks such as 9/11 are large and dramatic, involve many players, and are the result of many complex, sometimes poorly understood causes. Others, such as Ted Kaczynski's solitary bombing campaign, are low-profile, small, isolated events. Spotting possible terrorist attacks beforehand and preventing them remains an exceedingly difficult endeavor because patterns can be difficult to recognize. Generalizations are notoriously difficult to make.[1]

The initial difficulty in assessing terrorism is the lack of a precise, uncontested definition of the term. Despite this unfortunate reality, several common elements are present. First, violence or the threat of violence exists. To distinguish between state-sanctioned actions, such as police actions or wartime activities, the threat or the violence must violate the law of the jurisdiction where the act occurs. Civilians must be harmed whether they are the focus of the act or serve as collateral damage. Finally, to distinguish the act from an ordinary criminal matter, the purpose must be to advance a broader moral, social, political, religious, or ethnic goal. Terrorist acts usually involve a weak individual or group expressing discontent with a real or perceived source of repression or a hated symbol of a corrupted society.

In each incident recounted within these pages, an individual or group of individuals felt compelled to employ violence to further a personal, religious, social, or political cause because they felt weak and marginalized. Understanding why an individual or group of individuals chooses to resort to violence is difficult. As Richard Hofstadter and Michael Wallace, two leading researchers into political violence, quite rightly observe, organized violence on American soil "lacks both an ideological and a geographical center; it lacks cohesion." Historians have struggled to understand and discuss political violence (apart from wartime activities) because typically "it is committed by isolated individuals, by small groups, and by large mobs" and "undertaken for a variety of purposes" not always easily explained.[2]

Despite historical differences, varying methods, and distinct objectives, all persons who engage in terrorist acts are united by a common bond: fear. Fear convinces terrorists that the status quo is unacceptable. They seethe with resentment about wrongs, real or imagined, visited on them by external forces. They believe they have few, if any, options available to combat those forces through the regular channels of reasoned discourse and political exchange. In their skewed view of the world, filtered through the lenses of ideology or religion or unknown personal grievances, terrorists are honoring their ideals, God's will, or their own private demons in snuffing out the lives of their transgressors, even if that means innocents—euphemistically labeled "collateral damage"—are injured or killed. In fact, sometimes injuring or killing innocents is the paramount objective.[3]

Since September 11, 2001, many books and articles have been published about terrorism and America's response to the problem of "nonstate actors" who engage in violence. Some works examine the psychology or sociology of terrorism. Others seek to develop a grand theory, develop typologies, or construct a meta-narrative to explain why terrorists do what they do. Many post–September 11 works analyze America's homeland security apparatus and discuss why it failed on 9/11 and where it continues to be vulnerable. Like most things, these works vary from the good to the bad to the ugly.[4]

A few of the more valuable works bear mentioning here. In *Terrorism versus Democracy: The Liberal State Response*, Paul Wilkinson explains why terrorism often is the strategy of choice among disaffected individuals. Because weak, numerically inferior groups can strike at a larger target and conduct a war of attrition, terrorist attacks are an enormously appealing enterprise. The attacks are high yield and low risk. The resultant overreaction by authorities calls attention to the plight of the terrorist group and aids in recruiting new members. Publicity magnifies the importance of the event, which encourages marginalized groups to plan for future spectacular episodes.[5]

Bruce Hoffman traces the history of the concept in his book *Inside Terrorism*. He explains that terrorists do not see themselves in a negative light. They are wrapped up in their activities and blind to desires and interests apart from their own. Terrorists act in accordance with a worldview that may be radically different from the mainstream view.[6]

Audrey Kurth Cronin's *How Terrorism Ends* explores the reasons why terrorism has evolved over time and how terrorism ends. According to Cronin, the modern perception that terrorism is on the rise is attributable to the evolution of the concept. During the twentieth century, groups labeled as terrorists enjoyed greater access to state sponsors. Terrorism seemed to accomplish a group's goals. Terrorists gained access to increasingly lethal weaponry. The public sees terrorist attacks through the media, and therefore terrorism can reach an ever-expanding audience, which heightens the public relations value of a dramatic attack on a symbolic target. Despite the apparent ascendancy of terrorism, however, terrorist episodes end as events change and the power of particular nation-states rises and falls.[7]

In the second edition of *Terrorism Today*, Christopher C. Harmon argues that terror groups cannot continue their activities indefinitely. They eventually falter owing to interrelated factors, including the cumulative effects of systematic police work, effective political and military leadership, enhanced methods of intelligence gathering, and the appropriation of adequate financial resources to fight terrorism, among other things. Because terrorists adapt their methods repeatedly, states must respond decisively and remain eternally vigilant.[8]

Loch K. Johnson's *Bombs, Bugs, Drugs, and Thugs: Intelligence and America's Quest for Security* is a prime example of a book that seeks to understand the subject by focusing on institutions. Johnson's book surveys the entire structure of American intelligence activities, ranging from the Central Intelligence Agency (CIA) to the Federal Bureau of Investigation (FBI) to the National Security Council (NSC), and it offers recommendations for improvement.[9] In *Terrorism, Asymmetric Warfare, and Weapons of Mass Destruction: Defending the U.S. Homeland*, Anthony S. Cordesman offers a range of recommendations for improving security and fighting terrorism, from reevaluating what constitutes a threat and bolstering homeland defense measures to improving resource allocation and sharpening intelligence.[10]

Some books focus on where the Bush administration (and, to be fair, its predecessors) failed to combat terrorism effectively. Ron Suskind's book *The One Percent Doctrine: Deep Inside America's Pursuit of Its Enemies Since 9/11* begins with Vice President Dick Cheney's assertion that if there is "a one percent chance" that a threat is real, "we have to treat it as a certainty in terms of our response." From there, Suskind explores the mistakes made by America's intelligence community in responding to twenty-first-century threats to homeland security.[11] Thomas E. Ricks has written several books on the mistakes made in fighting terrorism, especially the flawed decision to fight the Iraqi war. Probably his best known work is *Fiasco: The American Military Adventure in Iraq.*[12]

Other books explore terrorism as a means of understanding the concept separately and apart from specific failures in American public policy. Probably the best book to date on the history of terrorism, at least with respect to militant Islam, is Lawrence Wright's Pulitzer Prize–winning *The Looming Tower: Al Qaeda and the Road to 9/11*, which traces the series of events that led up to the September 11 attacks and serves as a major source for the narrative found in chapter 12 of this book. Although it discusses American policy and its defects, *The Looming Tower* primarily traces the bastardization of Islam through the thinking of the men who influenced al-Qaeda's rise and fall.[13] Steve Coll's masterful work *Ghost Wars: The Secret History of the CIA, Afghanistan, and Bin Laden, from the Soviet Invasion to September 10, 2001* is another excellent Pulitzer Prize–winning book about the events leading up to the September 11 attacks. Coll reviews the CIA's operations in Afghanistan, the origins of the Taliban and al-Qaeda, and U.S. intelligence agencies' attempts to capture or kill Osama bin Laden before the 2001 attacks.[14]

Caleb Carr, a well-known novelist and military historian, provides yet another excellent terrorism primer in *The Lessons of Terror: A History of Warfare against Civilians*. Carr's book is broad and panoramic; it focuses on terrorism in general throughout the centuries. According to Carr, terrorism employed by national armies as well as extremists is ultimately self-defeating. Instead of prompting submission, it stiffens enemy resolve and never leads to long-lasting success.[15] Joseph T. McCann's *Terrorism on American Soil: A Concise History of Plots and Perpetrators from the Famous to the Forgotten* is a treasure trove of information, an accessible, easy-to-read encyclopedia of terrorist attacks in the United States. The book discusses episodes from the assassination of President Abraham Lincoln in 1865 to the anthrax letters mailed to American political leaders and news outlets in the fall of 2001.[16] In lieu of focusing on foreign sources, Kevin Borgeson and Robin Valeri assemble a series of thoughtful, incisive essays on domestic terrorism in their compilation titled *Terrorism in America*.[17]

A voluminous body of scholarly articles on terrorism has appeared in recent years. In "What Terrorists Really Want: Terrorist Motives and Counterterrorism Strategy," Max Abrahms argues that terrorists do not readily adhere to a strategic model employed for understanding rational decision making. In fact, they tend to act in puzzling ways that sometimes undermine their own goals. Terrorist organizations that attack civilians unleash a backlash that frustrates their desires. They might achieve their objectives through traditional bargaining and negotiation, but they frequently reject compromises that are in their best interests. They fall prey to internecine squabbling that harms them and helps their enemies. They sometimes initiate violent attacks without accepting responsibility, which mutes their message and resembles traditional criminal activity.[18]

Martha Crenshaw supports this analysis in "The Logic of Terrorism." Although terrorist attacks can be useful in setting the national or international agenda, terrorists sometimes act irrationally. They become impatient for action and fail to plan appropriately. They lose popular support and occasionally seem to be elitists because they exclude outsiders and fail to drum up grassroots support. They assume their demands and interests supersede the demands and interests of non-group members. In the long run, they fail because they do not always act rationally, although their actions can be characterized as the result of a "collectively rational choice." They loosely attempt to accomplish their goals, but they get sidetracked by ancillary issues, personnel disputes, and a breakdown of group cohesiveness.[19]

Other helpful articles that contributed to this book include Muhammad Mahroof Khan and Afshan Azam, "Root Causes of Terrorism: An Empirical Analysis"; Walter Laqueur, "The Terrorism to Come"; Ariel Merari, "Deterring Fear: Government Responses to Terrorist Attacks"; and John P. Moran, "The Roots of Terrorist Motivation: Shame, Rage, and Violence in *The Brothers Karamazov*." Each of these articles, and dozens of others in a similar vein listed in the references, provides a scholarly treatment of the causes and consequences of terrorism. They present provocative, well-argued, and meticulously researched explorations of the issue.[20]

The works I have cited analyze the success and failure of anti-terrorism policies. As valuable as these books are, they generally focus either on a specific type of terrorism (religious fanaticism or al-Qaeda, for example) or they provide a sweeping theoretical review of terrorism across the centuries. In some instances, the tomes are relatively dry and written for a scholarly audience, or at least a readership that is well versed in the subject matter. Often the books offer theories and typologies for studying terrorism.

Terrorist Attacks on American Soil differs from the above-mentioned works. For readers interested in grand theories, psychological studies, or meta-narratives, this book will not fit the bill. The purpose here has been to recall emblematic, dramatic stories to recapture the human drama of terrorism. Scholarly works sometimes lack a sense of the drama and pathos found in terrorist attacks. Yet behind each episode recounted in this book is a tale of human woe and grief, an intensely personal story that no scholarly account fully captures. Accordingly, this book has focused on the human dimensions in each incident as well as the repercussions of the attacks.

Several lessons emerge from the incidents recounted here. First, terrorism has been around as long as governments have existed, and it will continue to be around as long as governments exist. After the September 11, 2001, terrorist attacks in the United States, many commentators as well as members of the public bemoaned the fact that they no longer felt safe. For citizens unaccustomed to reflecting on terrorism and its consequences, the September 11 attacks seemed to be something new and terrifying, perhaps even unprecedented. The reality is that terrorism on American soil is not unprecedented—far from it. A major premise of this book is that disaffected people have evolved into terrorists throughout history. Accordingly, September 11 was not unprecedented, even if the scope was larger than previous attacks and the carnage was beyond what many people could have imagined. September 11 focused new attention on an old problem.

The initial problem involves defining "terrorism." To paraphrase Justice Potter Stewart's famous definition of obscenity, most people know it when they see it. But what else can we say? For the purposes of this book, terrorism is defined as "an act of violence or a threat of violence undertaken by non-state, non-governmental agents against citizens and other non-combatants to achieve one's objectives," but even that designation is not precise. Lack of precision is exactly the difficulty in preventing, mitigating, and/or prosecuting terrorism. What we might define as terrorism if perpetrated by foreigners in another country can be seen, and in most cases should be seen, as a criminal matter if the perpetrators engage in impermissible violence in their home nation-state.

Just as crime and violence are ongoing, systemic problems, so too is terrorism. Alienated loners such as Ted Kaczynski will always feel an overwhelming desire to visit their pain on others. Anti-government zealots such as Weatherman, Timothy McVeigh, or Eric Rudolph will see acts of violence as the most efficacious means of calling attention to their grievances. Religious extremists such as the September 11 bombers will forever seek to grab headlines as a mechanism for combating their feelings of powerlessness. Political activists such as Luke Pryor Blackburn, the Puerto Rican nationalists who attempted to assassinate President Truman, and the McNamara brothers see violence as the quickest way to publicize their cause. Groups such as the Mormons, the anarchists who probably bombed Wall Street in 1920, the white power structure in nineteenth-century Louisiana, and the twentieth-century Ku Klux Klan members who bombed the Sixteenth Street Baptist Church feel oppressed and under fire; therefore they fight fire with fire.

This book explored some of the most dramatic terrorist attacks on American soil, but it was by no means an exhaustive treatment. If the total number of attacks could be agreed upon and examined in a single work, the book would stretch across multiple volumes and thousands upon thousands of pages. The lesson is that terrorism is not a new phenomenon. It may be more apparent after September 11, 2001, but terrorism has been with us since the founding of the republic, and even earlier.

A second insight is that terrorism is portable, relatively inexpensive, and garners a lot of attention for the resources expended. Unlike traditional warfare among nations, terrorism can be undertaken on the cheap and, depending on the nature of the contemplated acts, with comparatively little advance planning. To state the case crassly using a cost-benefit analysis, the costs typically are low and the return on investment is high. As Paul Wilkinson has noted, terrorist attacks present few risks and can yield many dividends. Consider the ease with which terrorist attacks can be undertaken compared with alternative forms of action. It requires fewer resources to tear down the feeling of safety and security that a society enjoys than to build up a genuine infrastructure that leads to positive societal change. One or two carefully staged attacks can be undertaken successfully, thereby triggering widespread panic. Al-Qaeda has generated much fear in the United States in the twenty-first century, fear that probably is disproportionate to the actual risk. Of course, that is exactly the point of terrorism. By planting a seed of doubt about what might occur next—al Qaeda sleeper cells might suddenly come to life and repeat the horrific events of September 11, 2001, or they might acquire weapons of mass destruction—the terror lingers long after the event has taken place. For some alienated parties, the sense of power that comes from striking fear into the hearts of persons and societies with whom they disagree is appealing, especially when we reflect on the types of people attracted to terrorism. Terrorists often are self-important, alienated, histrionic, macho young men (and occasionally women) looking for a sense of purpose that comes from a cause that appears larger than life.

I mentioned in the introduction that my eight-year-old stepdaughter had heard of Eric Rudolph. In fact, she asserted that "everybody knows about Eric Rudolph." In the normal course of events, no one would hear about Eric Rudolph. I have lived my entire life in the Deep South. Southerners (and persons from other parts of the country as well) typically refer to an Eric Rudolph as a "redneck." That term need not be derisive, but generally it designates a person of no special importance. Eric Rudolph was no one special, just another redneck in the neighborhood. Yet in the United States, fame is often the coin of the realm. For a person with no particular athletic prowess, intellectual horsepower, political aptitude, or artistic skills, it is a rare and perhaps precious coin. For the angry loner or politically alienated soul who feels hurt, offended, disenfranchised, and unappreciated, the fastest way to fame and a feeling of self-worth is to express dissatisfaction through violence. Most rednecks live and die with little or no attention from the outside world. Blow up an Olympic venue and suddenly eight-year-olds know your name.

This is not to suggest that Eric Rudolph sought martyrdom. If he had succeeded according to plan, he would have continued his serial bombing campaign indefinitely. Nonetheless, despite his desire to elude capture, he sought to call attention to his objectives. He became a self-mythologizing outlaw, a folk hero to the anti-government crowd. He shared this general goal with most of the terrorists portrayed in this book—he wanted his deeds and his legend to live on even as he escaped from the authorities.

Terrorism works for the substate actor who seeks to spread his or her misery to others quickly, affordably, and with maximum attention. This observation is especially true in an age when onlookers can capture the scene instantly on film or video, upload it on the Internet, and share the images in minutes or even seconds. The world is immediate, and people are hungry for stories that entertain, entice, or enthrall. Terrorist violence is perfectly suited to an era seeking interesting stories and images.

Another lesson is that terrorism can never be eradicated; it can only be contained. In conjunction with the previous point, because terrorism is cheap and garners quick attention, it will never be eradicated. Terrorists frequently act in small groups at the substate level; they can operate "under the radar." The variety of actions and the endless permutations and combinations available to would-be terrorists simply preclude the possibility of eliminating all nefarious plots. Although a vigilant citizenry and a vigorous law enforcement presence can reduce the number of incidents or the severity of an attack in most cases, invariably a determined band of marauders will succeed upon occasion. If nothing else, the laws of probability ensure that not all terrorists can be stopped. If the reasons that terrorists act and the methods by which they select targets can be understood, most attacks can be contained. Containment means that terrorists do not acquire weapons of mass destruction or engage in repeated acts of violence without answering to legal authorities. Although obviously foiling all terrorist plots is the ideal, if this goal is not attainable, at least it is preferable that terrorists engage in a solitary act of violence in lieu of acquiring and exploding a "dirty bomb," a nuclear weapon, or a biological agent.

If this assessment initially sounds flippant or disconcerting, the comment is not designed to be demoralizing. Any clear-eyed analysis of the causes and consequences of terrorism suggests that clever, determined terrorists willing to risk everything to inflict harm on others will occasionally succeed. The stories in this book attest to that sobering reality. The fact that terrorism exists cannot be denied, but it is also true that terrorism can be controlled as long as we remain vigilant and continually strive to understand the phenomenon.

Terrorism continues because for some groups it meets their needs. Some researchers suggest that terrorists ultimately fail in their quest to capture the hearts and minds of the citizenry because when the facts about the horrific damage done to innocents become known, all but the most zealous adherents will turn their back on the terrorists and their cause. The respected military historian Caleb Carr makes this point in his 2003 book *The Lessons of Terror: A History of Warfare against Civilians*. Max Abrahms and Martha Crenshaw reiterate these arguments, and others, in their works cited in this book. From a strictly rational, Enlightenment-era assessment, this conclusion rings true, assuming that capturing the hearts and minds of the citizenry is the goal.

Max Abrahms suggests that rational actors act pursuant to stable, consistent preferences by comparing costs and benefits among competing choices and selecting an option that offers the optimal expected utility. The problem with this rational strategic model is that terrorists often behave outside the traditional understanding of rationality. This observation is not to suggest that terrorists are irrational, although some may be, but that their sense of what constitutes a rational act varies from the mainstream perspective.[21]

Political terrorists may seek to maximize the number of adherents, but not all terrorists are motivated by a desire to effect changes in public policy. Some terrorists do not operate in accordance with a clearly discernible rational framework. Having rejected traditional methods of influencing public policy such as voting, lobbying, and attempting to influence public opinion through nonviolent means, terrorists may not wish to capture hearts and minds. Whatever disaffection drives them to engage in violence may propel them forward in spite of—or perhaps because of—the opprobrium of their fellow man. To an alienated terrorist such as Ted Kaczynski, Timothy McVeigh, or Eric Rudolph, the idea that the world looks on him as a pariah is perfectly consistent with his original sense of alienation and isolation. A terrorist who sees himself as an ascetic denying himself the pleasures of a corrupted world is not necessarily disheartened by condemnation. He may even thrive on it. Thus, for individuals or groups subjected to scorn and derision, terrorist acts may still be viewed as successful. For these small groups of people, terrorism will always be a powerful, compelling course of action because, according to their twisted sets of values, it works.

Terrorist attacks fulfill a human need—perhaps a need to cause pain in others. This conclusion contains an implicit premise about the psychology of terrorists and terrorism. The terrorist is someone who projects a psychological desire onto the world. He or she feels anger or resentment or a desire for attention that presumably cannot be fulfilled or satiated through other means. Making someone else hurt provides a sense of satisfaction. For some highly motivated terrorists, the desire to inflict pain on others is up close and personal. Slaughtering members of the Baker-Fancher party during the Mountain Meadows Massacre required the killers to watch as their victims crumpled to the ground and the survivors begged for their lives. A few accounts recorded the "hideous, demon-like yells" the ambushers emitted as they shot and clubbed unarmed men, women, and young children to death. Mormons had been persecuted for decades. Their anger, fear, and frustration poured out in one terrible episode of gratuitous violence.

Christopher Columbus Nash and his white supremacist paramilitary group that shot fleeing freedmen reputedly engaged in horrific violence with great glee during the 1873 massacre in Colfax, Louisiana, expressing their frustration and hostility toward blacks through an outlet that satisfied their base desires, at least until the recriminations commenced. The world of the 1860s and 1870s had changed radically. Blacks no longer knew their place in established society. Southern whites were fearful and angry at the loss of Southern pride and traditional social relations that stretched back for many generations. In all likelihood, the perpetrators were not thinking of long term consequences when they acted. They were caught up in that time and place. They sought a return to the Old South, a mythical land where whites exercised control over people of color.

Would be presidential assassins Griselio Torresola and Oscar Collazo exchanged gunfire with law enforcement officials up close and personal when they tried to kill President Truman in 1950. They would have shot down the leader of the free world if the incident had unfolded as planned. Their desire to publicize the plight of Puerto Ricans was bizarre when placed in a rational strategic model. Rather than generate sympathy for the cause, assassinating the American president probably would have caused heavy-handed reprisals.

It takes a special kind of gumption and zeal to confront one's enemies face to face. Far more terrorists prefer to revel in their destruction from afar. Luke Pryor Blackburn, the much-reviled "Dr. Black Vomit," sent infected garments into interstate commerce and hoped for the worst. He sought to ruin lives and undermine a nation, but, having striven to cure yellow fever–infected patients earlier in his career, he had no desire to witness the destruction he unleashed.

Bombers seem especially interested in wreaking havoc from safe environs. When the McNamaras booby-trapped the *Los Angeles Times* building, they sought to send a message to the odious Harrison Gray Otis, the newspaper's owner and publisher, but they set their charge and scampered to safety. The message need not bring harm to them or their interests. The unknown assailants on Wall Street in 1920 were more than willing to sacrifice a horse and the lowly minions who labored in the vicinity, but the perpetrators were not similarly interested in sacrificing themselves on an altar of public accountability. The Klansmen who snuffed out the lives of four little girls with a bomb inside the Sixteenth Street Baptist Church in 1963 were anxious to harm citizens of a darker hue, but they were equally anxious to avoid harm to themselves or neighbors sporting the preferred pigmentation. Weatherman members willingly marched to protest the war, but those who engaged in violent acts frequently went underground to avoid criminal prosecution. In a similar vein, Ted Kaczynski, Timothy McVeigh, and Eric Rudolph felt no compunction about harming victims, but each sought to escape punishment afterward. Even if Osama bin Laden convinced others to commit suicide in aid of his warped anti-American plots, he hunkered down inside a well-fortified compound and did everything he could to avoid detection when he was in harm's way.

Terrorism succeeds for terrorists who operate outside of a rational strategic model, but it works only insofar as terrorists can formulate and implement a plan. Even in light of the relative ease with which modern weaponry can be acquired or manufactured and the small expense involved, the logistics can be daunting. Moreover, as terrorists become more innovative and clever, so do the intelligence officials and law enforcement personnel who would foil their efforts.

In some cases, terrorist acts follow a traditional story line that can alert us to future attacks. Related to the preceding discussion, intelligence officials and police officers recognize that tell-tale patterns exist whenever terrorists threaten public order. We must learn to recognize the clues before an attack occurs. Regardless of their motivations and ideological or religious beliefs, all terrorists share some common characteristics, and their actions share common features. Almost all terrorists leave a paper trail. They talk with other would-be terrorists. They often write down their plans. In some cases, they espouse their views in public, although their ideas are usually ignored or ridiculed. Even loners such as Ted Kaczynski and Eric Rudolph left a trail; it just required sufficient time to find it.

Unfortunately, in other cases the story line is confusing and unclear. Sometimes terrorist behavior prior to an attack appears no different from the behavior of other persons. Because would-be terrorists do not always respond to the same motivations, ferreting out their activities beforehand becomes problematic. A leaderless attacker such as the Unabomber or Eric Rudolph acts very differently than an al-Qaeda member. After the fact, clues to their behavior may be visible, but often the story line is opaque in the months, weeks, and days leading to an attack.

Whatever else they share, terrorists all act from a position of weakness. They believe they cannot work within the existing public policy framework. Sometimes they have tried to engage in the policy process and have been unsuccessful in garnering attention. They frequently believe, rightly or wrongly, that formal participation will be detrimental to their cause because the government is too dictatorial or corrupt to respond favorably. Disaffected would-be terrorists generally are not crazy; they almost always come to rely on violence as the appropriate means of dissent after considering other options and rejecting them as unworkable. The challenge for law enforcement personnel and military strategists is to recognize the signs of potential terrorism and intervene appropriately. Intervention may require a military crackdown if a plot is uncovered in its late stages, or it may be less heavy-handed if the situation is not desperate and the danger is not clear and present.

Consider the episodes discussed in this book. In virtually every instance, the emotions underlying the incident strongly suggested that terrorists would emerge to lash out at their perceived oppressors. For example, the Mormons were repeatedly attacked as strange cultists who threatened traditional religious values. They fled westward and consolidated their forces into a tight-knit community. After founding father Joseph Smith fell victim to mob violence, his successor, Brigham Young, consistently employed incendiary rhetoric to defend the church. Luke Pryor Blackburn, the infamous "Dr. Black Vomit," was a staunch defender of the Southern Confederacy. That he would attempt to infect Northern partisans with yellow fever–infected garments was regrettable, but certainly in keeping with the desperate measures sometimes employed in those desperate times. White supremacists' attacks on armed black freedmen in Colfax, Louisiana, in 1873 were foreseeable. Labor violence in the early twentieth century, an assassination attempt on an American president, Ku Klux Klan violence in 1960s Mississippi, and political bombings are all actions that can be understood in context. Even the al-Qaeda terrorist plot was potentially discoverable during the summer of 2001, when the "system was blinking red."

The problem is that hindsight reveals the clues far better than foresight ever can. Sifting through data after the fact demonstrates where and why the clues failed to add up to actionable intelligence. We always view the future through a glass darkly. Perhaps the best we can do is to examine the past and seek to discern patterns that help us understand what the future might hold.

NOTES

1. Laqueur, *No End to War*, 22.

2. Quoted in Hofstadter and Wallace, *American Violence*, 1–2.

3. Crenshaw, "The Logic of Terrorism," 11–12; Lutz and Lutz, *Terrorism in America*, 2–3.

4. See, for example, Cronin, *How Terrorism Ends*, 3–5; DeNardo, *Power in Numbers*; Harmon, *Terrorism Today*, 172–87; Lutz and Lutz, *Terrorism in America*, 1–2; Richardson, *What Terrorists Want*.

5. Wilkinson, *Terrorism versus Democracy*, 3–7.

6. Hoffman, *Inside Terrorism*, 30–40.

7. Cronin, *How Terrorism Ends*.

8. Harmon, *Terrorism Today*, 172–87.

9. Johnson, *Bombs, Bugs, Drugs, and Thugs: Intelligence and America's Quest for Security*.

10. Cordesman, *Terrorism, Asymmetric Warfare, and Weapons of Mass Destruction: Defending the U.S. Homeland*.

11. Suskind, *The One Percent Doctrine*, 150.

12. Ricks, *Fiasco: The American Military Adventure in Iraq*.

13. Wright, *The Looming Tower*.

14. Coll, *Ghost Wars*.

15. Carr, *The Lessons of Terror*.

16. McCann, *Terrorism on American Soil*.

17. Borgeson and Valeri, *Terrorism in America*.

18. Abrahms, "What Terrorists Really Want," 82–93. See also Abrahms, "Why Terrorism Does Not Work."

19. Crenshaw, "The Logic of Terrorism," 8–20. See also Crenshaw, "Theories of Terrorism."

20. Khan and Azam, "Root Causes of Terrorism: An Empirical Analysis," 65–86; Laqueur, "The Terrorism to Come," 49–64; Merari, "Deterring Fear: Government Responses to Terrorist Attacks," 26–31.

21. Abrahms, "What Terrorists Really Want," 79–81.

REFERENCES

Abrahms, Max. "What Terrorists Really Want: Terrorist Motives and Counterterrorism Strategy." *International Security* 32, no. 4 (Spring 2008): 78–105.

———. "Why Terrorism Does Not Work." *International Security* 31, no. 2 (Fall 2006): 42–78.

Abuza, Zachary. "Tentacles of Terror: Al Qaeda's Southeast Asian Network." *Contemporary Southeast Asia* 24, no. 3 (December 2002): 427–65.

Adamic, Louis. *Dynamite: The Story of Class Violence in America*. Oakland, Calif.: AK Press, 2008.

Akhtar, Salman. "The Psychodynamic Dimension of Terrorism." *Psychiatric Annals* 29, no. 6 (June 1999): 350–55.

Allen, Charles. "The Hidden Roots of Wahhabism in British India." *World Policy Journal* 22, no. 2 (Summer 2005): 87–93.

Allen, David. "An Image from Oklahoma City." *Journal of American History* 94, no. 1 (June 2007): 172–78.

Anderson, S. Willoughby. "The Past on Trial: Birmingham, Bombing, and Restorative Justice." *California Law Review* 96, no. 2 (April 2008): 471–504.

Arrington, Leonard J. *Brigham Young: American Moses*. New York: Knopf, 1985.

Arrington, Leonard J., and David Bitton. *The Mormon Experience: A History of the Latter Day Saints*. Champaign: University of Illinois Press, 1992.

Assadi, Djamchid, and Britta Lorunser. "Strategic Management Analysis of al Qaeda: The Role of Worldwide Organization for a Worldwide Strategy." *Problems and Perspectives in Management* 5, no. 4 (2007): 57–71.

Avrich, Paul. *Sacco and Vanzetti: The Anarchist Background*. Princeton, N.J.: Princeton University Press, 1991.

Ayala, Cesar J., and Laird W. Bergad. "Rural Puerto Rico in the Twentieth Century Reconsidered: Land and Society, 1899–1915." *Latin American Research Review* 37, no. 2 (2002): 65–97.

Ayala, Cesar J., and Rafael Bernabe. *Puerto Rico in the American Century: A History since 1898.* Chapel Hill: University of North Carolina Press, 2007.

Aydinli, Ersel. "Before *Jihadists*, There Were Anarchists: A Failed Case of Transnational Violence." *Studies in Conflict and Terrorism* 31, no. 10 (October 2008): 903–23.

Ayers, Bill. *Fugitive Days: A Memoir.* Boston: Beacon Press, 2001.

Ayers, Bill, and Bernadine Dohrn. "What Race Has to Do with It." *Monthly Review* 60, no. 10 (March 2009): 50–55.

Bagby, Milton. "Two Arrested for 1963 Church Bombing." *American History* 35, no. 4 (October 2000): 6–7.

Bagley, Will. *Blood of the Prophets: Brigham Young and the Massacre at Mountain Meadows.* Norman: University of Oklahoma Press, 2002.

Baird, Nancy Disher. *Luke Pryor Blackburn: Physician, Governor, Reformer.* Lexington: University Press of Kentucky, 1979.

Bakeless, John. *Spies of the Confederacy.* Mineola, N.Y.: Courier Dover Publications, 1997.

Bancroft, Hubert Howe. *History of Utah, 1540–1886.* San Francisco: History Company, 1889.

Barber, David. *A Hard Rain Fell: SDS and Why It Failed.* Jackson: University Press of Mississippi, 2008.

Barkun, Michael. *Religion and the Racist Right: The Origins of the Christian Identity Movement.* Rev. ed. Chapel Hill: University of North Carolina Press, 1997.

Barnard, Jeff. "Artist Has Portfolio of Crimes; Jean Boylan Sketched the Unabomber Suspect. Another Prominent Case: Terry Nichols' Trial." *Philadelphia Inquirer*, November 29, 1997: A7.

Bartley, Abel A. "The Fourteenth Amendment: The Great Equalizer of the American People." *Akron Law Review* 36, no. 3 (2003): 475–90.

Bates, Tom. *RADS: The 1970 Bombing of the Army Math Research Center at the University of Wisconsin-Madison and Its Aftermath.* New York: HarperCollins, 1992.

Beale, Howard K. *The Critical Year: A Study of Andrew Johnson and Reconstruction.* New York: Frederick Ungar, 1958 [1930].

Being the Portraits and Biographies of the Progressive Men of the West. Charleston, S.C.: Nabu Press, 2010 [1923].

Belluck, Pam. "A Brother's Anguish: In Unabom Case, Pain for Suspect's Family." *New York Times*, April 10, 1996: A1, A14.

Belz, Herman. *Reconstructing the Union: Theory and Policy during the Civil War.* Ithaca, N.Y.: Cornell University Press, 1969.

Berger, Dan. *Outlaws of America: The Weather Underground and the Politics of Solidarity.* San Francisco: AK Press, 2006.

Berkowitz, Roger. "Assassinating Justly: Reflections on Justice and Revenge in the Osama Bin Laden Killing." *Law, Culture and the Humanities* 7, no. 3 (October 2011): 346–51.

Black, Jeremy. "1979: The Real Year of Revolution." *History Today* 59, no. 5 (May 2009): 5–6.

Blackmon, Douglas A. *Slavery by Another Name: The Re-enslavement of Black Americans from the Civil War to World War II*. New York: Doubleday, 2008.

Blanche, Ed. "After Bin Laden." *The Middle East* 423, no. 1 (June 2011): 20–23.

Blum, Howard. *American Lightning: Terror, Mystery, the Birth of Hollywood, and the Crime of the Century*. New York: Crown Books, 2008.

Booker, M. Keith. *A Martyr to His Cause: Film and the American Left; a Research Guide*. Santa Barbara, Calif.: Greenwood Press, an Imprint of ABC-CLIO, 1999.

Booth, William. "Kaczynski Resists the Insanity Defense." *Washington Post*, December 26, 1997, A1.

Borgeson, Kevin, and Robin Valeri. *Terrorism in America*. Sudbury, Mass.: Jones and Bartlett, 2009.

Borradori, Giovanna. "Beyond the Culture of Terrorism." *Philosophy Today* 49, no. 4 (Winter 2005): 397–407.

Boylan, Jeanne. *Portraits of Guilt: The Woman Who Profiles the Faces of America's Deadliest Criminals*. New York: Pocket Books, 2001.

Branch, Taylor. *Parting the Waters: America in the King Years, 1954–63*. New York: Simon & Schuster, 1988.

———. *Pillar of Fire: America in the King Years, 1963–65*. New York: Simon & Schuster, 1998.

Brands, H. W. "Hesitant Emancipator: Abraham Lincoln Endured Hours of Personal Anguish before He Unveiled the Proclamation That Ended Slavery." *American History* 44, no. 2 (June 2009): 54–59.

Brereton, Bridget, and Teresita Martinez-Vergne. *General History of the Caribbean: The Caribbean in the Twentieth Century*. New York: Macmillan Caribbean, 2003.

Brinkley, Douglas. *Rosa Parks*. New York: Viking, 2000.

Broad, William J. "Unabom Manifesto Echoes 60's Tumult." *New York Times*, June 1, 1996, A8.

Brooke, James. "New Portrait of Unabomber: Environmental Saboteur around Montana Village for 20 Years." *New York Times*, March 14, 1999, A20.

Brown v. Board of Education of Topeka, 347 U.S. 483 (1954).

Bryant, Douglas H. "Unorthodox and Paradox: Revisiting the Ratification of the Fourteenth Amendment." *Alabama Law Review* 53, no. 2 (Winter 2003): 555–81.

Brzezinski, Zbigniew. "Right Cause, Wrong Response." *Wall Street Journal*, September 9, 2011, A19.

Burg, Robert W. "Amnesty, Civil Rights, and the Meaning of Liberal Republicanism, 1862–1872." *American Nineteenth Century History* 4, no. 3 (Fall 2003): 29–60.

Burke, Jason. "Al Qaeda." *Foreign Policy* 142, no. 1 (May/June 2004): 18–26.

Burns, William J. *The Masked War: The Story of a Peril That Threatened the United States*. Charleston, S.C.: Nabu Press, 2010 [1913].

Bushman, Richard Lyman. *Joseph Smith: Rough Stone Rolling*. New York: Vintage, 2007.

Caeti, Tory J., John Liederbach, and Steven S. Bellew. "Police-Media Relations at Critical Incidents: Interviews from Oklahoma City." *International Journal of Police Science and Management* 7, no. 2 (Summer 2005): 86–97.

Calabresi, Steven G., and Christopher S. Yoo. "The Unitary Executive during the Second Half-Century." *Harvard Journal of Law and Public Policy* 26, no. 3 (Summer 2003): 667–801.

Callahan, James Morton. *A Diplomatic History of the Southern Confederacy*. New York: Frederick Ungar, 1964 [1901].

Campos-Flores, Arian, Catharine Skipp, and Frederick Burger. "How He Stayed Hidden." *Newsweek* 141, no. 24 (June 16, 2003): 36.

Caputi, Jane. "Guest Editor's Introduction: Of Towers and Twins, Synchronicities and Shadows; Archetypal Meanings in the Imagery of 9/11." *Journal of American Culture* 28, no. 1 (March 2005): 1–10.

Card, Claudia. "Recognizing Terrorism." *Journal of Ethics* 11, no. 1 (March 2007): 1–29.

Carr, Caleb. *The Lessons of Terror: A History of Warfare against Civilians*. New York: Random House, 2003.

Carson, Clayborne. "Between Contending Forces: Martin Luther King, Jr., and the African American Freedom Struggle." *Magazine of History* 19, no. 1 (January 2005): 17–21.

———. "To Walk with Dignity: The Montgomery Bus Boycott." *Magazine of History* 19, no. 1 (January 2005): 13–15.

Catsam, Derek Charles. "'Mister, This Is Not Your Fight!': The 1961 Montgomery Freedom Ride Riots." *Studies in the Literary Imagination* 40, no. 2 (Fall 2007): 93–109.

CBS News. *What We Saw: The Events of September 11, 2001—In Words, Pictures, and Video*. New York: Simon & Schuster, 2002.

Chalberg, John. *Emma Goldman: American Individualist*. 2nd ed. New York: Longman, 2008.

Chalmers, David M. *Hooded Americanism: The History of the Ku Klux Klan*. 3rd ed. Durham, N.C.: Duke University Press, 1987.

Chase, Alston. *Harvard and the Unabomber: The Education of an American Terrorist*. New York and London: Norton, 2003.

Clarke, James W. *American Assassins: The Darker Side of Politics*. Princeton, N.J.: Princeton University Press, 1990.

Cleary, Caitlin. "Bloggers Smell Conspiracy with Flight 93 Photo." *Pittsburgh Post-Gazette*, 6 August 2006: B1.

Clinton, Bill. *My Life*. New York: Knopf, 2004.

Cohen, Michael. "'Cartooning Capitalism': Radical Cartooning and the Making of American Popular Radicalism in the Early Twentieth Century." *International Review of Social History* 52, no. S15 (December 2007): 35–58.

Coll, Steve. *Ghost Wars: The Secret History of the CIA, Afghanistan, and Bin Laden, from the Soviet Invasion to September 10, 2001.* New York: Penguin, 2004.

Conlin, Joseph R. "William D. 'Big Bill' Haywood: The Westerner as Labor Radical." In *Labor Leaders in America,* edited by Melvyn Dubofsky and Warren Van Tine, 111–33. Champaign: University of Illinois Press, 1987.

Copeland, Larry. "Olympics Bomber Apologizes, but Not to All Victims." *USA Today,* August 23, 2005, 3A.

———. "Rudolph Ate Acorns, Lizards, Game." *USA Today,* June 4, 2003, 1A.

Cordes, Bonnie, Brian M. Jenkins, Konrad Kellen, Gail Bass, Daniel Relles, William Sater, Mario Juncosa, William Fowler, and Geraldine Petty. *A Conceptual Framework for Analyzing Terrorist Groups.* Santa Monica, Calif.: Rand Corporation (R–3151), 1985.

Cordesman, Anthony S. *Terrorism, Asymmetric Warfare, and Weapons of Mass Destruction: Defending the U.S. Homeland.* Westport, Conn.: Praeger, 2008.

Coulson, Danny O., and Elaine Shannon. *No Heroes: Inside the FBI's Secret Counter-Terror Force.* New York: Pocket Books, 1999.

Cowan, Geoffrey. *The People v. Clarence Darrow.* New York: Crown Books, 1993.

Cox, LaWanda Fenlason. *Lincoln and Black Freedom: A Study in Presidential Leadership.* Columbia: University of South Carolina, 1994.

Crenshaw, Martha. "The Logic of Terrorism: Terrorist Behavior as a Product of Strategic Choice." In *Origins of Terrorism: Psychologies, Ideologies, Theologies, States of Mind,* edited by Walter Reich, 7–14. Washington, D.C.: Woodrow Wilson Center Press, 1998.

———. "Theories of Terrorism: Instrumental and Organizational Approaches." In *Inside Terrorist Organizations,* edited by David C. Rapoport, 13–31. New York and London: Columbia University Press, 1988.

Cronin, Audrey Kurth. *How Terrorism Ends: Understanding the Decline and Demise of Terrorist Campaigns.* Princeton, N.J.: Princeton University Press, 2009.

Crook, John. "U.S. Special Operations Personnel Raid Compound in Pakistan, Kill Osama bin Laden." *American Journal of International Law* 105, no. 3 (July 2011): 602–5.

Crosby, Molly Caldwell. *The American Plague: The Untold Story of Yellow Fever, the Epidemic That Shaped Our History.* New York: Penguin, 2007.

Crothers, Lane. "The Cultural Foundations of the Modern Militia Movement." *New Political Science* 24, no. 2 (June 2002): 221–34.

Cunningham, David. *There's Something Happening Here: The New Left, the Klan, and FBI Counterintelligence.* Berkeley and Los Angeles: University of California Press, 2004.

Curriden, Mark. "Rebuilding a Reputation." *ABA Journal* 83, no. 1 (January 1997): 20.

Currie, David P. "The Reconstruction Congress." *University of Chicago Law Review* 75, no. 1 (2008): 383–495.

Darrow, Clarence. *The Story of My Life*. New York: Scribner, 1932.

DeNardo, James. *Power in Numbers: The Political Strategy of Protest and Rebellion*. Princeton, N.J.: Princeton University Press, 2006.

Department of Justice of the United States. Baltimore, Md.: Lord Baltimore Press for the Institute for Government Research, 1927.

Derbyshire, Stuart W. G. "The Execution of Timothy McVeigh: Must See TV?" *British Medical Journal* 322, no. 7296 (May 19, 2001): 1254.

DeWitt, David Miller. *The Impeachment and Trial of Andrew Johnson, Seventeenth President of the United States: A History*. New York: Macmillan, 1903.

Dietz, James L. *Economic History of Puerto Rico: Institutional Change and Capitalist Development*. Princeton, N.J.: Princeton University Press, 1986.

Dolbeare, Kenneth M. *American Political Thought*. Chatham, N.J.: Chatham House, 1984.

Donald, David Herbert. *Lincoln*. New York: Simon & Schuster, 1995.

Doran Michael. "The Pragmatic Fanaticism of al Qaeda: An Anatomy of Extremism in Middle Eastern Politics." *Political Science Quarterly* 117, no. 2 (Summer 2002): 177–90.

Douglas, John E., and Mark Olshaker. *Unabomber: On the Trail of America's Most-Wanted Serial Killer*. New York: Pocket Books, 1996.

Dowd, Maureen. "His Brother's Keeper." *New York Times*, April 11, 1996, A25.

Drabble, John. "The FBI, COINTELPRO-WHITE HATE, and the Decline of the Ku Klux Klan Organizations in Alabama, 1964–1971." *Alabama Review* 61, no. 1 (January 2008): 3–47.

Dray, Philip. *Capitol Men: The Epic Story of Reconstruction through the Lives of the First Black Congressmen*. Boston and New York: Houghton Mifflin, 2008.

Dubofsky, Melvyn. *"Big Bill" Haywood*. Manchester, U.K.: Manchester University Press, 1987.

DuBois, W. E. B. *The Souls of Black Folk: Essays and Sketches*. 8th ed. Chicago: A. C. McClurg, 1909.

Dwyer, Jim, and Kevin Flynn. *102 Minutes: The Untold Story of the Fight to Survive Inside the Twin Towers*. New York: Times Books, Henry Holt, 2005.

Editors of *Life*. *Brought to Justice: Osama Bin Laden's War on America and the Mission That Stopped Him*. New York, Boston, and London: Little, Brown, 2011.

Edwards, David B. "Bin Laden's Last Stand." *Anthropological Quarterly* 75, no. 1 (Winter 2001): 178–85.

Egan, Timothy. "Hiding Out Underneath the Big Sky." *New York Times*, April 7, 1996, E1, E4.

Ellis, Joseph J. *American Sphinx: The Character of Thomas Jefferson*. New York: Vintage, 1998.

Eskew, Glenn T. *But for Bombingham: The Local and National Movements in the Civil Rights Struggle*. Chapel Hill: University of North Carolina Press, 1997.

Faber, John. *Great News Photos and the Stories behind Them*. 2nd ed. New York: Dover, 1978.

Farrell, John A. "Darrow in the Dock." *Smithsonian* 42, no. 8 (December 2011): 98–111.

Ferkiss, Victor. "The FBI Comes Calling: My Encounter with the Unabomber." *Commonweal* 126, no. 16 (September 26, 1997): 9–10.

Fernandez, Anthony, III. "Remembering the Oklahoma City Bombing." *Journal of American History* 94, no. 1 (June 2007): 179–82.

Flaherty, Lois T. "Youth, Ideology, and Terrorism." *Adolescent Psychiatry* 27, no. 1 (2003): 29–58.

Flood, Charles Bracelen. *1864: Lincoln at the Gates of History*. New York: Simon & Schuster, 2009.

Flores, Lisa Pierce. *The History of Puerto Rico*. Santa Barbara, Calif.: Greenwood Press, a Division of ABC-CLIO, 2009.

Flowers, Deidre B. "The Launching of the Sit-In Movement: The Role of Black Women at Bennett College." *Journal of African American History* 90, no. 1–2 (Winter 2005): 52–63.

Fonda, Daren, Paul Cuadros, Greg Fulton, Greg Land, Constance Richards, and Frank Sikora. "How Luck Ran Out for a Most Wanted Fugitive." *Time* 161, no. 23 (June 9, 2003): 23–30.

Foner, Eric. *The Fiery Trial: Abraham Lincoln and American Slavery*. New York and London: Norton, 2010.

———. *Forever Free: The Story of Emancipation and Reconstruction*. Illustrations edited with a commentary by Joshua Brown. New York: Knopf, 2005.

———. *Reconstruction: America's Unfinished Revolution: 1863–1877*. New York: Francis Parkman Prize Edition, History Book Club, 2005 [1988].

Foner, Philip Sheldon. *The Spanish-Cuban-American War*. New York: Monthly Review Press, 1972.

Ford, Lacy K. "Reconfiguring the Old South: 'Solving' the Problem of Slavery, 1787–1838." *Journal of American History* 95, no. 1 (June 2008): 95–122.

Fouda, Yosri, and Nick Fielding. *Masterminds of Terror: The Truth behind the Most Devastating Terrorist Attack the World Has Ever Seen*. New York: Arcade, 2003.

"Four Little Girls, Nobody Knew Their Names: The Sixteenth Street Church Martyrs." *New Crisis* 107, no. 3 (May/June 2000): 34.

Franks, Lucinda. "From the Underground, a New Magazine." *New York Times*, March 20, 1975: 24.

———. "U.S. Inquiry Finds 37 in Weather Underground." *New York Times*, March 3, 1975: 38.

Frasier, Steve. *Every Man a Speculator: A History of Wall Street in American Life*. New York: HarperCollins, 2005.

Furniss, Norman F. *The Mormon Conflict: 1850–1859*. New Haven, Conn.: Yale University Press, 2005 [1960].

Gaddis, John Lewis. *Strategies of Containment: A Critical Appraisal of American National Security Policy during the Cold War*. 2nd ed. Oxford and New York: Oxford University Press, 2005.

Gage, Beverly. *The Day Wall Street Exploded: A Story of America in Its First Age of Terror*. Oxford and New York: Oxford University Press, 2009.

Gerges, Fawaz A. *The Rise and Fall of Al-Qaeda*. New York and Oxford: Oxford University Press, 2011.

Gitlin, Todd. *The Sixties: Years of Hope, Days of Rage*. New York: Bantam Books, 1989.

Glaberson, William. "Accepts Life Term without Parole and Forgoes Right to Appeal." *New York Times*, January 23, 1998, A1, A18.

Goodman, Brenda. "Falsely Accused Suspect Pursues Libel Case." *New York Times*, May 27, 2006: A11.

Goodwin, Doris Kearns. *Team of Rivals: The Political Genius of Abraham Lincoln*. New York: Simon & Schuster, 2005.

Graves, Kerry A. *The Spanish-American War*. Mankato, Minn.: Capstone Press, 2000.

Graysmith, Robert. *Unabomber: A Desire to Kill*. Washington, D.C.: Regnery, 1997.

Greater Oklahoma City Chamber of Commerce website. "Oklahoma City Accolades." http://www.okcchamber.com/page.asp?atomid=1789 (accessed July 15, 2011).

Green, Michael S. *Freedom, Union, and Power: Lincoln and His Party during the Civil War*. New York: Fordham University Press, 2004.

Greenstein, Paul, Nigey Lennon, and Lionel Rolfe. *Bread & Hyacinths: The Rise and Fall of Utopian Los Angeles*. Paso Robles: California Classics Books, 1992.

Guimond, James, and Katherine Kearney Maynard. "Kaczynski, Conrad, and Terrorism." *Conradiana* 31, no. 1 (Spring 1999): 3–25.

Gunaratna, Rohan. *Inside Al Qaeda: Global Network of Terror*. New York and London: Columbia University Press, 2002.

Gussow, Mel. "The House on West 11th Street." *New York Times*, March 5, 2000, 7–15.

Hahn, Steven. *A Nation under Our Feet: Black Political Struggles in the Rural South from Slavery to the Great Migration*. Cambridge, Mass., and London: Belknap Press of Harvard University Press, 2005.

Halberstam, David. *The Children*. New York: Random House, 1998.

Hambrick-Stowe, Charles E. *Charles G. Finney and the Spirit of American Evangelicalism*. Grand Rapids, Mich.: Eerdmans, 1996.

Hamill, Sean. "A Sept. 11 Photo Brings Out the Conspiracy Theorists." *New York Times*, September 11, 2007, A20.

Hamm, Mark S. *Apocalypse in Oklahoma: Waco and Ruby Ridge Revenged*. Lebanon, N.H.: Northeastern University Press, 1997.

Harmon, Christopher C. *Terrorism Today*. 2nd ed. London: Frank Cass, 2008.

Harrison, Robert. "New Representations of a 'Misrepresented Bureau': Reflections on Recent Scholarship on the Freedmen's Bureau." *American Nineteenth Century History* 8, no. 2 (June 2007): 205–29.

Hefner, Phil. "Jesus Wept." *Dialog: A Journal of Theology* 41, no. 1 (Spring 2002): 4–7.

Helprin, Mark. "We Can't Reform the Arab World." *Wall Street Journal*, September 9, 2011, A10.

Henley, William Ernest. *Poems*. 4th ed. London: David Nutt, 1900.

Henry, Robert Selph. *The Story of Reconstruction*. New York: Konecky & Konecky, 1999.

Henzel, Christopher. "The Origins of al Qaeda's Ideology: Implications for U.S. Strategy." *Parameters* 35, no. 1 (Spring 2005): 69–80.

Hernandez, Raymond. "Brother Who Tipped Off the Authorities Leads a Quiet, Simple Life." *New York Times*, April 5, 1996, A25.

Hertzberg, Hendrik. "Beyond the Palin." *New Yorker* 84, no. 33, (October 10, 2008): 29–30.

Hesseltine, William B. *Lincoln's Plan of Reconstruction*. Chicago: Quadrangle Books, 1967.

Hewitt, Christopher. *Understanding Terrorism in America: From the Klan to Al Qaeda*. New York and London: Routledge, 2003.

Hickey, John J. *Our Police Guardians: History of the Police Department of the City of New York, and the Policing of Same for the Past One Hundred Years, also an Account of My Travels through Europe and America, Visiting All of the Largest Cities, Covering Some Sixty-five Thousand Miles as a Police Propagandist; with Reminiscences of the Past Forty Years, Thirty-two Pages of Illustrations, and Ten Pages of Reproduction of Historical Letters and Much Other Interesting Information "Touching on and Appertaining to" This History*. Memphis, Tenn.: General Books, LLC, 2010 [1925].

Higgins, Michael. "A Difficult Client." *ABA Journal* 84, no. 1 (March 1998): 18.

Hmoud, Mahmoud. "Negotiating the Draft Comprehensive Convention on International Terrorism: Major Bones of Contention." *Journal of International Criminal Justice* 4, no. 5 (November 2006): 1031–43.

Hobbes, Thomas. *Leviathan*. Edited by Herbert W. Schneider. Indianapolis: Bobbs-Merrill, 1958.

Hoffman, Bruce. "The Global Terrorist Threat: Is Al-Qaeda on the Run or on the March?" *Middle East Policy* 14, no. 2 (Summer 2007): 44–58.

———. *Inside Terrorism*. New York and London: Columbia University Press, 1998.

Hofstadter, Richard, and Michael Wallace. *American Violence: A Documentary History*. New York: Knopf, 1970.

Hoodbhoy, Pervez. "Afghanistan and the Genesis of Global Jihad." *Peace Research* 37, no. 1 (May 2005): 15–30.

Horn, Stanley F. *Invisible Empire: The Story of the Ku Klux Klan, 1866–1871*. Montclair, N.J.: Patterson Smith, 1969.

Horton, James Oliver, and Lois E. Horton. *Slavery and the Making of America.* New York and Oxford: Oxford University Press, 2005.

Horwitz, Tony. *Midnight Rising: John Brown and the Raid That Sparked the Civil War.* New York: Henry Holt, 2011.

Howard, Lucy, and Arlyn Tobias Gajilan. "A New Link." *Newsweek* 131, no. 10 (March 9, 1998): 4.

Howe, Daniel Walker. *What Hath God Wrought: The Transformation of America, 1815–1848.* Oxford and New York: Oxford University Press, 2007.

Huhn, Wilson R. "The Legacy of *Slaughterhouse, Bradwell,* and *Cruikshank* in Constitutional Interpretation." *Akron Law Review* 42, no. 4 (2008–2009): 1051–80.

Hunt, William R. *Front-Page Detective: William J. Burns and the Detective Profession, 1880–1930.* Madison, Wisc.: Popular Press, 1990.

Hunter, Stephen, and Joseph Bainbridge Jr. *American Gunfight: The Plot to Kill Harry Truman—and the Shootout That Stopped It.* New York: Simon & Schuster, 2005.

Hyman, Harold M. *The Radical Republicans and Reconstruction, 1861–1870.* Indianapolis: Bobbs-Merrill, 1967.

Hynd, Alan. "The Great Wall Street Explosion." In *Disaster!,* edited by Ben Kartman and Leonard Brown, 191–95. New York: Farrar, Straus & Giroux, 1971.

Iftikhar, Arsalan Tariq. "Letter to the Editor: Home-Grown Terrorists." *New York Times,* June 11, 2002, A28.

"Infiltrating the Underground." *Time* 111, no. 2 (January 9, 1978): n.p.

Jacobs, Ron. "The New History of the Weather Underground." *Monthly Review* 58, no. 2 (June 2006): 59–64.

———. *The Way the Wind Blew: A History of the Weather Underground.* New York: Verso Books, 1997.

Jacobs, Ron, and Saul Landau, eds. *The New Radicals: A Report with Documents.* New York: Vintage, 1966.

Jansen, G. H. *Militant Islam.* New York: Harper & Row, 1979.

Jefferson, Thomas. *Notes on the State of Virginia.* Edited by William Peden. Chapel Hill: University of North Carolina Press, 1982 [1955, 1781].

Jimenez de Wagenheim, Olga. *Puerto Rico's Revolt for Independence: El Grito de Lares.* Princeton, N.J.: Markus Wiener Publishers, 1993.

Johnson, Loch K. *Bombs, Bugs, Drugs, and Thugs: Intelligence and America's Quest for Security.* New York and London: New York University Press, 2002.

Johnston, David. "A Device in Cabin Is Said to Match the Unabomber's." *New York Times,* April 9, 1996, A1, A18.

———. "Go-Between for Family Was in Dark." *New York Times,* April 8, 1996, B8.

———. "Terror in Oklahoma: The Overview; Two Are Detained in Bombing Case But Are Freed after Questioning." *New York Times,* May 3, 1995, A1.

Jones, Doug. "Justice for Four Little Girls: The Bombing of the Sixteenth Street Baptist Church Cases." *Young Lawyer* 14, no. 5 (February 2010): 4–6.

Jones, Stephen, and Peter Israel. *Others Unknown: Timothy McVeigh and the Oklahoma City Bombing Conspiracy*. New York: Public Affairs, 2001.

Jones, V. C. "The Rise and Fall of the Ku Klux Klan." *Civil War Times Illustrated* 2, no. 10 (February 1964): 11–17.

Jonsson, Patrik. "How Did Eric Rudolph Survive?" *Christian Science Monitor* 95, no. 132 (June 4, 2003): 1.

June, Dale L. *Introduction to Executive Protection*. Boca Raton, Fla.: CRC Press, 1999.

Kaczorowski, Robert J. "Congress' Power to Enforce Fourteenth Amendment Rights: Lessons from Federal Remedies the Framers Enacted." *Harvard Journal on Legislation* 42, no. 1 (Winter 2005): 187–283.

Kaczynski, Theodore. "Industrial Society and Its Future, by FC." Minneapolis, Minn.: Filiquarian Publishing, 2005. http://cyber.eserver.org/unabom.txt (accessed June 27, 2011).

Kane, Joseph Nathan. *Facts about the Presidents*. New York: Ace Books, 1976.

Kaplan, Justin. *Lincoln Steffens: A Biography*. New York: Simon & Schuster, 2002.

Kauffman, Michael. *American Brutus: John Wilkes Booth and the Lincoln Conspiracies*. New York: Random House, 2005.

Keith, LeAnna. *The Colfax Massacre: The Untold Story of Black Power, White Terror, and the Death of Reconstruction*. New York and Oxford: Oxford University Press, 2008.

Kendrick, Benjamin B. *The Journal of the Joint Committee of Fifteen on Reconstruction, 39th Congress, 1865–1867*. Clark, N.J.: Law Book Exchange, 2005 [1914].

Kennedy, Paul. "Truman Death Aim Denied by Collazo." *New York Times*, March 2, 1951, A32.

Kessler, Ronald. *The FBI*. New York: Pocket Books, 1993.

Khan, Muhammad Mahroof, and Afshan Azam. "Root Causes of Terrorism: An Empirical Analysis." *Journal of Interdisciplinary Studies* 20, nos. 1–2 (2008): 65–86.

Kifner, John. "Swirling around Unabom Suspect, an Environmental Dispute." *New York Times*, April 14, 1996, A27.

Kihss, Peter. "'Sublime Heroism' Cited in Shooting." *New York Times*, March 3, 1954, A14.

King, Martin Luther, Jr. "Letter from a Birmingham Jail." In *I Have a Dream: Writings and Speeches That Changed the World*, edited by James M. Washington, 83–88. New York: HarperCollins, 1992.

Kinshasa, Kwando M. "An Appraisal of *Brown v. Board of Education, Topeka KS* (1954) and the Montgomery Bus Boycott." *Western Journal of Black Studies* 30, no. 4 (Winter 2006): 16–23.

Klarman, Michael J. *From Jim Crow to Civil Rights: The Supreme Court and the Struggle for Equality*. New York and Oxford: Oxford University Press, 2004.

Klebanow, Diana, and Franklin L. Jones. *People's Lawyers: Crusaders for Justice in American History*. Armonk, N.Y.: M. E. Sharpe, 2003.

Kleinfield, N. R. "Getting Here from There: In the Years Since 2001, Neither Our Worst Fears Nor Our Highest Hopes Have Been Realized, But What Passes for Normal Has Exacted a Price." *New York Times—Supplement: The Reckoning*, September 11, 2011, 1–2.

Klubuchar, Lisa. *1963 Birmingham Church Bombing: The Ku Klux Klan's History of Terror*. Mankato, Minn.: Compass Point Books, 2009.

Knowles, Helen J. "The Constitution and Slavery: A Special Relationship." *Slavery and Abolition* 28, no. 3 (December 2007): 309–28.

Kraditor, Aileen S. *Means and Ends in American Abolitionism: Garrison and His Critics on Strategy and Tactics, 1834–1850*. New York: Vintage, 1969.

Krakauer, Jon. *Under the Banner of Heaven: A Story of Violent Faith*. New York: Doubleday, 2003.

Krug, Ronald S., Sara Jo Nixon, and Robert Vincent. "Psychological Response to the Oklahoma City Bombing." *Journal of Clinical Psychology* 52, no. 1 (January 1996): 103–5.

Laqueur, Walter. *No End to War: Terrorism in the Twenty-first Century*. New York: Continuum International Publishing, 2003.

———. "The Terrorism to Come." *Policy Review* 126, no. 1 (August/September 2004): 49–64.

Leebaert, Derek. *The Fifty-Year Wound: How America's Cold War Victory Shapes Our World*. Boston, New York, and London: Back Bay Books, 2002.

Leeper, Amy M. "An Adlerian Analysis of the Unabomber." *Journal of Individual Psychology* 58, no. 2 (Summer 2002): 169–76.

Lemann, Nicholas. *The Promised Land: The Great Black Migration and How It Changed America*. New York: Vintage, 1992.

———. *Redemption: The Last Battle of the Civil War*. New York: Farrar, Straus & Giroux, 2006.

Lempert, Michael. "The Unmentionable: Verbal Taboo and the Moral Life of Language; Avoiding 'The Issues' as Addressivity in U.S. Electoral Politics." *Anthropological Quarterly* 84, no. 1 (Winter 2011): 187–208.

Leonard, Elizabeth D. *Lincoln's Avengers: Justice, Revenge, and Reunion after the Civil War*. New York: Norton, 2004.

Lesch, Ann M. "Osama Bin Laden: Embedded in the Middle East Crises." *Middle East Policy* 9, no. 2 (June 2002): 82–91.

Lewis, John, with Michael D'Orso. *Walking with the Wind: A Memoir of the Movement*. Orlando, Fla.: Harcourt, Brace.

Lewy, Guenter. *America in Vietnam*. New York and Oxford: Oxford University Press, 1978.

Ling, Peter. "Racism for Lunch." *History Today* 50, no. 2 (February 2000): 36–38.

Logan, Rayford W. *The Betrayal of the Negro: From Rutherford B. Hayes to Woodrow Wilson*. Cambridge, Mass.: Da Capo Press, 1997 [1965].

Lopresti, Mike. "Unfounded Suspicion Took Cruel Toll on Atlanta Olympic Hero Jewell." *USA Today*, August 31, 2007, C8.

Luckovich, Mike. "I Couldn't Let an Injury Stop Me." [Editorial cartoon.] *Atlanta Journal-Constitution*, July 28, 1996: SS25.

Luse, Christopher A. "Slavery's Champions Stood at Odds: Polygenesis and the Defense of Slavery." *Civil War History* 53, no. 4 (December 2007): 379–412.

Lutz, Brenda J., and James M. Lutz. *Terrorism in America*. New York: Palgrave Macmillan, 2007.

MacLean, Nancy. *Behind the Mask of Chivalry: The Making of the Second Ku Klux Klan*. New York and Oxford: Oxford University Press, 1994.

Mandel, Bernard. *Samuel Gompers: A Biography*. Brentwood, Calif.: Antioch Press, 1963.

Mantell, Martin E. *Johnson, Grant, and the Politics of Reconstruction*. New York and London: Columbia University Press, 1973.

Marshall, Randall D., and Eun Jung Suh. "Contextualizing Trauma: Using Evidence-Based Treatments in a Multicultural Community after 9/11." *Psychiatric Quarterly* 74, no. 4 (Winter 2003): 401–20.

Martinez, J. Michael. *Carpetbaggers, Cavalry, and the Ku Klux Klan: Exposing the Invisible Empire during Reconstruction*. Lanham, Md.: Rowman & Littlefield, 2007.

McCann, Joseph T. *Terrorism on American Soil: A Concise History of Plots and Perpetrators from the Famous to the Forgotten*. Boulder, Colo.: Sentient Publications, 2006.

McCormick, Charles H. *Hopeless Cases: The Search for the Red Scare Terrorist Bombers*. Lanham, Md.: University Press of America, 2005.

McCullough, David. *Truman*. New York: Simon & Schuster, 1992.

McDermott, Terry. "A Perfect Soldier; Mohamed Atta, Whose Hard Gaze Has Stared from a Billion Television Screens and Newspaper Pages, Has Become, for Many, the Face of Evil Incarnate." *Los Angeles Times*, January 27, 2002: A1.

———. *Perfect Soldiers: The 9/11 Hijackers—Who They Were, Why They Did It*. New York: Harper, 2005.

McDougal, Dennis. *Privileged Son: Otis Chandler and the Rise and Fall of the LA Times Dynasty*. New York: Perseus, 2001.

McFadden, Robert D. "From a Child of Promise to the Unabom Suspect." *New York Times*, May 26, 1996, A1, A22.

McFarlane, Robert C. "Afghanistan Should Have Been the Focus." *Wall Street Journal*, September 9, 2011, A19.

McGirr, Lisa. "The Passion of Sacco and Vanzetti: A Global History." *Journal of American History* 93, no. 4 (March 2007): 1085–1115.

McKinstry, Carolyn Maull, with Denise George. *While the World Watched: A Birmingham Bombing Survivor Comes of Age during the Civil Rights Movement*. Carol Stream, Ill.: Tyndale House, 2011.

McPherson, Edward. *The Political History of the United States during the Great Rebellion*. 4th ed. Washington, D.C.: James J. Chapman, 1882.

McPherson, James M. *The Abolitionist Legacy: From Reconstruction to the NAACP*. Princeton, N.J.: Princeton University Press, 1976.

———. *Battle Cry of Freedom: The Civil War Era*. New York: Ballantine, 1988.

———. *The Struggle for Equality: Abolitionists and the Negro in the Civil War and Reconstruction*. Princeton, N.J.: Princeton University Press, 1964.

———. *Tried by War: Abraham Lincoln as Commander in Chief*. New York: Penguin, 2008.

McVeigh, Timothy. "An Essay on Hypocrisy." James Randi Education Foundation (JREF) website. http://forums.randi.org/showthread.php?t=10494 (accessed July 8, 2011).

———. "I Explain Herein Why I Bombed the Murrah Federal Building in Oklahoma City." WordPress.com website. http://truthinourtime.wordpress.com/2010/02/19/timothy-mcveighs-manifesto (accessed July 10, 2011).

McWhorter, Diane. "Fearing the Worst." *Smithsonian* 37, no. 2 (May 2006): 16–18.

———. "No Trial Closes Injustice's Wounds." *USA Today*, May 22, 2002: 12A.

Mead, Walter Russell. *Special Providence: American Foreign Policy and How It Changed the World*. Oxford and New York: Routledge, 2002.

Means, Howard. *The Avenger Takes His Place: Andrew Johnson and the 45 Days That Changed the Nation*. New York: Harcourt, 2006.

Melanson, Philip H. *The Secret Service: The Hidden History of an Enigmatic Agency*. New York: Carroll & Graf, 2005.

Mello, Michael. *The United States of America versus Theodore John Kaczynski: Ethics, Power, and the Invention of the Unabomber*. Madison, Miss.: Context Publishing, 1999.

Memon, Amina, and Daniel B. Wright. "Eyewitness Testimony and the Oklahoma City Bombing." *Psychologist* 12, no. 6 (June 1999): 292–95.

Merari, Ariel. "Deterring Fear: Government Responses to Terrorist Attacks." *Harvard International Review* 23, no. 4 (Winter 2002): 26–31.

Metress, Christopher. "Making Civil Rights Harder: Literature, Memory, and the Black Freedom Struggle." *Southern Literary Journal* 40, no. 2 (Spring 2008): 138–50.

Michel, Lou, and Dan Herbeck. *American Terrorist: Timothy McVeigh & the Tragedy at Oklahoma City*. New York: Avon, 2002.

Miles, Orvell. "After 9/11: Photography, the Destructive Sublime, and the Postmodern Archive." *Michigan Quarterly Review* 45, no. 2 (Spring 2006): 238–56.

Millard, Candice. *Destiny of the Republic: A Tale of Madness, Medicine and the Murder of a President*. New York: Doubleday, 2011.

Miller, Laura. "A Change in the Weather." *New York Times*, November 30, 2003: B31.

Mole, Phil. "9/11 Conspiracy Theories: The 9/11 Truth Movement in Perspective." *Skeptic* 12, no. 4 (2006): 30–42.

Monroe, Sylvester, and Timothy Roche. "The Forest Is His Ally." *Time* 152, no. 4 (July 27, 1998): 26–27.

Moran, John P. "The Roots of Terrorist Motivation: Shame, Rage, and Violence in *The Brothers Karamazov*." *Perspectives on Political Science* 38, no. 4 (Fall 2009): 187–96.

Morris, Michael. *The Madison Bombings: The Story of One of the Two Largest Vehicle-Bombings Ever.* London: Research House, 1988.

Morrison, Blake. "Special Report: 'Your Wayward Son, Eric Rudolph.'" *USA Today*, July 5, 2005, 1A.

Nacos, Brigitte L. "Terrorism as Breaking News: Attack on America." *Political Science Quarterly* 118, no. 1 (Spring 2003): 23–52.

Nasir, Sohail Abdul. "Al Qaeda, Two Years On." *Bulletin of the Atomic Scientists* 59, no. 5 (September/October 2003): 32–41.

National Commission on Terrorist Attacks upon the United States. *The 9/11 Commission Report.* New York and London: Norton, 2004.

Nelson, Larry E. "Thompson, Jacob." In *Macmillan Information Now Encyclopedia: The Confederacy*, edited by Richard N. Current, 607–9. New York: Macmillan Reference USA, 1993.

Oates, Stephen B. *To Purge This Land with Blood: A Biography of John Brown.* 2nd ed. Amherst: University of Massachusetts Press, 1984.

Obama, Barack H. "Remarks by the President on Osama Bin Laden. White House Website, May 2, 2011. http://www.whitehouse.gov/the-pressoffice/2011/05/02/remarkspresidentosamabin-laden (accessed November 15, 2011).

O'Donnell, Paul, and Lucy Howard. "The Hunt Intensifies." *Newsweek* 132, no. 17 (October 26, 1998): 6.

Oleinik, Anton. "Lessons of Russian in Afghanistan." *Society* 45, no. 3 (June 2008): 288–93.

Oleson, J. C. "'Evil the Natural Way': The Chimerical Utopias of Henry David Thoreau and Theodore John Kaczynski." *Contemporary Justice Review* 8, no. 2 (June 2005): 211–28.

"Oscar Collazo, 80, Truman Attacker in '50." *New York Times*, February 23, 1994, A16.

Oswell, Douglas Evander. *The Unabomber and the Zodiac.* Self-published, 2007.

"Out of the Woods." *The Economist* 367, no. 8327 (June 7, 2003): 26.

Packard, Jerrold M. *American Nightmare: The History of Jim Crow.* New York: St. Martin's, 2003.

Padover, Saul K., ed. *Thomas Jefferson on Democracy.* New York: New American Library, 1939.

Parks, Rosa, and Gregory J. Reed. *Quiet Strength: The Faith, the Hope, and the Heart of a Woman Who Changed a Nation.* Grand Rapids, Mich.: Zondervan Publishing House, 1994.

Pedersen, Daniel, Daniel Klaidman, and Vern E. Smith. "A Mountain Manhunt." *Newsweek* 132, no. 4 (July 27, 1998): 16–19.

Pernicone, Nunzio. "Luigi Galleani and Italian Anarchist Terrorism in the United States." In *Terrorism: Critical Concepts in Political Science.* Edited by David C. Rapport, 189–214. Oxford and New York: Routledge, 2006.

Peterson, Merrill D. *Lincoln in American Memory.* New York and Oxford: Oxford University Press, 1995.

Pico, Fernando. *History of Puerto Rico: A Panorama of Its People*. Princeton, N.J.: Markus Wiener Publishers, 2006.

Pittman, Benn, compiler and arranger. *The Assassination of President Lincoln and the Trial of the Conspirators*. New York: Moore, Wilstach & Baldwin, 1865.

Poll, Richard D., and Ralph W. Hansen. "'Buchanan's Blunder': The Utah War, 1857–58." *Military Affairs* 25, no. 3 (Autumn 1961): 121–31.

"The President Reports on the Death of Osama bin Laden." *Army* 61, no. 6 (June 2011): 6–7.

Pridemore, William Alex, Mitchell B. Chamlin, and Adam Trahan. "A Test of Competing Hypotheses about Homicide Following Terrorist Attacks: An Interrupted Time Series Analysis of September 11 and Oklahoma City." *Journal of Quantitative Criminology* 24, no. 4 (December 2008): 381–96.

Pryor, John P. "The 2001 World Trade Center Disaster: Summary and Evaluation of Experiences." *European Journal of Trauma and Emergency Surgery* 35, no. 3 (June 2009): 212–24.

Rable, George C. *But There Was No Peace: The Role of Violence in the Politics of Reconstruction*. Athens: University of Georgia Press, 1984.

Rappoport, Jon. *Oklahoma City Bombing: The Suppressed Truth*. Escondido, Calif.: Book Tree, 1995.

Rayback, Joseph G. *A History of American Labor*. New York: Free Press, 1966.

Remnick, David. *The Bridge: The Life and Rise of Barack Obama*. New York: Knopf, 2010.

———. "Mr. Ayers's Neighborhood." *New Yorker Blog*, 4 November 2008. http://www.newyorker.com/online/blogs/tny/2008/11/mr-ayerss-neighborhood.html (accessed May 27, 2011).

Richardson, Louise. *What Terrorists Want: Understanding the Enemy, Containing the Threat*. New York: Random House, 2006.

Ricks, Thomas E. *Fiasco: The American Military Adventure in Iraq*. New York: Penguin, 2006.

Ridgeway, James. *Blood in the Face: The Ku Klux Klan, Aryan Nations, Nazi Skinheads, and the Rise of a New White Culture*. 2nd ed. New York: Thunder's Mouth Press, 1995.

Rohrbach, Augusta. "'Truth Stronger and Stranger Than Fiction': Reexamining William Lloyd Garrision's *Liberator*." *American Literature* 73, no. 4 (December 2001): 727–55.

"Rosa Louise McCauley Parks 1913–2005." *Journal of Blacks in Higher Education* 49, no. 1 (Autumn 2005): 64–65.

Rosenthal, John. "Doing Justice to Zacarias Moussaoui." *Policy Review* 146, no. 1 (December 2007/January 2008): 39–61.

Rostow, Nicholas. "Before and After: The Changed UN Response to Terrorism since September 11th." *Cornell International Law Journal* 35, no. 3 (Winter 2002): 475–90.

Rowland, Tim. "John Brown's Moonlight March." *America's Civil War* 22, no. 4 (September 2009): 29–35.

Rudd, Mark. *Underground: My Life with SDS and the Weathermen*. New York: HarperCollins, 2009.

Runkle, Benjamin. *Wanted Dead or Alive: Manhunts from Geronimo to Bin Laden*. New York: Palgrave Macmillan, 2011.

Russakoff, Dale, and Serge F. Kovaleski. "An Ordinary Boy's Extraordinary Rage." *Washington Post*, July 2, 1995, A1, A21.

Sale, Kirkpatrick. *SDS*. New York: Random House, 1973.

Sale, Richard. *Clinton's Secret Wars: The Evolution of a Commander in Chief*. New York: Thomas Dunne Books, St. Martin's, 2009.

Saleh, Nivien. "Egypt: Osama's Star Is Rising." *Middle East Policy* 9, no. 3 (September 2002): 40–44.

Samaha, Joel. *Criminal Law*. 10th ed. Belmont, Calif.: Wadsworth Centate Learning, 2011.

———. *Criminal Procedure*. 8th ed. Belmont, Calif.: Wadsworth Cengage Learning, 2012.

Sapru, R. K. *Public Policy. Formulation, Implementation, and Evaluation* 2nd ed. New York: Sterling Publishers, 2004.

Scaturro, Frank J. *President Grant Reconsidered*. Lanham, Md.: University Press of America, 1998.

Scherer, John L. "Locating Bin Laden." *USA Today Magazine* 139, no. 2788 (January 2011): 22–25.

Schuster, Henry, and Charles Stone. *Hunting Eric Rudolph: An Insider's Account of the Five-Year Search for the Olympic Park Bomber*. New York: Berkley Books, 2005.

Shaw, Robert B. "Leadership Lessons from the Life of Ulysses S. Grant." *Leader to Leader* 42, no. 1 (October 2006): 29–35.

Shenon, Philip. "Report Claims That 9/11 Terrorists Were Identified before Attacks." *New York Times*, September 22, 2006: A15.

Sides, Hampton. *Hellhound on His Trail: The Stalking of Martin Luther King Jr. and the International Hunt for His Assassin*. New York: Doubleday, 2010.

Simba, Malik. "The Obama Campaign 2008: A Historical Overview." *Western Journal of Black Studies* 33, no. 3 (Fall 2009): 186–91.

Simkins, Francis Butler, and Charles Pierce Roland. *A History of the South*. 4th ed. New York: Knopf, 1972.

Simpson, Brooks D. *Let Us Have Peace: Ulysses S. Grant and the Politics of War and Reconstruction, 1861–1868*. Chapel Hill: University of North Carolina Press, 1991.

———. *The Reconstruction Presidents*. Lawrence: University Press of Kansas, 1998.

Singer, Jane. *The Confederate Dirty War: Arson, Bombings, Assassination and Plots for Chemical and Germ Attacks on the Union*. Jefferson, N.C., and London: McFarland, 2005.

Sinker, Mark. "Catcalling." *Film Quarterly* 63, no. 2 (Winter 2009/2010): 62–65.

Slaughter, Anne-Marie. "Resilience vs. Revenge." *Wall Street Journal*, September 9, 2011, A19.

Slonecker, Blake. "The Columbia Coalition: African Americans, New Leftists, and Counterculture at the Columbia University Protest of 1968." *Journal of Social History* 41, no. 4 (Summer 2008): 967–96.

Smith, Allen. "Present at the Creation and Other Myths: The Port Huron Statement and the Origins of the New Left." *Socialist Review* 27, nos. 1–2 (1999): 1–27.

Smith, Elbert B. "Shoot-out on Pennsylvania Avenue." *American History* 32, no. 3 (July/August 1997): 16–24.

Smith, Jean Edward. *Grant*. New York: Simon & Schuster, 2001.

Smith, Kyle. "The Day the Children Died." *People* 48, no. 7 (11 August 1997): 87–91.

Sokol, Jason. *There Goes My Everything: White Southerners in the Age of Civil Rights, 1945–1975*. New York: Vintage, 2006.

Soodalter, Rod. "Partisan, Terrorist, Soldier, Spy." *America's Civil War* 23, no. 2 (May 2010): 34–41.

Springer, Nathan R. "Patterns of Radicalization: Identifying the Markers and Warning Signs of Domestic Lone Wolf Terrorists in Our Midst." MA thesis, Naval Postgraduate School, 2009.

Stampp, Kenneth M. *The Era of Reconstruction, 1865–1877*. New York: Knopf, 1965.

Steers, Edward, Jr. *Blood on the Moon: The Assassination of Abraham Lincoln*. Lexington: University Press of Kentucky, 2001.

———. "Risking the Wrath of God." *North and South* 3, no. 7 (September 2000): 59–70.

Stephen, Andrew. "America: Eric Rudolph Is Alleged to Have Bombed Abortion Clinics, a Gay Club and the Olympic Games. So Why Do Swathes of Decent, Hard-working Americans Hail Him as a Folk Hero?" *New Statesman* 132, no. 4641 (June 9, 2003): 9–10.

Stephens, Bret. "9/11 and the Struggle for Meaning." *Wall Street Journal*, September 6, 2011, A19.

Stewart, David O. *Impeached: The Trial of President Andrew Johnson and the Fight for Lincoln's Legacy*. New York: Simon & Schuster, 2009.

Stewart, Sherrel. "Historic Church in Store for Revival: Site of 1963 Bombing to Become a National Landmark." *Black Enterprise* 36, no. 4 (November 2005): 42.

Stickney, Brandon M. *"All-American Monster": The Unauthorized Biography of Timothy McVeigh*. Amherst, N.Y.: Prometheus Books, 1996.

Stone, Irving. *Clarence Darrow for the Defense*. New York: Bantam Books, 1967.

Students for a Democratic Society. *SDS New Left Notes—National Convention Proposals*. Chicago: SDS, June 1969.

Suskind, Ron. *The One Percent Doctrine: Deep Inside America's Pursuit of Its Enemies since 9/11*. New York: Simon & Schuster, 2007.

Swazo, Norman K. "'My Brother Is My King': Evaluating the Moral Duty of Global Jihad." *International Journal on World Peace* 25, no. 4 (December 2008): 7–47.

Sweeney, James F., Diane Solov, and Rich Exner. "Pennsylvania Crash Carries Horror into Small Towns." *Cleveland Plain Dealer*, September 12, 2001, A6.

Symeonidou-Kastanidou, Elizabeth. "Defining Terrorism." *European Journal of Crime, Criminal Law and Criminal Justice* 12, no. 1 (2004): 14–35.

Szasz, Ferenc M., and Margaret Connell Szasz. "Religion and Spirituality." In *The Oxford History of the American West*, edited by Clyde A. Milner II, Carol A. O'Connor, and Martha A. Sandweiss, 361–91. New York and Oxford: Oxford University Press, 1994.

"Ten Years On." *Economist* 400, no. 8749 (September 3, 2011): 11–12.

"Terrorist Bill Ayers Misrepresents His Past." *New American* 24, no. 25 (December 8, 2008): 8.

Tharp, Mike. "Where Is Eric Rudolph?" *U.S. News & World Report* 125, no. 16 (October 26, 1998): 26.

Tidwell, William A. *April '65: Confederate Covert Action in the American Civil War*. Kent, Ohio: Kent State University Press, 1995.

Tidwell, William A., James O. Hall, and David Winfred Gaddy. *Come Retribution: The Confederate Secret Service and the Assassination of Lincoln*. Jackson: University Press of Mississippi, 1988.

TornadoChaser.Net. "Where Is Tornado Alley?" http://www.tornadochaser.net/tornalley.html (accessed July 15, 2011).

Trefousse, Hans L. *The Radical Republicans: Lincoln's Vanguard for Racial Justice*. New York: Knopf, 1969.

Trelease, Allen W. *White Terror: The Ku Klux Klan Conspiracy and Southern Reconstruction*. Baton Rouge: Louisiana State University Press, 1971.

Tulis, Jeffrey K. *The Rhetorical Presidency*. Princeton, N.J.: Princeton University Press, 1987.

———. "The Two Constitutional Presidencies." In *The Presidency and the Political System*, 3rd ed., edited by Michael Nelson, 85–115. Washington, D.C.: Congressional Quarterly Press, 1990.

Turk, Austin T. "Sociology of Terrorism." *Annual Review of Sociology* 30, no. 1 (2004): 271–86.

The Unabomber Pages: The Victims. http://www.francesfarmersrevenge.com/stuff/unabomber/victims.htm (accessed June 19, 2011).

"Underground on West Side." *New York Times*, February 16, 1982: B4.

United Nations Website. "Security Council Resolution 1566." http://www.un.org/Docs/sc/committees/1566/1566ResEng.htm (accessed March 20, 2012).

United States v. Cruikshank, 92 U.S. 542 (1876).

United States Court of Appeals for the Ninth Circuit, United States of America v. Theodore John Kaczynski, 239 F.3d 1108 (9th Cir. 2001).

United States of America v. Theodore John Kaczynski, 262 F.3d 1034 (9th Cir. 2001).

Valentine, Lonnie. "The Execution of Timothy McVeigh as Religious Sacrifice." *Peace Review* 13, no. 4 (December 2001): 531–36.

Van Elteren, Mel. "Workers' Control and the Struggles against 'Wage Slavery' in the Gilded Age and After." *Journal of American Culture* 26, no. 2 (June 2003): 188–203.

Vollers, Maryanne. *Lone Wolf: Eric Rudolph and the Legacy of American Terror.* New York: HarperPerennial, 2007.

Wade, Wyn Craig. *The Fiery Cross: The Ku Klux Klan in America.* New York and Oxford: Oxford University Press, 1987.

Wade-Lewis, Margaret. "I Remember Rosa Parks: The Impact of Segregation." *Black Scholar* 35, no. 4 (Winter 2005): 2–12.

Waits, Chris, and Dave Shors. *Unabomber: The Secret Life of Ted Kaczynski.* Helena, Mont.: FarCountry Press, 1999.

Walker, Ronald W., Richard E. Turley Jr., and Glen M. Leonard. *Massacre at Mountain Meadows.* New York and Oxford: Oxford University Press, 2008.

Ward, Ian. "Towards a Poethics of Terror." *Law, Culture, and the Humanities* 4, no. 2 (June 2008): 248–79.

Warmouth, Henry C. *War, Politics and Reconstruction: Stormy Days in Louisiana.* New York: Macmillan, 1930.

Watson, Bruce. *Freedom Summer.* New York: Viking, 2010.

———. *Sacco & Vanzetti: The Men, the Murders, and the Judgment of Mankind.* New York: Viking, 2007.

Weather Underground. *Prairie Fire: The Politics of Revolutionary Anti-Imperialism; Political Statement of the Weather Underground.* Brooklyn, N.Y., and San Francisco: Communications Company, 1974. http://www.usasurvival.org/docs/Prairie-fire.pdf (accessed May 27, 2011).

Weber, Cynthia. "Popular Visual Language as Global Communication: The Remediation of United Airlines Flight 93." *Review of International Studies* 34, S1 (January 2008): 137–53.

Weigel, George. "A Campaign of Narratives." *First Things: A Monthly Journal of Religion and Public Life* 191, no. 1 (March 2009): 21–27.

Weinberg, Arthur, and Lila Weinberg. *Clarence Darrow: A Sentimental Rebel.* New York: Putnam, 1980.

White, Ronald C., Jr. *A. Lincoln: A Biography.* New York: Random House, 2009.

Wieseltier, Leon. "Even Obama Embraces Drones." *Wall Street Journal*, September 9, 2011, A19.

Wilber, Del Quentin. *Rawhide Down: The Near Assassination of Ronald Reagan.* New York: Henry Holt, 2011.

Wilkerson, Cathy. *Flying Close to the Sun: My Life and Times as a Weatherman.* New York: Seven Stories Press, 2007.

Wilkinson, Paul. *Terrorism versus Democracy: The Liberal State Response.* 2nd ed. New York and London: Routledge, 2001.

Wilkinson, Peter. "The Making of a Maniac." *Rolling Stone* 926, no. 1 (July 10, 2003): 31–34.

Williams, T. Harry. *Lincoln and the Radicals.* Madison and Milwaukee: University of Wisconsin Press, 1965.

Wilson, Kirk H. "Interpreting the Discursive Field of the Montgomery Bus Boycott: Martin Luther King Jr.'s Holt Street Address." *Rhetoric and Public Affairs* 8, no. 2 (Summer 2005): 299–326.

Winik, Jay. *April 1865: The Month That Saved America*. New York: HarperCollins, 2001.

Wolffe, Richard. *Renegade: The Making of a President*. New York: Three Rivers Press, 2010.

Wolfowitz, Paul. "We Had to Address State Sponsors of Terror." *Wall Street Journal*, September 9, 2011, A19.

Woodward, C. Vann. *Origins of the New South, 1877–1913*. Baton Rouge: Louisiana State University Press, 1951.

———. *The Strange Career of Jim Crow*. 2nd ed. Oxford and New York: Oxford University Press, 1966.

Wright, Lawrence. *The Looming Tower: Al-Qaeda and the Road to 9/11*. New York: Knopf, 2006.

Wright, Robin. *Rock the Casbah: Rage and Rebellion across the Islamic World*. New York: Simon & Schuster, 2011.

———. "The Struggle within Islam." *Smithsonian* 42, no. 5 (September 2011). 104–14

Wright, Stuart A. *Patriots, Politics, and the Oklahoma City Bombing*. New York and Cambridge: Cambridge University Press, 2007

Yoo, John. "Ten Years without an Attack." *Wall Street Journal*, September 6, 2011, A21.

Zarate, Juan C., and David A. Gordon. "The Battle for Reform with Al-Qaeda." *Washington Quarterly* 34, no. 3 (Summer 2011): 103–22.

INDEX

Page numbers in italics refer to images

Abbottabad, Pakistan, 399–403
ABC News, 370
Abouhalima, Mahmud, 367, 368
Abrahms, Max, 421, 425, 426
Adair City, Oklahoma, 301
Adam and Eve, 324
Aden, Yemen, 366, 372
The Aeneid, 361
Afghan mujahedeen. *See* mujahedeen
Afghanistan, 363, 364, 365, 369, 371,
    372, 374, 375, 376, 378, 396, 397,
    398, 401, 404, 420
Africa, 48, 223, 370–71
Aiken, John, 32
Air Traffic Control (ATC) Center, 379,
    380
Ajaj, Ahmad, 367, 368
Akerman, Amos T., 81
Alabama, 53, 168, 176, 185, 187, 195,
    197, 198, 346, 351
Alabama State Police, 346
Albany movement, 176, 186

Alexander, George B., 101
Alexander, Kent, 336
Alexandria Democrat, 87
Alfred P. Murrah Federal Building,
    276, 291, 293, 294–95, 300, 301,
    305, 306, 308, 309
Algeria, 218
Al Jazeera, 370, 397
Allah, 376, 387
Allen, Charles, 65
Allen, Charles Herbert, 154
Alphia, 62
al-Qaeda, 307, 365–78, 394–400, 402,
    403–04, 417, 420–21, 422, 423, 428,
    429. *See also* bin Laden, Osama;
    September 11, 2001, attacks
Al-Thager Model School, 363
American Anarchist Fighters, 135–36
American Airlines, 380, 384; Flight 11,
    379–81, 382, 384, 385, 388, 390;
    Flight 77, 383–84, 385, 392; Flight
    444, 245; Flight Services Office,

380; Southeastern Reservations Office, 379
American Bridge Company, 98
American Federation of Labor (AFL), 101, 105, 106, 111, 134
American Institute for Scientific Research, 137
American neo-Nazis, 301
American Party ("Know Nothings"), 279
American Revolution, 279, 293
American Socialist Party, 134
American Student Union, 207
America's Kids Day Care Center, 294
America's Most Wanted, 348–49
ammonium nitrate, 290, 293, 300
anarchism, 123, 130, 132–34, 137, 138, 139, 140, 141, 142, 423
"anarcho-Islam," 363
Anderson, Eleanor, 256, 257
Andrews, North Carolina, 323, 325
Angelakos, Diogenes J., 247–48, 258
anthrax, 421
Anti-Saloon League, 194
Appel, Horace, 112
Arabian Sea, 371, 402
Area 51, 290
Arkansas, 25, 33, 38, 61, 66, 292
Arlington City, Virginia, 392
Arlington County Fire Department, 392
Arlington National Cemetery, 164, 165, 166
Army Commendation Medal, 284
Army of God, 2, 340–41, 354
Army of Northern Virginia, 54
Army Rangers, 281, 326
Arpey, Gerard, 384
"As I Sat Alone by Blue Ontario's Shores," 149
Ashcroft, John, 307, 384
Ashley, Karen, 213
Asheville, North Carolina, 346, 349

Asia, 150, 205, 212, 226, 229, 374, 378
Associated Press, 140
Atef, Mohammed, 397
Atlanta Compromise, 181
Atlanta Constitution, 194
Atlanta, Georgia, 1, 2, 98, 181, 194, 195, 319, 320, 321, 328, 329, 330, 331, 332, 334, 335, 337, 338, 339, 340, 341, 342, 344, 351, 352, 353
Atlanta Bomb Task Force, 341
Atlanta Committee for the Olympic Games (ACOG), 319, 329, 333
Atlanta Journal-Constitution, 333, 336, 333, 336, 340
Atlanta Police Department, 329, 330
Atta, Mohammed, 374–75, 376, 377, 378–79, 381, 394
Attas, Hamida al-, 362
Attas, Mohammed al-, 362
Avrich, Paul, 141
Ayers, Bill, 213, 220, 223–25, 227–31
Ayyad, Nidal, 367, 368
Azam, Afshan, 422
Azzam, Abdullah, 363, 364–65

"Bad Company," 283
Bain, Robert, 107, 108
Baker-Fancher party, 25–32, 35, 38, 39, 40, 426
Ballinger, Ed, 386
Bandy, Jody, 349
Banihammad, Fayez, 381
Bari, Judi, 256
Bateman, William, 29
Baxley, Bill, 197
Beamer, Todd, 387–88
Bearnson, Leroy Wood, 247
Beat Generation, 208
Bell, Griffin, 219
Benjamin, Judah P., 54
Bentley, Alvin, 168
Berger, Dan, 225
Bevel, James, 186

Bill of Rights, 124

BI-LO, 347

Billy the Kid, 348

bin Attash, Walid Muhammad Salih bin Roshayed. *See* Khallad

bin Laden, Mohammed bin Awad, 362

bin Laden, Osama, 397, 421, 428; death of, 402–3; early life, 362–65, 405n1; establishes al-Qaeda, 364–67; hunted by United States after September 11 attacks, 394–402; plans September 11 attacks, 372–78; targets United States, 366–72. *See also* al-Qaeda; September 11, 2001, attacks

Binalshibh, Ramzi, 374, 375–76, 377, 378, 385

Biossat, Edward, 87

Birdzell, Donald, 161–62, 163

Birmingham, Alabama: and civil rights movement, 24, 177, 178, 185, 187, 188, 190, 191, 196, 198; and Eric Rudolph, 321, 341–47, 351, 353

The Birth of a Nation, 193

Bisceglie, Anthony, 261

Bissell, Judith, 222

Bissell, Silas, 222

Bisset, George, 111–2

Black, Cofer, 396

Black Hawk helicopters, 366, 400, 401

Black Liberation Army (BLA), 223

Black Panther Party, 212, 213, 215, 218, 219, 223

Black Power movement, 205, 209, 285

Blackburn, Churchill, 49

Blackburn, James, 60

Blackburn, Luke Pryor, 4, 9, 47; and service to the Confederate States of America, 53–54; early life, 49–54; as Kentucky governor, 46, 66; as medical doctor, 45–46, 50–52, 66, 268; postbellum years, 65–66; and prison reform, 46, 66; and yellow

fever plot, 46–47, 59–68, 423, 427, 429

Blackman, William, 63

Blair, Ezell A. Jr., 185

Blair House, 150, 160, 161–62, 163, 164–165

Blake, William, 417

Blanton Jr., Thomas, 189, 196, 198

Boda, Mario "Mike," 141, 142

Boeing 767, 379

Bombingham. *See* Birmingham, Alabama

Bombs, Bugs, Drugs, and Thugs: Intelligence and America's Quest for Security, 420

Book of Mormon. *See* Smith, Joseph Jr.

Booth, John Wilkes, 65, 150–51, 293

Borgeson, Kevin, 421

Boring, Floyd, 161, 162

Boston, Massachusetts, 62, 63, 369, 378, 379, 380, 381, 382, 383

Boswell, Ella Gist, 51, 52

Boudin, Kathy, 215, 223

Bowen, Bill, 351

Boylan, Jeanne, 251

Bradley, Ed, 307

Bradley fighting vehicle, 282–83

Brailovsky, Alexander, 137

Branch Davidians (Waco), 287–88, 289, 291, 293, 341

Brandeis, Louis, 303

Branham, Thomas Wayne, 322–24, 325, 326

Brant, Harry, 141

Bridson, Nadia, 249

Briggs, John, 222, 223

British Israelism. *See* Christian Identity movement

Brooklyn, New York, 368

Brotherhood of Eternal Love, 217

Brown v. Board of Education of Topeka, 183, 195

Brown, H. Rap, 307

Brown, John, 221, 230
Brown, William Wells, 179
Bryant, Watson, 335–36
Bryant & Stratton College, 278
Bryce, J. B., 102
Buchanan, James, 23, 24, 55
Buffalo, New York, 126, 151, 280, 286, 287
Bureau of Alcohol, Tobacco, Firearms, and Explosives (ATF), 244, 246, 291, 321, 326, 336, 338, 339, 340, 341, 344, 392
Bureau of Investigation (BOI). *See* Federal Bureau of Investigation (FBI)
Bureau of Refugees, Freedmen and Abandoned Lands. *See* Freedmen's Bureau
Burger King restaurant, 278, 347
Burke Armored Car Service, 280
Burlingame, Charles F., 383
Burns, Jerry, 262
Burns, William J.: and *Los Angeles Times* bombing case, 101–3, 114, 115; and Wall Street bombing case, 129, 130, 137, 140, 142
Burnside, Ambrose, 57
Burrell, Garland E. Jr., 264, 265–66
Burson-Marsteller ("Burston Marsteller"), 254, 255, 256
Bush administration, 4, 395, 398, 401, 404, 420
Bush, George W., 3, 388, 395, 396, 398
Butcher, Hans, 309
Butcher, Torrey, 309
Butler, Benjamin, 60

Cable News Network (CNN), 336, 349, 370
Cain and Abel, 324
Cairo University, 374
Calhoun, William Smith, 82–83

California, 217, 218, 222, 256, 264, 289, 373, 377
California Forestry Association (CFA), 256
Camp Douglas prison camp, 63
Campos, Pedro Albizu, 155, 156, 157, 158, 159
Canada, 20, 54–59, 61, 62, 64, 65, 245
Cape Canaveral, 322
Caplan, David, 102
Capone, Al, 36, 142
Carl Dittmars Powder Company, 128–29
Carleton, James Henry, 33
Carmichael, Stokely, 186
Carr, Caleb, 421, 425
carpetbaggers, 78, 81, 83, 193
Carter, Jimmy, 167, 168, 219, 400
Case, Stewart, 245
Cash, Herman Frank, 189, 196, 198
Castro, Fidel, 167
Catholic Church, 131, 194, 322
Catholic Worker movement, 322
CBS News, 340, 388
Centennial Olympic Park, 98, 320, 321, 328, 329–33, 338, 339
Central Intelligence Agency (CIA), 241, 365, 369–70, 371, 373, 396, 397, 400, 420
Cermak, Anton, 151
Chadwick, Minzor, 342–43, 344
Chambliss, Robert "Dynamite Bob," 189, 196, 198
Chaney, James, 176
Charlebois, David, 383
Cheney, Dick, 420
Cherney, Darryl, 256
Cherokee County Jail, 349, 350
Cherokee County Police Department, 349
Cherry, Bobby Frank, 189, 196, 198
Chiang Kai–shek, 150

Chicago, Illinois, 36, 58, 59, 63, 102, 103, 104, 110, 113, 133, 135, 151, 167, 212, 214, 222, 223, 224, 240, 244, 245, 246, 247, 261, 268, 382

China, 35, 150

Chinook helicopters, 401

cholera, 46, 49–50

Christ, Jesus, 15, 16, 190, 193–94

Christian Identity movement, 321, 324–25, 326

Church of Israel, 326

Church of Jesus Christ of Latter-Day Saints (LDS), 13–14; origins, 16–19; and Mountain Meadows Massacre, 25–34, 423, 426; and movement to Utah, 22–23; persecution against, 19–20, 21, 35, 36, 37, 38, 426, 429; polygamy, 18, 19, 21, 23, 37; and Quorum of the Twelve Apostles, 20, 21; and Utah War, 23–25. *See also* Mountain Meadows Massacre; Smith, Joseph Jr.; Young, Brigham

Churchill, Julia, 53

Citizens' Commission to Investigate the FBI, 219

Civil Rights Bill of 1866, 75

Civil War, American, 9, 46, 65, 66, 72, 83, 86, 88, 91, 151, 179, 192, 193, 279

The Clansman, 193, 194

Clark, Judith Alice, 223

Clarke, Edward Young, 194

Clarke, Judy, 264, 351

Clay, Clement C., 62–63

Clay, Henry, 49

Cleere, Ray, 335

Clinton, Bill, 298, 371, 372

Coffelt, Leslie, 163, 164–65, 167

COINTELPRO, 4, 219, 221, 228. *See also* Federal Bureau of Investigation (FBI)

Cold War, 208, 226, 279

Cole, James "Catfish," 195

Coleridge, Samuel Taylor, 1

Colfax Massacre, 9, 84–86, 89–91, 180, 427, 429

Coll, Steve, 420–21

Coll y Cuchi, José, 155

collateral damage, 6, 48, 116, 124, 143, 189, 228, 284, 295, 418, 419

Collazo, Oscar, *162*; assault on Truman, 159–67, 168, 168, 169–70, 427; death, 167; early life, 158–59

Collins, Addie Mae, 190, 196

Columbia University, 210, 215, 260

Columbus, Christopher, 48

communism, 133, 137, 140, 150, 164, 177, 187, 207, 208, 219, 222, 226, 229, 260, 270, 322, 340, 363, 364

Company A, Second Battalion, 327th Infantry Regiment, 326–27

Company C, Second Battalion, Sixteenth Regiment of the First Infantry Division, 282

Company E, Fourth Battalion, 281

Comprehensive Convention on International Terrorism. *See* United Nations

Computer Assisted Passenger Prescreening System (CAPPS), 379, 383

Connor, Eugene "Bull," 24, 187, 188

Confederate States of America (CSA), 4, 46, 47, 53–59, 61, 64, 66–67, 72, 74, 77, 429; Special and Secret Service Bureau, 54

Congress of Racial Equality (CORE), 185, *199*

Congress of the United States, 32, 55, 73–80, 124, 153, 154, 157, 168, 219, 388, 396

Constitution, United States, 73, 75, 76, 78, 79, 219, 278, 290, 291

Cooke, Jay, 81–82

Cooper, D. B., 348

Copperheads. *See* Northern Peace
　　Democrats
Cordero, Andres Figueroa, 168
Cordesman, Anthony S., 420
Cory Hall Mathematics Building, 247,
　　248
Cotton States and International
　　Exposition, 181
Coune, Larry, 337
Counterterrorist Center (CTC), 369,
　　396
Cox, Sarah Collins, 190
Coyle, John W., 300
Cradlebaugh, John, 33–34
Crenshaw, Martha, 421, 425
Crist, Buckley, 244
Cronin, Audrey Kurth, 419
Cruikshank, William, 87
Cuba, 54, 153, 167, 208, 214, 226, 385,
　　400
Cuban missile crisis, 208, 226
Cuban Revolutionary Party, 153
Cullowhee, North Carolina, 326
Cumming, Alfred, 23–24, 33
Cummins, R. W., 24
Curtis, Marc, 222
Czolgosz, Leon, 151

Dahl, Jason, 385, 386
Dahl, Sandy, 385
Dallas, Texas, 151, 298, 361
Dame, William H., 28, 39
Dante Alighieri, 71
Dar es Salaam, Tanzania, 370
Darrow, Clarence, 98, *118*, 134; early
　　years, 103–4; and jury tampering
　　charge, 107–9, 111–14, 117–19; and
　　McNamara defense, 104–7, 110
Davidson, Joseph, 161, 162
Davis, Clifford, 168
Davis, Henry Winter, 74
Davis, Jefferson, 51, 54–55, 64–65, 187
Davis, LeCompte, 105

Davis, Nord Jr., 324, 325
Davis, Tom, 320, 330–31, 334, 337
Days of Rage. *See* Weatherman
Debs, Eugene V., 103, 207
Declaration of Independence, 132
"The Declaration of Jihad on the
　　Americans Occupying the Country
　　of the Two Sacred Places," 369
Democratic Party, 89, 207
Dehm, Harry, 112
dengue fever, 49
Dennison, Bill, 256, 257
Denver, Colorado, 276, 301
Denvir, Quin, 264
Desert Storm, Operation, 282–84
"Deterring Fear: Government
　　Responses to Terrorist Attacks," 422
Detroit, Michigan, 57, 102, 217
Dhahran, Saudi Arabia, 367
DiMucci, Dion, 277
The Divine Comedy, 71
Dixon, Thomas Jr., 193, 194
Dohrn, Bernadine, 213, 214, 220,
　　223–24, 225
Domino's Pizza, 344
Douglas, John, 246
Douglass, Frederick, 179
Downs, Joseph, 163
Doyle, Stephen, 141
Dr. Black Vomit. *See* Blackburn, Luke
　　Pryor
Dreamland Motel, 293, 297, 300
DuBois, W. E. B., 181, 182
Dulles International Airport, 245, 369,
　　383, 384
du Pont de Nemours Company, E. I.,
　　128–29
Dylan, Bob, 205–6

"18 West 11th Street," 205, 216
E pluribus unum, 325
Early, Jubal, 54
Earth First!, 256

Earth First! Journal, 254

Easton Police Department, 382

"Eco-Fucker Hit List," 254

Economic Research and Action Project (ERAP), 209. *See also* Students for a Democratic Society (SDS); Weatherman

Edwards Air Force Base, 290

Egypt, 284, 363, 365, 374, 375, 394, 397

Eisenhower, Dwight D., 195, 208, 226

Ellis, Joseph J., 132

Elohim City, 301

Enderson, Woody, 341

Enforcement Act of 1870, 86, 88

Enid, Oklahoma, 300

The Enlightenment, 425

Enright, Richard E., 129–30

Epstein, Charles, 252, 253, 264

Espionage Act of 1917, 134–35

"An Essay on Hypocrisy," 304–5

An Essay on Man, 45

Eugene O'Neill stamps, 244, 247, 249

Europe, 49, 52, 53, 59, 123, 125, 150, 374, 378

Evanston, Illinois, 244

Evers, Medgar, 176, 186

Exclusionary rule, 118

Exxon, 255

Exxon Valdez incident, 255

Fairfield, New Jersey, 378

Fallon, George Hyde, 168

Fancher, Alexander, 29. *See also* Baker-Fancher Party

Farouq mosque, 368

Faulkner, William, 90

Faust, 175

"FC." *See* Freedom Club

Federal Aviation Administration (FAA), 379, 380, 386

Federal Bureau of Investigation (FBI), 307, 322, 326, 332, 420; Behavioral Sciences Unit, 246; and Branch Davidians (Waco), 287–88, 289; and Centennial Olympic Park bombing, 332, 334–37; definition of terrorism, 6, 223, 229–30, 240; and Eric Robert Rudolph, 321, 338, 339, 340, 341, 349; and Oklahoma City bombing, 279, 290, 291, 296–98, 302, 307; and Ruby Ridge, 288–89; and September 11 attacks, 373, 392, 394; and the Sixteenth Street Baptist Church bombing, 196–97; Ten-Most-Wanted List, 217, 349; and the Unabomber, 239, 245, 246, 253, 256, 261, 262, 341; and the Wall Street bombing case, 115, 130, 131–32, 138, 140, 141; and Weatherman, 216, 217, 218, 219–20, 221, 222, 223, 228, 229; and World Trade Center bombing (1993), 368. *See also* COINTELPRO

Federal Bureau of Prisons, 307

Federal Correctional Complex, 307

Federal Emergency Management Agency (FEMA), 392

Federal Highway Administration, 295

Federal Public Defender Program, 351

Federal Rules of Criminal Procedure, 264

Felicani, Aldino, 138

Felipe, Luis, 307

Fessenden, William P., 80

Fiasco: The American Military Adventure in Iraq, 420

Field of Empty Chairs, 308, *309*

Fifteenth Amendment, 81

Finney, Charles Grandison, 15

Fire Department of New York (FDNY), 389, 390, 391–92

First Amendment, 88

First Great Awakening, 14–15

First Reconstruction Act of 1867, 77

Fischer, Enoch, 247
Fischer, Patrick, 247
Fishburn, Jason, 337
Fisher, Edwin, 136–37, 141
Florence, Colorado, 307, 353
Florida, 322, 378
Florida Flight Training Center, 377
Flynn, John, 261
Flynn, William J., 130–32, 134, 135, 137, 138, 140, 142
Foraker, Joseph B., 153
Foraker Act, 153–54
Forbes, 275
Ford, Gerald R., 151, 223
Ford, W. Joseph, 103
Forney, Jacob, 33
Forrest, Nathan Bedford, 193
Forsyth, Bill, 330
Fort Benning, Georgia, 281, 290, 326
Fort Campbell, Kentucky, 327
Fort Dix, New Jersey, 215
Fort Lauderdale, Florida, 322
Fort Myer Fire Department, 392
Fort Riley, Kansas, 281
Fort Sumter, South Carolina, 55, 73
Fort Worth, Texas, 380
Fortier, Lori, 290, 299, 300, 302, 304
Fortier, Michael, 290–91, 299, 300, 302, 304
Fourteenth Amendment, 76–77, 88
Fourth Amendment, 117–18, 219
Franklin, Bert, 107–9, 111, 112–13, 119
Fredericks, John D., 103, 106–7, 108, 109, 113, 114, 115, 117–18
free speech movement, 209–10
Freedmen's Bureau, 75
Freedom Club (FC), 250, 255, 257, 258, 259, 263
Freedom Riders, 176, 185–86
Freeh, Louis, 332, 335
Fremont, John C., 23
French Revolution, 5, 132

Gaddafi, Muammar Muhammad Abu Minyar al-, 370
Gage, Henry, 109
Gaithersburg, Maryland, 378
Galleani, Luigi, 133, 134
Galleanists, 133–34, 138, 139
Gandhi, Mohandas, 37, 184, 206
Garfield, James A., 151
Garrett (police dog), 347
Garrison, William Lloyd, 230
Gayman, Don, 326
Geary Lake, 293
Gelernter, David, 252–53, 264
Geisler, Jerry, 112
Georgia, 330, 334
Georgia Bureau of Investigation (GBI), 320, 330, 339, 341
Georgian, 64
Germany, 35, 376
Ghamdi, Ahmed al, 381
Ghamdi, Hamza al, 381
Ghamdi, Saleed al, 384
Ghanem, Alia. *See* Attas, Hamida al-
Ghost Wars: The Secret History of the CIA, Afghanistan, and Bin Laden, from the Soviet Invasion to September 10, 2001, 420–21
Gianotti, Richard J., 222
Gilbert, David, 223
Gilded Age, 9
Gill, Sir John, 164
Goethe, Johann Wolfgang von, 175
Gold, Ted, 215
Goldman, Emma, 133, 136
Goodman, Andrew, 176
Gompers, Samuel, 98, 101, 103, *104*, 104–5, 110, 111, 113
Gordon, George, 192
Graff, Harry, 102
Graham, Billy, 298
Grant, Ulysses S., 80–81, 82, 83, 86, 193
Grant, Wade, 336

Grant Parish, 82, 84
Great Britain, 324, 352
Great Compromise, 76
Great Depression, 226
Great Migration, 182
Great War. See World War I
Greatest Generation, 226
Greeley, Horace, 55–56, 80
Green, Keith, 300
Greensboro, North Carolina, 185
Greenwich Village, 215, 220, 228
Griffith, D. W., 193
Grimm, Jeanette, 256, 257
Gross, Samuel David, 52
Guadalupe Hidalgo, Treaty of, 22
Guam, 153
Guantanamo Bay, Cuba, 3, 385, 400
Guiteau, Charles J., 151
Gulf War, 281, 282–84
Gulfport, Mississippi, 290
Gumbel, Bryant, 388
Gutierrez, Mary, 244

Haber, Alan, 208
Hadnot, James, 84, 85, 87
Hadnot, J. P., 87
Hafs, Abu. See Atef, Mohammed
Haight, Isaac, 26–27, 28, 34, 39
Hale, Isaac, 17
Halifax, 62
Hamas, 362
Hamburg, Germany, 374, 375, 376, 377
Hampton, Fred, 212
Hanjour, Hani, 377, 378, 383
Hanson, Christine, 382
Hanson, Lee, 382
Hanson, Peter, 382
Hanson, Sue, 382
Hanssen, Robert, 307
Harding, Warren G., 195
Harmon, Christopher C., 419–20
Harrelson, Charles, 307

Harriman, Job, 104, 105
Harrington, John, 113, 119
Harris, John G., 245
Harris, Kevin, 288, 289
Harvard University, 130, 155, 217, 241, 242, 265, 268, 344
Hauser, John, 248
Hawthorne, Alice, 331–32
Hawthorne, John, 332
Hayden, Tom, 208
Haymarket riot, 133, 214
Haywood, William Dudley "Big Bill," 103, 134–35, 136, 137
Hazara region, 399
Hazmi, Nawaf al, 373, 374, 377, 383
Hazmi, Salem al, 383
Haznawai, Ahmad al, 384–85
Helena, Montana, 262, 263
hemorrhagic disease, 48
Henley, William Ernest, 280, 308
hepatitis, 49
Herblock, 298, 299
Herington, Kansas, 292, 293
Hezbollah Al–Hejaz (Party of God in the Hijaz), 362, 367
Higbee, John, 29, 30, 34
High Times, 327
Highlander Center, 184
Hill, James, 252
Hinckley, John, 151
Hiroshima, 304
Hitler, Adolf, 35, 195
Hobbes, Thomas, 132, 177, 178
Hodge, Steve, 290
Hoffman, Abbie, 300
Hoffman, Bruce, 5, 419
Hoffman, Dustin, 216
Hofstadter, Richard, 418
Holcombe, James P., 62–63
Hollywood, 98, 387, 402
Holocaust, 325
Holt, Joseph, 65
Homer, Leroy Jr., 385

Hoover, J. Edgar, 115, 141, 196–97, 219. *See also* Federal Bureau of Investigation (FBI)
Horiuchi, Lon, 288–89, 291
Horrocks, Michael, 381
Horsley, Albert Edward, 134
How Terrorism Ends, 419
Hudson Corridor, 378
Hudson River, 378
Huff, Nancy, 31
Huffman Aviation, 377
Hughes, Jermaine Jerome (WN–1), 344–46
Hussein, Saddam, 282, 284, 304, 370
Hyams, Godfrey Joseph, 60–66
Hylan, John, 130
"Hyperion," 123

"I Explain Herein Why I Bombed the Murrah Federal Building in Oklahoma City," 305–6
Ice Brothers, 247
Idaho, 134, 279
improvised explosive device (IED), 327
Independence Party. *See* Partido Independentista
Indianapolis, Indiana, 102, 384
Indianapolis Air Traffic Control Center, 384
Indochina, 209, 229
"Industrial Society and Its Future, by FC." *See* Kaczynski, Theodore (Ted)
Industrial Workers of the World (IWW), 134, 135
Inside Terrorism, 419
International Association of Bridge and Structural Workers, 97, 102
International Business Machines (IBM), 325
International Islamic Front for Jihad Against Jews and Crusaders, 370
International Olympic Committee, 334

Internet, 258, 349, 374, 399, 425
Interstate 35, 296
"Invictus," 280, 308
Invisible Empire. *See* Ku Klux Klan
Iowa, 22, 168
Iran, 370, 400
Iranian hostages (1979–1981), 400
Iraq, 282–85, 286, 304, 305, 306, 366, 370, 396, 420
Ireland, 324
Irizarry, Luis, 157
Islam (militant), 362–63, 364, 365, 366, 368, 370, 375, 420
Islamabad, Pakistan, 399
Islamic Jihad, 362, 365
Ismoil, Eyad, 367, 368
Israel, 17, 37, 319, 324, 326, 365, 373
Israel Identity. *See* Christian Identity movement

Jack the Ripper. *See* Tumblety, Francis
Jackson, Andrew, 4, 151
Jackson, Mississippi, 186
Jacobs, John "J. J.," 213, 214
Jaffe, Richard, 351
Jarrah, Ziad, 374, 376, 377, 378, 385, 386, 387
Jayuya Uprising, 157–58
Jeddah, Saudi Arabia, 363
Jefferson, Lisa, 387–88
Jefferson, Thomas, 132–33, 293–94
Jensen, Ben, 168
Jersey City, New Jersey, 368
Jewell, Richard, 320, 321, 330, 334–36, 337, 344, 347, 352
Jews, 194, 324, 327, 370, 376
JFK. *See* Kennedy, John F.
Jim Crow, 180, 181, 182, 183, 185, 186. *See also* segregation
John Birch Society, 325
John Does #1, 298
John Doe # 2, 304

Johnson, Andrew, 59, 65–66, 72–73, 74, 75–77, 78–79, 81, 82; and impeachment, 79–80
Johnson, Lyndon B., 210
Johnson, Loch K., 420
Johnson, Nelphi, 27, 30–31
Johnson's Island prison camp, 57, 64
Joint Chiefs of Staff, 402
Joint Committee on Reconstruction, 76
Jones Act of 1917, 154–55
Jones Aviation School, 377
Jones, Doug, 346
Jones, Jeff, 213, 220
Jones, Stephen, 300–301, 302, 303
Julius Caesar, 239
Junction City, Kansas, 293, 296, 297
Junkyard Bomber, 245
Jurassic Park, 254
Justesen, Thomas "Michael," 222–23
Justice Department, U.S. *See* United States Department of Justice

Kabul, Afghanistan, 397
Kaczynski, David, 240, 243, 250, 260–62
Kaczynski, Linda, 260–61
Kaczynski, Theodore (Ted), 98, *263*, 277, 305, 307, 310, 311, 337, 341, 351, 353, 423, 426, 428; arrest and indictment, 262–64; assessment of, 267–69; early life, 240–44; estrangement from brother David, 260–61; and "Industrial Society and Its Future, by FC," 258–60, 261; *The United States v. Theodore John Kaczynski*, 263–66; and violent activities, 239–58, 418
Kaczynski, Wanda, 262
Kahtani, Mohamed al, 385
Kansas, 221, 276, 281
Keats, John, 123
Kellogg, William Pitt, 83–84, 85

Kennedy, John F., 3, 151, 186, 206, 298, 361
Kennedy, Joseph P., 128
Khaldan training camp, 375
Khallad, 373, 374
Khan, Muhammad Mahroof, 422
Khartoum, Sudan, 365
Khobar Towers, 367
Kilby, Charles, 349
King, A. D., 187
King, Martin Luther Jr., 176, 177, 178, 184, 186, 187, 188, 190, 305
Kingdom Message. *See* Christian Identity movement
Kingman, Arizona, 290
Kirtland, Ohio, 17, 20
Kling, Robert, 293, 296–97, 299
Klonsky, Mike, 212
Kloppenburg, Ralph C., 249
KNBC Television, Los Angeles, 330
Knight, Dick, 240
Koran, 375
Korean War, 149, 150, 163–64, 322
Koresh, David, 287, 289, 291
Ku Klux Klan (KKK): and civil rights movement, 185, 186; during Reconstruction era, 81, 83, 192–93, 194; and Sixteenth Street Baptist Church bombing, 177, 178, 189–90, 198, 199, 200, 423, 427; during the twentieth century, 191, 193–96, 219, 285, 429
Kuwaiti, Abu Ahmed al-, 399, 400

laetrile, 323
Lakeland, Florida, 375
Laqueur, Walter, 422
Latin Kings, 307
Lawler, Oscar, 103
League for Industrial Democracy (LID), 207, 209. *See also* Student League for Industrial Democracy (SLID)

Leary, Timothy, 217–18
Lebanon, 374, 376, 394
Lebron, Lolita, 168–69
Lee, Edwin Gray, 59
Lee, John D., 29, 30, 31, 32, 33, *34*, 36, 39
Lee, Mary Jane, 252
Lee, Robert E., 54, 72
Leggio, Vinzenio. *See* Ligi, Tito
Lenin, Vladimir, 268
Leopold, Nathan, 268
The Lessons of Terror: A History of Warfare Against Civilians, 421, 425
"Letter from Birmingham Jail," 305
Leverknight, Kelly, 394
Lewis, John, 186
Lexington and Concord, 293
Ley de la Mordaza, 157
Liberal Republicans, 81, 83
Life, 186
Ligi, Tito, 139–40
Lincoln, Abraham, 4, 46, 57–58, 59, 61, 62, 64–65, 67, 72, 73, 74, 75, 78, 82, 151, 180, 293, 421
Lincoln Memorial, 187
Lincoln, Montana, 239, 243, 261, 262
Linde, William. *See* Lindenfeld, Wolfe
Lindenfeld, Wolfe, 140
Little Rock, Arkansas, 195
Liuzzo, Viola, 176
Llewellyn Iron Works, 103, 109
Lockwood, George, 108, 109
Loeb, Richard, 268
Logan International Airport, 381
"The Logic of Terrorism," 421
London, England, 61, 385
Long, Gerry, 213
The Looming Tower: Al Qaeda and the Road to 9/11, 420
Los Angeles, California, 99, 100, 101, 102, 103, 105, 106, 107, 108, 109, 111, 112, 114, 330, 334, 369, 377, 379, 381, 384

Los Angeles Times, 97, 99, 100, 109, 112, 115, 116
Los Angeles Times bombing, 9, 97–98, 100–101, 102, 112, 114, 115–17, 119, 123, 125, 129, 143, 427
Louisiana, 88–89, 423; and Reconstruction, 82–86, 180
Lovejoy, Elijah, 19
Luckovich, Mike, 332–33
Luddite, 239, 246, 263
Lumbee Indians, 195
Lyons, Emily, 342–43, 353

M-1 tank, 282
Ma'alim fi-l-Tariq, 363
MacArthur, Douglas, 163
MacDonald, Andrew. *See* Pierce, William Luther
MacDonald, William L. "Larry," 64
Machtinger, Howie, 213
Magoffin, Beriah, 53
malaria, 49
Manasseh, 324
Manhattan, 124, 388, 390
Mao Tse-tung, 35, 150
Marble, North Carolina, 347
March on Washington, 186–87, 188
Marker, Terry, 244
Martin, Jack, 336
A Martyr to His Cause, 105
Massachusetts, 74, 134, 325, 382
Matsch, Richard P., 301, 303
Matthews, Sean, 349
May 19 Communist Organization, 222
McCain, Franklin, 185
McCain, John, 225
McCann, Joseph T., 421
McClatchey, Val, 394
McClellan, George B., 59
McConnell, James V., 249
McDaniel, Tom, 262
McDonald's, 345, 346
McDonnell Douglas, 322

McEnery, John, 83, 84
McGown, Lea, 293, 297, 300
McGuinness, Thomas, 379
McKinney, Jesse, 84
McKinley, William, 151, 153, 154
McManigal, Ortie, 102, 105, 114
McMurty, Samuel, 30
McNair, Denise, 190, 196
McNamara, James B., *114*,
   117, 118, 134, 143, 423, 427;
   aftermath of the case, 109–11,
   113, 115; investigation, arrest,
   and arraignment, 102–5; trial
   preparations and plea bargain,
   106–7, 109
McNamara, John J., *114*, 117, 118, 134,
   143, 423, 427; aftermath of the case,
   109–11, 113, 115; investigation,
   arrest, and arraignment, 102–5;
   trial preparations and plea bargain,
   106–7, 109
McNeil, Dan, 399
McNeil, Joseph, 185
McNutt, Cyrus F., 105
McRaven, William, 402
McVeigh, Ed, 276, 277–78, 292
McVeigh, Jennifer, 292, 302, 303
McVeigh, Mildred "Mickey" Hill, 276,
   303
McVeigh, Timothy James, 116, 297,
   319, 347, 353, 368, 423, 426, 428;
   aftermath of bombing, 303–7;
   alienation of, 286–92; arrest and
   prosecution, 296–303, 350–51;
   assessment of, 309–11; and Branch
   Davidians (Waco), 287–88, 289,
   290, 291, 293, 294, 341; early life,
   276–80; execution, 308; military
   service, 280–86, 287; racism of, 280,
   285; and violent activities, 292–95.
   See also Oklahoma City bombing
McVeigh, William "Bill," 276, 303
Mecca, Saudi Arabia, 369, 375

Mektab al Khidmat (MAK), 365. *See
   also* al-Qaeda
Mellon, Jim, 213
Memorandum of Notification (MON),
   371
Merari, Ariel, 422
Merchants and Manufacturers
   Association, 100
Meredith, James, 186
Merrill, Charles, 216
Merrill, James, 205, 216
Merrill Lynch, 216
Mes Aynak training camp, 374
Metropolitan Washington Airports
   Authority, 392
Mexico, 218, 323, 348
Miami International Airport, 322
Michigan, 168, 286, 287
Mihdhar, Khalid al, 373, 374, 377, 383
militia movement, 278, 279–80, 305,
   310, 311
Milton, John, 13
Minh, Ho Chi, 212, 218, 229
Miranda, Rafael Cancel, 168
Miranda rights, 335
Mississippi, 51, 52, 53, 54, 55, 59, 176,
   186, 429
Missouri, 17, 19, 20, 21, 24, 326
Mohammed, Khalid Sheikh, 367, 372,
   373–74, 377, 383, 394, 400
Montana, 243, 264, 279
Montgomery, Alabama, 183, 184,
   185–86
Montgomery Improvement
   Association, 184
Moore, Roger, 292
Moqed, Majed, 383
Moran, John P., 422
Morgan, J. P., 124, 140
Mormons. *See* The Church of Jesus
   Christ of Latter-Day Saints
Moroni. *See* Smith, Joseph Jr.
Mossad, 365

Moses, Bob, 186
Mosser, Kelly, 255
Mosser, Kim, 255
Mosser, Susan, 254–55
Mosser, Thomas J., 254–55, 264
Mountain Meadows, 13, 27, 32, 33–34
Mountain Meadows Massacre, 9, 24, 25–40, 417, 426
Moussaoui, Zacarias, 377, 385
Mujahedeen, 364, 366
Mullin, Leslie Anne "Esther," 223
Munich, Germany, 319
Murphy, North Carolina, 328, 347, 349
Murphy, J. M., 126
Murphy Police Department, 349
Murray, Gilbert, 256–57, 264
Murray, Henry, 241–42, 265
Muslim Brotherhood, 375
Murtagh, John, 215
Muslim fundamentalism, 116

9/11. See September 11, 2001, attacks
9/11 Commission, 368, 395, 404
9/11 Commission Report, 395
Nairobi, Kenya, embassy bombing, 370
Nami, Ahmed al, 384
Nantahala High School, 325
Nash, Christopher Columbus, 84, 85, 427
Nash, Diane, 186
Nashville, Tennessee, 247
The Nation, 79
Nation of Islam, 219
National Association for the Advancement of Colored People (NAACP), 176, 181, 182, 183, 184, 186
National Erectors' Association, 99, 101
National Islamic Front, 365, 370
National Knights of the Ku Klux Klan, 195
National Medical Response Team, 392
National Science Foundation, 242

National Security Council (NSC), 420
National Student League, 207
National Union Party, 76
Native Americans, 13, 17, 27, 28, 36, 37, 47, 75, 76, 325
Native Forest Network, 254
Nauvoo, Illinois, 19, 21
Nauvoo Expositor, 19
Nauvoo Legion, 14, 19, 24, 26, 28, 29, 30, 31, 32; See also Church of Jesus Christ of Latter Day Saints
Nazi Party, 195, 268, 301, 325
NBC Television, 336, 340, 398
Nebraska, 22, 276
Nelson, Levi, 86, 87
Neruda, Pablo, 319
New Bern, North Carolina, 62
New Jersey, 264, 385
New Orleans, Louisiana, 49, 52, 53, 60, 65, 82, 85, 185
New Woman, All Women Health Care Clinic, 342–44, 351, 353
New York City, New York, 3, 59, 61, 123, 124, 129, 130, 131, 133, 136, 138, 158, 159, 210, 217, 223, 254, 367, 369, 373, 382, 388, 389, 392, 393, 417
New York Post, 336
New York State, 278, 287, 325, 340
New York Stock Exchange, 127
New York Sun, 139
New York Times, 246, 253, 255, 257, 258
New York Tribune, 77, 80
New Yorker, 266
Newark International Airport, 369, 377, 385
Newsweek, 305
Nichols, Terry Lynn, 281–82, 286, 287, 290, 292–93, 294, 299, 300, 303, 304
nitromethane, 293, 300
Nixon, Richard M., 220–21, 300
Noble County jail, 296

Noel, "Mad Max," 262
Nordmann, Bobo (dog), 348
Nordmann, George, 348
North Carolina, 55, 195, 266, 285, 321, 346, 347, 348
North Atlantic Treaty Organization (NATO), 150
North Caldwell, New Jersey, 254
North Carolina Agricultural & Technical College, 185
North Carolina Knights of the Ku Klux Klan, 195
Northern Alliance, 397
Northern Peace Democrats, 57–59, 61, 75
Northpoint Tactical Teams, 325
Northside Family Planning Services, 337–38, 339, 353
Northwestern University, 223, 244, 245
Notes on the State of Virginia, 132. *See also* Jefferson, Thomas
Nuremberg War Trials, 291

101st Airborne, 327
Obama, Barack H., 224–25, 400, 401, 402–03
Oberlin College, 15
Office of Strategic Services (OSS), 241
Ogonowski, John, 379
Ohio, 15, 17, 19, 57, 58, 74, 103, 153, 349
Oklahoma City bombing, 9, 140, 257, 284, 286–87, 291, 294–96, 300, 301, 305, 307, 347. *See also* McVeigh, Timothy James
Oklahoma City, Oklahoma, 275–76, 291, 292, 293, 294, 295, 296, 298, 300, 305, 306, 308
Oklahoma City Memorial, 308, *309*
Oklahoma State University, 300
Old Testament, 324
Olmstead Amendment, 154
Olson, Barbara, 384

Olson, Theodore, 384
Olympic Games (Atlanta, 1996), 319, 328–34, 342, 344, 352, 424
Olympic Games (Los Angeles, 1984), 334
Olympic Games (Munich, 1972), 319
Omari, Abdul Aziz al, 379
"On Another's Sorrow," 417
The One Percent Doctrine: Deep Inside America's Pursuit of Its Enemies Since 9/11, 420
Ong, Betty, 379–80, 381
Operation Infinite Reach, 371
Operation Rescue, 337
Orchard, Harry. *See* Horsley, Albert Edward
the Order, 326
Order of the Sons of Liberty, 57, 58
Original Ku Klux Klan of the Confederacy, 195
Orlando International Airport, 385
Osawatomie (magazine), 221–22
Oswald, Lee Harvey, 297–98
Otherside Lounge, 339, 340, 344, 353
Otis, Harrison Gray, 99–100, 101, 110, 427
Otto, Susan, 300
Oughton, Diana, 215
Outlaws in America, 225

Pacific Ocean, 163, 374
pacifism, 133
Pakistan, 364, 366, 371, 399–404
Pakistan Military Academy, 399
Palin, Sarah, 224–25
Palmer, A. Mitchell, 131, 137, 139, 142
Panic of 1873, 81–82
Panther 21. *See* Black Panther Party
Paradise Lost, 13
Parks, Rosa, 183–84
Partido Independentista, 154
Pathfinder, 258
Patrik, Linda. *See* Kaczynski, Linda

Patriot Movement, 285, 289

Peace Corps, 206, 223

"The Peaceful Revolutionist," 133

Pearl Harbor attack, 3, 4, 361

Pearson, Jimmy, 334

Pendleton, New York, 276, 286, 292

Pennsylvania, 54, 74, 103

Pennsylvania State University, 247

Pentagon, 98, 217, 218, 373, 378, 384, 392, 393, 403. *See also* September 11, 2001, attacks

Penthouse, 258

Perry, Marc. *See* Curtis, Marc

Perry, Oklahoma, 296, 297

Peterson, Eric, 393

Pettus, John J., 53, 54

Philippines, 153, 301, 304

Piedmont College, 334, 335

Pierce, William Luther, 278. See also *The Turner Diaries*

Piñero, Jesús T., 157

Politically Incorrect, 384

polygamy. *See* Church of Jesus Christ of Latter-Day Saints

Ponce Massacre, 156

Pope, Alexander, 45

Port Authority of New York, 389, 391, 392

Port Huron Statement (PHS), 208–9

Portland, Maine, 378

Postell, Jeff, 349

Pot, Pol, 35

Powell, Colin, 398

Prairie Fire Collective, 222

Prairie Fire Organizing Committee, 222

Prairie Fire: The Politics of Revolutionary Anti–Imperialism, 220–21

Pratt, Parley, 25, 38, 40

President's Daily Brief (PDB), 395

Price, Sterling, 53

Prince, Walter F., 137

Prince William Sound, Alaska, 254

Pritchett, Laurie, 186

Public Act 600, 157

Puerto Rico, 150; history of, 152–58; and nationalism, 151, 152–58, 159–60, 167–70, 427

Puerto Rican Cultural Center, 167

Puerto Rican Nationalist Party, 8, 151, 152, 154, 155, 156–57, 158, 159, 423

Pulaski, Tennessee, 192

Putnam, Michael T., 351

Quorum of the Twelve Apostles. *See* Church of Jesus Christ of Latter-Day Saints

Qutb, Sayyid, 363

Radical Republicans, 73–74, 75, 76, 81, 82, 83; and impeachment of Andrew Johnson, 79–80

Rahman, Omar Abdel, 365, 368

Rand Corporation, 6–7

Rathbun, Bill, 333

Reagan, Ronald, 151

Reagan, William, 222

Reconstruction, 72–82, 88, 90, 91, 180, 192–93, 194

Red Cross, 194

Reed, Walter, 48

Reid, Richard, 307

Reno, Janet, 258, 259, 264, 291

Republican Party, 23, 81, 82, 84, 180, 207, 222, 225, 300

Resolution 1566. *See* United Nations

Reuters news service, 339–40

Revolutionary Youth Movement, 207

Rice, Condoleezza, 395

Rice, Thomas Dartmouth, 180

Richmond, David, 185

Ricks, Thomas E., 420

Rigdon, Sidney, 17, 21

Riggs, Elisha Francis, 156

The Rime of the Ancient Mariner, 1

Ripley, Edward Hastings, 64
Riyadh, Saudi Arabia, 362, 366
Robbins, Terry, 213, 215
Roberts, Kenneth A., 168
Robertson, Carole, 190, 196
Robin Hood, 240
Robinson, James C., 58
Robinson, Stuart, 61
Rodriguez, Jesús, 282, 283
Rodriguez, Irving Flores, 168
Roe v. Wade, 342
Rogers, Earl, 103, 112–13
Rolling Stones, 231
Ronay, James C. "Chris," 245–46, 250
Roosevelt, Franklin, D., 149, 151
Roosevelt, Theodore, 151
"Root Causes of Terrorism: An
    Empirical Analysis," 422
"The Roots of Terrorist Motivation:
    Shame, Rage, and Violence in *The
    Brothers Karamazov*," 422
Ruby Ridge, Idaho, 288–89, 291, 302
Rudd, Mark, 210, 213, 223
Rudolph, Daniel, 328, 348
Rudolph, Eric Robert, 2, 3, 9, 10,
    98, 307, 321, 350, 423, 424, 426,
    428; alienation of, 325–26, 328;
    arrest and prosecution, 349–53;
    assessment of, 353–54; and
    Christian Identity movement, 321;
    disappearance of, 347–49; early life,
    322–23, 325–26; identification of,
    344–47; and marijuana business,
    327–28; military service, 319, 326–
    27; political views, 319, 352–53; and
    violent activities, 320–21, 330–32,
    337–47
Rudolph, Joel, 328
Rudolph, Patricia (Murphy), 322, 323,
    328
Rudolph, Robert Thomas, 322, 323
Rumsfeld, Donald, 396
Russell, David L., 300

Russia, 133, 137, 138, 140, 307. *See
    also* Soviet Union
Russky Golos, 137
Ryan, Frank M., 102, 104
Ryder truck, 293, 296, 300, 304, 367,
    368
RYM I. *See* "Toward a Revolutionary
    Youth Movement" (RYM)
RYM II. *See* "You Don't Need a
    Weatherman to Know Which Way
    the Wind Blows" (RYM II)

60 Minutes, 307, 336
Sacco, Nicola, 134, 138, 141, 142
Sacramento, California, 249, 252, 253,
    263, 264
Salameh, Mohammad, 367, 368
Samaranch, Juan Antonio, 334
San Diego, California, 351, 377
San Francisco, California, 215, 254,
    369, 385
San Quentin prison, *114*, 115
Sanderson, Robert "Sande," 342–43,
    353
Sandy Springs, Georgia, 337, 340, 342
Saracini, Victor, 381
Sarasota, Florida, 377
Satan, 324, 372, 398
Saudi Arabia, 281, 282, 362, 363, 364,
    366, 367, 369, 394, 404
Saudi National Guard, 366
Saudi royal family, 362, 366
Savio, Mario, 209
Saxon, Kurt, 325
scalawags, 78, 187, 193
Scheele, Walter T., 136
Schmidt, A. M., 102
Schmidt, Steve, 337
Schwerner, Michael, 176
Scrutton, Hugh, 249–50, 263
SEAL Team 6, 401
SEALs. *See* United States Navy Sea,
    Air and Land teams (SEALs)

Second Amendment, 88, 278, 279

"The Second Coming," 97

Second Great Awakening, 14, 15

Second Reconstruction Act of 1867, 77–78

Secret Service. *See* United States Secret Service

segregation, 180–87, 188, 193, 196, 208

Seligman, Arizona, 289

Senguen, Aysel, 376

Senior Executive Intelligence Brief (SEIB), 395

September 11, 2001, attacks, 3, 9, 98, 100, 116, 119, 140, 144, 175, 218, 361, 362, 378, 417, 418, 420–21, 422, 423, 424; aftermath, 394–403, 419; in the air, 378–88; on the ground, 388–94

Seward, William H., 61, 66

Shakespeare, William, 239

Shanksville, Pennsylvania, 3, 387, 393, 403, 417

Shehhi, Marwan al, 374, 376, 377, 378, 381

Shehri, Wail al, 379

Shehri, Waleed al, 379

Shelton, Robert, 195

Sheri, Mohand al, 381

Sherman, William T., 80

Sierras, 256

Simmons, William Joseph "Doc," 194

Sixth Amendment, 240

Sixteenth Street Baptist Church, 177, 178, 187, *191*; bombing of, 189–91, 195, 198, 200, 423, 427; history of, 188–89

slavery, 23, 73, 75–76, 86, 178–79, 230

smallpox, 46, 63

Smith, C. Lynwood, 351

Smith, E. J., 244

Smith, Elias, 34

Smith, George A., 24

Smith, Gerald L. K., 324

Smith, Hyrum, 20, 21, 25

Smith, Janet, 247

Smith, Joseph Jr., 14, *18*, 39; and Book of Mormon, 17, 20, 35; early years, 14–17; encounters Moroni, 16; and gold plates, 16–17; Midwest years, 17–19; murder of, 19–20, 21, 22, 25, 37, 429. *See also* Church of Jesus Christ of Latter-Day Saints

Smith, Walter Bedell, 164

Smith, Walter S. Jr., 291

Social Security, 150, 326

Sojourn, Celia, 220

Soldier of Fortune, 278

Somalia, 366, 400

The Souls of Black Folk, 181

South Carolina, 81, 193

Soviet Union, 35, 141, 150, 221, 226, 268, 363–64

Spain, 152–53, 324, 378

Spanish American War, 153

Spanish National Assembly, 156

Special Forces, U.S. Army, 281, 285, 321, 326, 397

Special Target Information Development program, 219. *See also* Federal Bureau of Investigation (FBI)

"Speedo Boys," 337

"Splendid Little War." *See* Spanish American War

Spooner, Lysander, 133

Stalin, Josef, 35

Stanton, Edwin M., 79

Star of the West, 55

Steffens, Lincoln, 106

Sterling Hall incident, 228

Steunenberg, Frank, 134

Stevens, Thaddeus, 74, 80

Stewart, Potter, 422

Stiles, Cal, 347

Stubbs, Fallon, 331–32

Student League for Industrial
Democracy (SLID), 207. *See also*
League for Industrial Democracy
(LID)
Student Nonviolent Coordinating
Committee (SNCC), 185–86, 209
Students for a Democratic Society
(SDS), 205, *211*, 223; early history
of, 207–10, 212, 216; splits into
Weatherman, 212–13, 214–15, 226,
231. *See also* Weatherman
"Subterranean Homesick Blues," 206
Suino, Nicklaus, 249
Sumner, Charles, 74
"Supermax" prison, 307, 353
Survivor Tree, 308
Suskind, Ron, 420
Swan, Edward, 62
Swango, Michael, 307
Swanson, Susan, 261
Sweeney, Brian David, 382
Sweeney, Louise, 382
Sweeney, Madeline "Amy," 379, 380,
381
Swift, Wesley, 324
Szabo, David, 337

Taliban, 369, 372, 397, 421
Tappis, Steve, 213
Taylor, Bob, 256, 257
Ten Days of Resistance, 210
Tenet, George, 395, 404
Tennessee, 55, 77, 79, 168, 176, 184
Tennessee Valley Authority police, 349
Tenure of Office Act, 78–79
terrorism: definition of, 4–10, 418,
422–23; lessons learned, 422–29.
See also specific episodes
Terrorism in America, 421
*Terrorism on American Soil: A Concise
History of Plots and Perpetrators
from the Famous to the Forgotten*,
421

*Terrorism, Asymmetric Warfare, and
Weapons of Mass Destruction:
Defending the U.S. Homeland*, 420
"The Terrorism to Come," 422
Terrorism Today, 419–20
*Terrorism versus Democracy: The
Liberal State Response*, 419
Terrorist Attacks on American Soil,
422
Texas, 217, 276
Third Reconstruction Act of 1867. *See*
Tenure of Office Act
Thirteenth Amendment, 75, 86, 178
Thompson, Jacob, *56*; and Canadian
cabal, 54–59, 62–63, 64, 65; early
years, 55, postbellum years, 59
Thompson, James, 55
Thoreau, Henry David, 133, 243
Thurston, David, 61
Tickal, Jeff (WN–2), 345, 346
Tillman, "Pitchfork Ben," 279
Time Warner, 258
Tojo, Hideki, 268
Topton, North Carolina, 322, 323, 325
Tora Bora, 397, 398, 399
Torres, Damian, 158
Torresola, Griselio, *164*; assault on
Truman, 159–65, 169–70, 427; early
life, 158, 159; death, 164–65, 167
"Toward a Revolutionary Youth
Movement" (RYM I), 212
Trail of Tears, 4
Treaty of Paris, 153
Truman, Harry S, 8, 157, *166*;
aftermath, 165–67, 169–70;
assassination attempt, 150, 151,
159–65, 423, 427, 429; presidential
accomplishments, 149–50
Trumbull, Lyman, 75
Truth, Sojourner, 179
Tumblety, Francis, 65, 70n53
Turabi, Hassan al, 365
Turner, Earl, 279

The Turner Diaries, 278–79, 281, 288, 293

Twin Towers. *See* World Trade Center

Tyler, Elizabeth, 194

typhus, 49

Unabomber. *See* Kaczynski, Theodore (Ted)

Union College, 260

Union League, 78

Union of Soviet Socialist Republics (USSR). *See* Soviet Union

United Airlines, 247, 381, 382, 384, 385, 386; Flight 93, 384–88, 393, 394, 403; Flight 175, 381–383, 385, 388, 390

United Arab Emirates, 374, 376, 394

United Klans of America (UKA), 189, 195

United Mine Workers, 103

United Nations, 5–6, 290, 368

United States v. Cruikshank, 88, 90–91

United States Air Force, 217, 222, 223, 248, 290, 306, 385

United States Army, 24, 25, 31, 32, 33, 36, 38, 40, 82, 130, 155, 276, 280, 282, 285, 287, 306, 321, 326–27

United States Capitol building, 168, 373, 378, 387

United States Department of Defense, 218, 392. *See also* Pentagon

United States Department of Homeland Security, 395, 404

United States Department of Justice, 86–87, 131, 135, 287, 289

United States Drug Enforcement Agency (DEA), 327

United States Marine Corps, 189, 306

United States Marshals Service, 75, 87, 263, 340

United States Navy, 152, 168, 306, 322, 371, 400,

United States Navy Sea, Air and Land teams (SEALs), 400, 401–2

United States Secret Service, 101, 131, 165, 167, 384

United States Special Operations Command, 400

United States Supreme Court, 71, 78, 80, 88, 91, 183, 195, 342

The United States v. Theodore John Kaczynski. *See* Kaczynski, Theodore (Ted)

University of Alabama at Birmingham (UAB), 341, 342, 344

University of California, Berkeley, 209, 242, 247, 248, 250

University of Illinois at Chicago, 223, 244

University of Michigan, 208, 242, 249

University of Mississippi, 186

University of Washington, 222, 223

University of Wisconsin–Madison, 228

"Upon the Punishment of Death," 275

Urbrock, Don, 186

U.S. Steel Corporation, 98

USA Patriot Act, 3, 4, 396

USS *Cole*, 372–73, 394

USS *Maine*, 153

USS *Michigan*, 57

Utah Territory, 14, 22–25, 36, 38

Utuado Massacre, 158

Uzunyol, Melih, 332

Valeri, Robin, 421

Vallandigham, Clement L., 57–58

Van Lydegraf, Clayton, 222, 223

Van Zandt, James, 168

Vanderbilt University, 247

Vanzetti, Bartolomeo, 134, 138, 141, 142

Venable, James, 195

Venice, Florida, 377

Vietnam War, 205, 206, 207, 210, 216, 218, 220, 221, 226, 227, 229, 304, 322, 364

Virgil, 361

Virginia, 54, 293, 392

Vollers, Maryanne, 323

Waco, Texas, 287, 288, 290, 291, 293, 294, 299, 302, 306, 341

Wade, Benjamin, 74

Wager, Susan, 215

Wahhab, Muhammad ibn Abd al-, 362–63

Wahhabism, 362–63

Waite, Morrison, 88

Walker, David, 170

Walker's Appeal in Four Articles, 179

"Walking Around," 319

Wall Street, 123, 124–25, 127, 135, 136, 138, 139–40, 143

Wall Street bombing: as cold case, 140–41; the incident, 8, 123–24, 125–28, 423, 427; the investigation, 128–45

Wall Street Journal, 130

Wallace, George, 187

Wallace, Michael, 418

Ward, William, 83, 84, 85

Warmouth, Henry C., 83, 84

Warren, Josiah, 133

Washington, Booker T., 180–81

Washington, George, 124

Washington, D.C., 3, 22, 39, 54, 62, 65, 160, 164, 168, 185, 199, 218, 245, 261, 279, 322, 340, 352, 373, 378, 387, 392, 402, 417

Washington National Airport, 245, 392

Washington Post, 258, 298

Watson, Tom, 279

weapons of mass destruction, 304, 424

Weather Underground Organization (WUO). *See* Weatherman

Weatherman, 205–6, 259, 423, 427–28; aftermath, 223–31; and Days of Rage, 213, 214; demise, 221–23; origins, 207, 212–14; and violent activities, 214–21. *See also* Students for a Democratic Society (SDS)

Weaver, Randy, 288–89

Weaver, Vicki, 289

Wesley, Cynthia, 190, 196

West, J. B., 165

Western Federation of Miners (WFM), 103, 134

"What Terrorists Really Want: Terrorist Motives and Counterterrorism Strategy," 421

White, C. E., 108–9

White House, 150, 160, 161, 163, 165, 195, 373, 378, 384, 387, 402

White League, 83, 89

White Power, 285, 423

Whitman, Walt, 149

Wickersham, George W., 106

The Wild One, 227

Wilkerson, Cathy, 215

Wilkinson, Paul, 419, 423

Williams, David, 302

Williams, George, 86

Wilson, Sloan, 247

Winship, Blanton, 156–57

Wood, Lin, 336

Wood, Percy, 247, 258

Wood, Robert W., 136

Woods, Arthur, 130

Woodward, Michael, 380, 381

Wordsworth, William, 275

World Trade Center: and 1993 attacks, 304, 307, 367–69; North Tower, 381, 382, 383, 385, 388, 389, 390, 391; 7 World Trade Center, 388; South Tower, 383, 385, 388, 389, 390, 391; and September 11, 2001, attacks, 98, 100, 373, 378, 381–86, 388–89, 394. *See also* September 11, 2001, attacks

World War I, 123, 125, 127, 130, 131,
    134, 142, 155, 183, 194, 207
World War II, 141, 182, 195, 226, 304,
    324
World War III, 164
Wright, Gary, 250
Wright, Lawrence, 420

Yale University, 252, 254
Yasin, Abdul Rahman, 367
Yeats, William Butler, 97
yellow fever, 46, 47–49, 52, 60, 65, 66,
    67, 427
yellow fever plot. *See* Blackburn, Luke
    Pryor
Yemen, 372, 374, 375, 376, 377
Yemeni, Abu Bara al, 373, 374
"You Don't Need a Weatherman to
    Know Which Way the Wind Blows"
    (RYM II), 212–13

Young, Bennett H., 63
Young, Brigham, *26*, 429; early years,
    20–22; move to Utah, 22–23, 39;
    role in the Mountain Meadows
    Massacre, 25–26, 27, 28, 31–33,
    34, 39; and Utah War, 23–25,
    32–33, 38, 39–40. *See also* Church
    of Jesus Christ of Latter-Day
    Saints; Mountain Meadows
    Massacre
Yousef, Ramzi Ahmed, 304, 307,
    367–68, 369, 373

Zawahiri, Ayman al-, 365
Zeehandlaar, Felix J., 100
Zelenko, Florian. *See* Zelenska,
    Florean
Zelenska, Florean, 138–39
Zoeller, Steve, 330
Zwerg, James, 186

ABOUT THE AUTHOR

J. Michael Martinez works in Monroe, Georgia, as corporate counsel with a manufacturing company. He also teaches political science, criminal justice, and public administration courses as a part-time faculty member at Kennesaw State University, the University of South Dakota, and the University of Georgia, respectively. He has written numerous academic articles as well as five previous books.